"Yun Ma's fascinating book examines how China and the United States manage national parks and other protected areas. The study of China is especially important because the various classes of protected areas there are relatively new and little understood. Her account of traveling to southwestern China to visit Pudacuo National Park, the country's first, demonstrates how even local officials often know far less about such protected areas than we would expect."

John C. Nagle, University of Notre Dame, USA

"This important comparative study of how US and Chinese legal institutions address national park recreation controversies offers valuable insights into the role law, politics, and economics play in shaping each nation's nature conservation policies, while providing a realistic assessment of the many challenges park managers face in both countries."

Robert B. Keiter, University of Utah, USA and author of
To Conserve Unimpaired: The Evolution of the National Park Idea

"The 'Protected Area' is a very important field of environmental law in China, but one somehow lacking due consideration. This book presents one of the earliest comprehensive studies on protected areas from a legal perspective. By comparing the situation in China with that in the US, the author provides many constructive suggestions for improving Chinese law."

Tianbao Qin, Wuhan University, China

Conservation and Recreation in Protected Areas

This book provides a comprehensive and up to date comparative study of the management and resolution of conflicts between conservation and recreation in protected areas in the US and China. Competing claims on the use of nature, increasing regulation of land use and recreational activities, and the conflicting goals between conservation and development have led to a rise in conflicts in the designation and management of protected areas. How to effectively manage and resolve these conflicts has become a challenge for both legislators and managers.

By adopting an institutional dimension in legal interpretation, this book critically examines how such conflicts are dealt with in the legal regimes of the US and China while exploring interactions between legislatures, agencies, and courts. The book searches for a plausible solution to improve the legal framework of protected areas in China by emulating pertinent mechanisms developed in the US, whilst also presenting legal and policy recommendations to the US.

This informative book will be useful for legal scholars in Chinese law, nature conservation law, administrative law, and comparative law.

Yun Ma is a lecturer in administrative law at the Law School of China University of Political Science and Law (CUPL), Beijing, China. She graduated cum laude from the Law School of CUPL with the bachelor's degree in law, and obtained a 'free pass' to the master studies in constitutional and administrative law at CUPL. Funded by the China Scholarship Council, she worked as a PhD candidate at the Department of Constitutional and Administrative Law and Erasmus China Law Center at the Erasmus School of Law since September 2011 and obtained her doctoral degree in 2015. She worked as a visiting researcher at Maurer School of Law of Indiana University and S.J.Quinney College of Law of University of Utah in the United States between September 2013 and February 2014. Her research interests include administrative law, natural resources law and environmental governance. She has authored and co-authored articles and book chapters on administrative litigation, private land conservation, national parks and other topics.

The Rule of Law in China and Comparative Perspectives
Series Editors:
Yuwen Li, Erasmus University Rotterdam, The Netherlands and
Fu Hualing, University of Hong Kong, Hong Kong

There is no doctrine more effective than the rule of law in portraying the complex transformation of Chinese society from the rule of men towards the rule of law – a process inaugurated in post-Mao China which is continuing to advance legal reforms to the present day. In other parts of the world, striving for the rule of law is also evident: countries in transition face a similar mission, while the developed democratic countries are forced to tackle new challenges in retaining the high benchmark of the rule of law that has been established.

Research on the legal system in China and in comparison with other countries in the framework of the rule of law covers broad topics of public and private law, substantive law and procedural law, citizens' rights and law enforcement by courts. Based on this broad understanding of the rule of law, the series presents international scholarly work on modern Chinese law including: comparative perspectives, interdisciplinary, and empirical studies.

Other titles in this series:

The Judicial System and Reform in Post-Mao China
Yuwen Li

Administrative Litigation Systems in Greater China and Europe
Edited by Yuwen Li

Legal Reforms and Deprivation of Liberty in Contemporary China
Edited by Elisa Nesossi, Sarah Biddulph, Flora Sapio and Susan Trevaskes

Conservation and Recreation in Protected Areas

A Comparative Legal Analysis Of Environmental Conflict Resolution In The United States And China

Yun Ma

LONDON AND NEW YORK

First published 2016
by Routledge
2 Park Square, Milton Park, Abingdon, Oxon OX14 4RN

and by Routledge
711 Third Avenue, New York, NY 10017

First issued in paperback 2018

Routledge is an imprint of the Taylor & Francis Group, an informa business

© 2016 Yun Ma

The right of Yun Ma to be identified as author of this work has been asserted by her in accordance with sections 77 and 78 of the Copyright, Designs and Patents Act 1988.

All rights reserved. No part of this book may be reprinted or reproduced or utilised in any form or by any electronic, mechanical, or other means, now known or hereafter invented, including photocopying and recording, or in any information storage or retrieval system, without permission in writing from the publishers.

Trademark notice: Product or corporate names may be trademarks or registered trademarks, and are used only for identification and explanation without intent to infringe.

British Library Cataloguing in Publication Data
A catalogue record for this book is available from the British Library

Library of Congress Cataloging in Publication Data
Ma, Yun, (Law teacher)
Conservation and recreation in protected areas : a comparative legal analysis of environmental conflict resolution in the United States and China / By Yun Ma.
pages cm. — (The rule of law in China and comparative perspectives)
Includes bibliographical references and index.
1. Environmental mediation—United States. 2. Environmental mediation—China. 3. Conservation of natural resources—Law and legislation—United States. 4. Conservation of natural resources—Law and legislation—China. 5. Dispute resolution (Law)—United States. 6. Dispute resolution (Law)—China. I. Title.
K3585.M3 2016
344.5104'6—dc23
2015036442

ISBN 13: 978-1-138-60561-9 (pbk)
ISBN 13: 978-1-4724-7527-5 (hbk)

Typeset in Times New Roman
by Swales & Willis Ltd, Exeter, Devon, UK

Contents

Figures	ix
Tables	x
Cases	xi
Abbreviations	xii
Preface and Acknowledgments	xiv

1	Introduction	1

PART 1
Conflicts in Theory: Concepts, Institutions and Rationale   13

2	Schemes of Protected Areas: Historical, Structural and Institutional Perspectives	15
3	Resolving Conflicts in Protected Areas: Rationale, Principles and the Institutional Approach	41

PART 2
Country Studies: United States   69

4	The Legal Framework of Protected Areas in the United States	71
5	The Formation of Conflicts in Public Land Designation and Management	88
6	Resolution of Conflicts in Legislation and Policies: Assessing the Legal Foundations	111
7	Resolution of Conflicts: A Judicial Perspective	126

PART 3
Country Studies: China   155

8	The Legislative and Policy Frameworks of Protected Areas in China	157

9	The Formation of Conflicts in the Designation and Management of Protected Areas in China	180
10	The Resolution of Conflicts in Law and Practice in China	210
11	Pudacuo National Park and Beyond in Yunnan Province: National Parks Envisioned and National Parks in Practice	240
12	Comparative Observations, Conclusions and Recommendations	259

Appendix I The List of Applicable Laws on Protected Area Management in China   288
Bibliography   290
Index   304

Figures

3.1	Illustration of the relationships between use, conservation and preservation	43
3.2	Typology of conflicts among the three pillars of ecology, equity and economy	49
5.1	Recreational visitation to all national park units (1904–2010)	93
5.2	Number of units of the National Park System and national parks by decade (1872–2013)	94
5.3	Recreational visits to units of the National Park System per year (1979–2014)	95
5.4	Enacted budgets of the NPS and their percentages in federal outlays (fiscal years 2000–14)	97
5.5	Photo of a private house constructed on inholdings in Zion National Park	103
6.1	The process of determining appropriate uses in the National Park System	123
7.1	The geographic map of the Merced River and Yosemite National Park	146
8.1	The hierarchy of legislative documents in China	159
8.2	Classification of primary functional zones and their functions in China	174
9.1	Tourism revenues and their percentage of GDP in China (2000–13)	181
11.1	Visitors walking on the trails in Pudacuo National Park, September 2012	244
11.2	Institutional structure associated with the establishment and management of Pudacuo National Park	245
11.3	Income and tourist visitation of Pudacuo National Park (2005–11)	246
11.4	Perceptions of the relationship between national parks and other PAs in terms of biodiversity protection and income generation	250

Tables

2.1	Categorization of PAs (I–VI) by the IUCN-WCPA	18
2.2	Overview of different systems of public land designations in the US	23
2.3	Number and acreage of nature reserves in China (1956–2013)	32
2.4	Institutional structure of PA designation in China	33
2.5	The number and area of nature reserves, SHAs and forest parks, and their percentage of territorial area in China	35
2.6	Management of various types of nature reserves by different authorities (2009)	37
3.1	Classification of conflicts in PA designation and management	50
5.1	The status quo of regulations on motorized use within the National Park System (as of February 2013)	108
6.1	Comparison of the designated use patterns of four types of federal land designations	123
8.1	The typology of legislative documents in China	158
8.2	The types and formats of EIAs in China	163
9.1	Comparison of the average PA budget in selected countries	186
9.2	Sources of income in nature reserves and their respective percentages	188
9.3	Overview of the self-generated income of nature reserves and its percentage of total income	189
9.4	Different models of governance structure of SHAs in China	197
10.1	Comparison of designated use patterns among nature reserves, SHAs and forest parks	216
10.2	Number of judicial cases on PA-related issues, based on their causes of action	230
10.3	Number of letters and visits related to environmental issues in China (1996–2012)	236
11.1	Comparison between the models of SHAs, nature reserves and national parks envisioned in Yunnan	251
12.1	The main forms of conflict in PA management in the US and China	263

Cases

1	*Chevron USA, Inc. v. Natural Resources Defense Council, Inc.* (1984)	129
2	*United States v. Mead Corp* (2001)	130
3	*Southern Utah Wilderness Alliance v. Dabney* (1998)	130
4	*National Rifle Association of America v. Potter* (1986)	133
5	*Bicycle Trails Council of Marin v. Babbitt* (1996)	134
6	*Bluewater Network v. Salazar* (2010)	135
7	*National Parks Conservation Association v. Jewell* (2013)	136
8	*Fund for Animals v. Babbitt* (1997)	139
9	*Fund for Animals v. Norton* (2003)	140
10	*International Snowmobile Manufacturers Association (ISMA) v. Norton* (2004)	140
11	*Fund for Animals v. Norton* (2004)	141
12	*Greater Yellowstone Coalition v. Kempthorne* (2008)	142
13	*Grand Canyon Air Tour Coalition v. FAA* (1998) *(Grand Canyon I)*	144
14	*US Air Tour Association v. FAA* (2002) *(Grand Canyon II)*	145
15	*Friends of Yosemite Valley v. Norton* (2002) *(Yosemite I)*	147
16	*Friends of Yosemite Valley v. Scarlett* (2006) *(Yosemite II)*	148
17	*Friends of Yosemite Valley v. Kempthorne* (2008) *(Yosemite III)*	148
18	*Wang et al. vs. The Government of Lin'an City* (2003)	231
19	*All-China Environment Federation (ACEF) vs. the Lihu Lake and the Huishan Mountain Management Committee of Wuxi City* (2012)	232
20	*Shi and Gu vs. the Urban Planning Bureau of Nanjing* (2001)	232
21	*Jin Kuixi vs. the Bureau of Urban Planning of Hangzhou City* (2003)	233

Abbreviations

ACEF	All-China Environment Federation
ALL	Administrative Litigation Law (China)
APA	Administrative Procedure Act (US)
BAT	Best Available Technology (US)
BLM	Bureau of Land Management (US)
CBD	Convention of Biodiversity
CCCPC	Central Committee of the Communist Party of China
CPC	Communist Party of China
DOA	Department of Agriculture (US)
DOI	Department of Interior (US)
ECBP	European Union – China Biodiversity Program
EFZ	Ecological Functional Zoning (China)
EFZs	Ecological Functional Zones (China)
EIS	Environment Impact Statement (US)
EPL	Environmental Protection Law (China)
ESA	Endangered Species Act (US)
FLPMA	Federal Land Policy and Management Act (US)
FONSI	Finding of No Significant Impact (US)
FWS	Fish and Wildlife Service (US)
FYP	Five-Year Plan (China)
ICJ	International Court of Justice
ISMA	International Snowmobile Manufacturers Association
IUCN	International Union for Conservation of Nature and Natural Resources
LL	Legislation Law (China)
LWCF	Land and Water Conservation Fund
MoC	Ministry of Construction (China)
MoEP	Ministry of Environmental Protection (China)
MoHURD	Ministry of Housing and Urban-Rural Development (China)
MoLR	Ministry of Land and Resources (China)
MUSYA	Multiple-Use, Sustained-Yield Act (US)
MP	Management Policies (US)
NEPA	National Environment Protection Agency (China)
NEPA	National Environmental Protection Act (US)
NFMA	National Forest Management Act (US)
NPC	National People's Congress (China)
NPCA	National Park Conservation Association

NPMO	National Park Management Office (Yunnan, China)
NPS	National Park Service (US)
NRA	National Recreation Area (US)
NRAA	National Rifle Association of America (US)
NWPS	National Wilderness Preservation System (US)
OECD	Organization for Economic Co-operation and Development
ORRC	Outdoor Recreation Review Commission (US)
ORV	Off-road Vehicles
PA	Protected Area
PEFZ	Primary Ecological Functional Zone (China)
PFZ	Primary Functional Zoning (China)
PIL	Public Interest Litigation
PNPMB	Pudacuo National Park Management Bureau (China)
PRC	People's Republic of China
RMB	Renminbi
SCNPC	Standing Committee of the National People's Congress (China)
SD	Sustainable Development
SDPC	State Development Planning Commission (China)
SEPA	State Environmental Protection Administration (China)
SFA	State Forestry Administration (China)
SFAR	Special Federal Aviation Regulations (US)
SHA	Scenic and Historic Area (China)
SPC	Supreme People's Court (China)
SPPC	Supreme People's Procuratorate (China)
STA	State Tourism Administration (China)
UN	United Nations
UNESCO	United Nations Educational, Scientific, and Cultural Organization
UNWTO	United Nations World Tourism Organization
USA/US	United States of America
US$	United States dollar
USFS	United States Forest Service (US)
VERP	Visitor Experience and Resources Protection (US)
WSRA	Wild and Scenic River Act (US)
YMMC	Yellow Mountain Management Committee (China)

Preface and Acknowledgments

My academic interests in the fields of environmental governance and natural resources law could be traced back to the period of my master studies when I chose the 'public trust doctrine' in the US as the topic of my master's dissertation. Since then, I have been deeply attracted by how the relationship among the government, the public and the property can be arranged under a delicately designed and effectively enforced legal system, and how the government can and should play a role when governing nature-and-environment-related matters. Meanwhile, studying in the capital city of China, Beijing, I strongly feel that China can never deviate from the trend of internationalization and globalization, and the Chinese legal system is no exception. I started to ponder how the two countries, namely the US and China, may establish a dialogue and communicate with each other on those issues that have enchanted me since my master's studies. During the period of my doctoral research at the Erasmus China Law Center (ECLC) at the Erasmus School of Law (ESL) of Erasmus University Rotterdam, I chose the comparative perspective between the US and China on their public land and protected area systems as the topic of my research. These four years' studies in the Netherlands provide me with a unique perspective to stand 'outside' China and observe the country's ongoing transition process and its accompanying problems. Insightful academic training and communication with scholars and experts from Europe and the US further provide me with ample knowledge and experiences from the outside world to draw lessons for China.

I am honored to be accompanied and helped by many people during the long march of completing this book. My particular appreciation first goes to my two supervisors at ESL, Professor Roel de Lange and Professor Yuwen Li. Without their constant encouragement and inspiring supervision, I could not have explored this research field with so much freedom and independence. Special thanks go to Professor Yuwen Li, who has taken care of me and other Chinese PhD students wholeheartedly. From her, I obtained not only the knowledge of legal studies, but also the wisdom of living a life, the courage of facing uncertainties and the enthusiasm of exploring the unknown. Her insights in Chinese law and her diligent scholarship will benefit me in my future academic career.

I would like to give my deep appreciation to my supervisor, Professor Zhang Shuyi, during my master's studies. His persistent academic pursuit, especially his insightful perspectives of social transformation in China and its dynamic interaction with Chinese law, has significantly influenced my way of thinking when conducting my doctoral research. His inconceivable courage and perseverance in combating illness have greatly inspired and encouraged me to have a brave heart regardless how enormous the difficulty may be.

I am deeply grateful to Professor Robert Fischman and Professor Robert Keiter for their great help and care during my visit to the US. Many thanks for receiving me at their universities on the basis of a plain email written by a student like me whom they had never met. This trust is definitely a great encouragement to a young researcher who is on her way to pursue her academic career. I spent the happiest Thanksgiving and Halloween ever due to the warm reception by Professor Fischman, his family and friends.

There are many people in and around the ESL to whom I owe my sincere gratitude: Professor Maarten Kroeze who has decisively welcomed Chinese PhD candidates with the fellowship from the CSC and thus provided me with this gorgeous opportunity to pursue my studies in the Netherlands, Professor Suzan Stoter, the current Dean of the ESL, who has provided great care and support to Chinese PhD students, Professor Martijn Scheltema and Professor Aletta Blomberg who are members of the inner committee and have kindly approved my dissertation, Professor Lodewijk Rogier, Professor Michael Faure, Professor Elaine Mak, Dr. Nick Efthymiou, Dr. Joke de Wit and other colleagues at my department. Great appreciation also goes to Professor Liu Daqun, Professor Chris Backes and Professor Martin de Jong who sat in my defense committee and raised marvelous questions at my defense.

I would also like to give my deep appreciation to Professor John Nagle at Notre Dame University, Professor Ben Boer at the University of Sydney, Professor Jean-Bernard Auby at SciencePo, Professor Colin Reid at Dundee University, John Zinda at Brown University, Professor Cai Shouqiu and Professor Qin Tianbao at Wuhan University, and others whom I have met on different occasions, for their kind help with my research.

I am deeply grateful to those legal scholars, administrative officials, NGO staff members and lawyers who provided me with great assistance and generously shared their experiences and opinions with me during my field studies in both China and the US, especially Professor Yang Shilong and Mr. Wang Jiangang from Kunming University of Science and Technology, Ms. Jin Tong and Ms. Wang Yue from TNC, Ms. Leslie Crossland and Mr. Jim Ireland from the NPS, and Ms. Erika Pollard and Ms. Cory MacNulty from the NPCA.

I am also grateful to Professor Robert Fischman and Professor Qin Tianbao for their kind comments on some chapters of this book. Furthermore, Alison Kirk at Ashgate Publishing has showed her great patience and support in bringing this book out.

I am lucky to have met many friends from China, Europe, the US and elsewhere. Your company has made my life abroad warm, colorful and memorable. My deepest appreciation goes to my father Ma Minghua, my mother Gao Chunyan, my sister Ma Xiaobo and my husband Zhao Shiheng. Thank you for your unconditional love, unparalleled understanding and perpetual support. This book is written for you.

While acknowledging the great help of many, any errors and deficiencies that remain are my sole responsibility.

August 2015
Beijing, China

1 Introduction

> Everyone needs to play, and to play out of doors. Without parks and outdoor life all that is best in civilization will be smothered.
>
> Enos Mills[1]

Research Topic

Nature, gifted with grandeur and a bounty of resources, has long been revered by human beings and continually shaped by our footprints. The way we perceive nature and our current interactions with nature have changed significantly over the past century. Nature demonstrates different facets: it is not only a reservoir of resources for conventional commodity use but also a popular tourist destination, a pleasurable playground, a laboratory for scientific research, a wildlife paradise, a basis of world heritage and a revenue generator for local economies.[2] The demand for various uses of nature has increased and diversified. This situation has produced a transformative process for public land[3] that has continued to the present day. Two dominant features of this transformation process can be identified across different jurisdictions: one feature is an increase in public awareness of nature conservation and the other is an increase in recreational demands and the accompanying blossoming of the tourism industry.

In terms of the first feature (i.e. conservation awareness), environmental protection has become a foundational tenet of the current political, social and legal discourses at the international and domestic levels.[4] To protect the natural landscape from derogating behaviors by humans, particular geographic areas are carved out of the public domain and receive dedicated protection. This idea underpinned the establishment of Yellowstone National Park in 1972 in the United States (US), which was the first national park in the world. Since then, the designation of protected areas (PAs) has emerged and become a dominant and effective conservation tool worldwide.[5] In terms of the second feature (i.e. the boom of recreation

---

1 Enos Mills, *Your National Parks* (Boston, MA: Houghton Mifflin, 1917), p. 379.
2 Eight facets of the national park idea in the US are displayed by Robert Keiter in his book *To Conserve Unimpaired: The Evolution of the National Park Idea* (Washington, DC: Island Press, 2013). He describes national parks as 'Nature's Cathedrals', 'A Pleasuring Ground', 'The Nation's Playground', 'A Commercial Commodity', 'Ancestral Lands', 'Nature's Laboratory', 'Fountains of Life' and 'A Vital Core'.
3 This book particularly focuses on public land. For a discussion of the ownership structure in China and clarification of the research scope, see pp. 28–9 of Chapter 2.
4 This is featured by adopting 'sustainable development', which will be discussed in Chapter 3 (see pp. 51–7).
5 See generally Barbara Lausche, *Guidelines for Protected Areas Legislation* (Gland, Switzerland: IUCN, 2011), and Alexander Gillespie, *Protected Areas And International Environmental Law* (Leiden and Boston, MA: Martinus Nijhoff Publishers, 2007).

2 Introduction

and tourism), recreational use, including traditional activities such as hiking, camping and fishing, and new activities such as kayaking and snowmobiling, has emerged as a crucial component of the overall public land use pattern. This boom has occurred not only in developed countries such as the US but also in developing countries such as China, as indicated by the burgeoning nature-based tourism markets in both countries.[6] Numerous activities collectively make tourism 'the largest industry on the planet'.[7]

The transformation of public land-use patterns presents challenges to PA managers, who must manage various expectations to shape nature, accommodate different interests and claims to use nature and reconcile potential conflicts. Natural resources in PAs are usually subject to common access; they are managed collectively and are interrelated with the ecological process.[8] Due to these features, different uses of nature may physically interact and unavoidably compete with each other in both temporal and spatial dimensions. Therefore, trade-offs are needed to balance the allocation of different uses of public lands. The three most important types of uses that have tilted this balance are commodity use, conservation use and recreational use.[9]

Various dynamics exist in the interactions among these three types of uses. Conservation and recreation have demonstrated a symbiotic relationship. Recreation was the foundation of the original constituencies for the idea of national parks, which can be observed in the case of the US. A well-conserved environment is the basis for sustainable tourism development and guarantees the quality of recreational experiences.[10] Therefore, a coalition has been formed between conservationists and recreationists against the exploitative commodity use of nature. For example, both groups may oppose the construction of dams for energy purposes because dams may not only cause ecological derogation but also deprive whitewater enthusiasts of rafting. However, this traditional coalition has gradually collapsed due to the emergence of mass recreation and industrial tourism. Recreational overuse and high-impact recreational use, particularly motorized recreation, have had considerably negative impacts on the surrounding environment. Relentless people pressure coupled with advances in recreation technology make conservationists increasingly cautious about escalating recreational demand. Moreover, recreationists have also been greatly divided, especially between low-impact recreational users, such as hikers and bird watchers, and high-impact recreational users, such as off-road vehicle drivers and snowmobilers. For example, snowmobile users may destroy snow trails previously used by skiers, and swimmers may lose access to rivers if these waters are designated for whitewater rafting.

Partly to mitigate the potential conflicts arising from different uses of nature, modern conservation law has focused on the management and regulation of the use of PA resources. Exploitative use is categorically prohibited or intensively regulated within PAs. Attempts have been made to control, decrease, or even eliminate some forms of recreation. To realize

---

6 For discussions of the recreational use pattern and nature-based tourism markets in the US and China, see *infra* Chapters 5 and 9.

7 John Terborgh et al., *Making Parks Work: Strategies for Preserving Tropical Nature* (Washington, DC: Island Press, 2002), p. 383. Statistical information about the tourism industry around the world is available at the United Nations World Tourism Organization, http://www2.unwto.org/. Last visited January 2015.

8 Aagaard identifies three features of environmental resources, i.e. they are public, physical and natural, and pervasively interrelated, in order to show that environmental problems are intrinsically conflicts between different uses instead of a traditional perception of 'environmental harm'. See Todd Aagaard, 'Environmental Harms, Use Conflicts, and Neutral Baselines in Environmental Law', 60.7 (2011) *Duke Law Journal*, pp. 1505–64.

9 For a clarification of different sets of terms such as 'use, preservation and conservation' and 'recreation and tourism', see *infra* pp. 41–3 of Chapter 3.

10 For a discussion about 'sustainable tourism' at length, see *infra* p. 57 of Chapter 3.

these goals, some legal and managerial instruments have been broadly adopted across different jurisdictions, such as environmental impact assessments, environmental standards and permits, the delineation of carrying capacities and setting caps on visitor numbers.

However, designing and implementing a regulatory framework that can satisfy all stakeholders is no easy task. The key to regulation lies in deciding which forms of recreational use are appropriate, as well as the scale and degree to which a proposed type of use is permissible. Any activity may unavoidably have an impact on the natural environment. Therefore, the baseline of regulation is 'how much intrusion upon the untrammeled ecosystem we are prepared to tolerate'.[11] Different groups have their own preferences for delimiting such a baseline. As a result, disputes about what constitutes appropriate and sustainable use and how management authorities should behave in making such a judgment flourish.

Conflicts may not only arise from competing claims to the use of nature but also from different objectives and goals that PAs must serve. In addition to providing ecosystem services, PAs may serve development goals, such as economic development, poverty alleviation and the improvement of local livelihoods, especially in developing countries.[12] On the one hand, tourism benefits are deemed the most environmentally friendly way to contribute to local economies, mitigate the financial loss of local communities and improve local communities' livelihoods. On the other hand, the designation and management of PAs may cause 'people–park conflicts', which manifest in the resentment of local communities toward PA designation and the enforcement of conservation law.[13] Strict regulations of traditional uses of natural resources by local communities may deteriorate these communities' livelihoods. Increasing numbers of visitors may deprive local communities of access to and control of natural resources. An unbalanced distribution of tourism benefits and conservation burdens may marginalize the local population and create injustice. To solve these problems, some fundamental inquiries need to be made: should nature be preserved for its intrinsic value per se, or should it serve human needs and development goals? How should human beings be situated in natural settings?

Old problems and new challenges are intertwined, making the issue of PAs a battlefield. The effective management of conflicts in PAs calls for a robust, adaptive and resilient application of the law. The kernel of the law lies in identifying potential uses, recognizing potential conflicts, determining a designated use pattern based on the selection and assessment of values, regulating uses and managing conflicts that arise from the uses of PA resources. Aagaard argues that 'environmental law is better understood as a way of managing conflicting uses of environmental resources'[14] and proposes the 'use-conflict' framework as 'a way of organizing thinking about environmental problems and lawmaking'.[15] In the context of this 'use-conflict' framework, the types of uses and conflicts, the regulatory patterns and the ways that disputes are adjudicated may be similar or different in different jurisdictions. Thus, the degree to which conflicts may be effectively managed and resolved may differ under different domestic legal frameworks.

This book chooses the US and the People's Republic of China (hereinafter, China) as two examples of jurisdictions for comparative study. Both countries have designated a variety

---

11 Joseph Sax, 'Fashioning a Recreation Policy for Our National Parklands: The Philosophy of Choice and the Choice of Philosophy', 12 (1979) *Creighton Law Review*, p. 974.
12 Lea Scherl et al. (eds.), *Can Protected Areas Contribute to Poverty Reduction?: Opportunities and Limitations* (Gland, Switzerland and Cambridge: IUCN, 2004).
13 For general discussion of people-park conflicts, see *infra* p. 48 of Chapter 3. For a discussion of people–park conflicts in the context of China, see *infra* pp. 205–8 of Chapter 9.
14 Todd Aagaard, *supra* note 8, p. 1507.
15 Ibid., p. 1527.

of PAs across their considerably vast territories. Abundant natural and scenic resources have created many recreational opportunities, together with burgeoning nature-based tourism markets in both countries. As the flagship designation of American public land, the concept of the national park has evolved for more than a hundred years in the US. The National Park Service, the federal management agency of the National Park System, celebrates its centennial in 2016. Winks claims that the American National Park System is the 'most complex, the most carefully articulated, and thus the most specific system in the world'.[16] In addition to accumulating abundant experience in the management of national parks, the US offers a great opportunity to examine how its legal system for national parks is structured: 'Legislation passed with respect to the [National Park System] . . . whether generic to the system as a whole or specific to an individual unit, has more extensive application than any other park system in the world.'[17] Congressional statutes, agency regulations and management policies, and judicial case law have shaped the conservation and recreation patterns of national park lands.

In China, a complicated conservation scheme has been formulated since the 1950s. The opening up of China since the 1980s has led to a great liberation of the economy and a blossoming of the tourism industry. The tremendous transformation of China in the last two decades at the economic, societal and political scales provides fresh insights for the current research. In addition to its 'economic miracle', China has astonished the world with its serious environmental problems that have been exposed in recent decades.[18] Committed to fighting environmental deterioration and creating a green economy, the Chinese government has hastened its pace of environmental law making. PA designation, nature conservation, biodiversity protection and the maintenance of ecological security have gained considerable weight in the political agenda. However, because China has a poor reputation for its rule of law and lacks a legal culture in general, it continues to struggle to translate the letter of the law into practice. Ingrained problems accumulated during decades of legal practice cannot be resolved overnight. There is still a long way to go and much to learn. These are the preliminary contexts and perspectives for the comparative studies that follow.

In addition to filling the gap in the literature on comparative legal studies between the US and China on domestic PA law, this research intends to add to the literature (1) a sustainability test of tourism in terms of realizing sustainable development in PAs, and (2) the application of the institutional theory advocated in the field of statutory interpretation in framing and analyzing PA law.

First, the principle of sustainable development has been broadly endorsed at the international level and has become a paradigm for legislation and policy making on the economy, society and the environment.[19] There is a need to examine whether sustainable development can be a governing legal principle in the field of PA management and whether it may be used as a comparative benchmark for assessing the legal foundations of both the US and China. Considering the blossoming of the recreational use of PA resources, the need to conduct sustainability tests in the field of tourism also arises. Closely linked to the tourism industry and

---

16 Robin Winks, 'The National Park Service Act of 1916: "A Contradictory Mandate"?', 74.3 (1997) *Denver University Law Review*, p. 576.
17 Ibid.
18 There is no need to provide more evidence, as the serious problem of air pollution is obvious. Heavy haze dramatically engulfs parts of Northern China, including Beijing, in the beginning of 2013, and this situation continues until now. For a vivid depiction, see Brian Stallard, 'See the Heavy Haze That is Choking China', October 29, 2014. Available at http://www.natureworldnews.com/articles/9946/20141029/see-heavy-haze-choking-china.htm. Last visited January 2015.
19 For more discussion on the principle of sustainable development, see *infra* p. 51 et seq. of Chapter 3.

environmental justice appeals, recreation in PAs involves three pillars upon which the concept of sustainable development is based: the environment, the economy and society. Therefore, this situation facilitates an integral perspective with which to examine the realization of sustainability in PA-based tourism activities. By examining tourism policy making and practices in PAs in the US and China, this book adds to the literature on how the sustainability test can be processed in the field of tourism development and how to translate sustainable tourism into a legal principle that governs tourism-related decision making in PAs.

Second, the effective management of conflicts by law can be a co-effort by different legal institutions. Legislatures, agencies and equivalent government institutions (hereafter, agencies) and courts may be the three most recognizable key players, although the roles of other institutions such as the legal profession and civil society may also be vital. The interactions among the three institutions occur on various scales, one of which is the interpretation of statutes. To facilitate the flexibility of administration, discretion may be delegated to agencies by congressional statutes. When conducting the balance exercise required by sustainable development, law-enforcement bodies must construct and interpret statutes to weigh different interests. When making judicial judgments, courts may take a hard look at agencies' discretionary decision making, or choose to defer to agencies out of respect for their profession. Therefore, when analyzing conflict management and resolution in law, institutional interactions among legislatures, agencies and courts cannot be overlooked. To approach a normative way of thinking about how institutions should be structured in managing conflicts, the institutional theory of statutory interpretation proposed and elaborated by Vermeule[20] can provide clarity. This theory outlines variables of institutional construction and proposes a 'formalism' of statutory interpretation that may have methodological implications for the current research. This book is an attempt to adopt the institutional dimension and to analyze how legislatures, agencies and courts interact with each other in managing and resolving conflicts that arise from PAs in domestic contexts.

Research Questions and Sub-questions

Various forms of conflicts have arisen due to PA designation and management. Legal frameworks are structured in the US and China to manage and resolve conflicts in their domestic contexts. Adopting a comparative perspective, this book aims to answer the following research question: *how are conflicts between conservation and recreation in PAs managed and resolved in the legal regimes of the US and China through institutional interactions among legislatures, agencies and courts, and how should these conflicts be managed and resolved?*

The central research question can be further broken down into three sub-questions:

1   What roles do recreation and tourism play in shaping the use-conflict framework of PA designation and management? Before examining the legal frameworks and instruments that facilitate conflict resolution, a preliminary step is to examine the factors that give rise to conflicts in PAs and the resulting forms of conflicts. This requires the identification of potential uses of nature, the interaction between different uses, the consequences of this interaction, and different stakeholders and their respective interests. How recreation and tourism shape the use pattern of nature and invoke the generation of conflicts is the starting point for analyzing how these conflicts can be managed and resolved by the law. The identification of this role is also the premise for placing tourism under the

---

20 For more discussion on the institutional theory of statutory interpretation, see *infra* pp. 65–6 of Chapter 3.

6 *Introduction*

sustainability test, namely, examining why recreation and tourism entail the need for a sustainability test and what stakes must be integrated and balanced in a sustainable development framework.

2   What are the main forms of conflict in PAs in the US and China? How did their current statuses evolve? The formulation of conflicts in PAs is situated in domestic social-economic contexts. The structure of the legal system also has a decisive influence on the format of conflicts, for example, what is written in statutes and who has the authority to interpret these statutes. Investigation of the main forms of conflicts and their evolutionary processes reveals why different legal instruments and approaches are employed by the two countries to address their respective problems.

3   How and to what degree is the resolution of conflicts achieved through institutional interactions mainly among legislatures, agencies and courts? How should a desirable legal framework be designed from an institutional perspective? Based on the institutional approach developed by theoretical analysis, follow-up questions involve examining how conflicts are addressed by each institution, namely, what legislatures say, how statutes are interpreted and implemented by agencies and how courts interpret statutes and review agencies' actions. The distinctive capacities and limitations of each institution can be identified, and the way the current legal framework adjudicates and resolves conflicts can be assessed. Based on this identification and assessment, a desirable legal framework that optimizes the interactions between different institutions can be proposed based on domestic contexts.

In addition to approaching the answers to these three questions by comparative studies, a further concern of this research lies in the extent to which China can learn from the experiences of the US. The respective contexts of the two countries are assessed by identifying the unique features and conditions of each country's approach. The transferability of the US's experiences is examined based on the divergences observed in comparative studies and the variables related to these divergences.

Methods and Materials

The methodologies applied in this book are mainly classic legal analysis, comparative legal study and field study.

Classic legal analysis is used to analyze how the legal system may provide a common ground for conflict resolution in PA management. The focus of legal analysis is how different institutions, particularly legislatures, agencies and courts, interpret statutory language and how their interpretations interact with each other. To serve this purpose, congressional statutes, legislative records and intent statements, agency regulations and rules, policy documents and judicial cases are reviewed for both countries. In the context of the US, some common-law doctrines, such as the public trust doctrine, are also discussed.

In addition to a review of legal documents and literature, field studies were conducted for this research. During my visit to China in September 2012, I visited Yunnan Province with a focus on its pilot project of introducing the 'national park model' to China. I joined a guided tour to the site of Pudacuo National Park, the 'first' national park in China. In a semi-structured way, I interviewed some governmental officials, staff members working at operation enterprises, non-governmental organizations (mainly The Nature Conservancy) and several local residents. These conversations helped me to better understand the concerns and pursuits of different organizations and individuals and their perceptions of each other.

My previous findings obtained from the literature review were verified and sharpened. I also obtained some unpublished materials from the interviewees. The methods that I adopted in this field study and the materials I obtained will be discussed further in Chapter 11.

During my second visit to China in August 2014, I visited several nature reserves and scenic and historic areas located in Fujian Province. My intention was to better understand the role of tourism in local governments' policy-making agendas and the relationship between PA authorities and local communities. I interviewed various people from management agencies for nature reserves, investment companies in scenic and historic areas, tourism departments within local governments, real estate companies and several local residents. Conversations with these people provided me with some intuitive knowledge on how the tourism economy is promoted at the local level and how tourism benefits are generally distributed among the government, companies and local residents. This first-hand information is not available in publications. The knowledge I obtained from this visit is largely presented in Chapter 9, in which the dominant forms of conflicts in PA management in China are discussed, especially those conflicts that arise between conservation authorities and local communities.

During my visit to the US from September 2013 to February 2014, I interviewed legal scholars, officials working for the National Park Service, national park superintendents,[21] environmental organizations (mainly the National Park Conservation Association) and some gateway community members. Updated information and materials about the on-the-ground management of national parks were obtained. I learned how NGOs interacted and worked with the National Park Service and local communities and what their concerns and pursuits were when bringing about lawsuits or starting negotiations. This knowledge assisted me in deepening and verifying my understanding from the literature review.

With regard to comparative studies, some clarifications are necessary. Regarding their functions, the comparative studies on conservation laws and policies conducted in this book can have informative as well as critical functions: they not only assist in knowledge and system building but also may help in determining better laws and providing tools for the critique of law.[22] With regard to the process of comparison, Kamba identified three phases: the description of norms, concepts and institutions; the identification or discernment of differences and similarities, and the explanation of the identified divergences and resemblances.[23] In his detailed review of comparative constitutional law, Hirschl classified four types of comparative inquiries:

1   Freestanding and descriptive inquiry into a single country with little or no reference to comparable practices in other countries;
2   Comparative references that aim to find 'the best' or most suitable rule through 'analogy, distinction and contrast' across legal systems;

---

21 Leslie Crossland was then the Superintendent of the Golden Spike National Historic Site and Jim Ireland was then the Superintendent of Timpanogos Cave National Monument in Utah. Both of them have worked at other national park units as well.
22 When examining the functional method of comparative law, Ralf Michaels summarizes seven functions: (1) the epistemological function of understanding legal rules and institutions, (2) the comparative function of achieving comparability, (3) the presumptive function of emphasizing similarity, (4) the formalizing function of system building, (5) the evaluative function of determining the better law, (6) the universalizing function of preparing legal unification, and (7) the critical function of providing tools for the critique of law. See Ralf Michaels, 'The Functional Method of Comparative Law', in Mathias Reimann and Reinhard Zimmermann (eds.), *The Oxford Handbook of Comparative Law* (Oxford: Oxford University Press, 2006), p. 363.
23 Walter Joseph Kamba, 'Comparative Law: A Theoretical Framework', 23.3 (1974) *The International and Comparative Law Quarterly*, pp. 511–12.

3 'Concept formation through multiple descriptions' of the same phenomena across different countries, and
4 Controlled comparison and inference-oriented case selections that aim to generate or support causal arguments and explain the observed phenomena.[24]

The current research is mainly motivated by the second type of inquiry: the search for a plausible solution to improve the legal framework of China by emulating pertinent mechanisms developed elsewhere. This aim more or less echoes the utilitarian function of comparative studies, which is to extend and enrich the 'supply of solutions'.[25] Baker stated that a comparative approach can provide a laboratory for evaluating alternative policy options to similar problems and can allow us to hold a mirror to the national context of those 'apparent success stories'.[26] This statement applies to the current research.

With regard to the selection of the US as a comparative sample, a general selection principle of a 'prototypical case', in Hirschl's words, is adopted.[27] As the birthplace of the concept of national parks, the US has become a 'flagship' country in PA studies. The US-based national park concept has not only gained great popularity in the US but also flourished worldwide. The American people are often proud to claim that national parks are the 'best idea' that they ever had.[28] Given the country's considerably complex and developed legal framework of national park management and its enshrinement of the rule of law in a constitutional context, it seems that the US has much to offer as an 'apparent success story'. With the aim of seeking a 'supply of solutions', this research is predominantly China-oriented and aims to learn from the US example to solve Chinese problems. Nevertheless, it is conceivable that the research could lead to legal and policy recommendations that might be relevant to the US.[29]

Of course, there is a commensurability problem.[30] Due to differences in the political regimes, social contexts, legal development and even languages of the two nations, salient differences can be easily found in terms of the domestic legal and regulatory frameworks of PAs. For example, although the linguistic problem is common in a comparative context, it becomes more salient in the context of nature conservation between the US and China. One of the core concepts in American conservation law – 'wilderness' – remains largely an American phenomenon. A parallel translation cannot be easily found in Chinese or in other languages such as Japanese or French.[31] Considering these contextual differences, questions remain regarding how the current research can yield a meaningful comparison.

---

24 Ran Hirschl, 'On the Blurred Methodological Matrix of Comparative Constitutional Law', in Sujit Choudhry (ed.), *The Migration of Constitutional Ideas* (Cambridge: Cambridge University Press, 2007), pp. 40–47.
25 Konrad Zweigert and Hein Kötz, *An Introduction to Comparative Law* (Oxford: Oxford University Press, 1998), p. 15.
26 Randall Baker (ed.), *Environmental Law and Policy in the European Union and the United States* (Westport, CT: Praeger, 1997), pp. 6–7.
27 Hirschl summarizes five principles of case selection in inference-oriented comparative studies, which are the 'most similar cases' principle, 'the most different cases' principle, the 'prototypical cases' principle, 'the most difficult cases' principle and the 'outlier cases' principle. See Ran Hirschl, *supra* note 24, pp. 47–58.
28 Wallace Stegner, 'The Best Idea We Ever Had', 46 (1983) *Wilderness*, pp. 4–13 ('National parks are the best idea we ever had. Absolutely American, absolutely democratic, they reflect us at our best rather than our worst.')
29 See *infra* section 'Conclusions' of Chapter 12.
30 About the commensurability problem, see generally Nicholas Robinson, 'IUCN as catalyst for a law of the biosphere: acting globally and locally', 35.2 (2005) *Environmental Law*, p. 281.
31 J. Baird Callicott, 'Contemporary Criticisms of the Received Wilderness Idea', in David Cole et al. (eds.), *Wilderness Science in a Time of Change: Changing Perspectives and Future Directions* (Ogden, UT: US Department of Agriculture, Forest Service, Rocky Mountain Research Station, 2000), p. 24. For more discussions on the idea of wilderness in the US, see *infra* pp. 116–17 of Chapter 6.

Comparison in this book is premised on the 'universality of problems', which is the basis for the functional method of comparative law.[32] Notwithstanding contextual differences, similar problems arise across jurisdictions regarding how to effectively manage conflicts that arise from PA designation and management by law. An ideal and unique model of conservation law that is universally applicable to different countries may not exist. The choice of a legal system is largely context-specific. Nevertheless, lessons can still be learned regarding how similar problems are addressed in different domestic contexts.

This research also conducts comparative inquiries classified as the third type by Hirschl, namely, 'thick concept' formation through multiple descriptions of the same phenomenon across different countries. Through the comparison (albeit a limited and selective comparison) of conflict generation and conflict management in PAs between the US and China, some basic concepts can be formulated and tested, such as 'conflict', 'conflict management' and 'institutional interaction'. These 'thick' concepts formulated in the current research may inform audiences on a broader scale about the rationale for a specific phenomenon.

The current research aims not only to describe phenomena but also to explain them. Instead of stating what happens, it is more important to show the way that things happen.[33] In this book, effort is devoted to understanding the laws and policies of the US and China by connecting them to their social-economic contexts. As will be elaborated in Chapter 12, specific contextual elements are identified to explain the divergences that are found between the US and China. However, this can only be a first step. No complete inventory or comprehensive analysis can be achieved. The present study aims to clarify the factors that might be relevant in comparative studies. In this sense, the current research is not systematically inference-oriented, the fourth type of comparative inquiry classified by Hirschl. Nonetheless, the clarification of these relevant factors still has merit because it can indicate the potential risks of legal borrowing and transplantation. These risks have become explicit in the transplantation of the concept of 'national parks' into China.[34] In addition to being considered the 'best idea' by Americans, national parks are also claimed to be an 'American paradigm'.[35] Previous literature has shown that 'the American model is more often than not inappropriate and difficult to implement in less developed countries.'[36] The current comparative studies may verify the presumed uniqueness of the American national park model and the plausibility of transplanting it into other contexts.

Limitations and Areas for Future Study

First, the selection of the US and China as comparative samples may be challengeable. Some skeptical concerns may be rooted in an antagonistic attitude toward the methodology of comparative studies itself. The differences between the US and China in terms the development of their legal systems are so huge that a problem of comparability may emerge during the research. This is intensively reflected in the asymmetry of the available literature, legislative documents and judicial cases in the two countries. Nevertheless, the ongoing legal development

---

32 Ralf Michaels, *supra* note 22, pp. 368–9 (the author notices that 'comparability is attained through the construction of universal problems as *tertia comparationis*').
33 Randall Baker, *supra* note 26, p. 7.
34 For more details, see *infra* Chapter 11.
35 Denise Antolini, 'National Park Law In The US: Conservation, Conflict, And Centennial Values', 33 (2009) *William and Mary Environmental Law and Policy Review*, p. 859.
36 M.I. Jeffrey, 'National Parks and Protected Areas – Approaching the Next Millennium', (1999) *Acta Juridica*, p. 163.

10 *Introduction*

in China and the progress China has made can be observed. The Chinese legal system is undergoing a remarkable process of modernization and rationalization.[37] This process has occurred throughout the period of this research project. The decisions adopted by the Communist Party of China in 2014 that enthusiastically embrace the idea of national parks can be considered a vital step toward changing the landscape of PA designation in China. The establishment of an environmental chamber within the Supreme People's Court in 2014 shows a gratifying judicial commitment to dispute resolution in environmental issues. The amendment to the Environmental Protection Law with substantive changes became effective in 2015.[38] Addressing the latest legal developments in China and comparing them with the legal system of the US may add value to the current research because this examination may contribute to updating obsolete previous studies, indicating the trends in legal development in China and better understanding current Chinese problems. Nevertheless, it is recognized that other jurisdictions' experiences may also be beneficial to China, such as some European countries and some developing countries that share similar development problems with China. This can be a potential field for further studies, whose findings may also be beneficial and enlightening to further the development of China.

Second, the selection of field study sites and the coverage of interviewees are mainly based on the accessibility of information and on my contacts. There is a lack of cooperation with academia in Chinese bureaucracies that makes field studies difficult and unavoidably limited. Given this selective choice of field study samples, the observations reflected in this book may be partial or even inaccurate. However, the empirical studies in this research do not aim for quantitative data collection or to provide a comprehensive picture of the status quo of PA management in China and the US. These studies are mainly used to complement the literature review and provide updated information. In this sense, these field observations may add value.

Third, with regard to the research on China, limitations emerge from the potential exclusion of legal documents and inaccuracies in the statistical data. There is an absence of an environmental code, and administrative regulations undergo constant and inconsonant amendments in China. Not all governmental documents are publicly accessible, even though a legal mandate requires them to be available.[39] Although many databases can be utilized, no single method can guarantee that all applicable regulations are identified or whether a given version of a regulation is the most updated.[40] Furthermore, statistical data are incomplete and sporadic. There may also be inconsistencies in the data collected, which may negatively influence the conclusions. Nevertheless, this research has made every effort to minimize these limitations. All published and publicly accessible official documents released by the central authority on PA management were examined. The sections relating to the management of nature reserves and other types of PAs in various yearbooks in China were consulted. Data from different sources were double-checked and compared to ensure their reliability. Online sources, particularly media coverage, were used to illustrate the problem and provide the most updated information.

Finally, although this book ambitiously targets all types of PAs in the US, the discourse is focused on national parks. This selective discussion may have negative effects on the conclusions from a comparative perspective. For example, national parks are a federal product.

---

37 See generally Bin Liang, *The Changing Chinese Legal System, 1978–Present: Centralization of Power and Rationalization of the Legal System* (New York: Routledge, 2008).
38 For these latest developments, see *infra* Part III, Country Studies of China.
39 State Council, 政府信息公开条例 (Regulations on the Disclosure of Government Information), May 1, 2008.
40 Charles McElwee, *Environmental Law in China: Mitigating Risk and Ensuring Compliance* (New York: Oxford University Press, 2011), p. 14.

The fact that the management of refuges and forests may face more pressure from local interests may make this subject more meaningful for comparison between the US and China because the central-local relationship in managing PAs is problematic in China. Other types of public land designations in the US, such as national wildlife refuges and national forests, can be potential fields for future studies.

The Structure and Design of the Research

This book is structured in three parts in addition to the introduction and conclusion.

Part I provides the conceptual and theoretical frameworks of the book. It consists of two chapters. Chapter 2 provides a conceptual framework of PAs to bridge the gap in a terminological sense and to facilitate the comparative studies that follow. It first reviews the history of the designation and development of PAs at the international and regional levels. Then, the schemes of PAs and the institutional structures of PA management in the US and China are examined under their current legal and regulatory frameworks. Finally, a conceptual framework for this book is provided with some clarifications.

Chapter 3 provides a theoretical framework and has three objectives. First, to facilitate the examination of how conflicts are resolved in the US and China, the factors that contribute to the rise of these conflicts, the rationale for different types of conflicts and the merits of conflict management are elaborated. Second, to identify the necessity and plausibility of a sustainability test for tourism, the principle of sustainable development and its associated principles of sustainable tourism and ecotourism are analyzed. Whether these principles can serve as comparative benchmarks for assessing the legal foundations of the US and China and how they can contribute to conflict resolution are examined. Third, in the analysis of how conflicts are resolved under domestic legal regimes, the institutional theory of statutory interpretation is elaborated to identify how institutional interactions, mainly those among legislatures, agencies and courts, can affect conflict resolution. Whether this theory has methodological implications in the construction of PA law and conflict resolution in PA management is also examined.

Part II and Part III present separate country studies. They are devoted to discussing the current legal and policy frameworks of PAs and the main forms of conflicts arising from PA designation and management. In addition, the way such conflicts are addressed within the framework of institutional interaction among legislatures, agencies and courts is elaborated, and whether such interactions have resulted in a desirable resolution of conflicts is examined.

Part II, the country study of the US, consists of four chapters. Chapter 4 reviews the current legal and regulatory frameworks that govern the management of national parks and other types of public land designations in the US. Chapter 5 presents the transformation of public land use patterns and the regulatory framework for recreational activities. The main forms of conflicts arising from such a transformation are identified and discussed. Particular attention is paid to the role of recreational use in invoking these conflicts. Chapter 6 discusses how statutes and agency policies adjudicate conflicts between conservation and recreation and the degree to which a solution is achieved. It first analyzes three types of statutes that Congress has enacted for national park management, the Organic Act, modern environmental statutes and enabling acts. The way that conflicts between conservation and recreational are adjudicated in these three types of statutes is examined with a particular focus on how the latter two types of statutes influence the application of the Organic Act. The chapter then discusses how the management policies issued by the NPS interpret the purpose statement of the Organic Act and restate the non-impairment standard prescribed therein. Chapter 7 analyzes how the

12 Introduction

courts interpret congressional statutes, evaluate agencies' interpretations of these statutes, and choose the deference standard in reviewing agencies' management decisions. Symbolic cases in the application of the Organic Act are examined to determine whether there is established case law on how the Organic Act should be read. Several high-profile and long-lasting national park-related litigations are discussed to illustrate the role the courts may play in resolving highly political policy conflicts.

Part III is composed of four chapters regarding the country study of China. Chapter 8 reviews the legal, regulatory and policy frameworks of PA management in China and discusses the ongoing controversies over the enactment of the Natural Heritage Law. Chapter 9 discusses the evolution of tourism policies and the dominant forms of conflict in PA management. The chronic problem of funding shortfalls and the resulting consequences are discussed. Particular focus is given to how China's current economic development model has influenced the generation of conflicts. Chapter 10 first reviews the legal instruments provided by the law to adjudicate and reconcile conflicts and then discusses the compliance and enforcement of law in practice. Reasons for the implementation gap and potential solutions are explored. Finally, the role of courts in solving PA-related disputes is scrutinized. The predicament of the courts in fully playing their role is analyzed. Recent developments such as the establishment of environmental courts and the opening of public interest litigation are critically reviewed. Chapter 11 is mainly based on field observations of the pilot project for national parks promoted in Yunnan Province. It aims to explore how different actors involved in the project have co-shaped the blueprints of national parks and how the national park model is translated into practice. It also examines the way the experiences and lessons gained from this pilot project can inform ongoing efforts to escalate the designation of national parks in China.

Chapter 12 provides comparative observations between the US and China by identifying the convergences and divergences between them. Variables for each domestic context are examined to explain why there are divergences and how these divergences emerge. Findings and conclusions are presented based on the research questions proposed above. Finally, legal and policy recommendations for China are provided.

Part 1
Conflicts in Theory
Concepts, Institutions and Rationale

2 Schemes of Protected Areas
Historical, Structural and Institutional Perspectives

Introduction

To study protected areas (PAs) in the US and China, a preliminary step is necessary to clarify several concepts and definitions. This chapter approaches these issues from the perspective of internationally accepted terminology and then examines whether there are differences between US and Chinese law and how these differences can be addressed.

First, the history of the designation and development of PAs at the international and regional levels is reviewed. The definition and categorization of PAs as formulated by the International Union for Conservation of Nature and Natural Resources (IUCN) is particularly emphasized. This section also discusses how the system of PAs embodies the idea of the intentional shaping of nature and reflects different management philosophies based on different degrees of naturalness and human intervention. Second, the schemes for PAs in the current legal and regulatory frameworks of the US and China are examined. This section examines the histories of public land conservation and PA designation in the two countries and investigates how their conservation policies have evolved over time and how the institutional frameworks of PA management were formulated. Due to differences in land tenure and governmental structures between the two countries, the schemes of PAs in the US and China are quite complex, with various titles and governance structures. To clarify these structural differences, the procedures and authorities for PA designation are also discussed. The conceptual framework used in this book is provided in the summary.

The Intentional Shaping of Nature: From National Parks to Protected Areas

Definitions

The intentional shaping of natural landscapes can be traced to the ancient history of human beings. It is said that the Persians established the first 'parks' in the world. These parks were known as '*paradeisoi*' in Greek, a term that has evolved into the modern word 'paradise'.[1] Parks were born out of the idea of revering the awesomeness and grandeur of nature. This idea was epitomized by the establishment of the first national park in the world, Yellowstone, in 1872.[2] The American idea of designating a parcel of land and separating it from human intervention provided the world with the so-called 'Yellowstone Model'.[3] Since then, national parks and other types of special designations have successively emerged. In different regimes,

---

1 Barry Strauss, *Salamis: The Greatest Naval Battle of the Ancient World, 480 B.C.* (London: Arrow, 2005), p. 45.
2 Details of the history of national parks in the US will be provided *infra* in on pp. 24–5 of Chapter 2.
3 About the distinctiveness of the Yellowstone Model, see *infra* pp. 44–6 of Chapter 3.

a variety of titles for these designations have been adopted, such as parks, reserves, natural sites, sanctuaries, wildlife refuges and wilderness areas, to name a few examples in English. The designation of areas with specific protected status has become the most broadly applied conservation tool around the world.[4] A multi-layered regulatory framework at the national, regional and international levels with a particular focus on designating various types of protected areas has been formulated.

At the international level, the Convention Concerning the Protection of the World Cultural and Natural Heritage adopted in 1972 was an important milestone. This convention used the concept of 'world heritage' to selectively inscribe sites of 'outstanding universal value', which is a high threshold.[5] With the aim of wetland conservation and the 'wise use' of wetlands and wetland resources, the Convention on Wetlands of International Importance, Especially as Waterfowl Habitat (the 'Ramsar Convention'), which became effective in 1975, established a list of 'Wetlands of International Importance'.[6] The United Nations Educational, Scientific and Cultural Organization (UNESCO) launched the Man and the Biosphere Programme in the early 1970s. This initiative established the World Network of Biosphere Reserves, which currently consists of 631 'biosphere reserves' in 119 countries.[7] In 1992, the Convention on Biological Diversity (CBD) was adopted at the 'Rio Earth Summit' and came into force in 1993. It addresses the pressing problems of the 'conservation of biological diversity, the sustainable use of its components and the fair and equitable sharing of the benefits arising out of the utilization of genetic resources'.[8] The designation of a system of protected areas to achieve the objectives stated above is deemed the responsibility of each contracting party.[9]

Agreements and networks have also been established at regional levels. Examples are the Convention on Nature Protection and Wild Life Preservation in the Western Hemisphere of 1940, the Convention on the Conservation of Nature in the South Pacific of 1976 and the Association of South East Asian Nations Agreement on the Conservation of Nature and Natural Resources of 1985. In the European context, a series of regional conventions have been established, including the Convention on the Conservation of European Wildlife and Natural Habitats of 1979 (the 'Bern Convention') and the European Landscape Convention of 2000 (the 'Florence Convention'). Two directives have been issued by the Council of Europe: Council Directive 79/409/EEC on the Conservation of Wild Birds of 1979 and the Council Directive 92/43/EEC on the Conservation of Natural Habitats and of Wild Fauna and Flora of 1992. These are commonly known as the 'Bird' and 'Habitat' directives. The 'Natura 2000 Network' was subsequently established based on these two directives. Two specific sites were designated under the Natura 2000 Network: the Special Protection Areas for birds and Special Areas of Conservation for other species and habitats.[10]

---

4 See generally Alexander Gillespie, *Protected Areas And International Environmental Law* (Leiden and Boston, MA: Martinus Nijhoff Publishers, 2007); Nigel Dudley (ed.), *Guidelines for Applying Protected Area Management Categories* (Gland, Switzerland: IUCN, 2008).
5 See Preamble of the Convention. Full text is available at http://whc.unesco.org/archive/convention-en.pdf. Last visited January 2015.
6 The concept of 'wise use' is specifically adopted in the Ramsar Convention. See Articles 2, 3 and 6 of the Convention.
7 UNESCO, *World Network of Biosphere Reserves* (WNBR), available at http://www.unesco.org/new/en/natural-sciences/environment/ecological-sciences/biosphere-reserves/world-network-wnbr/. Last visited January 2015.
8 Article 1 of the CBD.
9 Article 8 of the CBD.
10 For more information, see European Commission, 'Natura 2000 Network', available at http://ec.europa.eu/environment/nature/natura2000/index_en.htm. Last visited January 2015.

The fact that there is a multi-layered conservation framework has resulted in thematic overlap, with overlapping jurisdictions and management objectives, a diversity of designations and confusing acronyms. This situation has been described as 'a sea of incompatible frameworks and paradigms',[11] and has created difficulties in determining benchmarks and standards for comparative purposes. To solve these problems, proposals have been made to unify the concepts and develop a categorization scheme that is internationally applicable. The most remarkable achievement in this regard is the definition and categorization of PAs developed by the IUCN, which has gained international recognition.[12] In 1962, at the first World Parks Congress, it was recommended that the Commission on National Parks and Protected Areas (now the World Commission on Protected Areas (WCPA)) and the IUCN establish an internationally applicable classification of terms for national parks and equivalent reserves. The definition and classification of PAs was subsequently addressed at the Second World Parks Congress in 1972, the third one in 1982 and the fourth one in 1992.[13] After thirty years of elaboration, in 1994, the *Guidelines for Applying Protected Area Management Categories* were finally published by the IUCN. After a slight revision in 2008, the current definition of a PA provided by the IUCN is as follows: 'A clearly defined geographical space *recognized*, *dedicated* and *managed* through legal and other effective means, to achieve the *long-term conservation of nature* with associated ecosystem services and cultural values' (emphasis added).[14]

PAs are thus defined in a strict sense. The IUCN explicitly states that only those areas whose main objectives are to 'achieve the long-term conservation of nature' can be deemed PAs. Other objectives can also be achieved, such as ecosystem services and cultural values, but they should not 'interfere with the aim or outcome of nature conservation'.[15] This means that in the case of conflict, nature conservation should be the priority.[16]

Categories and Categorization

In addition to providing the definition of PAs, the IUCN has formulated a matrix of the categorization of PAs that ranges from Category I to VI and identifies different management objectives (Table 2.1 below). Generally, the degree of naturalness decreases and the extent to which the area is open to human intervention (such as use and management activities) increases in conjunction with the categories I to VI. A 'national park' is categorized in Category II of PAs. The primary objective of national parks is to 'protect natural biodiversity along with its underlying ecological structure and supporting environmental processes, and to promote education and recreation'. 'Other objectives' of national parks include 'to manage visitor use; to take into account the needs of indigenous people and local communities; and to contribute to local economies through tourism'.[17] These objectives differ from those in Category I, which aim for strict preservation, including 'strict nature reserves' and

---

11 See Alexander Gillespie, *supra* note 4, p. 29.
12 Several international inventions have adopted the IUCN's categorization of PA, such as the CBD. The United Nations Environment Programme World Conservation Monitoring Centre (UNEP-WCMC) uses the 2008 definition of PA for the World Database on Protected Areas (WDPA), available at http://www.protectedplanet.net/. Last visited January 2015.
13 Nigel Dudley, *supra* note 4, pp. 3–4; and Alexander Gillespie, *supra* note 4, pp. 29–30.
14 Nigel Dudley, *supra* note 4, p. 8.
15 Ibid., p. 9.
16 Ibid., p. 10.
17 Ibid., p. 16.

18 Conflicts in Theory

'wilderness areas'. Moreover, national parks will not generally allow resource uses that are permitted in Category VI, except for subsistence or minor recreational purposes.[18] In other words, the categorization of 'national parks' ranges in the middle of the conservation spectrum elaborated by the IUCN.

Several titles of categories in this table can also be found in domestic laws, such as national parks, national monuments and wilderness areas in American law, and national parks and monuments in British law.[19] Although different jurisdictions have legislated with the same title, these designated areas may not necessarily fall into the same category of PAs according to the IUCN's criteria. Areas with the same title of 'national parks' may be managed in different ways by different nations. This is reflected in the classification of these areas into the PA categories by the IUCN. Scholars generally observe that 'most of the area protected in North America falls into Category II', whereas 'most of the area protected in Europe falls into Category V or VI.'[20] For example, all 15 national parks in the United Kingdom are classified and managed in accordance with Category V (protected landscape/seascape).[21] Units of the National Park System in the US are classified into different categories ranging from I to V based on the different management objectives of each unit.[22] In contrast, Pudacuo National Park in China, which will be discussed in Chapter 11, has not yet been classified as a separate PA unit.

The IUCN's definition of PAs provides a conceptual common ground that facilitates a comparison between different jurisdictions. Its categorization matrix also provides a benchmark to contextualize some easily-taken-for-granted concepts, such as national parks.[23] A preliminary step for establishing a comparative framework is therefore to contextualize existing types of designations into the general scheme of PA studies.

Table 2.1 Categorization of PAs (I–VI) by the IUCN-WCPA

Category	Title	Description
Ia	Strict nature reserves	• Strictly protected areas • Set aside to protect biodiversity and also possibly geological/geomorphological features, where human visitation, use and impacts are strictly controlled and limited to ensure protection of the conservation values • Can serve as indispensable reference areas for scientific research and monitoring
Ib	Wilderness areas	• Large unmodified or slightly modified areas • Retain their natural character and influence, without permanent or significant human habitation • Protected and managed so as to preserve their natural condition
II	National parks	• Large natural or near-natural areas • Set aside to protect large-scale ecological processes, along with the complement of species and ecosystems characteristic of the area

---

18 Ibid., p. 17.
19 See National Parks and Access to the Countryside Act 1949, 1949 c. 97 (Regnal,12_13_and_14_Geo_6); and Ancient Monuments and Archaeological Areas Act 1979, 1979 c. 46.
20 Federico Cheever, 'British National Parks for North Americans: What We Can Learn from a More Crowded Nation Proud of Its Countryside', 26.2 (2007) *Stanford Environmental Law Journal*, p. 252.
21 Nigel Dudley, *supra* note 4, p. 11.
22 As will be shown on p. 26, the National Park System consists of more than twenty types of designations in the US. They cover a broad range of categories of PAs according to the IUCN's standard.
23 This is of particular importance considering the fact that there have been practices in China at local levels to introduce the national park model based on the IUCN's categorization. For more details, see *infra* Chapter 11.

Table 2.1 (continued)

		• Provide a foundation for environmentally and culturally compatible spiritual, scientific, educational, recreational and visitor opportunities
III	National monuments or features	• Set aside to protect a specific natural monument, which can be a landform, a seamount, a submarine cavern, a geological feature such as a cave, or even a living feature such as an ancient grove • Generally quite small protected areas that often have high visitor value
IV	Habitat/species management areas	• Protect particular species or habitats, and management reflects this priority • May need regular, active interventions to address the requirements of particular species or to maintain habitats (not a requirement)
V	Protected landscapes/ seascapes	• Interaction of people and nature over time has produced an area of distinct character with significant ecological, biological, cultural and scenic value • Safeguarding the integrity of this interaction is vital to protecting and sustaining the area and its associated nature conservation and other values
VI	Protected areas with sustainable use of natural resources	• Conserve ecosystems and habitats, together with associated cultural values and traditional natural resource management systems • Generally large, with most of the area in a natural condition, where a proportion is under sustainable nature resource management and where low-level non-industrial use of natural resources that is compatible with nature conservation is seen as one of the main aims of the area

Source: Adapted from Nigel Dudley[24]

The Scheme of Protected Areas in the US

The US has not incorporated the term 'PA' into its legal framework. This does not necessarily mean that there is no American PA law. PA is mostly discussed in the framework of public land and natural resource law in the American context. National parks, the 'crown jewels' of federal landholding,[25] are deemed the flagship of American PAs. However, 'national parks are merely the tip of the federal iceberg.'[26] Currently, American public lands are mainly classified into five categories managed by four federal agencies in two executive departments.[27] At the state and local levels, states and local municipalities may designate PAs, such as state and city parks, refuges and forests, based on state and local laws. Considering the diversity of state law and practices in the US, the research in this book mainly focuses on federal land, though PAs designated below the federal level are occasionally discussed for complementary purposes. In terms of federal land, not all public land designations fit into the definition of PAs provided by the IUCN. For example, some federal forests are mainly designated for timber production instead of nature conservation. These forests cannot be deemed PAs according to the IUCN criteria.[28] In the following text, 'PAs' and 'public lands' are used interchangeably, with a focus on public lands that solely or partly serve the purpose of nature conservation.

24 Nigel Dudley, *supra* note 4, pp. 13–23.
25 George Coggins, Charles Wilkinson and John Leshy, *Federal Public Land and Resources Law* (New York: Foundation Press, 2007), p. 1.
26 Ibid.
27 See *infra* p. 21 et seq.
28 For more discussion on the difference between a forest and a forest PA, see Nigel Dudley, *supra* note 4, pp. 52–3.

Conflicts in Theory

The Evolution of Public Land Policies: An Introductory Remark

The evolution of public land policies in the US is well chronicled. In short, it has undergone four distinct stages: acquisition, disposal, retention and intensive management.[29]

Acquisition (Birth of the US)

The formation of the geographical territory of the US is a history that abounds with the acquisition of lands from original colonies, foreign nations, American Indian tribes, the State and private landowners through treaties, conquests and purchases.[30] All these acquisition activities have resulted in both federal ownership and sovereignty over what is now known as the 'public domain'.[31] The acquisition of the public domain during the years from 1781 to 1867 accounted for 81 percent of all US land. It also created thirty American states that are commonly known as 'public land states'.[32]

Disposal (Nineteenth Century)

During the nineteenth century, a disposal policy was embraced to promote settlement and development in the West. Private ownership of land and resources was the core element of the national land strategy during this period. A series of statutes were enacted to serve this purpose, such as the Homestead Act of 1862 and the General Mining Law of 1872. The principle of 'first in time, first in right'[33] was adopted to allocate the vast West of this newly born nation. This policy was rooted in the idea of inexhaustible natural bounty, and flaws gradually manifested. Dubbed the 'Great Barbeque' in the West, this policy was accompanied by the depletion of resources such as timber and wildlife. Therefore, the necessity of an adjustment to the national land policy was gradually recognized.

Retention (1872–1964)

With the end of the nineteenth century approaching, and the emergence of the Progressive Movement, government ownership of land and resources was promoted in accordance with the Progressive idea that government better served as a guardian of the public welfare and interests.[34] Some observers stated that 'progressivism, as applied to natural resources through

---

29 Jan G. Laitos and Thomas A. Carr. 'The Transformation on Public Lands', 26.2 (1999) *Ecology Law Quarterly*, p. 147; James Huffman, 'The Inevitability of Private Rights in Public Lands', 65 (1994) *University of Colorado Law Review*, pp. 245–54, and Robert Keiter, 'Public Lands and Law Reform: Putting Theory, Policy, and Practice in Perspective', 3 (2005) *Utah Law Review*, p. 1131. For a discussion about the history of public lands development, see Paul Wallace Gates and United States Public Land Law Review Commission, *History of Public Land Law Development* (Washington, DC: Government Printing Office, 1968).
30 Paul Smyth, 'Conservation and Preservation of Federal Public Resources: A History', 17 (2002) *Natural Resources & Environment*, p. 77.
31 About the relationship between property and sovereignty, especially in terms of American tribal property, see Joseph Singer, 'Legal Theory: Sovereignty and Property', 86 (1991) *Northwestern University Law Review*, pp. 1–56.
32 Bureau of Land Management, 'Public Land Statistics (2012)', June 2013, p. 3. Available at http://www.blm.gov/public_land_statistics/pls12/pls2012-web.pdf. Last visited January 2015.
33 Robert Keiter, *supra* note 29, p. 1132.
34 Samuel Hays, *Conservation and the Gospel of Efficiency: the Progressive Conservation Movement, 1890–1920* (Cambridge, MA: Harvard University Press, 1959), pp. 122–46 and 261–76. Cited from Robert Keiter, *supra* note 29, p. 1134.

its conservationist offshoot, was so central to the history of the federal land management agencies.'[35] The goal of efficiency exalted in the Progressive Era subsequently influenced the management philosophy for public lands. By adopting a series of congressional legislations, the federal government began to set aside parts of the public domain as specially protected areas, such as national parks, national monuments and wildlife refuges. The first national park, Yellowstone, was established by Congress in 1872. The first national forest, Shoshone (part of what was then called the 'Yellowstone Timberland Reserve'), was created by Congress in 1891. The first national wildlife refuge, Pelican Island, was established by an executive order in 1903. Through the specific designation of PAs, the traditional culture of 'land alienation and consumptive use in American history' was seriously challenged.[36] In 1934, with the passage of the Taylor Grazing Act, the lands that are now managed by the Bureau of Land Management were intentionally removed from herding, settlement and grazing and placed under federal control. This marked the waning of the era of public land disposal.

Intensive Management (1964–present)

Once the federal government retains ownership of federal lands, it must allocate them among competing uses. During the 1960s, when the environmental movement emerged in the US, intensive management activities began to take place on public lands, including resource use and visitor management. This trend was accompanied by a series of environment-related legislations enacted by Congress, such as the Wilderness Act of 1964, the National Environmental Policy Act of 1969, the Endangered Species Act of 1973 and the Clean Water Act of 1977.[37] These congressional statutes reflected a growing federal commitment to public land and natural resource conservation.

The path of the evolution of public land policies in the US is illustrated by remarkable events and the enactment of symbolic legislation. The advent of each distinctive era reflects changing values and norms regarding public land, including its function in fulfilling national purposes and its relation to nature conservation.

The Current Institutional Framework of Public Land

Public lands are now mainly legislated in four distinct systems: the National Park System, the National Forest System, the National Wildlife Refuge System, and remaining public lands that do not fall into any of the former three systems. Public land management institutions were established somewhat later than were the different types of public land designations.[38] These four public land systems are now governed and managed by the National Park Service (NPS), the United States Forest Service (USFS), the Fish & Wildlife Service (FWS), and the Bureau of Land Management (BLM), respectively. Among these four agencies, the USFS is affiliated with the Department of Agriculture (DOA) and the remaining three are operated under the Department of Interior (DOI). The directors/chiefs of these four agencies are nominated by the president and approved by the Senate.

---

35 Robert Nelson, 'The Federal Land Management Agencies', in Richard Knight and Sarah Bates (eds.), *A New Century for Natural Resources Management* (Washington, DC: Island Press:1995), p. 42.
36 Lary Dilsaver (ed.), *America's National Park System: The Critical Documents* (Boston, MA: Rowman & Littlefield, 1994), Chapter 1 'The Early Years, 1964–1918', available at http://www.cr.nps.gov/history/online_books/anps/index.htm. Last visited February 2015.
37 For more details of environmental statutes enacted during this period, see *infra* Chapter 4.
38 Robert Nelson, *supra* note 35, p. 40.

22   Conflicts in Theory

Currently, these four agencies administer approximately 95 percent of the approximately 650 million acres of federally owned lands.[39] Each of them is given distinctive authority for public land management.[40] To carry out this authority, each agency has formulated its own management policies and built its own constituencies, for example, outdoor recreationists and the NPS, timber companies and the USFS, hunters and the FWS, and oil and gas enterprises and the BLM.

In addition to the designations shown above, which are managed by parallel federal agencies, there are other types of designations of public lands. The most prominent designations are wilderness areas and national recreational areas.

Wilderness Areas

The designation of 'wilderness areas' and the National Wilderness Preservation System (NWPS) were established by the Wilderness Act of 1964.[41] Unlike the National Park System or the Wildlife Refuge System, the NWPS is not managed by a single agency. If Congress designates a parcel of land as a 'wilderness area', the agency with jurisdiction over that parcel of land prior to the wilderness designation retains its management authority. The agency must manage the land in accordance with the purpose stated in the Wilderness Act. In other words, the Wilderness Act provides management authority to administer wilderness areas to the four federal agencies: the NPS, USFS, BLM and FWS.[42]

Statistics show that as of February 2015, there were 796 wilderness areas designated in the US. Among them, the USFS holds the most units (442), which accounts for 56 percent; the BLM holds 222 units (28 percent); the FWS holds 71 units (9 percent); and the NPS holds the remaining units (61), which accounts for 8 percent. In terms of size, more than 109 million acres of federal lands are protected by their wilderness status.[43] This equals approximately 4.5 percent of the nation's entire territory, which is as large as the state of California. Although this number is large, Congress is still criticized by wilderness advocates for its slow pace of wilderness designation.[44] This slow pace is apparent in the unsatisfactory record of wilderness designation by the 112th Congress (2011–13), which was the first since the 89th Congress (1965–67) not to protect a single acre of wilderness.[45] The only wilderness bill enacted into law by the 112th Congress reduced the acreage of a wilderness area by 222 acres.[46]

---

39 Kori Calvert et al., 'Recreation on Federal Lands', *Congressional Research Service Report for Congress*, RL33525, September 22, 2010, p. 1. Full text is available at http://cnie.org/nle/crsreports/10Oct/RL33525.pdf. Last visited April 2015.

40 For more discussion about each agency's management authority, see *infra* pp. 72–80 of Chapter 4.

41 16 USC §§ 1131–6. For more details, see *infra* pp. 80–2 of Chapter 4.

42 Originally, the Wilderness Act of 1964 did not include BLM lands in the wilderness inventory requirement. The Federal Land Policy and Management Act later added the wilderness use and inventory requirement onto BLM lands in 1976. See *infra* p. 124 of Chapter 6.

43 See Wilderness.net, 'Wilderness Statistics Reports', available at http://www.wilderness.net/NWPS/chart. Last visited February 2015. In 1980, Congress passed the Alaska National Interest Lands Conservation Act (16 USC §§ 3101–233). Over 56 million acres of lands in Alaska were designated wilderness areas that had doubled the size of the NWPS.

44 John D. Leshy, 'Contemporary Politics of Wilderness Preservation', 25.1 (2005) *Journal of Land, Resources & Environmental Law*, p. 1, and Sandra Zellmer, 'A Preservation Paradox: Political Prestidigitation and an Enduring Resource of Wildness', 34.4 (2004) *Environmental Law*, pp. 1017–18.

45 Max Greenberg, 'How Congress Dropped the Ball Again on Wilderness This Week', February 7, 2014, available at http://wilderness.org/blog/how-congress-dropped-ball-again-wilderness-week. Last visited February 2015.

46 P.L.112–97. For more details, see Katie Hoover, Kristina Alexander and Sandra Johnson, 'Wilderness: Legislation and Issues in the 113th Congress', Congressional Research Service R41610, April 17, 2014, p. 18. Full text is available at http://nationalaglawcenter.org/wp-content/uploads/assets/crs/R41610.pdf. Last visited February 2015.

National Recreational Areas

Along with the increasing conservation and recreational demands of public lands, Congress began to designate parcels of public lands primarily for recreational and conservation use.[47] Generally, extractive uses that may impede recreation and conservation are strictly controlled in such areas. The labels that Congress has used for these areas are diverse, such as national recreation areas, national scenic areas and national seashores. These areas are generically named 'National Recreation Areas' (NRAs).

Like the NWPS, NRAs may be managed by different agencies, including the NPS, the USFS and the BLM.[48] For example, the first NRA under the administration of the NPS, Lake Mead, was established in 1964, and the first NRA under the USFS, the Spruce Knob-Seneca Rocks NRA, was designated in 1965. Unlike the NWPS, NRAs are established by individual congressional statutes and are not systemized into one particular system. Furthermore, in the NWPS, the designation of wilderness areas has priority over existing designations, which means that these specific areas must be managed according to the standard prescribed by the Wilderness Act. In contrast, the designation of an NRA does not negate the application of existing generic laws. In this sense, NRAs cannot be deemed a *sui generis* system of separate designations that are distinguished from existing ones; instead, they are a loose combination of different designated areas with the same title or purpose. The five distinctive systems of public land designations are shown in Table 2.2.

Table 2.2 Overview of different systems of public land designations in the US

	Type	Management agency	Number of units	Acreage	Percentage (%)
Quadripartite public land systems	National park system	NPS	401	79,691,484	13.08
	National forest system	USFS	175	192,880,840	31.65
	National wildlife refuge system	FWS	820	88,948,699	14.60
	BLM lands	BLM	–	247,859,076	40.67
	Total			609,380,099	100
Other designation	NWPS	NPS, USFS, FWS and BLM	792	109,546,170	–

Source: USFS, FWS, and Ross Gorte et al.[49]

47 For more details of this tendency, see *infra* p. 92 et seq. of Chapter 5.
48 Since the FWS manages the national wildlife refuge system under a dominant use mandate, i.e. wildlife-dependent recreational use, there seems to be no necessity to designate special national recreational areas under the FWS. In practice, there is no such designation managed by the FWS. For a discussion of the dominant use mandate, see *infra* pp. 77–8 of Chapter 4.
49 The total units of National Forest System consist of 155 national forests and 20 national grasslands. The total units of NWRS consist of 561 National Wildlife Refuges, 209 Waterfowl Production Areas and 50 Coordination Areas. See USFS, 'About Us – Meet the Forest Service', available at http://www.fs.fed.us/aboutus/meetfs.shtml; FWS, 'Statistic Data Tables for Lands Under Control of the Fish and Wildlife Service', available at http://www.fws.gov/refuges/realty/archives/pdf/2013_Annual_Report_of_LandsDataTables.pdf. Other information is collected from Ross Gorte et al., 'Federal Land Ownership: Overview and Data', *Congressional Research Office Report for Congress*, R42346, February 8, 2012, p. 16. Available at https://www.fas.org/sgp/crs/misc/R42346.pdf. All were last visited in February 2015.

Shaping the National Park System: A Historical Perspective

This section focuses on the evolution of the National Park System. Three distinctive stages in this history can be identified: the birth of the concept of national parks, the establishment of the NPS, and the formulation of the National Park System.

The Birth of National Parks in the US (1872–1916)

In 1864, President Lincoln signed a bill granting to California the Yosemite Valley and land including the Mariposa Grove of Giant Sequoias to be held for the public 'in perpetuity'.[50] This bill was the basis for the idea of national parks and arguably created the first national park in the US,[51] though the first commonly acknowledged national park was Yellowstone National Park, designated by Congress in 1872.[52] Congress set aside more than one million acres as 'a public park or pleasuring ground for the benefit and enjoyment of the people'.[53] Unlike Yosemite, which was granted to the state of California, the territory of Yellowstone stretched over three different states: Wyoming, Idaho and Montana. The idea of designating an area as a 'national' park that enjoyed federal protection was thus born.

The birth of the concept of national parks was closely related to merchants and large enterprises. The designation of national parks in the West was expected to increase the transportation of eastern tourists by train. For example, Jay Cooke, who helped finance the Northern Pacific Railroad, and others who were related to the railroad business, proved to be influential during the establishment of Yellowstone.[54] National identity is also considered one of the incentives for the American establishment of national parks. The US, which was then a young country compared to its European ancestors, attempted to symbolize its unparalleled natural beauty in 'national parks' that would rival the monuments that Europe had developed.[55]

After Yellowstone, Congress continued this pattern. By the time the NPS Organic Act was passed in 1916, 14 national parks had been established.[56] However, the time span of 44 years (i.e. 1872–1916) indicates that the idea of national parks was not enthusiastically promoted within this period.

In addition to the designation of national parks, Congress explored other means to protect the scenic, historic and cultural treasures of the US. In 1890, Congress designated the first

---

50 Linda Greene, *Historic Resource Study (Yosemite: The Park and Its Resources; A History of the Discovery, Management, and Physical Development of Yosemite National Park, California)*, Washington, DC: US Department of the Interior/National Park Service, 1987, p. xxxvi.
51 Harmony Mappes, 'Comment. National Parks: For Use and "Enjoyment" or for "Preservation"? and the Role of the National Park Service Management Policies in That Determination', 92 (2007) *Iowa Law Review*, p. 604.
52 Aubrey Haines, *Yellowstone National Parks: Its Exploration and Establishment* (Washington, DC: US National Park Service, 1974).
53 Yellowstone National Park Act (1872), in Lary Dilsaver (ed.), *supra* note 36, Chapter 1.
54 Dennis Herman, 'Loving Them to Death: Legal Controls on the Type and Scale of Development in the National Parks', 11 (1992) *Stanford Environmental Law Journal*, p. 6; Harmony Mappes, *supra* note 51, p. 606; see also George Coggins and Robert Glicksman, 'Concessions Law and Policy in the National Park System', 74.3 (1997) *Denver University Law Review*, p. 731 (they mentioned the Northern Pacific Railroad was an enthusiastic booster of the Yellowstone bill because it foresaw that lots of people would need rail transport to visit the Yellowstone).
55 Nathan Scheg, 'Preservationists vs. Recreationists in Our National Parks', 5 (1998) *Hastings West-Northwest Journal of Environmental Law and Policy*, pp. 49–50, and William Shutkin, 'The National Park Service Act Revisited', 10 (1991) *Virginia Environmental Law Journal*, p. 351.
56 Harmony Mappes, *supra* note 51, p. 605. See also Benjamin Kline, *First Along the River: A Brief History of the US Environmental Movement* (Lanham, MD: Rowman & Littlefield, 2011), p. 68.

National Battlefield Park.[57] In 1906, Congress passed the Antiquities Act, which authorized the president to 'declare . . . objects of historic or scientific interest that are situated upon the lands owned or controlled by the Government of the United States to be national monuments'.[58] Compared to Congress's slow pace of designating national parks, the president showed more interest in exercising his power to designate national monuments. Within ten years, by 1916, 21 national monuments had been established by the president's executive orders.[59]

The Creation of the NPS and the Hetch Hetchy Debate (1916–70)

Many different designations occurred on public lands after the establishment of Yellowstone, and their management authority was scattered. For example, the management of national monuments was divided between the DOI, the DOA and the Department of War. This distribution was deemed uneconomical and inefficient.[60] The call for a consolidated federal institution to manage these scattered areas was consistently heard, beginning in the early 1900s.

In 1910, Richard Ballinger, the then-Secretary of the DOI, recommended in his annual report that Congress should create a 'bureau of national parks and resorts' to ensure the competent administration of parks.[61] In February 1911, President Taft recommended the establishment of a bureau of national parks as essential to the 'proper management of those wondrous manifestations of nature which were so startling and so beautiful that everyone recognizes the obligations of the Government to preserve them for the edification and recreation of the people'.[62] After three hearings before Congress in 1912, 1914 and 1916,[63] the NPS was finally created by the enactment of the Organic Act of 1916.[64]

The protracted process of creating the NPS was partly attributed to the Hetch Hetchy Valley debate.[65] This debate is considered the first national debate on nature preservation and a symbol of environmental activism. In 1908, San Franciscans proposed damming the Hetch Hetchy Valley inside Yosemite to provide a steady water and power supply. This proposal stirred controversy between utilitarians and preservationists. The frequently cited argument by the utilitarians that supported this bill was that 'only a few thousand people visited Hetch Hetchy every year, while nearly 500,000 San Franciscans were thirsty for the water the

---

57 Chickamauga and Chattanooga National Military Park, see http://www.nps.gov/chch/index.htm, last visited February 2015.
58 Section 2, Antiquities Act (1906), 16 USC §§431–3.
59 Harmony Mappes, *supra* note 51, p. 605. It is noteworthy that, in the judgment of *National Rifle Asso. v. Potter*, it was stated that by 1916, there were 13 national parks and 19 national monuments established in total (628 F. Supp. 903 (D.C. Court, 1986), p. 905).
60 Harlan Unrau and G. Frank Williss, *Administrative History: Expansion of the National Park Service in the 1930s* (Denver, CO: Denver Service Center, National Park Service, 1983), Chapter 2, Introduction, available at http://www.cr.nps.gov/history/-online_books/unrau-williss/adhi2.htm. Last visited February 2015.
61 Bills to Establish a National Park Service and for Other Purposes: Hearing on H.R. 434 & H.R. 8668 Before the House Comm. On the Public Lands, 64th Congress, 1st Session 3 (1916). See Robin Winks, 'The National Park Service Act of 1916: "A Contradictory Mandate"?', 74 (1997) *Denver University Law Review*, p. 585.
62 President William Howard Taft (February 11, 1911) in Hearing 1916. See Robin Winks, ibid., p. 586.
63 Ibid., pp. 587, 590, 594.
64 For more details of this Organic Act, see *infra* p. 72 et seq. of Chapter 4.
65 The influence of Hetch Hetchy Valley on the passage of the Organic Act is noted by many scholars. See Nathan Scheg, *supra* note 55, pp. 50–51; Richard Ansson and Dalton Hooks, 'Protecting and Preserving our National Parks in the Twenty First Century: Are Additional Reforms Needed Above and Beyond the Requirements of the 1998 National Parks Omnibus Management Act?', 62.2 (2001) *Montana Law Review*, p. 218, and Michael Mantell, 'Preservation and Use: Concessions in National Parks', 8.1 (1979) *Ecology Law Quarterly*, pp. 11–12.

26 Conflicts in Theory

Valley could provide.'[66] Preservationists, led by John Muir, believed that nature should be saved from destruction and human interference. In 1913, Congress passed a bill agreeing to flood the valley. Although preservationists lost the valley in this debate, the Hetch Hetchy debate greatly raised public awareness of nature conservation. Preservationists began to craft a more comprehensive scheme to better protect nature, leading to a successful lobby that passed the Organic Act, which established the NPS.

Shaping the National Park System: 1970 and Beyond

After establishing the NPS, the designation of national park units witnessed steady growth. Due to the government's reorganization in 1933, nearly fifty national military parks, national parks, battlefield sites and national monuments that were previously under the control of the Department of War were transferred to the DOI and placed under the NPS.[67] By 1970, 217 units were designated with different titles under the control of the NPS.[68] To unify management standards across different types of designations, Congress passed the General Authorities Act in 1970, which clearly established the National Park System and defined it as follows: 'any area of land and water now or hereafter administered by the Secretary of the Interior through the [NPS] for park, monument, historic, parkway, recreational, or other purposes'.[69]

The National Park System has developed into a complicated system of federally designated areas including more than twenty types of designations, including national battlefields, national lakeshores, national monuments, national reserves and others.[70] Within the 401 units, only 59 are called 'national parks'. The National Park System has evolved from 'the basic bipartite design of parks and monuments to a diverse taxonomy'.[71] There is no established rule to clarify each type of designation. Congress has discretion over designating a type to each unit. According to the nomenclature of the NPS, generally speaking, 'a national park contains a variety of resources and encompasses large land or water areas to help provide adequate protection of the resources', whereas 'a national monument is intended to preserve at least one nationally significant resource. It is usually smaller than a national park and lacks its diversity of attractions.'[72] Both Congress and the NPS have attempted to simplify the nomenclature and establish basic criteria for these titles.[73]

The expansion of the National Park System in terms of both number and size is considered to have been random and piecemeal. Scholars argue it has failed to deliver a unified federal commitment to nature conservation.[74] This can be further seen from the designation authorities and procedures discussed below.

---

66 Dennis Herman, *supra* note 54, p. 6; Michael Mantell, ibid., pp. 11–12, and Richard Ansson and Dalton Hooks, ibid., p. 218.
67 Harlan Unrau and G. Frank Williss, *supra* note 60, Chapter 2, 'C. Reorganization of 1933'.
68 NPS Statistics, 'Annual Summary Report (1970)', available at https://irma.nps.gov/Stats/Reports/National. Last visited February 2015.
69 Section 2 of the General Authorities Act of 1970.
70 For the twenty types of designations, see NPS, 'Units in the National Park System', available at http://www.nps.gov/news/upload/CLASSLST-401_updated-03-27-13.pdf. Last visited February 2015.
71 Robert Fischman, 'The Problem of Statutory Detail in National Park Establishment Legislation and Its Relationship to Pollution Control Law', 74 (1997) *Denver University Law Review*, p. 790 (he notes that the National Park System also includes a miscellaneous category for *sui generis* units such as the White House and Prince William Forest Park, Virginia).
72 NPS, 'Nomenclature of Park System Areas', available at http://www.nps.gov/parkhistory/hisnps/NPSHistory/nomenclature.html. Last visited February 2015.
73 Ibid.
74 Robert Keiter, *To Conserve Unimpaired: The Evolution of the National Park Idea* (Washington, DC: Island Press, 2013), p. 232.

Designation of PAs: Authorities and Procedures

The federal government may directly designate a parcel of public land as a particular type of PA, such as a national park. It can also acquire lands that are not owned by the federal government, such as state or privately owned lands, and designate them as federal PAs. A federally designated PA may include parcels of state-owned and privately owned land. As of September 2009, there were 84.3 million acres of land within the National Park System; 80.4 million were federally owned, and the remaining 3.9 million were privately owned or owned by other public bodies, such as states.[75] This patched ownership arrangement has created tension between different landowners.[76] The federal acquisition of land for designation purposes is mainly achieved through the Land and Water Conservation Fund (LWCF), created by the LWCF Act of 1965. The fund is derived from revenues from offshore oil and gas leases. It was created especially for federal and state governments to acquire land and water to preserve outdoor recreation resources.[77]

With regard to the national park designation, the NPS Organic Act is silent regarding the role of the NPS in expanding the National Park System.[78] As of 1978, when the Redwood Amendment to the Organic Act was passed, the NPS was required 'to investigate, study, and continually monitor the welfare of areas whose resources exhibit qualities of national significance and which may have potential for inclusion in the National Park System'.[79] The National Park Omnibus Management Act of 1998 further added that the NPS should not initiate new studies without specific congressional authorization.[80]

The designation of a unit within the National Park System is mainly accomplished by acts of Congress. The president was given the power to designate national monuments by the Antiquities Act of 1906, so the power to designate a national monument is shared between Congress and the president. Different administrations have shown different interests in designating national monuments. Several active presidents, such as Carter and Clinton, designated millions of acres of public lands as monuments, whereas other presidents, such as Nixon, Ford and Reagan, did not designate any parcels of land as national monuments.[81] Controversies arise regarding whether the president should be entitled to this discretion to dispose of large tracts of public land. On March 26, 2014, Republicans promoted a bill passed in a 222-to-201 vote in the House to amend the Antiquities Act by requiring that any presidential national monument designation of 5,000 acres or larger undergo public scrutiny.[82] Although it is unlikely that the Senate will endorse this bill and make it into law, there is a political

---

75 Carol Vincent, 'National Park System: Establishing New Units', *Congressional Research Service Report for Congress*, RS20158, July 22, 2010. Full text is available at http://crs.ncseonline.org/nle/crsreports/10Aug/RS20158.pdf. Last visited February 2015.
76 For more details, see *infra* p. 100 et seq. of Chapter 5.
77 §460 l–4.
78 Robert Keiter, *supra* note 74, p. 75.
79 16 USC. §1a–5.
80 National Parks Omnibus Management Act (title III, §303).
81 President Jimmy Carter (in office 1977–81) designated 15 national monuments up to 54,125,000 acres, and President Bill Clinton (in office 1993–2001) designated 19 national monuments up to 5,031,391 acres. The acreages of the designated monuments during the tenures of these two Presidents rank the top two among all Presidents in the US. For more information, see Senator Tom Coburn, 'PARKED! How Congress' Misplaced Priorities are Trashing Our National Treasures', www.novoco.com/.../resource.../coburn_parked_how_congress_misplaced . . . , October 2013, p. 15. Last visited January 2016.
82 See Ed O'Keefe and Juliet Eliperin, 'How Republicans are Using National Monuments to Fight President Obama', March 26, 2014, available at http://www.washingtonpost.com/blogs/the-fix/wp/2014/03/26/can-republicans-stop-obama-from-creating-national-monuments/?tid=pm_politics_pop. Last visited January 2015.

divergence, especially between Congress and the president, on the disposal of public land for conservation purposes.

The Scheme of Protected Areas in China

The Ownership Structure of Lands and Natural Resources: A Preliminary Context

Because the US section of this book focused on PAs designated as public lands, it is necessary to clarify the ownership structure of land and natural resources in China. Generally, there are two types of ownership with regard to land and natural resources: state ownership and collective ownership. Although private individuals are excluded from owning lands and natural resources, they may have the usufruct of and benefit from them.

The ownership of lands is mainly distinguished by their location, and the ownership of natural resources is distinguished by their type. In terms of lands, according to the latest amended Constitution in 2004:

> . . . lands in the cities are owned by the State, lands in the rural and suburban areas are owned by collectives except for those portions that belong to the State as prescribed by law, and house sites and privately farmed plots of cropland and hilly land are also owned by collectives. (Article 10)

In terms of natural resources, it is provided that

> . . . all mineral resources, waters, forests, mountains, grasslands, unclaimed land, beaches and other natural resources are owned by the State, that is, by the whole people, with the exception of the forests, mountains, grasslands, un-claimed lands and beaches that are owned by collectives as prescribed by law. (Article 9)

The general principle is that natural resources are owned by the State unless otherwise provided. Mineral resources and waters can only be owned by the State, whereas other areas, including forests, mountains, grasslands, unclaimed lands and beaches, can be owned by the State or by collectives.

The tenure structure of forest-related resources is more complicated. The Forest Law and its implementing regulations identify three types of forest-related resources: forests (森林), forestlands (林地) and forest woods (林木). The State or collectives may have ownership of all three types. Private individuals cannot have ownership of forests, but they can have usufruct of forestlands and ownership of forest woods.[83] Currently, state-owned forestland accounts for 42.45 percent of all forestland and is managed by state-owned forest enterprises and farms. Collectively owned forestland accounts for 57.55 percent, with diverse models of governance structures.[84]

The pattern of land ownership in PAs may be diversified. A PA may be totally state owned or totally collectively owned, or it may have a mixed ownership structure.[85] This pattern is the

---

83 NPC, 中华人民共和国森林法 (Forest Law of PRC), April 29, 1998, Article 3; State Council, 中华人民共和国森林法实施条例 (Implementing Regulations of the Forest Law of PRC), January 29, 2000, Article 2.

84 Li Ping and Zhu Keliang, *A Legal Review and Analysis of China's Forest Tenure System with an Emphasis on Collective Forestland* (Washington, DC: Rights and Resources Initiative, 2008), p. 7.

85 Li Jianquan et al., 我国自然保护区林权改革问题与对策探讨 (Problems and Counter-measures on Collective Forest Tenure Reform in the Nature Reserves in China), 12 (2009) 林业资源管理 *(Forest Resources Management)*, p. 3.

same case as the forest tenure in PAs. A survey conducted in 2007 showed that in all forest-type nature reserves[86] in China, there were 79,054.9 square kilometers collectively owned forestlands, which accounted for 6.52 percent of the total area of nature reserves. In some eastern provinces, such as Zhejiang and Fujian, this percentage could be as high as 74.66 and 80.13 percent, respectively.[87] In some nature reserves, forestlands were entirely owned by collectives, such as Huangsang in Hunan and West Eerduos Nature Reserves in Inner Mongolia.[88]

One can see from the statistics that collective ownership accounts for a considerable percentage of the overall ownership pattern of PAs. In practice, as a result of previous traditions, some collective lands and forests were designated as nature reserves without consulting relevant stakeholders and considering their interests. This situation resulted in numerous conflicts regarding how to clarify the ownership of lands and resources within PAs.[89] Furthermore, since the early 2000s, the central government has sponsored pilot projects and initiatives at the provincial level on 'collective forest tenure reform' (集体林权改革).[90] This reform, inspired by the Household Responsibility System (家庭联产承包责任制) in the agriculture field in the 1980s,[91] aimed to contract out collectively owned forestlands to individual households to enable and encourage them to operate forest-related resources. Due to this reform, there is an explicit discrepancy between those individual households that live within nature reserves and those outside of nature reserves regarding their capacities to benefit from forest products. Therefore, proposals have been made to initiate such reforms within nature reserves as well.[92]

Nature Conservation in the People's Republic of China: A Historical Review

The Establishment of the First Nature Reserve and Its Sluggish Development (1956–78)

The notion of protecting nature with a specific designation was born in the People's Republic of China (PRC, hereafter, China) in the 1950s. The first nature reserve, Dinghu Mountain Nature Reserve, was established in Guangdong Province by the approval of the State Council in 1956.[93] It was advocated by several scientists from the China Academy of Science who

---

86 For a discussion of different types of nature reserves and their respective management institutions, see *infra* pp. 36–8.
87 Liu Wenjing et al., 我国自然保护区集体林现状问题与分析 (Problems and Analysis of the Status Quo of Collectively Owned Forest Lands in Nature Reserves in China), 24.3 (2011) 世界林业研究 (*World Forestry Research*), p. 74.
88 Xu Jiliang et al., 'A Review and Assessment of Nature Reserve Policy in China: Advances, Challenges and Opportunities', 46.4 (2012) *Oryx*, p. 559.
89 For a discussion of such conflicts, see *infra* p. 205 et seq. of Chapter 9.
90 Jintao Xu, Andy White and Uma Lele, 'China's Forest Land Tenure Reforms: Impacts and Implications for Choice, Conservation, and Climate Change', *Rights and Resources Initiative*, 2010, available at http://www.rightsandresources.org/documents/files/doc_1403.pdf. Last visited February 2015.
91 It was first adopted in agriculture in 1981 and later extended to other sectors of the economy in China. The household responsibility system, which allows households to contract land, machinery and other facilities from collective organizations, replaces the production team system as the unit of production and income distribution. This institutional change resulted in remarkable growth in agricultural productivity. See generally Justin Yifu Lin, 'The Household Responsibility System in China's Agricultural Reform: A Theoretical and Empirical Study', 36.3 (1988) *Economic Development and Cultural Change*, p. 199.
92 Liu Wenjing et al., *supra* note 87, p. 75. For more discussion on the conflicts between nature reserve designation and local communities' development, see *infra* p. 205 et seq. of Chapter 9.
93 See Yao Jiawei, 第一个自然保护区50年"保卫战" (50 Years' 'Guardian War' for the First Nature Reserve), in 南方周末 (*Southern Weekly*), February 14, 2007, available at http://www.infzm.com/content/5913. Last visited April 2015.

30 *Conflicts in Theory*

were also deputies of the National People's Congress (NPC). Without a congressional mandate as there was in the US, only one announcement was posted in *Southern Daily* on June 23, 1956, stating that 'the Dinghu Mountain in Gaoyao County is a nature reserve; from now on, timber logging, hunting, smoking, firing and other activities would be prohibited in this area'.[94] The first nature reserve in China was thus born.

Following the designation of Dinghu Mountain, the Chinese government issued several rules to protect forest and wildlife resources. In October 1956, the Ministry of Forestry formulated the *Draft of Designating a Logging Ban Zone of Natural Forest (Nature Reserve)* and designated more than 40 areas in 15 provinces (/regions) as 'logging ban zones' (禁伐区).[95] In 1960, the State Council issued the *Instructions on Active Protection and Rational Utilization of Wild Animals Resources* and proposed to establish nature reserves and no-hunting zones to protect rare wildlife.[96]

The nascent nature reserve system was situated in a less poetic social and economic backdrop than in the US, where national parks were born out of the desire to admire natural beauty. The campaign of the 'Great Leap Forward' occurred in China from 1958 to 1961 and called for the development of socialism 'greater, faster, better, and more economically' (多快好省).[97] Under the irrational and even frantic goal of industrialization and collectivization during this period, the protection of forests and nature went explicitly against the call for 'backyard furnaces' in China. From 1966 to 1976, the Cultural Revolution struck another serious blow at efforts toward nature conservation.[98] During this period, the problem of environmental management was addressed for the first time by the Chinese government when China prepared for the 1972 United Nations Conference on the Human Environment in Stockholm.[99] Nevertheless, the process of environmental protection and nature conservation still suffered significantly from the overall political turbulence.[100] Judith Shapiro made a keen observation about the devastating impact of Maoist politics on China's environment. She noted that the traditional Chinese ideal of 'harmony between the heavens and humankind' (天人合一) was abrogated in favor of Mao's insistence that 'man must conquer nature' (人定胜天).[101] During this period, nature was deemed an object to be conquered and tamed instead of something to be revered and protected.

---

94 Ibid.
95 Ministry of Forestry, 关于天然林禁伐区(自然保护区)划定草案 (Draft of Designating a Logging Ban Zone of Natural Forest (Nature Reserve)), October 1956. See Ke Shuifa and Zhao Tiezhen, 中国的自然保护区 (Nature Reserve in China), 11 (2001) 地理教学 (*Geographical Teaching and Study*), p. 10.
96 State Council, 关于积极保护和合理利用野生动物资源的指示 (Instructions on Active Protection and Rational Utilization of Wild Animals Resources), 1960. See ibid.
97 Hong Jiang, 'Grassland Management and Views of Nature in China since 1949: Regional Policies and Local Changes in Uxin Ju, Inner Mongolia', 36.5 (2005) *Geoforum*, p. 645.
98 For more information about the history of China in the 1950s–1970s, see generally R. Keith Schoppa, *The Columbia Guide to Modern Chinese History* (New York: Columbia University Press, 2000), pp. 119–54.
99 In 1973, the National Conference on Human Environment was held in which the first country-wide discussion on environment protection was launched. See Organization for Economic Co-operation and Development (OECD), *Governance in China* (Paris: OECD, 2005), p. 497.
100 For scholarly discussion about the environmental history of China during Mao's era, see Richard Edmonds, *Patterns of China's Lost Harmony: A Survey of the Country's Environmental Degradation and Protection* (London and New York: Routledge, 1994); Vaclav Smil, *China's Environmental Crisis: An Inquiry into the Limits of National Development* (Armonk, NY: M.E. Sharpe, 1993), and Hong Jiang, supra note 97.
101 Judith Shapiro, *Mao's War Against Nature: Politics and The Environment in Revolutionary* China (Cambridge and New York: Cambridge University Press, 2001), p. 9.

The tumultuous relationship between humans and nature under Mao's ideology caused stagnation in the development of nature reserves. As of 1978, there were only 34 nature reserves, accounting for 0.13 percent of the total area in China.[102]

The Renaissance of the Policy Significance of Nature Conservation in the Post-Mao Era

In the post-Mao era, along with the shift in the nation's emphasis from class struggle to economic development, there was a growing awareness of the significance of nature protection. The development of nature reserves flourished. The symposium on agricultural and natural resources held in 1979 heralded a new era for nature conservation.[103] The enactment of the Environmental Protection Law (for trial implementation) in 1979 was a landmark of the renaissance of environmental protection on the nation's agenda. In 1985, the then-Department of Forestry issued the Measures on the Administration of the Forest and Wildlife Nature Reserves.[104] This was the first legal document with a particular focus on nature reserves. Since then, a series of relevant laws, regulations and policies have been enacted to govern issues such as the protection of wildlife, grassland, forests and maritime environments.[105]

China also began to actively participate in programs launched at the international level and to join international and regional conventions on nature conservation.[106] One of the most remarkable achievements took place in 1992, when China became one of the first developing countries to ratify the CBD.[107] As a contracting party, China agreed to establish a system of PAs and to take specific measures to conserve biodiversity. The legal framework for nature conservation in China has been further improved by the Chinese government's fulfillment of its conventional responsibilities.

Situated in this beneficial policy environment, both the number and the area of nature reserves have witnessed great growth in the post-Mao era. As shown in Table 2.3, from the 1980s onward, the growth rate of nature reserves has skyrocketed in China. As of the end of 2013, the most recent year for which statistics are available, there were 2,697 nature reserves established, which represented a 79-fold increase in terms of quantity and a 116-fold increase in terms of the area covered in 1978.

---

102 Ke Shuifa and Zhao Tiezhen, *supra* note 95, p. 10.
103 Xu Jiliang et al., *supra* note 88, p. 557.
104 Department of Forestry, 森林和野生动物类型自然保护区管理办法 (Measures on Administration of the Forest and Wildlife Nature Reserve), July 6, 1985.
105 For more discussion, see *infra* Chapter 8.
106 In 1973, China became a member of the 'Man and Biosphere' Programme (MAB). China is a contracting party of a series of international conventions, such as the Convention Concerning the Protection of the World Cultural and Natural Heritage (ratified in 1985) and the Ramsar Convention (ratified in 1992). Currently, there are 28 nature reserves included in the MAB network and designated as 'Biosphere Reserves', 45 sites listed in the 'World Heritage List', 46 wetlands listed as 'The Ramsar List of Wetlands of International Importance', and 29 designated 'World Geological Park'.
107 Jerry McBeath and Jennifer Huang McBeath, 'Biodiversity Conservation in China: Policies and Practice', 9–4 (2006) *Journal of International Wildlife Law & Policy*, p. 300.

32 Conflicts in Theory

Table 2.3 Number and acreage of nature reserves in China (1956–2013)

Year	Total number	Total area (sq. km)	Increase rate of area (%)	Average area (sq. km)	Percentage of territorial area in China (%)
1956	1	11.33	/	11.33	–
1965	19	6,488.74	/	341.51	0.07
1978	34	12,650.00	/	372.06	0.13
1982	119	40,819.35	/	343.02	0.40
1985	333	193,300.00	/	580.48	2.10
1987	481	237,000.00	/	492.72	2.47
1989	573	270,630.17	/	472.30	2.82
1991	708	560,666.50	/	791.90	5.54
1993	763	661,791.28	/	867.35	6.89
1995	799	718,500.00	/	899.25	7.19
1997	926	769,790.00	/	831.31	7.64
1998	926	769,790.00	0.00	831.31	7.64
1999	1,146	881,524.30	14.51	769.22	8.80
2000	1,227	982,079.67	11.41	800.39	9.85
2001	1,551	1,298,900.00	32.26	837.46	12.9
2002	1,757	1,329,450.00	2.35	756.66	13.2
2003	1,999	1,439,800.00	8.30	720.26	14.4
2004	2,194	1,482,260.00	2.95	675.60	14.8
2005	2,349	1,499,490.00	1.16	638.35	15.0
2006	2,395	1,515,350.00	1.06	632.71	15.8
2007	2,531	1,518,818.00	0.23	600.09	15.19
2008	2,538	1,489,400.00	−1.94	586.84	15.13
2009	2,541	1,477,500.00	−0.80	581.46	14.72
2010	2,588	1,494,400.00	1.14	577.43	14.90
2011	2,640	1,497,114.64	0.18	567.09	14.93
2012	2,669	1,497,900.00	0.05	561.22	14.94
2013	2,697	1,463,098.00	−2.32	542.49	14.60

Source: Ministry of Environmental Protection[108]

However, examining the figures more carefully, several phenomena are noteworthy. First, although the quantity of nature reserves has shown an absolute increase, the growth rate of the area of these reserves is much lower. This tendency is particularly apparent after the 2000s. For example, the average area of nature reserves in 2000 was approximately 800 square kilometers, whereas in 2013, the number decreased to approximately 542 square kilometers. In other words, nature reserves in China are becoming smaller and smaller. This has caused the effect of an 'ecological island'; which means that the designation of nature reserves is piecemeal and patched and cannot reflect the entire ecological process. Scholars criticize the excessive

---

108 The data from 1956–91 is from Ministry of Environmental Protection, 中国环境状况公报2000 (Environmental Situation Bulletin in China (2000)), available at http://jcs.mep.gov.cn/hjzl/zkgb/2000/200211/t20021125_83824.htm; the data of 1982, 1987 and 1993 is cited from Li Jingwen, Cui Guofa and Li Junqing, 'Income and managing problems of the protected areas in China', 12.3 (2001) *Journal of Forestry Research*, p. 196; the data from 1995–2012 is from 全国环境统计公报 (1995–2013) (Environmental Statistics Bulletin in China (1995–2013)) (the most updated data is until 2013), available at http://www.mep.gov.cn/zwgk/hjtj/qghjtjgb/; the data in 2011 is from the website of the MoEP, http://sts.mep.gov.cn/zrbhq/zrbhq/201208/P020120824531200801316.pdf. All were last visited January 2015.

emphasis on the quantitative increase of nature reserves and inadequate attention to the quality of nature reserve management.[109]

Second, the total area saw a decrease in 2008 and 2009. In fact, despite a small increase in the total area in 2007, 136 new nature reserves were established in that year. This means that there has been a considerable shrinkage of existing nature reserves. This phenomenon is partly due to the enactment of the Regulations on Scenic and Historic Areas in 2006. Because regulations on scenic and historic areas (SHAs) are less strict than regulations on nature reserves, some local nature reserves were re-designated as SHAs, which resulted in a decrease in the total area of nature reserves.[110]

An Increasing Variety of PA Designations and Management Bodies

In addition to paying increasing attention to the development of nature reserves, China has gradually diversified the types of PA designations and applied different management strategies to them. For example, the system of SHAs was established under the authority of the construction department in 1982,[111] the system of maritime nature reserves was established by the oceanic administration in 1983, and the system of forest parks was established by the forestry administration in 1993. There are currently more than a dozen types of designations of PAs in China (Table 2.4).

Table 2.4 Institutional structure of PA designation in China

Authority	Designation	Enabling legislation	Effective date (amendment date)
Ministry of Housing and Urban-Rural Development (MoHURD)	SHA	Regulations on Scenic and Historic Areas	June 7, 1986 (December 1, 2006)
	Park	Opinions on Strengthening the Administration of Parks	February 3, 2005
	Key national park	Interim Measures on Administration of Key National Parks	March 31, 2006
	Urban wetland park	Measures on Administration of Urban Wetland Parks at the National Level (Trial)	February 2, 2005
Ministry of Environmental Protection (MoEP)	Nature reserve	Regulations on Nature Reserves	December 1, 1994
	Ecological functional zone	Outline for the Protection of the National Ecological Environment	November 26, 2000
State Forestry Administration (SFA)	Forest and wildlife-type nature reserve	Measures on Administration of Forest and Wildlife-type Nature Reserves	July 6, 1985

(continued)

---

109 D.Q. Zhou and R. Edward Grumbine, 'National Parks in China: Experiments with Protecting Nature and Human Livelihoods in Yunnan Province, People's Republic of China (PRC)', 144 (2011) *Biological Conservation*, p. 1315.
110 See Xu Jiliang et al., *supra* note 88, p. 558. More details of this phenomenon of de-designation of nature reserves is discussed on pp. 221–3 of Chapter 10.
111 In November 1982, the State Council approved 44 SHAs as the first batch of SHAs at the national level. This marked the formal establishment of the system of SHAs in China. It is noteworthy of notice that the Interim Regulations on SHAs were not issued until 1986. See the MoHURD, 中国风景名胜区事业发展公报 (1982–2012) (Bulletin of the Development of Scenic and Historic Areas in China (1982–2012)), December 2012, p. 1. Full text is available at http://www.mohurd.gov.cn/zxydt/w02012120419937414971793750.doc. Last visited February 2015.

34   *Conflicts in Theory*

Table 2.4 (continued)

Authority	Designation	Enabling legislation	Effective date (amendment date)
	Forest park	Measures on Administration of Forest Parks	December 11, 1993
		Opinions on Accelerating the Development of Forest Parks	December 21, 2006
		Measures on Administration of Forest Parks at the National Level	August 1, 2011
	National wetland park	Measures on Administration of National Wetland Parks (Trial)	February 28, 2010
Ministry of Land and Resources	Mineral park	Announcement on Strengthening the Construction of National Mineral Parks	January 11, 2006
	Geological park	Announcement on Strengthening the Construction of International Geological Parks in China	April 9, 2009
Ministry of Water Resources	Irrigational scenic area	Measures on Administration of Irrigational Scenic Areas	August 1, 2004
State Administration of Cultural Heritage	Cultural relics Archeological site parks	Law on Protection of Cultural Relics Measures on Administration of National Archeological Site Parks (Trial)	June 29, 2013 December 17, 2009
State Oceanic Administration	Maritime special protected area	Measures on Administration of Maritime Special Protected Area	August 31, 2010

One of the most important factors that have led to the diversification of PA designations is the increasing recreational use of PAs. Table 2.4 shows that most new designations are based on the notion of 'parks'. New types of designations usually develop out of scenic resources in terms of geological, irrigational, or mineral resources. Different departments claim their respective management authority over these new types of designations. Alford and Shen note that 'national agencies vie with one another to develop new laws that will . . . justify their continued call on state resources'.[112] This has largely complicated the overall institutional structure of PA management. As will be discussed below, the problem of overlapping designations exists, and the issue of the best way to coordinate different management authorities remains to be solved.[113]

Among these designations, the three most common and important types of terrestrial PAs are nature reserves, SHAs and forest parks in terms of their number, size and legislative significance. At the level of 'administrative regulation', which is enacted by the State Council, there are only two types of PAs: nature reserves and SHAs. Other types of PAs are designated by the regulations and rules issued by each department.[114]

As of 2013, there were more than 6,600 units of these three types of PAs in China, which covered approximately 18.26 percent of the territorial land (Table 2.5). It is noteworthy that in contrast to the management of forests in the US by the USFS, the forest park is a special

---

112 William Alford and Yuanyuan Shen, 'Limits of the Law in Addressing China's Environmental Dilemma', 16 (1997) *Stanford Environmental Law Journal*, p. 139.
113 See *infra* pp. 225–6 of Chapter 9.
114 About the legislative hierarchy in China, see *infra* pp. 158–60 of Chapter 8.

designation that differs from the designation of forests in general.[115] Both forests and forest parks are managed by the SFA; however, they differ in terms of allowable uses and regulated activities, which can be seen from the strict regulation of timber production in forest parks.[116] According to the latest statistics, there are 2.08 million square kilometers of forest vegetation in China.[117] The area of forest parks accounts for approximately 8.5 percent of the total area of forests.

Table 2.5 The number and area of nature reserves, SHAs and forest parks, and their percentage of territorial area in China

Type	Number	Area (sq. km)	Percentage of territorial land (%)
Nature Reserves	2,697	1,463,098	14.58
SHAs	962	193,700	1.93
Forest Parks	2,948	175,800	1.75
Total	**6,607**	**1,832,598**	**18.26**

Source: Data are collected from official releases[118]

Local Initiatives to Introduce National Parks

In addition to the types of PAs discussed above, there have been attempts to designate 'national parks' at the local level.[119] In 2007, under the auspices of international NGOs (especially The Nature Conservancy), local governments and the SFA, the 'first' national park, Pudacuo National Park, was inaugurated in Shangri-La County, Diqing Tibetan Autonomous Prefecture, Yunnan Province. Yunnan claims that Pudacuo was established in accordance with the international standards for PAs set by the IUCN, and it differs from existing types of PA designations, particularly nature reserves and SHAs. The operation of Pudacuo has experienced great economic success. However, Yunnan's initiative to introduce the national park model has been criticized for lacking the legitimate power to designate a 'national' park. Due to the lack of statutory stipulations at the national level, consensus has not been achieved among

---

115 Forest is defined as land having no less than 20 percent tree canopy cover. See Xu Jianchu and David Melick, 'Rethinking the Effectiveness of Public Protected Areas in Southwestern China', 21.2 (2006) *Conservation Biology*, p. 8.
116 See SFA, 森林公园管理办法 (Measures on Administration of Forest Parks), Article 12, and SFA, 国家级森林公园管理办法 (Measures on Administration of Forest Parks at the National Level), Article 14.
117 See SFA, 中国森林资源 (2009–13) (Forest Resources in China (2009–13)), available at http://www.forestry.gov.cn/main/58/content-660036.html. Last visited January 2015.
118 The data of nature reserve are from MoEP, 全国环境统计公报 (2013) (Environmental Statistics Bulletin in China (2013)), available at http://zls.mep.gov.cn/hjtj/qghjtjgb/201503/t20150316_297266.htm; the data of SHA are from the MoHURD, 中国风景名胜区事业发展公报 (1982–2012) (Bulletin of the Development of Scenic and Historic Areas in China (1982–2012)), available at http://www.mohurd.gov.cn/zxydt/w02012120419937414971793750.doc; the data of forest parks are from SFA, 2013年度森林公园建设经营情况 (Construction and Operation of Forest Parks in 2013), available at http://zgslgy.forestry.gov.cn/portal/slgy/s/2452/content-669504.html. All last visited January 2015.
119 In the relevant English literature, the use of the term 'national park' is chaotic. In some scholarly writing, the term includes 'national forest parks, national key scenic resorts, national natural reserves, national geo-parks, national wetland parks, national mining parks and national water reserve parks', see Guangyu Wang et al., 'National Park Development in China: Conservation or Commercialization?', 41 (2012) *AMBIO*, p. 249. In other cases, it refers specifically to SHAs at the national level, nature reserves at the national level, or both in China. See Ma Xiaolong, Chris Ryan and Bao Jigang, 'Chinese National Parks: Differences, Resource Use and Tourism Product Portfolios', 30 (2009) *Tourism Management*, p. 21. The usage of the term 'national park' is no more accurate in these contexts considering the fact that Pudacuo has been operating for more than eight years now. For more details, see Chapter 11.

central agencies about who should have the power to manage this new model of national parks. Therefore, disputes have arisen. Although the latest policy from the CPC has shown keen interest in establishing national parks across China, further measures have not yet been specified.[120] Thus, the plan for the development of national parks in China remains unclear.

The Institutional Framework of PA Designation and Management

A General Overview and the Proposed 'Natural Heritage System'

There is no integrated system of PAs in China. Although many scholars advocated the adoption of the concept and categories of 'PAs' developed by the IUCN into law to integrate diverse designations in China, their efforts were thwarted when the draft of the 'Law on Natural Heritage' was released to replace the former draft of the 'Law on Protected Areas'.[121] The enactment of the Law on Natural Heritage is still under debate, especially with regard to the definition and scope of 'natural heritage'. Whether the 'Natural Heritage System' could be a governing concept for PA management in China remains questionable. The proposed 'Natural Heritage System' did not unify the management authority across different departments, nor did it comprehensively cover different types of PA designations in China. According to the latest draft, the National Heritage System is mainly a combination of existing systems of SHAs and nature reserves that leaves their management authority unchanged. Whether the Chinese legislatures will adopt the IUCN's definition and categorization of PAs into their national legislation remains to be seen.

The Institutional Structure of Nature Reserve Designation and Management

The institutional structure of nature reserve management is mainly formulated on two sets of criteria: different types and different levels of nature reserves. Nature reserves are divided into three categories (natural ecosystems, species and natural relics) that include nine specific types.[122]

Before 1994, nature reserves were separately managed by different departments. There was no unified authority in charge of the overall supervision of nature reserve management. The Regulations on Nature Reserves of 1994 adopted a system that combined 'integrated management' and 'separate management by departments' (综合管理与分部门管理相结合) to manage nature reserves. At the central level, the MoEP (the then-National Environment Protection Agency (国家环保局)) is in charge of the integrated management of nature reserves. Competent departments of forestry, agriculture, geology and mineral resources, water conservancy, marine affairs and other departments are responsible for relevant types of nature reserves within their jurisdictions (Article 8). This combined system was confirmed by an official interpretation by the MoEP (the then-State Environmental Protection Agency, SEPA, (国家环保总局)) in 2001 in response to an inquiry by Guangdong Province on the application of Article 8 of the Regulations.[123] Three reasons were provided in this explanation:

---

120 Central Committee of the Communist Party of China (CCCPC), 中共中央关于全面深化改革若干重大问题的决定 (Decisions of the CCCPC on Several Major Issues Concerning Comprehensively Deepening Reforms), November 12, 2013, para. 52. For more details, see *infra* Chapter 11.

121 The draft of the 'Law on Natural Heritage' will be further discussed on *infra* pp. 163–5 of Chapter 8.

122 State Environmental Protection Administration, 自然保护区类型与级别划分原则 (Principles for Categories and Grades of Nature Reserves), GB/T 14529–93, July 19, 1993.

123 SEPA, 关于《中华人民共和国自然保护区条例》有关条款具体应用问题的复函 (Reply of the SEPA on Application of Relevant Articles Provided in the Regulations of the Nature Reserves of the P.R.C.), *Huanhan* No. 268 [2001], November 13, 2001.

1 The complexity of the categorization of nature reserves makes separate management necessary,
2 Practices before the 1990s indicated that coordination between different departments and supervision needed to be established to mitigate potential inter-departmental conflicts, and
3 Practices after the Regulations took effect in 1994 indicated that such a combinative management system was effective and thus necessary.

Table 2.6 shows the composition of authorities on nature reserve management and the numbers of nature reserves that are under their control.

Table 2.6 Management of various types of nature reserves by different authorities (2009)

Authority	Number	Percentage (%)
SFA	1,879	73.9
MoEP	253	10.0
MoHURD	11	0.4
State Oceanic Administration	102	4.0
Ministry of Agriculture	85	3.3
Ministry of Land and Resources	69	2.7
Ministry of Water Resources	44	1.7
Other	98	3.9
Total	**2,541**	**100**

Source: Megan Kram et al.[124]

Although the MoEP is in charge of the overall management of all nature reserves, only 10 percent of all nature reserves are under its direct control. Instead, the SFA manages the majority of Chinese nature reserves, namely, the forest- and wildlife-type nature reserves. In addition, the SFA manages other types of PAs, such as forest parks and national wetland parks (see Table 2.4). In this way, the SFA plays a crucial role in China's nature conservation scheme.

Nature reserves are divided into four levels: at the national level, the provincial level, the city level, and the county level.[125] The criteria to be listed as a nature reserve at the national level are 'of typical significance nationally or internationally, of significant international influence in terms of science, or of special scientific research value'.[126]

The designation of nature reserves is based on a procedure of 'application, examination and approval'. To be listed as a nature reserve at the national level, first, governments at the provincial level where the proposed nature reserve is located or competent departments under the State Council apply to the National Nature Reserves Appraisal Committee, which is affiliated with the MoEP. After the appraisal by the Committee, competent departments of environmental protection under the State Council coordinate with relevant departments and decide whether to approve the application. Their comments are submitted to the State

---

124 Megan Kram et al., *Protecting China's Biodiversity: A Guide to Land Use, Land Tenure, and Land Protection Tools* (Beijing: The Nature Conservancy, 2012), p. 157.
125 The Regulations on Nature Reserves only prescribe two levels, i.e. national and local levels (Article 11). According to an official explanation made by the Legislative Affairs Office of the State Council in 2002, nature reserves at the local level are further divided into provincial, city and county levels. See State Council, 国务院法制办关于如何适用《中华人民共和国自然保护区条例》第十二条的请示的复函 (Reply of the Legislative Affairs Office of the State Council on How to Apply Article 12 of the Regulations on Nature Reserves of PRC), 国法秘函 [2002]190号, *Guofamihan* No. 190 [2002], October 16, 2002.
126 Article 11 of the Regulations on Nature Reserves of 1994.

38   Conflicts in Theory

Council for final approval. The designation of nature reserves at local levels follows similar procedures and depends on approval by provincial governments.[127]

The Institutional Structure of SHA Designation and Management

The Interim Regulations on the Administration of Scenic and Historic Areas of 1985 (the Interim Regulations) classify SHAs into three levels: national, provincial and city-county levels. The Regulations on Scenic and Historic Areas of 2006 (the Regulations) abridge the third level, and SHAs are currently classified as either national or provincial. The institutional structure has been adjusted accordingly.

In the 1980s, the institutional framework of SHA management was not fully established in China. The Interim Regulations provide that 'a level of government should be established where the SHA is located' (Article 5). This means that all branches of a government, including the legislature, executive bodies and judiciary, are established for an SHA. In reality, several governments were specifically created for SHAs during the 1980s in China. The establishment of the government of Wulingyuan District is such an example.[128] If no ad hoc government is established within the domain of an SHA, it is generally provided that a management body for an SHA should be established.

After the Regulations were promulgated in 2006, the institutional structure of SHA management was more or less stabilized. At the central level, the management of SHAs was assigned to the construction department (i.e. the MoHURD). This department is responsible for supervising the management of SHAs throughout the country. The Regulations also require that other departments at the central level are responsible for 'relevant aspects' of the supervision and management of SHAs. In contrast to nature reserves, other relevant departments play a cooperative and assisting role in SHA management, and they have management authorities that are delegated by legislatures in particular types of nature reserves under their control.

The criteria to be listed as an SHA at the national level are generally based on a 'national representativeness' standard (Article 8), which is similar to the 'national significance' standard of nature reserves. The designation of SHAs at the national level shares similar procedures with the designation of nature reserves (Article 10).

At the local level, competent departments of construction within governments at the provincial level are empowered to manage SHAs at the local level (Article 5). At the ground level, SHAs are managed by individual SHA administrations with different titles, such as administrative committees or bureaus. These administrations have various institutional arrangements with local governments. Therefore, the institutional structure of individual SHAs at the local level may differ significantly from one another.

The Institutional Structure of Forest Park Designation and Management

According to the Measures of the Administration of Forest Parks of 1993, forest parks are divided into three levels: national, provincial and city-county levels (Article 6). The designation procedures for forest parks differ from those for nature reserves and SHAs.

---

127   Article 12 of the Regulations on Nature Reserves of 1994.
128   The State Council approved the establishment of the Wulingyuan government in 1988, at the same time as the SHA of Wulingyuan was designated as a SHA at the National Level. The district of Wulingyuan is subordinated to the city of Zhangjiajie in Hunan Province and is in charge of managing the SHA of Wulingyuan that consists of Zhangjiajie National Forest Park, Tianzi Mountain Nature Reserve, Suoxiyu Nature Reserve and Yangjiajie Nature Reserve.

First, because there is no 'administrative regulation' or law that enables the establishment of forest parks, forest parks are a product of the forestry department. The SFA, instead of the State Council, is in charge of approving the application of the establishment of 'forest parks at the national level'.

Second, the scope of qualified applicants for this designation differs. The owners and users of forests, forest woods and forestlands are entitled to apply to establish forest parks at the national level.[129] These differ from relevant administrative authorities as qualified applicants in the case of nature reserves and SHAs. This is partly due to the particular tenure structure of forest-related resources in China discussed above.

Third, the criteria for designating a forest park at the national level are more specific and include the following:

1 The quality of forest scenic resources must reach the first level of the relevant national standard and must achieve a score of at least 40,
2 The area to be designated must accord with the development plan of forest parks at the national level,
3 The ownership of forest resources must be clear, without any disputes, and
4 There must be a qualified operation and management body with clear duties and responsibilities that is equipped with relevant technological and managerial staff.[130]

According to the Measures of the Administration of Forest Parks of 1993, 'a management body of forest parks should be established if such parks are established by the forestry administration, state-owned forest farm, state-owned forest nursery or collective forest farm'. It is noteworthy that if such forest parks are established by state-owned forest farms or nurseries, these farms or nurseries would become the management bodies of forest parks. Unlike other management agencies that are part of governments, these administration bodies are *public institutions sponsored by governments* (事业单位), which are similar to NGOs (Article 4).

Summary

First, the previous discussion shows that the designation of PAs has become a dominant strategy to protect nature around the world. The rationale for PAs is to separate valuable landscapes, fauna and flora, resources and ecosystems from those factors that might threaten them. A myriad of international, regional and national instruments has come into existence with a particular focus on designating certain parcels of land as specifically protected areas.

Second, the definition and categorization of PAs developed by the IUCN and the domestic practices of PAs in the US and China demonstrate the complexity of formulating a PA scheme. A 'one-size-fits-all' tactic does not suffice to address site-specific issues of different types of natural areas, different types of needs from different user groups and different degrees of need for human intervention. Therefore, a diversified and hierarchical structure of PA designation is necessary to accommodate PAs to fit into these complexities.

---

129 'SFA, 国家级森林公园设立、撤销、合并、改变经营范围或者变更隶属关系审批管理办法 (Administrative Measures on Examination and Approval of the Establishment, Revocation, Merger, Change of Business Scope or Change of Subordination Relationship of Forest Parks at the National Level), 国家林业局令第16号 (Decree No. 16 of the SFA), July 20, 2005, Article 3. Full text is available at http://www.gov.cn/gongbao/content/2006/content_303591.htm. Last visited February 2015.
130 Ibid., Article 3.

40   Conflicts in Theory

Third, there has been an evolution of public land policies in both the US and China. In the US, public land policies have undergone four distinctive stages. These stages reflect changing perceptions of and underlying values in relation to nature, the development needs of the nation, influences from the environmental movement and improved environmental science. In China, nature conservation has suffered setbacks due to political turbulence and has witnessed a renaissance in the post-Mao era. PA designation has gradually diversified; however, it has not been systemized and legalized. Compared to the US, where the institutional structure of public land management is considerably formalized and stabilized, the scheme of PAs in China is still undergoing experimental and contingent changes due to initiatives from both the local and departmental levels.

Fourth, the roles of local governments in managing public land differ significantly between the US and China. In the US, the designation of PAs on federal lands indicates a federal solution to land and resource protection. Federal public land management agencies are direct managers of public lands, although they may cooperate with states and local governments on certain issues. In China, due to the hierarchical designation structure, departments at the central level are not directly involved in the management of PAs. Instead, they function as policy makers and supervisors. PAs at all levels in China are managed in practice by local governments, even though they possess a 'national' title. In this way, local governments play an important role in the management of national PAs.

Following this examination of the definition and categorization of PAs at the international level and the schemes of PAs in the US and China, I will now provide some clarifications on the concepts to be used in this book and the scope of this research. The term 'PA' with particular reference to the IUCN is used as a governing concept throughout the book. Regarding the scope of this research,

1. It only focuses on terrestrial PAs due to the particularities of maritime PAs;[131]
2. Country studies of the US mainly focus on PAs designated at the federal level on public lands, with a specific focus on national parks, whereas other types of designations will serve for comparative and complementary purposes, and
3. In the case of China, attention is focused on the three dominant types of PAs: nature reserves, SHAs and forest parks.

---

131 The particularities of maritime PAs include that they are always exceptionally large areas, areas beyond national jurisdiction, vastly extended areas within national jurisdiction, less well understood, have large-scale connectivity of natural processes, three-dimensional spaces, with high environmental variability and have long-standing traditional tenure and resource rights regimes. Thus maritime PAs have received special legislative treatments around the world. See Barbara Lausche, *Guidelines for Protected Areas Legislation* (Gland, Switzerland: IUCN, 2011), pp. 209–64.

3 Resolving Conflicts in Protected Areas
Rationale, Principles and the Institutional Approach

Introduction

To examine how conflicts are resolved in the legal systems of the US and China, preliminary questions to address include what are the conflicts in PA management, why there are conflicts, what the goal of conflict resolution is and how law can contribute to conflict resolution. This chapter approaches these preliminary questions in three ways. It first elaborates the *rationale* for conflict and conflict resolution scenarios with a particular focus on the role of recreation and tourism. Second, it outlines the *principles* that govern how an optimal balance would look and how it can be achieved. Third, it develops an *institutional* approach to analyze how a desirable legal regime can be constructed.

First, a preliminary clarification of three sets of terms used in this book is provided, including use, preservation and conservation; recreation and tourism; and conflict and dispute. Then, the reasons conflicts arise and the contexts in which conflicts are situated are discussed. By applying Campbell's triangle model, conflicts in PAs are classified into three types: resource conflicts, development conflicts and property conflicts.

Second, the principle of sustainable development (SD) and its associated principles, including sustainable tourism and ecotourism, are investigated. The requirements established in these principles to balance interests and make decisions that affect the environment are examined. Through a presentation of the normative influences of these principles on nature conservation law, this study examines how the legal system can better integrate the substance of these principles to resolve conflicts in PA management.

Third, this study investigates how legal interpretation may play a role in the resolution of conflicts in PA management. Based on an elaboration of Vermeule's institutional theory of legal interpretation, an institutional approach is proposed to frame the issues of conflict and conflict resolution in PA management. The potential of Vermeule's theory to frame the interpretation of PA-related laws and its limitations are examined.

A Preliminary Clarification of Basic Concepts

The following three sets of terms are used throughout this book: (1) use, preservation and conservation; (2) recreation and tourism; and (3) conflict and dispute. Clarification of these terms is provided below.

Use, Preservation and Conservation

In spoken and written English, the words 'preservation' and 'conservation' are used interchangeably. They share meanings, such as the protection and care of nature. However, in particular contexts, differences between them may be apparent or even crucial, such as in environmental philosophy and the legislative language used in the NPS Organic Act.[1]

From a linguistic perspective, Webster's Dictionary defines 'conservation' as 'to care or keep supervision of something by a governmental authority or by a private association or business, [such as] planned management of a natural resource to prevent exploitation, destruction, or neglect'.[2] To 'preserve' is defined as 'to keep safe from injury, harm, or destruction; [or] to keep alive, intact, in existence, or from decay'.[3] Some subtle differences can be found: conservation indicates a certain type of activity, such as management and supervision, whereas preservation refers to an intact status.

In the field of nature studies, especially in the context of the US, conservation refers to a protective status of nature in which affirmative management activities (such as predator eradication and fire extinguishing) exist and the controlled use of natural resources is allowed. In contrast, preservation elevates the value of natural processes per se. It refers to a 'step-out' approach with as little human interference as possible. In the early history of nature management in the US, preservationists and conservationists were considered two distinct groups of people that possessed different, even opposing, attitudes toward the human-nature relationship.[4]

Another concept that is frequently used in nature studies is 'use'. The scenario of conflicts between 'use and preservation' is applied broadly in the literature.[5] However, this dichotomy is not always tenable. Some scholars deem preservation a type of 'use' for its provision of ecological services, such as the maintenance of climates, habitats and species. These services can even be quantified into economic value. In 1997, Costanza et al. estimated the economic value of 17 ecosystem services, which fell in the range of US$16–54 trillion per year, with an average of 33 trillion dollars per year.[6] Federal public land statutes in the US also deem 'preservation' one of 'multiple uses'.[7]

---

1 The Organic Act mandates the NPS to 'conserve' nature and provide for enjoyment. The adoption of the term 'conserve' instead of 'preserve' is used by scholars to argue against the 'museum' perception of nation parks. For more discussion of the semantic reading of the Organic Act, see *infra* p. 113 of Chapter 6.

2 Philip Babcock Gove et al., *Webster's Third New International Dictionary of the English Language, Unabridged* (Springfield, MA: G. & C. Merriam Co., 1981), p. 483.

3 Ibid., p. 1794.

4 For a comprehensive list of literature on the 'conservation-preservation' debate in the US, see Adam Rome, 'Conservation, Preservation, and Environmental Activism: A Survey of the Historical Literature', NPS online publication, 2003, available at http://www.cr.nps.gov/history/hisnps/NPSThinking/nps-oah.htm. Last visited February 2015. In literature, many commentators have drawn a firm distinction between conservation and preservation, see A. Dan Tarlock, 'For Whom the National Parks?', 34 (1981) *Stanford Law Review*, pp. 256–7; Harmony Mappes, 'Comment. National Parks: For Use and "Enjoyment" or for "Preservation"? and the Role of the National Park Service Management Policies in That Determination', 92 (2007) *Iowa Law Review*, pp. 612, 628, and Denise Antolini, 'National Park Law In The US: Conservation, Conflict, And Centennial Values', 33 (2009) *William and Mary Environmental Law and Policy Review*, p. 856.

5 See Bill Carter and Gordon Grimwade, 'Balancing Use and Preservation in Cultural Heritage Management', 3.1 (1997) *International Journal of Heritage Studies*, pp. 45–53; Oumar Bouare, 'A Policy Tool for Establishing a Balance between Wildlife Habitat Preservation and the Use of Natural Resources by Rural People in South Africa', 44 (2006) *African Journal of Ecology*, pp. 95–101; Michael Mantell, 'Preservation and Use: Concessions in National Parks', 8.1 (1979) *Ecology Law Quarterly*, pp. 1–54, and Kamron Keele, 'Preservation and Use: Road Building, Overcrowding, and the Future of Our National Parks', 11 (1998) *Tulane Environmental Law Journal*, pp. 441–59.

6 Robert Costanza et al., 'The Value of the World's Ecosystem Services and Natural Capital', 387 (1997) *Nature*, pp. 253–60.

7 See multiple-use mandates on BLM and national forest lands. For more details, see *infra* pp. 78–80 of Chapter 4.

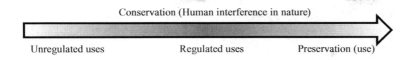

Figure 3.1 Illustration of the relationships between use, conservation and preservation

If we situate conservation within a value-free context and understand it on a spectrum of different degrees of human interference in nature, the relationships between use, preservation and conservation can be described as shown in Figure 3.1 below. At the left-hand extreme lie unregulated uses of nature, and at the right-hand extreme lies pure preservation, leaving nature in a pristine state. In reality, the intensity of conservational activities occurs between these two extremes, which means that most uses are under a certain degree of regulation.

Recreation and Tourism

The second question lies in the conceptual differences between recreation and tourism. Both recreation and tourism may occur in various forms. This book focuses on outdoor recreation in the natural environment, such as hiking, mountain climbing and skiing. In general, recreation refers to experiences of refreshment, relaxation and enjoyment. Recreation is not necessarily costly and does not depend on commercial services, whereas the perception of tourism is always connected to the market as a sector of industry. Distinguishing between the two might help in clarifying their roles in PA designation and management. Recreational use by the public is often enshrined as one of the fundamental purposes of PA designation; however, the tourism industry can only be deemed a 'by-product'. In low-income developing countries, recreational needs may rank lower than basic livelihoods in the hierarchy of human needs. However, because tourism may generate benefits for local communities and because it has the potential to improve livelihoods, PAs' political and economic functions become more explicit in this context. In the relevant literature, the phrase 'recreation and tourism' is often used to cover a broad range of topics.[8] In this book, the terms 'recreation' and 'tourism' are used interchangeably, based on different contexts: recreation generally refers to a specific type of land use together with other types of use, whereas tourism is used to discuss the economy, industry, market and benefits.

Conflict and Dispute

The last pair of concepts to be clarified is conflict and dispute. Schmid defines conflict as follows:

> Conflict is present when two or more parties perceive that their interests are incompatible, express hostile attitudes, or . . . pursue their interest through actions that damage the other parties . . . Interests can differ over: i) access to and distribution of resources (e.g. territory, money, energy sources, food); ii) control of *power* and participation in political

---

8 For example, see John Tribe, *The Economics of Recreation, Leisure and Tourism* (London: Routledge, 2012); Stephen Williams, *Tourism and Recreation* (Harlow, England: Prentice Hall, 2003), and John Edington and M.A. Edington, *Ecology, Recreation, and Tourism* (Cambridge: Cambridge University Press, 1986).

decision-making; iii) *identity* (cultural, social and political communities); iv) *status*, particularly those embodied in systems of government, religion, or ideology.[9]

In terms of the relationship between conflict and dispute, 'a dispute occurs when a conflict over a specific issue or event becomes public.'[10] In this sense, 'all disputes reflect conflict, but not all conflicts develop into disputes.'[11]

Compared to the terms 'dispute' and 'dispute resolution', which are broadly used and discussed in the legal arena, *conflict* analysis has not been similarly acknowledged. Conflict is not necessarily bad; it can 'represent the productive interaction of competing interests and values'.[12] It is 'to be expected in pluralist democracies, and is often a sign that democracy is working'.[13] It precedes the discovery of and solution to problems. Engel and Korf identify three key steps of 'conflict management':

1 Identify latent conflict and address it constructively;
2 Prevent existing conflict from escalating; and
3 Make use of conflict in promoting positive social change.[14]

Therefore, the steps mentioned above may be of particular importance for the objective of settling disputes. This also applies to legal studies. Because interests may differ over a broad range of issues, legal remedy, especially judicial remedy, may not be universally applicable to all types of conflicts. By identifying the main forms of conflicts and whether they are judicable disputes, conflicts can be better understood and managed, and directed resolution mechanisms can be provided by the law.

The Rationale for Conflict and Conflict Resolution in PA Management

To examine how conflicts are managed and resolved in the legal regime, a preliminary step is to investigate why there are conflicts, the contexts in which such conflicts are embedded, the interplay between different types of conflicts and the key concerns in resolving a particular conflict. This section examines the rationale for conflict and conflict resolution in PA management. The particular features of these conflicts are identified, a classification model is proposed, and some key concerns in resolving different types of conflicts are identified.

The Rise of Conflicts: Reasons and Contexts

The Rise of Conflicts in the Context of the Plurality of Values

How people view nature and their interactions with nature is the starting point to formulate rules that guide their behaviors and choices of actions. However, nature management is rarely consensus based. Different philosophies and values guide behaviors in many different ways. This plurality is found not only between different groups of individuals but

---

9 Alex Schmid, *Thesaurus and Glossary of Early Warning and Conflict Prevention Terms (abridged version)* (London: Fewer, 1998). Cited from Antonia Engel and Benedikt Korf, *Negotiation and Mediation Techniques for Natural Resource Management* (Rome: Food and Agriculture Organization of the United Nations, 2005), pp. 8–9.
10 Antonia Engel and Benedikt Korf, ibid., pp. 19–20.
11 Ibid., p. 20.
12 Connie Lewis, *Managing Conflicts in Protected Areas* (Gland, Switzerland: IUCN, 1996), p. 2.
13 Martin Nie, 'Drivers of Natural Resource-Based Political Conflict', 36 (2003) *Policy Science*, p. 333.
14 Antonia Engel and Benedikt Korf, *supra* note 9, p. 3.

also as a remarkable feature of institutions. Tension exists among different groups in society and institutions that pursue different goals and hold different management strategies toward nature.

In general, a fundamental divergence that guides environmental philosophical thinking is the tension between anthropocentrism and non-anthropocentrism.[15] The former regards human beings as the only or main source of moral standing. It emphasizes human domination over nature and the instrumental value of nature to the welfare and benefit of human beings. In contrast, the latter recognizes the intrinsic value of nature and embodies the ethic of 'reverence for life'. This difference may provide different justifications for nature conservation and PA designation. Kalamandeen and Gillson identified four distinctive periods that involved four models of conservation and distinctive justifications for designating PAs:[16]

1. Wilderness conservation and the Yellowstone model,
2. 'Wise use' and the Game Reserve model,
3. Wildlife and biodiversity conservation, and
4. Ecosystem management.[17]

In the first model, PAs are mainly designed to preserve the wild and pristine status of nature and its recreational and scientific value. The NPS in the US embodied this wilderness ethic, which was symbolized with the establishment of Yellowstone National Park. In contrast to the wilderness ethic, the 'wise use' model is advocated by people considered utilitarians. This wise use ideology has become the governing management philosophy for the USFS in managing national forests. It is epitomized in the expression of Glifford Pinchot, the first director of the USFS: the 'greatest good for the greatest number'.[18] 'Wise use' is not based on an anti-conservation rationale. Though it does not cherish the value of conservation per se, it endorses the instrumental value of conservation for the purpose of 'better use' by human beings. A typical example of the wise use model is the game reserve, in which wildlife is conserved not for wildlife per se but for purposes of sustainable hunting by maintaining populations. In the third model, animal welfare and biodiversity are enmeshed with ethical concerns. PA designation is a crucial means to curb the extinction of biodiversity and to support the welfare of wildlife or, for 'animal rights' advocates, to protect animal rights. Each species has its *raison d'être* and deserves respect and reverence.

The first three models are based on the assumption that human intervention is detrimental to nature: it may derogate wilderness, cause the overexploitation of game species, or accelerate the extinction of biodiversity. The fourth ecosystem management model adopts a 'people-in-nature' approach and deems human beings part of the ecological process to be protected.[19]

---

15. See generally Katie McShane, 'Anthropocentrism vs. Nonanthropocentrism: Why Should We Care?', 16.2 (2007) *Environmental Values*, pp. 169–86.
16. Michelle Kalamandeen and Lindsey Gillson, 'Demything "Wilderness": Implications for Protected Area Designation and Management", 16 (2007) *Biodiversity Conservation*, p. 170. Similar findings were also made by Gamborg et al. by looking into the reason why we should protect while managing and conserving wildlife, they notice a plurality of values exists: the instrumental value of wildlife to human beings, the well-being of individual wild animals (animal welfare), biodiversity protection, ecosystem protection and protection of wild nature. See Christian Gamborg, Clare Plamer and Peter Sandoe, 'Ethics of Wildlife Management and Conservation: What Should We Try to Protect?', 3.10 (2012) *Nature Education Knowledge*, p. 8.
17. Michelle Kalamandeen and Lindsey Gillson, ibid., pp. 167–74.
18. Ibid., p. 170.
19. For an illustrative comparison between these four models, see ibid., p. 175.

46 Conflicts in Theory

The foregoing discussion demonstrates that on the one hand, a pluralism of values exists, as argued by Norton in his sustainability studies.[20] On the other hand, the tension between different values is inevitable. A simple example of hunting may illustrate this tension. Deemed a 'blood sport', recreational hunting is strongly opposed by animal rights advocates, whereas hunters enjoy the adventurous atmosphere and trophies. This tension is also reflected in different agencies' management strategies, simply conceptualized as pro-development and pro-conservation ideologies. As will be shown below, examples include the tension between the NPS and the USFS in the case of the US and the tension between the MoHURD and the MoEP in the case of China. Inter-agency rivalry and inconsistencies between different agencies have created a patched and fragmented management pattern of PAs.

The Rise of Conflicts in a Changing Use Pattern of Land and Resources

Land-use patterns have undergone gradual change worldwide. In addition to traditional commodity uses, such as timber and mineral resources, new types of uses are burgeoning.

One of the most prominent changes in public land use is the increasing recognition of conservation. By recognizing the significance of biodiversity and ecosystem services, nature conservation has become a leading scenario in land and resource management. This can be seen in the increasing use of PA designation as a conservation tool. In addition to setting aside land for conservation, other types of land and resource uses have emerged: genetic resources are used in bioprospecting for scientific research and medicine production; scenic resources are used for filming and outdoor recreation, and forests are used to provide carbon sinks that are further traded on the market. These uses have enlarged our perceptions of what nature can provide.

Within the geographical boundaries of PAs, due to the scarcity of land and resources and the common access to them, different types of uses unavoidably interact with each other on both temporal and spatial dimensions. Conflicts arise in this process of interaction, especially among commodity use, preservation and recreational use. A coalition between preservationists and recreational users used to exist among these three groups. Because recreation and tourism largely rely on the positive qualities of the environment and scenic resources, preservationists and recreational users are in agreement with each other in opposing exploitative commodity users, such as miners and lumberjacks. However, this coalition has gradually collapsed. An increasing variety of motorized recreational uses, such as snowmobiles, personal watercraft and other off-road vehicles, has intensified the conflicts between the recreational use of nature and preservation. Compared to traditional non-motorized recreational activities, such as hiking, bird watching and camping, motorized recreation has greater negative environmental impacts. Therefore, the traditional coalition between preservationists and recreationists has been weakened. As will be shown below, in the US, conflicts among motorized recreationists, non-motorized recreationists and preservationists have become an overwhelming concern in public land policy making and have been frequently debated in courts.[21]

This divergence can also be seen in studies of the tourism-environment interaction. Tourism used to be considered a 'zero-pollution' industry. According to Jafari, from the 1950s to the 1960s, tourism was deemed an ideal activity and was enthusiastically promoted. By the

---

20 Bryan Norton, *Sustainability: A Philosophy of Adaptive Ecosystem Management* (Chicago, IL: University of Chicago Press, 2005).
21 See *infra* Chapter 5.

1970s, the negative impacts of tourism were gradually acknowledged. This situation resulted in a paradigm shift of tourism from an 'advocacy platform' to a 'cautionary platform'.[22] Budowski classified the relationship between nature conservation and tourism into three categories:

1. Coexistence: both pursue individual goals and have minimal interaction;
2. Conflict: detrimental effects of tourism on the environment and the encroachment of tourism on local communities emerge; and
3. Symbiosis: the two exist in a mutually beneficial relationship due to their advantageous interaction.[23]

The Rise of Conflicts under the Regulatory State

To mitigate conflicts arising from competing claims to use land and resources, management has been put in place for resources and tourists. In the context of the rise of the regulatory state,[24] a product of the Progressive Era, uses of land and resources are intensively regulated. This regulation is made possible via intensive rule making, rule monitoring and rule enforcement.[25] There are generally two sets of criteria that are adopted by regulations. The first is the environmental impact and consequences of a proposed use, and the second is the nature of such uses (e.g. whether it is a commercial use or a self-reliant use). The former can be deemed a quantitative standard, whereas the latter is a qualitative standard.

Due to the designation of PAs, exploitative use has been strictly regulated across different jurisdictions within PAs, such as mining and timbering. This regulation also extends to recreational use in terms of either the scale or the degree of use. For example, some forms of recreational activities in PAs, such as hunting, may be explicitly outlawed or allowed with a permit. Alternately, such activities may be restricted to a certain period (e.g. closed fishing season) or to a certain area (e.g. hunting ban area) or capped (e.g. quotas on permissible snowmobile use).

However, making management decisions that are acceptable and satisfactory to all parties is not an easy task. Allowing one type of use while banning another is not always justifiable, especially considering the general legislative mandate to 'promote recreation' in the legislative practices of some countries, such as the US.[26] Preservationists complain about the delay and weakness in regulating uses that may cause adverse impacts on nature, whereas recreational users may be disgruntled by management agencies' restriction of their recreational opportunities or the overly strict regulations placed on them. Different parties hold

---

22 Jafari proposed a four-platform model of tourism development in the post-WWII era, which are advocacy platform (1950s–1960s), cautionary platform (1970s), adaptancy platform (1980s) and knowledge-based platform (1990s onwards). This four-platform model has become the most well-known in tourism studies. See Jafar Jafari, 'Research and Scholarship: The Basis of Tourism Education', 1.1 (1990) *Journal of Tourism Studies*, pp. 33–41.
23 Gerardo Budowski, 'Tourism and Environmental Conservation: Conflict, Coexistence, or Symbiosis?', 3.1 (1976) *Environmental Conservation*, pp. 27–31.
24 For an early discussion on 'regulatory state', see James Anderson, *The Emergence of the Modern Regulatory State* (Washington, DC: Public Affairs Press, 1962). For a comprehensive review of the concept of the 'regulatory state', see David Levi-Faur, 'The Odyssey of the Regulatory State: From a "Thin" Monomorphic Concept to a "Thick" and Polymorphic Concept', 35.1 (2013) *Law & Policy*, pp. 29–50.
25 David Levi-Faur, ibid., p. 39.
26 The NPS Organic Act of 1916 requires the NPS to 'promote and regulate' the use of national parks (16 USC §1). For more discussion, see *infra* p. 73 of Chapter 4.

differing opinions on how nature should look and how management agencies should behave. Therefore, conflicts arise between the regulators, the regulated and third parties. In the US, disputes arise between agencies and citizen groups (both environmental NGOs and recreational clubs). Both substantive and procedural aspects of agencies' management decisions are frequently debated in court.[27]

The Rise of Conflicts under the Development-Conservation Paradox

In addition to providing ecosystem services, PAs serve other goals, especially development goals. The relationship between conservation and local communities that live within or around PAs is always a contentious issue, especially in developing countries. This is because a considerably large population resides within economically impoverished but biologically rich areas. These areas are the places where nature most needs to be conserved, biodiversity most needs to be protected, poverty most needs to be eliminated, and people's livelihoods most need to be improved. PA designation and management usually accompany the restriction of local communities' use of natural resources and a decrease in the quality of their livelihoods. This has resulted in the problem of poverty and the degradation of livelihoods. Poverty is one of the decisive factors that results in the deterioration and derogation of the natural environment.[28] Therefore, conflicts between conservation and development arise.

In terms of the relationship between conservation and development, some argue that 'only development will make conservation possible in the poorest countries'.[29] They view development, especially poverty alleviation, as a precondition of conservation. Others refute the idea of incorporating development into conservation by arguing that 'it is unlikely that development will in itself stop the destruction of biological diversity, because its value to the economy and to development is only potential and cannot be evaluated in monetary terms'.[30]

To cope with conservation-development conflicts, a new idea of a 'people-oriented' approach has been adopted since the 1980s. This idea embraces practices such as community-based management and Integrated Conservation with Development Projects (ICDPs).[31] These projects aim to realize a win-win situation in which the natural landscape and resources are conserved and the poverty and hardship of local communities is alleviated by increasing their income. However, studies cast doubt on the real effects of ICDPs and cite their failures.[32] In addition to initiatives in managerial ideas, a paradigm shift in law can be observed, the most explicit of which is the proposal of a rights-based approach to nature conservation law. Increasing importance is attached to human rights in conservation-related issues at the UN or domestic levels.[33]

---

27 See *infra* Part II.
28 See Sairam Bhat, *Natural Resources Conservation Law* (Los Angeles, CA: SAGE, 2010), p. 9 (the author identifies poverty as one of the reasons of environmental deterioration in India).
29 Cyrille de Klemm and Clare Shine, *Biological Diversity Conservation and the Law: Legal Mechanisms for Conserving Species and Ecosystems* (Gland, Switzerland and Cambridge: IUCN, 1993), p. xvii.
30 Ibid., p. xvii.
31 The first batch of ICDPs was initiated by the World Wide Fund for Nature in 1985. Today, there have been more than three hundred ICDPs around the world. For more information, see Ross Hughes and Fiona Flintan, *Integrating Conservation and Development Experience: A Review and Bibliography of the ICDP Literature* (London: International Institute for Environment and Development, 2001).
32 Ibid., p. 7; Ralph Winkler, 'Why do ICDPs fail?: The Relationship Between Agriculture, Hunting and Ecotourism in Wildlife Conservation', 33.1 (2011) *Resource and Energy Economics*, pp. 55–78.
33 HRBA Portal, 'The Human Rights Based Approach to Development Cooperation: Towards a Common Understanding Among UN Agencies', 2003, available at http://hrbaportal.org/the-human-rights-based-approach-to-development-cooperation-towards-a-common-understanding-among-un-agencies. Last visited

The Typology of Conflicts: Application of the Triangle Model

The conflicts described above are centered on three pillars – economic growth, nature conservation and social equity – which have been well identified and recognized in the current scenario of SD.[34] Various conflicts arise in the interaction between these three pillars of concern.

Campbell identifies three types of conflicts in his discussion of urban planning. To achieve the three goals of urban planning, i.e. 'green, profitable and fair', he contends that the planner must reconcile three conflicting interests: 'to "grow" the economy, distribute this growth fairly, and in the process not degrade the ecosystem'.[35] By taking advantage of the three pillars of the concept of SD, he classifies three types of conflicts:

1 Property conflict (economic growth-equity conflict) arises from competing claims on and uses of property by private property owners and government. Its prerequisite is the 'intrinsically contradictory nature of property' as both a private commodity and a public good.
2 Resource conflict (economic-ecological conflict) arises from competing claims on the consumptive use of natural resources and the preservation of nature for present and future demands. Its prerequisite is the tension between the economic and ecological utility of nature.
3 Development conflict (equity-preservation conflict) arises from competing needs to reduce poverty through economic growth and protect the environment through growth management.[36]

The relationship between these three types of conflict is shown in Figure 3.2.

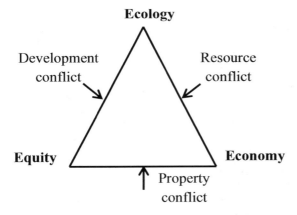

Figure 3.2 Typology of conflicts among the three pillars of ecology, equity and economy
Source: Adapted from Scott Campbell, 1996[37]

February 2015. See also Thomas Greiber (ed.), *Conservation with Justice: A Rights-based Approach* (Glad, Switzerland: IUCN, 2009).
34 See *infra* p. 51 et seq.
35 Scott Campbell, 'Green Cities, Growing Cities, Just Cities?: Urban Planning and the Contradictions of Sustainable Development', 62.3 (1996) *Journal of the American Planning Association*, p. 297.
36 Ibid., pp. 298–99.
37 Ibid., p. 298.

Although Campbell's model is established in the context of urban-rural planning, it is beneficial for the current research. Similar conflicts are observed in the area of PA designation and management. Applying Campbell's analytical framework, a framework of classification of conflicts in PAs is proposed below that governs the following discussion of the US and China.

Table 3.1 Classification of conflicts in PA designation and management

Type of conflict	Content	Prerequisite	Core concerns in conflict resolution
Resource conflict	Conflicting claims on uses of natural resources, e.g. commodity use vs. preservation of nature Competing claims on a particular type of use, e.g. non-motorized vs. motorized recreational use	Scarcity of natural resources, including scenery resources	Substantive: to clarify the fundamental purposes that PAs intend to serve; to set a baseline of management criteria; to identify the scale and degree of permissible use Procedural: Environmental Impact Assessment (EIA)
Development conflict	Competing goals of PAs, e.g. poverty reduction and the improvement of local communities' livelihoods vs. strict nature conservation	Multiple goals of PAs; dynamics in people-park relationship	Substantive: to equitably distribute burdens and benefits; to adopt a localized strategy of PA management Procedural: to guarantee procedural justice in decision-making (e.g. access to information, participatory rights)
Property conflict	*Jus dispodendi* of private/ collective ownership vs. state intervention in property right; State vs. collective vs. private/ federal vs. states vs. private	The public good nature of private/ collective property in PA-based resources	To clearly demarcate boundaries of different property arrangements; to promote public-private partnership and incentive-based mechanisms

This research does not go into detail about every type of conflict. The subject of this research includes PAs designated on publicly owned lands, with a particular focus on the role of government in managing these PAs. Therefore, nature conservation on private land, state land (in the context of the US) and collective land (in the context of China) are sporadically mentioned,[38] but they have not received full attention.[39] Furthermore, because the need

---

38 For example, on *infra* p. 100 et seq. of Chapter 5, the conflicts between private inholdings within national parks and management agencies and between state right-of-way and federal agencies in the US are discussed. On *infra* p. 205 et seq. of Chapter 9, the collective ownership within PAs and the conflicts between collectives and the state are discussed.
39 Preliminary research is also done about private land conservation. See Yun Ma, 'Working in Concert: Regulation and Incentives for Private Land Conservation in the United States', in A. McCann et al. (eds.), *When Private Actors Contribute to Public Interests: A Law and Governance Perspective* (The Hague: Eleven International Publishing, 2014), pp. 155–76. In this chapter, I discuss various legal mechanisms on private land for the purpose of conservation, with a particular focus on the tension and possible integration between regulation

for poverty alleviation is not as salient in the US as it is in China, as will be shown below,[40] development conflict is not commonly observed in the context of the US. Therefore, the discussion on the US is mainly focused on resource conflicts.

Attainment of an Optimal Balance: Seeking Principles

The various conflicts discussed above require a balance to be reached among different values and interests. Numerous efforts have been devoted to assessing how such a balance can be attained and how an optimal balance might look. The most prominent achievement in this field is the formulation of the principle of SD. Although this concept involves ambiguities and even though it has received criticism, as will be shown below, the concept of SD has become an underpinning tenet of legislation and policy making on the economy, society and the environment at both the international and domestic levels. In this section, SD and its associated principles of sustainable tourism and ecotourism are examined to determine how they perceive and resolve conflicts that arise from competing interests. The evolution of SD at the international level, the essences and core legal principles embodied in SD and the endorsement of this principle in the domestic legal systems of the US and China are examined. Finally, the legal implications of these principles and the extent to which they may facilitate the attainment of a balance in PA management are analyzed.

Sustainable Development: Evolution and Substance

The Evolution of SD at the International Level

Sustainable development has been broadly endorsed by a large number of states, NGOs and intergovernmental organizations,[41] and has great significance in international legal instruments, both binding and non-binding. The evolution of SD is a result of intense UN-led activities. It is continually shaped by actions at the international level, mainly the World Summit,[42] and remains an evolutionary concept.

The Stockholm Declaration of 1972 first noted the link between the environment and development.[43] It was not until 1987, when the World Commission on Environment and Development issued the so-called 'Brundtland Report' (*Our Common Future*), that the term 'SD' was used for the first time to integrate the environment and development. For this reason, the Brundtland Report is deemed a watershed in thinking about the environment and

---

and incentive-based mechanisms, including conservation easement agreements concluded between authorities, NGOs and private landowners.
40 See *infra* pp. 55–7 for a discussion on the endorsement of sustainable development in the US and China.
41 For example, the IUCN, the World Bank, the International Monetary Fund and the World Trade Organization. For more information on how these organizations endorse SD, see generally John Drexhage and Deborah Murphy, 'Sustainable Development: From Brundtland to Rio 2012', p. 10, background paper prepared for consideration by the High Level Panel on Global Sustainability at its first meeting, September 19, 2010. Full text is available at http://www.un.org/wcm/webdav/site/climatechange/shared/gsp/docs/GSP1-6_Background%20on%20Sustainable%20Devt.pdf. Last visited February 2015.
42 For a discussion on the functions of World Summit and International Consultation in developing the idea of SD, see Nico Schrijver, *The Evolution of Sustainable Development in International Law: Inception, Meaning and Status* (Leiden: Martinus Nijhoff, 2008), pp. 99–101.
43 Declaration of the United Nations Conference on the Human Environment, June 16, 1972, A/CONF.84/14.

development.[44] The definition of SD it provided has now become the most frequently quoted one: SD is the 'development that meets the needs of the present generation without compromising the ability of future generations to meet their own needs'.[45]

The Brundtland Report provided the momentum for convening the landmark 1992 UN Conference on Environment and Development (also known as the Rio Earth Summit) that further elevated the role of SD in the international community. The Rio Declaration elaborated 27 principles of SD for joint fulfillment at the international scale and called for the integration of the environment and development.[46]

The World Summit on Sustainable Development held in Johannesburg in 2002 represented another landmark in the evolution of SD. Proposed in the Johannesburg Declaration and Implementation Plan,[47] the third pillar of 'social development' was added to the previous 'bipolar components' of SD, namely, economic development and environment protection.[48] Since then, the three pillars of SD that are now broadly accepted – economic development, environmental protection and social equity[49] – have been established. The three pillars are recognized as 'non-hierarchical objectives'.[50]

The Substance of SD: Intrinsic SD-based Principles

Although SD is broadly acknowledged, it is criticized for its vagueness and elusive definition of sustainability,[51] its all-encompassing nature[52] and its 'politically expedient compromise'.[53] Therefore, SD is sometimes deemed 'empty of substance or incapable of legal classification'.[54] However, these criticisms do not bar SD from penetrating environmental

---

44 Chris Sneddon, Richard Howarth and Richard Norgaard, 'Sustainable Development in a post-Brundtland World', 57.2 (2006) *Ecological Economics*, p. 253.

45 World Commission on Environment and Development, *Our Common Future* (Oxford: Oxford University Press, 1987), p. 43.

46 Rio Declaration on Environment and Development, 1992: UN doc. A/CONF.151/26.

47 Johannesburg Declaration on Sustainable Development and the Plan of Implementation of the World Summit on Sustainable Development: UN doc. A/CONF.199/20.

48 Michael Healy, 'The Sustainable Development Principle in Untied States Environmental Law', 2 (2011) *George Washington Journal of Energy & Environmental Law*, p. 22. It is noteworthy that before Johannesburg, in 1997, during the Rio+5 Conference, the UN added social development as one of the three pillars of SD. It was during the Johannesburg Conference in 2002 that such a notion was confirmed and generalized. See UN doc. A/RES/S-19/2, June 28, 1997.

49 This is reflected in both scholarly research and UN documents. For example, Jacob Scherr and Judge Gregg, 'Johannesburg and Beyond: The 2002 World Summit on Sustainable Development and the Rise of Partnership', 18 (2005–06) *Georgetown International Environmental Law* Review, p. 429, and UN, 'The Future We Want' (adopted at the United Nations Conference on Sustainable Development in 2012): A/CONF.216/16.

50 The comment on 'non-hierarchical objectives' is from Alhaji Marong, 'From Rio to Johannesburg: Reflections on the Role of International Legal Norms in Sustainable Development', 16 (2003) *Georgetown International Environmental Law Review*, p. 31.

51 Michael Redclift, *Sustainable Development: Exploring the Contradictions* (London: Methuen, 1987), and Yosef Jabareen, 'A New Conceptual Framework for Sustainable Development', 10.2 (2008) *Environment, Development and Sustainability*, pp. 179–92.

52 See Sharachchandra Lele, 'Sustainable Development: A Critical Review', 19.6 (1991) *World Development*, p. 607.

53 Lamont Hempel, *Environmental Governance: The Global Challenge* (Washington, DC: Island Press, 1996), p. 39. Cited from David Hodas, 'The Role of Law in Defining Sustainable Development: NEPA Reconsidered', 3 (1998) *Widener Law Symposium Journal*, p. 5.

54 See Virginie Barral, 'Sustainable Development in International Law: Nature and Operation of an Evolutive Legal Norm', 33.2 (2012) *European Journal of International Law*, p. 383.

law at both the international and national scales. It has been broadly incorporated into international conventions,[55] applied in international and domestic adjudication,[56] and reflected in national constitutions.[57]

Some legal principles have been identified and deemed intrinsic components of the concept of SD. Barral considers SD a combination of two principles, intergenerational equity (equity between generations) and intragenerational equity (equity within one generation), via the means of integration. In his words,

$$SD = (\text{Intergenerational equity} + \text{Intragenerational equity}) \times \text{Integration}.^{58}$$

Atapattu categorizes the components of SD into substantive and procedural ones. The former include (1) the right to equity, (2) intra- and intergenerational rights, and (3) the principle of integration. The procedural components include (1) the right to information and to participate in the decision-making process, (2) the EIA process, and (3) the right to effective remedies.[59]

In 2002, the International Law Association adopted the New Delhi Declaration of Principles of International Law Relating to Sustainable Development.[60] These include the following:

1 The duty of States to ensure sustainable use of natural resources;
2 The principle of equity and the eradication of poverty;
3 The principle of common but differentiated responsibilities;
4 The principle of the precautionary approach to human health, natural resources and ecosystems;
5 The principle of public participation and access to information and justice;
6 The principle of good governance, and
7 The principle of integration and interrelationship, in particular in relation to human rights and social, economic and environmental objectives.

The components and connotations of SD are not static; instead, the concept of SD is evolving and continues to shape the formulation of legal principles. Just as Barral noted, the list of principles connected to the achievement of SD cannot be *exhaustive* due to the 'concept's intrinsically evolutive nature'.[61] Overall, SD requires the adoption of the principle of integration to fulfill the state's commitment to environmental protection, to ensure the sustainable use of natural resources and to realize intra- and intergenerational equity.

---

55 For example, the 1992 Climate Change Convention, the 1992 Convention on Biodiversity Protection, the 1994 Anti-Desertification Convention, the 1998 Convention on Access to Information, Public Participation in Decision-making and Access to Justice in Environmental Matters (Aarhus Convention), etc. For a detailed discussion on the adoption of 'sustainable development' in treaty law, see Nico Schrijver, *supra* note 42, pp. 102–41.
56 For a detailed discussion about the application of SD in international jurisprudence and selected cases in domestic jurisprudence, see ibid., pp. 141–53.
57 These nations include South Africa, Qatar, Ecuador, Jamaica, etc. La Charte de l'environnement de 2004 of France, incorporated into the Constitution, also includes sustainable development as a goal of public policy making. For more details, see ibid., pp. 153–61.
58 Virginie Barral, *supra* note 54, pp. 380–81.
59 Sumudu Atapattu, 'Sustainable Development, Myth or Reality: A Survey of Sustainable Development Under International Law and Sri Lankan Law', 14 (2002) *Georgetown International Environmental Law Review*, p. 273.
60 International Law Association, 'New Delhi Declaration of Principles of International Law Relating to Sustainable Development', April 2, 2002. Full text is available at http://cisdl.org/tribunals/pdf/NewDelhiDeclaration.pdf. Last visited February 2015.
61 Virginie Barral, *supra* note 54, p. 382.

54 Conflicts in Theory

Does SD Have Normative Status?

SD has become an 'unavoidable paradigm of environment/development relations'.[62] However, the debate over its normativity continues unabated: is SD a legal norm, or is it merely an idea, a concept or an objective?

Both international jurisprudence and academia have profiled different facets of SD and its normative status. For example, in the *Gabcikovo-Nagymaros* case of 1997, the International Court of Justice (ICJ) deemed SD a *concept*.[63] However, Judge Weeramantry, in his separate opinion of this case, argued that SD was 'more than a mere concept, but . . . a principle with normative value'.[64] In the *Pulp Mills* case of 2010, the ICJ refined SD as an *objective* to be achieved.[65] In contrast to the previous cases by the ICJ in which the customary status of SD was denied, in the *Iron Rhine* case in which the Permanent Court of Arbitration delivered the award, SD was deemed 'a principle of general international law'.[66]

In academia, opinions on the normative status of SD also vary. Two extremes can be observed: SD is nothing more than an empty concept, and SD is an established international legal norm. McCloskey once used the metaphor of SD as the Emperor's new clothes because it is 'a fine phrase without much meaning'.[67] Despite recognizing the influence of SD in guiding the decision-making process, Atapattu deems SD 'neither precise nor coherent enough . . . to be applied by courts as a legal principle'.[68] Marong argues that although there is 'legitimate international expectation that States and other actors should conduct their affairs in accordance with the norms, ideals, and objectives of [SD]', SD cannot deemed a binding legal obligation.[69] Barral argues that in addition to the hermeneutical function of SD that assists judicial bodies in the interpretation of conventions, it has the function of 'obligation of means or of best efforts' for states to achieve SD.[70] Vagit deems SD a general principle with normative values in international law, which is legitimized by the widespread use of SD in both domestic and international legal systems.[71]

Though controversies remain on the status of SD as customary international law, scholars agree that SD has contributed intensively to the establishment of key principles of decision making in both substantive and procedural ways, such as the EIA, the precautionary principle, inter-and intragenerational equity and public participation.[72] Through these principles,

---

62 Ibid., p. 379.
63 See Gabcikovo-Nagymaros Project (Hungary v. Slovakia), Judgment, ICJ Reports 1997, p. 78 ('this need to reconcile economic development with protection of the environment is aptly expressed in the concept of sustainable development').
64 Ibid., p. 88, Separate Opinion of Vice-President Weeramantry.
65 See Pulp Mills on the River Uruguay (Argentina v. Uruguay), Judgment, ICJ Reports 2010, p. 64 ('the need to strike a balance between the use of the waters and the protection of the river consistent with the objective of sustainable development').
66 Award in the Arbitration regarding the Iron Rhine ('Ijzeren Rijn') Railway between the Kingdom of Belgium and the Kingdom of the Netherlands, May 24, 2005, 27 (2005) *Reports of International Arbitral Awards*, p. 67.
67 Michael McCloskey, 'The Emperor Has No Clothes: The Conundrum of Sustainable Development', 9 (1998) *Duke Environment Law & Policy Forum*, p. 157.
68 Sumudu Atapattu, *supra* note 59, p. 281.
69 Alhaji Marong, *supra* note 50, p. 22.
70 Virginie Barral, *supra* note 54, p. 377.
71 Christina Voigt, *Sustainable Development As a Principle of International Law: Resolving Conflicts between Climate Measures and WTO Law* (Leiden: Martinus Nijhoff Publishers, 2009), p. 75.
72 Michelle Barnard, 'The Role of International Sustainable Development Law Principles in Enabling Effective Renewable Energy Policy – A South African Perspective', 15.2 (2012) *Potchefstroom Electronic Law Journal*, pp. 207–43 (the author adopts the legal principles developed by the *New Delhi Declaration of Principles of International Law Relating to Sustainable Development* as criteria in a principled assessment of renewable energy law and policy).

law can make a difference and contribute to the realization of SD.[73] Marong refers to these intrinsic principles of SD as 'good conduct terms' that should be incorporated into domestic legal systems toward the attainment of SD in different contexts.[74]

Endorsement of SD in the Legal Systems of the US and China

Although SD has a paramount influence at the international level, the way that domestic countries endorse the principle of SD in their domestic legal systems varies substantially. This can be seen in the examples of the US and China.

THE UNITED STATES

When examining the implementation of SD in the US, Bryner claims that 'the US has basically remained aloof from the sustainable development agenda'.[75] At the level of federal environmental statutes in the US, the term 'sustainable development' is entirely missing, according to a Westlaw search.[76] This indicates that the principle of SD is not enthusiastically embraced in the US at the legislative level for reasons that are twofold: SD is still deemed 'a problem for developing countries',[77] and SD is partially perceived as equal to pro-environmental actions.[78] However, this does not necessarily mean that the essence of the principle of SD is not reflected in American law.

Given the overwhelming consideration of poverty reduction embodied in the concept of SD at the level of international law, this problem might not be as pressing for the US, an affluent and industrialized nation, as it is for developing countries.[79] Therefore, in the literature addressing the problem of SD in the US, the central concern is between economic development and environmental protection.[80] It is even asserted that the only criterion to assess whether American law conforms to SD requirements is '[whether the] environment [is] protected sufficiently, if such protection is available at a reasonable cost'.[81]

By adopting the criteria on 'the degree to which statutes reference environmental protection alone ... economic impact alone, or a balance of environmental protection and economic impact', Healy summarizes three approaches to SD in American environmental statutes:[82]

1. The 'thumb on the scale' approach, which favors environmental protection or economic development in regulating impacts on the environment;[83]
2. The balancing approach, which addresses the concerns of SD on a case-by-case basis; examples of this approach include the following:

73 Alhaji Marong, *supra* note 50, p. 76.
74 Ibid., p. 59.
75 Gary Bryner, 'The United States: "Sorry – Not Our Problem"', in William Lafferty and James Meadowcroft, *Implementing Sustainable Development: Strategies and Initiatives in High Consumption Societies* (Oxford: Oxford University Press, 2000).
76 Thirty-five hits are found in the database of Westlaw; however, none of them relates to the incorporation of 'sustainable development' in environmental law. The data are cited from Michael Healy, *supra* note 48, p. 22 and footnote 35.
77 Gary Bryner, *supra* note 75.
78 Michael Healy, *supra* note 48, p. 19.
79 Ibid., p. 21 and footnote 17.
80 See ibid.; David Hodas, *supra* note 53, p. 5 (noting that 'the key element of sustainable development is the recognition that economic and environmental goals are inextricably linked').
81 Michael Healy, *supra* note 48, p. 39.
82 Ibid.
83 Respective examples are the Clean Air Act and the Clean Water Act.

56 *Conflicts in Theory*

- o The National Environmental Policy Act (NEPA),[84] in which agencies consider expected adverse environmental impacts before proposing development activities;
- o The Federal Insecticide, Fungicide, and Rodenticide Act, in which regulatory action is required when environmental harm outweighs social benefits (cost-benefit analysis), and
- o 'Exemption procedures' in the Endangered Species Act (ESA),[85] in which development is permitted when 'its benefits clearly outweigh important harms to the environment'.

3 The approach of 'shifting the applicable regulatory regime along the sustainable development spectrum', in which statutes show more than one specific approach to addressing environmental issues due to variances such as costs and phases of regulation.

Healy concludes that 'U.S. environmental law appears to be quite inconsistent in its approach to [SD].'[86] By applying the criterion of whether protection is sufficiently protected if it is available at a reasonable cost, he concludes that the Clean Water Act fails to meet the requirement of a balance embodied in SD because it mandates environmental protection 'only to the extent that the protection is affordable'.[87] In contrast, though the Clean Air Act also imposes controls on the basis of available technology, as in the Clean Water Act, it provides a second phase of regulation based on the standard of 'minimal risk to human health'.[88] Therefore, it conforms to the requirements of SD.

Other scholars also assess American laws to determine whether they conform to the principle of SD. For example, by pointing out the structural defect of the NEPA, namely, 'no after-the-fact responsibility for substantive errors', Hodas argues that 'NEPA not only fails to promote sustainable development, it allows decision-makers to dress up unsustainable proposals with a veneer of sustainability.'[89] His criteria seem more stringent than Healy's criteria because procedural mechanisms do not suffice to bring about a substantive balance, according to Hodas.

CHINA

In contrast to the US's aloof attitude, China enthusiastically welcomes the idea of SD into its domestic scenario of development. Shortly after the Rio Conference in 1992, China became the first developing country to embrace this concept by issuing the Ten Strategies for Environment and Development.[90] To fulfill its obligation made at the Rio Conference to implement the Agenda 21, China made its own Agenda 21 in 1994. This was the first Agenda 21 at the national level worldwide.

SD has been written into both legislation and policies as a governing principle.[91] It has obtained a paramount position on political agendas, especially when the idea of 'scientific

---

84 For more discussion of the NEPA, see *infra* pp. 82–3 of Chapter 4.
85 For more discussion of ESA, see *infra* pp. 83–4 of Chapter 4.
86 Michael Healy, *supra* note 48, p. 39.
87 Ibid., p. 27.
88 Ibid., p. 39.
89 David Hodas, *supra* note 53, p. 7.
90 CCCPC and State Council, 中国环境与发展十大对策 (Ten Strategies for Environment and Development), August 1992.
91 For a discussion about incorporation of SD in legislation and policies in China, see *infra* p. 160 et seq. of Chapter 8 and p. 210 et seq. of Chapter 10.

development' (科学发展观) was proposed by the CPC as a guiding ideology to direct the development of the nation.[92]

In contrast to the various approaches to SD in American environmental statutes, it seems that China simply adopts the 'thumb on the scale' approach, as Healy calls it, to fulfill the requirements of SD. The 'priority of protection' (保护优先) is prescribed as a fundamental principle in the Environmental Protection Law of 2014.[93] Concerning the governing status of the Environmental Protection Law in the field of environmental protection, the principle of 'priority of protection' equally applies to each sector of environmental management, including PA management. Caution is still necessary regarding how this legislative commitment can be translated into practice.[94]

Sustainable Tourism and Eco-tourism

Sustainable Tourism

SD has become a 'parental paradigm' for tourism management.[95] Tourism development should also be based on the criterion of sustainability. Therefore, an important concept for tourism is proposed: sustainable tourism. As defined by the United Nations Environmental Programme (UNEP) and the United Nations World Tourism Organization (UNWTO), sustainable tourism is 'tourism that takes full account of its current and future economic, social and environmental impacts, addressing the needs of visitors, the industry, the environment and host communities'.[96]

In addition to the economic and environmental aspects of tourism, the social aspects of tourism have received increasing attention within the international community, as seen in the call for a responsible and universally accessible tourism and the aim of poverty elimination through good practices of sustainable tourism.[97]

Tourism in PAs has specifically been addressed. In a non-binding charter, the European Charter for Sustainable Tourism in Protected Areas issued by the EUROPARC Federation, a pan-European and non-governmental umbrella organization of PAs in Europe, defined 'sustainable tourism in PAs' as

> . . . any form of tourism development, management or activity which ensures the long-term *protection and preservation* of natural, cultural and social resources and contributes in a positive and equitable manner to the *economic development* and *well-being* of individuals living, working, or staying in protected areas. (emphasis added)[98]

---

92 For more discussion of China's adoption of SD and scientific development, see *infra* pp. 171–2 of Chapter 8.
93 Article 5. See *infra* p. 210 et seq. of Chapter 10 (discussing the fundamental purpose of PA designation and management).
94 For more discussion, see *infra* p. 219 et seq. of Chapter 10.
95 Richard Sharply, 'Tourism and Sustainable Development: Exploring the Theoretical Divide', 8.1 (2000) *Journal of Sustainable Tourism*, p. 1 (though by comparing the two concepts, he argues that the principles of sustainable development cannot be transposed onto tourism as a specific economic and social activity).
96 UNEP and UNWTO, *Making Tourism More Sustainable – A Guide for Policy Makers* (Paris: UNEP, 2005), p. 12.
97 See UNWTO, Global Code of Ethics for Tourism: For Responsible Tourism, October 1999 (promoting 'responsible, sustainable and universally accessible tourism') and UNWTO, 'Sustainable Tourism – Eliminating Poverty', available at http://step.unwto.org/. Last visited February 2015.
98 EUROPARC Federation, 'European Charter for Sustainable Tourism in Protected Areas', first published in 1999 and updated in 2007 and 2010, p. 4. Full text is available at http://www.europarc.org/uploaded/documents/460.pdf. Last visited February 2015.

58 *Conflicts in Theory*

Like the term SD, the definition of the term 'sustainable tourism' is vague, which causes difficulties in applying it in practice.[99] Nevertheless, several key elements can be identified in the call for sustainable tourism:

1 Compliance with the principle of SD;
2 Protection of natural and cultural heritage;
3 A high-quality tourist experience;
4 Partnership among authorities, industry, tourists and local communities at the local, national, regional and international levels;
5 Public participation and consensus building in tourism-related decision making;
6 Equitable distribution of the benefits and burdens of tourism, and
7 Improvement of the quality of life of local residents and contributions to local economic development.

Ecotourism

A related concept in the literature and in management practice is ecotourism. The International Ecotourism Society defines ecotourism as 'responsible travel to natural areas that conserves the environment, sustains the well-being of the local people, and involves interpretation and education'.[100] The IUCN defines ecotourism as 'environmental responsible travel and visitation to relatively undisturbed natural areas, in order to enjoy and appreciate nature ... that promotes conservation, has low visitor impact, and provides for beneficially active social-economic involvement of local populations'.[101] Ecotourism is generally understood as a responsible way to conduct tourism. Several common elements can be identified: conservation-based tourism, community-based tourism and equity-and-justice-oriented tourism.

First, sustainable tourism aims to realize a balance between the environment, the economy and society, whereas ecotourism presents itself as a solution to these competing interests, that is, 'environmentally sustainable tourism'.[102] Williams states that ecotourism must incorporate notions of sustainable tourism; however, 'sustainable tourism does not necessarily encapsulate the value of ecotourism, but rather, represents the attempted reconciliation of environmental, economic, and social considerations.'[103] In this sense, sustainable tourism, like SD, represents a balancing approach, whereas ecotourism emphasizes the priority of conservation.

Second, ecotourism ensures that economic benefits from tourism remain at the local level within communities instead of flowing to external stakeholders.[104] Scheyvens argues that 'ecotourism ventures should only be considered "successful" if local communities have some measure of control over them and if they share equitably in the benefits emerging from

---

99 For relevant discussion, see Axel Marx, 'Towards Sustainability? The Case of Tourism and the EU', 6 (1997) *European Environmental Law Review*, pp. 181–2, and Karen Woodward, 'Loving the Environment to Death: Can Law Protect the Environment from the Leisure Threat?', 5 (1996) *European Environmental Law Review*, pp. 149–50.
100 The International Ecotourism Society, 'What is Ecotourism?', available at http://www.ecotourism.org/what-is-ecotourism. Last visited February 2015.
101 Héctor Ceballos-Lascuráin, *Tourism, Ecotourism, and Protected Areas: The State of Nature-based Tourism Around the World and Guidelines for its Development* (Gland, Switzerland and Cambridge: IUCN, 1996), p. 20.
102 Angela Williams, 'Reconciling Tourism and the Environment: A Task for International Environmental Law?', 9 (2007) *Vermont Journal of Environmental Law*, p. 32.
103 Ibid., p. 33.
104 Sangkwon Lee and Tazim Jamal, 'Environmental Justice and Environmental Equity in Tourism: Missing Links to Sustainability', 7.1 (2008) *Journal of Ecotourism*, p. 58.

ecotourism activities.'[105] However, empirical studies have shown that the benefits of tourism flow to the state and state-sponsored enterprises, whereas local communities receive the fewest benefits from tourism.[106]

Third, ecotourism embodies both distributive and procedural aspects of justice.[107] It requires that the benefits and costs of tourism development and nature conservation are equitably and fairly distributed among different stakeholders and that the public is provided with sufficient opportunities to participate in tourism policy-making and decision-making processes.

There is confusion regarding whether ecotourism should be deemed a principle or a product.[108] It is sometimes misused as a *product* of nature-based tourism without considering the criteria stated above. For example, it has been stated that there is a trend in China toward turning ecotourism into an income earner.[109]

Implications of SD for the Construction of PA Laws and Policies

A Principle of Integrated Policy Making

An inherent requirement of SD is to integrate environmental, social and economic goals instead of treating them as separate issues. The reference to integration in SD is straightforward because if environmental factors are not taken into consideration in the formulation and implementation of other sectors of policy that regulate economic and social activities, the development model cannot be environmentally sustained and vice versa.

Integrated policy making aims to ensure that 'policy issues are appropriately defined, potential solutions compared, the solution that increase synergies and reduces trade-offs adopted, and the adopted solution implemented, monitored, and evaluated.'[110] A baseline of integrated policy making is that different policies should 'at least not hinder the achievement of each other's objectives', and an ideal situation is that different policies would even 'contribute to each other's objectives'.[111] The principle of integrated policy making has two implications: it not only aims to ensure that all environmental, social and economic goals are considered, but also intends to ensure that sustainability is achieved. In other words, it requires both procedural and substantive integration.[112]

---

105 Regina Scheyvens, 'Ecotourism and the Empowerment of Local Communities', 20.2 (1999) *Tourism Management*, p. 245.
106 Susan Stonich, 'Political Ecology of Tourism', 25.1 (1998) *Annals of Tourism Research*, pp. 25–54 (the author adopts a political ecological approach to analyze the relationship between tourism development, water and environmental health in Honduras). See also John Zinda, 'Hazards of Collaboration: Local State Co-optation of a New Protected Area Model in Southwest China', 25.4 (2012) *Society & Natural Resources*, pp. 384–99 (the author examines the national park project in Yunnan, China and concluded that local communities are sidelined from tourism development).
107 Sangkwon Lee and Tazim Jamal, *supra* note 104, pp. 47–8; see also Blanca Camargo, Katy Lane and Tazim Jamal, 'Environmental Justice and Sustainable Tourism: The Missing Cultural Link', 24.3 (2007) *The George Wright Forum*, pp. 70–80.
108 Erlet Cater, 'Introduction', in Erlet Cater and Gwen Lowman (eds.), *Ecotourism: A Sustainable Option?* (London: Wiley and the Royal Geographical Society, 1994), pp. 3–5, and Angela Williams, *supra* note 102, p. 34.
109 Han Nianyong and Ren Zhuge, 'Ecotourism in China's Nature Reserves: Opportunities and Challenges', 9.3 (2001) *Journal of Sustainable Tourism*, pp. 228–42. For more discussion, see *infra* Chapter 10.
110 United Nations Environmental Programme, *Integrated Policymaking for Sustainable Development: A Reference Manual* (Geneva, Switzerland: UNEP, 2009), p. 5.
111 Sander Hees, 'Sustainable Development in the EU: Redefining and Operationalizing the Concept', 10.2 (2014) *Utrecht Law Review*, p. 66.
112 John Dernbach, 'Sustainable Development as a Framework for National Governance', 49.1 (1998) *Case Western Reserve Law Review*, pp. 50–58.

60 *Conflicts in Theory*

To formulate laws and policies that are geared toward SD, the principle of integration needs to be incorporated in the processes of law making, policy making and decision making. Equilibrium needs to be achieved among different interests and stakeholders without one disproportionately trumping the other. The application of the principle of integration can have a harmonizing impact on the effects of the fragmentation of laws and policies. It may also promote coordination between different law-implementation bodies.

PA management involves multiple agencies, each of which possesses a distinguishing management philosophy and objective. Because each agency is empowered with authority over policy making, the field of PA management has many choices of policies. Integrated policy making is crucial because inter-agency rivalry and a lack of coordination between governmental agencies are likely to produce fragmented policies or policies that give one or more factors disproportionate weight. Adding environmental concerns to sector policy making that may influence PA management, such as tourism policies, at an early stage may contribute to the detection, prevention and mitigation of the negative environmental impacts of such policies. Furthermore, the integration should be equitable, which requires that the burdens and interests that arise from PA designation and management are equally and fairly distributed within the community and between current and future generations.

A Rule of Conflict Resolution

The goals of SD may conflict with each other. Different legal norms that aim to attain different goals of SD may also conflict with each other. For example, the provisions in environmental statutes may conflict with rules related to the economy and trade. Therefore, a balancing exercise needs to be conducted between the different goals of SD. To achieve such a balance, different weights need to be attached to each goal that SD aims to promote. Different arguments can be made regarding the weighting process. It may be argued that the objective of policy integration is to find 'win-win' solutions to different goals, and environmental interests do not necessarily prevail over other social and economic interests. It may also be argued that there is a hierarchy of priorities between different goals. Voigt argues for a consideration of respect for ecological thresholds as the inherent component of SD. Among the three pillars of SD, environmental factors should be given priority over others, and environmental protection is the prerequisite for any development to be conducted in a sustainable manner.[113]

Recognizing the status *primus inter pares* of ecological functions among the various aspects of SD, the principle of SD can have the potential to be an 'arbiter' of conflicts between different legal norms.[114] Lower provides an analytical framework of SD as an 'interstitial norm'. In his words, SD 'does not seek to regulate the conduct of legal persons directly', which is the distinguishing feature of a *primary norm* in Hart's words,[115] but can '[push] and [pull] the boundaries of true primary norms when they threaten to overlap or conflict with each other'.[116] In this sense, the principle of SD can be functional for legal practitioners, particularly judges, to solve conflicts of norms. The application of SD may produce a hierarchical

---

113 Christina Voigt, *supra* note 71, pp. 38–41.
114 Ibid., p. 54.
115 H.L.A. Hart, *The Concept of Law* (Oxford: Clarendon Press, 1994), Chapter V 'Law as the Union of Primary and Secondary Rules'.
116 Vaughan Lowe, 'Sustainable Development and Unsustainable Arguments', in Alan Boyle and David Freestone (eds.), *International Law and Sustainable Development: Past Achievements and Future Challenges* (Oxford: Oxford University Press, 1999), p. 31.

systemization of values by which the conformity of a particular norm to SD can be assessed and the rule to choose the most appropriate applicable norm can be established. Courts may invoke the principle of SD to invalidate laws and policies that prove to be *unsustainable*. The application of the principle of SD can also work as a way to correct unsustainable development practices. All of these potential functions of SD are of crucial significance in attaining sustainability in PA management.

A Framework of Good Governance

Good governance is a key element of the principle of SD.[117] Partnership among multiple stakeholders and a 'localized' strategy of tourism management are also associated with the concept of sustainability in tourism. The application of SD in PA law requires conformity with the requirements of good governance.

Endowing SD with the essence of good governance occurs in the far-reaching context of the transition from government to governance. Governance is 'a process whereby societies or organizations make their important decisions, determine whom they involve in that process and how they render account'.[118] As opposed to government, governance 'involves the full range of individuals and organizations involved with policy decisions and implementation'.[119]

According to the Organization for Economic Cooperation and Development (OECD), the key elements of good governance in environmental policies include the following:

1 Consensus/science-based objectives (differentiated by time) appropriately reflected in policies, laws and regulations;
2 An appropriate institutional framework for policy development and implementation, including a clear allocation of responsibilities and powers to national and sub-national levels of government;
3 Institutions and instruments for policy integration and coherence that embrace the three pillars of SD: the environment, the economy and society, and
4 The provision of information, public participation and access to an impartial judiciary in the development and implementation of environmental policies.[120]

The application of the requirements of good governance in PA management requires an appropriate institutional framework in which power and responsibility are clearly allocated at both vertical (central-local) and horizontal (intra-department and inter-department) levels. It requires a legislative guarantee to the right to information and participatory rights during

---

117 Thomas Wälde, 'Natural Resources and Sustainable Development: from "Good Intentions" to "Good Consequences"', in Nico Schrijver and Friedl Weiss (eds.), *International Law and Sustainable Development: Principles and Practice* (Leiden and Boston, MA: Martinus Nijhoff Publishers, 2004), p. 148; Konrad Ginther, Erik Denters and P.J.I.M. De Waart, *Sustainable Development and Good Governance* (Dordrecht: Martinus Nijhoff, 1995), and John Graham, Bruce Amos and Timothy Plumptre, *Governance Principles for Protected Areas in the 21st Century* (Ottawa: Institute on Governance, 2003), available at http://iog.ca/wp-content/uploads/2012/12/2003_June_pa_governance2.pdf. Last visited February 2015.
118 P.F.J. Eagles, 'Governance of Recreation and Tourism Partnerships in Parks and Protected Areas', 17.2 (2009) *Journal of Sustainable Tourism*, pp. 231–48, at p. 231.
119 Ryan Plummer and David Fennell, 'Managing Protected Areas for Sustainable Tourism: Prospects for Adaptive Co-management', 17.2 (2009) *Journal of Sustainable Tourism*, p. 153.
120 OECD, *China in the Global Economy: Governance in China* (Paris: OECD, 2005), p. 495.

the decision-making process.[121] It also requires an independent and professional judiciary to provide effective and fair remedies to afflicted interests and to practice the judicial review of agencies' decision-making.

An Indicator of Contextual Differences

The application of SD varies across different times, areas and subjects. Barral categorizes three dimensions in which SD varies: *ratione temporis*, *ratione personae* and *ratione materiae*.[122] These dimensions refer, respectively, to variance in intergenerational understanding and the interpretation of SD, variance between developing and developed countries in terms of their state capacities and levels of development, and variance of SD in terms of the area or type of activity concerned, such as forestry and fishery activities.

The temporal dimension requires the adoption of a future-oriented perspective to understand current issues. The personal dimension requires a trans-jurisdictional perspective to examine domestic issues that might be similarly confronted in other countries. The material dimension necessitates caution against the universal applicability of a particular standard or interpretation when it occurs across areas or activities.

From the foregoing discussion of the endorsement of SD in the domestic legal systems of the US and China, one can see that the term 'SD' may not be explicitly endorsed in domestic law, and different nations may approach and interpret SD in their own ways. Nevertheless, the principle of integrated decision making and the need to balance different interests are unanimously acknowledged. Thus, a comparative perspective is necessary to examine how sustainability is interpreted and perceived in domestic contexts. This perspective is adopted in the current research.

Formulating a Legal Arena: Toward an Institutional Approach

The key to formulating a legal arena lies in how to design a legal framework that facilitates an optimal balance between conflicting interests. The key issues are who (to balance) and how (to balance). In terms of the 'who' issue, different players are involved in constructing law, mainly legislatures, administrative agencies and courts. Each institution has its own capacities and concerns that determine how these players interact and what consequences this interaction may produce. It is necessary to clarify the term 'administrative agencies' as used in this book. In the US, the institutional structure of the federal executive branch is diverse and possesses different titles, such as departments, bureaus and administrations within departments, executive independent agencies, independent regulatory commissions, government corporations, and other agencies and entities.[123] Nevertheless, they are all included under the umbrella term 'agencies'. A broad definition of 'agency' is provided in the Administrative Procedure Act of 1946: 'each authority of the Government of the United States, whether or not it is within or subject to review by another agency', excluding Congress, courts and the

---

121 This call is intensively reflected in the Convention on Access to Information, Public Participation in Decision-making and Access to Justice in Environmental Matters ('Aarhus Convention'), which was adopted in 1998 and became effective in 2001. It has 47 parties up to now, including 46 countries and the European Union who ratified the Convention in 2005. For more information, see United Nations Economic Commission for Europe, 'Aarhus Convention', available at http://www.unece.org/env/pp/introduction.html. Last visited February 2015.
122 Virginie Barral, *supra* note 54, p. 382.
123 For more details, see Miroslava Scholten, *The Political Accountability of EU and US Independent Regulatory Agencies* (Leiden: Martinus Nijhoff Publishers, 2014), p. 197.

Resolving Conflicts in Protected Areas 63

governments of the territories or possessions of the US.[124] In the current research, the term 'agencies' specifically refers to the four federal land-management agencies. In China, a definition of 'agency' is not similarly provided in law. The term 'agency' used in this research generally refers to all administrations that exercise administrative power, including governments at all levels, their executive departments, and management bodies that exercise on-the-ground management authority of PAs.

In terms of the 'how' issue, a balancing decision necessitates a certain degree of discretion. Discretionary decisions are subject to the substantive and procedural requirements prescribed by law. Statutory instructions are not always clear. In addition to carrying out the mandates of the statutes, it is increasingly recognized that agencies need to interpret statutes in the event of ambiguities. Therefore, legal rules involve not only how to ensure agencies' compliance with statutory stipulations but also how to delimit permissible room for agencies' own construction of statutes.

Both the *who* and the *how* issues indicate the significance of interactions among different legal institutions in constructing a desirable legal framework. Identification of what the legislation says and how agencies carry out and interpret legislation is the key process of doctrinal legal analysis. Conflict resolution largely relies on how the statutes are to be interpreted by different institutions. Therefore, in this section, the perspective of administrative discretion in making balancing decisions is adopted to analyze how a legal arena is constructed. The resolution of conflicts that arise from vague or ambiguous statutory language relies on how a statute is to be interpreted. Theories of statutory interpretation, particularly the institutional theory of statutory interpretation, are applied to determine how different institutions have interpreted and should interpret a particular text.

The Raison D'être *of Administrative Discretion and the Means of Statutory Interpretation*

Discretion is a power that is inherently possessed by administrative agencies. It is conferred to agencies to achieve flexibility of administration. Agencies exercise their discretionary power to weigh different interests to best fulfill legislative goals. Departing from the traditional view that deems administrative discretion against the rule of law,[125] modern administrative law that arises from the regulatory state has broadly recognized the inevitability of administrative discretion due to the broad delegation of power from Congress to the executive bodies.[126]

Despite its inevitability, discretion is not unfettered. Instead, it is subjected to the principles and mechanisms of administrative law. There are generally three methods to control administrative discretion:

1 The enactment of laws by Congress to clarify indefinite legal terms and reduce the room for discretionary decision making;
2 Control of the process of discretionary decision making, such as requirements for due process and public participation, and

---

124 5 USC §551 (1). For more details about the Administrative Procedure Act, see *infra* p. 84 of Chapter 4.
125 See John Locke, *Two Treatises on Government* (London: Awnsham Churchill, 1690).
126 See generally Kenneth Davis, *Discretionary Justice: A Preliminary Inquiry* (Baton Rouge: Louisiana State University Press, 1969). See also Robert Rabin, 'Federal Regulation in History Perspective', 38 (1986) *Stanford Law Review*, p. 1189.

3 Judicial review of administrative decision making, which includes 'scrutiny of the substantiality of the evidence supporting agency fact-finding', procedural safeguards and requirements of reasoned consistency in agency decision making.[127]

According to Stuart, discretion has two sources: (1) an agency is endowed with plenary responsibilities by the legislature and has free choice; and (2) an agency's choice is controlled among alternatives dictated by the legislature, but the 'generality, ambiguity, or vagueness' of statutes makes this choice unclearly determined.[128] The factors that contribute to the lack of specificity of statutes include, among others, a 'lack of legislative incentives to clarify directives', 'legislators' desire to avoid resolution of controversial policy issues', 'the inherent variability of experience' and 'the limitations of language'.[129] Statutory ambiguity is a common problem across jurisdictions. Because the legislature cannot foresee every potential circumstance that may occur in the future, the usage of 'indefinite legal terms' is broadly observed in statutes. Typical examples of these terms include 'state secrets' and 'public order'. This entails the need for statutory interpretation of these terms.

An agency's interpretation of statutes is a crucial means of exercising its discretion. A paradigm shift is therefore found in terms of administrative agencies' functions, from strictly carrying out statutes (in Stewart's words, the 'transmission belt' model)[130] to actively interpreting statutes. Sunstein even asserts that statutory interpretations by agencies have replaced judicial interpretation, and federal agencies have become 'America's common-law courts, with the power to adapt statutory regimes to new facts and new values when the underlying statute is ambiguous'.[131]

Compared with the pragmatic approach in American academia that generally refers to discretion in terms of statutory ambiguities, a distinction is made between discretion and 'indefinite legal terms' in continental-law countries, such as Germany. It is stated that 'completing an indefinite legal term is a question of law, whereas the exercise of discretion is a matter of convenience.'[132] The most crucial difference between indefinite legal terms and discretion is their reviewability by the judiciary. The judiciary has full power to review administrative agencies' interpretations of indefinite legal terms, whereas it must show deference to discretionary decision making.[133] Chinese academia also accepts this distinction, though this distinction is not firmly established by law.[134]

It is generally accepted that in both continental-law and common-law countries, courts should not replace the discretionary decisions made by administrative agencies with their

---

127 Richard Stuart, 'The Reformation of American Administrative Law', 88.8 (1975) *Harvard Law Review*, pp. 1679–80.
128 Ibid., p. 1676 and footnote 25.
129 Ibid., p. 1677 and footnote 27.
130 The 'transmission belt' metaphor refers to the functions of administrative agencies that they are mainly for implementing legislative directives made by Congress. See ibid., p. 1675.
131 Cass Sunstein, 'Is Tobacco a Drug? Administrative Agencies as Common Law Courts', 47 (1998) *Duke Law Journal*, p. 1013.
132 René Seerden (ed.), *Administrative Law of the European Union, its Member States and the United States: A Comparative Analysis* (Antwerp: Intersentia, 2007), p. 130.
133 Ibid., p. 130 (the case of Germany) and p. 194 (the case of the Netherlands).
134 For a discussion of indefinite legal term and discretion in Chinese academia, see generally Zheng Chunyan, 取决于行政任务的不确定法律概念定性—再问行政裁量概念的界定 (The Nature of 'Indefinite Legal Term' Inferred from Administrative Tasks – Re-questioning the Definition of Administrative Discretion), 37.3 (2007) 浙江大学学报 (*Journal of Zhejiang University*), pp. 166–74.

own decisions; that is, the 'judicial usurpation of agency discretion'[135] is not allowed. In the US, the 'arbitrary and capricious standard' prescribed in the Administrative Procedure Act is generally used for the judicial review of administrative discretion. The principle of judicial deference on agencies' interpretation of statutes is established in the *Chevron* case.[136] In continental-law countries such as Germany, courts only review whether administrative agencies have made mistakes in exercising their discretion. Such mistakes include exceeding their discretion and abusing their discretion.[137] In the Netherlands, courts may only intervene 'if the weighing of interests [is] manifestly incorrect (prohibition against arbitrariness, *willekeur*)'.[138] In the Administrative Litigation Law in China, a general judicial review standard for administrative discretion is not established. Instead, two separate standards are generally referred to as legislative standards on the judicial review of administrative discretionary decision making. First, Chinese courts are entitled to review discretionary administrative punishments that are 'obviously unjust' (行政处罚显失公正); second, the standard of 'abuse of power' (滥用职权) is used to annul an administrative action (Article 70).[139]

Toward an Institutional Theory of Legal Interpretation

There is abundant theoretical framing for the way statutes can and should be interpreted. Influential approaches include the positivism proposed by Hart, the integral interpretation proposed by Dworkin and the textualism proposed by Manning.[140] In a critical review of these traditional interpretation theories for their 'institutional blindness', Vermeule's book *Judging under Uncertainty* proposes an institutional argument for the 'formalism' of legal interpretation.[141] He argues that any approach to statutory interpretation should rest on the empirical premises of two variables: the institutional capacities and systematic effects that an interpretative choice may entail. He contends that the right question is not 'how, in principle, should a legal text be interpreted?' but 'how should certain institutions, with their distinctive abilities and limitations, interpret certain texts?'[142]

135 Termed by Nie in Martin Nie, *supra* note 13, p. 259.
136 *Chevron USA., Inc. v. Natural Resources Defense Council, Inc.*, 467 US 837 (1984). For more details, see *infra* p. 129 of Chapter 7.
137 René Seerden (ed.), *supra* note 132, p. 130.
138 Ibid., p. 194.
139 NPC, 中华人民共和国行政诉讼法 (Administrative Litigation Law of the People's Republic of China), January 1, 2015. For analysis of the judicial application of these two review standards, see Zheng Chunyan, "隐匿"司法审查下的行政裁量观及其修正 – 以《最高人民法院公报》中的相关案例为样本的分析 (Judicial Perception of Administrative Discretion and its Rectification from the Perspective of 'Hidden' Judicial Review: Analysis Based on Relevant Cases Released in the Supreme People Court's Gazette), 1 (2013) 法商研究 (*Studies in Law and Business*), p. 61, and Shen Kui, 行政诉讼确立"裁量明显不当"标准之议 (Analysis on Establishing the Standard of 'Obvious Inappropriate Discretion' in Administrative Litigation), 4 (2004) 法商研究 (*Studies in Law and Business*), pp. 27–37.
140 Herbert L.A. Hart, *The Concept of Law, 3rd edition* (Oxford: Oxford University Press, 2012) (he argues that the legality of a given norm depends on its sources instead of merits); Ronald Dworkin, *Law's Empire* (Cambridge, MA: Harvard University Press, 1986) (Dworkin's theory is often taken to be antagonistic to Hart's; he argues for treating law as integrity and assumes that the law is structured by a coherent set of principles about justice and fairness and procedural due process), and John Manning, 'Textualism as a Nondelegation Doctrine', 97.3 (1997) *Columbia Law Review*, pp. 673–739 (he urges that courts should interpret statutes according to the ordinary meaning of their texts). See generally Frank Cross, *The Theory and Practice of Statutory Interpretation* (Stanford, CA: Stanford University Press, 2008).
141 Adrian Vermeule, *Judging under Uncertainty: An Institutional Theory of Legal Interpretation* (Cambridge, MA: Harvard University Press, 2006).
142 Ibid., p. 36.

66 Conflicts in Theory

In fact, scholars have long recognized the relevance of institutional capacities for interpretation theories, such as William Eskridge's dynamism and Richard Poser's pragmatism theories of statutory interpretation. Vermeule insists that both of these have subtle forms of institutional blindness and rebuts them as a 'nirvana fallacy' for holding an overly idealized view of courts.[143] Eskridge argues for the flexible judicial treatment of statutory texts by incorporating a broad range of public values and updating obsolete statutes.[144] Posner argues for 'practical reasoning' in directing statutory interpretations toward the most beneficial outcome for society and is thus deemed a consequentialist.[145] Vermeule states that this is 'overestimat[ing] the judiciary's capacity to succeed at dynamic updating and flexible interpretation'.[146] He identifies two problems that may cause institutional dilemmas for judges: uncertainty (i.e. judges do not have enough information to make an interpretive choice) and bounded rationality (i.e. judges have limited capacity to understand and use information even if it is accessible).[147] Instead, he advocates a dramatic shift of interpretive authority from courts to agencies.[148] By using the method of cost-benefit analysis, he argues that an optimal interpretive approach should minimize the collateral costs of decision and uncertainty. In a nutshell, his institutional argument indicates that judges should do the following:

1   'Follow the clear and specific meaning of the legal texts, where those texts have clear and specific meanings; and
2   Defer to the interpretations offered by legislatures and agencies, where legal texts lack clear and specific meanings.'[149]

Vermeule's institutionary theory has incurred criticism. Opponents question his negative view of the judiciary's capacities and his overly optimistic view of agencies' capacities.[150]

Developing an Institutional Approach to PA Law

Institutional theory informs a particular approach and dimension that may be used to interpret and construct PA law in the current research.

First, to set the context, the scenario of conflict and conflict resolution that was previously framed falls into the general context of the discussion on administrative discretion and statutory interpretation. Statutory vagueness and ambiguities are prevalent in the field of nature conservation law. Terms such as 'rational use' and 'appropriate use' are used broadly in legislation to define the standard for the allowable use of natural resources, not to mention

---

143 Ibid., p. 40.
144 William Eskridge, 'Dynamic Statutory Interpretation', 135 (1987) *University of Pennsylvania Law Review*, pp. 1479–555.
145 Richard Posner, *Law, Pragmatism, and Democracy* (Cambridge, MA: Harvard University Press, 2003). In an article of 2003, Posner explicitly proposed the institutional dimension of his statutory interpretation theory. See Richard Posner, 'Reply: The Institutional Dimension of Statutory and Constitutional Interpretation', 101 (2003) *Michigan Law Review*, pp. 954–5.
146 Adrian Vermeule, *supra* note 141, p. 10.
147 Ibid., pp. 154–5.
148 For example, Vermeule states that 'specialist agencies . . . are far better positioned to comprehend the complex legislative histories of their particular statutes than the generalist judges': ibid., p. 215.
149 Ibid., p. 1.
150 Caleb Nelson, 'Statutory Interpretation and Decision Theory', 74 (2007) *University of Chicago Law Review*, pp. 329–406, and Jonathan Siegel, 'Judicial Interpretation in the Cost-benefit Crucible', 92 (2007–08) *Minnesota Law Review*, pp. 387–433.

the term 'sustainability', upon which consensus is hardly ever achieved. Influenced by the Progressive idea, it has been advocated that the 'science of conservation must be left to the professionally trained and apolitical experts' in agencies.[151] As the daily, on-the-ground managers of PAs, agencies must make discretionary decisions on which uses are rational and appropriate and which are not. Agencies are therefore empowered with the discretion to determine the meanings of these terms that Congress has presented.

Second, the institutional arguments toward statutory interpretation emphasize the role of interactions among different institutions in fostering a desired interpretation of law. In the current research, the issue boils down to how the term 'sustainability', in a general sense, can and should be interpreted by different institutions, mainly legislatures, agencies and courts, with their distinctive abilities and limitations.

Vermeule argues that his institutional theory has both methodological and substantive implications.[152] Adopting his thesis as a methodology, the current research takes as its starting point the premise that all institutions, particularly legislatures, administrative agencies and courts, have distinctive institutional capacities and limits, such as uncertainty and bounded rationality. When controversies occur in PA management, especially political conflicts, a premised question is who should be primarily responsible for dealing with such issues: Congress, agencies or courts? Vermeule states that institutional design matters in interpreting statutes and solving conflicts. What Congress should say in law, how agencies should carry out and interpret statutes and how courts should oversee agencies' management decisions are key issues to be addressed when designing a legal framework for PA management.

In the context of US public land law, scholars have discussed how institutional interaction influences agencies' decision making. For example, Michael Mortimer argues that 'Congress has . . . [continued] to avoid responsibility for difficult resource management decisions', and that the USFS's 'attempts at resource management have been plagued by controversy and litigation' due to 'ambiguous management goals' enacted by Congress.[153] As will be shown below, similar situations can be found in the context of national park management.

Summary

PA designation and management is rife with various types of conflicts. These conflicts involve issues such as how to use natural resources, how to distribute the benefits and burdens that arise from PA management, and how to protect the property rights of land and resources within PAs. These conflicts arise due to the plurality of values that govern how people view nature and interactions with nature, the changing land- and resource-use patterns, the transforming tourism-environment relationship, the increasing regulations on land use and recreational activities, and the conflicting goals of PAs between conservation and development.

Various conflicts necessitate a balance among conflicting interests. The principle of SD, despite its ambiguities, has become an underpinning tenet for what an optimal balance looks like and how it can be reached. The tourism industry also needs to undergo a sustainability test to realize sustainable tourism. SD requires the integration of environmental, social and economic factors in decision making, the sustainable use of natural resources and the

---

151 See generally Samuel Hays, *Conservation and the Gospel of Efficiency: The Progressive Conservation Movement, 1890–1920* (Cambridge, MA: Harvard University Press, 1959). Cited from Martin Nie, *supra* note 13, p. 260.
152 Adrian Vermeule, *supra* note 141, p. 1.
153 Michael J. Mortimer, 'The Delegation of Law-Making Authority to the United States Forest Service: Implications in the Struggle for National Forest Management', 54 (2002) *Administrative Law Review*, pp. 912, 910.

realization of intra- and intergenerational equity. Although the US and China show different attitudes toward the inclusion of the concept of SD in their domestic legal frameworks, this does not necessarily exclude SD from being a comparative benchmark for the assessment of domestic legal construction. SD confers the principle of integrated decision making in both substantive and procedural respects. It can be a rule for resolving conflicts between different legal norms, and it provides criteria for courts to eliminate unsustainable state conduct. It places good governance requirements on the construction of legal frameworks for PA management in domestic contexts. It also necessitates a comparative perspective to examine how sustainability is interpreted and realized in different contexts.

The key issue in formulating a legal arena as a common ground lies in how to accommodate conflicting interests and reach an optimal balance. Due to the prevalence of statutory vagueness and ambiguities in conservation law, agencies are empowered with the discretion to interpret and determine the meanings of statutory language. The institutional theory of statutory interpretation states that the institutional design of legislatures, agencies and courts matters when there is a need for statutory interpretation. A normative setting for a legal framework needs to take into account the capacities and limits of each institution.

The rationale, principles and approaches discussed above lead to the next two country studies of the US and China. Parts II and III will examine how conflicts in PA management, particularly conflicts between conservation and recreation, are formed and resolved under the current legal frameworks of the US and China. Normative questions on how an institutional arrangement to resolve these conflicts should be designed and implemented are also explored and analyzed.

Part 2
Country Studies
United States

4 The Legal Framework of Protected Areas in the United States

Introduction

A preliminary step in analyzing how conflicts that arise from protected area (PA) management are resolved in the legal system is to identify what the applicable laws are, how they evolve into the current status, and how PA law is situated in the general environmental law framework. This chapter aims to provide an overview of the legislative framework of PAs in the US. First, applicable congressional statutes related to PA management are analyzed with a particular focus on the National Park System. Second, legislative frameworks for other types of public land designations are discussed, and the differences in congressional mandates on different public land management agencies are identified. Third, overarching and generic legislation that applies to all types of public lands is discussed. Fourth, in addition to these statutory legislations, common law plays a role, albeit a controversial role, in public land management. Common-law principles are discussed, with a particular focus on the public trust doctrine.

Before moving forward, some introductory remarks are presented on the sources and hierarchies of law in the US.[1] The Constitution of the US, the 'supreme law of the land',[2] is the fundamental law of the federal government. The principles of the separation of power and checks and balances are adopted as the foundation of government formation. Three branches are established under the federal government: the legislative, executive and judicial branches. Federal courts have the sole authority to interpret the Constitution and to review the constitutionality of federal laws and state laws. Congress has the power to enact federal statutes, which are compiled in the United States Code (USC). Congress may grant federal agencies the authority to issue rules and regulations that have a quasi-legislative character. Valid federal rules and regulations possess the force of law and preempt state laws and rules similarly to the preemptive effect of federal statutes.[3] The president has the power to issue executive orders to direct the actions of federal agencies, and these executive orders possess a force equal to the law. Rules, executive orders and other executive branch notices are first published in the Federal Register and are subject to public comments, and then, they are codified in the Code of Federal Regulation (CFR). Courts produce case law with binding effects. Common law, which evolves from courts' decisions, is also part of the legal system in the US.

---

1 See generally William Burnham, *Introduction to the Law and Legal System of the United States* (St. Paul, MN: West/Thomas Reuters, 2011).
2 Article VI, Clause 2 of the Constitution of the US.
3 For general discussions of the 'preemption doctrine' and the 'supremacy clause' in the Constitution of the US, see William Bratton, 'The Preemption Doctrine: Shifting Perspectives on Federalism and the Burger Court', 75 (1975) *Columbia Law Review*, pp. 623–54, and Viet Dinh, 'Reassessing the Law of Preemption', 88.7 (1999) *Georgetown Law Journal*, pp. 2085–118.

The Legislative Framework of the National Park System

The characteristics of a national park, such as its wild fauna and flora, natural resources, wilderness features and historical structures, subject national park management to a series of relevant legal documents. The National Park System is governed by a long list of hierarchical legal documents ranging from the Constitution, international treaties and statutes to executive orders, regulations, directives and management policies. This complicated legal framework has become a distinguishing feature of the National Park System in the US. Winks commented that 'legislation passed with respect to the Park System . . . whether generic to the system as a whole or specific to an individual unit, has more extensive application than any other park system in the world.'[4]

The 'Property Clause' in the Constitution

The constitutional basis for enacting laws on federal land lies in Article IV, Section 3, Clause 2 of the US Constitution, which is commonly referred to as 'the Property Clause', which states, 'Congress will have the power to dispose of and make all needful rules and regulations respecting the territory or other property belonging to the United States.'[5] Congress is thus empowered with two types of powers: one to dispose of properties belonging to the US, including federal lands, and the other to make all necessary rules and regulations for that purpose. By contrast, under the scenario of the dichotomy of natural resources law and environmental law,[6] it is generally accepted that the constitutional basis for the former lies in the 'Property Clause', whereas the basis for environmental law, which is roughly defined as 'pollution control law', lies in the 'Commerce Clause', in which Congress is empowered to regulate pollution activities that have a substantial relation to interstate commerce.[7]

Congressional Mandates to the National Park Service

Under the empowerment of the 'Property Clause', quite a long list of statutes has been enacted by Congress to govern national park management. As of January 2015, this list of applicable statutes covered 72 acts enumerated by the Office of Policy of the National Park Service (NPS).[8]

These 72 acts can be generally categorized into three categories. The first category refers to those acts specifically directed to the NPS and the National Park System it manages, such as the Organic Act of 1916, the General Authorities Act of 1970, and the National Parks Omnibus Management Act of 1998. This category also includes the 'enabling legislation'

---

4 Robin Winks, 'The National Park Service Act of 1916: "A Contradictory Mandate"?', 74 (1996–97) *Denver University Law Review*, p. 576.
5 Article IV, Section 2, Clause 2 of the Constitution of the US.
6 See Robert Fischman, 'What is Natural Resources Law?', 78.2 (2007) *University of Colorado Law Review*, pp. 717–50 (the author argues that natural resources law has distinctive attributes that distinguish it from pollution control law or property law).
7 Article 1, Section 8, Clause 3 of the Constitution ('The Congress shall have power . . . to regulate commerce with foreign nations, and among the several states, and with the Indian tribes'). For discussions of this general distinction, see Paul Smyth, 'Conservation and Preservation of Federal Public Resources: A History', 17 (2003) *Natural Resources & Environment*, p. 77, and Robert Fischman, 'The Problem of Statutory Detail in National Park Establishment Legislation and Its Relationship to Pollution Control Law', 74 (1996) *Denver University Law Review*, pp. 784–5.
8 NPS Office of Policy, 'Policy Related Laws', available at http://home.nps.gov/applications/npspolicy/getlaws.cfm. Last visited January 2015.

formulated for each unit of the National Park System by Congress. The second category refers to the broad-ranging acts enacted by Congress relating to the protection of the environment and natural resources, such as the Wilderness Act of 1964, the Endangered Species Act of 1973 and the National Environmental Policy Act of 1970. The third category refers to acts that are universally applicable to all federal agencies including the NPS, such as the Administrative Procedure Act of 1946. This section focuses on the first category, specific legislation on national parks. The other two are discussed in the following sections.

The Organic Act of 1916: The Birth of the NPS

As previously discussed, the direct result of the Organic Act of 1916 was the birth of the NPS. This is the main reason this act is titled 'Organic'.[9] Until now, the Organic Act has acted as the most important congressional statute for the NPS, and legal scholarship has focused almost exclusively on it. The statement of the fundamental purpose of national parks has become the kernel of the Act, which reads as follows:

> ... which purpose is to conserve the scenery and the natural and historic objects and the wild life therein and to provide for the enjoyment of the same in such manner and by such means as will leave them unimpaired for the enjoyment of future generations.[10]

Several key words can be identified in this statement, including 'conserve', 'enjoyment' and 'unimpaired'. Because explanations of these terms are not provided in the Act, this statement has stirred ongoing controversy.[11] In addition to this controversial statement, the Act empowers the NPS to 'promote and regulate' the use of park land and resources by 'means and measures as conform to the fundamental purpose'.[12] A dual task of the promotion and regulation of use is thus assigned to the NPS. Potential tension exists between the two tasks, which has mired the NPS in a management dilemma.[13] Reaching a balance requires a proper explanation of the 'fundamental purpose' that the NPS is instructed to fulfill. In practice, debates on both of the NPS's promotion and regulation of park uses always refer to the explanation of the fundamental purpose stated above. Literally speaking, this congressional delegation is quite broad. Cheever states that the NPS is 'getting "carte blanche" from Congress'.[14]

The General Authorities Act of 1970: Toward the Unification of the 'National Park System'

Since the late 1930s, Congress has designated different types of park areas, such as national lakeshores, national seashores and national scenic riverways, most of which are specifically for recreational purposes.[15] The NPS itself also developed a taxonomy of 'management categories' (i.e. natural, historical and recreational areas) to distinguish different areas based on

---

9 Fischman traces the meaning of 'Organic' and proposes five requisite components of a modern organic act, which include a systematic purpose, designated uses, comprehensive planning, substantive management criteria and public participation. See Robert Fischman, 'National Wildlife Refuge System and the Hallmarks of Modern Organic Legislation', 29 (2002) *Ecology Law Quarterly*, pp. 514–92.
10 16 USC §1.
11 See *infra* p. 111 et seq. of Chapter 6.
12 16 USC §1.
13 This can be seen from numerous lawsuits against the NPS's management decisions. See *infra* Chapter 7.
14 Federico Cheever, 'United States Forest Service and National Park Service: Paradoxical Mandates, Powerful Founders, and the Rise and Fall of Agency Discretion', 74 (1996–97) *Denver University Law Review*, p. 632.
15 See *infra* pp. 92–3 of Chapter 5.

their natural conditions and management requirements.[16] Accordingly, in some recreational areas, traditionally prohibited activities such as hunting, trapping and fishing were allowed by the NPS. To clarify the mission it expressed in 1916 and the management standards across different categories of park areas, Congress passed an act in 1970 that is generally referred to as the 'General Authorities Act'.[17]

In addition to re-confirming the mission stated in the Organic Act of 1916, the General Authorities Act attempted to unify the scattered national park units into one cohesive 'National Park System'. It stated, 'natural, historic, and recreation areas ... though distinct in character, are united through their inter-related purposes and resources into one national park system as cumulative expressions of a single national heritage.'

This statement indicated that no matter whether a park unit was a natural, historic, or recreational area, it would be integrated into the 'National Park System' and protected equally with other units under the Organic Act.[18] After this Act, the NPS gradually phased out its usage of 'management categories'. Thus, the less restrictive management standards enjoyed in recreational areas were no longer valid. This shift triggered litigations against the NPS.[19]

The 1970 Act also made several visible moves by stating

> [National park units] derive increased national dignity and recognition of their superb *environmental quality* through their inclusion jointly with each other in one national park system *preserved* and managed for the *benefit and inspiration* of *all the people* of the United States. (emphasis added)

This was the first time that the significant role of national parks in environmental protection was recognized. Ross notes that the 1970 Act used the term 'preserve' to supplant the use of 'conserve' in the Organic Act, and the phrase 'benefit and inspiration' has 'trumped, or at least embellished' the word 'enjoyment' in the Organic Act.[20] Winks reads the wording of 'all the people' in this sentence as an indication that requires management decisions to serve the purpose of national benefits instead of localized and specified interests or those 'historically vested bodies that [lack] clear national significance'.[21]

The Redwood Amendment of 1978: Adjacent Development and the Derogation Standard

The Redwood Amendment of 1978 was originally enacted to amend the Redwood National Park Act of 1968, with the purpose of expanding the Redwood National Park.[22] Originally created in 1968, Redwood was an enclave surrounded by both public and private timberlands. The environment and landscape within the park suffered dramatically from extensive

---

16 See *National Rifle Association v. Potter*, 628 F. Supp. 903 (D.D.C. 1986), p. 905.
17 Pub. L. No. 91–383; 84 Stat. 825 (1970) (codified as amended at 16 USC §1a-1–1a-7).
18 For an in-depth examination of the 1970 and the following 1978 amendment, see Robin Winks, *supra* note 4, pp. 577–9.
19 See *Bicycle Trails Council of Martin v. Babbitt*, 82 F. 3d 1445 (9th Cir. 1996) (the NPS's decision to close bicycle trails in a national recreational area was upheld by the court). For more details, see *infra* pp. 134–5 of Chapter 7.
20 Molly Ross, 'The Requirement to Leave Park Resources and Values "Unimpaired"', 30.1 (2013) *The George Wright Forum*, pp. 68–9.
21 Robin Winks, *supra* note 4, p. 578.
22 Pub. L. 95–250, Title I, §101(b), Mar. 27, 1978; 92 Stat. 166; 16 USC §1a-1.

upstream logging activities. In 1978, despite opposition from the timber industry, Congress acquired up to 48,000 acres of these upstream lands to expand the park and restore the ecosystem.[23] Because this act added two important sentences after the first section of the General Authorities Act of 1970, it was considered an amendment to the Act of 1970 and thus was named 'The Redwood Amendment'. These two important sentences read as follows:

> Congress further reaffirms, declares, and directs that the promotion and regulation of the various areas of the National Park System . . . shall be consistent with and founded in the purpose established by the first section of [the Organic Act], to the common benefit of all the people of the United States. The authorization of activities shall be construed and the protection, management, and administration of these areas shall be conducted in light of *the high public value* and *integrity of the National Park System* and shall not be exercised in *derogation* of the values and purposes for which these various areas have been established, except as may have been or shall be directly and specifically provided by Congress. (emphasis added)

The first sentence is a reaffirmation of the mandate set forth in the Organic Act. The importance of this amendment is shown in the second sentence, which sets a standard for the NPS to manage the National Park System (i.e. the 'derogation standard'). On the one hand, the NPS is empowered to prohibit any activities that could 'derogate' the values and purposes of parks. On the other hand, the NPS is required to safeguard parks and manage them in a manner that would not 'derogate' them. However, the prescribed 'derogation' standard does not differ substantially from the 'impairment' standard embodied in the Organic Act. This is reflected in the NPS's interpretation of these two standards in its Management Policies of 2006. The NPS explicitly emphasizes that derogation and impairment are not two different standards; there is only one management standard.[24] It seems that the importance of the Redwood Amendment lies in its initial concern for external threats and development adjacent to national parks, which has produced considerable challenges for park managers.[25]

The National Parks Omnibus Management Act of 1998

Facing the problems of overcrowding and funding shortages, Congress enacted the National Parks Omnibus Management Act in 1998.[26] As an omnibus act, many management issues are addressed in it, such as the reform of the concession industry,[27] budget and fundraising problems, encouragement for cooperative agreements with universities and scientific communities, and the reform of the criteria for admission to the National Park System.[28]

23 For more information of the Redwood National Park, see Edwin Bearss, *History Basic Data: Redwood National Park, Delnorte and Humboldt Counties, California* (Washington, DC: USDOI, NPS, Division of History, Office of Archeology and Historic Preservation, 1982).
24 Section 1.4.2 of the Management Policies of 2006. For more information, see *infra* p. 120 et seq. of Chapter 6.
25 James Agee, 'Issues and Impacts of Redwood National Park Expansion', 4.5 (1980) *Environmental Management*, pp. 407–23.
26 16 USC §5901; Pub. L. 105–391; 112 Stat. 3497 (1998).
27 The content of concession reform is separately referred to as the 'Concession Management Improvement Act' to be discussed in the next section.
28 See generally Richard Ansson and Dalton Hooks, 'Protecting and Preserving our National Parks in the Twenty First Century: Are Additional Reforms Needed Above and Beyond the Requirements of the 1998 National Parks Omnibus Management Act?', 62.2 (2001) *Montana Law Review*, p. 217.

This Act is the latest comprehensive congressional legislation on national parks. Compared to previous acts, it provides more substantive criteria on the management of national parks.[29] For example, it requires the inventory and monitoring of resource conditions in the National Park System (Section 204) and the consideration of resource studies for management decisions on administrative record (Section 206).

The Concession Policy Act of 1965 and the Concession Management Improvement Act of 1998

The Organic Act empowers the Secretary of the Interior to grant 'privileges, leases, and permits and enter into contracts relating to the same with responsible persons, firms, or corporations'.[30] To systematize concession policies across the border, in 1965, Congress enacted the Concession Policy Act and stated that the development of

> ... public accommodations, facilities, and services ... shall be limited to those that are necessary and appropriate for public use and enjoyment of the national park area in which they are located and that are consistent to the highest practicable degree with the preservation and conservation of the areas.[31]

This Act proved to be an effective tool to attract investment.[32] However, the NPS did not benefit significantly from the concessioners' success, and the royalties it received were quite limited.[33] To improve the concession practices and solve the problem of the profit-sharing imbalance, the Concession Management Improvement Act[34] was enacted by Congress as part of the Omnibus Management Act of 1998. The 1998 Act confirmed the purpose statement expressed in the 1965 Act, which limited park accommodations and services to those that are 'necessary and appropriate'.[35] The main changes introduced by the 1998 Act included adding competitive bid requirements, reducing preferential rights possessed by concessioners[36] and changing the franchise fee distribution pattern.[37]

The reform accomplished by the 1998 Act was not welcomed by concessionaires, whose statutory advantages shrunk. The Act was challenged in the courts by two Yellowstone concessionaires.[38]

---

29 Compared to BLM land and national park lands, substantive management criteria are more explicitly prescribed in National Forest Management Act of 1976 and the National Wildlife Refuge System Improvement Act of 1997. The 'non-impairment standard' prescribed in the NPS Organic Act seems not to be 'substantive' enough. See Robert Fischman, *supra* note 9, p. 545.
30 16 USC. §3.
31 Section 1, 16 USC §20–20g; 79 Stat. 969 (1965).
32 The concession industry earned $800 million in 1998 alone. See Richard Ansson and Dalton Hooks, *supra* note 28, p. 220.
33 Ibid., p. 222.
34 112 Stat. 3503; 16 USC §5951 *et seq.*
35 16 USC §5951.
36 It is stated that 'except as provided in subparagraph (B), the Secretary shall not grant a concessioner a preferential right to renew a concessions contract, or any other form of preference to a concession contract' (§5952). This provision nearly ended the preferential rights that concessionaires had enjoyed under the 1965 Concession Policy Act.
37 The 1998 Act distinguished the 'special account' and 'subaccount for each unit' for distribution of franchise fees. The parks were allowed to retain 80 percent of the franchise fees collected at the unit under the concession contracts, rather than turning all of them over to the special account established in the 'Treasury of the United States', which was required under the 1965 Concession Policy Act. See 16 USC §5956(c), (d).
38 'Yellowstone Concessionaires File Suit Over New Bidding Law', *Associated Press Newswires*, December 17, 2000. Cited from Richard Ansson and Dalton Hooks, *supra* note 28, p. 229.

Enabling Legislation for Units within the National Park System

The congressional mandates presented above are generally applied to the entire range of the National Park System. Nevertheless, each unit within this system is created by Congress through an individual 'enabling legislation'. In this way, Congress addresses specific goals and instructions with regard to the particular unit within the system. The sources of legislation that are applicable to each unit within the National Park System vary. For example, hunting is prohibited in most national park units; however, through enabling legislation, Congress explicitly prescribes that hunting is allowed in Grand Teton National Park.[39] Congress also makes it clear that enabling legislation has precedence over the general Organic Act in case of a conflict between them.[40] Consequently, park managers need to manage the parks not only in accordance with the overarching congressional mandates but also in accordance with the park's own enabling legislation, which has been specifically formulated. The NPS's managerial discretion is thus limited. This legislative model is named 'place-based legislation',[41] meaning that site-specific legislation trumps generic laws.

Congressional Mandates for Other Types of Public Land Designations

In contrast to the impairment standard for national park management, the Fish and Wildlife Service (FWS) manages the national wildlife refuge system according to a dominant use mandate, and the United States Forest Service (USFS) and the Bureau of Land Management (BLM) manage their public lands based on multiple-use mandates.

A Dominant Use Regime: The National Wildlife Refuge System

One of the original congressional mandates on the National Wildlife Refuge System is the Migratory Bird Treaty Act of 1918,[42] which aims to implement the 1916 Convention between the US and Great Britain to sustain populations of migratory birds. In 1929, Congress enacted the Migratory Bird Conservation Act,[43] which promoted the development of the fledgling Refuge System by authorizing the newly established Migratory Bird Conservation Commission to purchase or rent lands to serve as waterfowl refuges.[44] This Act set a general standard for this type of acquisition, which was to be 'suitable for use as an inviolate sanctuary' for migratory birds.[45]

After a precipitous decline in waterfowl populations in the early 1930s, in 1934, Congress enacted the Migratory Birds Hunting and Conservation Stamp Act, which is commonly known as the Duck Stamp Act.[46] To acquire more lands for waterfowl refuges, this Act created a dedicated Migratory Bird Conservation Fund by selling federal hunting stamps to waterfowl hunters, who were required to affix such stamps to their hunting licenses.

---

39 An Act to Establish A New Grand Teton National Park in the State of Wyoming and for Other Purposes, 64 Stat. 849 (1950), Section 6(b).
40 16 USC §1c(b) (stating that 'the provisions of the Organic Act . . . shall, to the extent such provisions are not in conflict with any such specific provision, be applicable to all areas within the national park system').
41 Martin Nie and Michael Fiebig, 'Managing the National Forests through Place-based Legislation', 37.1 (2010) *Ecology Law Quarterly*, p. 14.
42 40 Stat. 755;16 USC §§703–12.
43 45 Stat. 1222; 16 USC §§715–15d, 715e, 715f–715r.
44 16 USC.§715a.
45 16 USC.§715d.
46 48 Stat. 452; 16 USC §§718–718(j).

78 *Country Studies: United States*

The Duck Stamp funding remains the major source of funds for purchasing lands and expanding the refuge system.[47]

As recreational demands in refuges mounted, in 1962, Congress enacted the Refuge Recreation Act,[48] which heralded the beginning of the modern trend. It authorized the FWS to administer refuges, hatcheries and other conservation areas for recreational use. For the first time, it employed a compatibility standard that has now become the touchstone of refuge administration.[49] The 1962 Act prohibited 'those forms of recreation that are not directly related to the primary purposes' of the refuge until the Secretary of the Interior determines that

1 Such recreational use will not interfere with the primary purposes for which the areas were established; and
2 Funds are available for the development, operation, and maintenance of these permitted forms of recreation.[50]

In 1966, Congress passed the National Wildlife Refuge Administration Act,[51] which consolidated disparate national wildlife refuges into a unitary Refuge System[52] and established a uniform compatibility standard to govern all refuge activities instead of the specific recreational uses addressed by the 1962 Act.

In 1997, Congress enacted the National Wildlife Refuge System Improvement Act,[53] which further elaborated the compatibility standard and clarified the FWS's mission. It provided that

> . . . the mission of the System is to administer a national network of lands and waters for the conservation, management, and where appropriate, restoration of the fish, wildlife, and plant resources and their habitats within the United States for the benefit of present and future generations of Americans.[54]

The Act enshrines compatible wildlife-dependent recreation uses as the priority general public uses. Wildlife-dependent recreation use is defined and limited to the use of a refuge 'involving hunting, fishing, wildlife observation and photography, or environmental education and interpretation'.[55]

A Multiple-use Mandate for National Forests

The Organic Administration Act of 1897 stipulated the purpose of the national forest designation, which was 'to improve and protect forest within the boundaries, or . . . [to secure]

---

47 Robert Fischman, *supra* note 9, p. 474.
48 76 Stat. 653; Pub. L. 87–714; 16 USC §§460k–460k-4.
49 16 USC §460k.
50 Section 1 of the 1962 Act. The adoption of these two determinations, i.e. 'interference' and 'fiscal availability', was quite unusual compared to other congressional mandates on other public lands at that time. See Robert Fischman, *supra* note 9, pp. 478–9.
51 80 Stat. 927; Pub. L. 89–669; 16 USC §668dd–ee.
52 16 USC §668dd ('all lands, waters, and interests therein administered by the Secretary as wildlife refuges, areas for the protection and conservation of fish and wildlife that are threatened with extinction, wildlife ranges, game ranges, wildlife management areas, or waterfowl production areas are hereby designated as the 'National Wildlife Refuge System').
53 Pub. L. 105–57; 16 USC §§668dd, 668ee. It was codified as the amendment of the 1966 Act.
54 National Wildlife Refuge System Improvement Act of 1997, Section 4.
55 Ibid., Section 5.

favorable conditions of water flows, and to furnish a continuous supply of timber for the use and necessities of citizens of the United States'.[56] National forests were directed to be managed for productive purposes. In the case of *United States* v. *New Mexico*,[57] the Supreme Court stated that there were only two purposes established for the national forest system in this Act: watershed protection and timber production.

However, this utilitarian philosophy was soon challenged by emerging environmental concerns. Conflicts between preservation and timber production led to the enactment of the Multiple-Use, Sustained-Yield Act (MUSYA)[58] in 1960 to clarify the USFS's mission, which read as follows: 'It is the policy of the Congress that the national forests area established and shall be administered for outdoor recreation, range, timber, watershed, and wildlife and fish purposes'.[59]

This was the first time that Congress asked the USFS to manage its lands for purposes of outdoor recreation and wildlife rather than merely for timber and watershed. Since then, the 'multiple use' of national forests has been affirmed in statutory language. The MUSYA defined 'multiple use' as the management of national forests to ensure that they are

> ... utilized in the combination that will best meet the needs of the American people; making the most judicious use of the land for some or all these resources or related services over areas large enough to provide sufficient latitude for periodic adjustments in use to conform to changing needs and conditions.[60]

It also emphasized that multiple use did not necessarily mean the 'combination of uses that [would] give the greatest dollar return or the greatest unit output'.[61]

The MUSYA did not specify the priority among these five uses or provide a solution for the competitive use of forest lands. This situation led to the case of *Sierra Club* v. *Hardin*,[62] in which the plaintiffs argued that the USFS's large-scale timber sale violated the MUSYA because the USFS failed to consider and balance uses other than timber production. The district court denied the plaintiffs' claims, and the circuit court vacated and remanded the judgment.[63]

In 1976, Congress enacted the National Forest Management Act (NFMA) to address the problem of over-exploitation and to further clarify how the USFS should balance the industrial use of timber and nature conservation in national forests.[64] The NFMA created a new planning process and imposed strict environmental constraints, including biodiversity protection, on the USFS.[65]

A Multiple-use Mandate on BLM Lands

The BLM received its multiple-use mandate until 1976 through the Federal Land Policy and Management Act (FLPMA).[66] The FLPMA states that public lands should be 'retained in

---

56 30 Stat. 35; 16 USC §§473–8, 479–82 and 551.
57 *United States v. New Mexico*, 438 US 696 (1978).
58 16 USC §§528–31.
59 16 USC §528.
60 16 USC §531.
61 16 USC §531.
62 325 F. Supp. 99 (D. Alaska, 1971).
63 *Sierra Club v. Butz*, 3 Envtl. L. Rptr. 20292 (9th Cir. 1973).
64 16 USC §§1600–1687.
65 16 USC §1604(g)(3)(B).
66 Pub. L. 94–579; 43 USC §§1701–2.

Federal ownership... disposal of a particular parcel will serve the national interest'.[67] The federal government's long-established policy of retaining public lands was thus recognized.

Although the FLPMA largely followed the definitions of 'multiple use' and 'sustained yield' provided in the MUSYA, the most important difference was that the FLPMA did not specify five uses, as in the MUSYA, but provided an open-ended number of uses, which read as follows:

> The term 'multiple use' means... a combination of balanced and diverse resource uses that takes into account the long-term needs of future generations for renewable and non-renewable resources, including, but not limited to, recreation, range, timber, minerals, watershed, wildlife and fish, and natural scenic, scientific and historical values.[68]

This statement shows that more permissible uses were allowed on BLM lands than USFS lands, such as use for minerals. Furthermore, in defining 'multiple use', the MUSYA cited the 'harmonious and coordinated management of the various resources... without impairment of the productivity of the land'.[69] By contrast, the wording of the FLPMA was 'without permanent impairment of the productivity of the land and the quality of the environment'. The FLPMA included 'the quality of the environment' in its impairment standard, which was a product of the emerging environmental movement in the 1970s. The expression 'permanent impairment' shows that the criteria of permissible land use for BLM lands were lower than the criteria for USFS lands. In other words, uses that cause minor impairment are allowed on BLM lands as long as there is no permanent impairment.

Overarching and Generic Legislation on Federal Land Management Agencies

In addition to congressional statutes that specifically address federal land management, other environmental statutes and administrative acts may impose requirements on the four federal land agencies' management decisions.

The Wilderness Act of 1964

The idea of keeping nature in its wild state originates from the USFS's management practices in 'primitive areas', which date back to the 1920s. The USFS's management of these areas was then without statutory backing[70] and thus incurred litigation.[71] To legalize the idea of wilderness protection, the first wilderness bill was heard in Congress in 1956. However, both the USFS and the NPS initially opposed the idea of designating wilderness areas on the lands they

---

67 Section 102, 43 USC 1701.
68 43 USC §1702(c).
69 16 USC §531.
70 Before 1964, Congress enacted legislation requiring some specific federal lands to be managed as roadless, such as the Shipstead-Nolan Act in 1930. It is also deemed to be the first congressional recognition of the wilderness idea. However, most of the USFS's primitive areas were not granted by Congress.
71 See *Perko v. United States*, 204 F. 2d 446 (8th Cir. 1953) (The President's Executive Order decreed that the airspace below 4,000 feet above sea level in roadless areas of the Superior National Forest was reserved and set aside as an airspace reservation. Private landowners of resorts challenged the validity of this Order and argued that this was unconstitutional taking of their property as it deprived them of a commercial aviation service. The Appeal Court affirmed the judgment and ruled for the US.)

managed.[72] After several years of negotiation and debates, the Wilderness Act[73] was finally enacted by Congress in 1964. This Act imposed the strictest legal protection for federal lands.

Four concrete steps were taken by Congress in the Wilderness Act. First, the Act established the new designation of wilderness areas, which composed the National Wilderness Preservation System on federal lands. It also specified the procedures and standards to expand the System by adding new units.[74]

Second, it provided a definition of wilderness and wilderness areas that, like other American statutes, guided the judiciary to review agencies' management decisions.[75] Terms such as 'untrammeled by man', 'man as a visitor', 'primeval character', and 'unnoticeable human imprint' were used in the definitions. These definitions were formed in a quite poetic, idealistic and romantic sense.[76] Vagueness in the statutory language also resulted in subsequent suits.[77]

Third, the Act instructed management agencies to take an inventory of their primitive areas or road-less areas to assess the suitability of these areas to be designated as wilderness areas within ten years.[78] In fact, this requirement is not well implemented in practice due to opposition from agencies. For example, the NPS did not finish the inventory by the deadline of 1974, and it remains to be completed.

Finally, the Act listed prohibitive uses and management standards within wilderness areas.[79] The Act completely proscribed 'commercial enterprise and permanent road' and conditionally prohibited 'temporary road and use of mechanical transport and structure or installation' within wilderness areas.[80] This strict prohibition has incurred controversies and resistance. For example, when the Act was considered in the 1950s, it was opposed by Western officials who feared that the prohibition of economic activities in wilderness areas would deprive local interests.[81]

To quell interagency rivalries between the USFS and the NPS and to balance wilderness protection and commercial interests, the Wilderness Act also made some compromises. These are reflected in three respects:

---

72 The USFS argued that the statutory wilderness would be contrary to its multiple-use management practices. Congress passed the MUSYA in 1960 and recognized the compatibility. For relevant discussions, see *infra* section 3.1 and section 6 of Chapter 6.
73 16 USC §§1131–6.
74 16 USC §1131(a) and §1132(d)).
75 16 USC §1131(c).
76 George Coggins, Charles Wilkinson and John Leshy, *Federal Public Land and Resources Law* (New York: Foundation Press, 2007), p. 1012.
77 See *Wilderness Society v. US Fish and Wildlife Service* (353 F. 3d 1051 (9th Cir. 2003) (en banc), amended by 360 F. 3d 1374 (9th Cir. 2004) (en banc)). Judge Graber pointed out two ambiguities embodied in the statutory language of 'wilderness': (1) wilderness is not absolutely off limits to all human interference because some human activities are to be allowed, and (2) there are two kinds of conflicting interpretations on how an agency should protect and manage an area so as to preserve its natural conditions: to protect against the introduction of artificial propagation programs that alter the natural ecological processes, or to preserve the natural ecological processes as they would exist in their wild state, in the absence of artificial disturbance from outside the wilderness area.
78 16 USC §1132(b)–(c). This inventory instruction was originally made to the NPS, the USFS and the FWS. Until Congress passed the FLPMA in 1976, wilderness inventory requirements were placed on the BLM (43 USC §1782(a)).
79 16 USC §1133(b)–(d).
80 16 USC §1132(c). For more discussion on regulation of commercial use within wilderness areas, see *infra* section 3.1 of Chapter 6.
81 John Nagle, 'The Spiritual Values of Wilderness', 35 (2005) *Environmental Law*, p. 961.

82 *Country Studies: United States*

1   It provided that any wilderness area would continue to be managed by the previous agency that had managed it before the designation.[82]
2   Congress reserved the right to designate new wilderness areas by clearly stating that 'no Federal lands shall be designated as "wilderness areas" except as provided for in this chapter or by a subsequent Act.'[83]
3   It generally prohibited construction of roads and commercial uses, and it also provided quite a few exceptions to have the Act passed.[84] It protected some existing uses and allowed for limited commercial use and resource exploitation within wilderness areas.[85]

The National Environmental Policy Act of 1969

The enactment of the National Environmental Policy Act (NEPA)[86] launched the modern environmental law era. The aim of the NEPA is to ensure that the decisions made by federal agencies are environmentally sound. Instead of creating an elaborate regulatory scheme, the NEPA adopts an 'unusual strategy'[87] to change the decision-making procedures used by federal agencies. It requires all federal agencies to take a close look at environmental consequences before they make decisions. The core requirement of the NEPA is outlined in its Section 102, which states that all federal agencies

> . . . include in every recommendation or report on proposals for legislation and other major federal actions significantly affecting the quality of the human environment, a detailed statement by the responsible official on:
>
> (i)   The environmental impact of the proposed action;
> (ii) Any adverse environmental effects which cannot be avoided should the proposal be implemented;
> (iii) Alternatives to the proposed action;
> (iv) The relationship between local short-term uses of man's environment and the maintenance and enhancement of long-term productivity; and
> (v)   Any irreversible and irretrievable commitments of resources which would be involved in the proposed action should it be implemented.[88]

This detailed statement is commonly known as an 'Environmental Impact Statement' (EIS). This model of assessing environmental impact has become 'the most widely emulated form

---

82 Section 2(b).
83 Section 2(a).
84 For a thorough discussion of wilderness exceptions, see John Nagle, 'Wilderness Exceptions', 44 (2014) *Environmental Law*, pp. 373–414 (the author identifies four types of exceptions: 1. Congress decided not to designate an area as wilderness even though the area possesses wilderness characteristics; 2. Congress draws the boundaries of a wilderness area to exclude land that possesses wilderness characteristics because Congress wants to allow activities there that would be forbidden by the Act; 3. Congress specifically authorizes otherwise prohibited activities when it establishes a new wilderness area, or 4. Congress acts to approve contested activities in response to a controversy that arises after a wilderness area has already been established.)
85 Section 4(c) and (d).
86 42 USC §§4321–70a.
87 Robert Percival et al., *Environmental Regulation: Law, Science, and Policy (sixth edition)* (New York: Aspen Publishers, 2009), p. 858.
88 42 USC §4332(C).

of environmental regulation' around the world.[89] The section also specifies the circumstances under which EIS should be prepared, that is, proposals for legislation and other major federal actions that significantly affect the quality of the human environment.[90] Among the five requirements, the consideration of alternatives is deemed the heart of the EIS.[91]

In addition to the EIS requirement, the NEPA provides for other two types of environmental review, 'environmental assessment'[92] and 'finding of no significant impact' (FONSI).[93] The former is a concise document prepared by agencies to determine whether to prepare an EIS or a FONSI. If it is found that significant impacts will result, an EIS is prepared. If it is determined that there will be no significant impact, a FONSI is prepared.

The Endangered Species Act of 1973

The Endangered Species Act (ESA)[94] was enacted to protect America's endangered and threatened wildlife. The implementation of the ESA is mainly governed by the FWS. One of the most remarkable provisions is Section 9, the so-called 'taking provision', which prohibits anyone from taking any endangered or threatened species. Section 3 defines 'taking' as 'to harass, harm, pursue, hunt, shoot, wound, kill, trap, capture, or collect, or attempt to engage in any such conduct'. The ESA also sets a bottom line for the federal government by requiring all federal agencies to consult with the FWS before they take any action. Section 7 requires federal agencies to consult with the FWS Secretary to ensure that any agency action 'is not likely to jeopardize the continued existence of any endangered species or threatened species or result in the destruction or adverse modification of habitat of such species'.[95] This consultation requirement is applicable to the NPS's species and habitat management decisions within the National Park System.

Congress intended to use this consultation procedure to 'reduce conflicts between economic development and endangered species protection'.[96] However, the record of consultation decisions is not satisfying. The Government Accountability Office report in 1992 showed that 90 percent of the FWS inquiries led to informal resolution, and 90 percent of the formal consultations resulted in no-jeopardy decisions.[97] Another report showed that among the 14,004 consultations completed by the FWS Region 1 in 2001, only 863 (6 percent) were

---

89 It is said that more than a hundred countries around the world require some form of EIA. See Alan Gilpin, *Environmental Impact Assessment (EIA): Cutting Edge for the Twenty-first Century* (Cambridge: Cambridge University Press, 1997), and Robert Percival, 'Law, Society and the Environment', in Robert Gordon and Morton Horowitz (eds.), *Law, Society and History: Themes in the Legal Sociology and Legal History of Lawrence M. Friedman* (Cambridge: Cambridge University Press 2011), p. 220 (noticing that 'nearly every country on the globe now requires some form of environmental assessment').

90 The courts have parsed these circumstances word by word, such as 'major federal actions', 'proposal for' and 'significantly affecting the quality of the human environment'. See *Lange v. Brinegar*, 625 F. 2d 812 (9th Cir. 1980); *Swain v. Brinegar*, 542 F. 2d 364 (7th Cir. 1976); *Kleppe v. Sierra Club*, 427 US 390 (1976), and *Hanly v. Kleindienst*, 471 F. 2d 823 (2nd Cir. 1972).

91 40 CFR §1502.14 (stating that [alternatives including the proposed action] is the heart of the EIS).

92 40 CFR §1508.9.

93 40 CFR §1508.13.

94 16 USC §§1531–44.

95 16 USC §1536(a)(2).

96 John Steiger, 'The Consultation Provision of Section 7 (a)(2) of the Endangered Species Act and Its Application to Delegable Federal Programs', 21 (1994) *Ecology Law Quarterly*, p. 256.

97 US Government Accountability Office, 'Endangered Species Act: Types and Number of Implementing Actions', May 8, 1992, GAO/RCED-92-131BR.

formal consultations, with three (0.02 percent) resulting in a finding of jeopardy.[98] These findings show that the FWS tries to 'avoid completely abandoning a proposed project' and attempts to find alternatives when implementing Section 7 consultations.[99]

The Administrative Procedure Act of 1946

The Administrative Procedure Act (APA)[100] was enacted as a response to the increasing scale of the administrative state during the New Deal era. It sets the ground rules for all federal agencies. The NPS and other federal public land agencies are no exception. They must conform to the 'notice and comment' requirements for informal agency rule making as well as other well-established rules for agency decision making.

In the context of public land, the APA is of particular importance in terms of its guidance in the judicial review of agency actions. It allows courts to set aside agency actions that are 'arbitrary, capricious, an abuse of discretion, or otherwise not in accordance with law',[101] which is usually referred to as the 'arbitrary and capricious standard'. Actions taken through formal adjudication or formal rule making are reviewed under a different standard, which is called the 'substantial evidence test'.[102]

Because some environment-related legislation, such as the Wild and Scenic River Act, does not authorize citizen suits, a judicial review of agency action is proposed under the APA based on its 'arbitrary and capricious' standard.

Common-law Doctrines

In addition to legislative mandates, common law plays a role in public land management. Two common-law doctrines are generally referenced: the public nuisance doctrine and the public trust doctrine (PTD). The public nuisance doctrine empowers members of the public whose rights are infringed by a 'nuisance'[103] to bring a lawsuit to enjoin the offending activities. The federal government is also empowered to enjoin activities that create nuisances on federal lands. In the specific context of national parks, Scheg notes the potential of this doctrine to control recreational activities by stating that

> ... if one considers the use of the national parks to be a right common to all, a public nuisance theory would seem to be ideally suited as authority for the government to bring lawsuits to control the detrimental activities of recreational users of the parks.[104]

In contrast, the PTD was and remains the most widely debated and discussed common-law doctrine in relation to natural resources management. Since the resurgence of the PTD in the 1970s as a result of the article by Professor Joseph Sax, 'The Public Trust Doctrine

---

98 US Government Printing Office, 'Endangered Species Act: Review of the Consultation Process Required by Section 7; Hearing before the Subcommittee on Fisheries, Wildlife, and Water', June 25, 2003, S. Hrg. 108–356.
99 John Steiger, *supra* note 96, p. 259; Mark Schwartz, 'The Performance of the Endangered Species Act', 39 (2008) *Annual Review of Ecology, Evolution, and Systematics*, p. 287.
100 5 USC §§551–706.
101 5 USC §706(2)(A).
102 5 USC §706(2)(E) (2000).
103 The Second Restatement of Torts defines a public nuisance as 'an unreasonable interference with a right common to the general public'. Restatement (Second) of Torts §821B (1979).
104 Nathan Scheg, 'Preservationists vs. Recreationists in Our National Parks', 5 (1998) *Hastings West-Northwest Journal of Environmental Law & Policy*, pp. 58–9.

in Natural Resources Law',[105] it has been lauded as a doctrine with the potential for environmental and natural resources protection, and it has also been subject to significant criticism.[106] Although there is hardly an undisputable definition, the PTD, at its core, is 'the idea that there are some resources, notably tidal and navigable waters and the lands under them that are forever subject to state ownership and protection in trust for the use and benefit of the public'.[107]

The judiciary plays a crucial role in expanding the scope of the PTD in terms of both geography and protected activities. The PTD traditionally confines itself to the field of tidal land and navigable waters. By active judicial promotion, it has extended to inland lakes, tributaries[108] and resources above high watermarks, such as dry land, beaches, parkland and wildlife.[109] In addition to geological expansion, there is an explicit expansion of activities to which PTD is applicable. The PTD was originally adopted to protect the activities of navigation, fishery and commerce. It is currently also used to protect recreational activities.[110]

The PTD is now broadly used in various causes of actions.[111] Generally, these can be classified into four categories:

1. The guarantee of citizens' access to natural resources,
2. Environmental and resource protection,
3. Limitation on the government's alienation of trust property, and
4. Limitation on the government's diversion of uses of trust property.[112]

However, the application of the PTD is deemed a matter of state law. Whether the PTD could be equally applied to federal lands, such as national parks (i.e. whether the federal government has the same trust duty and obligation as state governments do) is still controversial

---

105 Joseph Sax, 'The Public Trust Doctrine in Natural Resources Law: Effective Judicial Intervention', 68 (1970) *Michigan Law Review*, pp. 471–566. This article ranked 46 in Shapiro and Pearse's compiling of the most cited legal review articles. See Fred Shapiro and Michelle Pearse, 'The Most-Cited Law Review Articles of All Time', 110 (2012) *Michigan Law Review*, pp. 1483–553.
106 See Richard Lazarus, 'Changing Conceptions of Property and Sovereignty in Natural Resources: Questioning the Public Trust Doctrine,' 71 (1986) *Iowa Law Review*, pp. 631–716; William Araiza, 'Democracy, Distrust and the Public Trust: Process-Based Constitutional Theory, the Public Trust Doctrine and the Search for a Substantive Environmental Value', 45 (1997) *UCLA Law Review*, pp. 385–452, and James Huffman, 'Speaking of Inconvenient Truths: A History of the Public Trust Doctrine', 18 (2007) *Duke Environment Law & Policy Forum*, pp. 1–371.
107 Alexandra Klass, 'Modern Public Trust Principles: Recognizing Rights and Integrating Standards', 82 (2006) *Notre Dame Law Review*, p. 699.
108 For a thorough analysis of the expansion of PTD to inland lakes and tributaries in California, see Sarah Smith, 'A Public Trust Argument For Public Access To Private Conservation Land', 52 (2002) *Duke Law Journal*, pp. 631–4.
109 Mackenzie Keith, 'Judicial Protection for Beaches and Parks: The Public Trust Doctrine above the High Water Mark', 16 (2010) *Hastings West-Northwest Journal of Environmental Law & Policy*, pp. 165–191, and Susan Morath Horner, 'Embryo, Not Fossil: Breathing Life into the Public Trust Doctrine in Wildlife', 35 (2000) *Land & Water Law Review*, pp. 23–75.
110 Bertram Frey, 'The Public Trust in Surface Waterways and Submerged Lands of the Great Lakes States', 40 (2007) *University of Michigan Journal of Law Reform*, pp. 907–1055.
111 Plater et al. summarized three causes of actions: resource-defense or prevention-of-derogation, alienation and diversion. Moss summarizes three: diversion of use or alienation, diversion of trust assets to another agency and resource defense or derogation cases. See Zygmunt Plater et al., *Environmental Law and Policy: Nature, Law, and Society* (New York: Aspen Publishers: 2004), p. 1068, and Kenneth Moss, 'Public Trust Doctrine in South Carolina', 7 (1998) *South Carolina Environmental Law Journal*, p. 31.
112 See Yun Ma, 美国公共信托理论评介 (Review of the Public Trust Doctrine in the United States), unpublished master's dissertation of China University of Political Science and Law of 2011.

in literature.[113] Furthermore, federal courts differ in their opinions on this issue.[114] There is still no decisive and universal implication of the doctrine's applicability to federal land, including designated PAs. Scheg notes two disadvantages of the PTD. The first is its dependence on judicial interpretation. Courts may freely determine whether the NPS has affirmative trustee duties. The second is the uncertainty of what duties the public trusteeship may entail. Unless Congress explicitly imposes trustee duties on public land agencies by statutes, uncertainties remain with regard to the agencies' trustee duties in public land management.[115]

Considering the controversies and uncertainties stated above, this book mainly focuses on the statutory laws of public land management, which have been discussed in the previous sections.

Summary

First, law, especially the enactment of statutes, is employed as the principal tool to regulate and guide public land management. In addition to the trend of enacting environmental statutes such as the NEPA, due to the environmental movement in the 1970s, a comprehensive legislative framework on public land management has been in place since the beginning of the specific designation of public lands. In this context, national parks are governed by a complicated legislative framework. Congress has enacted several dozens of acts that govern national park management. Compared to most other countries, including China, congressional legislation governing national parks in the US is well developed and mature.

Second, different public land management agencies receive distinctive congressional mandates. In contrast to the BLM and the USFS's multiple-use mandate and the FWS's dominant-use mandate, the NPS is instructed to provide both conservation and enjoyment and to manage park lands based on a non-impairment standard.

Third, federal public land legislation has elevated environmental values to a prominent position. This is not only reflected in the Organic Acts for each management agency but also in overarching environmental legislation, such as the Wilderness Act and the NEPA. This tendency carries visible consequences: an increasing federal commitment to preservation, stricter management criteria, the extensive regulation of public land uses, broader civic involvement and a 'harder look' by the judiciary at agencies' decisions that may affect the environment.

Fourth, the legislative framework of the National Park System has been continually diversified and fragmented by enabling legislation. The core federal policy is reflected in the Organic Act, which remains the governing statute for the NPS and the entire system. However, it is seldom amended. Congress enacts enabling legislation for each unit of the

---

113 See Eric Pearson, 'The Public Trust Doctrine in Federal Law', 24 (2004) *Journal of Land Resources & Environmental Law*, p. 177 (the author refutes the inapplicability of PTD on federal land by stating that 'assuming the [PTD] should exist at all . . . the outstanding question is why it should not take on parallel contours at both the state and federal levels). See also Michael Blumm and Lynn Schaffer, 'The Federal Public Trust Doctrine: A Law Professors' Amicus Brief', Lewis & Clark Law School Legal Studies Research Paper No. 2014–18 (this amicus brief was signed by more than fifty law professors arguing a district court's interpretation of the PTD as a product of state law erroneous).
114 In *Sierra Club v. Department of the Interior*, the Sierra Club alleged that the NPS failed to protect Redwood National Park from private lumber companies and breached its duties as a public trustee of the park. The court supported the 'trustee' scenario. See *Sierra Club v. Department of the Interior*, 376 F. Supp. 90 (N.D. Cal. 1974). However, in another case, *Sierra Club v. Andrus*, the court denied that the NPS had special trustee obligations beyond those 'statutory duties'. See *Sierra Club v. Andrus*, 487 F. Supp. 443 (D.D.C. 1980).
115 Nathan Scheg, *supra* note 104, p. 60.

system, which makes the legislative framework quite diversified. Congress intends to specify management requirements in greater detail in the enabling legislation, which indicates the 'expanding role of congressional involvement in national park system management'.[116] This detailing tendency produces at least three consequences. First, managers must first look into enabling legislation to determine whether a specific issue has been addressed by Congress in the particular unit. Second, the NPS's power to make discretionary management decisions may shrink due to specific congressional instruction. Third, it makes courts' adjudicative work easier, which means courts may easily find 'the' answer prescribed in enabling legislation. For these reasons, Fischman argues that the Organic Act cannot serve as an indicator of trends, and enabling legislation deserves more academic attention to consider national-park-related issues.[117]

---

116 Robert Fischman, *supra* note 7, p. 781.
117 Ibid.

5 The Formation of Conflicts in Public Land Designation and Management

Introduction

The use pattern of public land in the US has witnessed a remarkable transformation. On the one hand, the early policy of promoting the recreational use of public land ushered in the arrival of mass recreation and industrial tourism, which incurred the increasing regulation of recreational activities. On the other hand, the increasing awareness of environmental protection calls for a stronger state commitment to nature conservation and both necessitates and justifies the more intensive regulation of the use of natural resources. Conflicts arising from both the changing land-use pattern and increasing regulation have perplexed public land managers.

This chapter discusses the transformation occurring on public land and the regulatory pattern of recreational use and reveals the main forms of conflicts arising from the transformation. First, key changes in public land use patterns are identified. Second, the evolution of recreational policies is revealed. Challenges in recreation management, especially overcrowding and underfunding, are addressed. Third, the regulation of recreational activities is discussed, with a particular focus on the regulation of the motorized recreational use of public land. Fourth, the main forms of conflict over recreation in modern times are presented. Examples include conflicts arising from extractive use and adjacent development, the construction of recreational amenities and the commercialization of park services, motorized recreational activities and hunting. Conflicts between recreational use and nonfederal rights are also examined to determine how 'property conflict' may be formulated in the context of the US.

A Changing Land Use Pattern of Public Lands

Public land in the US has been long exploited for commercial use, such as timber felling, grazing, hard rock mining and oil and gas drilling. This is especially the case for national forests and BLM lands that are managed on multiple use mandates,[1] whereas the total acreages of forest lands and BLM lands account for more than 70 percent of public lands. This public land-use pattern has undergone tremendous changes in recent decades. The most prominent two are increasing preservation and the recreational use of public land.

More than a decade ago, in their article 'The Transformation on Public Lands', Laitos and Carr observed two-fold changes to the use of public lands: the rise and fall of traditional commodity uses of public lands and the growth of recreation and preservation uses of public lands.[2] Based on this observation, they further argued that the multiple-use pattern had

---

[1] See *supra* pp. 78–80 of Chapter 4, the MUSYA of 1960 for the USFS and the FLPMA of 1976 for the BLM.
[2] Jan Laitos and Thomas Carr. 'The Transformation on Public Lands', 26.2 (1999) *Ecology Law Quarterly*, pp. 140–242.

failed to accomplish the goal of simultaneously producing compatible resources.[3] They also predicted that 'the looming conflict in public land use will be between two former allies – recreation and preservation interests.'[4] The main type of conflict on public land was between 'low-impact, human powered recreational users (preservationists) and high impact, motorized recreational users (recreationists)'.[5] Five years later, in another article, Laitos and Reiss took their conclusions one step further. They proclaimed that there was a 'recreational war' for natural resources on public land,[6] and argued that public land was shifting from a paradigm of a multiple-use system to a dominant-use one. Recreation and preservation had become new forms of dominant uses of public lands.[7] They further specified that the dominant forms of conflicts on public land were those among three groups, preservationists, 'high impact, non-motorized recreationists' and motorized recreationists.[8]

These observations of the transformation of public land are echoed by other scholars. Stevens and Frank note two phenomena currently occurring on public lands: the exalted place that environmental preservation has occupied and the rise of recreation as a major use of public lands.[9] The academic observation also echoes public opinion on the desired use pattern of public lands. According to a poll in 2013, on the list of 'very important priority' areas for public lands managed by the federal government, two choices were at the top: the first was 'permanently protect/conserve public lands for future generations', accounting for 65 percent, and the second was 'ensure access to public lands for recreation', accounting for 63 percent.[10]

A consensus has been achieved on the rising role of preservation and recreation. However, whether it is accurate to claim that recreation has replaced traditional commodity use and thus has become a dominant or major use of public lands remains controversial.[11] Laitos and Carr argue that the commodity uses of public lands are in decline. However, there may be some limitations to this argument. Currently, 15 years after Laitos's first article was written, oil and gas drilling is still one of the most lucrative activities occurring on public lands. Federal lands produce 11 percent of the nation's natural gas supply and 5 percent of its oil.[12] Statistics show that sales of oil and gas leasing on public lands grew by 20 percent in 2011. Among all of the leases, the BLM brought in $256 million compared to $213 million in 2010.[13] Though the data show a decrease in 2012 and 2013, the total earnings remained above

---

3 Ibid., p. 145.
4 Ibid., p. 144.
5 Ibid.
6 Jan Laitos and Rachael Reiss, 'Recreation Wars for Our Natural Resources', 34 (2004) *Environmental Law*, pp. 1091–122.
7 Ibid., p. 1091.
8 Ibid., pp. 1108–14.
9 Jan Stevens and Richard Frank, 'Current Policy and Legal Issues Affecting Recreational Use of Public Lands in the American West', Resources for the Future Discussion Paper 09–23, July 2009, p. 2. Full text is available at http://www.rff.org/RFF/Documents/RFF-DP-09-23.pdf. Last visited January 2015.
10 Hart Research Associates, 'Equal Ground – Balancing Conservation and Drilling on America's Public Lands', June 12, 2013. Full text is available at http://cdn.americanprogress.org/wp-content/uploads/2013/06/MEMO-Hart-Research-Equal-Ground-06-2013.pdf. Last visited January 2015.
11 Robert Fischman and Robert Keiter expressed their concerns about the so-called 'dominant use' paradigm. The author's personal interview with them was in January 2014.
12 See US Department of the Interior, BLM, 'Oil and Gas', available at http://www.blm.gov/wo/st/en/prog/energy/oil_and_gas.html. Last visited January 2015.
13 Puneet Kollipara, 'Oil and Gas Leases on Public Lands Up 20 Percent in 2011, Feds Say', January 20, 2012. Available at http://fuelfix.com/blog/2012/01/10/oil-and-gas-leases-on-public-lands-up-20-percent-in-2011-feds-say/. Last visited January 2015.

$200 million.[14] These figures do not necessarily indicate that oil and gas drilling activities have more monetary value than preservation and recreation because their measuring methods may differ substantially. It is difficult or even meaningless to compare the two groups solely in monetary terms. However, they show that the commodity use of nature still possesses an important role in the overall public land-use pattern.

Compared to 15 years ago, when Laitos's article was written, the process of shifting from commodity use to preservation and recreational use seems to have been tempered. In addition to the steady role of commodity use that was previously clarified, recreational visits have maintained a moderately stable level since the 1990s.[15] The overwhelming environmental pursuit to curb economic development has encountered a counterforce composed of private business and local communities, which, to a certain extent, has pushed back this shifting process. Transformation has thus become more dynamic and locked in a fluctuating struggle.

No matter how recreational use and commodity use are portioned, a simple observation is that there is a growing demand for the recreational use of public land. Recreational use has become a crucial, if not dominant, component of public land use. The Department of Interior (DOI) estimates that hunting, fishing, and other outdoor recreation contributes an estimated $730 billion to the US economy each year.[16] A NPS report shows that park visitors spent $12.95 billion in gateway regions. This amounts to '251,600 jobs, $9.34 billion in labor income, and $16.50 billion in value added'.[17] A recent report by the Fish and Wildlife Service (FWS) shows that wildlife-refuge-based recreation has a significant influence on local economies. In the fiscal year 2011, recreational spending in the National Wildlife Refuge System generated '$2.4 billion of sales in regional economies'.[18] A second observation is that there is a corresponding commitment, either political or legal, toward nature conservation, which is seen in the frequent enactment of environmental statutes since the late 1960s. Furthermore, Laitos's observation of the division between recreationists and preservationists is largely verified by increasing regulation on recreational activities and the follow-up disputes heard in courts.[19]

Burgeoning Recreational Use and the Intensive Management of Recreational Activities

Promotion of Recreation in the Early Period

When the NPS was established, recreation was viewed an important component of the national park experience and was extensively promoted in park policies. The rationale was that the new national parks needed 'a strong political constituency to ensure congressional

---

14 The total receipts in 2012 were US$233 million, and US$202 million in 2013. See BLM, 'Oil and Gas Lease Sales, Calender Years 2009–2013'. Available at http://www.blm.gov/wo/st/en/prog/energy/oil_and_gas/statistics.html. Last visited January 2015.
15 For details, see *infra* p. 95.
16 DOI, 'Fiscal Year 2013, The Interior Budget in Brief (February 2012)', p. DO 7. Full text is available at http://www.doi.gov/budget/appropriations/2013/highlights/upload/2013_Highlights_Book.pdf. Last visited January 2015.
17 Yue Cui et al., 'Economic Benefits to Local Communities from National Park Visitation, 2011', February 2013, Natural Resource Report NPS/NRSS/ARD/NRR–2013/632 , p. v. Full text is available at http://www.nature.nps.gov/socialscience/docs/NPSSystemEstimates2011.pdf. Last visited January 2015.
18 Erin Carver and James Caudill, 'US Fish & Wildlife Service – Banking on Nature: The Economic Benefits to Local Communities of National Wildlife Refuge Visitation', October 2013, p. ii. Available at http://www.fws.gov/refuges/about/RefugeReports/pdfs/BankingOnNature2013.pdf. Last visited January 2015.
19 For more details, see *infra* p. 130 et seq. of Chapter 7.

protection, and that constituency would primarily be the American citizens who visited the parks and developed lasting ties with them'.[20] The first director of the NPS, Stephen Mather, aimed to promote the accessibility of national parks to the public.[21] This aim is evident in the Lane Letter, which instructed the NPS to approve luxurious hotels and to collaborate with railroad and highway companies to promote park visitation.[22] The NPS welcomed people to visit, and the more the better.

Congress confirmed public recreation as part of the mission of the newly established NPS in the Organic Act of 1916 by using the word 'enjoyment'. The NPS's strategy was to promote recreation and make national parks more accessible to the public. Since the beginning, the NPS has been working in tandem with railroad companies to construct roads to and within parks. The arrival of the automobile era in the 1920s further broadened the accessibility of national parks to the general public. Economic prosperity and greater leisure time stimulated more recreational visitation to national parks. In addition, nature was actively manipulated by the NPS to provide better visiting experiences to visitors, such as the eradication of 'bad' animals and the extinguishing of wildfires.[23]

National parks witnessed an intensive expansion of recreational amenities throughout the period from the 1930s to the 1960s. This expansion was largely accomplished by two programs: the Civilian Conservation Corps (CCC) from 1933 to 1942 and Mission 66 from 1956 to 1966.

The CCC operated as part of Roosevelt's New Deal programs. It largely expanded the role of the NPS in providing recreational services.[24] The CCC helped the NPS to construct public recreational facilities, such as roads, camps, trails, cabins, swimming pools, and picnicking and camping facilities. It is calculated that when the CCC ended, '2,186 miles of road, 188 new water lines, 5,310 new campground acres, and various other building projects were added to the national parks.'[25]

After World War II, recreational visits to national parks skyrocketed. Facing the need to renovate park facilities and recognizing the opportunity of the upcoming fiftieth anniversary, the NPS launched the so-called 'Mission 66' program to be completed by 1966. This program aimed to expand park facilities and attract more visitors. Congress showed great support for the NPS's ambition: it 'responded with everything Wirth [the then NPS Director] asked for, and initially Mission 66 was hailed as a great success'.[26] This was a symbol of the shift of national park management policy toward industrial tourism and intensive recreational

---

20 Robert B. Keiter, *To Conserve Unimpaired: The Evolution of the National Park Idea* (Washington, DC: Island Press, 2013), pp. 15–16.
21 Ibid., p. 15.
22 The Lane Letter was written from the Secretary of the Interior Franklin Lane to Stephen Mather in 1918. This letter is deemed the first official interpretation of the Organic Act after its enactment in 1916 and therefore gains broad academic attention. See 'Secretary Lane's Letter on National Park Service Management', May 13, 1918, in Lary Dilsaver (ed.), *America's National Park System: The Critical Documents* (Lanham, MD: Rowman and Littlefield, 1994), pp. 48–52.
23 Robert Keiter, *supra* note 20, p. 46.
24 See generally Richard Sellars, 'New Deal Impacts on the Park Service', in idem, *Preserving Nature in the National Parks* (New Haven, CT and London: Yale University Press, 2009), pp. 140–42; Conrad Wirth, *Parks, Politics, and People* (Norman: University of Oklahoma Press, 1980), pp. 128–57, and John Paige, *The Civilian Conservation Corps and the National Park Service, 1933–1942: An Administrative History* (Washington, DC: National Park Service, 1985).
25 Robert Keiter, *supra* note 20, p. 47.
26 Ethan Carr, 'Park, Forest and Wilderness', 17.2 (2002) *The George Wright Forum*, p. 22.

development.[27] Large-scale construction in the Mission 66 program incurred criticism from preservationists, especially the Sierra Club, which questioned the appropriateness of prioritizing new construction in national parks instead of preservation activities.[28]

Responses to the Arrival of Mass Recreation

In the post- World War II era, public demand for outdoor recreation surged, and an era of mass recreation arrived. Figure 5.1 shows that recreational visits in 1960 increased 24 times over the 1930s, before the war. Current recreational visitation has experienced another 3.5-time increase from the 1960s.

In addition to the increasing recreational use of national park lands, other public land management agencies also experienced burgeoning recreational demands. The BLM reports that eight out of every ten contacts between the BLM and the public relate to recreation.[29] The latest report from the USFS shows that there were approximately 165.9 million annual recreational visits to national forest lands throughout the fiscal years 2007 to 2011.[30] In 2010, there were approximately 439 million recreational visits to DOI-administered sites, which included nearly 58 million visits to BLM public lands, more than 281 million to NPS units, more than 47 million to national wildlife refuges, 2 million to fish hatcheries, and 90 million to Bureau of Reclamation recreation sites.[31]

In response to mass recreation, several visible moves have been made on the congressional, executive or agency levels. These changes can be seen in the establishment of new recreation-based institutions, the expansion of the National Park System, new types of recreation-oriented designations and specific congressional legislation on recreation issues.

First, from an institutional perspective, Congress created the first Outdoor Recreation Review Commission (ORRC) in 1958 to complete another inventory of recreational resources and to recommend ways to meet surging demand over the next several decades. Following the ORRC's recommendation in its 1962 report, two explicit changes occurred: first, the Bureau of Outdoor Recreation was specifically created in 1962 to focus on recreational issues,[32] and second, Congress passed the Land and Water Conservation Fund Act of 1964 to acquire lands for recreational purposes.[33] The ORRC also introduced the notion of charging user fees for recreational activities. Since then, charging user fees has been gradually incorporated into federal policy.

By a presidential executive order, the President's Commission on Outdoor Recreation Resources Review, later renamed the President's Commission on Americans Outdoors,

---

27 See generally Richard Sellars, *supra* note 24, pp. 180–85; Conrad Wirth, *supra* note 24, pp. 266–70, and Robert Keiter, *supra* note 20, pp. 47–9.
28 Ethan Carr, *supra* note 26, p. 23.
29 BLM, 'People, Places, & Partners: Planning, Managing, and Enhancing Recreational Experiences on BLM Public Lands', available at http://www.blm.gov/pgdata/etc/medialib/blm/wo/Communications_Directorate/general_publications/ppp.Par.31679.File.dat/blmRecHandout.pdf. Last visited January 2015.
30 USFS, 'National Visitor Use Monitoring Results USDA Forest Service National Summary Report', May 22, 2012, available at http://www.fs.fed.us/recreation/programs/nvum/nvum_national_summary_fy2011.pdf. Last visited January 2015.
31 DOI, 'Fiscal Year 2013, The Interior Budget in Brief (February 2012)', p. DO 22, available at http://www.doi.gov/budget/appropriations/2013/highlights/upload/2013_Highlights_Book.pdf. Last visited January 2015.
32 The Bureau of Outdoor Recreation was short-lived. It was replaced by the Heritage Conservation and Recreation Service in 1977. The latter was again reorganized to be governed by the NPS in 1981.
33 16 USC §§4601–4 *et seq.*

Conflicts in Public Land Designation: the US 93

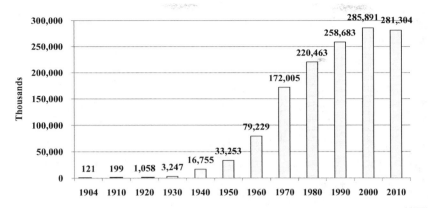

Figure 5.1 Recreational visitation to all national park units (1904–2010)
Source: NPS statistics, 'Annual Abstracts and Forecast Reports' (1904–2010)

was established in 1985 to review existing public outdoor recreation policies, programs and opportunities.[34]

Second, Congress has significantly expanded the park system to meet escalating recreational demands. Figure 5.2 shows that from less than fifty national park units in the 1930s, Congress and the president designated hundreds of new units to the National Park System, which resulted in more than four hundred units currently within the system.

Third, new types of designations were created by Congress, which diversified the components of the National Park System. Some new designations were especially created for recreational purposes, such as national recreational areas and national scenic trails. The first National Recreation Area was designated in 1936, and the first National Seashore was created soon after that.[35] There are now more than twenty different types of designations within the system. Congress has added 18 national recreation areas, 14 national lakeshores and seashores, 3 national scenic trails, 15 national rivers and others to the National Park System.

Fourth, several acts were enacted by Congress specifically targeting outdoor recreation, such as the Outdoor Recreation Act of 1963 to promote outdoor recreation programs[36] and the National Trails System Act to preserve outdoor historic resources and provide for recreation needs.[37] The Land and Water Conservation Act in 1964 made substantive funding available for federal, state and local governments to acquire land, water and wetlands for recreational use.

---

34 Executive Order 12503, January 28, 1985. See also George Siehl, 'The Policy Path to the Great Outdoors: A History of the Outdoor Recreation Review Commissions', Resources for the Future Discussion Paper 08–44, October 2008. Full text is available at http://www.rff.org/Documents/RFF-DP-08-44.pdf. Last visited January 2015.
35 Respectively, the Lake Mead on the Colorado River, 16 USC §460(n) *et seq.* and the Cape Hatteras (renamed the Cape Hatteras National Seashore Recreational Area in 1940), 16 USC §§459 a-1 *et seq.*
36 Pub. L. 88–29 ('all American people of present and future generations be assured adequate outdoor recreation resources' and federal government should 'promote the coordination and development of effective programs relating to outdoor recreation').
37 Pub. L. 90–543; 82 Stat. 919; 16 USC §1241 *et seq.* ('provide for the ever-increasing outdoor recreation needs of an expanding population and . . . promote the preservation of, public access to, travel within, and enjoyment and appreciation of the open-air, outdoor areas and historic resources of the Nation').

94   *Country Studies: United States*

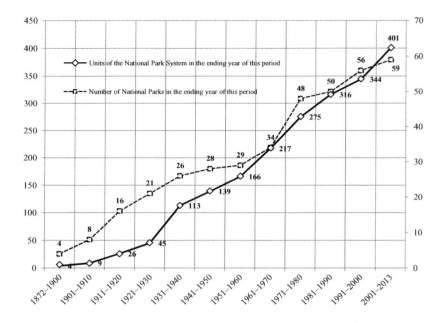

Figure 5.2 Number of units of the National Park System and national parks by decade (1872–2013)
Source: NPS Statistics; Harpers Ferry Center and NPS[38]

Challenges to Recreation Management: Overcrowding and Underfunding

The arrival of mass recreation has brought considerable challenges to park managers. The most visible problem is overcrowding. It has been claimed that 'the American people are loving their national parks to death.'[39] Rapidly increasing park visitation has placed relentless pressure on maintaining landscapes, habitats and resources inside parks. The NPS's conventional strategy to accommodate increasing visitors is to build more accommodation facilities, instead of capping them.[40] However, underfunding and budget cuts have further increased the difficulty of construction projects and effective visitor management.

In addition to a first-glance observation of the overcrowding problem, some recent tendencies shed light on this old problem and bring new challenges to park managers. Figure 5.3 shows that although recreational visits have skyrocketed since the 1940s, in recent years,

38 NPS Statistics, 'Annual Summary Report (1904 – Last Calendar Year)', available at https://irma.nps.gov/Stats/SSRSReports/National%20Reports/Annual%20Summary%20Report%20(1904%20-%20Last%20Calendar%20Year), and Harpers Ferry Center and NPS, *The National Parks: Shaping the System* (Washington, DC: US DOI, 2005), appendix 'Park Origins Chronological Summary', available at http://www.cr.nps.gov/history/online_books/mackintosh1/sts3.htm. Both were last visited in January 2015. Due to re-name, re-designation, combination and de-designation of certain park units, the number in total may not equal the sum of individual items.
39 Dennis Herman, 'Loving Them to Death: Legal Controls on the Type and Scale of Development in the National Parks', 11 (1992) *Stanford Environmental Law Journal*, pp. 3–67, and Federico Cheever, 'The United States Forest Service and National Park Service: Paradoxical Mandates, Powerful Founders, and the Rise and Fall of Agency Discretion', 74 (1997) *Denver University Law Review*, p. 637.
40 This strategy is challenged in courts. See *infra* p. 146 et seq. of Chapter 7 (Merced River 'user capacity' controversy).

national park visitation has not experienced a sharp increase as it did before. Instead, park visitation has been maintained at approximately 280 million per year. Some commentators even assert that park visitation has experienced a 'steep decline'. This is seen in the decrease of the number of overnight stays and camping.[41] This decrease can be partly attributed to the NPS's failure to attract young people and minorities outdoors.[42] Park visitors are largely well-paid older generations who have long been park lovers; however, younger generations and minority groups are losing interest in outdoor recreation. Another phenomenon, along with the overall decrease of park visitation, is the unbalanced distribution of visitation among different park units. Some popular sites, such as Yellowstone and Yosemite, have been under great pressure due to overcrowding. However, visitation to less well-known and remote park sites is limited and even decreasing.

These phenomena have caused some consternation among members of Congress and the NPS. They consider declining numbers of visitors to be a symbol of eroding constituencies to national parks and envision budget cuts to the NPS. There have been calls in recent years to promote greater industrial recreation and commercialized recreational activities in parks to reconnect national parks to the American people.[43] In April 2010, President Obama launched the America's Great Outdoor initiative to reconnect Americans, especially youth, with outdoor recreation.[44] Therefore, the NPS is struggling, on the one hand, to ease the pressure of overcrowding in certain areas; on the other hand, it is struggling to promote and encourage more people to go outdoors. If the NPS's latter strategy turns out to be successful, it could be expected that the overcrowding problem within national parks may become more serious.

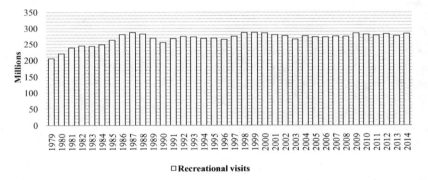

Figure 5.3 Recreational visits to units of the National Park System per year (1979–2014)
Source: NPS Statistics[45]

---

41 Julie Cart, 'Camp? Outside? Um, No Thanks', *Los Angeles Times*, November 24, 2006 (overnight stays fell 20 percent, tent camping and backcountry camping each decreased 24 percent during the period 1995–2005). Available at http://articles.latimes.com/2006/nov/24/local/me-natparks24. Last visited January 2015.
42 Denise Antolini, 'National Park Law In The US: Conservation, Conflict, And Centennial Values', 33 (2009) *William and Mary Environmental Law and Policy Review*, p. 878.
43 Julie Cart, *supra* note 41.
44 See AGO, 'About America's Great Outdoor', available at http://www.doi.gov/americasgreatoutdoors/whatwedo/index.cfm. Last visited January 2015.
45 NPS Statistics, 'Annual Visitation Summary Report (1979 – Last Calendar Year)', available at https://irma.nps.gov/Stats/Reports/National. Last visited April 2015.

In terms of the budget, although the Land and Water Conservation Act was enacted to assist in the acquisition of lands for recreational use, Congress only fully funded these projects once. Throughout the 1970s, 1980s and early 1990s, national parks incurred a $3.5 million backlog in maintenance projects.[46] Underfunding produces three potential consequences: first, the daily management budget is decreased, so parks lack sufficient staff for visitor-related work; second, the decaying infrastructure cannot be repaired in time, which poses safety risks to visitors; and third, research programs may be discontinued or postponed, which leads to insufficiencies in the scientific research and monitoring of ecological processes.

There are multiple reasons for the current situation. Since the 1970s, Congress has approved more than a hundred units to the National Park System. Most of these new parks were created solely because members of Congress wanted new parks in their districts.[47] The NPS is reluctant to refuse Congress members' proposals for 'park pork barrel' projects because it depends on Congress's appropriation of funding.[48] As of March 2013, only one state, Delaware, did not have a national park designation. Urged by Delaware politicians, who stated that they 'also want to have a national park', the First State National Monument was finally designated by the president in March 2013, and the National Park System was finally spread across all fifty states.[49] However, whether there is a true need to designate so many parks and whether these proposed parks truly meet the 'national significance' standard to be included in the system is overlooked. The NPS has also spent money on extravagantly overpriced construction projects, such as the toilets at Delaware Gap National Recreation Area, which cost $333,000.[50]

Partly to address the underfunding problem, in 1996, Congress enacted the 'fee demonstration program', which allowed 100 out of 375 park units to charge higher entrance fees and keep 80 percent of the revenues.[51] The Omnibus Management Act of 1998, as discussed above, was also a response to the funding problem by increasing concession fees and conducting budget and funding reforms. However, due to recent government retrenchment, funding for public lands has been greatly reduced. Figure 5.4 shows that after reaching a peak in 2010 of $3.15 billion, the NPS budget has continually decreased since 2011, with a slight increase in 2014. In terms of the percentage of the NPS budget to federal outlays, there is a tendency toward a continuous decrease, and the percentage has fluctuated approximately 0.08 percent in recent years. Although compared to most developing countries and even most developed countries, the US allocates a considerable amount of money to PA management,[52] there are still increasing concerns about the negative consequences of budget cuts for parks.[53]

---

46 Richard Ansson and Dalton Hooks, 'Protecting and Preserving Our National Parks in the Twenty First Century: Are Additional Reforms Needed Above and Beyond the Requirements of the 1998 National Parks Omnibus Management Act?', 62.2 (2001) *Montana Law Review*, p. 215.
47 Ibid., p. 216; Richard Ansson, 'Our National Parks-Overcrowded, Underfunded, and Besieged with a Myriad of Vexing Problems: How Can We Best Fund Our Imperiled National Park System', 14 (1998) *Journal of Land Use & Environmental Law*, p. 19.
48 Richard Ansson, ibid., p. 20.
49 Brad Scriber, 'Delaware Gets Its First National Monument', *National Geographic News*, March 26, 2013. Available at http://news.nationalgeographic.com/news/2013/03/130326-delaware-first-state-national-monument-science-nation/. Last visited February 2014.
50 Richard Ansson, *supra* note 47, p. 21.
51 Omnibus Consolidated Rescissions and Appropriations Act of 1996, P.L. 103–104.
52 For a comparison among countries in PA funding, see *infra* p. 186 of Chapter 9.
53 For a recent discussion on the budget of the NPS, see Tom Coburn, 'PARKED! How Congress' Misplaced Priorities are Trashing Our National Treasures', October 2013, pp. 33–82, available at http://www.novoco.com/historic/resource_files/research/coburn_parked_how_congress_misplaced_priorities_are_trashing_our_national_treasures_110713.pdf. Last visited January 2016.

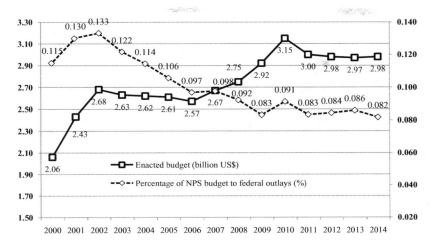

Figure 5.4 Enacted budgets of the NPS and their percentages in federal outlays (fiscal years 2000–14)
Source: DOI, Office of Budget; NPS, Budget Justifications (Green Book) and White House, 'Historical Tables'[54]

Conflicts in Public Land Management

Controversy over how to manage and use public lands is described as being 'as American as apple pie and as old as the nation'.[55] Old conflicts gradually shift in their focus and intensity, and new conflicts emerge. These conflicts mainly focus on three types of public land uses: development, conservation and recreation.

Adjacent Development and Extractive Use vs. Conservation and Recreation

Adjacent Development

Extractive industrial uses in national parks are generally banned. However, national parks are not islands; instead, they are part of a shared landscape. The original boundary of a national park may be a product of political negotiation and compromise. Therefore, it may not fully represent a complete ecological system. Because ecological processes occur across boundaries, activities occurring within park boundaries may have impacts outside of these boundaries, and the activities occurring on adjacent lands may significantly affect a park's resources and value.

Extractive uses outside park boundaries threaten the effective conservation of national parks.[56] It is recognized that more than 50 percent of the approximately 5.7 million acres of habitats suitable for grizzly bears in the Greater Yellowstone Ecosystem lies within USFS lands

---

54 In terms of the enacted budget of the NPS, most of the data in the table is from the website of DOI, Office of Budget, available at http://www.doi.gov/budget/appropriations/index.cfm. In the case that the number of enacted budgets in a specific fiscal year is not provided in the DOI website, the number provided by the NPS Greenbooks is used, which is available at http://www.nps.gov/aboutus/budget.htm. The data of federal overlays is from White House, 'Summary of Receipts, Outlays, and Surpluses or Deficits: 1989–2019', available at http://www.whitehouse.gov/OMB/BUDGET/HISTORICALS. All were last visited in January 2015.
55 Jan Stevens and Richard Frank, *supra* note 9.
56 The initial concern of adjacent development was addressed in the Redwood Amendment of 1978. See *supra* p. 75 of Chapter 4.

that are under a multiple-use mandate.[57] The destructive use of BLM lands also threatens adjacent national parks. For example, the landfill project on BLM lands near Joshua Tree National Park was supposed to receive 20,000 tons of trash every day.[58] Oil- and gas-drilling activities on adjacent BLM lands may damage park resources and visitors' experiences by producing constant noise, uncertain and unstudied air and water impacts, and visible rigs from park trails day and night. Using the technology of hydraulic fracturing, or fracking, oil and natural gas are extracted from shale formations buried deep beneath the surface, producing considerable harm to air, water and wildlife.[59] Furthermore, oil- and gas-drilling activities may have destructive influences on gateway communities' tourism economies. Conflicts are thus intensified.

Political controversies arise from the issue of adjacent development. The shift of energy policy during the transition from the Bush Administration to the Obama Administration may illustrate this type of controversy. In December 2008, the Bush Administration issued six auction plans for oil and gas leases on BLM lands in Utah that were near two iconic national parks, Arches and Canyonlands. To protect the national parks and prevent the industries from obtaining a lease, a university student bid on several of the lease parcels with no intention of paying for them. He was sentenced to jail for civil disobedience.[60] Following six lawsuits brought by the NPCA and other groups, the BLM was ordered by the courts to remove the most controversial parcels in the proposed plans. In 2009, the Obama Administration agreed to remove an additional 77 offending leases from the Moab auction. A new leasing process, called the 'Master Leasing Plans', was also launched. It specifically examined how oil and gas was leased in particular controversial areas, such as lands with high recreational and ecological value, including many lands near national parks.[61]

To cope with the problem of adjacent development, academics have proposed to expand the boundaries of national parks by annexing adjacent lands.[62] Such practices have also taken place. In the 1960s, Walt Disney proposed to build a ski resort in the Mineral King Valley that was previously managed by the USFS. This project called for 27 ski lifts for 2 million visitors per year. After decades of disputes and lawsuits,[63] in 1978, Congress added the proposed ski lands to the Sequoia National Park and thus ended the dispute.[64]

---

57 Craig Shafer, 'The Unspoken Option to Help Safeguard America's National Parks: An Examination of Expanding US National Park Boundaries by Annexing Adjacent Federal Lands', 35 (2010) *Columbia Journal of Environmental Law*, p. 58.
58 After being disputed in courts, this project was finally revoked by a court ruling in 2009. See NPCA, 'Joshua Tree National Park', available at http://www.npca.org/parks/joshua-tree-national-park.html. Last visited January 2015.
59 In 2013, the NPCA issued a special report on what large-scale oil and gas development adjacent to national parks could mean for these parks. See NPCA, 'A Responsible Process: Using Master Leasing Plans to Balance Sensible Energy Development and the Protection of National Parks', 2013, available at http://www.npca.org/assets/pdf/A-Responsible-Process-web-spreads.pdf. Last visited January 2015.
60 Nick Lund, 'The DeChristopher Effect: How Years of Controversy over Drilling for Energy in the Southwest Could Result in Compromise', January 22, 2014; available at http://www.parkadvocate.org/the-dechristopher-effect-how-years-of-controversy-over-drilling-for-energy-in-the-southwest-could-result-in-compromise/. Last visited January 2015.
61 See NPCA, *supra* note 59.
62 Craig Shafer, *supra* note 57.
63 See *Sierra Club v. Morton*, 405 US 727 (1972).
64 16 USC §45f ('Mineral King Valley addition authorized'). For more information, see Nathan Masters, 'In the '60s, Disney Almost Built a Ski Resort in Sequoia National Park', February 18, 2014. Available at http://southland.gizmodo.com/a-mountain-disneyland-how-disney-almost-built-a-ski-re-1525286740. Last visited January 2015.

Mining, Oil and Gas Drilling and Abandoned Mines

Due to the low cost (nearly free) and exclusive rights to mining provided in the General Mining Act of 1872,[65] numerous mines were developed, especially in the Western region. Mining activities inside parks are currently under intense regulation. New mining claims under the 1872 General Mining Act are prohibited in all park units. However, existing mining rights within national parks continue to threaten the protection of park land and resources. In 1976, in response to controversies over ongoing mining activities in the Death Valley and Denali National Parks, Congress enacted the Mining in the Parks Act to put these existing mining rights under NPS regulation.[66] It is generally required that prospective operators should obtain the approval of their plans of operation from the NPS.

Similarly, nonfederal oil- and gas-drilling activities inside national parks are under federal regulation. Prospective operators are required to obtain approval from the NPS for their operation plans.[67] However, as a compromise, approximately 60 percent of the 534 nonfederal oil and gas operations in twelve units are exempted from such regulations.[68] These exemptions continue to threaten park conservation.

Furthermore, after they were exploited to their maximum economic potential, mines were abandoned, leaving behind rotting structures and hazardous materials. Though mining in national parks has been intensively regulated, these abandoned mines have not been cleaned up, and they have become hazards for recreationists.[69] As of 2008, there were 'at least 161,000 [hardrock mine] sites in [12 Western states] with at least 332,000 features that may pose physical safety hazards and at least 33,000 sites that have degraded the environment'.[70] After inspecting the management of abandoned mines on BLM and NPS lands,[71] the DOI released an audit report in 2008 and concluded that the BLM and NPS have 'put the public's health and safety at risk by not addressing hazards posed by abandoned mines on their lands'.[72]

Abandoned mines also present the risk of contaminating ground water, which adversely influences swimming, fishing and other water-related recreational activities. For example, the long-abandoned Pennsylvania Mine in Colorado causes continuous pollution to the Peru Creek through toxic metals. The creek flows downstream to the Snake River, which winds through the White River National Forest. The pollution has caused the decimation of trout

---

65 It provides that 'all valuable mineral deposits in lands belonging to the United States, both surveyed and unsurveyed, shall be free and open to exploration and purchase ... by citizens of the United States' (30 USC §22).

66 16 USC §1901 *et seq*. The Act governs activities 'resulting from the exercise of valid existing mineral rights on patented or unpatented mining claims within any area of the National Park System,' and makes such activities subject to 'regulations prescribed by the Secretary of the Interior as he deems necessary or desirable for the preservation and management of those areas' (16 USC §1902).

67 36 CFR. Part 9, Subpart B (the so-called '9B regulations').

68 NPS, 'Oil and Gas Management', available at http://www.nature.nps.gov/GEOLOGY/oil_and_gas/index.cfm. Last visited January 2015.

69 Jan Stevens and Richard Frank, *supra* note 9, p. 7.

70 See Government Accountability Office, 'Hardrock Mining: Information on Abandoned Mines and Value and Coverage of Financial Assurances On BLM Land', GAO-08-574T (2008), front page and p. 13. Full text is available at http://www.gao.gov/assets/120/119391.pdf. Last visited January 2015.

71 Most of the abandoned mines are located on BLM and USFS lands. The vast majority of abandoned mines on NPS lands are located in the California desert areas, specifically at the Death Valley National Park, Mojave National Preserve and Joshua Tree National Park. See DOI, Office of Inspector General, 'Audit Report: Abandoned Mine Lands in the Department of the Interior', *C-IN-MOA-0004–2007*, July 2008, p. 2, available at https://www.blm.gov/epl-front-office/projects/nepa/31261/37258/39058/OIG-AML_Report_7-08.pdf. Last visited January 2015.

72 Ibid., p. 1.

stocked for fishing purposes and has led to considerable losses to local communities because tourism is the primary source of revenue in adjacent areas.[73]

Nonfederal Rights vs. Public Land Control

Due to the disposal of public lands throughout the nineteenth century in American history, such as railroad land grants, homestead claims and mining patents, American public land presents a checkerboard feature. Though a large part of national park lands is federally owned, parcels of private and state lands are scattered within the system.[74] The NPS must contend with these nonfederal claims when conserving and accommodating visitors inside parks.

Rights of Way

As part of the Mining Law of 1866, the Revised Statute 2477, commonly known as R.S. 2477, was enacted by Congress to grant 'the right-of-way for the construction of highways across public lands not otherwise reserved for public purposes'.[75] R.S. 2477 was repealed by the enactment of the Federal Land Policy and Management Act (FLPMA) in 1976; however, the FLPMA did not terminate 'valid existing rights' on the date of its approval.[76] During the period from 1866 to 1976, R.S. 2477 granted thousands of rights of way across federal lands in states and counties, with more than 5,600 in Utah alone.[77]

Because federal agencies adopt a conservation-oriented management policy on public lands, states and counties have increasing concerns that their access to federal lands for motorized recreation and extractive industries may be impaired. Therefore, relying on R.S. 2477, they frequently challenge federal agencies' management of public lands. Different courts possess different opinions regarding the right-of-way claims.[78] This issue has not been settled in legislation or in case law.

Most right-of-way controversies have occurred in Utah. In 2000, when President Clinton declared the Grand Staircase-Escalante a national monument, several Utah counties filed lawsuits asserting roadway claims under R.S. 2477.[79] In 2005, Kane County in southern Utah passed an ordinance opening all Class B and D roads in the county to off-road vehicle (ORV) use.[80] Many of these roads that Kane opened were previously closed to ORV due to the designation of national parks, wilderness areas and national monuments. Kane removed federal signs that prohibited ORV access and placed its own signs. Though some roads that Kane claimed did not account for a de facto 'road',[81] Kane adopted the ordinance as open

---

73 For details, see Scott Streater, 'Abandoned Mines: Water Supply, Fish Stocks, Recreation Propel Efforts to Clean Colo.'s Peru Creek', in *Land Letter*, December 4, 2008. Available at http://www.eenews.net/stories/71923. Last visited January 2015.
74 For the relevant discussion, see *supra* p. 27 of Chapter 2.
75 Mining Act of 1866, ch. 262, §8, 14 Stat. 251.
76 Pub. L. No. 94–579, §701(a); 43 USC §1701 note (a).
77 US DOI, 'Report to Congress on R.S. 2477: The History and Management of R.S. 2477 Right-of-Way Claims on Federal and Other Lands', June 1993. Available at https://archive.org/details/reporttocongress8278unit. Last visited January 2015.
78 Matthew Squires, 'Note: Federal Regulation of R.S. 2477 Rights-of-Way', 63 (2008) *N.Y.U. Annual Survey of American Law*, pp. 566–90 (noticing that the 9th and 10th Circuit Courts have adopted different approaches to interpret the R.S. 2477 right-of-way, i.e. the legislative approach and the proprietary approach).
79 *Norton v. Southern Utah Wilderness Alliance*, 542 US 55 (2004).
80 Kane County Ordinance No. 2005–3 Off-Highway Vehicles, August 8, 2005, available at http://www.highway-robbery.org/documents/Kane_County_ORV_ordinance_August_2005_signed.pdf. Last visited January 2015.
81 See Matthew Squires, *supra* note 78, p. 550.

defiance against the federal government in spite of objections from federal land management agencies. A lawsuit was soon presented by the Wilderness Society against this ordinance.[82] The district court supported the Wilderness Society's claim by holding that Kane must first establish the validity of its R.S. 2477 claims, and, until it did so, federal law preempted any ordinances and actions. However, the appellate court dismissed the Wilderness Society's action for its lack of prudential standing to pursue the claims.[83]

Another example relates to the NPS's management of the Salt Creek inside Canyonlands National Park. The NPS used to open Salt Creek to ORV use. The Southern Utah Wilderness Alliance sued the NPS in 1995.[84] As a result, the NPS finally prohibited vehicles in Salt Creek in June 2004. However, San Juan County and the State of Utah sued the NPS and asked for a right-of-way for motorized use under R.S. 2477.[85] After several years of lawsuits, in 2011, the district court of Utah finally ruled in favor of the NPS that Salt Creek was not a R.S. 2477 right-of-way.[86]

In addition to state right-of-way claims, private sectors may claim the right of way to access private property or to allow utilities to pass over, under, or through federal lands. In the case of *Hale* v. *Norton*,[87] private landowners requested a right-of-way permit from the NPS to bring a trailer and bulldozer across national park lands multiple times to rebuild a home. The NPS informed them that a document of Environmental Assessment would be needed. The court supported the NPS's decision to require the document by stating that it was 'appropriate for the NPS to apply a NEPA analysis to the Hales' request'.[88]

Rails-to-trails Controversies

Railroad companies obtained the right of way to thousands of miles of land from the federal government to build rails on federal lands.[89] With the advent of automobile tourism, the role of railroads has experienced a decline. This change in transportation patterns has led to the question of how to address thousands of miles of unused railroads. A proposed solution is to convert these unused or disused railroads to recreational trails for hikers, skiers, bikers and horseback riders. In 1965, the first recreational trail, Eiroy-Sparta State Trail in Wisconsin, was created from an abandoned rail corridor. This rail-to-trail idea was backed by Congress with the enactment of the National Trails System Act in 1983.[90] Congress encouraged state and local agencies and private actors to establish appropriate trails through the interim use of railroad rights of way. Following this, states have actively converted abandoned railroad

---

82 *The Wilderness Society v. Kane County, Utah*, 470 F. Supp. 2d 1300 (D. Utah, 2006); *The Wilderness Society v. Kane County, Utah*, 581 F. 3d 1198 (10th Cir. 2009), rev'd by 632 F. 3d 1162.
83 *The Wilderness Society v. Kane County, Utah*, 632 F. 3d 1162 (10th Cir. 2011).
84 *Southern Utah Wilderness Alliance v. Dabney*, 7 F. Supp. 2d 1205 (D. Utah 1998), rev'd, 222 F. 3d 819 (10th Cir. 2000). For more details, see *infra* p. 130 et seq. of Chapter 7.
85 *San Juan County v. United States*, 420 F. 3d 1197 (10th Cir. 2005); *San Juan County v. United States*, 503 F. 3d 1163 (10th Cir. 2007).
86 *San Juan County v. United States*, Civil No. 2:04-CV-0552BSJ (D.C. of Utah, 2011).
87 *Hale v. Norton*, 476 F. 3d 694 (9th Cir. 2007).
88 Ibid., p. 701.
89 These rights of way were granted under the 1875 General Railroad Right of Way Act. For more information on federal railroad rights of way, see Pamela Baldwin and Aaron Flynn, 'Federal Railroad Rights of Way', CRS Report for Congress, May 3, 2006, available at http://congressionalresearch.com/RL32140/document.php. Last visited January 2015.
90 P.L. 98–11, 97 Stat. 42; codified as 16 USC §1247(d). Implementing regulations of this Act is codified into 49 CFR §1152.29 'Prospective use of rights-of-way for interim trail use and rail banking'.

rights of way to recreational trails. However, thousands of lawsuits were brought by private landowners who claimed that such a conversion amounted to unconstitutional taking without compensation.[91]

In addition to state governments, federal agencies face similar claims. Recently, the USFS was sued by a private owner, Brandt, and the case went all the way to the Supreme Court.[92] In 2005, the USFS proposed to convert a railroad corridor that was abandoned in 2004 into a bicycle trail that bisected Brandt's land where the railroad formerly operated. Brandt stated that his view was ruined by these bikers. He claimed that once the railroad abandoned the government-issued right of way, he gained ownership of that land. Therefore, the USFS's conversion amounted to an unconstitutional taking of this property. In contrast, the USFS claimed that the abandoned railroad right of way reverted to the US and became federal property. These conflicting interpretations have significant political implications. This is why the Obama Administration took the 'unusual step' of asking the Supreme Court to review this case, even though lower courts had ruled for the USFS.[93] The Supreme Court finally ruled in March 2014 that Brandt obtained full rights over the right of way, which was an easement terminated by the railroad's abandonment.[94]

Construction on Park Inholdings

Private lands that are located within national parks and other federal lands are called 'inholdings'. Private landowners are free to build houses or other buildings on their inholdings. At Gettysburg National Military Park, a private landowner built a 390-foot observation tower on private land within the park in 1974.[95] In Zion National Park in Utah, such inholdings amount to 3,490 acres.[96] The following photo shows a private mansion constructed by a private landowner near one of the most scenic spots, Tabernacle Dome, in Zion.

These construction activities may impair the ecosystems of parks. They may also impair the overall park atmosphere because private houses are easily visible by visitors. With the concern that inholdings might lead to subdivisions sprouting inside parks, the NPS and environmental groups have sought to acquire these sandwiched personal properties based on the Land and Water Conservation Fund of 1964. However, due to financial retrenchment, the NPS has seldom been sufficiently funded to acquire these personal properties.[97] Though some successful examples have been achieved by resorting to private donors and charities,[98] how to handle these inholdings and curb landowners' desires to dispose of their properties in a manner incompatible with the park environment remains a concern for park managers.

---

91 For example, *Lawson v. Washington*, 107 Wash. 2d 444, 730 P. 2d 1308 (1986). The figure is from Jeremy P. Jacobs, 'Wyo. man takes "rail trail" fight with Forest Service to Supreme Court', December 3, 2013, available at http://www.eenews.net/stories/1059991197. Last visited January 2015.
92 *United States v. Brandt*, 496 Fed. Appx. 822 (10th Cir. 2012); *Marvin M. Brandt Revocable Trust v. United States*, 572 US (2014).
93 Jeremy P. Jacobs, *supra* note 91.
94 *Marvin M. Brandt Revocable Trust v. United States*, 572 US (2014).
95 This private land was finally purchased by the NPS and the building was condemned in 2000. See Richard Ansson and Dalton Hooks, *supra* note 46, p. 260.
96 NPS, 'Zion National Park General Management Plan', August 2001, p. 3.
97 Richard Ansson and Dalton Hooks, *supra* note 46, pp. 256–8.
98 Thomas Burr, 'Anonymous donor preserves the view of Zion's Tabernacle Dome', *Salt Lake Tribune*, October 12, 2012. Available at http://www.sltrib.com/sltrib/politics/55065830-90/park-national-zion-private.html.csp. Last visited January 2015.

Conflicts in Public Land Designation: the US 103

Figure 5.5 Photo of a private house constructed on inholdings in Zion National Park
Source: © Cory MacNulty/National Parks Conservation Association

Use of Motorized Vehicles vs. Use of Non-motorized Vehicles

Over the last several decades, motorized recreation, such as the use of snowmobiles, personal watercrafts and other ORVs, has gained great popularity. Between 1999 and 2008, the number of four-wheeled all-terrain vehicles in use almost tripled, increasing from 3.6 million to 10.2 million.[99] These vehicles interfere with traditional forms of recreation, such as fishing, bird-watching, camping and hiking. Conflicts between motorized users and non-motorized users arise. Some scholars refer to this conflict as a conflict between 'passive recreational use' and 'active recreational use'.[100]

ORV use on national park lands is one of the most contentious issues in park management. This is partly due to the diversity of stakeholders, including motor clubs, outfit producers and groups of environmentalists who pursue quieter and wilder natural experiences. The opponents of ORV use assert that these vehicles damage the natural landscape, destroy habitats, present safety risks, harass wildlife and cause conflicts with non-motorized

---

99 Robert Keiter, *supra* note 20, p. 81.
100 Jan Stevens and Richard Frank, *supra* note 9, p. 13.

recreational users.[101] Bluewater Network, an organization dedicated to reducing environmental damage from motor vehicles, denounces snowmobiling as 'one of the most environmentally devastating recreational activities permitted by the [NPS]'.[102] Statistics show that snowmobile use accounts for 97.9 percent of carbon monoxide emission in West Yellowstone during the winter season.[103] Supporters contend that motor vehicles provide outdoor recreation opportunities for seniors and the disabled, allow visitors to access hard-to-reach areas and bring economic benefits to gateway communities. Moreover, snowmobiles can make parks accessible during harsh winters. They also assert that technological advances continue to limit the noise and pollution of motor vehicles.[104]

Partly to minimize potential conflicts arising from ORV use, strict regulations have been placed on motorized recreation.[105] These regulations have resulted in numerous lawsuits among the NPS, the motor clubs and the environmental groups that possess respective interests in this matter.[106]

The Commercialization and Construction of Recreational Amenities vs. Conservation

In 2013, the NPS launched a pilot project in five national parks to increase Wi-Fi availability and cellular phone coverage in national parks.[107] This project was intended to invite more Americans to visit national parks by providing them with an opportunity to be connected while enjoying nature. Though the proposed plan only covered areas of park entrances, lodges, visitor centers and major traffic corridors, unexpected objections still arose. Concerns included the damage to the environment from the 100-foot-tall cell towers, the loss of solitude and the disturbance of the wilderness experience. Because this project was a joint effort between the NPS and the National Park Hospitality Association, a concessioner organization, opponents also contended that this project was intended to serve commercial subscribers and that it constituted a private use of public lands.[108]

This event reveals several problems that have plagued park managers, such as the appropriateness of facility construction and the relationship between concessioners and the NPS. It also touches upon fundamental inquiries into recreational policy making, including what types of park experiences should be provided to visitors and how to reconcile different demands and perceptions of park experiences, for example, being connected to or disconnected from Wi-Fi.

---

101 Laura Comay, Carol Vincent and Kristina Alexander, 'Motorized Recreation on National Park Service Land', February 8, 2013, *Congressional Research Service Report for Congress*, p. 1. Full text is available at http://www.fas.org/sgp/crs/misc/R42955.pdf. Last visited January 2015.
102 Witness Statement of Sean Smith, the public lands director for Bluewater Network, before the House Subcommittee on National Parks and Public Lands, Oversight Hearing on Snowmobile Recreation in National Parks, particularly Yellowstone National Park, May 25, 2000, pp. 4–5. The testimony is available at http://naturalresources.house.gov/uploadedfiles/sean_smith_testimony_5.25.00.pdf. Last visited January 2015.
103 James McCarthy, 'Snowmobiles: Environmental Standards and Access to National Parks', *Congressional Research Service*, RL 31149, 2002, p.CRS6. Available at http://cnie.org/NLE/CRSreports//RL31149.pdf. Last visited January 2015.
104 Laura Comay et al., *supra* note 101, p. 1.
105 See *infra* pp. 106–9.
106 For more details, see *infra* p. 138 et seq. of Chapter 7.
107 Charlie Brennan, 'Pilot Will Boost Cell Coverage, Wi-Fi at 5 National Parks by Summer', January 2, 2013, available at http://www.denverpost.com/ci_22503196/pilot-will-boost-cell-coverage-wifi-at-5. Last visited January 2015.
108 Randi Minetor, 'Proposed Wi-Fi Pilot Project in National Parks Spurs Controversy', April 4, 2013; available at http://www.examiner.com/article/proposed-wifi-pilot-project-national-parks-spurs-controversy?cid=rss. Last visited December 2014.

To promote the recreational use of national parks, the NPS actively cooperates with concessioners to provide accommodations and recreational services to visitors. These large companies have deeply influenced the shaping of park policies, especially in promoting tourism within parks. As visitors' demands for better and more diversified services increase, concessioners begin to build more luxurious facilities within park boundaries. This not only threatens the protection of park resources but also raises questions about the appropriateness of such amenities in the national park setting. The NPS's enthusiastic promotion of recreation and the follow-up phenomenon of the commercialization of national parks placed the NPS under harsh criticism. Newton Drury criticized the NPS as the 'Super-Department of Recreation' and a 'glorified playground commission'.[109] The Leopold Report of 1963 stated that 'it seems incongruous that there should exist in the national parks mass recreation facilities such as golf courses, ski lifts, motorboat marinas, and other extraneous developments which completely contradict the management goal.'[110] It urged the NPS to reverse its policy of permitting these nonconforming uses. The Vail Agenda report of 1992 further stated that the NPS 'is in danger of becoming merely a provider of "drive through" tourism or, perhaps, merely a traffic cop stationed at scenic, interesting or old places'.[111]

In addition to the pressure of commercialization from concessioners, pressure also comes from gateway communities. After the establishment of the NPS, private enterprises, most of which were large railroad companies, were allowed to monopolistically provide accommodations to visitors inside parks. This situation has, to some extent, marginalized local small businesses that previously provided rudimentary services. Due to the advent of automobile tourism, increasing numbers of tourists visit national parks in their own automobiles, which has fundamentally challenged the monopolistic position of concessioners.[112] Automobile visitors bring commercial opportunities for gateway communities that may provide local hotels or motels instead of concessioner-run lodges inside parks. National parks have therefore become a cash cow for gateway communities. Similar to concessioners inside park boundaries, there is a tendency among communities to commercialize their services and accommodate as many visitors as possible. Keiter describes this commercialized atmosphere in gateway communities outside parks as the 'Glitter Gulch' syndrome.[113] While the NPS is alert to retrenching facilities and commercial services, it is also confronted with resistance from both concessioners and gateway communities, which pursue the maximization of their interests.

Recreational Use vs. Regulation Sui Generis

Some particular types of recreational activities are under *sui generis* regulation within national parks. They are not regulated based on their detriment to the environment but are generally deemed inconsistent with the national park setting. Examples include hunting and thrill-seeking recreational activities, such as hang gliding and base jumping.

---

109 Robert Keiter, *supra* note 20, p. 70.
110 The Wildlife Management in the National Parks, often referred to as the 'Leopold Report', is a paper composed of a series of ecosystem management recommendations that were presented by the Special Advisory Board on Wildlife Management to the Secretary of the Interior in 1963.
111 NPS, *National Parks for the 21st Century: The Vail Agenda* (Washington, DC: NPS, 1992). The Vail Agenda was the report and recommendations from the 75th Anniversary Symposium convened by the NPS in Vail, Colorado in 1991.
112 Robert Keiter, *supra* note 20, p. 96.
113 Ibid., p. 110.

Recreational hunting is generically prohibited in national parks, except for specific congressional mandates provided in enabling acts.[114] In contrast, recreational hunting is generally allowed in wildlife refuges because hunters are the original constituencies of the FWS. Issues regarding whether hunting should be allowed in national parks and whether trapping is an allowable hunting method have been raised in courts.[115] The fundamental divergence between hunters and wildlife preservationists is whether recreational hunting, a so-called 'blood sport', should be allowed. Wildlife lovers oppose any form of killing animals to amuse human beings. This divergence is more sympathetic than scientific.

Thrill-seeking activities are also under strict regulation in national parks. Parachuting, or base jumping, is generally prohibited by NPS regulations.[116] As of 2013, more than forty units, approximately 10 percent of the total units of the National Park System, allowed off-road mountain bicycling.[117] Similarly, rock climbing is under intensive management based on a permit system. These thrill-seeking activities may not be detrimental to the environment (or, at least, they may be less detrimental than motorized activities). The NPS prohibits these activities on the grounds that these sports are inappropriate inside parks. However, the NPS shows inconsistencies in its management policies on thrill-seeking activities. Regulations are mainly made on a park-by-park basis. For example, base jumping is permitted once a year at the New River Gorge National River, but it is prohibited elsewhere.[118] The extent to which the individual judgment of the NPS is based on site-specific conditions and whether a system-wide management policy should be adopted are still disputable issues.

The Increasing Regulation of Recreational Activities

Joseph Sax stated that 'parks and wilderness areas are not the product of the modern growth of regulatory government or of the expansion of the federal role in American life.'[119] Traditionally, the public land system is not under intensive management and regulation. In Sax's words, 'the [traditional] governance of the national parks and national forests was so open-ended that it cannot be usefully compared with any example drawn from the contemporary structure of administrative law.'[120] Currently, however, this is no longer the case. Increasing recreational use has fundamentally changed the regulatory pattern of public lands.

The Organic Act instructs the NPS to both 'promote and regulate' the use of national parks.[121] In an era of mass recreation, the NPS no longer needs to promote park visitation, with exceptions to this promotion among the younger generation and minority groups. The recreational use of parks has caused the derogation of the environment and harassment to wildlife. It has also produced conflicts between different user groups. To protect nature and reconcile these conflicts, the management and regulation of certain recreational activities are necessary.

---

114 For a discussion of exceptional mandate of hunting in enabling acts, see *infra* p. 118 of Chapter 6.
115 *National Rifle Association of America v. Potter*, 628 F. Supp. 903 (D.D.C. 1986) (the court upheld the NPS's generic regulations on the prohibition of hunting and trapping throughout the National Park System). For more details, see *infra* p. 133–4 of Chapter 7.
116 36 CFR 2.17(a)(3).
117 Laura Comay et al., *supra* note 101, p. 17.
118 Robert Keiter, *supra* note 20, p. 85.
119 Joseph Sax, 'Parks, Wilderness, and Recreation', in Michael Lace (ed.), *Government and Environmental Politics: Essays on Historical Developments since World War Two* (Washington, DC: Woodrow Wilson Center Press: 1989), p. 115.
120 Ibid., p. 116.
121 16 USC §1. See *supra* p. 73 of Chapter 4.

The regulation of recreational use did not occur until the 1960s. According to Keiter's survey, in 1960, park officials issued a 'backcountry management plan' to address the problem of environmental damage caused by increasing recreational activities at the Sequoia and Kings Canyon backcountry meadows.[122] This document represents an early agency effort to intervene in growing recreational demands and heralds the era of the intensive recreation management of public lands. Currently, the regulation of recreational activities takes place in various forms and to a significant extent.

The key to regulation lies in the question of whether a certain type of use is permissible, as well as the scale and degree of such use.[123] To make such judgments, two standards may be applied: the appropriateness of a proposed use in the national park context and the environmental impacts of this use. For example, snowmobiling is prohibited or limited largely due to its consequences for the natural environment. The reason that base jumping is regulated is not its adverse impacts on the environment, but its thrill-seeking nature. However, a bright line is not easily drawn to determine which type of use is appropriate, which is not and how much use is too much. Regulation on recreation is accompanied by continuous controversies and resistance. Nearly every effort made to curb particular forms of recreation has been politically resisted and frequently litigated.[124]

The current regulation of recreational activities in national parks can be classified into three patterns:

1. *'Opened unless closed'*: recreational activities are generally allowed unless otherwise specified. For example, recreational fishing is allowed in parks when it is authorized or not specifically prohibited by federal law.[125]
2. *'Closed unless opened'*: recreational activities are generally prohibited unless otherwise specified. Examples include hunting, trapping,[126] base jumping, and personal watercraft and off-road vehicle use.
3. *'Case-by-case regulation'*: recreational activities are neither generally allowed nor prohibited but are to be decided on a case-by-case evaluation. Examples include recreational pack and saddle stock use.[127]

Currently, the most volatile controversy concerns the regulation of motorized recreational use, which falls into the second pattern. In general, the federal government has broad control over motorized recreation. This includes the federal control of the use of motorized vehicles on private lands that may have adverse impacts on public lands.[128]

There are two main executive orders that compose the general regulatory framework governing the recreational use of motorized vehicles on public lands: the E.O. 11644 adopted by President Nixon in 1972 (the 1972 Order)[129] and the E.O. 11989 adopted by President Carter in 1977 (the 1977 Order), which amended the 1972 Order.[130] The 1972 Order was issued to

---

122 Robert Keiter, *supra* note 20, p. 71.
123 Dennis Herman, *supra* note 39.
124 Robert Keiter, *supra* note 20, p. 74.
125 NPS Management Policies of 2006, Section 8.2.2.5. For more details about the Management Policies, see *infra* p. 120 et seq. of Chapter 6.
126 Ibid., Section 8.2.2.6 ('hunting, trapping, or any other methods of harvesting wildlife by the public will be allowed where it is specifically mandated by federal law').
127 Ibid., Section 8.2.2.8.
128 Byron Kahr, 'The Right to Exclude Meets the Right to Ride: Private Property, Public Recreation, and the Rise of Off-Road Vehicles', 28 (2009) *Stanford Environmental Law Journal*, pp. 98–9 (discussing federal regulations of ORV use on private lands).
129 Exec. Order 11644, 37 FR 2877 (February 8, 1972).
130 Exec. Order 11989, 42 FR 26959 (May 24, 1977).

... ensure that the use of [ORVs] on public lands will be controlled and directed so as to protect the resources of those lands, to promote the safety of all users of those lands, and to minimize conflicts among the various uses of those lands. (Section 1)

The Order directed each agency to designate areas and trails in which ORVs might be permitted and areas in which such uses might not be permitted (Section 3). The most significant amendment to the 1972 Order appeared in Section 9 of the 1977 Order, which authorized agencies to immediately close areas or trails if the use of ORVs would cause or was causing considerable adverse effects on the environment. Each agency was authorized to adopt the policy to close the areas stated above except for those areas or trails that were suitable and specifically designated as open to such uses.

These two executive orders are applicable to all types of federal lands. On national park lands in particular, routes and areas for ORV use can only be designated into four types of National Park System units: national recreation areas, national seashores, national lakeshores and national preserves.[131] Table 5.1 shows the status quo of regulations on motorized recreational use within the National Park System. It can be seen that the regulation of motorized recreation presents a piecemeal feature and adopts a park-by-park approach. Different types of motorized activities are subjected to different degrees of regulation in different park units. This approach has caused site-specific conflicts, such as the snowmobile controversy in Yellowstone and the overflight controversy in the Grand Canyon.[132]

Table 5.1 The status quo of regulations on motorized use within the National Park System (as of February 2013)

Type of motorized use	Status quo
All-terrain vehicles (ATVs) and oversand vehicles	Twelve of the 398 units are open to ATVs, four-wheel-drive vehicles, and/or dune, sand and swamp buggies.
Snowmobiles	Forty-three units are open to snowmobile use. Disputes are primarily focused on winter-use plans developed by the NPS in Yellowstone about setting the numerical limits of snowmobiles.
Aircraft overflights	The main dispute is about how to limit air tours and restore the natural quiet in the Grand Canyon. The NPS and the Federal Aviation Administration work together to implement congressional statutes on reducing noise within national parks.
Personal watercraft (PWC)	PWC use is allowed in designated areas in 13 units. PWC bans in two units were challenged by environmental groups in court in 2010.

Source: Adapted from Laura Comay et al., 2013[133]

Although over-snow vehicles were defined as ORVs in both executive orders[134] and the NPS Management Policies recognized snowmobiles as a form of ORV,[135] the regulation of snowmobiles was distinct from general ORV regulation. The rule that ORV permits

---

131 36 CFR §4.10 (b).
132 For more details, see *infra* p. 138 et seq. of Chapter 7.
133 Laura Comay et al., *supra* note 101.
134 In the 1972 Order, ORV was defined as 'any motorized vehicle designed for or capable of cross country travel on or immediately over land, water, sand, snow, ice, marsh, swampland, or other natural terrain' (Section 2(3)). The 1977 Order also modified the definition of ORV excluding military, emergency and law enforcement vehicles.
135 NPS, Management Policies of 2006, §8.2.3.2.

could only be issued in four specific types of park units did not apply to snowmobiles.[136] Therefore, snowmobile use can also be permitted in 'national parks' under certain conditions. Nevertheless, the regulation of snowmobiles falls into the second pattern of 'closed unless opened'.[137] Snowmobiles are categorically prohibited 'except where designated and only when their use is consistent with the park's natural, cultural, scenic and aesthetic values, safety considerations, park management objectives, and will not disturb wildlife or damage park resources'.[138] During the 1970s, the snowmobile regulation strategy was to designate certain routes for snowmobiles through special regulations without entry limits.[139] In recent years, the NPS has begun to set a cap on the numbers of snowmobiles in parks.

The NPS adopted a park-by-park approach to snowmobile regulation. After the 1972 Order, Anderson, the then-superintendent of Yellowstone, first responded to the order by designating all of Yellowstone's interior roads as snowmobile routes.[140] However, other national park superintendents did not respond in the same manner. For example, in 1975, Glacier National Park decided to ban snowmobiles, and this ban was formalized in 1977. Other national parks, such as Yosemite, Sequoia/Kings Canyon, and Lassen National Parks, eliminated snowmobile use in the same period.[141]

Summary

The public land use pattern has witnessed a gradual transformation. Apart from traditional commodity uses of public land, diversified uses have mushroomed. The two most prominent issues are burgeoning recreational demands across different types of public land designations and an increasing commitment to conserving nature. Recreational use in national parks was previously associated with a preferential legislative and policy-making tendency. The resulting mass recreation and industrial tourism produced considerable challenges for park managers, especially the overcrowding problem. The budget shortfall further exacerbated this problem. It is noteworthy that the tendency to shift from commodity use to recreational use has been tempered in recent years, as evidenced by the fact that the role of commodity use on public land has remained steady and that recreational visitation has maintained a stable level since the 1990s. Nevertheless, the regulatory and management frameworks of public lands have been extensively influenced by the interaction between different uses, particularly commodity, conservation and recreation.

Various conflicts are formulated in diverse forms, both internal and external. New forms of conflicts continue to emerge due to technological, social and economic variations. Extractive uses of adjacent lands outside national park boundaries threaten conservation and the enjoyment of park resources. Existing mining rights and abandoned mines within parks place the preservation of park resources and the provision of recreational opportunities in jeopardy. Property conflicts are also found between nonfederal rights and public land control. States and individuals claim the right of way on public land for development or recreational

---

136 Laura Comay et al., *supra* note 101, p. 3.
137 See *Wyo. v. Dept. of Interior*, 587 F. 3d 1245, p. 1248 (10th Cir. 2009) (characterizing the NPS's regulatory framework as 'closed unless opened').
138 36 CFR §2.18(c).
139 36 CFR §4.10 (designating routes for ORVs, but providing no limits on maximum access).
140 39 FR 16151 (May 7, 1974).
141 Michael Yochim, 'The Development of Snowmobile Policy in Yellowstone National Park', 7.2 (1999) *Yellowstone Science*, p. 6. See also Robert Keiter, *supra* note 20, p. 77.

purposes. Private inholdings inside park boundaries also have negative impacts on both park environments and resource protection.

Interest groups have been significantly divided by recreational uses. The former alliance between environmental preservationists and recreational users deteriorated due to the emergence of high-impact motorized recreational use. Conflicts between motorized and non-motorized recreational activities are frequently debated in courts and have become the dominant form of conflict in park management. Partly to reconcile and mitigate conflicts arising from recreational use, intensive regulation has been gradually placed on recreational activities by restricting the type or scale of recreational activities. However, these regulations also incur controversies regarding whether regulation is needed for certain activities and how strict the regulation should be. This is evident from the resistance and discontentment of recreational groups on *sui generis* regulation, such as regulations of hunting and thrill-seeking activities. Furthermore, the commercialization of parks and the construction of recreational amenities cause increasing concerns and tension among concessioners, gateway communities and the NPS. Currently, the NPS's management emphasis has shifted from the active promotion of recreational visitation to the intensive management of recreational uses and the reconciliation of conflicts arising therein.

6 Resolution of Conflicts in Legislation and Policies

Assessing the Legal Foundations

Introduction

Having reviewed the rise of conflicts on public land in the previous chapter, this chapter examines how these conflicts are resolved in law and the extent to which such a solution has been achieved. Both Congress and the NPS have established their respective understandings of how a national park should look and how conflicts arising from park management should be resolved. Therefore, the assessment of the legal foundations is two-fold: it involves what Congress states in law and how the agency interprets the statutory language.

First, three types of statutory mandates are scrutinized. By examining the purpose statement embodied in the NPS Organic Act, the congressional intent to balance the weight of conservation and enjoyment is identified. The management criteria prescribed therein, the non-impairment standard, is analyzed, and the controversies arising from how the purpose statement should be interpreted are examined. Then, modern environmental statutes, particularly those statutes associated with wilderness protection, are subsequently discussed. These statutes have, to a certain extent, repositioned the human-nature relationship that was established in the Organic Act. The third type of congressional statutes is the enabling act, which marks a subtle shift of the congressional attitude in establishing such a balance.

Second, regulations and management policies issued by the NPS are examined with a particular focus on the Management Policies of 2006. How the Organic Act is interpreted by the NPS and how such an interpretation accords with or deviates from congressional mandates are examined.

Based on both congressional mandates and agency management policies, the designated use pattern of national parks is finally proposed with a comparison to other types of public land designations. The role of recreation in these designated use patterns is given particular focus.

The NPS Organic Act and Its Impairment Standard

The Purpose Statement of National Parks: A Contradictory Mandate?

As mentioned earlier, there is a long-standing controversy about the fundamental purpose of national parks prescribed in the Organic Act, which reads as follows:

> [The fundamental purpose of national parks] is to *conserve* the scenery and the natural and historic objects and the wild life therein and to provide for the *enjoyment* of the same in such manner and by such means as will leave them *unimpaired* for the enjoyment of future generations.

This sentence has several key terms, namely, 'conserve', 'enjoyment' and 'unimpaired'. The Organic Act seems to contain multiple purposes: (1) to conserve scenery, natural and historic objects and wildlife; (2) to promote the public enjoyment of them; and (3) to leave them unimpaired for the enjoyment of future generations.[1]

Similar conflicting statements are found in the purpose statements of specific national parks. For example, the General Management Plan for Grand Canyon National Park explicitly states that the purpose of the Grand Canyon is to 'preserve and protect its natural and culture resources and ecological processes, as well as its scenic, aesthetic, and scientific values' and to 'provide opportunities for visitors to experience and understand environmental interrelationships, resources, and values of the Grand Canyon without impairing the resources'.[2]

The application of the Organic Act may be useful to solve easy questions. A management decision that promotes both enjoyment and conservation would fit into the Act's mandate, such as the maintenance of the landscape and wildlife population. Similarly, a decision that impairs both conservation and enjoyment opportunities would be directly outlawed, such as the construction of dumpsites. However, the real challenge that this statement may produce is whether conservation and enjoyment are compatible with each other and whether there are inherent conflicts between the two. Taking it one step further, if such conflicts exist, how can we reconcile them?

For this reason (i.e. the coexistence of conservation and enjoyment in the purpose statement), the Organic Act is frequently referred to as a 'dual mandate'. Antolini held that the Organic Act had 'a soft or silent dual mandate that leaves the NPS "broad discretion" in making its specific management decisions'.[3] Cheever labeled the Organic Act a 'paradoxical mandate'.[4] Orr and Humphreys phrased the Act as embodying a 'mission rivalry'.[5] Herman stated that . . . in passing the [NPS] Organic Act, Congress saddled the [NPS] with a schizophrenic mandate: the park system was to be managed both to preserve its resources "unimpaired" for future generations and to allow for "free pass" by members of the public.[6]

Abundant literature has shed light on the debate about how this statement should be read. Opinions have conflicted: some see that conservation trumps enjoyment, whereas others see tourism and the recreational use of park resources as having an explicit congressional sanction. The analytical approaches that have been adopted also vary. Some adopt a linguistic method to interpret the statutory language, some compare the purpose statement of national parks with those of other types of public land designations, and others analyze the intent of Congress by tracing the legislative history and records.

---

1 John Lemons and Dean Stout, 'A Reinterpretation of National Park Legislation', 15 (1984) *Environmental Law*, p. 50.
2 US DOI, NPS and Denver Service Center, 'General Management Plan of the Grand Canyon National Park', August 1995, pp. 6–7, available at http://www.nps.gov/grca/parkmgmt/upload/GRCA_General_Management_Plan.pdf. Last visited January 2015.
3 Denise Antolini, 'National Park Law In The US: Conservation, Conflict, and Centennial Values', 33 (2009) *William and Mary Environmental Law and Policy Review*, p. 891.
4 Federico Cheever, 'The United States Forest Service and National Park Service: Paradoxical Mandates, Powerful Founders, and the Rise and Fall of Agency Discretion', 74 (1997) *Denver University Law Review*, p. 625.
5 Shannon Orr and Rebecca Humphreys, 'Mission Rivalry: Use and Preservation Conflicts in National Parks Policy', 12.1 (2012) *Public Organization Review*, pp. 85–98.
6 Dennis Herman, 'Loving Them to Death: Legal Controls on the Type and Scale of Development in the National Parks', 11 (1992) *Stanford Environmental Law Journal*, p. 17.

Textual Interpretation of the Organic Act

Opinions based on a semantic reading of the legal text vary. Herman notes that 'the plain language of the Organic Act implies that preservation trumps use whenever the two are in conflict.'[7] Arguments for the pro-conservation[8] reading of the Organic Act include the following:

1. In terms of the sequence of the words, 'the conservation clause comes before the use clause, suggesting a primary, overarching emphasis on preservation and conservation';[9]
2. Because the condition of 'leaving them unimpaired for the future generation' is particularly placed on use and enjoyment, this 'non-impairment' standard 'indicates that resource preservation responsibilities should take precedence over public use in the event of conflict.'[10]

However, by reading the language of the Organic Act in a different way, the conclusion that use and enjoyment are prioritized as the purpose of national parks can also be drawn. In contrast to reading 'non-impairment' as a *requirement* of use and enjoyment, it is argued that the term before non-impairment is 'for the enjoyment of future generations'. Therefore, enjoyment is the *purpose* of non-impairment, not the other way around: 'The restrictions on use are not purely for the sake of preservation as an end; they are to ensure that use and enjoyment will continue in perpetuity.'[11] In this way, preservation can be read as the *means* that serves the *end,* which is to guarantee the availability of recreational opportunities to all.

Implications of Other Types of Designations

The arguments *a contrario* and by analogy that compare national parks with other types of public land designations also contribute to identifying the fundamental purpose of national parks. The two most frequently adopted objects of reference are national forests and wilderness areas.

As soon as the national park idea was proposed, the distinct value of the preservation of national parks was noted by legislators, with comparisons to the then-existing national forest system. As previously shown, the Organic Administration Act of 1897, the so-called 'Organic Act for the USFS', articulated two purposes of the national forest system, watershed protection and timber production, which were later confirmed by the Supreme Court.[12] In the House Report on the NPS Organic Act, it was stated that 'the segregation of national park areas necessarily involves the question of the preservation of nature as it exists', whereas the 'primary objects and purposes [of national forests] are the utilitarian use of land, of water, and of timber, as contributing to the wealth of all the people.'[13] This Report was adopted by the Supreme Court to illustrate the distinctive purpose of national forests.[14] The Supreme

---

7 Ibid.
8 As previously discussed, the terms of conservation and preservation are not explicitly distinguished in some literature. See *supra* p. 42 of Chapter 3. Though a proper distinction does make a big difference, as will be demonstrated in Chapter 12, conservation and preservation are not strictly distinguished in this chapter. They are used interchangeably especially in the context of direct citation.
9 Harmony Mappes, 'National Parks: For Use and "Enjoyment" or for "Preservation"? and the Role of the National Park Service Management Policies in That Determination', 92 (2007) *Iowa Law Review*, p. 611.
10 Robert Keiter, 'Preserving Nature in the National Parks: Law, Policy, and Science in a Dynamic Environment', 74 (1996–97) *Denver University Law Review*, p. 675.
11 Harmony Mappes, *supra* note 9, p. 617.
12 *Supra* p. 79 of Chapter 4.
13 H.R. Rep. No. 700, 64th Cong., 1st Sess. 3 (1916).
14 *United States v. New Mexico*, 438 US 696 (1978), fn. 18.

114   Country Studies: United States

Court also noted that in 1906, Congress transferred the jurisdiction of the national forests to the Department of Agriculture, whereas national parks remained exclusively under the jurisdiction of the Department of the Interior (DOI). This separation of jurisdictions also proved that the purpose of national parks and the purpose of national forests were different: one was to preserve nature and the other was to utilize national assets.[15]

Different opinions may be formulated when comparing national parks to wilderness areas. Because the Wilderness Act adds additional protection to previously designated national parks, it is argued that this does not detract from the purposes of the Organic Act or the enabling legislation of a particular park unit.[16] This means that the status of the non-use of a park area accords with the Organic Act. The Organic Act should consequently be read as a preservation mandate. However, the Wilderness Act can also be read in a different way, which might support the opposite argument: 'The fact that Congress saw a need to specially designate land . . . as "wilderness" . . . implies, by mere existence that such protection did not already exist in parks.'[17] This reading belies the previous construction of the Organic Act because if there were already a preservation mandate, there would be no need to add additional protection to national parks. In this sense, use and enjoyment should be interpreted as the fundamental purposes of national parks.

The Review of the Legislative History: Intent of the Framers

The review of the legislative history is the most frequently used method to explore congressional intent, though this method of statutory interpretation is controversial in adjudication.[18] Similar to other interpretation methods, tracking legislative history produces conflicting opinions.

After exhaustively reviewing the legislative records of the Organic Act and the personal papers of congressmen who were involved in enacting the Act, Robin Winks, a Yale historian, found that there was and is no inherent contradiction in the Act. The mission of the NPS, to conserve the scenic, natural and historic resources in such a way as to leave them unimpaired, takes precedence over providing means of access.[19] Winks's research has become the most widely cited work on the legislative history of the Organic Act.

However, by referring to the personal statements of Frederick Law Olmsted, Jr., the drafter of the original language of the Act, scholars also note that the framers did not always prioritize conservation. Instead, they intended to attract more visitors to national parks and had a 'compelling interest in and sympathy with, the people using the parks'.[20] The park historian Richard Sellars's statement that Congress reaffirmed the NPS's authority in the Organic Act 'with its emphasis on public use' is also used as support.[21]

---

15 Ibid.
16 John Lemons and Dean Stout, *supra* note 1, p. 59.
17 Harmony Mappes, *supra* note 9, p. 620.
18 See *Hall v. US*, 132 S. Ct. 1882 (2012), p. 1892 (cautioning 'against allowing ambiguous legislative history to muddy clear statutory language') (quoting *Milner v. Department of Navy*, 131 S. Ct. 1259 (2011), p. 1266).
19 Robin Winks, 'The National Park Service Act of 1916: "A Contradictory Mandate"?', 74 (1997) *Denver University Law Review*, p. 623.
20 John Nagle, 'How National Park Law Really Works', 86 (2015) *University of Colorado Law Review*, p. 880. This article is available as Notre Dame Law School Legal Studies Research Paper No.1430. The citation is on page 14 in this research paper.
21 Richard Sellars, *Preserving Nature in the National Parks: A History* (New Haven, CT: Yale University Press, 1997), p. 285. Cited from Martin Nie, 'Statutory Detail and Administrative Discretion in Public Lands Governance: Arguments and Alternatives', 19 (2004) *Journal of Environmental Law & Litigation*, p. 234 and footnote 54.

The Softness of the Organic Act: True Congressional Intent?

The previous discussion shows that each interpretation method may yield conflicting conclusions. To some extent, the problem of how to prioritize conservation and enjoyment remains unsolved. Recognizing this conundrum of legal interpretation, some scholars deny the value and benefits of continuing to interpret the Organic Act because it is inherently ambiguous and of little help in solving the use-preservation conflicts.[22] For example, Everhart claims that the instruction from the Organic Act to the NPS is 'ambiguous, perhaps even meaningless, as a guideline'.[23]

On the contrary, other scholars disagree that the ambiguities embodied in the Organic Act should be deemed a legislative defect. Instead, they argue that it is Congress's true intent to avoid answering difficult questions and leave the NPS with the discretion to make management decisions.[24] Mappes notes that the 'legislators even used the term "purpose" in the singular form, acknowledging that the two mandates were inextricably intertwined.'[25] Therefore, conservation and enjoyment cannot be intentionally separated even through meticulous legislative deliberation. It is left to the NPS to decide in particular instances. Nagle even asserts that unlike the *presumed* discretion, as the Court recognized it in the famous *Chevron* case,[26] there is evidence that 'Congress purposefully delegated broad management authority to the NPS.'[27] In this sense, the administrative discretion received by the NPS should not be deemed a *given* by Congress; instead, congressional mandates should not impose excessive restrictions on the NPS's discretion lest they fail to produce a proper balance with full empowerment.

Regardless of whether the ambiguities in the Organic Act were part of the congressional intent, the ambiguities make the *Chevron* test meaningful in judicial review of the NPS's management decisions. The essence of the *Chevron* test is how much judicial deference should be afforded to agencies in the case of statutory ambiguities. The case law discussed in Chapter 7 shows that the courts afford substantial deference to the NPS in its management decisions regarding balancing conservation and enjoyment.

Hardening the Organic Act: The Role of Wilderness-oriented Statutes

The Organic Act leaves the potential conflict between conservation and enjoyment unresolved. It is asserted that 'the softness of the Organic Act becomes clearer when its dual mandate is matched up against a similar statute with a clarion conservation mandate.'[28] Modern environmental statutes, especially those statutes that embody a feature of wilderness protection, have played such a role. The idea of wilderness is closely related to nature

---

22 See John Lemons and Dean Stout, *supra* note 1, pp. 44–5 ('an examination of the history and meaning of park legislation was of limited value because Congress had never resolved the difficult questions of competing uses or the dilemma of preservation versus development'); see also Michael Mantell, 'Preservation and Use: Concessions in National Parks', 8.1 (1979) *Ecology Law Quarterly*, p.1; Nathan Scheg, 'Preservationists vs. Recreationists in Our National Parks', 5 (1998) *Hastings West-Northwest Journal of Environmental Law and Policy*, p. 51.
23 William Everhart, *The National Park Service* (New York: Praeger, 1972), p. 80.
24 Robin Winks, *supra* note 19, pp. 593–4.
25 Harmony Mappes, *supra* note 9, p. 621.
26 For a discussion of administrative discretion and the *Chevron* case, see *infra* p. 129 of Chapter 7.
27 John Nagle, *supra* note 20, Research Paper , p. 18.
28 Denise Antolini, *supra* note 3, p. 903.

conservation in the American context,[29] though this is not necessarily the case elsewhere.[30] Wallace Stegner stated that 'if the national park idea is . . . the best idea America ever had, wilderness preservation is the highest refinement of that idea.'[31]

Compared to these wilderness-oriented statutes, the influences of the NEPA – a crucial modern environmental statute – on the Organic Act are not as salient as those of the wilderness statutes. This is partly due to the nature of the NEPA as a procedural guarantee instead of substantive requirements. The NEPA does not adjudicate substantial conflicts between conservation and enjoyment. In some cases, the NEPA can even undermine the conservation mandate of the Organic Act.[32] This section discusses two wilderness-oriented statutes, the Wilderness Act and the Wild and Scenic Rivers Act, and reveals how their preservation mandates influence national park management.

The Wilderness Act: A Stronger Preservation Mandate

The enactment of the Wilderness Act was initially advocated by the Wilderness Society, a main player in the Wilderness Movement. The Wilderness Society argued that national parks, as administered under the NPS Organic Act, were deficient in protecting the wilderness value of these areas. In response, the NPS initially opposed the extension of the wilderness designation to park lands. It contended that the Organic Act provided it with sufficient authority to conserve park lands and resources; thus, an additional wilderness designation would be unnecessary.[33] Keiter notes that the NPS's concern was actually twofold: first, the Act would 'undercut [its] management prerogatives', by making it more difficult to build roads and other facilities, for example; second, because it has always been the practice that the USFS lands are taken to create new or expand existing national parks,[34] it would be difficult for the NPS to ask the USFS to transfer any more lands.[35] Under such circumstances, as previously shown, the Wilderness Act turns out to be a product of compromise.[36]

29 For a classic reading of American wilderness and its criticism, see Jan Laitos and Rachael Gamble, 'The Problem with Wilderness', 32 (2008) *Harvard Environmental Law Review,* pp. 503–97; J. Baird Callicott and Michael Nelson, *The Great New Wilderness Debate* (Athens: University of Georgia Press, 1998), and J. Baird Callicott, 'Contemporary Criticisms of the Received Wilderness Idea', 1 (2000) *Wilderness Science in a Time of Change Conference Proceedings.*
30 Though the model of national parks has received popularity worldwide, the concept of wilderness remains largely an American phenomenon. One of the reasons is that there is no wilderness left in many countries around the world. Another reason is due to the resistance from local cultures. See J. Baird Callicott, *ibid.*, p. 24.
31 Wallace Stegner, 'A Capsule History of Conservation', in Wallace Stegner, *Where the Bluebird Sings to the Lemonade Springs: Living and Writing in the West* (New York: Random House, 1992), p. 128. Cited from Curt Meine, *Wallace Stegner and the Continental Vision: Essays on Literature, History, and Landscape* (Washington, DC: Island Press, 1997), p. 174.
32 Denise Antolini, *supra* note 3, pp.896–902. For more discussion on the application of NEPA in judicial process, see *infra* pp. 137–8 of Chapter 7.
33 Robert Keiter, *To Conserve Unimpaired: The Evolution of the National Park Idea* (Washington, DC: Island Press, 2013), p. 21.
34 The original transfer occurred during the 1933 government re-organization. All national monuments previously managed by the USFS were transferred to the DOI and placed under the management authority of the NPS. The establishment of Olympus National Park also derives from the previous designation of Olympus National Monument managed by the USFS. For more details of inter-agency battle between the USFS and the NPS on national monument management, see Gerald Williams, 'National Monuments and the Forest Service', NPS, November 18, 2003. Available at http://www.cr.nps.gov/history/-online_books/fs/monuments.htm. Last visited January 2015.
35 Robert Keiter, *supra* note 33, p. 22.
36 See *supra* pp. 80–2 of Chapter 4.

The Wilderness Act states that wilderness areas should be 'administered for the use and enjoyment of American people in such manner as will leave them unimpaired for future use and enjoyment as wilderness'.[37]

Compared to the purpose statement in the NPS Organic Act, which is to 'conserve, provide for the enjoyment and leave them unimpaired for the enjoyment of future generations', both Acts emphasize the use and enjoyment of the American people and adopt the so-called 'non-impairment' standard. In this sense, the statutory language in the Wilderness Act and the Organic Act do not differ substantially. The major difference is reflected in the strict regulation of commercial and motorized vehicle use and road construction.

The Wilderness Act generally prohibits the construction of any 'permanent road' except as specifically provided for in this Act and subject to existing private rights. It also provides limited authorization for 'temporary roads' unless they are 'necessary to meet minimum requirements for the administration of the wilderness area'. The same requirement applies to the use of motor vehicles, motorized equipment, or motorboats, the landing of aircraft, other forms of mechanical transport, and structures or installation.[38]

The Wilderness Act categorically proscribes commercial enterprise but allows a narrow exception for the authorization of 'commercial services' by stating that 'commercial service may be performed within the wilderness areas . . . to the extent necessary for activities which are proper for realizing the recreational or other wilderness purposes of the areas.'[39]

In this sense, the Wilderness Act adds a layer of protection to national park lands that were originally under the protection of the Organic Act.

The Wild and Scenic Rivers Act of 1968

Congress passed the Wild and Scenic Rivers Act (WSRA)[40] in 1968 to counterbalance decades of dam, diversion and other river-related development. Today, there are 203 rivers and creeks with a total length of 12,600 miles protected by the WSRA as units of the National Wild and Scenic Rivers System.[41]

Generally speaking, the WSRA adds another layer of legal protection to the outstanding rivers that are located within existing public land designations such as national parks. The WSRA mandates the protection of some outstanding rivers in their natural and free-flowing state 'for the benefit and enjoyment of present and future generations'. It aims to protect American rivers with 'outstandingly remarkable value', including 'scenic, recreational, geologic, fish and wildlife, historic, cultural, or other similar values'.[42] River managers are required to 'protect and enhance' this value without 'limiting other uses that do not substantially interfere with public use and enjoyment of these values'.[43] In other words, recreational use, insofar as it is consistent with public use and enjoyment and does not substantially interfere with them, is allowed in the National Wild and Scenic River System.

---

37 Section 2(a).
38 Section 4(c).
39 Section 4(d)(6). The distinction between commercial enterprise and commercial service is debated in *High Sierra Hikers Association v. Blackwell*, 390 F. 3d 630 (Court of Appeals, 9th Circuit 2004).
40 Pub. L. No. 90–542, 82 Stat. 906 (1968), codified at 16 USC §1271 *et seq.*
41 US National Wild and Scenic River System, 'River Mileage Classification for Components of the National Wild and Scenic Rivers System', September 2012. Available at http://www.rivers.gov/documents/rivers-table.pdf. Last visited January 2015.
42 16 USC §1271.
43 16 USC §1281.

Managers are required to delineate river boundaries and classify the river or its various segments as wild, scenic, or recreational,[44] the three levels of WSRA protection. First and foremost, every wild, scenic, or recreational river must be free-flowing. Wild rivers are free from impoundment such as dams and other water resource projects. They represent vestiges of primitive America and are generally not accessible except by trail. Scenic rivers are also free from dams and other water resource projects. They have shorelines or watersheds that are still largely primitive and undeveloped, but that are accessible in places by roads. Recreational rivers or segments are accessible by road or railroad, may have some development along their shorelines, and may have been dammed or diverged in the past.[45]

Because both the designations of 'wilderness' and 'wild and the scenic river' are additions to existing public land designations, the WSRA provides a solution to the potential overlap between them. It prescribes that in case of conflict between the Wilderness Act and the WSRA, the more restrictive provisions should apply.[46]

To summarize, compared to the NPS Organic Act, the WSRA establishes a clearer preservation mandate but allows uses, including recreational uses, that do not adversely affect a river's 'outstandingly remarkable values'. The WSRA is considered a model for improving the mandate of the NPS because it considerably heightens the judicial scrutiny of the agency's actions.[47]

A Tendency to Push Back: Enabling Acts and Congressional Intervention

Although environmental statutes have hardened the soft Organic Act by showcasing clearer preservation mandates, there are counterbalancing forces that swing the pendulum back toward enjoyment. Nagle shows that such forces mainly come from statutory provisions that Congress enacts for specific parks. These provisions can be either prospective or responsive. The former refers to enabling acts made by Congress when new national park units are established, and the latter refers to specific statutes Congress enacts to 'mandate a different management policy that had been adopted by the NPS'.[48]

With regard to enabling acts, as previously shown, they may alter the general provisions in the Organic Act and have priority of application over the Organic Act. The most explicit example is hunting and trapping. These activities are generically prohibited by the Organic Act; however, they may be explicitly allowed by the individual enabling acts of particular units, such as the Great Sand Dunes National Park.[49] Congress shows a tendency to detail its instructions in enabling acts,[50] which curtails the NPS's discretion. For example, it permits the use of snowmobiles on one particular trail in Rocky Mountain National Park.[51] The enabling act for the Lake Mead National Recreation Area specifies in detail permissible recreational uses, such as bathing, boating, camping, picnicking, and vacation cabin site use.[52]

---

44   16 USC. §1273(b).
45   Ibid.
46   16 USC §1281(b).
47   Denise Antolini, *supra* note 3, p. 906. For judicial elaboration of the WSRA, see the controversy of the Merced River, discussed in *infra* p. 146 et seq. of Chapter 7.
48   John Nagle, *supra* note 20, Research Paper, p. 31.
49   Great Sand Dunes National Park and Preserve Act of 2000, Pub. L. No. 106–530.
50   See generally Robert Fischman, 'The Problem of Statutory Detail in National Park Establishment Legislation and Its Relationship to Pollution Control Law', 74 (1996) *Denver University Law Review*, pp. 779–814.
51   16 USC §192b-9(g).
52   16 USC §460n-3(b).

In the case of a specific management controversy within national parks, Congress is also inclined to step in and provide a particular solution. These are the so-called 'responsive provisions' made by Congress, as Nagle calls them. Nagle noted three recent disputes in which local congresses actively intervened in specific management controversies, mostly between local communities' desires, such as the development of the local economy, and the NPS's enforcement of conservation laws, such as the regulation of motorized recreation and noise control.[53] These controversies and the way Congress was involved showed strong political influences on the NPS's decision making and enforcement of law. It also raised the concern of how to maintain the integrity of the National Park System without Congress providing too many exceptional rules to each park unit.[54] In addition to the examples of local congresses' interventions mentioned by Nagle, a recent bill regarding boating activities in rivers shows a similar tendency. Despite long-standing bans on canoes, rafts and other boating vehicles in rivers, Yellowstone and Grand Teton were recently forced to open their rivers to paddlers by a bill passed in the House of Representatives.[55]

Should Congress act in this way? Does it place too much political maneuvering on the NPS's professional judgment? Nagle holds a considerably tolerant attitude toward this type of congressional intervention. Three reasons are provided:

1   'Disputes between conservation and enjoyment often feature parties with equal political power.' The congressional endorsement of local communities and economy is equally armed with those *powerful* environmental groups;
2   Congressional intervention does not undercut the authority of the NPS, especially on its professional judgment, or the integrity of the federal judiciary. Congress has the last say on how the *value* of conservation and enjoyment should be balanced instead of *knowledge* that the NPS is better equipped, and
3   The integrity of the National Park System should not preclude site-specific rules that guarantee the flexibility of the system.[56]

In contrast, Nie shows a more conservative attitude toward such congressional intervention with regard to the risk of exacerbating park conflicts. Enabling legislation may 'hamper comprehensive planning and dilute the importance of administrative and scientific expertise' and create a 'less cohesive, integrated, and unified' national park system.[57]

Agency Regulations and Policies on National Park Management

The Framework of NPS Regulations and Guidance Documents

Delegated by Congress in the Organic Act, the Secretary of the DOI is authorized to 'make and publish such rules and regulations as he may deem necessary or proper for the use and

---

53   The first dispute is about control of ORV use in Cape Hatteras National Seashore which is against development of the local tourism economy, the second dispute is about boat inspection by the NPS personnel in Yukon Charley National Preserve in Alaska, and the third dispute is about permissible use of an air museum in the Fort Vancouver National Historic Site. See John Nagle, *supra* note 20, Research Paper, pp. 36–45.
54   Robert Fischman, *supra* note 50, p. 808.
55   Matthew Brown, 'Bill to Open Yellowstone, Grand Teton to More Paddling Advances in US House', January 28, 2014. Available at http://missoulian.com/news/state-and-regional/bill-to-open-yellowstone-grand-teton-to-more-paddling-advances/article_48860ff6-885e-11e3-abb1-001a4bcf887a.html. Last visited January 2015.
56   John Nagle, *supra* note 20 , Research Paper, pp. 45–6.
57   Martin Nie, 'Statutory Detail and Administrative Discretion in Public Lands Governance: Arguments and Alternatives', 19 (2004) *Journal of Environmental Law & Litigation*, pp. 237–8.

management of the parks, monuments, and reservations under the jurisdiction of the [NPS]'.[58] Most national-park-related regulations are now codified into Title 36 of the Code of Federal Regulations under the title 'Parks, Forests, and Public Property'.[59] These regulations stipulate how policies prescribed by the NPS Director will be applied to the public who uses the parks. They are the roadmap for park managers to decide whether a proposed use will be allowed, limited, or prohibited. These regulations can be enforced against violators, which is why these policies are published in the form of 'regulations'.

The guidance documents that the NPS has formulated for park managers are called the 'NPS Directive System'.[60] This system consists of three types of documents. The first is the 'Management Policies' (MP), a recent version of which was released in 2001 and revised in 2006. The second is the 'director's orders' to accomplish interim updates and amendments of the MP. The third is usually found in the form of 'handbooks or reference manuals' to assist employees in carrying out the MP and the director's orders.[61] Among these three types, the MP is of the highest academic importance.

The Management Policies of 2006

The MP is applicable service-wide. It sets the general framework and prescribes parameters for making management decisions. The current 2006 MP is mainly divided into ten sections, which cover park system planning, resource management, wilderness management, park use, commercial visitor services and other management issues.

The History and Controversies of Policy Making: A Roller Coaster?

The original version of the MP was released in 2001.[62] The 2001 MP recognized that there was only a single standard regarding the promotion and regulation of the National Park System: the non-impairment standard. The derogation proposed in the General Authorities Act of 1970 was simply a different wording, not a different standard (1.4.2). It was also made clear that in the case of conflict between conserving resources and value and providing for the enjoyment of them, conservation would be predominant (1.4.3).

In 2005, the Bush Administration released a draft to amend the 2001 MP. After Paul Hoffman took the position of deputy assistant secretary in the DOI, he proposed a significant change to the previous MP. Aiming to water down the definition of impairment, the proposal required that 'any impairment finding be judged not just by the proposal's effect on park resources but also by its effect on visitor enjoyment'.[63] The draft deleted conservation as an independent goal, specifically removed all uses of the term 'preservation' and emphasized use and recreation.[64] It showed a strong user-friendly tendency and was considered to have rewritten the long-accepted interpretation of the Organic Act that deemed resource conservation

---

58 16 USC §3.
59 36 CFR 1, *et seq.*
60 NPS, 'The Directive System', in NPS, 'Management Policies 2006: The Guide to Managing the National Park System'. Available at http://www.nps.gov/policy/mp/policies.html. Last visited January 2015.
61 Ibid.
62 Early NPS policy making can be traced back to the 'Lane Letter', which was written by Secretary Franklin Lane to Director Stephen Mather in 1918. The 2001 MP was discussed as the original version in the sense that it was the previous version of the current 2006 MP.
63 Robert Keiter, *supra* note 33, p. 75.
64 Harmony Mappes, *supra* note 9, pp. 629–30.

the NPS's primary responsibility.[65] Jon Jarvis, the current NPS director nominated by President Obama, openly criticized the proposed changes as 'the largest departure from the core values of the National Park System in its history, posing a threat to the integrity of the entire system'.[66] Madeline Kass suggested that the proposed management policies reflected political priorities and threatened a long-standing alliance between preservationists and recreational park vacationers.[67]

After the draft was released for public comment, it lit a fire among the public and park supporters. More than 45,000 comments arrived at the NPS. Under pressure, the NPS reversed its opinions and finalized the MP in 2006, which is the one currently in use. The 2006 MP shows a shift from the 2005 draft, which is considered 'roller-coaster' policy making.[68]

Restatement of the Impairment Standard

The 2006 MP retains the impairment standard articulated in the 2001 MP.[69] First, the MP reiterates that derogation and impairment are not two different standards; there is only one single standard governing national park management (1.4.2). It is also emphasized that 'when there is a conflict between conserving resources and values and providing for enjoyment of them, conservation is to be predominant' (1.4.3).

Second, 'enjoyment' is defined in a broad manner. It is not merely recreational experiences by those who actually visit parks; instead, it includes broader recipients, such as those 'who appreciate [national parks] from afar' (1.4.3). The question arises regarding whether the impairment of enjoyment is deemed the impairment that is outlawed. According to the NPS's interpretation, the standard of impairment of park resources and value is not likewise applied in determining the impairment of enjoyment. The impairment of park resources may impair others' opportunity to enjoy national parks.[70] The opportunity of future generations to experience enjoyment should be protected under the impairment standard.

Third, the MP provides a definition of 'impairment': 'an impact that, in the professional judgment of the responsible NPS manager, would harm the integrity of park resources or values, including the opportunities that otherwise would be present for the enjoyment of those resources or values' (1.4.5).

The impacts of visitor activities, NPS administrative activities and concessioners' activities may lead to impairment. These activities should be governed under the impairment test. This definition is of crucial importance because it is the clearest articulation of the agency's interpretation of the term 'impairment' that is not defined in the statute.

Finally, with regard to how the NPS should make decisions to identify and avoid impairments, the MP proposes a 'professional judgment' requirement.[71] Decision makers are thus

---

65 Ibid., pp. 623–4.
66 Robert Keiter, *supra* note 33, p. 75.
67 Madeline Kass, ' The National Park Service Management Policies Controversy', 20 (2006) *Natural Resources & Environment*, p. 70.
68 Denise Antolini, *supra* note 3, p. 866.
69 Section 1.4. For relevant academic discussion, see Thomas Duncan, 'Driving Americans' Perception of Recreation: Awaiting the Park Service's Long-Term Solution to Access in Yellowstone National Park', 19.2 (2012) *Jeffrey S. Moorad Sports Law Journal*, p. 713; James Rasband et al., *Natural Resources Law and Policy* (New York: Foundation Press, 2009), p. 618 (claiming that revised 2006 MP reiterated the interpretation of impairment provided for in the 2001 MP).
70 See NPS, 'The Impairment Issue: Questions and Answers', '20. Is the impairment of enjoyment prohibited?', August 2007. Available at http://www.nps.gov/protect/q_and_a.htm. Last visited January 2015.
71 According to the MP's definition, professional judgment means 'a decision or opinion that is shaped by study and analysis and full consideration of all the relevant facts, and that takes into account the decision-maker's

required to take into consideration the environmental impact assessment required by the NEPA, the consultations required under the National Historic Preservation Act, relevant scientific and scholarly studies, advice, or insights offered by subject matter experts and others who have relevant knowledge or experience, and the results of civic engagement and public involvement activities (1.4.7).

Appropriate Use, Unacceptable Impact and Impairment

In addition to restating the impairment standard, greater assurance is proposed by the MP, which is the test of 'unacceptable impacts'. This is the most prominent achievement of the 2006 MP.

The NPS requires managers to prohibit uses that would cause unacceptable impacts, that is, those impacts that 'fall short of impairment, but are still not acceptable within a particular park's environment' (1.4.7.1). By applying both the 'impairment' and the 'unacceptable impact' tests, the NPS may allow 'appropriate uses' in national parks, which are 'suitable, proper, or fitting for a particular park, or to a particular location within a park' (1.5). Such appropriate uses may be hierarchical. Because providing opportunities for public enjoyment is a crucial component of the NPS's mission, 'appropriate public enjoyment' is deemed a preferred form of use that the NPS actively promotes, whereas 'other uses' are allowed when they are considered appropriate upon regulation. 'Preferred forms of enjoyment' should satisfy two requirements:

1   Be uniquely suited to the superlative natural and cultural resources found in the park, and
2   Foster an understanding of and appreciation for park resources and values, or promote enjoyment through a direct association with, interaction with, or relation to park resources (1.5).

Figure 6.1 shows the process of determining whether a proposed use is an appropriate use.

Designated Use Patterns on Public Land: The Role of Recreation

Designated use is one of the hallmarks of the modern Organic Act for public land management agencies.[72] It refers to those categories or types of activities that are to be prohibited, preferred, encouraged, or merely tolerated in a certain type of public land designation. Based on the discussions above, the designated use patterns of public lands can be summarized as shown in Table 6.1.[73]

The National Wildlife Refuge System typically features a hierarchically designated use pattern. The initial image of refuges was that of an 'inviolate sanctuary for migratory birds' as prescribed by the Migratory Bird Conservation Act of 1929. Until 1962, when the Refuge Recreation Act was enacted, recreational use was authorized as an appropriate use of wildlife refuges. The National Wildlife Refuge System Improvement Act of 1997 established priority for wildlife-dependent recreational use; thus, the dominant-use regime for wildlife refuges was formulated. Other types of uses are also conditionally allowed in wildlife refuges, such as

   education, training, and experience; advice or insights offered by subject matter experts and others who have relevant knowledge and experience; good science and scholarship; and, whenever appropriate, the results of civic engagement and public involvement activities relating to the decision', 2006 MP, Glossary.
72 Fischman summarizes five hallmarks including purpose statements, designated uses, comprehensive planning, substantive management criteria, and public participation. See Robert Fischman, 'National Wildlife Refuge System and the Hallmarks of Modern Organic Legislation', 29 (2002) *Ecology Law Quarterly*, pp. 514–92.
73 The hierarchy of designated uses within the wildlife refuge system is adapted from Fischman's research. See Robert Fischman, ibid., p. 531.

other recreational activities that meet the compatibility standard and the economic uses of natural resources that contribute to the achievement of a refuge purpose or the system mission.[74]

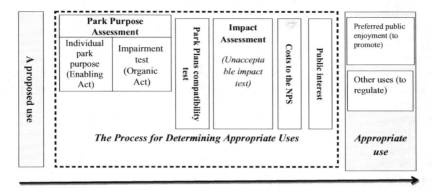

Figure 6.1 The process of determining appropriate uses in the National Park System
Source: Adapted from the NPS MP 2006, section 8.1.2

Table 6.1 Comparison of the designated use patterns of four types of federal land designations

	NPS	FWS
Primary use	1 Individual park purpose 2 Conservation 3 *Wilderness*	1 Individual refuge purpose 2 Conservation 3 *Wilderness*
Secondary use	4 Preferred public enjoyment	4 Wildlife-dependent recreation
Tertiary use	5 Other recreational uses	5 Other recreational uses
Quaternary use	6 Concession-related activities 7 Other appropriate uses	6 Refuge management economic activities (e.g. timber thinning, trapping, hay cropping) 7 Economic uses of natural resources (e.g. logging, grazing, oil/gas production, electricity transmission)

USFS

| Outdoor recreation | Range | Timber | Watershed | Wildlife and fish | *Renewable surface resources* | *Wilderness* |

BLM

| Recreation | Range | Timber | Minerals | Watershed | Wildlife and fish | Natural scenic, scientific and historic values | Other uses | *Wilderness* |

Source: Adapted from relevant statutes and policies

74 50 CFR §29.1.

Because the National Park System does not have a dominant-use mandate, as the wildlife refuge system does, the characteristic of hierarchy among different designated uses is not as salient as it is in the wildlife refuge system. Nevertheless, some hierarchical features can be observed from both the Organic Act and the MP of 2006. Similar to the refuge system, the primary uses are those prescribed in individual park purposes established by enabling acts and conservation, which is clarified by the MP and underpinned by wilderness-oriented statutes. Wilderness use is added to both national parks and wildlife refuges by the Wilderness Act in the case of wilderness designations within these areas. The secondary use is the so-called 'preferred public enjoyment' provided for in the MP, which satisfies the two requirements discussed above. The tertiary uses are other forms of recreational uses, such as snowmobiling and ORV uses. As a means to promote public enjoyment, concession-related activities are deemed quaternary uses together with other uses that have satisfied the 'appropriateness test'.

Unlike park and refuge systems, the designated use patterns of the lands administered by the USFS and the BLM do not show a hierarchal structure. As previously discussed, the MUSYA of 1960 and the FLPMA of 1976 provide multiple-use mandates for the USFS and the BLM, respectively.[75] Recreation is listed as one of these multiple uses in both national forests and BLM lands. Furthermore, the MUSYA authorized and directed the Secretary of Agriculture to 'develop and administer the *renewable surface resources* of the national forests for multiple use and sustained yield of the several products and services obtained therefrom'. It further specified that 'the establishment and maintenance of areas of wilderness area consistent with the purposes and provisions of [the MUSYA]'.[76] The FLPMA added the wilderness use and inventory requirement on BLM lands.[77] In this sense, there are seven types of designated uses of forest lands and eight enumerated types with one open-ended type of use of BLM lands.

Summary

The ambiguous statutory language in the NPS Organic Act can be considered the cause, or one of the causes, of conflicts. Its instruction to the NPS to both promote and regulate enjoyment has directly caused management dilemmas on national park lands. The NPS can be accused of not fulfilling its mandate either to preserve park land and resources or to provide optimal recreational opportunities to visitors. In this sense, the Organic Act itself does not adjudicate potential conflicts between conservation and enjoyment. The ongoing debate over the fundamental purpose shows that there is room left for statutory interpretation.

Modern environmental statutes, such as the Wilderness Act and the NEPA, burden agencies' decision-making processes in either a substantive or a procedural manner. These wilderness-oriented statutes clearly adjudicate conservation-enjoyment conflicts by showcasing a clearer preservation-oriented attitude. Due to the additional layer of protection of national parks provided by these statutes, the NPS's discretion in balancing conservation and enjoyment shrinks. Nagle asserts that 'they act as a check on any temptation that the NPS would encounter to prioritize enjoyment over conservation in certain instances.'[78] These environmental statutes may provide the judiciary with a stronger weapon for judicial review by enabling courts to take a 'hard look'[79] at the NPS's management decisions.

75 See *supra* pp. 78–80 of Chapter 4.
76 Section 2, 16 USC §529.
77 Section 603, 43 USC §1782 (a).
78 John Nagle, *supra* note 20 , Research Paper, pp. 30–31.
79 For the hard look doctrine, see *infra* p. 128 of Chapter 7.

The NPS's MP explicitly recognizes the priority of conservation over enjoyment as its management responsibility and thus relieves the tension between the two. It further elevates the protection standard prescribed by Congress by proposing the 'unacceptable impact' test. This strict threshold provides a clearer guideline for the NPS to make environmentally friendly decisions. However, when considering the rewriting of the MP in 2005, anxiety about the agency and the executive power remains compelling. A close connection between the agency's conservation policy and the political environment can be observed.

Although a conservation mandate of the Organic Act is clarified by environmental statutes and the NPS's own interpretation in the MP, there is a tendency by Congress to push back toward enjoyment in the form of either enabling acts or *ad hoc* intervention in management conflicts. The active involvement of Congress has created dynamics and uncertainties in the balance between conservation and enjoyment. Therefore, the assessment of the legal foundations for adjudicating the conservation-enjoyment conflicts increasingly depends on site-specific conditions.

7 Resolution of Conflicts
A Judicial Perspective

Introduction

Enshrined by the principle of the separation of powers, the judiciary is empowered by the Constitution to exercise judicial review and determine how Congress intends for statutes to apply to disputes. Having assessed the congressional statute and the NPS's interpretation of it in the previous chapter, the questions that follow address how to evaluate the judiciary's role in the resolution of conflicts and how different national park management would be today without courts.[1] This chapter approaches these questions by reviewing how the judiciary interprets congressional statutes, including the Organic Act and other environmental statutes, how it interplays with Congress, agencies and other interest groups, and how conflicts in public land management are perceived and resolved in the judicial sphere.

First, some characteristics and tendencies of public land lawsuits are identified to provide a context for the courts' role in adjudicating national-park-related disputes in general. Then, a brief overview of the standard of judicial review, especially in the field of environment-related cases, is provided.

Second, the judicial interpretation of the purpose statement embodied in the Organic Act is analyzed. A crucial question is whether case law has firmly established that the Organic Act should be read as a conservation mandate. The symbolic *Southern Utah Wilderness Association* case, its precedents and subsequent cases are examined to approach the answer to this question. Furthermore, the way that courts apply other environmental statutes in adjudicating public-land-related disputes, particularly the Wilderness Act and the NEPA, is analyzed. The influences of the application of these statutes on a review of the NPS's management decisions are presented.

Third, several high-profile controversies and hotly debated cases are further discussed, such as the Merced River controversy at Yosemite, the Yellowstone snowmobile policy case and the Grand Canyon overflight policy case, to identify the role of the courts in adjudicating politically controversial issues and the challenges it may encounter.

---

1 Farber proposes this question when he reviews the relevance of the Supreme Court in environmental law: how different would environmental protection be today if without judicial cases? He concludes that the Supreme Court has failed to play a 'constructive' and effective role in environmental law. See Daniel Farber, 'Is the Supreme Court Irrelevant – Reflections on the Judicial Role in Environmental Law', 81(1996) *Minnesota Law Review*, pp. 547, 569.

The Characteristics and Tendencies of Public Land Lawsuits

Some key characteristics and tendencies of public land lawsuits can be outlined. First, there has been more litigation on public lands since the 1970s. Prior to that time, it was not routine for the judiciary to intensively examine public land and natural resource-related decision making by federal agencies. Before the 1970s, the USFS, the NPS and the FWS did not appear frequently in federal courts. The BLM was an exception; however, the cases arose out of private disputes rather than claims against agency actions.[2] There are several reasons that explain the litigation boom in the 1970s:

1. Congress provided detailed management criteria in statutes and created enforceable rights for private parties, which facilitated bringing suits to courts;
2. Standing requirements were more relaxed, which enabled environmental groups to bring lawsuits to courts.[3] Litigation proposed by environmental groups has become commonplace;
3. Different interest groups were emerging, such as recreational user organizations. These groups were willing and ready to assert their rights as environmental groups do, which diversifies the components of plaintiffs, and
4. Courts are active in reviewing all kinds of administrative actions and are more inclined to impose judicial skepticism on administrative decision making.

Second, increasing numbers of claims are brought to courts based on procedural grounds, especially on the NEPA-based environmental impact assessment requirements. Though it is noted that NEPA is 'merely a procedural statute' and does not dictate any particular conservation result for the NPS,[4] it is frequently adopted and serves as an effective litigious tool for plaintiffs. The agency's management plans are increasingly sued by plaintiffs on the grounds of NEPA violation and procedural deficiencies. The NEPA is also used by agencies to legitimate their decisions against recreational demands, with the result of enhancing their conservation mandates.

Third, plaintiffs regularly claim that agencies have violated multiple statutes.[5] The NPS Organic Act does not itself create a private right of action. Therefore, plaintiffs seeking to enforce the values that the Organic Act protects need to base their claims on the APA in order for their cases to arrive in court. They usually allege the violation of other statutes, such as the NEPA, the ESA, the Wilderness Act and the WSRA.

Fourth, the NPS is frequently involved in lawsuits in which it has to defend itself against 'flying allegations from opposite sides',[6] that is, conservationists and user groups. When the NPS is sued by environmental groups for its lenient policy on motorized recreation, organized recreational groups may participate in litigation as interveners and

---

2 George Coggins, Charles Wilkinson and John Leshy, *Federal Public Land and Resources Law* (New York: Foundation Press, 2007), p. 207.
3 See *Sierra Club v. Morton*, 405 US 727 (1972) (the Supreme Court held that the Sierra Club might sue on behalf of any of its members who had individual standing when government actions caused injury to their particularized interests).
4 Denise Antolini, 'National Park Law In The US: Conservation, Conflict, And Centennial Values', 33 (2009) *William and Mary Environmental Law and Policy Review*, p. 901.
5 Ibid., p. 889.
6 Ibid.

128 *Country Studies: United States*

vice versa.[7] Therefore, the NPS is alternatively seen as parallel to both environmental groups and recreational groups before courts.

Standards of Judicial Review in General and in Particular

Judicial review of administrative decisions is generally differentiated into the review of questions of fact and the review of questions of law. Three levels of review standards are established with regard to the former, which are *de novo*, substantial evidence and the 'arbitrary and capricious' standard. With regard to the judicial review of questions of law, the most well-known standard is the *Chevron* doctrine.[8]

The 'Arbitrary And Capricious' Standard and the 'Hard Look Doctrine'

As previously discussed, the APA of 1946 provides the foundation for decision making for all federal agencies in the US. The scope of judicial review is stipulated in section 706, and the most well-known standard is presented in section 706(2) (a), which allows courts to strike down informal agency action that is 'arbitrary, capricious, an abuse of discretion, or otherwise not in accordance with law'.[9]

During the New Deal era, courts usually treated this standard essentially as a reasonableness standard[10] and showed a deferential attitude toward agencies. However, since the 1970s, courts have reviewed agency actions with greater scrutiny, which is termed a 'hard look doctrine'. This is intensively reflected in the *Overton Park* case,[11] in which the Supreme Court ruled that the Secretary of Transportation's sole reliance on litigation affidavits was insufficient to justify its decision to build highways through Overton Park. This case established a heightened standard to review agency actions than that provided in the APA. For example, the Supreme Court required agencies to create a full administrative record in their informal procedures and to base their decision on that record. Stipulated in the APA, such a requirement only applies to formal rule making and adjudication. The Supreme Court also stated that the judicial review should be a 'thorough, probing, in-depth review'.[12]

This heightened standard was later solidified in the *Motor Vehicle Manufacturers Association* case.[13] The Supreme Court required that agencies provide a satisfactory explanation for their actions, including a 'rational connection between the facts found [in the record] and the choice made'.[14] Since then, the so-called 'hard look doctrine' has been established, which requires courts to more closely scrutinize informal rulemaking by agencies.

---

7 See the case of *Southern Utah Wilderness Alliance v. Dabney*, 222 F. 3d. 819 (2000) (ORV groups intervened in support of the NPS's decision to allow continued motorized access to Salt Creek).
8 For a general discussion about American administrative law and judicial review standards, see Ronald Cass et al., *Administrative Law: Cases and Materials, sixth edition* (New York: Wolters Kluwer Law & Business, 2011). For literature in Chinese, see generally Zhang Qianfan, 司法审查的标准与方法—以美国行政法为视角 (Tests and Methods of Judicial Review: A Perspective from the Administrative Law of the United States), 6 (2006) 法学家(*The Jurist*), pp. 36–44 (the author reviews the standard of *de novo* trial, the reasonableness standard, the arbitrary and capricious standard, the hard-look doctrine, the standard of clear error and others).
9 5 USC §706(2)(a).
10 Alfred Aman, *Administrative Law and Process: Cases and Materials* (Newark, NJ: LexisNexis Matthew Bender, 2006), p. 803.
11 *Citizens to Preserve Overton Park v. Volpe*, 401 US 402 (1971).
12 Ibid., p. 415.
13 *Motor Vehicle Manufacturers Association v. State Farm Mutual Automobile Insurance Co.*, 463 US 29 (1983).
14 Ibid., p. 43.

The Chevron and Skidmore Deference and the Mead Standard

Case 1: *Chevron USA, Inc. v. Natural Resources Defense Council, Inc.* (1984)[15]

The central issue of the *Chevron* case was

> ... whether [the Environmental Protection Agency (EPA)]'s decision to allow states to treat all of the pollution-emitting devices within the same industrial group as though they were encased within a single "bubble" is based on a reasonable construction of the statutory term "stationary source".[16]

The Supreme Court found that the EPA's interpretation of the Clean Air Act was reasonable. This case is of crucial importance in American administrative law because it articulates the doctrine of 'administrative deference'.[17]

The *Chevron* case proposed a two-step test for courts to evaluate whether to defer to an agency's interpretation of a statute:

> Step 1: the court must first determine whether the statute is ambiguous. If Congress has unambiguously answered the question, then 'that is the end of the matter'.
>
> Step 2: If the courts determine that the statute is ambiguous, then the courts must defer to the agency if 'the agency's answer is based on a permissible construction of the statute.'[18]

The Supreme Court also noted that 'the court need not conclude that the agency construction was the only one it permissibly could have adopted to uphold the construction, or even the reading the court would have reached.'[19]

Chevron establishes the basic rule for statutory interpretation. In Sunstein's words, it grants agencies two important 'common-law functions': 'specifying statutory terms' in the case of ambiguities and 'adapting those terms to new facts and values'.[20] Due to the two-step test it established, the *Chevron* case has become the most frequently cited case in subsequent judgments. Sunstein states that

> *Chevron*, a kind of counter-*Marbury*[21] for the administrative state, has been cited more frequently than *Marbury v. Madison*, *Brown v. Board of Education*, or *Roe v. Wade* . . . [and] has become the framework through which agency interpretations of law are reviewed.[22]

The so-called '*Chevron* deference' has witnessed a gradual evolution. In 2001, the Supreme Court delivered another judgment in the *Mead* case that further elaborated the principle of 'administrative deference'.

---

15 467 US 837 (1984).
16 Ibid., p. 840.
17 The influences of the *Chevron* case on the American administrative law is so far-reaching that the *Journal of Administrative Law Review* has a special issue of commemoration of the thirtieth anniversary of the *Chevron* case in 2014. See *Administrative Law Review* 66.2 (2014).
18 *Chevron*, pp. 842–3.
19 Ibid., note 11.
20 Cass Sunstein, 'Is Tobacco a Drug? Administrative Agencies as Common Law Courts', 47 (1998) *Duke Law Journal*, p. 1058.
21 *Marbury v. Madison*, 5 US (1 Cranch) 137 (1803).
22 Cass Sunstein, *supra* note 20, p. 1058.

Case 2: *United States v. Mead Corp* (2001)[23]

The central issue of the *Mead* case is whether the tariff classification rulings made by the US Customs Service deserve *Chevron* deference. The Supreme Court ruled that *Chevron* deference was not applicable to such rulings. It set the standard for *Chevron* deference as follows: an administrative interpretation of a particular statutory provision qualifies for *Chevron* deference when 'It appears that Congress delegated authority to the agency generally to make rules carrying the force of law, and that the agency interpretation claiming deference was promulgated in the exercise of that authority.'

It further clarified that even if the agency action 'may be precedent in later transactions, precedential value alone does not add up to *Chevron* entitlement' (p. 232). In the alternative, administrative interpretations 'not meeting these standards are entitled not to deference, but to a lesser respect based on the persuasiveness of the agency decision' (p. 228). This lesser degree of deference is established in the *Skidmore v. Swift & Co.*[24] case, which is generally referred to as the *Skidmore* deference as compared to the *Chevron* deference. The *Mead* judgment distinguished these two types of deference: *Chevron* deference was established in delegated law-making power under a constitutional structure, whereas *Skidmore* deference was established under the scenario of 'prudential exercise of administrative discretion' by agencies.[25]

Based on the *Mead* judgment, courts should first review whether the agency is entitled to receive *Chevron* deference for its action before they can apply the first step of the *Chevron* test. For this reason, Cass Sunstein called the *Mead* test '*Chevron* step zero.'[26]

Judicial Interpretation of Congressional Statutes

Courts' Interpretation of the Organic Act

The core of the judicial interpretation of the Organic Act is focused on the following questions: whether there are ambiguities in the statutory language of the Organic Act (i.e. whether Congress explicitly establishes the priority of conservation over enjoyment) and whether the NPS is mandated with the discretion to balance conservation and enjoyment. If ambiguities and the NPS's discretion can be recognized, the question arises regarding how much judicial deference should be given to the NPS's interpretation of statutes.

Case 3: *Southern Utah Wilderness Alliance v. Dabney* (1998)[27]

The *Southern Utah Wilderness Alliance* (SUWA) case is symbolic in the case law regarding the interpretation of the Organic Act. It was the first time that the district court ruled against

---

23 533 US 218, 121 S. Ct. 2164, 150 L. Ed. 2d 292 (2001).
24 *Skidmore v. Swift & Co.*, 323 US 134 (1944).
25 Jerry Mashaw, 'Norms, Practices, and the Paradox of Deference: A Preliminary Inquiry into Agency Statutory Interpretation', 57 (2005) *Administrative Law Review*, p. 505.
26 Cass Sunstein, 'Chevron Step Zero', 92 (2006) *Virginia Law Review*, p. 187.
27 *Southern Utah Wilderness Alliance v. Dabney*, 7 F. Supp. 2d 1205 (D. Utah 1998), rev'd, 222 F. 3d 819 (10th Cir. 2000). A subsequent case is *Southern Utah Wilderness Alliance v. NPS*, 387 F. Supp. 2d 1178 (D. Utah 2005). In the following discussion, these three litigations are respectively referred to as *SUWA* 1998, *SUWA* 2000 and *SUWA* 2005. For a thorough study of the Canyonlands disputes, see generally David Watts, 'Canyonlands National Park and the Organic Act: Balancing Resource Protection and Visitor Use', NPS, September 2008. Full text is available at http://www.nps.gov/parkhistory/online_books/cany/resource_protection.pdf. Last visited January 2015.

the NPS's management decision on the basis of its violation of the Organic Act instead of other environmental statutes.[28]

In 1995, the NPS issued a backcountry management plan (BMP) for Canyonlands National Park that allowed the use of motor vehicles on jeep tracks or trails in a ten-mile segment of park road. The plaintiffs challenged the BMP, arguing that it violated the APA, the NPS Organic Act, the Canyonlands National Park Enabling Act and the NEPA. The plaintiffs argued that the Organic Act was a preservation mandate and protected park resources against any impairment. In contrast, the NPS contended that its decision was a 'reasonable accommodation of conflicting mandates that is to be afforded considerable deference'.[29]

The district court delivered its judgment in 1998 and found for the plaintiffs. It stated that 'the first *Chevron* inquiry [was] determinative' in the current case. The court phrased the central issue as 'whether the [NPS] is authorized to permit activities within national parks that permanently impair park resources'.[30] It ruled that Congress's answer to this question was clearly no. The Utah Shared Access Alliance[31] appealed. The NPS did not appeal, but it submitted a brief 'to advise the Court of the Department's views as to the proper legal construction of the [Organic] Act'.[32]

The 10th Circuit reversed and remanded. By citing precedents of the cases of *Bicycle Trails Council vs. Babbitt* and the *Sierra Club vs. Babbitt*,[33] the circuit court concluded that the Organic Act was inherently ambiguous. Therefore, the case was a *Chevron* Two case rather than a *Chevron* One case. The question before the circuit court was 'whether the agency's answer is based on a permissible construction of the statute'.[34]

In the judgment delivered by the 10th Circuit, the purpose statement of the Organic Act was elaborated. The circuit court first corrected the central issue that the district court had framed and rephrased it as

> ... whether the BMP, in particular the portion of the BMP allowing vehicle use on the ten-mile segment of the Salt Creek Road from Peekaboo Spring to Angel Arch, is inconsistent with a clear intent of Congress expressed in the Organic Act and the Canyonlands enabling legislation'.[35]

In contrast to the district court's view, the circuit court interpreted the Organic Act as 'permitting the NPS to balance the sometimes conflicting policies of resource conservation and visitor enjoyment in determining what activities should be permitted or prohibited'.[36] The court also elaborated the test for examining whether the NPS had properly established

---

28 John Nagle, 'How National Park Law Really Works', 86 (2015) *University of Colorado Law Review*. This article is available as Notre Dame Law School Legal Studies Research Paper No. 1430, see p. 16 and footnote 79. The NPS also singles out the *SUWA* case 'the first case to find that the Service's actions in a park had violated the Organic Act'. See NPS, 'The Impairment Issue: Questions and Answers', '3. Since similar lawsuits have been adjudicated before, why has the SUWA case been singled out?', August 2007. Available at http://www.nps.gov/protect/q_and_a.htm. Last visited January 2015.
29 *SUWA* 1998, p. 1211.
30 Ibid.
31 During the litigation in the first instance, the Utah Shared Access Alliance, a combination of motor vehicle recreation associations, intervened as co-defendants, together with the NPS.
32 *SUWA* 2000, p. 822
33 *Bicycle Trails Council v. Babbitt*, 82 F. 3d 1445 (9th Cir. 1996); *Sierra Club v. Babbitt*, 69 F. Supp. 2d 1202 (E.D. Cal. 1999). More details about these two cases will be provided later.
34 *Chevron* case, p. 843.
35 *SUWA* 2000, p. 826.
36 Ibid.

132 Country Studies: United States

such a balance, which was 'whether the resulting action leaves the resources "unimpaired for the enjoyment of future generations"'.[37]

At the time of the appellate case, the NPS was drafting its Management Policies, which would provide its construction of the 'impairment' standard. Because this draft policy lacked the formality that was required for *Chevron* deference, the circuit court ruled that 'there [was] currently no valid agency position worthy of deference.'[38] Therefore, the case was remanded to the district court to 're-examine the evidence in the record regarding impairment caused by vehicles in that area'.[39] The circuit court also required the lower court to examine the nature of the NPS Management Policies that might be released by the time of the re-trial, namely, whether they were 'legislative rules worthy of *Chevron* deference' or 'interpretative rules [that] should be evaluated pursuant to the less deferential standard'.[40]

After this appeal, the NPS issued its MP in 2001 and articulated the impairment standard (Section 1.4). In 2002, the NPS made a new environmental assessment of the use of motorcycles and issued a 'finding of no significant impact' (FONSI). The FONSI selected the alternative that would prohibit all motor vehicle access for implementation. A final rule was released by the NPS in 2004 that prohibited all motor vehicle use in this disputed area. This rule was totally different from its previous 1995 BMP. This time, the Utah Shared Access Alliance and other recreational groups disagreed. They relied on the Organic Act and argued that the final rule violated the Act because 'it [deprived] members of the public the ability to use and enjoy significant portions of Salt Creek Canyon.' They also challenged the validity of the 2001 NPS MP, arguing that it would make 'use and enjoyment . . . a secondary consideration'.[41]

This time, the district court learned the lesson from previous litigations. It recognized the inherent ambiguities in the Organic Act's impairment standard and adopted a *Chevron* Two approach to analyze the issue, as instructed by the circuit court. Three steps can be identified in the district court's analysis:

1   The 2001 MP was 'the type of agency decision intended to carry the force of law' that satisfied the *Mead* standard and was entitled to *Chevron* deference.
2   The NPS's construction of the statute was permissible under the second step of the *Chevron* test, which deserved judicial deference. The court read the Organic Act as not '[mandating that] the NPS equally balance preservation with public use in making its management decision'; instead, impairment was the test for providing conservation and enjoyment. Therefore, the court concluded that the NPS's 2001 MP was 'not manifestly contrary to the express language of the Organic Act'.[42]
3   The final rule '[fell] well within the NPS's broad grant of discretion and constitute[d] a permissible interpretation of the Organic Act and the Enabling Act'.

For these reasons, the district court ruled for the NPS and supported its prohibition of motor vehicle use in this disputed area.

It is clear that the district court delivered its judgment mainly based on a deference scenario instead of making a substantial judgment itself. In demonstrating that the NPS's construction of the Organic Act was permissible, it cited several precedents that were claimed to support the

37   Ibid., p. 827.
38   Ibid., p. 828.
39   Ibid., p. 830.
40   Ibid., p. 829.
41   *SUWA* 2005, p. 1181.
42   Ibid., p. 1190.

conservation mandate of the Organic Act. By citing the *National Rifle Association of America* case, it ruled that the legislative history of the Act suggested that the 'overriding purpose of the bill was to preserve "nature as it exists"'. By citing the *Bicycle Trails Council* case, it stated that 'the majority of courts that have interpreted the "no-impairment" mandate have interpreted it as placing an "overarching concern on preservation of resources".'[43] With these citations, it ruled that 'the [MP's] interpretation therefore is consistent with over twenty years of federal court decisions confirming that conservation is the predominant facet of the Organic Act.'

This logic seemed to create a *prima facie* contradiction. The district court ruled for the NPS because the NPS's interpretation of the Organic Act deserved *Chevron* deference. However, the precedents it quoted seemed to indicate that there was a long-established judicial interpretation of the Organic Act, that is, that it should be read as a conservation mandate. The question of whether this is an established case law that supports the conservation mandate of the NPS Organic Act remains unanswered. To approach this answer, it is necessary to examine the cited precedents and the cases that followed.

Examination of the Precedents

CASE 4: *NATIONAL RIFLE ASSOCIATION OF AMERICA V. POTTER* (1986)[44]

The court upheld the NPS's generic regulations on the prohibition of hunting and trapping throughout the National Park System. The National Rifle Association of America (NRAA) asserted that the Organic Act did not prohibit 'properly regulated hunting and trapping' activities, whereas the NPS argued that conservation of wildlife meant 'safeguarding it from harm, whether from natural or human causes.'[45] The most frequently cited sentence of the judgment is that 'in the Organic Act, Congress speaks of but a single purpose, namely, conservation.'[46] This statement is used by many scholars to support the court's recognition of the conservation mandate of the Organic Act.[47]

It is necessary to examine how this decision was reached by the court in its reasoning process. The court rejected the NRAA's argument by stating that its interpretation of the Organic Act was 'inconsistent with that principle of statutory interpretation known as *expression unius est exclusion alterius*'.[48] Because Congress authorized hunting and trapping in individual enabling acts, this led to 'a supposition that it expected that they would not be allowed to take place elsewhere'.[49] Though the court iterated the frequently cited 'single purpose statement' in its reasoning process,[50] this statement cannot be deemed a direct judicial argument to rebut the NRAA's claims. In other words, the value of this frequently cited statement is overestimated.

43 Ibid., 2005, p. 1191.
44 628 F. Supp. 903 (D.D.C. 1986).
45 Ibid., p. 909.
46 Ibid.
47 Robert Keiter, 'Revisiting the Organic Act: Can It Meet the Next Century's Conservation Challenges?', 28.3 (2011) *The George Wright Forum*, p. 243 ('The courts . . . have consistently found that resource conservation takes priority over public enjoyment or other interests'), and Frank Buono, 'The Wilderness Act of 1964: Its Relationship to the NPS Organic Act', 11.1 (1994) *The George Wright Forum*, p. 51.
48 The principle of '*expression unius est exclusion alterius*' means that 'omissions from enumerated specifics are generally presumed to be deliberate exclusions from the general unless otherwise indicated'. Cited from 628 F. Supp. 903 (D.D.C. 1986), p. 909.
49 Ibid.
50 In the latter part of the judgment, the court re-emphasized the 'single purpose of conservation' by stating that the Redwood Amendment mandated the NPS to manage parks according to the 'purpose' instead of 'purposes' of the Organic Act. See 628 F. Supp., p. 909.

This statement was not articulated as a direct answer to the conflict between conservation and visitor enjoyment. In fact, the judgment was silent on which one should be prioritized. Instead, the court concluded that hunting and trapping activities, even properly regulated hunting and trapping activities, did not fall into the category of 'visitor enjoyment' that deserves protection through the Organic Act. What the court had claimed to be the 'single purpose' was not conservation but rather the unimpaired status of park land and resources. Furthermore, the court ruled that it was 'satisfied that the [NPS]'s reading of the statutory law comports with the apparent legislative intent'.[51] This sentence shows that the court still relied on a 'deference' scenario. This statement echoed the 10th Circuit Court's attitude in the *SUWA* case: the case was a *Chevron* Two instead of a *Chevron* One issue.

CASE 5: *BICYCLE TRAILS COUNCIL OF MARIN V. BABBITT* (1996)[52]

Another precedent is the *Bicycle Trails Council* case, in which the NPS's closing of bicycle trails in a national recreational area was upheld. The frequently cited statement was that 'resource protection [was] the overarching concern [of the Organic Act].'[53] It should be noted that what the circuit court phrased as the 'overarching concern' was 'resource protection' instead of 'conservation'. Rather than saying that the court prioritized conservation over enjoyment, it is more accurate to say that the court actually defined the term 'resource protection' as 'non-impairment', as enshrined in the Organic Act. The circuit court also stated, 'The Organic Act is silent as to the specifics of park management and . . . the [NPS] has broad discretion in determining which avenues best achieve the Organic Act's mandate.'[54] One can observe that, similar to the previous case, courts showed deference to the NPS's discretion in making management decisions.

In addition to referring to these two cases, scholars refer to other judicial cases in which they claim that courts have consistently found the Organic Act to be a preservation mandate.[55] However, these cases do not necessarily preclude the conclusion that the judiciary first established its own interpretation of the Organic Act in such a way that conservation is to be prioritized. Though some excerpts from the judgments show a *prima facie* judicial attitude indicating this conclusion, putting them in context may make it clear that the courts recognized that the NPS has broad discretion in balancing conservation and enjoyment. Furthermore, courts show considerable deference to the NPS's interpretation. An examination of the cases after the *SUWA* case also helps to verify this conclusion.

Examination of the Cases Following the SUWA *Case*

Antolini conducted a quantitative study on the approximately forty reported national-park-related federal cases (twenty district court cases and twenty circuit court of appeal cases) adjudicated from 2000 to 2008.[56] She showed that courts found that the Organic Act gave the NPS broad

---

51 628 F. Supp. 903 (D.D.C. 1986), p. 912.
52 82 F. 3d 1445 (9th Cir. 1996).
53 Ibid., p. 1453.
54 Ibid., p. 1454.
55 For example, *Michigan United Conservation Clubs vs. Lujan*, 949 F. 2d. 202 (6th Cir. 1991), *Organized Fishermen of Florida v. Hodel*, 775 F. 2d 1544 (11th Cir. 1985);*Wilderness Public Rights Fund v. Kleppe*, 608 F. 2d 1250 (9th Cir. 1979). In these cases, courts upheld the NPS's regulations that limit hunting, fishing, whitewater rafting and other recreational activities. See Robert Keiter, *supra* note 47, p. 243 and footnote 20.
56 Denise Antolini, *supra* note 4, pp. 851–971.

discretion in making balancing decisions, and courts were inclined to show considerable deference to the NPS's discretion-based decision making. She also noted that several pre-2000 decisions showed that courts were inclined to provide great deference to the NPS's decisions.[57]

In accordance with judicial deference to the NPS, judgments show both pro-conservation and pro-enjoyment results. Especially before the 2000s, case law shows that courts usually upheld the NPS's conservation-oriented decisions challenged by user groups.[58] However, according to Antolini's survey during the period from 2000 to 2008, a stunning conclusion was that under the dualism of the Organic Act, there was a shift in case law toward a more user-driven mandate.[59] Examples included the series of cases regarding the snowmobile policy in Yellowstone in which courts favored a pro-user policy by the NPS,[60] the series of cases about commercial rafting on the Colorado River in which the NPS plan favoring commercial boaters was upheld,[61] and the case of *Davis v. Latschar*[62] in which the NPS's decision to conduct a controlled hunt of deer in Gettysburg National Military Park was upheld. The period that Antolini's research covered largely spanned the two terms of the Bush Administration. Previous discussions about the draft MP of 2005 and the oil and gas drilling policy in Utah have shown that the Bush Administration indicated an explicit pro-user tendency. Antolini's conclusion demonstrated a strong connection between the political commitment to national parks and the court record in this regard.

Following Antolini's quantitative research, this research conducted a further survey of reported national park-related federal cases adjudicated during the period from 2009 to 2014. Through a Westlaw search, 33 such cases, including 18 district court cases and 15 circuit court cases, were found with a combination of the key words 'National Park Service' and 'Organic Act'. By a further filter, ten cases, including seven district court cases and three court of appeal cases, were related to the NPS's management decisions.[63] However, limited rulings are based on elaborating the Organic Act; other environmental statutes, such as the NEPA and Wilderness Act, are more frequently used. Two examples of cases in which the Organic Act is referred to are discussed below.

CASE 6: *BLUEWATER NETWORK V. SALAZAR* (2010)[64]

Environmental groups challenged the NPS's decision to reintroduce personal watercrafts to two national seashores. The district court recognized that the NPS had to interpret the Organic Act to 'reconcile values that may at times be in tension with one another'.[65] It also stated that

57 Ibid., p. 895.
58 For example, the two precedents discussed in the previous section.
59 *Voyageurs Region National Park Association v. Lujan*, 966 F. 2d 424, 427 (8th Cir. 1992) (allowing snowmobiles in corridors of national park); *Wilderness Public Rights Fund v. Kleppe*, 608 F. 2d 1250, 1254 (9th Cir. 1979); *South Utah Wilderness Alliance v. Dabney*, 7 F. Supp. 2d 1205, 1211 (D. Utah 1998).
60 Different courts delivered conflicting judgments with regard to the snowmobile policy. For more details, see *infra* p. 139 et seq.
61 *Wilderness Public Rights Fund v. Kleppe*, 608 F. 2d 1250 (9th Cir. 1979), cert. denied, 446 US 982 (1980); *River Runners for Wilderness v. Martin*, 593 F. 3d 1064 (9th Cir. 2010).
62 *Davis v. Latschar*, 202 F. 3d 359 (D.C. Cir. 2000).
63 For example, in the case of *Sierra Club North Star Chapter v. LaHood*, 693 F. Supp. 2d 958 (D. Minnesota, 2010), it was ruled that the Organic Act and General Authorities Act did not apply in the current case as the proposed bridge was located in the lower segment of the Lower St. Croix which was a state-administered area (p. 983). This case is not taken into consideration in the current analysis. Other cases that are not included include those whose causes of actions are not based on the Organic Act, but based on other statutes, such as NEPA and APA. For example, *High Sierra Hikers Association v. U.S. DOI*, 848 F. Supp. 2d 1036 (N.D. Cal. 2012).
64 721 F. Supp. 2d 7 (D.C. Court, 2010).
65 Ibid., p. 20.

136 *Country Studies: United States*

> ... there can be no doubt, as NPS and the courts have concluded, that the overriding aim of the Organic Act, as well as the purpose of NPS's oversight and management of the park system, is to conserve the natural wonders of our nation's parks for future generations.[66]

The court finally ruled for environmental groups because the NPS failed to provide a reasoned analysis of how the facts it found led to the conclusion that no impairment was caused by reintroducing personal watercrafts.

CASE 7: *NATIONAL PARKS CONSERVATION ASSOCIATION V. JEWELL* (2013)[67]

The NPS approved an expanded electric transmission line across an existing right of way in the Delaware River Gap National Recreation Area. The NPS found that this would not bring impairment to the area. The National Parks Conservation Association sued the NPS, claiming that the transmission line would 'permanently scar the landscape and degrade the visitor experience in some of the most visited national parks in the country'. The district court showed considerable deference to this NPS decision. It stated that 'because the Organic Act is silent as to the specifics of park management, the Secretary has especially broad discretion on how to implement his statutory mandate.' It finally ruled that the NPS provided a sufficient rational basis for its non-impairment decision under the Organic Act and was thus not 'arbitrary and capricious'.

One can observe that in both Antolini's research and the follow-up studies discussed above, there seems to be no definite statutory standard for courts to apply in terms of interpreting the Organic Act. There are still inconsistencies in courts' interpretation of precedents and the Organic Act: some courts state that a strong preservation mandate has been firmly established by case law, whereas others recognize great discretion possessed by the NPS in balancing conservation and enjoyment. This creates difficulties in summarizing a universal standard of judicial review. With regard to the review of fact, the 'arbitrary and capricious' standard seems to be the one to which courts frequently refer, if there is any; this standard is more or less easy for the agency to satisfy. The requirement of a 'harder look' placed on the agency is not universally applied by courts. With regard to the review of agency's interpretation of statutes, which are concentratedly reflected in the NPS MP, courts have recognized its entitlement to *Chevron* deference via the landmark *SUWA* case. It is worthy of notice that recognition of MP's entitlement to *Chevron* deference does not necessarily mean that courts have recognized the enforceability of the MP. This difference between eligibility for *Chevron* deference and enforceability was explicitly pointed out in the case of *River Runners for Wilderness*, in which MP was ruled to be unenforceable because they do not 'prescribe substantive rules, nor were they promulgated in conformance with the procedures of the APA'.[68]

Courts' Application of Other Environmental Statutes

Courts seldom adjudicate national park-related disputes based solely on the Organic Act. Instead, other environmental statutes are more frequently applied. This section examines how the application of the Wilderness Act and the NEPA has influenced the courts' adjudication in national-park-related disputes.

---

66 Ibid., p. 21.
67 965 F. Supp. 2d 67 (D.C. Court, 2013).
68 593 F. 3d 1064 (Court of Appeals, 9th Circuit 2010), p. 1073.

Wilderness Act: A Less Deferential Judiciary

As previously shown, the Wilderness Act shows a strong preservation mandate, and the agency's discretion to make management decisions is therefore reduced. Sax deems the Wilderness Act 'the single most significant congressional enactment separating the old era of administrative discretion and expertise from the modern period of legislative skepticism toward the federal land-management bureaucracy'.[69] This legislative skepticism is also reflected in judicial attitudes.

Appel traces the 94 wilderness cases that courts at all levels have tried from the enactment of the Wilderness Act in 1964 to 2010. The data show that when wilderness advocates challenge agencies' decisions by seeking more protection or less use within a wilderness area, they tend to win with a success rate of 52 percent. When land agencies defend their decisions against wilderness users who argue that agencies are protecting wilderness too stringently, they almost never lose, with a high success rate of 86.4 percent. Appel depicts this phenomenon as the judiciary's 'one-way ratchet in favor of wilderness protection'.[70] By comparing other figures that show judicial deference to agency decisions, either generally in administrative law or particularly in environmental law, he asserts that the judiciary in wilderness cases stands in stark contrast; it shows less deference and a pro-wilderness tendency.[71] He provides six reasons that might explain the courts' attitude, including the language in the Wilderness Act that invites strict judicial construction, long-standing and widespread political support for wilderness protection, the risk-averse nature of judges, excellent attorneys in wilderness advocacy organizations, the correction of biased agencies' management decisions and broader popular support.[72]

In terms of national park-related cases, previous discussions indicate that courts show considerable judicial deference to the NPS's interpretation of the Organic Act. However, when the disputed decision is challenged against the Wilderness Act, courts are more inclined to adopt the standard of a 'hard look' at the NPS's wilderness-related decisions and show less deference. This echoes a previous finding that the soft Organic Act is hardened when it is matched by the Wilderness Act, which shows a clearer preservation mandate.[73]

NEPA: A Harder Look Requirement

After being applied for more than forty years, the NEPA became one of the most frequently litigated statutes in American environmental law.[74] The NEPA requires agencies to take a harder look at environmental consequences before taking major actions. The NEPA does not mandate a particular result, but it prescribes the necessary process to be followed. Courts have established four NEPA requirements to evaluate whether such a hard look is taken:

---

69 Joseph Sax, 'Parks, Wilderness, and Recreation', in Michael Lace (ed.), *Government and Environmental Politics: Essays on Historical Developments since World War Two* (Washington, DC: Woodrow Wilson Center Press: 1989), p. 120.
70 Peter Appel, 'Wilderness and the Courts', 29 (2010) *Stanford Environmental Law Journal*, pp. 111–19. The author mentioned in his introduction to this article the two figures as 56 percent and 88 percent which were inconsistent with the figures he used later in Table 1 of his article. Cf. pp. 66–7 and p. 113.
71 Ibid.
72 Ibid., pp. 119–25.
73 See *supra* p. 116 of Chapter 6.
74 Heather Ross, 'Using NEPA in the Fight for Environmental Justice', 18 (1994) *William and Mary Journal of Environmental Law*, p. 362 and note 41.

First, the agency [has] accurately identified the relevant environmental concern. Second, once the agency has identified the problem it must have taken a 'hard look' at the problem in preparing the [Environmental Assessment]. Third, if a finding of no significant impact is made, the agency must be able to make a convincing case for its finding. Last, if the agency does find an impact of true significance, preparation of an [Environmental Impact Statement (EIS)] can be avoided only if the agency finds that the changes or safeguards in the project sufficiently reduce the impact to a minimum.[75]

The relationship between the NEPA analysis and the Organic Act analysis is discussed in the case of *Bluewater Network v. Salazar*.[76] The court ruled that the NPS overwhelmingly relied on the 'impairment' reasoning to serve the purpose of its NEPA analysis. This did not fulfill the requirement of a 'hard look' under the NEPA.[77] In other words, the hard look requirement in the NEPA is more stringent than the impairment reasoning prescribed in the Organic Act.

By analyzing the application of the NEPA in national park cases, Antolini finds that the NEPA's influences can be two-fold: in some cases, the NEPA backstops the NPS's conservation mandate; however, in other cases, the NEPA may undermine the conservation mandate.[78] Because the NEPA is merely a procedural statute, in some cases, the NEPA is 'simply a litigation tool wielded by the NPS or private-use groups to justify agency decisions that promote the use and enjoyment of the National Parks over conservation'.[79] This finding echoes scholars' criticism of the NEPA for failing the sustainable development requirements because it lacks 'after-the-fact responsibility for substantive errors'.[80]

By reviewing courts' application of the Wilderness Act and the NEPA, one may find that the judicial review of national park-related issues becomes more complex. Compared to the deferential attitude in interpreting the Organic Act, the judiciary shows a more skeptical attitude to the NPS when other environmental statutes are applied.

In the following sections, several typical and influential judicial cases on national park-related management decisions are discussed to examine how the judiciary interprets the statutory terms, how it selects the deference standard in reviewing the agency's management decision, and the pitfalls and challenges of the judicial approach in adjudicating conservation-related disputes.

Case Study: The Use of Motorized Recreational Vehicles on Federal Land

Lawsuits centered on motorized recreation use, such as ORV use, have accounted for a significant proportion of the overall public land litigation. One of the earliest cases on the regulation of ORVs occurred at the Cape Cod National Seashore as early as 1981.[81] The district court required the NPS to 'more thoroughly consider whether ORV use . . . [was] an appropriate public use of the Seashore'.[82] However, this judicial protection was only procedural. After conducting a survey of 1,300 visitors, the NPS concluded that ORV use was

---

75 *Town of Cave Creek, Arizona v. Federal Aviation Administration*, 325 F. 3d 320 (2003), p. 327.
76 721 F. Supp. 2d 7 (D.C. Court, 2010).
77 721 F.Supp. 2d 7, pp. 39–40.
78 Denise Antolini, *supra* note 4, pp. 896–902.
79 Ibid., p. 901.
80 David Hodas, 'The Role of Law in Defining Sustainable Development: NEPA Reconsidered', 3 (1998) *Widener Law Symposium Journal*, p. 7.
81 *Conservation Law Foundation of New England, Inc. v. Clark*, 590 F. Supp. 1467 (D. Mass. 1984).
82 Ibid., p. 1489.

appropriate on the seashore, though on a limited basis. The plaintiff brought another case in 1989 and further argued that 'any use which alters the scenery from its original character is *per se* inappropriate.'[83] The circuit court rejected its claims.

Some controversies regarding motorized recreation have become symbolic in national park-related lawsuits. These include the snowmobile controversy in Yellowstone and the overflight controversy in the Grand Canyon.

The Snowmobile Controversy in Yellowstone National Park

After opening its doors to the first snowmobiles in 1963, Yellowstone witnessed an explosion of snowmobile use.[84] It admitted more snowmobiles than all of the other national parks combined.[85] This situation produced management problems, including air and noise pollution and wildlife harassment. Complaints mounted, and the NPS began to manage snowmobile use. The snowmobile controversy came to a head in the early 1990s and was reflected in the time-consuming process of winter-use planning along with numerous lawsuits. Keiter stated that 'few national park recreation controversies have evoked the passionate response that has driven the Yellowstone snowmobile imbroglio.'[86]

The Evolution of the Snowmobile Policy at Yellowstone

In 1971, the NPS issued the first regulation addressing 'oversnow vehicle' use in Yellowstone,[87] in which snowmobiles were generally allowed under some conditions. At the same time, the NPS began to groom snow-covered roads to facilitate oversnow vehicle use. After the 1972 Order issued by President Nixon regulating ORV use on public land,[88] Anderson, the then-superintendent of Yellowstone, first responded to the order by designating all of Yellowstone's interior roads as snowmobile routes.[89] Snowmobile use in Yellowstone burgeoned, and environmental groups were ignited.

CASE 8: *FUND FOR ANIMALS V. BABBITT* (1997)[90]

In 1997, the Fund for Animals sued the NPS for violating the NEPA and the ESA by grooming snowmobile trails in Yellowstone, which led bison to follow these trails out of the park. This eventually resulted in the slaughter of more than a thousand bison to prevent the spread of brucellosis to livestock outside the park. The two parties reached a settlement agreement several months later in which the NPS agreed to prepare an environmental impact statement (EIS) 'addressing a full range of all alternatives for all types of visitor winter use, including snowmobiling and trail grooming'.[91]

83 *Conservation Law Foundation of New England, Inc. v. Secretary of the Interior*, 864 F. 2d 954 (1st Cir. 1989).
84 NPS, 'Yellowstone in Winter: A History of Winter Use', available at http://www.nps.gov/yell/parkmgmt/timeline.htm. Last visited January 2015.
85 Michael Yochim, 'The Development of Snowmobile Policy in Yellowstone National Park', 7.2 (1999) *Yellowstone Science*, p. 2.
86 Robert Keiter, *To Conserve Unimpaired: The Evolution of the National Park Idea* (Washington, DC: Island Press, 2013), p. 76.
87 36 FR 12014 (June 24, 1971); 36 CFR §7.13.
88 For details of the 1972 Order, see *supra* pp. 106–8 of Chapter 5.
89 39 FR 16151 (May 7, 1974).
90 *Fund for Animals v. Babbitt*, No. 1: 97-cv-01126 (D.D.C. 1997).
91 *Fund for Animals v. Babbitt*, No. 1: 97-cv-01126 (D.D.C. September 23, 1997) (settlement agreement).

140 *Country Studies: United States*

In 1999, Bluewater Network, an NGO devoted to stopping environmental damage from motor vehicles, petitioned to the NPS, demanding that it ban recreational snowmobiling in Yellowstone and all other national park units that allowed it. In response, in December 2000, the NPS under the Clinton Administration issued a proposed rule that aimed to phase out snowmobiles from Yellowstone, Grand Teton and other nearby park units by the winter of 2003–2004 and to substitute the use of multi-passenger snowcoaches for snowmobiles. The NPS received 5,273 comments during the 30-day public comment period, of which more than 4,300 supported this phase-out rule.[92] In January 2001, the NPS released the final plan (the 'Clinton Plan') and decided to implement the snowmobile phase-out.[93] This plan was published the day after President Bush took office and was thus pending. In reality, this effort to eliminate snowmobiles proved to be short-lived.

Despite public support for this phasing out, the NPS's attitude toward snowmobiles has changed since November 2002, when the Clinton Rule was scheduled to go into effect. The NPS issued a rule and delayed the implementation for an additional year.[94] The shift of the NPS's attitude went further. In December 2003, the NPS issued a final plan in which the snowmobile ban in the Clinton era was eliminated and a daily entry limit of up to 950 snowmobiles was established (the 'Bush Plan'). This plan indicated a clear departure from the Clinton-era no-snowmobile policy and was soon debated in court.

CASE 9: *FUND FOR ANIMALS V. NORTON* (2003)[95]

The plaintiff argued that the NPS's decision to allow the continuation of snowmobiling and trail grooming violated the APA and the NEPA. The NPS gave two defenses: first, the new plan was based on the availability of 'cleaner, quieter snowmobiles' due to the implementation of the best available technology (BAT) requirements; second, the use of guided group tours and the maximum limit of 950 snowmobiles served as mitigation measures to prevent negative impacts on wildlife and their habitats.[96] However, the court rebutted both defenses, finding neither of them convincing.

The District Court for the District of Columbia (the 'D.C. court') found that the NPS's decision '[amounted] to an 180-degree reversal' 'in a relatively short period of time and conspicuously timed with the change in administrations'.[97] The NPS had the responsibility to supply a reasoned explanation; however, it failed to do so. Consequently, the 2003 Bush Plan was vacated and remanded. The 2001 Clinton Plan was confirmed to remain in effect.

After this judgment, the litigation centered on the Yellowstone snowmobile policy underwent dramatic chaos. Conflicting court rulings created confusion. The tension among the NPS, different interest groups, and the courts intensified.

CASE 10: *INTERNATIONAL SNOWMOBILE MANUFACTURERS ASSOCIATION (ISMA) V. NORTON* (2004)[98]

Unsatisfied with the D.C. court's judgment and failing to request a stay of the judgment in the D.C. Circuit Court of Appeals, in 2004, the ISMA, the Wyoming State Snowmobile

---

92 Cited from *Fund for Animals v. Norton*, 294 F. Supp. 2d 92 (2003), p. 100.
93 66 Fed. Reg. 7260, January 22, 2001.
94 Final Delay Rule, 67 Fed. Reg. 69473, citing from ibid.
95 *Fund for Animals. v. Norton*, 294 F. Supp. 2d 92 (D.D.C. 2003).
96 Ibid., pp. 106–7.
97 Ibid., p. 105.
98 304 F. Supp. 2d 1278 (D. Wyo. 2004).

Association, Wyoming state and local residents sued in the District Court of Wyoming, seeking to enjoin the implementation of the 2001 Clinton Plan. They asserted that the ban on snowmobiles would have caused irreparable harm, including significant financial loss, the loss of goodwill and the potential bankruptcy of businesses and concessionaires.[99]

The Wyoming District Court first claimed that it had jurisdiction over the validity of the 2001 Clinton Plan instead of the validity of the D.C. court's judgment. It ruled for the plaintiffs and issued an injunction relief by stating that 'any harm from issuing the injunction is less than the harm which would occur if the injunction is not granted.'[100] The NPS was

> ... temporarily restrained from enforcing the 2001 Snowcoach Rule ... [and required to] promulgate temporary rules for this 2004 snowmobile season that [would] be fair and equitable to snowmobile owners and users, to the business community, and to the environmental interests'.[101]

A simple fact was that until February 2004, the 2001 Clinton Plan was set aside. After this Wyoming judgment, crowds gathered at the D.C. District Court and asked for various types of relief or injunctions. The following case was heard.

CASE 11: *FUND FOR ANIMALS V. NORTON* (2004)[102]

The NPS sought relief by stating that it was 'left in the impossible position of having to satisfy two irreconcilable court orders'.[103] In contrast, the Fund for Animals and the Greater Yellowstone Coalition sought to enjoin trail grooming and snowmobiling.

Instead of scaling up the inner-judiciary conflict, the D.C. court made some compromises. It did not ask the NPS to enforce the 2001 Clinton Plan, but it asked the NPS to formulate a new one. It stated that a rule governing snowmobile use in the 2004–05 winter season did not exist because the 2003 Plan was enjoined by the D.C. court, the 2001 plan was subsequently enjoined by the Wyoming court, and the temporary plan ordered by the Wyoming court was only interim for this 2004 snowmobile season. Therefore, the environment groups' motion of injunction was denied for prematureness.

By June 2004, after a series of lawsuits, the snowmobile policy in Yellowstone returned to the starting line. The question arose regarding how a new snowmobile policy should be formulated.

In December 2004, the NPS published a 'Temporary Winter Use Plan' that was to be in effect through 2007 and was to be replaced with a long-term winter-use plan in the 2007–08 winter season.[104] This temporary plan allowed a daily limit of 720 snowmobiles. Two separate lawsuits followed: the Fund for Animals sued in the D.C. court on November 4, 2004, and the Wyoming Lodging and Restaurant Association sued in the District Court of Wyoming on November 10, 2004.[105] This time, neither court vacated the 2004 temporary plan. Therefore, the dispute continued until 2007.

99 Ibid., p. 1293.
100 Ibid., pp. 1293–4.
101 Ibid., p. 1294.
102 323 F. Supp. 2d 7 (D.D.C. 2004).
103 Ibid., p. 10.
104 69 Fed. Reg. 65348, November 10, 2004.
105 *Fund for Animals v. Norton*, 390 F. Supp. 2d 12 (D.D.C. 2005); *Wyoming Lodging and Restaurant Association v. US Department of Interior*, 398 F. Supp. 2d 1197 (D. Wyo. 2005).

142 *Country Studies: United States*

In December 2007, as promised, the NPS published the long-term winter-use plan.[106] This plan allowed up to 540 commercially guided and grouped (from size 1 to 11) BAT snowmobiles and 83 snow coaches into the park each day. Not surprisingly, this plan was simultaneously challenged by different groups in two courts, one in D.C. and the other in Wyoming.

CASE 12: *GREATER YELLOWSTONE COALITION V. KEMPTHORNE* (2008)[107]

In the D.C. court, the plaintiff alleged that the number allowed in the 2007 Plan was too high and violated the APA, the NEPA, the Organic Act and other regulations. In September 2008, the D.C. court delivered the judgment and found that the plan 'clearly elevate[d] use over conservation of park resources and values and fail[ed] to articulate why the Plan's "major adverse impacts" [were] "necessary and appropriate to fulfill the purposes of the park"'.[108] The 2007 plan was vacated and remanded to the NPS.

This time, the D.C. court delivered its judgment earlier than the Wyoming court. The Wyoming court issued an order stating its disagreement, but it declined to issue a ruling contrary to that of the D.C. court. The D.C. court's invalidation of the 2007 plan would remain undisturbed; however, the 2004 temporary plan that allowed 720 snowmobiles daily, as the last valid rule, would be reinstated until the NPS could promulgate an acceptable new one.[109] Therefore, while the litigation regarding the 2007 plan was ongoing, the NPS already began to formulate a new one.

On November 20, 2009, a final plan was issued by the NPS that allowed daily entry of up to 318 snowmobiles and 78 snowcoaches,[110] which was extended through subsequent winter seasons until the 2012–13 winter season.[111] Compared to the previous cap of 720 snowmobiles and 78 snowcoaches, this plan reduced the daily limit to a large extent. At the same time, the NPS was trying to formulate a permanent winter-use plan for Yellowstone that would govern the 2014–15 winter season onward.

The Latest Winter-use Plan for Yellowstone

Following extensive public review and comments, the most recent and final winter-use plan was issued by the NPS in February 2013. This final rule replaced the previous fixed maximum number of snowmobiles or snowcoaches with a flexible new concept, a 'transportation event', defined as one snowcoach or a group of up to ten snowmobiles, averaging seven seasonally. A maximum of 110 transportation events daily (with up to 50 transportation events for groups of snowmobiles) was prescribed. In contrast with the previous 'all commercial guiding' rule, the new plan provided some exceptions, allowing up to four transportation events to be non-commercially guided. According to the new calculation method, there may be up to 500 snowmobiles permitted, which is more than the current number of 318. Therefore, this change was applauded for its flexibility and simultaneously criticized for its tolerance of snowmobiling.[112]

106 72 Fed. Reg. 70781 (December 13, 2007).
107 577 F. Supp. 2d 183 (D.D.C. 2008).
108 Ibid., p. 210.
109 *Wyoming v. US DOI*, No. 07-CV-319 (D. Wyo. November 7, 2008).
110 74 Fed. Reg. 60159 (November 20, 2009).
111 77 Fed. Reg. 74027 (December 12, 2012).
112 See Phil Taylor, 'Yellowstone Releases Draft Snowmobile Plan', June 29, 2012 (citing that the Blue Ribbon Coalition supported the potential increase of snowmobile allowance by the new method), available at

The Overflight Controversy in Grand Canyon National Park

In contrast with the conflicts that arise from ground motor vehicles, the conflicts that arise from aircraft use are more complex due to the involvement of the aviation authority, business aircraft operators and concessioners of recreational air tours.

The Evolution of the Overflight Policy in Grand Canyon National Park

The Grand Canyon is closely connected to overflights. The first air tour company began operation in the Grand Canyon as early as 1927.[113] In June 1987, the Federal Aviation Administration (FAA) issued Special Federal Aviation Regulations (SFAR) No. 50–1, which regulated aircraft flying below 9,000 feet in the park.[114] This was the initial regulation on aircraft flying in the Grand Canyon.

In August 1987, Congress enacted the National Parks Overflights Act, in which overflights in the Grand Canyon were specifically addressed in Section 3.[115] Recognizing significant adverse effects of overflights on the 'natural quiet and experience of the park' and safety of park users, Congress made a *recommendation-plan-report* arrangement between the NPS and the FAA. First, the NPS was required to submit recommendations to the FAA regarding 'actions necessary for the protection of resources in the Grand Canyon from adverse impacts associated with aircraft overflights'. Such recommendations were required to 'provide for *substantial restoration* of the natural quiet'. Second, the FAA was required to issue a final plan for managing air traffic above the Grand Canyon. This plan should implement the recommendations from the NPS. Third, the NPS should submit a report to Congress discussing whether the plan had succeeded in 'substantially restoring the natural quiet'.[116]

THE 1994 NPS REPORT

As a response to the Overflights Act, recommendations were submitted by the DOI to the FAA in 1987, and they were adopted and implemented by the FAA in the form of SFAR 50–2 in 1988.[117] Minimum altitudes, four flight-free zones, four flight corridors and specified flight routes within the Grand Canyon were established. In 1994, the NPS submitted the report to Congress ('1994 NPS Report')[118] and provided three important definitions:

1. The appropriate measure of quantifying aircraft noise was the percentage of time that aircraft were audible;
2. An aircraft was audible if it increased the ambient noise level by three decibels; and
3. 'Substantial restoration of the natural quiet' meant that 50 per cent or more of the park achieved 'natural quiet' for 75–100 per cent of the day.[119]

      http://rlch.org/news/yellowstone-releases-supplemental-winter-use-plan, and Patricia Dowd, 'New Winter-use Plan for Yellowstone is a Step Backward', August 6, 2012, available at http://www.bozemandailychronicle.com/opinions/guest_columnists/article_ee578f1a-dfde-11e1-99ef-0019bb2963f4.html. Both were last visited January 2015.
113 See NPS, 'Overflights – Chronology of Significant Events', available at http://www.nps.gov/grca/naturescience/airoverflights_chrono.htm. Last visited January 2015.
114 *Special Flight Rules in the Vicinity of the Grand Canyon National Park*, 52 Fed. Reg. 22, 734 (1987).
115 Pub. L. No. 100–91;101 Stat. 674.
116 Section 3 (a)–(b).
117 *Special Flight Rules in the Vicinity of the Grand Canyon National Park*, 53 Fed. Reg. 20, 264 (June 2, 1988).
118 NPS, 'Report on the Effects of Aircraft Overflights on the National Park System', September 12, 1994.
119 Cited from *Grand Canyon Air Tour Coalition v. FAA*, 154 F. 3d 455 (1998), pp. 461–2.

Applying these definitions and standards, the NPS concluded that under the SFAR 50–2, only 34 percent of the Grand Canyon enjoyed a 'substantial restoration of the natural quiet,' which meant that only 34 percent of the park had aircraft noise no more than three decibels above ambient levels for at least 75 percent of the day. Moreover, with a recommendation to revise the SFAR 50–2, the report predicted that the SFAR 50–2 would cause the proportion of the park experiencing a substantial restoration of natural quiet to drop to less than 10 percent by the year 2010.[120]

THE 1996 FAA FINAL RULE

The FAA issued the final rule that adopted the definitions contained in the 1994 NPS Report in 1996 ('1996 Final Rule').[121] New flight-free zones were established, existing ones were modified, flight curfews for the eastern portion of the park were enacted, and a cap on the number of aircraft that could fly over the park was set.[122] However, the Final Rule did not set a cap on the number of flights. It turned out that the 1996 Rule significantly underestimated the actual number of aircraft: the estimated number was 136, and the actual number was 260. In 1997, the FAA clarified that the final rule would be less effective than previously thought, and it planned to re-assess the environmental impacts of aircrafts.[123]

CASE 13: *GRAND CANYON AIR TOUR COALITION V. FAA* (1998) *(GRAND CANYON I)*[124]

Four groups brought petitions against the 1996 Final Rule to the D.C. court. Among these four groups, three of them – the Grand Canyon Air Tour Coalition (a group of 13 air-tour operators), the Clark County Department of Aviation and the Las Vegas Convention and Visitors Authority, and the Hualapai Indian Tribe ('the Coalition') – argued that the FAA's rule did 'too much, too soon'. The fourth group, seven environmental groups led by the Grand Canyon Trust ('the Trust'), argued that the FAA's rule did 'too little, too late'.[125]

The Coalition contended that 'substantial restoration of the natural quiet' was defined overly restrictively by the NPS and the FAA ('too much'). The FAA should not have promulgated flight-free zones until it was ready to issue final routes and corridors and until it had more adequately assessed their environmental impact ('too soon'). In contrast, the Trust argued that the definition did not satisfy the Overflights Act's requirement. 'Substantial' should mean more than 50 percent instead of 37.5 percent yielded by the proposed measures (50 percent of the park for 75 percent of the day = 37.5 percent) ('too little'). It also contended that taking the needs of the air tour industry into consideration was not permissible. It urged the FAA to issue regulations that would 'immediately achieve the substantial restoration of natural quiet' ('too late').[126]

The court rejected petition requests from all four groups and upheld the final rule on the basis that it 'defer[red] to the agency's reasonable exercise of its judgment and technical expertise'. It also noted that the petitioners' requests were not yet ripe, and challenges might be raised again.[127]

---

120 1994 NPS Report, p. 13.
121 *Special Flight Rules in the Vicinity of Grand Canyon National Park*, 61 Fed. Reg. 69,302 (1996).
122 1996 Final Rule, pp. 69,317 and 69,332.
123 Cited from *Grand Canyon Air Tour Coalition v. FAA*, 154 F. 3d 455 (1998), p. 464.
124 154 F. 3d 455 (D.C. Cir. 1998).
125 *Grand Canyon I*, p. 460.
126 Ibid., p. 476.
127 Ibid., p. 478.

THE 2000 FAA LIMITATION RULE

In April 2000, the FAA published a rule to cap the number of commercial air tours that operators might run in the park ('the Limitations Rule'),[128] which prescribed that an air tour operator might not conduct more flights in the park than it conducted during the base year of May 1, 1997 through April 30, 1998.

CASE 14: *US AIR TOUR ASSOCIATION V. FAA (2002) (GRAND CANYON II)*[129]

In 2002, the US Air Tour Association ('the Association') sought the judicial review of the Limitations Rule, and the Grand Canyon Trust ('the Trust') intervened. The Association argued that the Limitation Rule was unlawful for five reasons:

1 Improper change in defining 'natural quiet' from 'three-decibels-above-ambient threshold' in the more developed area (*Noticeability standard*) to 'eight-decibels-below-ambient threshold' in backcountry areas (*Detectability standard*); this meant that the methodology to measure audibility was based on a 'vigilant and active listener' instead of a normal visitor;
2 Scientific flaws in choosing acoustic methodology;
3 The absence of a quiet technology rule in advance;
4 The violation of the Regulatory Flexibility Act, and
5 Ignorance of the elderly and disabled.[130]

The Trust contended that the FAA unlawfully altered the NPS's definition of the 'substantial restoration of the natural quiet' from '50% of the Park experiencing natural quiet for 75% of *any given* day' defined by the NPS to '50% of the Park experiencing natural quiet for 75% of the *average annual* day'. The FAA's methodology of noise measurement ignored noise from types of aircraft other than commercial air tours.[131]

The D.C. court rebutted the five arguments made by the Association and ruled that the agency had provided reasonable explanations of relevant change. However, the agency's change of definition from 'any given day' to 'the average annual day' was ruled to be arbitrary and capricious as argued by the Trust, similar to its ignorance of noise from other aircrafts. The case was finally remanded to the FAA for further consideration of the Trust's challenges.

Post-litigation Developments

As ordered by the Court, the NPS and FAA issued several clarifications and notices defining the controversial terms. However, the disputes between aircraft operators and environmental groups were not fundamentally solved.

In February 2004, the NPS and the FAA, under the auspices of the National Parks Overflights Advisory Group, a group co-founded in March 2001 by the NPS and FAA to implement the 1987 Overflights Act, began the 'alternative dispute resolution' (ADR) process. Mediation was conducted to resolve long-standing issues and improve interagency communication. Multiple stakeholders were involved in the mediation process, including the

---

128 *Commercial Air Tour Limitation in the Grand Canyon National Park Special Flight Rules Area*, 65 Fed. Reg. 17,708 (April 4, 2000).
129 298 F. 3d 997, 1015 (D.C. Cir. 2002).
130 *Grand Canyon II*, p. 1005.
131 Ibid., p. 1012.

two main adversaries (NPS and FAA), the FWS, which had concerns about the protection of endangered birds, tribes (e.g. the Hualapai, which had its own airtour company), hikers, commercial airline companies, airtour companies and others. A consensus was not easily achieved. Each agency prepared to release its own 'preferred alternative'.[132]

In January 2011, an agreement was reached between the Department of Transportation, with which the FAA was affiliated, and the DOI to delineate the responsibilities of the FAA and the NPS for the EIS process. In February 2011, the NPS released the Draft EIS for Grand Canyon overflights. Nearly 30,000 public comments arrived at the NPS. The final overflight management plan has still not been issued, and the airspace above the Grand Canyon remains a battlefield.

Case study: The Merced River Controversy in Yosemite Valley

Burgeoning recreational visits to national parks produce concern about limiting the number of visitors to parks. However, the NPS is reluctant to directly cap visitation limits. Its strategy is to add more accommodations, facilities and infrastructure to accommodate these increasing needs. Conflicts between construction projects and nature conservation frequently arise. The NPS is mired in the dilemma of whether to limit the number of visitors or to build more facilities to accommodate them. This dilemma was evident in a case regarding the Yosemite Valley.

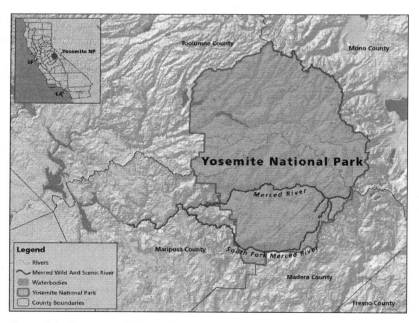

Figure 7.1 The geographic map of the Merced River and Yosemite National Park
Source: NPS[133]

---

132 Grand Canyon Trust, 'Oversight Hearing Outcomes', available at http://www.grandcanyontrust.org/grand-canyon/quiet_history_lawsuits_oversight-outcomes.php. Last visited January 2015.
133 NPS, 'Merced Wild and Scenic River Comprehensive Management Plan/DEIS', p. 1.1; available at http://www.nps.gov/yose/parkmgmt/upload/mrp-deis-chapter-1-web.pdf. Last visited January 2015.

WSRA and the Issue of 'User Capacity'

The Merced River flows through the seven-mile-long Yosemite Valley, and it is one of Yosemite National Park's most popular and scenic sites. Due to its designation as a 'National Wild and Scenic River' in 1987, the NPS was required to formulate a separate Merced River management plan and to revise the General Management Plan of Yosemite National Park (formulated in 1980) by 1990 to ensure that no inconsistent development or use of park lands would be undertaken.[134] The key statutory requirement of the management plan prescribed in the Wild and Scenic River Act (WSRA) is that it should address the issue of 'user capacities'.[135]

The 2000 Plan

The NPS had not finished the Merced River Plan in 1997 when a devastating flood wiped out the facilities at the Yosemite Lodge. After two lawsuits against the NPS's reconstruction activities,[136] the NPS released its initial Merced River Plan in 2000 ('the 2000 plan'). Two small local environmental groups – Friends of Yosemite Valley and Mariposans for Environmental Responsible Growth (the 'Friends') – brought a lawsuit and challenged this plan. These actions initiated an eight-year-long lawsuit on the Merced River Plan.

CASE 15: *FRIENDS OF YOSEMITE VALLEY V. NORTON* (2002) *(YOSEMITE I)*[137]

In the 2000 plan, the NPS proposed the Visitor Experience and Resources Protection (VERP) as the primary mechanism for addressing the issue of user capacity as required by the WSRA. Three features of this VERP framework later became the focus of court debate:

1. The VERP was an adaptive process. It required 'a continuing learning process, a reiterative evaluation of goals and approaches, and redirection based on an increased information base and changing public expectations'. A five-year timetable was proposed by the NPS to implement the VERP framework.
2. The VERP selected and monitored indicators and standards that reflected the desired conditions.
3. Management action would only be undertaken when the desired conditions were not being realized.[138]

The Friends claimed that the NPS failed to prepare a valid plan to protect and enhance the natural values of the Merced River and thereby violated the WSRA, the NEPA and the APA. However, the district court rejected all their claims. The Friends appealed to the 9th Circuit Court arguing that, among other issues, the plan failed to address the issue of user capacity.[139] The 9th Circuit reversed and remanded the case.

---

134 16 USC §1274(a)(62)(A).
135 16 USC §1274(d).
136 See *Sierra Club v. United States*, 23 F. Supp. 2d 1132 (N.D. Cal. 1998) and *Sierra Club v. Babbitt*, 69 F. Supp. 2d 1202 (E.D. Cal. 1999) (the court enjoined part of the NPS's road widening project within the Merced River corridor, and ordered the NPS to complete a valid Merced River Plan by July 2000).
137 *Friends of Yosemite Valley v. Norton*, 194 F. Supp. 2d 1066, 1127–8 (E.D. Cal. 2002), affirmed in part, reversed in part, 348 F. 3d 789 (9th Cir. 2003) (*Yosemite I*), clarified by 366 F. 3d 731 (9th Cir. 2004) (*Yosemite II*).
138 *Yosemite I*, p. 796.
139 Ibid., p. 793. The Friends also claimed that there were four deficiencies in the Plan: failure to address user capacity, inadequate protection of the El Portal section of the River by its demarcation of boundary, insufficient specific data and information provided in the Plan and its programmatic nature, and failure to cooperate with federal and state water pollution control agencies.

The court did not preclude the NPS from using the VERP to fulfill the user capacity requirement. However, it ruled that the 2000 plan failed to 'yield any actual measure of user capacities, whether by setting limits on the specific number of visitors, by monitoring and maintaining environmental and experiential criteria under the VERP framework, or through some other method'.[140] Recognizing that the WSRA did not provide a clear definition of 'user capacities', the 9th Circuit explained that the plain meaning of the statute was that the plan 'must deal with or discuss the *maximum number of people* that can be received'.[141] The NPS was also required to take temporary or provisional measures to avoid environmental degradation instead of waiting five years until the VERP would have been completed.[142]

In July 2004, following the circuit court's invalidation of the Merced River Plan, the district court ordered the NPS to develop a new or revised plan and enjoined certain Yosemite Valley construction projects by ruling that expanded development would inhibit the ability of the NPS to make decisions about user capacity.[143]

The 2005 Plan

In July 2005, the NPS released the second Merced River Plan ('the 2005 plan'), in which the VERP program was revised. An interim cap was established based on facility limits, including campsites, overnight lodging, day-visitor parking and bus parking spaces. Among these limits, the latter three were set at existing levels, whereas campsites were allowed to increase to match the level prior to the 1997 flood and 1987 designation.[144] The Friends challenged this 2005 plan again in the courts.

CASE 16: *FRIENDS OF YOSEMITE VALLEY V. SCARLETT* (2006) *(YOSEMITE III)*[145]

The district court found that the NPS continued to violate the WSRA, the NEPA and the circuit court's instructions in Yosemite I and II. It ruled that the new plan did not describe an actual level of visitor use that would not adversely impact the Merced's 'outstandingly remarkable values'.[146] The five-year timetable was also invalidated because it was 'a tentative plan of uncertain duration which adopts temporary limits, which will apply for an unknown length of time'.[147] The NPS appealed.

CASE 17: *FRIENDS OF YOSEMITE VALLEY V. KEMPTHORNE* (2008)[148]

The Ninth Circuit adjudicated on the validity of the Merced River management plan and invalidated it again. The NPS argued that 'sufficiently specific measurable limits on use' were provided, which could be found in

---

140 *Yosemite I*, p. 796.
141 Ibid.
142 Ibid., pp. 803–4.
143 *Friends of Yosemite Valley v. Kempthorne*, 464 F. Supp. 2d 993 (E.D. Cal. 2006), p. 1003 (quoting Judge Ishii's unpublished Memorandum Opinion and Order from July 6, 2004).
144 Cited from 520 F. 3d 1024 (9th Cir. 2008), p.1035.
145 *Friends of Yosemite Valley v. Scarlett*, 439 F. Supp. 2d 1074 (E.D. Cal. 2006), aff'd sub nom. 520 F. 3d 1024 (9th Cir. 2008) (*Yosemite III*).
146 Ibid., p. 1098.
147 Ibid., p. 1100.
148 *Friends of Yosemite Valley v. Kempthorne*, 520 F. 3d 1024 (9th Cir. 2008). The case was renamed as *Friends of Yosemite Valley v. Kempthorne* during the appeal.

1   the Wilderness Trailhead Quota System and the Superintendent's Compendium,
2   the new VERP indicators and standards and
3   the interim limits imposed by the User Capacity Management Program.[149]

However, none of these were accepted by the circuit court. Three reasons were provided:[150]

1   Neither the Wilderness Trailhead Quota System nor the Superintendent's Compendium was 'persuasive as to whether the 2005 Revised Plan adequately addresses user capacities', though the circuit court agreed that they were 'steps in the right direction'.
2   The VERP could be acceptable if implemented properly. However, it was reactive because it did not require a response to environmental degradation until after had occurred.
3   The NPS had a responsibility to address 'both past and ongoing degradation'. Degradation already existed due to existing construction of facilities, such as swimming pools, tennis courts, golf courses and rental facilities. These facilities did not meet the mandatory criteria for inclusion as a recreational 'outstandingly remarkable value', which are (1) a river-related or river-dependent value and (2) rare, unique, or exemplary in a regional or national context.[151] Therefore, holding facility levels to those in existence in 1987 was not protective of river values and thus did not satisfy the user capacity requirements.

The 2014 Plan

After eight years of litigation, the Friends and the NPS entered into mediation in 2008 and reached a court-mediated settlement agreement in 2009 that directed the NPS to complete a new Merced River Plan by July 2013.[152] A draft plan was issued in January 2013, and more than 30,000 written comments arrived at the NPS.[153]

Compared to previous plans, this draft plan seemed to be an overhaul. It called for a dramatic scaling-back of human activities and recreational facilities along and near the river, such as the closure of the swimming pool, removal of the ice rink and the closure of services for horseback riding and river rafting. These facilities and services were highly controversial in previous litigations. Furthermore, for the first time, the draft plan capped the number of visitors in East Yosemite Valley to 19,900 per day.[154]

This draft ignited another firestorm of controversy. This time, people were unsatisfied by the disappearance of so many recreational facilities. Critics noted that the current agenda of Yosemite could be best described as 'look, but don't touch'.[155] Gateway communities were displeased and worried about the potential loss of visitors. Even the framer of the WSRA,

149 Ibid., p. 1033.
150 Ibid., pp. 1033–5.
151 Ibid., p. 1035 and note 5.
152 NPS, 'Merced Wild and Scenic River Comprehensive Management Plan/DEIS', Chapter 2 'Purpose and Need for the "Merced River Plan"', pp. 2–7, available at http://www.nps.gov/yose/parkmgmt/upload/mrp-deis-chapter-2-web.pdf. Last visited January 2015.
153 The full draft was as long as 2,500 pages and criticized for not being reader friendly. For a summary of the draft Plan, see NPS, 'Summary Guide', available at http://www.nps.gov/yose/parkmgmt/upload/mrp-deis-sum-guide-web.pdf. Last visited January 2015.
154 Ibid., p. 14.
155 Tom McClintock, 'Yosemite National Park: Closed for Preservation', August 23, 2013. Available at http://online.wsj.com/news/articles/SB10001424127887324108204579020751582621362. Last visited January 2015.

150   Country Studies: United States

Tony Coelho, harshly attacked the draft plan by asserting that the Merced River had been recreational for almost 150 years and that the Yosemite Valley had never been wilderness. He argued that the draft should not 'change any infrastructure, or ban any activities traditionally carried on in Yosemite Valley'.[156] Others argued for removing the wild and scenic river designation from Merced,[157] and a congressman in California even threatened to introduce a bill that would force the park to keep its commercial services.[158]

On the other side, environmental groups were also unsatisfied. They stated that the NPS could have gone further to reduce recreational facilities and protect the river. Adair, from Friends of Yosemite, responded to the media by stating that 'optimism requires that we see movement in the right direction and we haven't seen that yet.'[159]

Facing the outcry from the public, the NPS applied for an extension from the court to submit the final plan to better incorporate public input. Released in February 2014, the final plan slightly increased the number of campsites and lodging units, retained the swimming pool and relocated the rental services.[160] A user capacity of 18,710 people at one time and 20,100 visitors per day in the East Yosemite Valley was established.

Implications of the Merced Controversy

First, the concept of visitor capacity has become a new and powerful tool for environmental groups to supervise and challenge the NPS's management decisions. Facing the overcrowding problem, the NPS has long avoided capping the number of visitors allowed in parks; instead, it has addressed this problem in an indirect way, such as by limiting available facilities, relocating facilities outside the parks and enticing visitors elsewhere.[161] The NPS's approach is reflected in the VERP program, on which it has primarily relied. However, in the Merced River case, the NPS was urged by the courts to face this problem in a more straightforward way.

In fact, there is no legal obstacle that impedes the NPS from capping the number of visitors. The easily ignited public at large placed the NPS in this dilemma. Strict limits on recreational visits unavoidably increase the risk of losing the NPS's constituencies that have accumulated throughout its century-long efforts to attract more people to parks. Any policy of limited access has political consequences and raises questions of equity by strongly implying

---

156 See open letter written by Tony Coelho to the NPS Director, April 13, 2013. Available at http://yosemiteforeveryone.com/wp-content/uploads/2013/04/4-14-Letter-From-Tony-Coelho.pdf. Last visited January 2015.
157 Peter Hoss, 'The Park is Fine Without the Merced River Plan', August 1, 2013. Available at http://www.nytimes.com/roomfordebate/2013/08/01/is-yosemite-national-park-for-all-or-some/yosemite-national-park-is-fine-without-the-merced-river-plan. Last visited January 2014.
158 Molly Peterson, 'Merced River Plan for Yosemite Draws Fire from Several Quarters', March 25, 2013, available at http://www.scpr.org/news/2013/03/25/36507/merced-river-plan-for-yosemite-draws-fire-from-sev/. See also Tom McClintock, 'Merced River Draft Comprehensive Management Plan and Environmental Impact Statement – Comments by Congressman McClintock', April 12, 2013, available at http://mcclintock.house.gov/2013/04/merced-river-draft-comprehensive-management-plan-and-environmental-impact-statement-comments-by-co.shtml. Both were last visited in January 2015.
159 Marc Boyd, 'Viewpoints: Plan is Best Chance to Restore Merced River', August 17, 2013. Available at http://www.sacbee.com/2013/08/17/5658046/plan-is-best-chance-to-restore.html. Last visited January 2014.
160 For details of this final Plan, see NPS, 'Merced River Plan', available at http://www.nps.gov/yose/parkmgmt/mrp_finalplan.htm. Last visited December 2014. For details of the changes between draft and final plan, see NPS, 'Executive Summary of the Merced River Final Plan', p. ES-5. Available at http://www.nps.gov/yose/parkmgmt/upload/MRP_Ch_Executive_Summary_web.pdf. Last visited January 2015.
161 Robert Keiter, *supra* note 86, p. 62.

'cultural elitism'.[162] As stated by Lemons and Stout, the NPS still faces the question of whether to 'preserve a high-quality experience for relatively few people or a less grand experience for greater numbers'.[163]

Second, the Merced River controversy stirs the question of how to interpret the term 'user capacity' stipulated in the WSRA. Though the NPS finally set a numerical limit in its 2014 plan, the 9th Circuit Court did not ultimately resolve whether the WSRA required a cap on the number of visitors.[164] This can be seen in subtle changes in the court's wording. Though the 9th Circuit interpreted 'user capacity' as the 'maximum number of people' in Yosemite I, it tempered its definition and suggested that a numerical cap *could* be a proper way to address 'user capacity' in Yosemite III. Finally, it left the decision of whether to cap the number of visitors to the NPS. It did not hold that the NPS must cap the number of visitors to satisfy the WSRA mandate. Instead, it suggested that a more flexible, adaptable framework of monitoring and maintaining conditions such as the VERP might satisfy the WSRA as well.[165]

Because the Merced River controversy occurred in the context of a 'wild and scenic river' designation, the Yosemite decisions did not have direct effects on the NPS's duties in identifying visitor capacities in national parks outside designated wild and scenic rivers. The 9th Circuit's decision did not 'threaten the [NPS's] widespread application of VERP outside of the wild and scenic river realm'.[166]

Summary

Considering the penchant for detail in the congressional instruction on the enabling acts, Fischman commented that 'courts play a relatively insignificant role in National Park System management, other than ensuring that the Service adhere to specific directives of Congress.'[167] He is certainly correct when a single, definite answer can be easily found in statutes, especially enabling acts. However, not all clear answers are available in statutes, particularly the conservation–enjoyment conflict in the purpose statement. Furthermore, Congress cannot fully foresee all problems and provide answers in advance (for example, problems arising from emerging forms of motorized recreation). Thus, the detailing tendency in congressional statutes lags behind the emergence of disputes to be solved. Therefore, before Congress gives specific instruction to agencies and courts (though whether Congress should do so remains controversial),[168] there is room for courts to maneuver.

Litigation has been used more frequently as a method of dispute resolution on public land-related cases since the 1970s. This has enabled the judiciary to play a more remarkable role in reviewing the agency's decisions, determining what Congress says in statutes and, finally, resolving disputes.

---

162 John Lemons and Dean Stout, 'A Reinterpretation of National Park Legislation', 15 (1984) *Environmental Law*, p. 48; see also John Cathcart-Rake, 'The Friends of Yosemite Valley Saga: The Challenge of Addressing the Merced River's User Capacities', 39 (2009) *Environmental Law*, p. 859.
163 John Lemons and Dean Stout, ibid., p. 48.
164 John Cathcart-Rake, *supra* note 162, p. 837.
165 *Yosemite III*, pp. 1034–5, n. 4.
166 John Cathcart-Rake, *supra* note 162, p. 838.
167 Robert Fischman, 'The Problem of Statutory Detail in National Park Establishment Legislation and Its Relationship to Pollution Control Law', 74 (1996) *Denver University Law Review*, p. 813.
168 See *supra* p. 118 et seq. of Chapter 6 discussing the role of Congress in pushing back towards enjoyment by enabling acts and intervention.

The discussion of the *SUWA* case, its precedents and the subsequent cases shows that there are still inconsistencies in courts' interpretations of the purpose statement of the Organic Act. The conclusion that the Organic Act should be read as a preservation mandate, as argued by scholars, has not been firmly established by case law. Instead, the judiciary recognizes the NPS has broad discretion in balancing conservation and enjoyment as mandated by Congress. Consequently, the judiciary has offered substantial deference to the NPS on its decisions regarding national park management based on the Organic Act and on its interpretation of the Organic Act that is reflected in its MP. Though the courts tend to be deferential to the NPS in its interpretation of the Organic Act, courts show less deference when other environmental statutes are involved, especially wilderness-related cases. The NEPA also enables the judiciary to take a harder look at agencies' environment-affecting decisions.

The finding of a deferential judiciary does not necessarily indicate that the courts play a limited role in interpreting statutes. Considering the conservation-enjoyment debate embodied in the purpose statement of the Organic Act, courts have at least clarified that Congress does not provide a clear-cut answer regarding whether conservation or enjoyment should be prioritized in the Organic Act. In other words, courts deem this issue a *Chevron* two issue instead of a first step, as elaborated in the *SUWA* case. In this sense, the judiciary already has a significant influence on how the Organic Act should be read – not as a spontaneous preservation mandate but as a 'dual mandate', based on which it was once seriously criticized.

The discussion of symbolic national park cases shows that the resolution of disputes largely relies on how statutory terms are to be interpreted. This is seen from both the interpretation of the 'substantial restoration of the natural quiet' of the Overflights Act in the overflight controversy in the Grand Canyon and the interpretation of the 'user capacity' of the WSRA in the Merced River controversy at Yosemite. On technical issues, such as the measurement of the audibility of aircrafts in the Grand Canyon, courts generally defer to agencies' professional and expertise-based judgments. On less technical issues, such as whether 'user capacity' requires a numerical cap on visitors, courts attempt to substantively assess agencies' interpretations and formulate their own.

The limitations of litigation become visible through these case studies. Litigation is protracted and costly. The Merced River Plan controversy has lasted for over a decade, and the dispute continues. It is estimated that litigations have cost approximately $15 million, and drafting the latest 2014 management plan has cost more than $1 million.[169] The Yellowstone snowmobile controversy has cost taxpayers more than $10 million in the last decade and produced upwards of 160,000 pages of documents.[170] Moreover, litigation is retroactive rather than proactive. Disputes sometimes cannot be completely resolved through litigious procedures, and courts are not totally value-free; they are vulnerable to political changes. This is reflected in the conflicting judgments delivered by the D.C. court and the Wyoming court in the snowmobile case in Yellowstone.

The rise of ADR demonstrates the limitations of the judicial approach to resolving disputes. During the ADR process, multiple stakeholders could be involved, which is otherwise difficult in the litigation process. In term of the overflight controversy in the Grand Canyon, after years of litigation, the NPS finally resorted to the mechanism of mediation. The Merced

---

169 See John Cathcart-Rake, *supra* note 162, p. 866 and note 273.
170 See Stephanie Simon, 'Battle Over Snowmobiles in Yellowstone Roars On', *Wall Street Journal*, October 21, 2011, at A6; Thomas Duncan, 'Driving Americans' Perception of Recreation: Awaiting the Park Service's Long-term Solution to Address Snowmobile Access in Yellowstone National Park', 19 (2012) *Villanova Sports & Entertainment Law Journal*, p. 701.

River Plan controversy was also finally settled by a court-led mediation agreement after a decade-long litigation. Another mediation example occurred in the Kenai Fjords National Park in Alaska. Skiers complained that snowmobilers ruined the snow-covered landscape and destroyed their recreational opportunities. Negotiations and mediation were attempted, and an agreement was finally reached among the different stakeholders.[171]

---

171 From the author's personal interview with Jim Ireland on February 11, 2014. Ireland is now the superintendent of Timpanogos Cave National Monument in Utah.

PART 3
Country studies
China

8 The Legislative and Policy Frameworks of Protected Areas in China

Introduction

China has witnessed increasing awareness of environmental protection in general and nature conservation in particular, and this awareness is reflected in both law making and policy making. This chapter aims, first, to present the current legislative and policy frameworks of protected area (PA) management and their evolutionary processes and then to summarize the characteristics and deficits of the current framework. Before moving forward, some introductory remarks on the general institutional structure, the typology and the hierarchy of legislative documents in China are provided to facilitate further discussion in the following chapters.

The Institutional Structure in China

The Chinese Constitution[1] creates a unitary State of China. In a strict sense, there is no 'separation of powers'; however, there does exist a 'separation of functions' between different State organs. At the national level, the National People's Congress (NPC) is the highest organ of State power in China. Its Standing Committee (SCNPC) is granted the power to interpret and supervise the enforcement of the Constitution and to enact and amend laws, with the exception of 'basic laws' that should be enacted by the NPC (Article 67). All administrative, judicial and procuratorial organs of the State are created by the people's congresses, to which these organs are responsible and under whose supervision they operate (Article 3). The State Council is the highest executive body. Ministries are organized under the State Council, and the ministers, among others, are components of the State Council (Article 86). The Supreme People's Court (SPC) is the highest judicial organ, and the Supreme People's Procuratorate (SPP) is the highest procuratorial organ. The State Council, the SPC and the SPP are responsible to the NPC and the SCNPC. The administrative division is based on a three-tiered structure of provinces, counties and townships. At each level, public sectors, namely, people's congresses, people's governments, people's courts and people's procuratorates, are organized.

1 China adopted its first Constitution in 1954. It has undergone significant revisions along with the flux of the political regime in China. The current Constitution was based on the version of 1982 which has been further amended in 1988, 1993, 1999 and 2004. In the text hereinafter, the Constitution of China will be referred to as the amended version of 2004.

The Typology and Hierarchy of Legislative Documents

The distribution of legislative power and the hierarchy of legislative documents in China are mainly stipulated in the Legislation Law of 2015 (the LL).[2] The legislative power of legislatures at both the central and local levels and the rule-making power of administrative bodies are distinguished and provided for in the LL. As shown in Table 8.1, in line with the Constitution, the LL classifies legislative documents into six categories: 'law' (法律), 'administrative regulations' (行政法规), 'local regulations' (地方性法规), 'autonomous regulations and separate regulations' (自治条例和单行条例), 'departmental rules' (部门规章) and 'local government rules' (地方政府规章).

Table 8.1 The typology of legislative documents in China

	Typology	Legislative authority
Central level	Law: Basic law	NPC
	Other law	SCNPC
	Administrative regulation	State Council
	Departmental rule	Ministries and commissions under the State Council
Local level	Local regulation	Local legislatures at the city level[3]
	Autonomous regulation and separate regulation	Legislatures of national autonomous areas[4]
	Local government rule	Local governments at the city level[5]

Source: Adapted from the Constitution and the LL.

As shown in Figure 8.1 below, the Constitution is at the top of the hierarchy chart, and law made by the NPC or the SCNPC follows. The administrative regulations by the State Council rank below the Constitution and the law and above other legislative documents. The most problematic issue arises with regard to the hierarchy between local regulations and departmental rules. According to the LL, when conflicts between local regulations and departmental rules arise, the State Council will make a preliminary decision. If it decides that the provisions of local regulations should be applied, local regulation will prevail in this case; if it decides that departmental rules should be applied, then the issue will be submitted to the SCNPC for a final ruling (Article 95).

---

2 NPC, Legislation Law of the P.R.C. (中华人民共和国立法法), adopted in July 2000 and amended in March 2015. A specific statute on legislation is not commonly seen in other countries. Scholars deem the Legislation Law 'a unique product among the world's major legal families'. See Chen Jianfu, *Chinese Law: Context and Transformation* (Leiden: Martinus Nijhoff Publishers, 2008), p. 180. For general information about law making in China, see Jan Michiel Otto, Maurice Polak, Jianfu Chen and Yuwen Li (eds.), *Law-making in the People's Republic of China* (The Hague, London and Boston, MA: Kluwer Law International, 2000).
3 The term 'local legislatures at the city level' refers to: 1. the people's congresses or their standing committees of the provinces, autonomous regions and municipalities directly under the central government, and 2. the people's congresses or their standing committees of cities with districts (设区的市). See Article 72 of the LL.
4 The term 'legislatures of national autonomous areas' refers to the people's congresses of the national autonomous areas (民族自治地方) including autonomous regions, autonomous prefectures and autonomous counties. See Article 112, 116 of the Constitution and Article 75 of the LL.
5 The term 'local governments at the city level' refers to: 1. the governments of the provinces, autonomous regions and municipalities directly under the central government, and 2. the governments of cities with districts. See Article 82 of the LL.

Legal Framework of Protected Areas in China 159

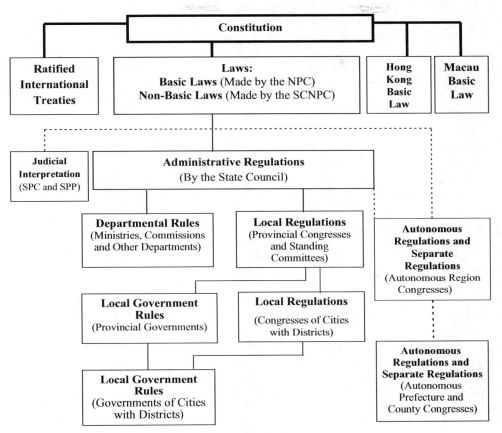

Figure 8.1 The hierarchy of legislative documents in China
Source: Adapted from the Constitution and the LL

However, the figure only illustrates part of the complete picture of the Chinese regulatory framework. There are other legal documents that are not stipulated in the LL, including numerous 'Opinions', 'Notices', 'Decisions', 'Instructions' and other normative documents (其他规范性文件)[6] that are issued by the ministries and commissions of the State Council, local governments and their organs. These documents are dubbed 'documents headed with red seals' (红头文件). There is no explicit distinction between 'government rules' (规章) that are part of governments' rule-making power and 'other normative documents' that are not.

---

6 The term of 'other normative document', as a specific legal concept in Chinese law, refers to the documents which are not stipulated in the LL and not listed in the 'legislative' system. It is not explicitly defined in any written law. In academic research, the provisions listed in Article 7 of Administrative Reconsideration Law of 1999 are generally deemed the scope of 'other normative documents'. Article 7 stipulates that the scope of legal documents that can be reviewed by administrative organs during the process of administrative reconsideration. It states that 'if citizens, legal persons or other organizations consider the following provisions illegal, upon which the concrete administrative actions are based, they may also apply for examination of these provisions when applying for administrative reconsideration of the said actions: 1. Provisions (规定) made by departments of the State Council, 2. Provisions made by local governments at or above the county level as well as the departments under them, and 3. Provisions made by government at the levels of villages and towns'.

Because the former category is beyond the scope of judicial review,[7] in reality, numerous normative documents that have violated citizens' rights and interests cannot be challenged before the courts.[8] The adoption of these 'documents headed with red seals' is pervasive in the government's administrative activities, and PA management is no exception. Due to the underdevelopment of the Chinese legal system, these normative documents have played the role of law to some extent and have sometimes even replaced the law. This phenomenon can be seen in the adoption of normative documents to regulate the rampant transfer of the operation rights of PAs.[9]

It is noteworthy that the LL empowers the SCNPC to interpret the law when further definition or clarification is needed under new circumstances and the SCNPC's interpretation has the same effect as the law (Articles 45 and 50). Besides the SCNPC's interpretation of the law, the SPC and the SPP are empowered to issue 'judicial interpretations' (司法解释) on the application of the specific provisions of the law during their adjudicative and procuratorial work.[10]

The Legislative Framework of PAs

The legislative framework of environmental protection can be generally categorized into pollution control law, environmental impact assessment law, marine protection law and natural conservation law.[11] The Environmental Protection Law is the basic law that is the foundation for other sectors of environmental laws. With regard to nature conservation law, until now, there has been no single act that comprehensively governs conservation-related issues. Instead, these issues are regulated by other applicable laws, such as laws on specific types of natural resources, spatial planning law, land administration law, and tourism law. At the level of 'administrative regulation', there are two regulations on nature reserves and scenic and historic areas (SHAs). At the lower level, specific 'departmental rules' are enacted to govern the administration of other types of PAs, such as forest parks. Other 'departmental rules' are issued to implement laws and regulations at a higher level.

Constitutional Clauses

The Constitution addresses the issue of PA in two respects: it confirms the state and collective ownership of land and natural resources (Articles 9 and 10)[12] and principally prescribes the State's responsibility in environmental and resource protection. It establishes that 'the

---

7 See Article 13 and 53 of Administrative Litigation Law of 2014 (explicitly excluding government rules in the scope of judicial review).
8 Generally see Yuwen Li and Yun Ma, 'The Hurdle is High: The Administrative Litigation System in the People's Republic of China', in Yuwen Li (ed.), *Administrative Litigation Systems in Greater China and Europe* (Farnham, England and Burlington, VT: Ashgate Publishing, 2014), pp. 15–40; see also Jiang Bixin, 行政诉讼法与抽象行政行为 (Administrative Litigation Law and Abstract Administrative Actions), 3 (2009) 行政法学研究 (*Administrative Law Review*), p. 13.
9 For more details, see *infra* p.192 et seq. of Chapter 9.
10 See 中华人民共和国各级人民代表大会常务委员会监督法 (Law on the Supervision of Standing Committees of People's Congresses at Various Levels), effective on January 1, 2007, Article 31; 全国人民代表大会常务委员会关于加强法律解释工作的决议 (Resolution of the SCNPC on Strengthening the Work of the Interpretation of the Law), adopted on June 10, 1981, and 中华人民共和国人民法院组织法 (Organic Law of People's Courts), adopted in 1979 and amended on October 31, 2006, Article 32.
11 Du Qun, 'The People's Republic of China', in Louis J. Kotzé and Alexander R. Paterson (eds.), *The Role of the Judiciary in Environmental Governance: Comparative Perspectives* (Alphen aan den Rijn, The Netherlands: Kluwer Law International, 2009), p. 414.
12 About the ownership structure of land and natural resources, see *supra* pp. 28–9 of Chapter 2.

State ensures the *rational use* of natural resources and protecting rare animals and plants; the encroachment or derogation of natural resources by any organization or individual by whatever means is prohibited' (Article 9), and that 'the State protects and improves the environment in which people live and the ecological environment. It prevents and controls pollution and other public hazards and organizes and encourages the afforestation and protection of forests' (Article 26). With regard to scenic areas that are culturally significant, the Constitution provides that 'the State protects sites of scenic and historic interests, valuable cultural monuments and other important historical and cultural heritage' (Article 22). Furthermore, concerning the nature of PAs as public property, the general proclamation that 'the State protects socialist public property' (Article 12) is applicable.

The Constitution itself does not specify which institution will represent the State in exercising State ownership and carry out the duty to protect PAs. Until the enactment of the Real Property Law (物权法) in 2007,[13] the State Council was entitled to exercise ownership of State-owned property on behalf of the State (Article 45).

Congressional Statutes

The Chinese legislature began to develop its environmental legislative framework at the end of the 1970s.[14] Environmental statutes account for more than 10 percent of all the statutes enacted by national legislatures, including the NPC and the SCNPC, in the past three decades.[15] A series of environmental statutes that were applicable to nature conservation and PA management were enacted in the 1980s, including the Marine Environmental Protection Law of 1982, the Forest Law of 1984, the Grassland Law of 1985, the Fisheries Law of 1986, the Land Administration Law of 1986, the Water Law of 1988 and the Wildlife Protection Law of 1988. These statutes underwent continuous amendments in the 1990s and the 2000s. The most symbolic legislation of the 2000s was the enactment of the Law on Environmental Impact Assessment in 2003.[16]

Environmental Protection Law

Increasing attention to nature conservation is seen in the continuous amendments to the Environmental Protection Law. In 1979, the SCNPC promulgated the Environmental Protection Law (for trial implementation) ('the 1979 EPL'). This was the first law to specifically address environmental problems in China, such as pollution and ecological degradation. It governs land and resource protection by regulating the use of soil, water, mineral resources, forests, grasses, wild animals and plants (Articles 10–15). This law has resulted in subsequent separate statutes, such as the Forest Law of 1984, the Grassland Law of 1985 and the Wildlife Protection Law of 1988. The 1979 EPL also sporadically addresses some specific types of PAs. For example, it includes 'scenic spots for sightseeing' and nature reserves in its definition

---

13 NPC, Real Property Law of PRC (中华人民共和国物权法), effective on October 1, 2007.
14 For a list of Chinese environmental legislation, see Appendix I.
15 Liu Jingjing, 'Environmental Justice with Chinese Characteristics: Recent Developments in Using Environmental Public Interest Litigation to Strengthen Access to Environmental Justice', Vermont Law School Research Paper, No.24-12, 2012, p. 16.
16 For a comprehensive review of environmental legislation in China, see Wang Shuyi and Wang Zaixiang, 中国环境法学三十年 (1978–2008) (Thirty Years of Environmental Law in China (1978–2008)), in Jiang Ming'an (ed.), 中国法学三十年 (1978–2008) (*Thirty Years of China Law (1978–2008)*) (Beijing: Zhongguo Renmin Daxue Chubanshe, 2008), pp. 463–89.

of 'environment' (Article 3) and prohibits the establishment and operation of polluting enterprises within these areas (Article 17). These provisions serve as the foundation for the subsequent regulations on SHAs and nature reserves enacted in 1985 and 1994, respectively. However, because the 1979 EPL was promulgated shortly after the turbulence in China, the provisions in its 33 articles are too brief and general and therefore lack enforceability.

After ten years of trial implementation, the 1979 EPL was amended in 1989 ('the 1989 EPL'), and the number of articles was increased to 47. Within this period, the level of environmental protection was strengthened, which can be seen in the elevation of the administrative level of authority for environmental protection. In 1982, the Environmental Protection Bureau (环境保护局) was established to replace the previous Leading Group of Environmental Protection (环境保护领导小组), an ad hoc coordination institution. This new bureau was then affiliated with the Ministry of Urban-Rural Construction and Environmental Protection. After two reorganizations in 1984 and 1988, the Environmental Protection Bureau was finally separated from the Ministry of Construction and renamed the National Environmental Protection Agency (国家环境保护局).[17] However, the increasing authority given to environmental protection has made departments of economic development and local governments anxious about the potential impairment of economic interests. Compromise on this issue is reflected by the fact that a pollutant discharge license was not adopted in the 1989 EPL. The 'Focus on Economic Development' (以经济建设为中心) was still the paramount concern.[18]

Although the 1989 EPL paid more attention to nature conservation issues, such as the protection of ecological environments (Article 19) and the designation of SHAs (Article 23), it was still criticized for adopting a partial approach to pollution control without providing enforceable rules on conservation.[19] For example, among the eleven articles that address the issue of liability, only one refers to the liability of damaging land and natural resources (Article 44). The gap between pollution control and ecological protection in the 1989 EPL was also recognized by the SCNPC when the draft of the amendment to the EPL was issued for the solicitation of public comments in 2012.[20]

In April 2014, after four rounds of deliberation, the amendment to the EPL was finally approved by the SCNPC ('the 2014 EPL'),[21] which intensively amended and expanded the 1989 EPL. In addition to the strengthened regulatory authority and liability for pollution that has been applauded by the media as 'the most stringent EPL ever',[22] the 2014 EPL also greatly elevates the significance of nature conservation. This change is reflected in the following aspects.

First, the 2014 EPL adds the 'building of ecological civilization' (生态文明建设) as one of the fundamental legislative purposes (Article 1), prescribes 'environmental protection' as 'the basic State policy'(基本国策) (Article 4) and proposes five fundamental principles

17 See Organisation for Economic Co-operation and Development (OECD), *Governance in China* (Paris: OECD, 2005), p. 498.
18 See Wang Jing, 从环境基本法的立法特征论我国《环境保护法》的修改定位 (Analysis on the Strategy of Amending the Environmental Protection Law of China Considering the Characteristics of the Fundamental Law), 16.4 (2004) 中外法学 (*Peking University Law Journal*), p. 476.
19 Xu Haigen, Wang Shunqing and Xue Dayuan, 'Biodiversity Conservation in China: Legislation, Plans and Measures', 8 (1999) *Biodiversity and Conservation*, pp. 834–5.
20 SCNPC, 关于<中华人民共和国环境保护法修正案(草案)>的说明 (Legislative Statement on the Draft of the Amendment to the Environmental Protection Law), August 31, 2012, para. 4 of section 3.
21 SCNPC, Environmental Protection Law of PRC (中华人民共和国环境保护法), effective on January 1, 2015.
22 See article 59 of the new EPL. For media coverage, see generally Jin Yu and Wang Shuo, 解读"史上最严格环保法" (Analysis of the Most Stringent Environment Protection Law Ever), May 1, 2014. Available at http://www.banyuetan.org/chcontent/sz/szgc/2014430/100433.html. Last visited January 2015.

of environmental protection: 'priority of protection, prevention first, integrated governance, public participation, and bearing of liability' (Article 5).

Second, the 2014 EPL establishes a set of legal instruments for ecological protection and nature conservation. For example, it delimits the 'ecological red lines' (生态红线) as environmental baselines and 'legalizes' the instrument of 'ecological functional zoning' (生态功能区划), which has been proposed in policy documents since 2000 (Article 29).[23] It also prescribes instruments such as ecological restoration (Article 30) and ecological compensation (Article 31). Furthermore, it establishes trans-boundary and cross-sector cooperation and coordination mechanisms to battle ecological derogation (Article 20).

Law on Environmental Impact Assessment

Since the NEPA of 1969 prescribed the instrument of environmental impact assessment (EIA) in the US,[24] EIA has been broadly endorsed by many countries. China followed this trend and enacted its own Law on EIA[25] in 2003. This law provides two types of EIA: EIA of plans and EIA of construction projects (Article 3). Four formats of EIA documents are prescribed, including a chapter or an explanation of environmental impacts in the plan (A), a report of environmental impacts (B), a statement on environmental impacts (C) and a registration form for environmental impacts (D).[26] The circumstances in which different types and formats of EIA are applied are shown in Table 8.2 below.

Table 8.2 The types and formats of EIAs in China

Type of EIA	Circumstances	Formats of EIA
Plan-based EIA	Land use plan; Construction, development and utilization of certain areas, river basins and sea areas	A (Article 7)
	Special plans for industry, agriculture, husbandry, forestry, energy, water infrastructure, transportation, urban construction, tourism and natural resources development	B (Article 8)
Construction project-based EIA	Projects that may cause significant impacts on the environment	B (Article 16)
	Projects that may cause mild impacts on the environment	C (Article 16)
	Projects that may cause very little impact on the environment, making it unnecessary to prepare EIA	D (Article 16)

Source: Adapted from the Law on EIA of 2003

The Draft of the Natural Heritage Law

Based on calls by both practitioners and scholars, PA legislation has been listed on the national legislature's agenda for more than ten years. The original proposal was to amend the existing Regulations on Nature Reserves. However, as time passed, the concept of 'natural heritage' emerged. This concept resulted in the draft of the 'Natural Heritage Protection Law'

---

23 For more details on ecological functional zoning, see *infra* p. 173 et seq.
24 See *supra* pp. 82–3 of Chapter 4.
25 SCNPC, 中华人民共和国环境影响评价法 (Law on EIA of PRC), effective on September 1, 2003.
26 Cf. three types of EIA documents in the US, i.e. EIS, environmental assessment and FONSI. See *supra* pp. 82–3 of Chapter 4.

released by the NPC in 2012 ('the Draft').[27] Although the Draft was optimistically expected to be approved during the plenary session of the NPC in March 2012, it encountered unexpectedly harsh criticism from both preservationists and scholars.[28] One of the sternest critics of this draft was Xie Yan, a prominent scientist from the Chinese Academy of Science. She launched an intensive campaign to thwart the legislation through the media and the Internet one month before the opening session of the NPC, which culminated in the postponement of the promulgation of this law.[29]

The title of the Draft itself changed several times: the Law on Nature Reserves, the Law on Protected Areas, the Law on Natural Protected Districts, and finally the Law on Natural Heritage.[30] These changes indicate that the final draft is, in reality, a product of compromise. The concept of 'natural heritage' was finally proposed to integrate the parallel systems of 'SHAs' and 'nature reserves'. According to Article 11 of the Draft, natural heritage is further divided into 'protected districts' and 'related protected districts'. The former includes core zones of nature reserves at the national level and core scenic spots of SHAs at the national level, whereas the latter is designated at the peripheries of the 'protected districts' based on different types of natural heritage and different measures of protection. Thus, the Draft only covers two types of PAs: SHAs and nature reserves. Furthermore, only SHAs and nature reserves at the national level are included.

Xie estimated that if the Draft were approved, the Natural Heritage Law would only cover approximately 600 PAs. This would leave more than 7,000 PAs unprotected, unregulated and, to some extent, illegal.[31] Gao and Cheng note that the integration of SHAs and nature reserves at the national level into a concept of 'natural heritage' creates legal disorder.[32] First, the scope of natural heritage is not in accordance with the understanding adopted in international conventions, especially the Convention for Protecting the World Cultural and Natural Heritage, which is much broader. Second, the draft is not in accordance with the existing legislative framework. According to the current legislation, SHAs consist of both natural sites and cultural sites. The definition of natural heritage in the Draft only pays attention to the natural

---

27 NPC, 中华人民共和国自然遗产保护法(征求意见稿) (Natural Heritage Protection Law of PRC (draft for soliciting public opinion)), March 6, 2012. Full text is available at http://green.sina.com.cn/2012-03-06/175124069634.shtml. Last visited January 2015.
28 Shen Qiaohong, 85名专家联名建议修改自然遗产保护法 (85 Experts Jointly Recommended to Revise the Natural Heritage Protection Law), in 南方周末 (*Southern Weekly*), September 15, 2012. Available at http://www.infzm.com/content/80785. Last visited January 2015.
29 Media coverage of Xie Yan's opinion can be found online, including several mainstream web portals in China. See Sina, 为什么反对《自然遗产保护法》 (Why I Oppose the Law on Natural Heritage Protection?), available at http://news.sina.com.cn/z/NaturalHeritage/; Sohu, 解焱：《自然遗产保护法》草案应推迟审议一年 (Xie Yan: The Deliberation of the Draft of the Law on Natural Heritage Protection should be Postponed for One Year), February 9, 2012, available at http://gongyi.sohu.com/20120209/n334242664.shtml, and Tencent, 女学者解焱"阻击"《自然遗产保护法》 (The Female Scholar Xie Yan 'Blocks' the Law of Natural Heritage Protection), February 7, 2012, available at http://news.qq.com/a/20120207/000445.htm. All were last visited January 2015.
30 See Zhang Hailin, 自然遗产保护法7年修改超10次，各方利益博弈 (More than 10 Revisions of the Natural Heritage Protection Law within 7 Years: The Game Among Different Stakeholders), December 20, 2010, available at http://news.sina.com.cn/c/sd/2010-12-20/150921675053.shtml. Last visited January 2015.
31 Xie Yan,《自然遗产保护法》草案存在的问题和通过后的后果 (Problems of the Draft of Natural Heritage Law and the Consequences if it should be Passed), February 5, 2012, available at http://xieyan07.blog.sohu.com/202820777.html. Last visited January 2015.
32 Gao Lihong and Cheng Fang, 我国自然遗产保护的立法合理性研究-兼评《自然遗产保护法》征求意见稿草案 (Research on the Appropriateness of the Legislation on Protection of Natural Heritage in China: Comments on the Draft of the Natural Heritage Law), 1 (2012) 江西社会科学 (*Social Science in Jiangxi*), pp. 153–62.

aspect, which results in the partial protection of SHAs. Furthermore, the Draft only focuses on the property value of natural heritage while leaving unprotected value that cannot be easily measured in monetary terms, such as ecological and aesthetic value.[33]

Moreover, according to the Draft, the department of environmental protection and the department of construction, which are in charge of managing nature reserves and SHAs, respectively, would become the two main authorities for natural heritage management. In this way, the Ministry of Housing and Urban-Rural Development (MoHURD) would become the largest beneficiary and replace the previous beneficial status of the SFA in terms of staffing and funding. This is why the SFA was the main stumbling block that impeded the drafting process.[34]

Opponents are unsatisfied with the proposed Natural Heritage Law, which selectively chooses particular types and levels of PAs to protect, and most opponents argue for the enactment of a 'Law on Protected Areas'. This law would be the 'Constitution' in the field of nature conservation and biodiversity protection. Fear has spread among scholars that if the Draft were passed, it would be extremely difficult to initiate the legislative process to enact another 'Law on Protected Areas'.[35]

Separate Legislation on Natural Resources

Because there is no comprehensive PA law, the protection and use of resources within PAs are governed by separate statutes on specific types of natural resources, such as the Forest Law, the Grassland Law and the Wildlife Protection Law.

First, these separate statutes place an obligation of PA designation on governments as a means to fulfill their responsibilities with regard to nature protection. For example, the Forest Law of 1998 specifically requires the designation of nature reserves to protect forestry resources. It states that

> . . . the competent forestry departments at the national and provincial levels *should* designate certain areas with typical forest ecosystems, habitats of rare and endangered animals and plants, natural tropical rain forests and other natural forest areas that are valuable for special protection as nature reserves. (Article 24)

The Wildlife Protection Law of 2004 also requires that 'competent wildlife departments at the national and provincial levels *should* designate the terrestrial and water areas where wildlife with special national and local protection inhabits and breeds as nature reserves' (Article 10). The Grassland Law of 2003 provides that

---

33 Gao Lihong and Cheng Fang, ibid., at p. 159.
34 See Oriental Outlook, 《自然遗产保护法》难产背后的"暗战" (Law on Natural Heritage Protection: 'The Dark War' Behind Its Dystocia), in 瞭望东方周刊 (*Oriental Outlook Weekly*), December 25, 2010, available at http://www.dooland.com/magazine/article_105458.html. Last visited January 2015.
35 See Zhou Ke and Hou Jiaru, 我国自然保护区分类体系的立法完善 (Improvement of Legislation on the Categorization System of Nature Reserves in China), 2 (2007) 首都师范大学学报(社会科学版) (*Journal of Capital Normal University (Social Sciences Edition)*), pp. 58–63; Gao Lihong and Cheng Fang, *supra* note 32; Xie Yan and Qin Tianbao, 为什么反对《自然遗产保护法》(Why I Oppose the Law on Natural Heritage Protection), March 13, 2012, available at http://talk.weibo.com/ft/201203084480; Lin Yan, 自然保护基本法：7年了，还在等! (Fundamental Law of Nature Protection: We are Still Waiting after Seven Years have Passed!), in 中国青年报 (*China Youth Daily*), November 24, 2010, available at http://zqb.cyol.com/content/2010-11/24/content_3450426.htm. Both were last visited in January 2015.

. . . competent grassland departments at the national and provincial levels *may* set up grassland nature reserves in the following areas: (1) grassland with representative significance; (2) areas in which rare and endangered species of wild animals and plants are concentrated; and (3) grasslands of significant ecological functions and economic and scientific research values. (Article 43)

It is worth noting that the specific word used in the Grassland Law is 'may', whereas the designation of nature reserves is obligatory in the former two areas.

Second, these statutes provide regulations on certain activities within PAs. The Wildlife Protection Law states that hunting and other activities that are detrimental to the habitation and breeding of wildlife are prohibited in nature reserves (Article 20). The Mineral Resources Law of 1996 states that unless approved by competent authorities, no one may mine mineral resources within nature reserves and important scenic spots designated by the State (Article 20). Forests within SHAs and nature reserves are categorized into 'forests for special use'[36] according to the Forest Law of 1998 (Article 4). Logging is prohibited within 'forests for specific use' (Article 31).

Other Applicable Statutes

The management of PAs is also governed by other statutes, mainly, the Tourism Law and general administrative statutes.

The Tourism Law[37] aims to protect tourists and tourist service providers' legal rights and interests and to protect and develop tourism resources (Article 1). It stipulates three principles of tourism development:

1 the integration of social benefits, economic benefits and ecological benefits;
2 the State encourages all market subjects to rationally utilize tourism resources under the precondition that tourism resources are effectively protected, and
3 scenic areas that are based on public resources should be public interest-oriented (Article 4).

To protect tourism resources, the Law requires that the necessary facilities for environmental protection and measures for ecological protection should be put into place before a tourist site can be opened to the public (Article 42). The Law also stipulates conditions on charging entrance fees to scenic areas, such as the requirement of a hearing before charging or increasing entry fees and additional fees, the requirement to decrease or cancel additional fees if the costs of the investment have already been covered (Article 43) and the requirement of a public announcement six months in advance of a fee increase (Article 44).

Another field of law that is applicable is general administrative statutes. Unlike the APA in the US, the Administrative Procedure Law has not been enacted in China, although different versions of drafts have been proposed by scholars.[38] Therefore, the principles of due

---

36 According to the current classification system, forests are classified into five categories: shelter forests, timber forests, economic forests, firewood forests and forests for special use. The last category refers to those forests in which forests and trees are primarily used for national defense, environmental protection and scientific purposes (Article 4).
37 SCNPC, 旅游法 (Tourism Law of PRC), effective on October 1, 2013.
38 Jiang Ming'an, 中华人民共和国行政程序法(试拟稿) (Administrative Procedure Law (draft)), 2002, available at http://www.publiclaw.cn/article/Details.asp?NewsId=248&Classid=&ClassName. Last visited January 2015, and Ma Huaide (ed.), 行政程序立法研究：《行政程序法》草案建议稿及理由说明书 (*Studies on Legislation of Administrative Procedure: Recommended Draft of the Administrative Procedure Law and its Explanations*) (Beijing: Falv Chubanshe, 2005).

process, public participation and procedural justice are not fully legalized in the current legal framework; instead, they are sporadically embodied in different sectors of administrative law.[39] Furthermore, because the APA grants a private right of action to bring lawsuits against federal agencies to courts in the US,[40] similar provisions are made in the Administrative Reconsideration Law of 1999[41] and the Administrative Litigation Law (ALL) of 2014.[42] The former grants private parties the right to apply for an administrative reconsideration within the administrative system (Article 2), and the recently amended ALL grants the right of action to private parties against administrative actions made by administrative bodies (Article 2).

Administrative Regulations

Regulations on Nature Reserves of 1994

In 1994, when the Regulations on Nature Reserves were issued, the number of nature reserves in China was mushrooming. To provide legislative support, the Regulations were enacted to 'strengthen the construction and management of nature reserves and protect the natural environment and resources' (Article 1). Although they introduced the basic principles and legal framework for the designation and management of nature reserves, the Regulations, with only 44 articles, were far from well-crafted.

The core mechanism adopted by the Regulations to manage nature reserves is the zoning mechanism, which divides nature reserves into three distinctive zones: the core zone, the buffer zone and the experimental zone (Article 18). In this way, different types and scales of designated and prohibited activities are specified. The degree of protection gradually increases from the outer experimental zone to the inner core zone.[43] Zoning is applauded as an effective means of nature reserve management; however, it triggers suspicion on the basis that it is overly rigid and not resilient. Local communities' livelihoods are negatively influenced by the designation and management of nature reserves, as is local economic development. Therefore, conflicts are intensified, leading to deficiencies in the implementation of the law.[44]

Regulations on Scenic and Historic Areas of 2006

In 2006, the State Council promulgated the Regulations on Scenic and Historic Areas ('the Regulations'), which repealed the Interim Regulations on Administration of Scenic and Historic Areas issued in 1985 ('the Interim Regulations').[45] The number of articles increased from 17 to 52, and the Regulations were enriched and became the main legal document for

---

39 These include Administrative Penalty Law of 1996, Administrative Licensing Law of 2004, Administrative Coercion Law of 2012. See NPC, 行政处罚法 (Administrative Penalty Law), effective on October 1, 1996; SCNPC, 行政许可法 (Administrative Licensing Law), effective on July 1, 2004, and SCNPC, 行政强制法 (Administrative Coercion Law), effective on January 1, 2012.
40 5 USC. §702.
41 SCNPC, 行政复议法 (Administrative Reconsideration Law), effective on October 1, 1999.
42 NPC, 行政诉讼法 (ALL), effective on January 1, 2015. The original ALL was enacted in 1989. It was for the first time amended in 2014.
43 For more discussion on designated use pattern within different zones of nature reserves, see *infra* pp. 215–16 of Chapter 10.
44 For details about the implementation gap, see *infra* p. 219 et seq. of Chapter 10 in general and p. 226 et seq. in particular for analysis of the reasons.
45 State Council, 风景名胜区条例 (Regulations on Scenic and Historic Areas), September 19, 2006, Decree No. 474 of the State Council, and 风景名胜区管理暂行条例 (Interim Regulations on Administration of Scenic and Historic Areas), June 7, 1985, *Guofa* No. 76 [1985].

regulating and managing SHAs. Compared with the Interim Regulations and the Regulations on Nature Reserves, the Regulations have made substantial improvements in terms of the establishment, planning, protection, utilization and management of SHAs.

First, the clear legal protection of property owners and users of land, resources and real estate within SHAs is provided, such as compulsory consultation requirements and compensation payments (Articles 9 and 11).[46]

Second, to regulate the rampant practice of transferring the operation rights of SHAs to individuals and enterprises at the local level, the Regulations establish a 'preliminary' concession system by stipulating the requirements for public bidding, the conclusion of a concession contract and the payment of compensation to use scenic resources (风景名胜资源有偿使用费) (Article 37). Furthermore, the management body of SHAs should not conduct for-profit commercial activities or authorize any enterprises or individuals to carry out the planning, management and supervision of SHAs. Staff members of the management body should not hold a concurrent post in any enterprise located within SHAs (Article 39).[47]

Third, the 'separation between revenue and expenditure' (收支两条线) is stipulated, which means that the income from the tickets of SHAs and compensation fees for the use of scenic resources paid by concessioners should be managed separately from their expenditures. The income should be exclusively used for the protection and management of scenic and historic resources and for compensating the losses of property owners and users within SHAs (Article 38).

Although the Regulations stipulate strict requirements for SHA management, criticism of law enforcement continues. The overuse and commercialization of scenic resources remain commonplace in practice.[48]

Departmental Rules

In addition to the two Regulations on nature reserves and SHAs, other sectors have developed 'departmental rules' to designate and manage PAs. These departmental rules, together with laws and administrative regulations, form the whole picture of the regulatory framework of PA designation and management at the national level.

These rules can be classified into two types. The first type includes rules enacted to implement congressional legislation and administrative regulations. To implement the Interim Regulations on Scenic and Historic Areas of 1985, the Ministry of Urban-Rural Construction and Environmental Protection (the MoHURD) issued the Implementation Measures of the Interim Regulations on Scenic and Historic Areas[49] in 1987 to specify and detail the provisions of the Interim Regulations. To implement the Regulations on Nature Reserves, the State Land Administration issued the Measures on the Administration of Land in Nature Reserves in 1995.[50] The second type includes rules that initially create new types of PAs. As shown above, there have been a variety of designations of PAs created by different departments, such as forest parks, wetland parks, mineral parks, irrigational scenic parks and archeological

---

46 For more discussion, see *infra* pp. 216–19 of Chapter 10.
47 For more discussion on 'transfer of operation right' and 'concession', see *infra* p. 192 et seq. of Chapter 9.
48 For more discussion on enforcement of the Regulations, see *infra* section 3.3 of Chapter 10.
49 Ministry of Urban-Rural Construction and Environmental Protection, 风景名胜区管理暂行条例实施办法 (Implementation Measures of the Interim Regulations on Scenic and Historic Areas), effective on June 10, 1987.
50 State Land Administration, 自然保护区土地管理办法 (Measures on the Administration of Land in Nature Reserves), effective on July 24, 1995.

site parks.[51] These two types of rules are generally referred to as 'implementing rule making' and 'innovative rule making' in Chinese academia.[52]

Local Regulations and Local Government Rules

At the local level, the legislative and regulatory frameworks are also diversified. Some scholars have argued for the goal of 'one protected area, one enabling act' (一区一法), that is, site-specific legislation for PA units.[53] However, this goal has not been fully achieved. By the end of 2012, 'local regulations' had been enacted by local people's congresses in 19 provinces and 'enabling legislation' had been adopted in 82 'SHAs at the national level'.[54] The statistics on nature reserves show that the number of enabling legislations for individual nature reserves stands at approximately fifty.[55] Compared to the total number of 2,669 nature reserves in 2012, this figure shows that a gap remains. Because legislative protection provided at the local level is one of the considerations for examiners in approving applications to become a 'PA at the national level', local legislatures have quickly advanced their 'enabling legislation' for PA units in recent years.

In the US, an enabling act for each national park unit is made by Congress. In contrast, the enabling legislation for each PA in China, if any, is usually made by the local legislature where the PA is located. According to the Legislation Law of 2015, local legislation must *accord* with the Constitution, laws and administrative regulations (Article 72). Therefore, most local legislation on PAs is enacted to implement the two regulations on SHAs and nature reserves by specifying and detailing them. In the US, a specific enabling act of a national park unit may contradict and take priority over the general law, i.e. the NPS Organic Act. The 'enabling legislation' for each PA in China must strictly follow the laws and regulations at the upper level. In practice, most local regulations repeat the regulations at the central level, which hardly reflects the place-based nature of PA management. Therefore, in contrast to the call for increasing academic attention to enabling acts in the US,[56] the academic significance of these local regulations in China is limited.

Overview of the Policy Framework of PAs

A General Overview of the Framework of Environmental Policy Making

Unlike the US, where agencies issue management policies to implement and interpret congressional statutes, policies in China are usually issued to fill a legislative vacancy. In China, there is no comprehensive policy manual on the management of PAs like the Management

---

51 See *supra* section 4.2.3 of Chapter 2.
52 See generally Yang Haikun, 论我国行政立法 (Analysis on Administrative Rule-making in China), 1 (1992) 北京社会科学 (*Beijing Social Science*), pp. 138–47.
53 Yan Shipeng and Luo Ying, 国家级自然保护区"一区一法"立法模式的理论分析 (The Theoretical Analysis on the Legislative Model of 'One Reserve, One Enabling Act' in Nature Reserves at the National Level), 20.5 (2007) 世界林业研究 (*World Forestry Research*), pp. 68–72.
54 MoHURD, 中国风景名胜区事业发展公报 (1982–2012) (Bulletin of the Development of Scenic and Historic Areas in China (1982–2012)), 2012, pp. 3–4. Full text is available at http://www.mohurd.gov.cn/zxydt/w02012120419937414971793750.doc. Last visited January 2015.
55 The data collection is from the database of Westlaw China and up to February 20, 2013. Concerning the overlap and amendments to enabling legislations, the number of 50 is calculated on an approximate basis.
56 Robert Fischman, 'The Problem of Statutory Detail in National Park Establishment Legislation and Its Relationship to Pollution Control Law', 74 (1996) *Denver University Law Review*, pp. 779–814.

170 *Country Studies: China*

Policies of 2006 issued by the NPS. Instead, policy documents are scattered in different fields, issued by different agencies and cover different issues. This section first discusses the composition and types of environmental policies and then reviews the evolution of policy making from a historical perspective.

Composition and Types of Environmental Policies

Environmental policies in China generally consist of two parts: pollution control and ecological protection. The latter part covers a broad range, such as ecological functional zoning, biodiversity and natural resources management. PA designation and management is a shared concern in these policies. In addition to its direct alignment with environmental policies, PA management is influenced by other relevant policies, such as urban-rural planning and tourism policies.

Among all types of policy documents, the most important and frequently used document involves various types of plans. These plans mainly include national economic and social development plans, territorial plans (mainly the urban-rural plan), pollution control plans, ecological protection plans and natural resources plans, such as plans for water resources, mineral resources and land use.[57]

The primary form of national economic and social development plans is the Five-Year Plan (FYP). FYPs are a series of plans made every five years. These plans map the development strategies and set the growth targets that will guide policy making for the following five years. Since 1953, there have been twelve FYPs.[58] PA planning was gradually formed during this process. Since the sixth FYP (1981–85), environmental protection has been listed as an independent chapter. The 1989 EPL requires that 'the plans for environmental protection formulated by the State must be incorporated into the national economic and social development plans' (Article 4). Since the eighth FYP (1991–95), a specific FYP on environmental protection has been issued or approved by the State Council. Beginning with the tenth FYP (2001–05), the NPC made an ad hoc plan for ecosystem construction and environmental protection.[59] Since the twelfth FYP (2011–15), a specific FYP for ecological protection has been issued.[60]

Environmental Protection as a Basic State Policy (Post-Mao–Early 1990s)

In the early 1970s, China began to take serious actions to combat environmental problems. Although these actions were comparatively late on a global scale, they nevertheless represented a courageous decision at that time because the economy of China was on the verge of

---

57 For a general overview of the planning for land utilization in China, see Tian Chunhua, 着眼未来的事业–我国土地利用规划工作30年历程回顾 (The Undertaking Aiming at the Future: Overview of the Land Utilization Planning in China in the Past 30 Years), in 中国国土资源报 (*News of the Land and Resources in China*), January 12, 2009. Full text is available at http://www.mlr.gov.cn/sy/gd1/200901/t20090112_113906.htm. Last visited January 2015.
58 It was named as the 'five-year plan' from the first to the tenth plans. Since the eleventh five-year period (2006–10), the name has been changed to 'five-year guideline (规划)' instead of 'five-year plan (计划)'. For purposes of expediency, the term of 'five-year plan' will be generally used in this book. Full texts of all five-year plans (guidelines) are available at http://dangshi.people.com.cn/GB/151935/204121/. Last visited January 2015.
59 NPC, 国民经济和社会发展第十个五年计划生态建设和环境保护重点专项规划 (National 10th Five-Year Plan for Ecosystem Construction and Environmental Protection), 2001.
60 See State Council, 国家环境保护"十二五"规划 (National 12th Five-Year Plan on Environmental Protection), 2011; and MoEP, 全国生态保护"十二五"规划 (National 12th Five-Year Plan on Ecological Protection), 2013.

bankruptcy and economic restoration was the top priority. China was facing a series of environmental problems, such as deteriorating quality of rivers, contamination of ground water, air pollution and industrial waste.[61] To some extent, these horrendous pollution problems detracted from attention to nature conservation. Therefore, the main focus of environmental policies was the prevention and control of pollution.

In 1983, at the Second National Environmental Protection Conference, then-Prime Minister Li Peng announced that environmental protection was a basic State policy (基本国策). The conference established three main policies: 'prevention first and integration between prevention and control of pollution', 'polluters pay' and 'strengthening environment management'.[62] Following this conference, environmental law making and institutional establishment were included on the agenda. In 1984, the State Council established the Environmental Protection Committee, which was dedicated to coordinating environment-related issues between different departments. The committee was headed by the prime minister, demonstrating the central government's resolution to seriously address environmental issues.[63]

Sustainable Development and Scientific Development as the Core of Environmental Policy-Making (1992–present)

EMBRACING SUSTAINABLE DEVELOPMENT

As previously discussed, China enthusiastically embraced the concept of sustainable development (SD) after the Rio Conference in 1992.[64] Since then, SD has gained a paramount position on the political agenda as well as in legislation and policy making. PA designation and management are no exceptions.

In 1993, the Environmental Action Plan of China (1991–2000) was approved by the State Council, and 7 percent of the total territorial area of the nation was reserved for the designation of nature reserves.[65] Other action plans were subsequently adopted, including the Action Plan for Biodiversity Protection in China in 1994, the Outline of the Development Plan for Nature Reserves in China (1996–2010) in 1997 and the National Plan for the Construction of the Ecological Environment in 1998.[66]

In 1995, China adopted the strategy of 'two fundamental transformations' (两个根本性转变), which marked the transition from a traditional planned economy to a socialist market

---

61 Zhang Kunmin and Wen Zongguo, 'Review and Challenges of Policies of Environmental Protection and Sustainable Development in China', 88.4 (2008) *Journal of Environmental Management*, p. 1250.
62 MoEP, 第二次全国环境保护会议 (1983年12月31日至1984年1月7日) (The Second National Environmental Protection Conference (December 31, 1983–January 7, 1984)). Available at http://www.zhb.gov.cn/ztbd/gzhy/diqicihbdh/ljhbdh/201112/t20111221_221579.htm. Last visited January 2015.
63 Li Ruinong, 贯彻环境保护基本国策 实现可持续发展—就我国改革开放以来环境保护事业发展访李鹏同志 (Implementing the Basic State Policy of Environmental Protection and Achieving Sustainable Development: Interview of Li Peng on the Development of Environmental Protection since the Opening-Up Reform of China), in 中国环境报 (*Newspaper of China Environment*), September 8, 2009. Available at http://www.cenews.com.cn/xwzx/zhxw/qt/200909/t20090908_622487.html. Last visited January 2015.
64 See *supra* section 4.1.3 of Chapter 3.
65 State Council, 中国环境保护行动计划 (1991–2000) (Environmental Action Plan of China (1991–2000)), 1994, p. 3. Full English text is available at http://documents.worldbank.org/curated/en/1994/03/698551/china-environmental-action-plan-china-1991-2000. Last visited January 2015.
66 State Council, 中国生物多样性保护行动计划 (Action Plan for Biodiversity Protection in China), 1994; SEPA, 中国自然保护区发展规划纲要 (1996–2010年) (Outline of the Development Plan for Nature Reserves in China (1996–2010)), 1997, and State Council, 全国生态环境建设规划 (National Plan for Construction of Ecological Environment), 1998.

economy as well as the transition from extensive growth to intensive growth.[67] This strategy was formed in the context of increasing concern about environmental pollution and demands for natural resource consumption in China.

The turning point for the significance of policy on ecological protection occurred in 1998, when a disastrous flood struck the southern part of China. The need for ecological environmental protection was acknowledged nationwide.[68] The lessons learned from this ecological disaster were reflected in the specific focus on ecological protection when China began to advance its strategy of Great Western Development (西部大开发) in the 2000s and the State Council approved the Six Primary Forestry Projects (六大林业重点工程) in 2001.[69] These enormous projects were conducted intensively across China, with an influence on a large population and a large amount of investment. For example, the project of returning farmland to forests (退耕还林) has influenced more than 25 provinces, 2,279 counties, 32 million peasant households and 124 million farmers.[70] One of the six projects, the project on wildlife protection and the construction of nature reserves, directly influenced PA management in China, as reflected in the substantial increase in the number of nature reserves since the new millennium (shown in Table 2.3).

Proposal of Scientific Development

Since 2003, the Outlook of Scientific Development (科学发展观)[71] has spread across China. This was initially an innovative ideology of the CPC, and it has become a guiding principle that governs the economy and society of the nation.

In December 2005, the State Council issued the Decision of the State Council on Implementing the Outlook of Scientific Development and Strengthening Environmental Protection (the Decisions),[72] which echoed the national development strategy of 'scientific development' and re-examined the issue of environmental protection under this strategy. The Environmental Rule of Law (环境法治) was proposed to strengthen the role of law in addressing environmental problems. The balance between economic and social development and environmental protection was established as the governing principle.

67 It was proposed during the Fifth Plenary Session of the 14th Central Committee of the Communist Party of China (CCCPC) held in 1995. See CCCPC, 中共中央关于制定国民经济和社会发展"九五"计划和 2010 年远景目标的建议 (Recommendations of the CCCPC on Drafting the 9th Five-Year Plan for National Economic and Social Development and Vision of 2010), September 28, 1995.
68 See Liu Yu et al., 'The Politics and Ethics of Going Green in China', in Joanne Bauer (ed.), *Forging Environmentalism: Justice, Livelihood, and Contested Environments* (Armonk, NY and London: M.E. Sharpe, 2006), p. 63.
69 *China Daily*, 国务院批准实施六大林业重点工程 (The State Council Approved the Six Primary Forestry Projects), February 16, 2001. Available at http://www.people.com.cn/GB/huanbao/55/20010216/396955.html. Last visited January 2015.
70 Xinhuanet, 中国退耕还林总投入将达4300多亿元 (The Total Investment in the Project of Returning Farmland to Forests would be 430 billion RMB), August 18, 2010. Available at http://politics.people.com.cn/GB/1026/12477229.html. Last visited January 2015.
71 The Outlook of Scientific Development was firstly put forward by the General Secretary of the CPC, Hu Jintao, in 2003 during his speech. It was further developed at the 3rd Plenary Session of 16th Central Committee of CPC held in October 2003. For more information, see Xinhuanet, 科学发展观 (Outlook of Scientific Development), available at http://news.xinhuanet.com/ziliao/2005-03/16/content_2704537.htm. Last visited January 2015.
72 State Council, 国务院关于落实科学发展观加强环境保护的决定 (Decision of the State Council on Implementing the Outlook of Scientific Development and Strengthening Environmental Protection), *Guofa* No. 39 [2005]. Full text is available at http://www.gov.cn/zwgk/2005-12/13/content_125680.htm. Last visited January 2015.

The Evolution of Policy-Making for PAs

Ecological protection carries considerable weight in the current policy-making agenda. This importance can be seen in the gradual acknowledgement of the equal priority of ecological protection and pollution control, and the adoption of the concepts of ecosystem and biodiversity protection along with the development of science in the research field. This section maps the evolution of policy making for ecological protection in general and then discusses policy making for nature reserves and SHAs in particular.

Ecological Functional Zoning

The most remarkable development of policy making for ecological protection in China is the proposal and practices of 'ecological functional zoning' (生态功能区划, EFZ) and the designation of 'ecological functional zones' (生态功能区, EFZs).

In 2000, the State Council issued the Outline of National Ecological Environmental Protection (the Outline),[73] in which the establishment of EFZs was proposed for the first time. The designation of EFZs was given the same priority as the designation of nature reserves as a conservation tool to protect the ecological environment. This policy initiative of establishing EFZs was underpinned by the Decision of the State Council on Implementing the Outlook of Scientific Development and Strengthening Environmental Protection in 2005 and the eleventh FYP (2006–10) (Chapters 20 and 23).

EFZ is officially defined as 'the process of dividing areas into different EFZs based on the factors of ecological environment, the sensitivity of ecological environment and the rule of regional differentiation of ecological services'.[74] EFZs, a new type of comprehensive designation, refer to those areas with crucial significance for ecological functions. EFZs are classified into three levels: national, provincial and prefectural. Similar to other designations of PAs, strict regulation is applied within EFZs, such as the prohibition of development activities and construction projects.

Given the policy-based practices of EFZ, since 2006, a broader context has been formulated under the concept of 'primary functional zoning' (PFZ) (主体功能区划).[75] PFZ aims to integrate ecological protection and spatial planning at the national level. The relationship between designations under PFZ and EFZs is shown in Figure 8.2 below. Primary EFZs are identified as either restricted exploitation zones (限制开发区) or prohibited exploitation zones (禁止开发区). The former refers to primary EFZs in which *large-scale* and *highly insensitive* industrialization and urbanization are restricted, and the latter refers to those in which all types of industrialization and urbanization are prohibited. A prohibited exploitation zone covers previous PA designations, such as SHAs, nature reserves, forest parks and other types of PAs.

EFZ has gained considerable weight in policy making and has developed into a comprehensive mechanism that guides the overall designation and management of PAs in China.

---

73 State Council, 全国生态环境保护纲要 (Outline of National Ecological Environmental Protection), *Guofa* No. 38 [2000].

74 Western Development Office of the State Council and State Environmental Protection Administration, 生态功能区划技术暂行规程 (Provisional Technical Specifications of Ecological Service Zoning), effective on September 1, 2002.

75 It was first proposed by the 11th FYP in 2006 and further developed in the National Plan of Primary Functional Zoning (全国主体功能区规划) issued by the State Council in 2010, *Guofa* No. 46 [2010].

As a new management tool that embodies the idea of 'integrated ecosystem management', which has been widely acknowledged around the world,[76] EFZ has several characteristics:

1 It emphasizes the significance of ecological service and ecosystem protection.
2 It functions as the scientific basis for land-use planning and other forms of ecological decision making.
3 It emphasizes coordinated management based on ecological services instead of the traditional criteria of individual factors of ecological environment.
4 It guides the industrial layout and structure and the exploitation of resources within EFZs.
5 It emphasizes public participation and the protection of community interests.

As discussed earlier, the new EPL of 2014 has generally endorsed EFZ, and EFZ has, to some extent, been 'legalized'. It is expected that the rules governing PA management that are proposed via the policy documents of EFZ discussed above will be incorporated into law in the short term.

Policy-Making for Nature Reserves

In addition to policy making on ecological protection in general, a series of policies and plans are specifically issued for nature reserve management.

In 1991, the former SEPA issued the National Eighth FYP and Ten-Year Plan on the Protection of Nature Reserve and Species.[77] This was the first specific plan for nature reserves.

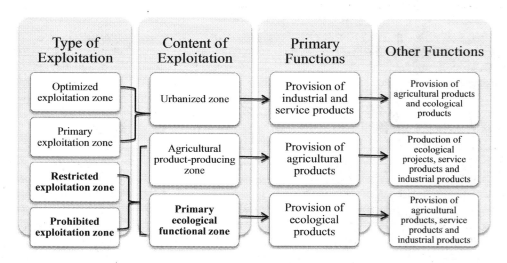

Figure 8.2 Classification of primary functional zones and their functions in China
Source: Adapted from the State Council, National Plan of Primary Functional Zoning (2010)

---

76 See Du Qun, 我国生态综合管理的政策与实践：生态功能区划制度探索 (Policies and Practices of Integrated Ecosystem Management in China: Exploration of the System of Ecological Functional Zoning), in 2007 年全国环境资源法学会(年会)论文集(第三册) (*Symposium of the Annual Conference of National Environmental Law and Natural Resources Law in 2007 (Volume 3)*).
77 SEPA, 全国自然保护区和物种保护八五计划和10年规划 (National 8th Five-Year Plan and Ten-Year Plan on Protection of Nature Reserves and Species), 1991.

To update this 1991 Plan, in November 1997, the State Council approved the Outline of the Development Plan for Nature Reserves in China (1996–2010) (the Outline).[78] The Outline summarized the major problems in nature reserve management, which included the limited number and area of nature reserves, overdevelopment within nature reserves, a shortage of funds, the deficiency of a national development plan and a dearth of professionalism in the management of nature reserves (Article 1 (3)). To handle these problems, two stages of goals were delimited in this Outline:

1. 1996–2000: establish 1,000 nature reserves (140–50 at the national level), accounting for approximately 9 percent of the total territorial area (10 percent plus SHAs), to improve the legal system of nature reserves, establish management authorities at 80 percent of total nature reserves and equip 50 percent of the total nature reserves.
2. 2001–2010: establish 1,200 nature reserves (160–70 at the national level), accounting for approximately 10 percent of the total territorial area (12 percent plus SHAs), to establish a comprehensive legal system of nature reserves, establish management authorities for 90 percent of the total nature reserves and equip 70 percent of the total nature reserves.

Based on these goals, the Outline further set goals for the number and area of nature reserves to be established by different departments. For example, the forestry department was required to set out more than 700 nature reserves by 2010.

A similar method of target setting is found in other plans issued on nature reserve management, such as the National Master Plan of Wildlife Protection and the Construction Project of Nature Reserves issued by the SFA in 2001, in which three stages of goals are delimited.[79]

Policy-Making for SHAs

The earliest policy making for SHAs can be dated to 1981, when the State Council approved and circulated a report by the Ministry of Construction and others.[80] The system of SHA designation and management was not established at that time. Destructive activities were not properly regulated, and the development of SHAs remained in a preliminary phase. This 1981 report proposed to designate SHAs, establish management authorities, make SHA plans and protect the natural resources of SHAs. Following this report, the State Council officially established the system of SHAs in 1982 by designating the first batch of 44 SHAs at the national level. This report also accelerated the enactment of the Interim Regulations on Administration of Scenic and Historic Areas issued by the State Council in 1985.

---

78 SEPA, 中国自然保护区发展规划纲要 (1996–2010年) (Outline of the Development Plan for Nature Reserves in China (1996–2010)), 1997.
79 SFA, 全国野生动植物保护及自然保护区建设工程总体规划 (National Master Plan of Wildlife Protection and the Construction Project of Nature Reserves), 2001. Full text is available at http://www.forestry.gov.cn/uploadfile/main/2010-11/file/2010-11-26-b2588ec7594b41f7a1a96e9990c3fd2d.pdf. Last visited January 2015.
80 State Council, 国务院批转国家城建总局等部门关于加强风景名胜保护管理工作的报告的通知 (Notice of the State Council on Approving and Circulating the Report of the State Administration of Urban Construction and Other Departments on Strengthening the Protection and Management of Scenic and Historic Areas), *Guofa* No. 38 [1981]. Full text is available at http://www.chinalawedu.com/news/1200/22016/22026/22263/2006/3/gu8537155721173600220570-0.htm. Last visited January 2015.

176 *Country Studies: China*

In 1992, the State Council circulated another report by the Ministry of Construction on SHAs.[81] Tourism had just begun to flourish in China at that time. Therefore, the construction and investment of SHAs were promoted to meet the needs arising from tourism and the opening-up of reforms in China. Following this policy, local governments promoted the development of SHAs on a broad scale. To attract investment, most local governments have engaged in an extensive campaign of transferring the operation rights of SHAs to private enterprises or individuals, and extensive construction projects within SHAs have begun to take place. The commercialization of SHAs that has arisen from these local practices has caused concern at the central level. Tension between central policies and their implementation at the local level has emerged.[82]

Unlike the ad hoc plan for nature reserves, the planning of SHAs is included in the general framework of urban-rural planning in China. Starting in 2000, the State Council, the MoHURD, the Ministry of Finance and other competent departments have issued a series of policy documents on SHA planning in the context of urban-rural planning.[83] This intensive policy making in SHA planning is mainly intended to regulate rampant construction activities, the transfer of SHA operation rights and the arbitrary change of SHA management plans occurring at the local level. These policy documents repetitively stipulate the prohibition of exploitative activities within SHAs, specify the procedures for SHA planning and provide the mechanisms for responsibility.[84]

These policy documents resulted in the enactment of the Regulations on SHAs in 2006. Most of the provisions provided in these policies were incorporated in the Regulations.

Summary

From the aforementioned law making and policy making on environmental protection in general and nature conservation in particular, some characteristics and defects can be identified.

At the legislative level, with regard to the overall environment-related legislation, a general observation by scholars is that China has established a complicated framework of environmental legislation that is relatively complete.[85] However, in spite of the broad coverage and number of statutes, China's environmental laws suffer from ineffective enforcement.

---

81 State Council, 国务院办公厅转发建设部关于加强风景名胜区工作报告的通知 (Circular of the General Office of the State Council on the Report of the Ministry of Construction on Strengthening the Work of Scenic and Historic Areas) 国务院办公厅转发建设部关于加强风景名胜区工作报告的通知), *Guobanfa* No. 50 [1992]. Full text is available at http://www.law-lib.com/law/law_view.asp?id=55150. Last visited January 2015.
82 For more details, see *infra* section 4.2 of Chapter 9.
83 State Council, 国务院办公厅关于加强和改进城乡规划工作的通知 (Notice of the General Office of the State Council on Strengthening and Improving the Work of Urban-Rural Planning), *Guobanfa* No. 25 [2000]. Full text is available at http://www.gov.cn/gongbao/content/2000/content_60113.htm; State Council, 国务院关于加强城乡规划监督管理的通知 (Notice on Strengthening the Supervision and Administration of Urban-Rural Planning), *Guofa* No. 13 [2002]. Full text is available at http://www.gov.cn/gongbao/content/2002/content_61538.htm. See also MoC et al., 关于贯彻落实《国务院关于加强城乡规划监督管理的通知》的通知 (Notice on Implementing the Notice of the State Council on Strengthening the Supervision and Administration of Urban-Rural Planning), *Jiangui* No. 204 [2002]. Full text is available at http://www.law-lib.com/law/law_view.asp?id=41223; MoC, 关于做好国家重点风景名胜区核心景区划定与保护工作的通知 (Notice on Improving the Work Affairs of Delimiting and Protecting the Core Scenic Spots of National Key Scenic and Historic Areas), *Jiancheng* No. 77 [2003]. Full text is available at http://www.china.com.cn/chinese/PI-c/320199.htm. All last visited January 2015.
84 For a discussion of these policies in details, partly see *infra* p. 192 et seq. of Chapter 9.
85 Alex Wang 'The Role of Law in Environmental Protection in China: Recent Developments', 8 (2006–07) *Vermont Journal of Environmental Law*, p. 203.

Both Chinese and foreign researchers regularly complain about the vagueness, brevity, ambiguity and lack of definition of important terminology in Chinese environmental law.[86] Alford and Shen note that China's environmental laws are more akin to policy statements than to laws in a western sense.[87] Consequently, a large amount of discretion in interpreting and applying these laws and regulations is vested in management agencies at the local level.

In the field of nature conservation, the defects of the current legislative framework are identified as follows.

First, to date, there has been no comprehensive law that covers all types of designations of PAs. Instead, the designation of PAs is quite diversified and lacks uniformity. A governing concept for PAs has not been adopted in the legislative framework. Furthermore, the legislative level of existing types of PAs is comparatively low. The enabling acts for nature reserves and SHAs are at the level of 'administrative regulation', and other types of PAs' enabling acts are below that level. Moreover, the speed of legislation is comparatively lower than the speed of establishing PAs. Therefore, PA management is not effectively regulated under a legal framework. This situation has resulted in the 'paper park syndrome'.[88]

Second, the current legislative framework is piecemeal and cannot meet the needs of PA management. The EPL is overwhelmingly focused on pollution control. Although the new EPL of 2014 has rectified this flaw to some extent, it remains challenging to attempt to rectify the long-unbalanced attention to pollution and conservation in practice, and this issue awaits an ideological change. Other laws, such as the Grassland Law and the Fishery Law, are oriented toward one specific type of resource. The concept of PA protection that is spatially and territorially integrated is not fully endorsed. Consequently, ideas such as ecosystem and biodiversity protection are not well incorporated into law. This situation is intensively reflected in wildlife protection. Flagship species, such as the giant panda, are well protected or even 'overprotected', whereas other unpopular but ecologically significant species do not have sufficient legal protection.

Third, the current legislative framework is department-dominant. This is reflected mainly in two aspects:

1   Departmental interests are the main stakes that dominate the legislative process, as reflected in the process of enacting the Natural Heritage Law. Departments are the main promoters of and active participants in the bargaining of legislation. Potential conflicts and friction between different departments have made the legislative process sluggish and the final draft a product of compromise.
2   Rule-making bodies are varied. Different departments have possessed the rule-making authority to designate and manage PAs, which has resulted in a diversified PA framework. Furthermore, these rules overlap and sometimes conflict with each other. However, the coordination mechanism is currently neither available nor sufficient.[89]

---

86 Charles McElwee, *Environmental Law in China: Mitigating Risk and Ensuring Compliance* (New York: Oxford University Press, 2011), p. 14.
87 William Alford and Yuanyuan Shen, 'Limits of the Law in Addressing China's Environmental Dilemma', 16 (1997) *Stanford Environmental Law Journal*, p. 135.
88 See *infra* p. 185 et seq. of Chapter 9.
89 For more discussion, see *infra* p. 225 et seq. of Chapter 10.

With regard to the characteristics and defects of the policy framework, one important observation is the frequent use of the policy-making instrument by the Chinese government. Because policies are more flexible and can be changed more easily compared to law making, policy making is a preferred choice. However, the heavy reliance on policies may impair the establishment of a stable and predictable legislative framework and the realization of the rule of law in China.

Fourth, in the evolution of environmental policies, a shift in focus from pollution control to equal attention to both pollution control and ecological protection can be identified, although ecological protection is still under-emphasized.[90] This situation is reflected in the allocation of funding and staffing and in the field of academic research. Most environmental lawyers, NGOs and scholars are concerned with the problem of pollution. Furthermore, public awareness of ecological protection is considerably lower than awareness of pollution problems.

Fifth, as a legacy of the period of a planned economy in China, the adoption of various plans is still used as the main instrument for policy making. Ranging from comprehensive FYPs to specific plans for nature reserves, plans have played a significant role in setting goals and guiding subsequent policy making. McElwee asserts that

> ... although China has permitted the market to control larger segments of its economy, the plan, though sporting a new name, continues to be an important tool in setting strategic goals, initiating broad reforms, and setting the targets upon which the performance of political cadres can be evaluated.[91]

The adoption of plans in China involves setting specific goals and targets, a process known as the 'target responsibility system' (目标责任制). Such targets are set by the central authority and distributed to different departments and provinces with a command-and-control nature. Moreover, most targets are set in terms of quantity instead of quality, such as a specific number and area of PA designations. This phenomenon is reflected in nearly every plan discussed above. Furthermore, in the process of planning, there is scarcely any public participation or comments. The FYP, as the most important State plan, is a State strategy with high political resolution rather than a product of sufficient public involvement and discussion.

Concerns arise about the legal basis for such plans, such as whether a plan is law, how a plan relates to law and how a plan is enforced with regard to the requirements set within it.[92] In reality, the targets set in the plans are to be followed by governments and their officials. Plans have played an equivalent role to the law. Guttman and Song even assert that 'in short, in a practical and authoritative sense the plan is law.'[93] However, the requirements in plans may be at odds with the requirements in the law or may lack comparable legal requirements. How to *legalize* planning remains a problem to be solved in China.

---

90 Cai Shouqiu and Wang Huanhuan, 改革开放30年：中国环境资源法、环境资源法学与环境资源法学教育的发展 (30 Years after the Open-up Policy: Development of Legislation on Environment and Natural Resources, Environment and Natural Resources Law and Legal Education on Environment and Natural Resource Law in China), 3 (2009) 甘肃政法学院学报 (*Journal of Gansu Institute of Political Science and Law*), pp. 1–9.
91 Charles McElwee, *supra* note 86, p. 72.
92 Dan Guttman and Song Yaqin, 'Making Central-local Relations Work: Comparing America and China. Environmental Governance Systems', 1.4 (2007) *Frontiers of Environmental Science & Engineering*, p. 423.
93 Ibid.

Sixth, the quality of the compliance with and implementation of policies is not satisfying. The previous discussion has shown that many policies that address the same issue have been enacted. This is reflected in the titles of policy documents, such as 'strengthening/further strengthening' and 'accelerating/further accelerating'. It is reasonable to doubt the effects of the enforcement of and compliance with these policies. Although insufficiencies also exist in the field of law enforcement, which will be discussed in Chapter 10, problems with the poor enforcement of policies might be worse, because most policies do not contain a clearly stated responsibility system.

9 The Formation of Conflicts in the Designation and Management of Protected Areas in China

Introduction

Due to diversified interests in the designation and management of PAs, various types of conflicts have arisen. This chapter examines the dominant forms of conflicts that arise from PA designation and management and how these conflicts formed and evolved. First, the status quo of the nature-based tourism industry and the evolution of tourism policies are discussed. Second, the chronic problem of the lack of sufficient funding for PA management is presented. Its consequences, such as the 'paper park syndrome', which means that parks only exist on paper, not in practice, and the 'ticket economy', which means that PA funding predominantly relies on the collection of entrance fees, are also discussed.

Based on these contexts, the most prominent forms of conflicts in PA management are examined. Conflicts between economic development and nature conservation are still fierce, as reflected in the construction of large-scale projects. The commercialization and industrialization of tourism have intensified the tension between the tourism industry and PA conservation. The resulting problems are reflected in the following three areas. First, the epidemic of the large-scale transfer of the operation rights of PAs has caused the de facto abdication of governments' management power over PAs. Second, as a result of private investment in PA operation, the construction of tourist facilities and amenities has become pervasive, and some of this construction has changed the natural landscape and derogated the ecosystem. Third, due to the lack of supervision and control, PAs have become a breeding ground for corruption and rent seeking. Finally, the 'development conflicts' between local communities and nature conservation are addressed.

The Flourishing Tourism Industry: Status Quo and Policies

Along with increases in the levels of income and leisure time, recreational demands have increased among citizens. As a result, since the 2000s, China has witnessed a flourishing tourism industry that constitutes a critical part of the Chinese economy. Nature-based tourism has also gained momentum across different types of PAs. In addition to its economic impacts, tourism has gradually had a social and environmental influence. Policy making is accordingly directed toward realizing sustainability in tourism development.

Prosperity of the Market of Nature-based Tourism

The success of the tourism industry mirrors the timeframe when China witnessed a rise in market force due to its 'opening up' policies. Both tourism revenue and the number of tourists have experienced stable growth since the 2000s. The tendency toward growth has become more apparent since the 2010s.[1] Figure 9.1 shows that tourism revenue has become an important component of China's GDP. This percentage has remained above 3.7 percent in the most recent decade and increased to 5.19 percent in 2013.

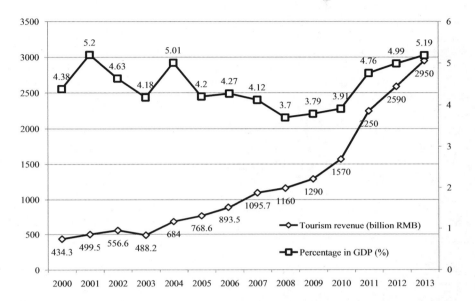

Figure 9.1 Tourism revenues and their percentage of GDP in China (2000–13)
Source: State Tourism Administration[2]

Nature-based tourism has seen corresponding growth. According to a survey conducted in 2011, among the 1,110 PA samples, 1,033 PAs were open for nature-based tourism, which accounted for 93 percent of the total number of PAs. The highest rate of increase occurred during the 1990s: 210 new PAs were opened to tourism, an increase of 156 percent compared to the 1980s.[3]

It is noteworthy that differences exist between the US and China in terms of their domestic tourism markets. These differences may result in different recreational policies and the main forms of conflict in PA management.

First, with regard to the components and purpose of visitors, most Chinese visitors travel to scenic spots for sightseeing.[4] Their preference for visiting destinations with well-constructed

1 For more details, see State Statistics Bureau, 国民经济和社会发展统计公报 (1979–2014) (Statistical Bulletin for National Economy and Social Development of PRC (1979–2014)), available at http://www.stats.gov.cn/tjsj/tjgb/ndtjgb/. Last visited January 2015.
2 State Tourism Administration, 中国旅游业统计公报 (2001–13) (Statistics Bulletin of Tourism Industry in China (2001–13)). Available at http://www.cnta.gov.cn/html/zh/index.html. Last visited January 2015. The figures of the year of 2000 in the table is calculated based on the figures of 2001.
3 Zhong Linsheng and Wang Jing, 我国保护地生态旅游发展现状调查分析 (Investigation and Analysis of the Situation of Ecotourism Development in Protected Areas of China), 31,24 (2011) 生态学报 (*Acta Ecologica Sinica*), p. 7, 452.
4 China Tourism Academy, 中国休闲旅游客户需求趋势研究 (Research on the Tendency of Recreational Customer Demands in China), March 2012. Summary of the research is available at http://www.ctaweb.org/html/2012–4/2012–4–13–11–34–48207.html. Last visited January 2015. The research shows that among

tourist facilities and the provision of convenient tourist services is unlike the pursuit of a wilderness experience in harsh natural conditions amongst recreational travelers within the US. Moreover, most Chinese recreational visitors are young and well educated,[5] in contrast to the 'elitism' of national park visitation in the US. Therefore, the NPS's recent efforts to attract younger generations to national parks do not suit the Chinese context.

Second, automobile use in China is not as popular as it is in the US. Self-driving tours were gradually popularized until the most recent decade. However, data show an increasing rate of motorized visitors to nature areas.[6] In 2012, there were 1.4 billion tourist visits in self-driving tours, accounting for 48 percent of the total number of tourist visits in 2012.[7] In 2013, sponsored by the State Tourism Administration (STA), the first official report with a particular focus on self-driving tourism was issued.[8] Statistics show that in 2012, there were 0.14 billion privately owned cars, 0.2 billion people with driver's licenses and more than 15,000 car clubs and motorcycle associations in China.[9] These figures indicate great potential for the motorized tourism market. The emergence of self-driving tourism is a symbol of the shift from 'sightseeing tourism' (观光旅游) to 'recreational tourism' (休闲旅游) in China.[10]

Third, similar to the trend in the US, new recreational forms are flowering in China, such as yachting, kayaking and the use of personal watercraft. This change accompanies a continuous increase in Chinese billionaires. For example, Hainan Province aims to promote high-end tourism products, such as personal aircrafts and watercrafts, to the super-rich. Some local governments spare no effort in promoting special products, particularly to serve the needs of these people, which has caused potential conflicts between private interests and public interests.[11]

Finally, with the advent of mass tourism, the enormous number of visitors has become a continuous challenge for tourism management. This problem has also perplexed park managers elsewhere. However, unlike in the US, due to the unsoundness of the system of paid annual vacations in China, the number of outdoor visitors has increased dramatically during several particular periods of public holidays. In the period October 1–7, 2014, there were

---

domestic individual visitors, 43.89 percent of them go for sightseeing, and 38.56 percent of them go for recreation and vacation. Among domestic group visitors, 47.03 percent of them go for sightseeing and 39.4 percent of them go for recreation and vacation.

5 See the research by China Tourism Academy, ibid.; see also Jin Xiaoqian, 我国休闲旅游者呈年轻化高学历特征 (Characteristics of Recreational Visitors: Young and Well-educated), March 15, 2012. Available at http://www.chinadaily.com.cn/hqcj/2012-03/15/content_14842023.htm. Last visited January 2015.
6 During the 'Golden Week' of the National Day holiday (October 1–7) in 2013, the SHA of Yueyanglou in Hunan Province received nearly 5,000 private motorized vehicles per day. The SHA of Wudang Mountain in Hubei Province received 12,700 private motor vehicles on October 3, 2013 alone. See China Tourism Academy, 中国区域旅游发展年度报告 (2013–14) (Annual Report of the Development of Regional Tourism in China (2013–14)), 2014. Available at http://www.ctaweb.org/html/2014–3/2014-3-31-8-18-21839.html. Last visited January 2015.
7 Liu Yang, 数据表明：中国2012年共有14亿2千人次选择自驾游 (Data Shows That There are in Total 1.4 Billion and 2,000 People Choosing Self-driving Tours in 2012 in China), May 24, 2013. Available at http://www.scopsr.gov.cn/whsh/mtjj/jklyms/ly/201305/t20130524_222732.html. Last visited January 2015.
8 China Tourism Automobile and Cruise Association and Tourism Research Center of Chinese Academy of Social Science, 中国自驾游发展报告 (Report on the Development of Self-driving Tourism in China), 2013.
9 Sun Changsheng, 中国自驾游发展趋势分析–暨自驾游数据简报 (Analysis of the Development Tendency of Self-driving Tourism in China-Brief Report of the Data of Self-driving Tourism), August 1, 2012. Available at http://blog.sina.com.cn/-s/blog_50a10c5c01019ikx.html. Last visited January 2015.
10 Liu Yang, *supra* note 7.
11 For details, see *infra* pp. 204–5.

31.69 million outdoor tourists.[12] This situation has caused concentrated and high-intensity derogation of the natural environment and scenic landscape.

From Tourism to Sustainable Tourism and Ecotourism: The Evolution of Policies

During the Mao period, tourism was politicized by receiving foreign diplomats and politicians. There were two main goals of tourism in this period: one was to increase the political influence of China, and the other was to earn revenues through foreign exchange.[13] The 'civilianization' and growth of the tourism industry only began in the post-Mao period.

Beginning with the Decision of the State Council on Strengthening the Work of Tourism issued in 1981,[14] the State Council has issued or co-issued a series of policy documents to promote the development of the tourism industry. The status of the tourism industry within the national economy has experienced a gradual increase from an 'important part of the tertiary industry'[15] to a 'new growth point of the national economy' (国民经济新的增长点)[16] to the current 'pillar industry' (支柱产业). In 2009, the State Council issued the Opinions of the State Council on Accelerating the Development of the Tourism Industry (the Opinions).[17] In the Opinions, the tourism industry was endowed with a dual status for the first time as a 'strategic pillar industry of the national economy' (国民经济的战略性支柱产业) and a 'modern service industry.'

In terms of the first status, the previous discussion shows that tourism revenue accounted for up to 5.19 percent of the nation's GDP in 2013. At the local level, until 2011, 27 of the 32 mainland provinces regarded the tourism industry as a pillar industry.[18] In terms of the second status, the role of tourism in providing public services in addition to boosting the national economy has been gradually recognized in policies.[19] As of 2004, the foreign exchange reserve of China reached US$610 billion, ranking the third largest in the world.[20] The percentage of foreign exchange from tourism in terms of the total foreign exchange

---

12 STA, 2014 年国庆假期假日旅游统计报告 (Statistic Report on Vocation Tourism during the National Holiday of 2014), October 8, 2014, available at http://www.cnta.gov.cn/html/2014-10/2014-10-8-16-47-45550.htmlhttp://www.cnta.gov.cn/html/2013-10/2013-10-8-%7B@hur%7D-37–44611.html. Last visited January 2015.

13 Du Jiang, 论中国旅游产业功能与产业政策的转变 (Analysis on the Transformation of the Function and Industrial Policy of Tourism in China), 5 (2005) 北京第二外国语学院学报 (*Journal of Beijing International Studies University*), p. 1.

14 State Council, 国务院关于加强旅游工作的决定 (Decision of the State Council on Strengthening the Work of Tourism), 1981.

15 Central Committee of the Communist Party of China & State Council, 中共中央、国务院关于加快发展第三产业的决定 (Decisions on Accelerating the Tertiary Industry), June 16, 1992. Full text is available at http://news.xinhuanet.com/ziliao/2005-02/17/content_2586400.htm. Last visited January 2015.

16 State Council, 国务院关于进一步加快旅游业发展的通知 (Announcement of the State Council on Further Accelerating the Development of Tourism Industry), *Guofa* No. 9 [2001]. Full text is available at http://www.gov.cn/gongbao/content/2001/content_60814.htm. Last visited January 2015.

17 State Council, 国务院关于加快发展旅游业的意见 (Opinions of the State Council on Accelerating the Development of the Tourism Industry), Guofa No. 41 [2009]. Full text is available at http://www.gov.cn/zwgk/2009-12/03/content_1479523.htm. Last visited January 2015.

18 Ban Ruochuan, 中国27省区市提出把旅游业发展为战略性支柱产业 (27 Provinces, Regions and Cities Propose to Develop Tourism Industry as a Strategic Pillar Industry), October 27, 2011. Available at http://www.china.com.cn/travel/txt/2011-10/27/content_23744833.htm. Last visited January 2015.

19 Tourism as part of the service industry was specifically addressed in the eleventh and twelfth FYPs. It is further underpinned by the STA in 2007. See STA, 关于进一步促进旅游业发展的意见 (Opinions on Further Improving the Development of the Tourism Industry), 2007.

20 Du Jiang, *supra note* 13, p. 3.

reserve decreased from 53.45 percent in 1979 to 4.22 percent in 2004.[21] In this context, the political function of tourism has faded, and the public service function of tourism has been highlighted.

In 2013, the State Council further issued the Outline of Civilian Tourism and Recreation (2013–20) (the Outline).[22] This was the first policy document with a specific focus on recreation instead of the previous focus on the tourism industry in policy making. The Outline emphasized the general interest embodied in public parks and encouraged the construction of infrastructure in scenic areas. It recommended several measures to promote tourism and recreation, such as guaranteeing employees' rights to vacation with pay, improving the quality and the public service of recreational use, improving infrastructure construction, and diversifying recreational products. The shift from tourism to civilian recreation indicates that the social effects of tourism, such as the equitable distribution of recreational opportunities, are taken into consideration in policy making.

In addition to the growing importance of tourism in the country's economic blueprint, the importance of nature protection and sustainable tourism is gaining increasing acknowledgment. The need for a balance between the development of tourism resources and the protection of nature is increasingly recognized in a series of policy documents.[23] Requirements have been established to include environmental protection in tourism planning, monitor environmental management within scenic spots and control pollution.[24] Measures such as coordination between different departments, the formulation of a social evaluation system for tourism plans, and the normalization of the development of tourism resources have been proposed.[25]

The related concept of ecotourism has also emerged in policy making. In 2008, the STA and the MoEP co-issued the National Outline of the Development of Ecotourism (2008–15).[26] Ecotourism refers to tourism based on ecological scenic resources within nature reserves, SHAs, or forest parks. Four basic principles were established for the development of ecotourism: strict protection, differentiated policies based on local conditions, the coordination and participation of stakeholders and the promotion of key pilot projects. The Outline also established requirements for the management of ecotourism-related scenic spots, such as the prohibition of destructive activities, the restoration of the ecosystem, the staggered opening of key tourist spots and key tourist routes, the development of a scientific zoning system and pollution control.

However, scholars have noted that the Chinese concept of 'ecotourism' (生态旅游) differs from the concept promoted in the West.[27] In most cases, ecotourism is understood as a tourism

---

21 Ibid., p. 4.
22 State Council, 国民旅游休闲纲要(2013–20年) (Outline of Civilian Tourism and Recreation (2013–20)), Guobanfa No. 10 [2013]. Full text is available at http://www.gov.cn/zwgk/2013-02/18/content_2333544.htm. Last visited January 2015.
23 STA and SEPA, 关于进一步加强旅游生态环境保护工作的通知 (Notice on Further Strengthening the Work of Tourist Ecological Environment Protection), Lvjicaifa No. 5 [2005]. Full text is available at http://www.mep.gov.cn/gkml/hbb/gwy/200910/t20091030_180689.htm. Last visited January 2015. See also STA, 2007, *supra* note 19.
24 STA and SEPA, ibid.
25 Shao Qiwei (Director of the STA), 国务院关于旅游业发展工作情况的报告 (Report of the State Council on the Development of Tourism Industry to the SCNPC), December 28, 2011. Available at http://www.npc.gov.cn/huiyi/ztbg/gylyygzqkbg/2011-12/28/content_1685797.htm. Last visited January 2015.
26 STA and MoEP, 全国生态旅游发展纲要 (2008–15) (National Outline of the Development of Ecotourism (2008–15)), Lvfa No. 61 [2008]. Full text is available at http://www.qhepb.gov.cn/hjgl/zrst/stbh/201003/t20100331_11815.html. Last visited January 2015.
27 Trevor Sofield and Fung Mei Sarah Li, 'China: Ecotourism and Cultural Tourism: Harmony or Dissonance?', in James Higham (ed.), *Critical Issues in Ecotourism: Understanding a Complex Tourism Phenomenon* (Amsterdam: Elsevier, Butterworth Heinemann, 2007), pp. 368–85.

product, namely, tourism activities based on an amenable ecological environment. This is very different from the understanding of ecotourism as a development idea. Sofield and Li note that in China, any tourism activity that is located in a natural setting is deemed ecotourism regardless of whether it is delivered in an environmentally, economically and socially sustainable way.[28]

The latest policy issued by the State Council in 2014[29] in response to the Decisions issued by the CPC[30] and the enactment of the Tourism Law in 2013 proposed the idea of 'scientific tourism development' (科学旅游观), which emphasized the realization of sustainability in tourism. It set the schedule for tourism development, with the establishment of 'national parks' scheduled for the end of 2015.

The Funding Structure of PAs and Its Consequences for Tourism Management

As in other developing countries, PA management in China is burdened by a shortage of funds. Therefore, the 'paper park syndrome' and the 'ticket economy' that the shortage has produced have become the most chronic problems and the greatest barriers to sustainable tourism in China.

The 'Paper Park Syndrome' and the Shortage of Government Funding

The number of PAs has grown in China since the 1990s. However, the designation of PAs lacks sufficient funding and effective management. Therefore, the 'paper park syndrome' has emerged.[31] According to an announcement issued by the State Council in 1998, it was estimated that 'at least one-third of the nature reserves have "three withouts" (without a management agency, without staff and without recurrent funding)' in China.[32] James Harness observed that 'the rapid growth of China's nature reserve system during the 1980s was not accompanied by a commensurate increase in state financial support for conservation.'[33]

The problem of funding shortfalls for PAs is chronic in China. Most PAs must 'fund themselves by themselves' (以区养区).[34] A cost-neutral approach is adopted in PA management, which means that managers must generate revenue to cover management costs through the collection of entry fees, concessions and the commercial operation of PAs.

PA funding in China is considerably lower than in other countries. According to two surveys conducted by the World Conservation Monitoring Center (WCMC) in 1993 and 1995, the average budget for PAs is US$893 per square kilometer, whereas the average PA budget

28 Ibid.
29 State Council, 国务院关于促进旅游业改革发展的若干意见 (Several Opinions of the State Council on Promoting the Reform and Development of Tourism), August 21, 2014, *Guofa* No. 31 [2014].
30 Central Committee of the Communist Party of China (CCCPC), 中共中央关于全面深化改革若干重大问题的决定 (Decisions of the CCCPC on Several Major Issues Concerning Comprehensively Deepening Reforms), November 12, 2013.
31 Guangyu Wang et al., 'National Park Development in China: Conservation or Commercialization?', 41 (2012) *AMBIO*, p. 248; James Harkness, 'Recent Trends in Forestry and Conservation of Biodiversity in China', 156 (1998) *The China Quarterly (Special Issue: China's Environment)*, p.918, and C.Y. Jim and Steve S.W. Xu, 'Recent Protected-Area Designation in China: An Evaluation of Administrative and Statutory Procedures', 170.1 (2004) *The Geographical Journal*, pp. 39–50.
32 State Council, 国务院办公厅关于进一步加强自然保护区管理工作的通知 (Announcement of the State Council on Further Strengthening the Management of Nature Reserves), *Guobanfa* No. 111 [1998].
33 James Harkness, *supra* note 31, p. 917.
34 Zuo Keyan, 'Management of Marine Nature Reserves in China: A Legal Perspective', 6.3 (2003) *Journal of International Wildlife Law & Policy*, p. 197.

in developed countries is US$2,058 and in developing countries is US$157.[35] According to a survey conducted in China based on 85 samples of nature reserves in 1999, the average funding for PAs was US$52.7 per square kilometer (including both national funding and self-generated income). The average funding for 46 nature reserves at the national level was US$113.1 per square kilometer.[36] Though comparative samples and methods may differ between studies, it can be observed that PA funding in China is considerably lower than the global average and even lower than PA funding in developing countries.

Table 9.1 Comparison of the average PA budget in selected countries

Country	Average PA budget (1996 US$ per km²)	Year of survey
US	2,560	1993
Canada	1,104	1991
Netherlands	9,775	1996
France	2,531	1993
United Kingdom	3,217	1995
Brazil	224	1995
India	277	1994
China	52.7 (all nature reserves)	1999
	113.1 (nature reserves at the national level)	

Source: Alexander James et al., 1999 and Han Nianyong, 2000[37]

Because there is no recent survey on this issue in China, the data used in this table are not up to date. China has not established a formal budgetary channel for supporting nature reserves.[38] Therefore, government funding is not allocated on a regular basis. This causes difficulties in scholarly research in ascertaining the degree of funding shortfalls in practice. Furthermore, accurate information on the amount of funding for each nature reserve is not publicly available.

Some sources show that state financial support for PAs has increased since the 2000s. This increase has mainly been achieved through ad hoc funding programs and projects, such as the Six Key Forestry Projects (六大林业重点工程) launched in 2001. One of these six projects is the project of 'wildlife protection and the construction of nature reserves'. The funding for this project reached US$62.87 million (2006 rate) in 2005, which indicates an average budget increase of US$41.93 per square kilometer.[39] Furthermore, since 2011, the central government

---

35 Alexander James, Michael Green and James Paine, *A Global Review of Protected Area Budgets and Staffing* (Cambridge: WCMC-World Conservation Press, 1999), p. V. Full text is available at https://www.cbd.int/financial/expenditure/g-spendingglobal-wcmc.pdf. Last visited January 2015. The survey covers 600 PAs in 108 countries around the world. However, the data of China was insufficient so that it was not included in this survey.
36 This survey was sponsored by the Chinese National Committee for Man and Biosphere Programme, the UNESCO and the Canadian International Development Agency in 1999. See Han Nianyong, 中国自然保护区可持续管理政策研究 (Research on the Policies of the Scientific Management of Nature Reserves in China), 15.3 (2000) 自然资源学报 *(Journal of Natural Resources)*, pp. 201–7.
37 Alexander James et al., *supra* note 35, pp. 5–7; Han Nianyong, ibid., p. 202. The data of the US provided by the WCMA survey is based on two federal agencies, i.e. the NPS and the FWS.
38 Li Jingwen, Cui Guofa and Li Junqing, 'Income and Managing Problems of the Protected Areas in China', 12.3 (2001) *Journal of Forestry Research*, p. 197.
39 The project funding on nature reserves in 2005 was 515 million RMB and the total area of nature reserves in that year was 1,499,490 square kilometers. The average exchange rate between USD and RMB was 8.1917 in 2006. See SFA, 六大林业重点工程建设统计公报 (2001–05) (Statistic Bulletin of the Construction

has allocated ad hoc transfer payments in the National Primary Ecological Function Zone to compensate those areas listed as prohibited or restricted exploitation zones, most of which are designated as PAs.

A recent study in 2011 also supports the notion that the deficiency in funding for nature reserves has been gradually alleviated.[40] The authors show that the total investment in nature reserves at the national level reached US$550 per square kilometer in 2009. Compared to US$113.1 per square kilometer in 1999, as shown in Table 9.1 above, the total investment in nature reserves at the national level increased by a factor of 2.3.[41] The report concludes that 65 percent of nature reserves at the national level received sufficient funding to cover their expenditures.[42] This result is not particularly satisfying considering that it only refers to nature reserves at the national level. The situation of reserves designated at the local level might be even worse.

Because central funding only accounts for a limited portion of the overall funding structure, a large part of funding for nature reserves must be supported by local financing. Local funding differs significantly from one area to another due to the different levels of development in different provinces and areas. According to a survey conducted in 1998, the Lingdingfutian Nature Reserve at the National Level received 2.9 million RMB from Guangdong Province, whereas the Maolan Nature Reserve at the National Level only received 280,000 RMB from Guizhou Province.[43]

How much money is really needed for the management of nature reserves? How huge is the gap? A rough estimation by the State Environmental Protection Agency (SEPA) shows that during the 2001–10 period, the total funds needed amounted to approximately 445 million RMB per year.[44] Other researchers have presented different estimations. Ma Zhong estimates that 1 billion RMB are needed per year to protect nature reserves at the national level, which is ten times the current amount of funding allocated for nature reserves.[45] Xie Yan and her research group estimate that at least 26 billion RMB are needed per year to guarantee ecological safety.[46] These results differ substantially. However, even if we ambitiously consider the highest amount (i.e. 26 billion RMB), it only accounts for less than 0.21 percent of the overall outlay in 2012.[47] Compared to the outlay for education, which accounts

---

of the Six Key Forestry Projects (2001–05)). Available at http://www.forestry.gov.cn/CommonAction.do?dispatch=index&colid=67. Last visited January 2015. The figures are no longer provided in the Bulletins issued by the SFA since 2006.

40 Li Yanbo et al., 'Current Status and Recent Trends in Financing China's Nature Reserves', 158 (2013) *Biological Conservation*, pp. 296–300.
41 The authors convert the data of 1999 to 1999 RMB and then adjust it to 2009 RMB as a benchmark for comparison to avoid the inaccuracies resulted from fluctuating exchange rate. See ibid., p. 298.
42 Ibid., p. 296.
43 Xu Haigen, 中国自然保护区经费政策探讨 (Discussion on the Funding Policy of Nature Reserves in China), 17.1 (2001) 农村生态环境 (*Rural Ecological Environment*), p. 14.
44 SEPA, 中国自然保护区发展规划纲要 (1996–2010年) (Outline of the Development Plan for Nature Reserves in China (1996–2010)), 1997.
45 Zhang Ke, 报告称守住生态安全底线每年需投入260亿 (Report Reveals that 26 Billion RMB is Needed per Year to Defend the Bottom Line of Ecological Safety), in 第一财经日报 (*China Business News*), November 9, 2012. Available at http://finance.qq.com/a/20121109/000350.htm. Last visited January 2015.
46 Ibid.
47 C.f. Shown in Figure 5.4, in recent years, the percentage of the NPS budget in terms of the federal outlay is between around 0.08 percent and 0.1 percent. In China, the estimation of 26 billion covers every aspect of ecological protection in which PA funding only accounts for a very limited part. The overall outlay in 2012 was 125,71 billion RMB in China. See Ministry of Finance, 2012 年财政收支情况 (Financial Revenue and Expenditure in 2012). Available at http://gks.mof.gov.cn/zhengfuxinxi/tongjishuju/201301/t20130122_729462.html. Last visited January 2015.

for more than 16.8 percent of the overall outlay, such a small amount of investment is not extravagantly beyond the nation's capacity. Thus, nature conservation still ranks considerably low on the nation's agenda of expenditures.

Comparing the figures between China and the US, a fundamental gap can be seen. The NPS receives its budget from the federal government up to approximately US$3,000 million per year (see Figure 5.4). Compared to the US, national funding in China seems trivial. This difference causes not only quantitative consequences but also qualitative ones, which are reflected in the operation structure of PAs and the resulting phenomenon of the 'ticket economy'.

Consequences of Funding Shortfalls: The Self-Funding Model and the Ticket Economy

Because most Chinese PAs must fund themselves with self-generated income, the commercial operation of PAs becomes unavoidable. Paul Mozur provided an example of the Datian National Nature Reserve in Hainan Province. Datian is famous for the endangered species it protects, the Eld's deer. Without sufficient funding to repopulate the deer, the reserve slaughtered a percentage of the deer to make blood wine, which was deemed a valuable medicine for the cure of diseases, and it sold this wine in stores on the reserve for a price of 100 RMB per bottle. Mozur indicated that there was an increase in deer harvesting as a result of the lack of the establishment of an adequate quota system.[48]

The phenomenon of the 'ticket economy' is prevalent. Based on a survey conducted in 1998 that included a sample of 77 nature reserves, Table 9.2 presents the main sources of income for nature reserves in China. From this table, it is clear that tourism services and resource exploitation account for a predominant percentage of the total income. Within the income of tourism services, income from tickets accounts for 82.72 percent. Local governments largely rely on selling entrance tickets to visitors to support PA management and to stimulate the local economy. This is directly reflected in the increase in entrance fees of scenic spots in recent years, which have stirred public outcry.[49] It has been calculated that one would need to spend 22,536 RMB to visit all 136 scenic spots in China certified at the AAAAA level.[50] This means that a Chinese resident would have to spend nearly eight months' income to visit all of these 5A scenic spots.[51]

Table 9.2 Sources of income in nature reserves and their respective percentages

Sources of income	Income (10,000 RMB)	Percentage (%)
Planting industry	1.95	4.41
Breeding industry	1.45	3.28
Tourism services	24.01	56.24
• Tickets	20.59	46.52
• Accommodation	3.42	7.73

48 Paul Mozur, 'Preserving China's Reserves', 171.2 (2008) *Far Eastern Economic Review*, p. 78.
49 Hexun News, 景区门票涨价：看不起的风景 (Increasing Entrance Fees: Unaffordable Scenery), 2012. Available at http://news.hexun.com/2012/jqmp/. Last visited January 2015.
50 Kuang Zhida and Fu Ying, 玩遍国内5A景区门票要花19085元 (You Must Spend 19,085 RMB to Enter All the 5A Scenic Spots), in 武汉晚报 (*Wuhan Evening News*), October 9, 2012, available at http://politics.people.com.cn/n/2012/1008/c1001-19184058.html. Last visited January 2015.
51 According to the World Bank, the Gross National Income per capita of China in 2012 was US$5,740. See World Bank, 'GNI per Capita, Atlas Method (Current US$)'. Available at http://data.worldbank.org/indicator/NY.GNP.PCAP.CD. Last visited January 2015.

Table 9.2 (continued)

Industrial production	1.48	3.34
Resource exploitation	10.19	23.02
• Sale of wood fallen from wind, dead woods and rotten woods	3.21	7.25
• Forest wood thinning	5.94	13.42
• Electricity fee from hydropower station	0.29	0.66
• Exploitation of mineral resources	0.20	0.45
• Other	0.55	1.24
• Resources compensation fee	5.18	11.70
Total	**44.26**	**100**

Source: Xu Haigen, 2001[52]

A survey conducted in 2000 provided similar findings. According to Han, self-generated income accounted for a considerable percentage of the total income of nature reserves. Based on a survey of 81 nature reserves in China, an overview of self-generated income and its percentage of total income is shown in Table 9.3.

Table 9.3 Overview of the self-generated income of nature reserves and its percentage of total income

Self-generated income/ total income (%)	Nature reserves at the national level		Nature reserves at all levels	
	Number	Percentage (%)	Number	Percentage (%)
0	9	17.3	14	17.3
1–20	12	23.1	19	23.5
21–40	11	21.2	14	17.3
41–60	10	19.2	13	16.1
61–80	7	13.5	6	7.4
81–100	3	5.7	15	18.5
Sum	**52**	**100.0**	**81**	**100.0**

Source: Han Nianyong, 2000[53]

Conflicts between Conservation and Recreation in PAs: Contexts, Origins and Formats

Conflicts between exploitative use and nature conservation remain paramount in PA management. These conflicts are reflected in various types of large-scale projects conducted within PAs. Moreover, the commercialization and industrialization of tourism have resulted in intense conflicts between the recreational use and conservation of PAs, as demonstrated by the involvement of the business sector in PA management, the construction of tourist amenities and the abusive use of administrative power in tourism development. Unlike the US, a particular type of conflict in China is that between nature conservation and local communities' livelihoods. This section discusses these types of conflicts, including their contexts, origins and formats.

Economic Development vs. Nature Conservation

Large-scale construction projects and the exploitation of natural resources have been and continue to be main contributors to China's rapid GDP growth. Although the significance of environmental protection has been gradually acknowledged, it occasionally conflicts with the

---

52 Xu Haigen, *supra* note 43, p. 15.
53 Han Nianyong, *supra* note 36, p. 203.

need for continuous economic growth. It has been noted that 'when real or perceived conflicts between economic development and the enforcement of environmental laws and regulations arose, economic development won.'[54] It is usually the case that nature is sacrificed to pave the road for economic development. Several examples can illustrate this phenomenon.

The first example is rapid urbanization. According to the strategy of 'Great Western Development' proposed since the 2000s, western China, whose ecologically sensitive areas used to be well protected, has been intensively reshaped.[55] Existing cities have expanded, and new cities have been created out of nowhere. For example, in 2012, the largest 'mountain-moving project' occurred in Gansu Province. An investment company was expected to spend up to 20 billion RMB to flatten 700 mountains in the area of Lanzhou, the capital city of Gansu Province, to build a new metropolis on the outskirts of the city. Critics argued that this project was unsuitable because Lanzhou is one of China's most chronically water-scarce cities.[56] However, because this project was sponsored by the State Council, such a large-scale transformation of the landscape obtained a free pass from public scrutiny and proceeded.[57]

The second example is damming activities. It is predicted that in 2022, there will be more than thirty dams constructed along the Yangtze River, with installed capacities four times that of the Three Gorges Dam.[58] Large-scale damming activities have raised concerns among environmental experts because the upstream watershed of the Yangtze River is a critical area of biodiversity and ecological protection. In practice, it is not unusual for the construction of dams to commence even before they are approved. For example, operators of the Xiangjiaba and Xiluodu Dams were punished by the SEPA in 2005 due to the lack of approval before the construction work started. In 2009, two dams began damming activities before they submitted documents for the environment impact assessment (EIA).[59] Though the MoEP issued injunctions for more than thirty dams on the Yangtze River at the beginning of 2005, which was labeled an 'unprecedented EIA storm', all suspended dams resumed their construction after paying a small penalty.[60] With pressure from the business sector and local governments, the MoEP currently faces a dilemma. The EIA is not as powerful as it

---

54 Charles McElwee, *Environmental Law in China: Mitigating Risk and Ensuring Compliance* (New York: Oxford University Press, 2011), p. 6.
55 For a discussion of the environmental effects of urbanization, see Li Bo, 高速城市化的环境代价与发展路径 (The Environmental Cost of Overheated Urbanization), in Friends of Nature, 中国环境发展报告 (2013) (*Annual Report on the Environmental Development of China (2013)*) (Beijing: Social Sciences Academic Press, 2013), pp. 1–23.
56 See Jonathan Kaiman, 'China to Flatten 700 Mountains for New Metropolis in the Desert', December 6, 2012, available at http://www.guardian.co.uk/world/2012/dec/06/china-flatten-mountain-lanzhou-new-area. Last visited January 2015.
57 Lanzhou New Zone (兰州新区) was the fifth 'New Zone at the National Level' approved by the State Council. See State Council, 国务院关于同意设立兰州新区的批复 (Approval and Reply of the State Council on Establishing the Lanzhou New Zone), August 20, 2012, *Guohan* No. 104 [2012]. Though this 'mountain-moving project' has incurred public criticism, the latest relevant media report in 2013 showed that this project was still proceeding then. Further information of this project is not available online.
58 Bao Zhiheng, 长江上游水电开发再现危局 (Hydropower Development Crisis in the Upstream of the Yangtze River), in Friends of Nature, 中国环境发展报告(2013) (*Annual Report on Environment Development of China (2013)*) (Beijing: Social Sciences Academic Press, 2013), p. 48.
59 Liu Shixin, 长江流域水电站陈旧规划如何变脸 (How could the Old Planning Document for the Dams in the Yangtze River Refresh Itself?), in 中国青年报 (*China Youth Daily*), June 15, 2009. Available at http://zqb.cyol.com/content/2009-06/15/content_2710376.htm. Last visited January 2015.
60 Meng Dengke, 环保复苏：金沙江水电站违规调查 (Revival of Environmental Protection: Investigation into the Illegal Behaviors of Hydropower Stations on the Jinshajiang River), in 南方周末(*Southern Weekly*), September 29, 2010. Available at http://www.infzm.com/content/30217. Last visited January 2015.

is supposed to be, and it sometimes becomes a shield for local governments to justify their development activities.[61]

Some appalling cases have been disclosed in the media. In early 2014, the illegal construction of a dam and hydropower station in a nationally designated poor county in Shaanxi Province was publicized. The construction project was not based on the EIA or on the examination and approval procedures from higher authorities. It was revealed that the planned inundated area covers the territory of a National Wetland Park inhabited by quite a few endangered species. The primary purpose of this project is not to generate electricity but to create human-made and dam-based scenery to facilitate the creation of a 'waterscape city' and the construction of water-based recreational facilities.[62]

The third example is the construction of transportation infrastructure. The density of railroads and freeways is an important indicator of the fragmentation of wildlife habitats and ecological systems. The density of freeways has experienced a steady increase since 1989 and a sharp increase since the 2000s. This is the same case with railroads. Due to the large-scale construction of freeways and railroads in China, the fragmentation of habitats and ecosystems is exacerbated. In its National Report on the Implementation of the Convention of Biodiversity, the MoEP claims that the Chinese government 'made every effort to keep railways and highways away from sensitive areas such as nature reserves and took measures to lower their environmental impacts'.[63] This may be true for the construction of some symbolic railroads with national significance, such as the Qinghai-Tibet railways. However, suspicion can be raised regarding the effects of the implementation of transportation infrastructure projects at the local level.[64]

The fourth example is the exploitation of mineral resources and oil and gas drilling. The exploitative use of nature resources remains a main engine of the Chinese economy. In 2012, 227 new large- and medium-sized mining sites were built. In 2013, another 67 sites were mined, and 1,337 mine-prospecting rights priced at 1.378 billion RMB and 1,962 mining rights priced at 5.289 billion RMB were transferred.[65] Although mining activities are strictly regulated inside PAs, there are still gaps in terms of their implementation. Mining activities inside PAs are occasionally disclosed in the media.[66] Furthermore, to facilitate road construction and the exploitation of natural resources in nature reserves, some local governments have adjusted the boundaries of nature reserves, making way for highways and mining sites. This phenomenon has become commonplace across China. To cope with this situation, the central government has issued a series of regulations to curb the rampant adjustment of nature reserves.[67]

61 Gong Gu, "环评风暴"的制度困境解析–以水电项目为例 (Analysis on the Institutional Dilemma of the 'EIA Storm': The Example of Hydro-electric Projects), 6 (2009) 法商研究 (*Studies in Law and Business*), pp. 122–30.
62 Chen Xingwang, 陕西国家贫困县为拦河造景花亿元建水电站 (A Nationally Designated Poor County in Shaanxi Province Spent Millions of Dollars to Build a Hydropower Station for Creating Human-made and Dam-based Scenery), in 东方早报 (*Oriental Morning Post*), May 8, 2014. Available at http://news.163.com/14/0508/08/9RN89R4800014AED.html. Last visited January 2015.
63 MoEP, 'China's Fourth National Report on the Implementation of the Convention on Biological Diversity', November 2008, p. 58. Full text is available at https://www.cbd.int/doc/world/cn/cn-nr-04-en.pdf. Last visited January 2015.
64 The gap between central policies and their implementation at the local level is commonplace in China. For more discussion on the enforcement of PA law in China, see *infra* p. 219 et seq. of Chapter 10.
65 Zong He, 全国新增大中型矿产地同比缩减七成 (The Number of Newly Added Large and Medium Sized Mining Sites Decreases to 30 Percent of Last Year's Total), in 中国矿业报 (*Chinese Mining News*), February 12, 2014. Available at http://app.chinamining.com.cn/Newspaper/E_Mining_News_2013/2014-02-12/1392200981d74020.html. Last visited January 2014.
66 See *infra* p. 219 et seq. of Chapter 10.
67 See *infra* pp. 221–3 of Chapter 10.

Consider the example of the Kalamaili Ungulate Nature Reserve in Xinjiang Province. The reserve was designated in 1982 with a size of 18,000 square kilometers. It functions as an important ecological belt to block sands from the Gobi Desert. In 1986, construction work on the National Highway 216, which traverses from north to south, divided the reserve in two. Even the core zone was divided. This development adversely influenced the migration of the main protected species of this reserve, the Mongolian wild ass.[68] This situation has worsened since the 2000s as abundant mineral resource deposits have been gradually discovered in this area. To facilitate and legalize the exploitation of coal resources, the size of the reserve has repeatedly decreased. In 2011, the size of the reserve was reduced by another 592.76 square kilometers. This was the fifth time that the government of Xinjiang Province agreed to curtail the protected areas of the reserve since the first adjustment in 2005. Currently, the reserve covers only 12,800 square kilometers, which means that almost one-third of its original size has been eliminated.[69] In 2010, a railway was constructed to transport the coal mined from the mining site inside the reserve. This railway split the reserve from west to east, and more challenges to wildlife and landscape protection emerged in this area. The Kalamaili Nature Reserve is not an exceptional case; more examples could easily be found.[70]

Commercialization and Industrialization of Tourism versus Nature Conservation

Involvement of the Private Sector: Transfer of the Operation Rights of PAs

The private sector has extensively intervened in the operation and management of PAs in China. The complex arrangements between the private sector and the governments have resulted in a variety of governance structures of PAs. The de facto abdication of management authority by transferring the operation rights of PAs to enterprises has stirred intensive regulation from the central government. Dynamics are found in such an interaction process among the central government, the local governments and the enterprises themselves.

DIFFERENT MODELS OF THE GOVERNANCE STRUCTURE OF PAs

Private investment in PA management, such as the construction of tourist facilities and the provision of visitor services, has commonly been adopted across jurisdictions. In the US, this issue is governed under the legal framework of concession, in which the private sector under the for-profit scheme is involved in national park management by entering into concession contracts with the relevant authority.[71]

The need for private investment is even more imminent in China due to the pervasive underfunding of PAs. However, rather than merely providing accommodations, facilities and

---

68 Sun Danping, 'Paper Protection in Western China', February 18, 2011. Available at https://www.chinadialogue.net/article/show/single/en/4113-Paper-protection-in-western-China. Last visited January 2015.

69 Wang Shanshan, 新疆卡拉麦里山自然保护区"被瘦身"调查 (Investigation into the Shrinkage of the Kalamaili Nature Reserve in Xinjiang Province), February 13, 2012. Available at http://finance.chinanews.com/ny/2012/02-13/3662469.shtml. Last visited January 2015.

70 For example, the size of the Luobupo Wild Camel Nature Reserve at National Level has been reduced by 16,800 square kilometers for the purpose of exploiting the sylvite resources in this area. This has adversely influenced the habitat for wild camels. See Zhao Mei, 新疆罗布泊野骆驼保护区面积缩减至6.12万平方公里 (The Size of the Luobupo Wild Camel Nature Reserve in Xinjiang Province is Reduced to 61,200 Square Kilometers), January 15, 2014. Available at http://www.huaxia.com/xj-tw/xjxw/2014/01/3704885.html. Last visited January 2015.

71 For a discussion of concession-related statutes, see *supra* p. 76 of Chapter 4.

services to visitors as it does in the US, the private sector in China intervenes in PA management to a greater degree. In practice, quite a few PA authorities have transferred the operation rights of the PA to private enterprises. The private sector is not only the service provider but also performs the functions that are associated with the administrative authority, such as the collection of entrance fees.

As early as 1997, the operation rights of two scenic spots in Zhangjiajie – Huanglong Cave and Baofeng Lake – were transferred to private enterprises by entering into a commission contract (委托经营) with a term of 50 years and a lease contract (租赁经营) with a term of 60 years, respectively.[72] Since then, various types of contracts have been adopted between governments and private enterprises in other PAs, and the large-scale transfer of operation rights has grown. For example, the operation rights of half of the scenic areas in Fujian Province have been transferred to enterprises.[73] In 2001, the government of Sichuan Province announced that it would publicly sell the operation rights of ten PAs, including more than a hundred scenic spots. One of the most famous Chinese tourist destinations, Jiuzhaigou, was also on this list.[74] Though accurate statistics are not available, it is estimated that the operation rights of more than three hundred scenic spots in more than twenty provinces have been transferred to private enterprises.[75]

Based on the practices of these transfers, scholarly research has classified different models of governance structures for PAs in China. Based on the theory of shared tenancy proposed by Zhang Wuchang, Tang Ling summarizes three models of PA operation:

1 dividing leases (分成租约),
2 fixed leases (固定租约), and
3 self-run models.[76]

Based on the degree of marketization, the ownership structure of operators and the link to administrative subordination, Peng Decheng classifies six models of PA governance:

1 compound operation (复合经营),
2 a self-run model (自营),
3 operation by State-Owned Enterprises (SOEs),
4 tenancy by the entirety (整体租赁),
5 operation by joint-equity enterprises, and
6 operation by listed companies.[77]

---

72 Wang Xiaorun and Huang Qiuli, 旅游景区经营权出让是祸是福 (Transfer of Operation Right of Tourist Spots: A Blessing or a Curse?), in 光明日报 (*Guangming Daily*), April 13, 2001, available at http://www.people.com.cn/GB/jinji/36/20010413/441406.html. Last visited January 2015.
73 Guo Hongpeng and Liu Baijun, 福建过半景区经营权转让给企业被指贱卖 (The Operation Rights of Half of the Scenic Areas, which are Accused of being Undervalued, have been Transferred to Enterprises in Fujian), in 法制日报 (*Legal Daily*), September 20, 2010, available at http://news.sina.com.cn/c/sd/2010-09-20/002121135799.shtml. Last visited January 2015.
74 Ibid.
75 Li Jiping, 景区"贱卖"质疑频出曝法规滞后 (Criticism of 'Undervalued' Scenic Spots Shows the Lagging Status of Legislation), September 20, 2010. Available at http://www.legaldaily.com.cn/index/content/2010-09/20/content_2294456.htm?node=22668. Last visited January 2015.
76 Tang Ling, 风景名胜区产权制度变迁研究 ('Research on the Evolution of the Property Right System of Scenic and Historic Areas'), unpublished PhD dissertation at Sichuan University in 2007, pp. 94–102.
77 Peng Decheng, 中国旅游景区治理模式研究 (*Research on the Governance Models of Tourist Spots in China*) (Beijing: Zhongguo Lvyou Chubanshe, 2003).

The Zhongjingyuan Research Institute further classifies ten models:

1 tenancy by the entirety,
2 public-listed company,
3 non-public-listed join equity enterprise,
4 compound operation with subordination to company groups,
5 SOE operation subordinated to local governments,
6 SOE operation subordinated to departments within local governments,
7 compound governance with the combination of the management committee and tourism administration,
8 compound governance with the combination of the management committee and resource administration,
9 a self-run model with subordination to tourism administration, and
10 a self-run model with subordination to resource administration.[78]

Based on the arrangement of property rights and the degree to which local governments transfer their managerial rights, Dan Su and colleagues summarize three models that are commonly adopted:

1 the leasing model,
2 the non-listed shareholding model and
3 the publicly listed shareholding model.[79]

Irrespective of the different methods of modeling, it is clear that a complex commercial arrangement has been formulated between government authorities and private enterprises. Some concrete examples are examined below to illustrate how private enterprises have 'taken' the PAs in China.

The Leasing Model

The first operation model occurs in the form of a lease contract. In practice, two types of lease contracts may be adopted. First, joint-equity enterprises, which are composed of both state-owned shares and public shares, may take over the authority and responsibility for PA management. The benefits arising from the operation of a scenic area are divided between different shareholders according to the shares they possess (Type A). In the second type, enterprises pay a fixed amount of money to government authorities in the name of land transfer fees, management fees, or other fees, and enjoy residual profits from the operation of a PA (Type B). Usually, such enterprises are not subordinated to governments as they are in Type A.

The first joint-equity enterprise that operated an SHA in China is the Fuchunjiang Tourist Company Limited by Shares in Tonglu, Zhejiang Province. The company was previously subordinated to the Tourism Bureau of Tonglu County and took charge of the overall development and operation of the tourism resources in Tonglu. Due to a shortage of funds, the company was transformed into a 'company limited by shares' (股份有限公司) in December 1993, with total capital up to 60 million RMB. More than 40 million was collected from

---

78 Beijing Zhongjingyuan Research Institute of Tourism Planning and Design, 中国旅游景区的经营管理模式 (Models of Operation of Tourist Areas in China), available at http://www.la-tourplanning.com/news/news.php?nid=54. Last visited January 2015.
79 Dan Su, Geoffrey Wall and Paul Eagles, 'Emerging Governance Approaches for Tourism in the Protected Areas of China', 39.6 (2007) *Environmental Management*, p. 749.

the public, with more than 300 shareholders.[80] The company performs all administrative functions of the scenic area and operates as a business unit with an equal rate of return on investment of more than 20 percent. This Tonglu model was followed by other provinces and areas, such as the Langyatai in Qingdao, the Keyan in Zhejiang, the Hailuogou in Sichuan, and the Wolong Panda Reserve in Sichuan.[81] All of them have established ad hoc enterprises to take over PA management. State-owned shares are usually dominant in the overall share structure, and various types of other shares coexist.

Another case is the Jinshanling Great Wall in Beijing. Since the 1990s, the government of Luanping County, where the Great Wall is located, could no longer afford expenditures for the maintenance and protection of the Great Wall. In 1997, the county signed a contract with a SOE, the Guangda Agriculture Development Ltd. ('Guangda'), which was subordinated to the Finance Bureau of Chengde City in Hebei Province. They co-founded a company ('the Company') to operate the Great Wall with each of them holding 40 percent and 60 percent of the total shares, respectively. The term of the contract was 50 years, from 1997 to 2047, and the income collected from entrance fees would be distributed between the two shareholders pro rata.[82] The Company thus substitutes for the government in managing and operating the scenic area.

These two examples are Type A. The benefits that state-owned shares obtain from the operating company are turned over to local financing, and all or some of these benefits are transferred to the management agency for the daily management of PAs.

In Type B, enterprises pay a fixed amount of money and monopolize the operation of a PA for a fixed term, which is usually more than 50 years. The operation of the Bifeng Canyon in Sichuan Province adopted this model. In 1998, a contract between Ya'an City, where the canyon is located, and the Sichuan Wanguan Company was concluded, through which the operation rights of the Canyon were exclusively transferred to Wanguan Bifeng Canyon Ltd. (the Company) for 50 years. A one-off payment of 10 million RMB was paid by the Company to Ya'an as the fee for the land transfer (土地转让费). Moreover, because there were 7,000 *mu* of state-owned forestry and 2,000 *mu* of collectively owned forestry within the PA, the company paid 3.5 million RMB to the local forestry agency to buy the land-use rights for the forests and paid more than 10 million RMB to local farmers for relocation. In addition to these one-off payments, the Company was obliged to pay 100,000 RMB annually to the PA management agency as a return.[83] This Bifeng model had many followers. Quite a few local governments have signed similar contracts with enterprises that paid a fixed amount of money and obtained monopolistic rights to operate complete scenic areas. For example, the Wanxiang Group invested 500 million RMB in Qiandao Lake, and Sanjia Ltd. obtained the operation rights to the Mianshan Mountain SHA in Shanxi Province for 50 years.[84]

In the leasing model, either Type A or Type B, the initial concern is to attract investment from the private sector to ease the underfunding problem of PAs. Local governments are the leading initiators of such contracts. In Type A, management agencies represent local governments in performing management duties and obtaining benefits from operating companies. This is a typical characteristic of the governance structure of China, which is dubbed 'unity between governments and enterprises' (政企不分). In Type B, management agencies are separated from operating companies. Agencies perform administrative functions, whereas

---

80 Peng Decheng, *supra* note 77, p. 86.
81 Tang Ling, *supra* note 76, p. 38.
82 Ibid.
83 Peng Decheng, *supra* note 77, pp. 67–70.
84 Tang Ling, *supra* note 76, p. 39.

companies perform operational functions. In the Chinese scenario, this phenomenon is called the 'separation between governments and enterprises' (政企分离) and has long been considered the goal of the reform of governmental structure.

The Self-run Model

In China, some scenic areas have been successfully commercialized and have become quite profitable. Therefore, in these areas, a shortage of funds is not as urgent as presented in the previous model. Instead, the primary concern is guaranteeing profitability and making government the largest beneficiary. The operation of these areas features a self-run model in which the government itself performs the function of an enterprise and retains all benefits arising from the operation of PAs. Examples of areas that use this model include the Yellow Mountain in Anhui Province and the Huangguoshu Waterfalls in Guizhou Province.

Before 1987, the government of Anhui Province directly took charge of the management of the Yellow Mountain. The city of Yellow Mountain at the prefecture level (地级市) was established in 1987. The Yellow Mountain Management Committee (YMMC) was established and given management authority by the provincial Congress in 1989. In 1996, the Yellow Mountain Tourism Development Company Limited by Shares ('the Company') was established. The previous Yellow Mountain Tourism Development Limited Liability Company (later renamed the Yellow Mountain Tourism Development Group ('the Group')), the single initiator of this new Company, subscribed for part of the shares with all of its business assets, including the Beihai Hotel and nine other enterprises, and raised money for the subscription of the remaining shares from both domestic and foreign investors. The Company was listed in the B-share market in 1996 and the A-share market in 1997. Because the business scope of the Company covers the development of scenic areas, hotels, ropeways and tourist agencies, it is applauded as 'the first tourist stock in a complete sense in China'.[85] The Group, the controlling shareholder of the Company, overlaps with the YMMC. The director and deputy director of the YMMC hold the posts of chairman and vice chairman of the board of directors of the Group. Other personnel and assets also overlap. This phenomenon is dubbed 'one team, two signboards' (一套人马,两块牌子). In reality, the YMMC commercially operates the whole PA in the name of the Company. The for-profit scheme of the administrative agency is thus legitimized through the intermediation of a commercial enterprise.

The Yellow Mountain model is considered a successful way to commercialize the operation of scenic areas. Thus, it was adopted by other areas. Many tourism companies listed by shares began to flourish in the stock market. For example, copying the Yellow Mountain model, the Ermei Mountain Tourism Company Limited by Shares was listed in the A-share market in 1997. Similar to the Yellow Mountain case, the Ermei Mountain Management Committee overlaps with the operating Company in terms of personnel and assets. This is also the case for Zhangjiajie in Hunan Province and Yulong Snow Mountain in Yunnan Province, though the structure of initiators and shareholders is slightly different. As of December 2014, there were 28 publicly listed companies in the tourism industry. The business scopes of most of them cover the investment and operation of a specific PA.[86]

85 For more information, see YMMC, 黄山旅游发展股份有限公司简介 (Introduction to Yellow Mountain Tourism Development Company Limited by Shares), available at http://www.tourmart.cn/otherinfo/stockContent.do?topid=7612. Last visited January 2015.
86 See Sina Finance, 旅游业的所有上市公司 (All Public-listed Companies in the Tourism Industry), available at http://vip.stock.finance.sina.com.cn/corp/view/vCI_CorpInfoLink.php?page=1&stockid=600054&Type=ZK34. Last visited January 2015.

Table 9.4 Different models of governance structure of SHAs in China

Models		Ownership	Management authority	Operation right	Right to benefits
Leasing model	Tonglu model	LG	OE	LG+OE	LG+OE (pro rata) +MA (fiscal allocation)
	Bifeng model	LG	MA	OE	LG (fixed rent) +OE (residual benefits) +MA (fiscal allocation)
Self-run model	Yellow Mountain model	LG	MA (≈OE)	OE (≈MA)	OE +MA LG (turnover from MA)
	Huangguoshu model	LG	MA	OE	OE (shareholder benefits) LG (shareholder benefits) MA (fiscal allocation)

In addition to the Yellow Mountain model, in which the government and enterprise are not separated,[87] there is another model in practice in which the two are separated. For example, in the SHA of Huangguoshu Waterfalls in Guizhou Province, the Huangguoshu SHA Management Committee and the Huangguoshu Tourism Group ('the Group') were established at the same time in 1999. The Group was established with its shares jointly held by the provincial, city and county governments. The Group is in charge of the SHA operation and assumes sole responsibility for its profits and losses. The Management Committee performs its administrative functions, such as drafting the management plan, examining and approving the investment projects, and coordinating different stakeholders. Though the Group and the committee are separated, due to the nature of the SOE of the Group, the Huangguoshu model is essentially a self-run model.

The cases discussed above demonstrate that a variety of governance structures of PAs have been put into practice. There are three main players in these operation models: local governments at different levels (LG), the management agency of a specific PA (MA) and operating enterprises (OE). They share management authority, the operation rights of the PA and the right to benefits in different combinations in different models, as shown in Table 9.4.

In reality, due to various initiatives and the constant adjustment of the operation structure by local governments in practice, the real picture is much more complex than the case shown in Table 9.4. The involvement of different departments, such as tourism and resource departments (land, water, forestry, etc.), and different company governance structures have added considerable complexity to the overall governance structure of PAs in China. Irrespective of the complexities, the common observation is that governments and business sectors are closely intertwined with each other under a for-profit scheme. This is the starting point to understand the Chinese problem, not only in specific PA management but also in other fields. Such a coalition is not without controversies. Supporters argue that introduction of enterprise-style management can activate the potential of PA development and solve the problems of underfunding and deficiencies of the professional management of the public sector.[88]

---

87 Due to new restrictions prescribed in Regulations on Scenic and Historic Areas in 2006, entry fees cannot be included in the income of a listed company. Therefore, 'asset stripping' and follow-up reforms were done in the Yellowstone Mountain operation structure after 2006.

88 Yan Youbing and Zhao Liming, 旅游景区经营权转让探析 (Analysis of Transfer of Operational Right of Scenic Areas), 5.3 (2005) 西北农林科技大学学报 (Journal of Northwest A&F University), pp. 92–6; Tang Ling, 论公共资源类旅游景区所有权与经营权分离 (Analysis on the Separation of the Ownership and the Operation Right of Public-resource-based Tourist Scenic Areas), 7 (2005) 西南民族大学学报 (Journal of Southwest University for Nationalities), pp. 275–7.

Opponents note that such a large-scale transfer of operation rights results in over-commercialization, and governments have de facto contracted out their authority and responsibility in managing and supervising PAs.[89]

THE EVOLUTION OF REGULATION: THE GAME BETWEEN CENTRAL AND LOCAL GOVERNMENTS

The transfer of operation rights to private enterprises is largely a local strategy, either for purposes of attracting investment or retaining tourism benefits by governments. In practice, some problems began to emerge during the process of large-scale transfer, such as the excessive exploitation of scenic resources and the unaffordable entrance fees charged by enterprises. It has also been claimed that such a transfer is a process of the privatization of State property, which results in a loss of State assets. The media report that some PAs with crucial ecological and biological significance have been 'sold' at relatively low prices. In some extreme cases, the term of the leasing contract may reach seventy years.[90] Coverage of the rampant transfer of operation rights is frequently seen in the media, and numerous streams of literature have been devoted to the discussion in this field.[91]

The central government began to intervene in local governments' transfer practices in the 2000s. This intervention is twofold: on the one hand, the central government strengthens the monitoring and regulation of the transfer; on the other hand, by learning about the experiences of concession in other countries, such as the US, the central government begins to promote standardized concession in PAs.

Regulation of the Transfer of the Operation Rights of SHAs

Before the 2000s, there was no legal or policy document that specifically addressed the issue of the transfer of operation rights. In 1995, the General Office of the State Council issued a notice that specified that 'no area or department shall be allowed to assign (出让), either overtly or in any disguised form, scenic resources and the lands within scenic areas in any name or any way.'[92] However, this notice only refers to the land and resources of SHAs; it is silent on the legality of transfer of the 'operation rights' of SHAs as a whole. In 2000, the General Office issued another notice on urban-rural planning in which the same statement as the 1995 Notice was made.[93] The same statement was repeated in the Notice on Strengthening the Supervision and Administration of Urban-Rural Planning made by the State Council in 2002.[94]

In 2001, in an official reply that quoted the previous documents issued by the General Office of the State Council in 1995 and 2000, the MoC explained that what the State Council meant was that 'no areas or departments shall be entitled to assign (出让) or transfer (转让),

---

89 Xie Ninggao, 国家风景名胜区功能的发展及其保护利用 (Development of Functions of Scenic and Historic Areas at the National Level and Their Protective Use), 4 (2002) 中国园林 (*Journal of Chinese Landscape Architecture*), pp. 16–20.
90 See Wang Xiaorun and Huang Qiuli, *supra* note 72, and Guo Hongpeng and Liu Baijun, *supra* note 73.
91 For a general list of relevant literature, see Liu Min, 中国景区经营权转让研究综述 (Literature Review of the Research on the Transfer of Operation Rights of Scenic Areas in China), 31.11 (2012) 地理科学进展 (*Progress in Geography*), pp. 1492–502 (during the period 2002–11, there were in total 143 articles published in 99 journals in Chinese on the topic of the transfer of the operation rights of scenic areas).
92 State Council, 国务院办公厅关于加强风景名胜区保护管理工作的通知 (Notice of the General Office on Strengthening Protection and Management of the Scenic and Historic Areas) *Guobanfa* No. 23 [1995].
93 State Council, 国务院办公厅关于加强和改进城乡规划工作的通知 (Notice of the General Office of the State Council on Strengthening and Improving the Work of Urban-rural Planning), *Guobanfa* No. 25 [2000].
94 State Council, 国务院关于加强城乡规划监督管理的通知 (Notice on Strengthening the Supervision and Administration of Urban-rural Planning), *Guofa* No. 13 [2002].

partially or as a whole, the operation rights of scenic and historic areas to individual enterprises.'[95] According to the MoC's interpretation, the assignment and transfer of 'the operation rights of a SHA' are a disguised form of the assignment and transfer of 'land and scenic resources', which is explicitly prohibited by the State Council.

In 2005, the Department of Construction in Fujian Province asked the MoC for instructions on whether it was allowed to transfer the operation rights of the key scenic spot of the Guanzhi Mountain SHA (a National Key SHA) to a private company. In its reply, the MoC explicitly refused Fujian's proposal.[96] It further specified that 'social investment in SHAs is encouraged under the conditions that the SHA is state-owned, supervised and managed by governments, and the investment accords with the planning of the SHA. The collection of entrance fees is an important method for governments to unify the management of scenic resources. Management agencies of SHAs may pay a certain amount of money from the benefits of entrance fees to enterprises as a return for its investment; however, it is prohibited to *assign* or *transfer* the monopolistic rights to operate scenic resources and collect entrance fees to enterprises'.

At a national conference on SHA management held in September 2005, the minister of the MoC, Qiu Baoxing, proposed four restrictions that could not be bypassed when local governments cooperated with private enterprises:

1   The government's management authority should not be impaired or transferred. SHAs should never be managed by enterprises.
2   Any form of the substantive transfer of operation rights in core spots of scenic areas is absolutely prohibited.
3   The transfer of operation rights in developed and mature scenic spots and other significant spots should not be allowed.
4   The collection of the *main* entrance fees of SHAs (instead of those fees for individual spots or facilities inside SHAS) should not be monopolized by enterprises or publicly listed in a bundle with other assets in the stock market (捆绑上市).[97]

These 'Four Baselines' were a summary of previous regulations and policies. However, some compromises were made by the MoC. The prohibition of the transfer of operation rights was confined to the scope of core spots, well-developed and mature spots, and the collection of *main* entrance fees. Some leeway was given to spots and items other than those stated above.

A previous discussion of the evolution of regulations and policies shows that the central government's attitude toward the local practices of the transfer of the operation rights of PAs is clearly negative. However, given that different policy documents were consecutively issued with exactly the same content, one can infer that the efficacy of enforcing these policies is not satisfactory. In reality, explicit prohibition from the central level does not curb local governments' rampant transfer practices. On the one hand, because some local practices have already become fait accomplis, the central government faces a dilemma when trying to enforce its regulations. On the other hand,

---

95 MoC, 于对四川省风景名胜区出让、转让经营权问题的复函 (Reply to Sichuan Province on Issues of Assignment and Transfer of Operation Rights of Scenic and Historic Areas), *Jianchenghan* No. 80 [2001]. Full text is available at http://china.findlaw.cn/lawyers/article/d2268.html. Last visited January 2015.
96 MoC, 建设部办公厅关于对国家重点风景名胜区经营权出让问题的复函 (Reply on the Issue of Transferring the Operation Rights of National Key Scenic and Historic Areas), *Jianbanchenghan* No. 225 [2005]. Full text is available at http://www.pkulaw.cn/fulltext_form.aspx?Gid=77452&Db=ch1. Last visited January 2015.
97 Kang Ning, 禁止转让核心景区经营权,建设部划四条"禁行线" (Transfer of Operation Right of Key Scenic Areas is Prohibited, Four Baselines are Scored by MoC), September 23, 2005, available at http://news.xinhuanet.com/fortune/2005-09/23/content_3530089.htm. Last visited January 2015.

even though some PAs were not transferred at the time of these regulations, local governments can still establish a complex arrangement with the business sector to dodge the central policy. A Chinese metaphor illustrates this situation well: 'where there is a rule, there is always a way to get around it' (上有政策，下有对策). These complexities have also subtly influenced the central government's attitude. This can be partly seen in the compromise made in the 'Four Baselines'. According to an anonymous interview with an official in the MoC, 'it is not a black and white thing. The "one size fits all" approach does not work.' Furthermore, the degree of monitoring by the central government has decreased in recent years. The MoC prefers to be silent unless there is whistleblowing. In the language of the media, there are too many mice, and there is only one cat.[98]

The Pilot Practices of Concession in Guizhou

In addition to strengthening the monitoring and regulation of the transfer of operation rights, the central government promoted the pilot program of concession in certain PAs.

In 2003, Guizhou Province was selected to be the first pilot province to introduce concessions in its core scenic spots. To proceed with the pilot project, in 2003, the Department of Construction in Guizhou Province delivered a draft report called 'Interim Measures on Administration of Concession of Scenic and Historic Areas in Guizhou Province' to the MoC. In its reply to Guizhou, the MoC stressed three opinions.

1 The object of concession should be defined as one or several specific *items* instead of the whole SHA. Therefore, the title of the draft should be revised accordingly.
2 It should be clarified that entrance fees are an important source of scenic resource protection, the exclusive right to the collection of entrance fees should not be transferred to enterprises, and service items, such as the maintenance of infrastructures, environmental sanitation, safety and other items within the categories of estate management could be transferred to enterprises. Enterprises could also be involved in the construction of infrastructure and newly developed scenic spots. Their investment could be rewarded from the income from entrance fees in the future.
3 The supervision and management of the planning and construction of SHAs should be strengthened.[99]

It can be seen from this reply that the MoC intentionally distinguished between the 'transfer of operation rights' of an SHA and 'concession' inside a SHA. The former was prohibited, whereas the latter was legal and encouraged.

After a revision in accordance with the MoC's reply, the government of Guizhou Province released Interim Measures of Administration of the Concession of Items of Scenic and Historic Areas in 2005 ('Interim Measures').[100] This was the first 'local governmental rule' about concession in SHAs in China. In the Interim Measures, concession is defined as

---

98 Yang Hongsheng, "景区经营权"转让挑战建设部"禁令"? (Transfer of Operation Rights of Scenic Areas: A Violation of the MoC's Prohibition?), in 新闻周报 (*News Weekly*), April 20, 2004. Available at http://www.landscapehr.com/career/detail-36443.htm. Last visited December 2014.
99 MoC, 建设部办公厅关于对《贵州省风景名胜区特许经营管理暂行办法》(征求意见稿)意见的复函 (Reply of the General Office of the MoC on Opinions of the 'Interim Measures on the Administration of Concessions of Scenic and Historic Areas in Guizhou Province' (draft for soliciting public comments)), September 1, 2003, *Jianbanchenghan* No. 411 [2003].
100 Provincial government of Guizhou, 贵州省风景名胜区内项目特许经营管理暂行办法 (Interim Measures of Administration of the Concessions of Items of Scenic and Historic Areas of Guizhou Province), Order No. 83 of the People's Government of Guizhou Province (2005).

... activities in which the citizens, legal persons and other organizations, within a specific term and scope, obtain the right to invest and operate one or all items in the scenic and historic area according to specific procedures, legal standards and conditions.

Moreover, the maximum term of the concession for all items is limited to 20 years, whereas the maximum term for an individual item is 15 years.

In reality, before the finalization of the Interim Measures in 2004, Guizhou Province had already conducted some 'concession' practices. The city of Xingyi, where the SHA of Malinghe Canyon at the National Level is located, signed a contract with Zhejiang Qingniao Group ('Qingniao') that obtained the exclusive concession rights to this SHA for 50 years. Qingniao would provide all profitable services, such as tourist coaches, sightseeing cruises, ropeways, drifting services, restaurants, accommodations, commodity sales and photography services, and pay the Xingyi Government franchise fees. This case was applauded as the first concession case in Guizhou and even the first concession case in China.[101] Although in this case the power to collect entrance fees was retained by the government, it was still not easy to distinguish between this 'concession' and the previous 'transfer of operation rights'. The term of this concession contract was 50 years, which violated the requirements prescribed by the new Interim Measures. The risk of policy change was still a main concern for investors. As discussed earlier, in 2005, the MoC began to strengthen the monitoring and regulation of the transfer of the operation rights of the SHA at the national level. This change caused anxieties in Qingniao, although it claimed to be a concession case instead of a case of the transfer of operation rights. Finally, in 2005, Qingniao decided to terminate the contract and withdrew all of its investment. This so-called first 'concession' case lasted only one year. The muddy situation in policy making and practice still requires clarification and improvement.

A 'Preliminary' Normalization

The confusion regarding 'concession' policy making and practice was normalized to a certain extent by the enactment of the Regulations on Scenic and Historic Areas ('Regulations') in 2006. As previously discussed, the Regulations established the systems of 'payment of compensation to use scenic resources' (Article 37), 'separation between revenue and expenditures' (Article 38), procedural requirements for concluding contracts to provide tourist services, such as public bidding (Article 37), and the prohibition of for-profit operations by management agencies (Article 39).[102]

Due to these requirements, several of the operation models of SHAs discussed above have lost their legality, such as the Tonglu Model and the Yellow Mountain Model, in which enterprises and governments are not separated. Local governments have gradually adjusted the operational structures of SHAs to fit the new regulatory framework. However, because this adjustment will alter the original benefit-sharing arrangement and affect the possessed interests, the process is sluggish and ongoing. MoHURD conducted an ad hoc campaign to inspect the enforcement of the Regulations in 2007. It was found that the transfer of management functions and the authority to collect entrance fees to enterprises was still commonly seen at the local level.[103] In some publicly listed tourism companies, the income from entrance fees

---

101 Shi Xinrong, 我国第一个风景区特许经营项目在贵州签约 (The First Concession Contract of a SHA in China was Signed in Guizhou), February 28, 2004, available at http://news.qq.com/a/20040228/000434.htm. Last visited January 2015.
102 See *supra* pp. 167–8 of Chapter 8.
103 For more details, see *infra* p. 223 et seq. of Chapter 10.

remains unseparated from the assets of the listed company. For example, in 2013, the Yellow Mountain Tourism Group was fined 30,000 RMB by competent finance authorities. This was partly due to its wrongdoings in accounting methods related to income from entrance fees.[104]

Though the Regulations established basic rules and regulations on SHA operation, there are still gaps to be addressed. The legislature hesitates to use the term 'concession' (特许经营 in Chinese) in the Regulations and avoids distinguishing between 'concession' and 'transfer of operation rights'. Instead, it only specifies that administrative agencies should retain the authority to collect entrance fees. It remains silent on specific issues, such as the maximum term of such contracts, the scope of service items that are allowed to be subjected to private operations, and the percentage of private operators' incomes for compensating the use of scenic resources. Furthermore, some prohibitions that have been repeatedly addressed in previous policies are not codified in the Regulations. These include the prohibition of transferring the operation rights of core spots of SHAs and the prohibition of including entrance fees in the company assets of a publicly listed company. The Regulations state that tickets should be exclusively 'sold' by administrative agencies, but this does not necessarily mean that entrance fees should be exclusively 'retained' by agencies. Therefore, some loopholes still exist. In this sense, the Regulations can only be deemed a 'preliminary' normalization of the disordered operation practices of SHAs beginning in the 1990s.

Though deficiencies remain in the Regulations, some achievements have been reached with regard to the pilot practices of concession in Guizhou Province. In September 2007, the Regulations on Scenic and Historic Areas in Guizhou Province were enacted, which repealed the Interim Measures issued in 2005. This new rule adds a separate chapter on the concession of SHAs with 13 articles, which enriches the regulatory framework on concession. It specifies the definition of concession (Article 39), the maximum terms of concession (Article 40), state ownership of newly added facilities after the termination of concession (Article 41), the formulation of the concession plan by administrative agencies (Article 42), the qualifications of bidders of concession (Article 43), the procedures for granting concession (Article 44), the prohibitive activities of concessioners (Article 46), the requirement of continuous operation by concessioners (Article 47), the preferential right of concessioners (Article 48), the right to terminate concession contracts in case of *force majeure* (Article 49), and the payment of compensation for using scenic resources (Article 50). A basic framework has been established that might be a transferable example of law making and policy making for other provinces and the central government. The limitation of this rule is that it does not have a retroactive effect on operation rights that were previously obtained (Article 51). Because many local governments have signed contracts with enterprises with terms up to 50 or even 70 years, addressing these operators seems more difficult than regulating future operators.

The Construction of Tourist Amenities and the Commercialization of PAs

The construction of tourist amenities and other facilities is prevalent in Chinese PAs. Though the adverse impact of vertical transportation facilities, such as ropeways and cable

---

104 See Yellow Mountain Tourism Development Company Limited by Shares, 黄山旅游发展股份有限公司关于财政部驻安徽省财政监察专员办事处对公司会计信息质量检查结论和处理决定的公告 (Announcement Regarding the Conclusion and Decision of the Office of Financial Ombudsman Affiliated to the Ministry of Finance in Anhui Province on the Issue of the Quality of Accounting Information), September 25, 2013. Full text is available at http://vip.stock.finance.sina.com.cn/corp/view/vCB_AllBulletinDetail.php?stockid=600054&id=1218124. Last visited January 2015. The accounting method was accordingly adjusted later in December 2013.

cars, on nature has been acknowledged,[105] the construction of such projects remains commonplace. One of the most notorious examples is the Bailong Sky Elevator in the SHA of Wulingyuan in Zhangjiajie, Hunan Province, which is a 330-meter glass elevator built into the side of a cliff.

According to the Master Plan of the Wulingyuan Scenic and Historical Area made by the Wulingyuan management agency in 1990 and approved by the MoC in 1992, 'an elevator [was] planned to be built in *Laowuchang*', the place where the Bailong Elevator is located now. Based on a financing contract signed between Sun Yingui and the government of the Wulingyuan District in 1992, construction work began in October 1999.

While the elevator was under construction, another large-scale program to rehabilitate the derogated landscape of Wulingyuan with an investment of up to 1 billion RMB was also in progress. The recovery program was a direct response to the negative report by UNESCO on Wulingyuan in 1998, which noted that the site was 'overrun with tourist facilities, having a considerable impact on the aesthetic qualities of the site'.[106] In this context, the construction of the Bailong Elevator was the topic of heated debates at the outset.

After construction was completed, the elevator began operation in May 2002. After 150 days, due to harsh criticism from society and the media, the operators of the elevator were ordered by the relevant authorities to suspend their operation. The criticism was twofold: the first concern was about the security issues of such a giant elevator, and the second criticism involved the legality of the construction work within PAs. The elevator operator claimed that the construction project fulfilled all of the compulsory procedures of examination and approvals and that the legal interests of the contractor should be respected and protected. Furthermore, elevator construction would be beneficial to the rehabilitation work. Because tourists had no need to stay overnight on the peak due to the convenience offered by the elevator, the demolition of accommodation facilities on the top of the mountain would be facilitated. Critics argued that the Master Plan on which the construction approval was based was seriously outdated and did not properly consider the environmental impacts of such a construction project. The construction derogated the scenic landscape, which was against the fundamental purpose of the World Heritage designation. The environmental protection bureau, which had previously approved the construction project, acknowledged the potential defects of the approval and proposed that the demolition of the elevator would be the best choice.[107]

Despite these environmental concerns, in August 2003, after ten months of suspension, the operation of the Bailong Elevator was resumed. This can hardly be deemed a settlement of the dispute. Instead, the close link between the revenue from the elevator's operation and the local economy is the dominant factor that underpins the legitimacy of this elevator. By charging 96 RMB per person to use the elevator, the operation of the elevator produced a turnover of more than 200,000 RMB per day. The accompanying tax from the operation

---

105 For example, see Xie Ninggao, 索道对世界遗产的威胁 (Threats of Ropeways on World Heritage), 6 (2000) 旅游学刊 (*Tourism Tribune*), pp. 57–60.
106 UNESCO, 'Decisions of the Twenty-second Extraordinary Session of the Bureau of the World Heritage Committee (Kyoto, 28–29 November 1998) with Regard to the State of Conservation of Properties Inscribed on the World Heritage List, Noted by the Committee', November 28–29, 1998. Available at http://whc.unesco.org/archive/repcom98a4.htm. Last visited January 2015. The Report evaluated three Chinese SHAs in total: Jiuzhaigou, Huanglong and Wulingyuan. Wulingyuan received the worst evaluation among the three.
107 Li Chunyan and Shou Beibei, 张家界观光电梯重新启动"上下"遭遇尴尬 (Operation of the Sightseeing Elevator in Zhangjiajie is Resumed; Dilemma Remains), August 21, 2003, available at http://www.people.com.cn/GB/huanbao/1074/2029784.html. Last visited January 2015.

accounted for 5 percent of the total tax income of Wulingyuan city.[108] The local government's interests and the developer's interests were closely tied. Furthermore, surveys showed that tourists and local communities supported the construction of this elevator because it was energy saving or because it could bring more income to them. Considering these factors, it will be difficult to demolish the elevator in the future.

Similar construction projects have occurred in other PAs. In 1983, one-third of the peak of the Taishan Mountain was dynamited for the construction of a ropeway. In 1987, the General Plan of the Taishan Mountain approved by the State Council recommended that 'the ropeway may be dismantled after the expiration of the maximum usage term.' The old ropeway was not dismantled as suggested until 2000. Instead, the large-scale expansion of the previous ropeway took place against strong criticism from society. For this expansion project, more than 15,000 cubic meters of mountain massif was dynamited. A new business street with hundreds of stores was constructed at the top of the Taishan Mountain.[109] In addition to the construction of transportation infrastructure, the construction of man-made scenery is prevalent, such as artificial fog and snow used to attract visitors. Commercial advertisements are also common; the most notorious example is the commercial billboard on the cliff of the SHA of the Three Gorges Dam.

The Abuse of Power in Tourism Development: The 'Privatization' of Scenic Resources

In practice, governments' power to develop tourism may be abused to serve a specific group of interests. Instead of improving tourist facilities and infrastructure for the general public, some PAs have become clubs for the super-rich. Some local governments zealously develop real estate and build golf courses inside PAs under the banner of 'ecological construction' or 'protective development'.

Golf is considered an upper-class sport in China. Along with the increasing number of Chinese billionaires, the need for golf-course construction has increased. Local governments consider this an indicator of economic development and thus approve quite a number of construction projects for golf courses. Because golf courses occupy a large amount of green land and need fresh water for daily maintenance, they have posed considerable threats to land and water protection. Since 2004, the State Council has issued a series of policy documents that categorically prohibit any new construction of golf courses and halt any construction that has not been approved.[110] However, this prohibition is not implemented in a satisfactory manner. In 2004, it was reported that there were 180 golf courses in China; by 2013, there were more than 600 golf courses. This means that more than 400 'illegal' golf courses have been constructed against explicit prohibitions in the last decade.[111] Most of these golf courses are constructed adjacent to or even inside PAs to take advantage of their scenic value and wetland resources.

---

108 Ibid.
109 Shen Xiaohui, 旅游 发乱象中的生态退化与文化缺失 (Ecological Degradation and Absence of Cultural Elements in Tourism Development), in Friends of Nature, 中国环境发展报告 (2013) (*Annual Report on Environment Development of China (2013)*) (Beijing: Social Sciences Academic Press, 2013), pp. 133–4.
110 State Council, 国务院办公厅关于暂停新建高尔夫球场的通知 (Notice of the State Council on Suspending New Construction of Golf Courses), January 10, 2004, *Guobanfa* No. 1 [2004]. Available at http://www.gov.cn/gongbao/content/2004/content_63138.htm. Last visited January 2015.
111 Chai Gang, 高尔夫球场"堵"与"疏" ('Interception' and 'Dredging' of Golf Courses), in 中国经营报 (*Chinese Business News*), May 18, 2013. Available at http://finance.sina.com.cn/roll/20130518/014715506105.shtml. Last visited January 2015.

It is reported that a company invested 15 billion RMB to construct a golf course in the Jiangshan Wetland Park in Shandong Province.[112] The construction of golf courses is not for golf per se; it is always combined with real-estate development because a golf course may increase the market value of the adjacent real estate. Together, golf and real estate have strongly spurred GDP growth, which is an important indicator of the performance of local officials.

It is reported that at the end of 2010, there were more than 50 real-estate companies investing in 'tourism real estate' at an amount of more than 300 billion RMB. In the first quarter of 2012, nearly 70 projects were established in tourism real estate, with a contracted amount of more than 100 million RMB. The total amount was more than 260 billion RMB.[113]

Furthermore, the construction of luxury hotels and conference centers within SHAs has become a breeding ground for corruption and rent seeking. To cope with potential corruption problems, as early as 1998, the General Office of the CPC and the State Council co-issued the Notice on Prohibiting Party Organs and Governmental Offices to Convene Conferences within Scenic and Historic Areas.[114] In September 2014, they issued another notice specifying the twelve SHAs in which the convention of conferences was prohibited.[115]

Through these dramatic examples, it is clear that administrative power and interests in developing tourism may be closely linked and may have severe consequences if the power is not properly controlled. There is a large gap in terms of the enforcement of central policies and regulations at the local level.

Conflicts between Conservation and Local Communities

As a developing country with a massive population, China has been forced to consider the fact that nature is not as 'wild' as it is, for example, in the US. There were approximately 30 million people living in and around China's nature reserves in 1997.[116] More importantly, these 30 million people were in considerable poverty, and their livelihoods needed drastic improvement.[117] The most recent literature shows that there were still approximately 10 million people living in approximately 2,000 nature reserves in China in 2008.[118]

---

112 Chai Gang, 首 集团被指投资150亿在国家自然保护区建高球场 (The Capital Development Group is Charged with Investing 15 Billion RMB in Constructing a Golf Course in a Nature Reserve), in 中国经营报 (*China Business News*), May 18, 2013. Available at http://finance.sina.com.cn/chanjing/gsnews/20130518/014515506096.shtml. Last visited January 2015.
113 Li Yue and Zhang Xinchen, 万达长白山超低价格圈地万亩，地方融资平台担保 (Wanda Group Buys More than 10,000 *mu* Lands of Changbai Mountain at Extremely Low Price; Local Government Provides Guarantee Using Its Financing Platform), in 第一财经日报 (*First Financial Daily*), June 1, 2012. Available at http://finance.qq.com/a/20120601/000960.htm. Last visited January 2015.
114 General Office of the CPC and State Council, 关于严禁党政机关到风景名胜区开会的通知 (Notice on Prohibiting Party Organs and Governmental Offices to Convene Conferences within Scenic and Historic Areas), 1998.
115 General Office of the CPC and State Council, 关于严禁党政机关到风景名胜区开会的通知 (Notice on Prohibiting Party Organs and Governmental Offices to Convene Conferences within Scenic and Historic Areas), September 2014. Full text is available at http://politics.people.com.cn/n/2014/0929/c1001-25755796.html. Last visited January 2015.
116 The figure was provided up to 1997 by Harkness. The latest figure is not available, but concerning the growth of population in the last decade in China, the author assumes that the current figure would be no less than 30 million. See James Harkness, *supra* note 31, p. 918.
117 Harkness also provided another figure for the purpose of contrast. The total number of people living in poverty in China in 1997 was around 58 million. See ibid.
118 Li Jianquan et al., 我国自然保护区林权改革问题与对策探讨 (Problems and Countermeasures on Collective Forest Tenure Reform in the Nature Reserves in China), 12 (2009) 林业资源管理 (*Forest Resources Management*), pp. 1–8.

For example, in the Sanjiangyuan Nature Reserve in Qinghai Province, there are more than 250,000 people living within the reserve's boundary.[119] Because more PAs have been established since the 1990s, conflicts between nature conservation and local residents have been exacerbated.

These conflicts are reflected in the following aspects:

1 Economic disenfranchisement and insufficient compensation to local residents due to the designation of PAs and the implementation of conservation programs,
2 Negative influences on nature by tourism-related activities conducted by local residents,
3 Unbalanced benefit-sharing schemes between different communities and between communities and governments, and
4 Insufficient participation by local communities in governments' decision making and lack of co-governance on issues of nature management on the local scale.

The designation of public PAs and the implementation of conservation programs usually accompany the displacement and economic disenfranchisement of local residents. Xu and Melik note that 'in China, displacement and resettlement of indigenous people are amongst the State's oldest continuous land-use policies.'[120] For example, 1,085 local villages were resettled from the core zone of the Wulingyuan Nature Reserve in Zhejiang Province. Similar programs were conducted in other nature reserves, such as Shennongjia in Hubei Province and Zhalong in Heilongjiang Province.[121] Meanwhile, due to the implementation of conservation laws, local residents' traditional uses of natural resources, such as fishing, timber cultivation and felling, hunting and plant collection, were strictly restricted. These resources comprise a large part of local residents' livelihoods; therefore, poverty is substantially exacerbated. Moreover, an increase in the wildlife population, such as bears and wolves, in PAs results in conflicts between humans and wildlife both inside and near PAs.

Compensation to local people for displacement, disenfranchisement and wildlife damage is not sufficiently funded and enforced.[122] Empirical studies indicate that local people show resentment toward the establishment of nature reserves.[123] Harkness gave an example: 'When the collective forest lands of Yuhu village were incorporated into the Yulongxueshan Nature Reserve in northwest Yunnan . . . farmers responded by cutting down trees they had previously managed on a sustainable basis.'[124]

Moreover, conflicts between governments and local communities may occur during the process of 'nationalization'. The designation of nature reserves sometimes accompanies the 'taking' of collectively owned lands. It has been stated that 'only 60% or so of nature and forest reserves are on land over which state agencies have clear control.'[125] In the Maolan Nature Reserve at the National Level in Guizhou Province, where the reserve was established in

---

119 Xu Jiliang et al., 'A Review and Assessment of Nature Reserve Policy in China: Advances, Challenges and Opportunities', 46.4 (2012) *Oryx*, p. 559.
120 Xu Jianchu and David Melick, 'Rethinking the Effectiveness of Public Protected Areas in Southwestern China', 21.2 (2006) *Conservation Biology*, p. 324.
121 Xu Jiliang et al., *supra* note 119, p. 559.
122 Xu Jianchu and David Melick, *supra* note 120, pp. 321–2.
123 Examples include the Changbai Mountain Biosphere Reserve in Jilin Province, Shennongjia National Nature Reserve in Hubei Province and Wolong Biosphere Reserve in Sichuan Province. See Guangyu Wang et al., *supra* note 31, p. 255.
124 James Harkness, *supra* note 31, p. 921.
125 Jerry McBeath and Jenifer Huang McBeath, 'Biodiversity Conservation in China: Policies and Practice', 9.4 (2006) *Journal of International Wildlife Law & Policy*, p. 310.

1986, the local government decided to *nationalize* forests within the boundaries of the nature reserves that were formerly collectively owned and privately used.[126] The 'nationalization' policy creates conflicts between the enforcement of conservation regulations and the protection of individual and collective property rights.

Although the designation of PAs may negatively influence local residents' traditional ways of life, the conservation of nature has also made it possible for nature to support alternative livelihoods for local communities. Along with the boom of nature-based tourism, income from tourism has become an important alternative for local residents. According to a survey conducted in Lashihai in Yunnan Province in the Meiquan village, which is located within the PA, income from traditional livelihoods was reduced to less than a quarter from 2005 to 2009 due to the implementation of conservation programs in this area. However, the percentage of income from tourism in terms of the total income of a family increased by 75 percent.[127] In this case, local residents formed horseback tourism teams and provided horse-riding services to visitors. However, this alternative also poses threats to the protection of the local ecosystem. The survey shows that wetlands in Lashihai are facing degradation and overuse due to the sharp increase in horse-riding services provided by local villagers.[128]

Another problem involves the benefit-sharing scheme in areas where nature-based tourism prospers. Such benefit-sharing arrangements exist not only between different communities but also between communities and the government. There is serious inequity in the distribution of tourism benefits within local residents and between local residents and outsider groups.[129] Because tourism activities are strictly restricted inside PAs, communities that reside inside PAs are, to some degree, deprived of benefiting from the profits of tourism; instead, communities that are peripheral to PAs (in the American sense, 'gateway communities') become the biggest beneficiaries. An example is found in the Zhangjiajie Forest Park at the National Level. It has been stated that 'many of the economic benefits of parks may be diverted to outside groups.'[130] A study of the Wolong Nature Reserve shows that there is still strong reliance on the exploitation of natural resources, such as the collection of medicinal herbs by local residents to maintain their livelihoods. The expected benefits of tourism are not explicit. This is largely due to the lack of skills and training among local residents to conduct tourism-related activities.

Previous discussions have shown that tourism income may contribute significantly to local revenues. Due to insufficient compensation for the economic losses suffered by local residents for the purpose of ecological protection, tourism benefits are not shared fairly between governments and local communities. Local people generally receive considerably fewer benefits in comparison with local governments' gains from the 'ticket economy'.[131] This is the case in the national park pilot project initiated by Yunnan Province. Zinda argues that 'while the national park flourishes, residents sit on the sidelines.'[132]

---

126 Ran Jingcheng, 中国自然保护56年 (56 Years of Natural Protection in China), 7 (2012) 中国国家地理 (*China National Geography*), p. 70.
127 Jian Wu *et al.*, 'The Governance of Integrated Ecosystem Management in Ecological Function Conservation Areas in China', 13.6 (2013) *Regional Environmental Change*, p. 1307.
128 Ibid., pp. 1309–10.
129 Liu Yang and Lv Yihe, 旅游活动对卧龙自然保护区社区居民的经济影响 (The Economic Impact of Tourism on Local Residents in Wolong Nature Reserve), 16.1 (2008) 生物多样性 (*Biodiversity Science*), pp. 68–74.
130 Guangyu Wang et al., *supra* note 31, p. 256.
131 See Xu Jianchu and David Melick, *supra* note 120, p. 321.
132 John Zinda, 'Hazards of Collaboration: Local State Co-optation of a New Protected-Area Model in Southwest China', 25.4 (2012) *Society & Natural Resources*, p. 396. For more discussions, see *infra* Chapter 11.

Finally, the local community's right to information and participatory rights is always bypassed when the government makes a decision related to nature conservation.[133] The absence of sufficient consultation with local people by governments at all levels is a decisive factor that intensifies the conflicts between governments and local communities.[134] Structural limits exist in terms of the insufficiencies of the legislative guarantee of participatory rights and the bureaucratic culture of elite domination.[135] In terms of the right to information, Chinese laws emphasize the obligation of governmental agencies to *open* and *disclose* information instead of empowering citizens with the *right* to information.[136] In terms of the right to participation, there is no explicit legal empowerment of citizens to participate in PA-related issues, and the scope of public participation in affairs related to environmental matters is not adequate in general.[137] Access to information is the precondition for effective participation. However, the deficiency of knowledge and the lack of incentives for local communities constrain their effective participation in PA management decisions.

Summary

Along with the liberation of the Chinese economy, tourism has become a pillar industry in the national economy, and it is situated in a favorable policy environment. The environmental and social aspects of tourism have gradually gained greater acknowledgment, as evidenced by the rise of sustainable tourism and ecotourism in China.

A shortage in PA funding has resulted in the 'paper park syndrome' in China. A self-funding model has been adopted to cover management costs, and tourism benefits have become the dominant component of the funding structure of PAs. The phenomenon of the 'ticket economy' has followed.

Conflicts between different interests in PA designation and management have accumulated in China. Confined by the stage of development, the conflicts between economic development and nature conservation in China are daunting. The process of urbanization and large-scale infrastructure construction has demonstrated the government's insatiable appetite to develop the economy. Though nature conservation has been elevated to a status with high political significance, it has been bypassed by the overwhelming goal of GDP growth. In addition to encroachment by economic development activities, the commercialization and industrialization of tourism has become a major threat to conservation. Incentivized by the GDP-based performance-assessment system, officials in local governments are inclined to commercialize and develop scenic resources in PAs as much as possible. Due to funding shortfalls, local governments spare no effort in attracting private capital to PA operations, which leads to the rampant construction of tourism amenities. From the discussion of complex government-business arrangements in PA operations, it can be observed that the business sector has intervened in PA management and, to some extent, has 'taken over' PAs. This situation has caused the de facto abdication of governments' management authority to commercial enterprises.

---

133 C.Y. Jim and Steve S.W. Xu, *supra* note 31, p. 40.
134 Guangyu Wang et al., *supra* note 31, p. 256.
135 Cevat Tosun, 'Limits to Community Participation in the Tourism Development Process in Developing Countries', 21.6 (2000) *Tourism Management*, pp. 613–33.
136 See State Council, 中华人民共和国政府信息公开条例 (Regulations on Disclosure of Government Information), May 1, 2008, and SEPA, 环境信息公开办法 (Measures on Disclosure of Environmental Information), May 1, 2008. For scholarly discussion, see generally Miao He and An Cliquet, 'Sustainable Development Through A Rights-based Approach to Conserve Protected Areas in China', 3 (2014) *China-EU Law Journal*, pp. 146–8.
137 See ibid., pp. 148–52. For more discussions, see *infra* pp. 216–19 of Chapter 10.

Lacking the rule of law and efficient supervision of governments' exercise of administrative power, administrative power in tourism development can easily be abused to serve private interests instead of the interests of the general public. The examples of the construction of golf courses, luxury hotels and conferences centers show that the enforcement of central policies at the local level is problematic.

Finally, conflicts between local communities and PA management remain pervasive in China. Local residents suffer from economic disenfranchisement due to PA designation, and they do not always receive sufficient compensation for their losses. In turn, the tourism-related activities and services provided by local residents may also have negative influences on nature. Due to the imbalance in sharing benefits that arises from nature-based tourism between different communities and between communities and local finance, the issue of justice emerges, and a more equitable and fair benefit-sharing scheme is necessary. Local communities' rights to information and to participation are not legislatively guaranteed or translated into practice. This causes problems with the acceptability of management decisions at the community level and intensifies people–park conflicts.

10 The Resolution of Conflicts in Law and Practice in China

Introduction

This chapter aims to show how the conflicts discussed in the previous chapter have been addressed in law and in practice and examines the extent to which a resolution has been achieved. First, to assess the legal foundations of conflict resolution, some key legal instruments are examined, including the purpose statement, designated use pattern, compensation and participation. Although a preliminary normative framework is established in law, the real problem in China does not lie in legal expression but rather in legal practices. The enforcement of conservation law is subsequently discussed, and ad hoc law enforcement campaigns launched by the central authorities are critically examined. In this way, several paramount examples of enforcement deficiencies are identified, such as the rampant adjustment of nature reserves and the overlapping designation and management of PAs. Reasons for the enforcement gap in environmental law in general and in PA regulation in particular are identified and analyzed.

Finally, this chapter examines the role of the judiciary in adjudicating PA-related disputes. The status quo of conservation-related lawsuits in China is discussed. The result shows that courts play a limited, even dormant, role in the resolution of disputes. The predicament of the judiciary regarding the full performance of its functions is discussed and analyzed. Recent developments in the establishment of environmental courts and the empowerment of public interest litigation are critically examined.

The Resolution of Conflicts in Law

Conflicts are addressed in many aspects of Chinese law. The general legal attitude can be observed in the purpose statement of law. Unlike the controversies over 'conservation and enjoyment' embodied in the Organic Act in the US, Chinese legislation has explicitly embraced the principle of the 'priority of protection', which replaces the previous 'principle of coordination'. A designated use pattern is also formulated in the law, which serves to adjudicate conflicts that arise from different uses of resources. The establishment of legal instruments to mitigate 'development conflict' in either procedural or substantive forms can also indicate the degree to which such conflicts have been resolved in law.

The Statement of Fundamental Purpose in Law

From the 'Principle of Coordination' to the 'Priority of Protection'

In the Constitution, both the *rational utilization* and *protection* of nature and resources are included as the State's duties (Articles 9 and 26). Although these articles are used by scholars as a constitutional basis for the principle of the 'priority of ecological protection' in framing natural conservation law,[1] there is no explicit recognition of the 'priority of protection' in the Constitution.

Instead, in the beginning stage of environmental legislation in China, the 'principle of coordination' (协调发展) is deemed a basic principle of environmental law and management practice. Though worded in different ways, its essence is to 'coordinate between economic development, social development and environmental protection'. For example, the Environmental Protection Law (EPL) (for trial implementation) of 1979 provided that 'in making national economic development plans, [governments] should *give overall consideration to* (统筹安排) protection and improvement of the environment and take practical measures for its implementation' (Article 5). At the National Environmental Protection Conference held in 1983, the principle of 'three synchronization, three benefits' (三同步，三效益) was proposed, which suggested that there should be synchronization in terms of planning, enforcement and development between economic construction, urban-rural construction and environmental construction to realize the unification of economic benefits, social benefits and environmental benefits.[2] This conference provided the foundation for the amendment of the EPL in 1989. In the 1989 EPL, the 'coordination principle' was legally established by stating that 'environmental protection plans formulated by the State must be incorporated into national economic and social development plans.' The State adopts economic and technological policies and measures that are favorable for environmental protection to 'coordinate the work of environmental protection with economic construction and social development' (Article 4).

This 'coordination principle' is also reflected in the relevant legislation on specific resources, such as the Forest Law of 1998, the Grassland Law of 2003 and the Land Administration Law of 2004. All of the fundamental purpose statements in Article 1 of these statutes use the terms 'rational utilization' (合理使用) and 'environmental protection'. Both the protection and utilization of natural resources are prescribed in one sentence as an integrated purpose. There is no explicit recognition of the priority of environmental protection. The overall criterion for regulating resource use is the so-called 'rationality' standard.

With regard to the relationship between 'coordinated development' and 'sustainable development', the academic literature suggests that 'coordinated development' is, in reality, the Chinese version of the principle of 'sustainable development'. The only difference is that the former principle emphasizes the horizontal relationship between protection and development, whereas the latter emphasizes a vertical intergenerational relationship.[3] Although the principle of coordination is applauded and enshrined as the basic principle of Chinese environmental law, scholars note that environmental protection is only one of many indicators that need to be considered when developing the economy. The essence of coordination is still the priority of economic development.[4] It requires environmental protection to be

---

1 Wang Jiheng, 论生态环境保护优先原则 (Analysis of the Principle of Priority of Ecological Protection), 5.6 (2011) 河南省政法管理干部学院学报 (*Journal of Henan Administrative Cadre Institute of Politics and Law*), p. 81.
2 Wu Weixing, 从协调发展到环境优先—中国环境法制的历史转型 (From 'Coordinated Development' to 'Priority of Environment': The Historical Turn of the Chinese Environmental Law System), 10.3 (2008) 河海大学学报(哲学社会科学版) (*Journal of Hehai University*), p. 29.
3 Jin Ruilin (ed.), 环境法学 (*Textbook of Environmental Law*) (Beijing: Peking University Press, 1999), p. 122.
4 Zhao Xudong and Huang Jing, 俄罗斯"环境保护优先性"原则：我国环境法"协调发展"原则的反思与改进 (Analysis on the Principle of 'Priority of Environmental Protection' in Russia: Re-thinking and Improvement of the 'Coordination Principle' in China), 6 (2000) 河北法学 (*Hebei Law Science*), p. 131; Cao Mingde, 论生态法的基本原则 (Analysis on the Fundamental Principles of Ecological Protection Law), 6 (2002) 法学评论 (*Law Review*), p. 63.

'coordinated' with economic and social development, not the other way around; that is, economic and social development should be 'coordinated' with the environment. Without the explicit acknowledgment of the priority of protection, the 'coordination principle' has created leeway and has caused the peripheralization of environmental interests and environmental law in practice.[5]

The shortcomings of this 'coordination principle' have been gradually perceived. The principle of the 'priority of protection' has emerged in both policy making and academic research. A 2005 decision by the State Council proposed that 'economic and social development must be coordinated with environmental protection.'[6] By revising the wording of this principle, the primary and secondary status between environmental protection and economic-social development was reversed, at least in theory. The decision also explicitly proposed that priority should be given to protection in ecologically sensitive areas and primary ecological functional zones.

In Chinese academia, the significance of the fundamental principles of environmental law is advocated by scholars. Cao Mingde considers the 'principle of coordination' incongruent with the principle of sustainable development and proposes the 'priority of ecological protection' as one of the fundamental principles of conservation law.[7] Yang Qunfang proposes that the 'priority of environment' should consist of two parts: the priority of protection and the priority of restoration.[8] Wang Canfa proposes adding a specific article to the EPL that elaborates the fundamental principles of environmental law.[9]

The principle of the 'priority of protection' was finally legalized in the EPL of 2014. Together with four other principles, including the prevention first, integrated governance, public participation and liability principles, 'priority of protection' was established as one of the five fundamental principles of environmental law (Article 5). Article 5 was not added to the initial version of the draft amendment to the EPL but rather to the later versions based on public comments.[10] Scholars expressed concern about adding the principle of the 'priority of protection' to the draft.[11]

First, the expression of the 'priority of protection' is seldom seen in environmental legislation in other countries. Chinese scholars who support the addition of this principle usually refer to the Russian Federal Environmental Protection Act of 2002, which has a similar expression in Article 3.[12] Therefore, there is limited legislative precedent on how to define, interpret and apply this principle.

---

5 Wu Weixing, *supra* note 2, p. 29.
6 State Council, 国务院关于落实科学发展观加强环境保护的决定 (Decision of the State Council on Implementing the Outlook of Scientific Development and Strengthening Environmental Protection), *Guofa* No. 39 [2005].
7 Cao Mingde, *supra* note 4.
8 Yang Qunfang, 论环境法的基本原则之环境优先原则 (Analysis of the Principle of Priority of the Environment as a Fundamental Principle of Environmental Law), 2 (2009) 中国海洋大学学报(社会科学版) (*Journal of Ocean University of China (Social Science Edition)*), pp. 62–5.
9 See Yang Chaofei (ed.), 通往环境法制的道路: <环境保护法>修改思路研究报告 (*Path to Environmental Rule of Law: Research report on Amending the Environmental Protection Law*) (Beijing: Zhongguo Huanjing Chubanshe, 2013), p. 85.
10 Zhu Xiao, 论中国环境法基本原则的立法发展与再发展 (Analysis on the Development and Further Development of the Fundamental Principles of Environmental Law in Legislation in China), 3 (2014) 华东政法大学学报 (*Journal of East China University of Political Science and Law*), p. 8.
11 Ibid. (Zhu Xiao reviews the legislative history of the article of fundamental principles, and details scholars' opinions when the draft was passed to the scholarly circle for the purpose of soliciting opinions).
12 Zhao Xudong and Huang Jing, *supra* note 4. Due to the author's limitations of language ability, the way this term is used and defined in its original context of Russian law is not checked.

Second, because Article 4 of the newly amended EPL prescribes that 'environmental protection is a basic State policy' and 'economic and social development should be coordinated with environmental protection'. it is unclear how the principle of the 'priority of protection' can be coordinated with these two provisions. Zhu Xiao argues that the provisions in Article 4 clarify the relationship between protection and development; therefore, there is no need to add the principle of the 'priority of protection' as a fundamental principle in Article 5. Instead, he argues for the addition of the 'precautionary principle' as a governing principle to replace the 'priority of protection' and 'prevention first'.[13]

Although problems remain with regard to the way the principle should be defined and interpreted, it has now been established as a fundamental principle of environmental law. Thus, this principle has become an overarching mandate for all relevant fields that address environmental protection, and PA management is no exception. In reality, in addition to the new EPL, the principle of the 'priority of protection' has already been included in separate congressional statutes, such as the Sea Island Protection Law of 2009 (Article 3) and the amended Soil and Water Conservation Law of 2010 (Article 3).

Purpose Statements of PA Designation and Management

This section reviews the evolution of purpose statements in the regulations of PA designation and management and discusses how the principle of the 'priority of protection' may apply to them.

SHAs

The Interim Regulations on Scenic and Historic Areas (1985) stated, 'These regulations are enacted to strengthen the management of SHAs, better *protect, utilize and develop* the scenic and historic resources' (Article 1). In the amended Regulations on Scenic and Historic Areas (2006), the wording was slightly different: 'to *effectively* protect and *rationally* utilize scenic and historic resources'. The general requirements for the effectiveness of the protection and rationality of utilization were added, and the 'development of resources' was excluded from the purpose statement. The amended Regulations also added one article to the fundamental principle of regulation of SHAs: 'the State adheres to the principle of scientific planning, integrated management, strict protection and perpetual utilization (永续利用)' (Article 3).

Although the 'priority of protection' is not enshrined as a fundamental principle in the Regulations, one article uses the term 'priority of protection' by stating that 'the master plans of SHAs should accord with the principle of "protection first and development second"' (Article 13). Furthermore, although 'sustainable development' is not prescribed as one of the fundamental principles of SHA management, it provides that 'the landscape and natural environment within SHAs should be strictly protected in light of the principle of sustainable development' (Article 24).

NATURE RESERVES

Article 1 of the Regulations on Nature Reserves (1994) states that these regulations are enacted 'to strengthen the establishment and management of nature reserves and protect the natural environment and natural resources'. Aiming for strict protection, the regulations do

---

13 Zhu Xiao, *supra* note 10, p. 9.

not even list 'utilization' as one of the purposes. Furthermore, unlike section 5, which is titled 'Utilization and Management' in the Regulations on SHAs, there is no single section on the utilization of resources in the Regulations on Nature Reserves. A strong pro-preservation feature of nature reserve management is found therein.

FOREST PARKS

In the Measures of the Administration of Forest Parks issued by the SFA in 1993 (1993 Measures), the legislative purpose was stated as follows: 'to strengthen the management of forest parks, *rationally utilize* the scenic resources of forests and *develop* the forest-related tourism industry' (Article 1). The purpose of 'protection' was not mentioned. This statement was amended when the Measures of the Administration of Forest Parks at the National Level was issued by the SFA in 2011 (2011 Measures), in which the legislative purpose was defined to 'normalize the management of forests parks at the national level, *protect and rationally utilize* scenic resources of forests, develop ecological tourism in forests and promote the development of ecological civilization' (Article 1). The 2011 Measures explicitly enshrine the 'coordination principle' as a governing principle of forest park management (Article 5).

Unlike nature reserves, other types of PAs have addressed both protection and utilization in their legislative purposes. A general requirement of 'rational utilization' is provided. A dominant feature of embracing the 'principle of coordination' is seen across these types of PAs. Because the new EPL explicitly adopts the principle of the 'priority of protection', this has become a governing principle in PA management as well. Therefore, considering the ongoing efforts to enact a fundamental law for PAs, the principle of the 'priority of protection' should be explicitly recognized. However, the draft of the Natural Heritage Law prescribes principles of 'sufficient protection, proper use (适度利用) and perpetuity for future generations' (Article 4). Although it shows a strong pro-protection feature, a more explicit incorporation of the principle of 'priority of protection' is needed to maintain consistency and unity within the legal system.

The Designated Use Pattern in PAs

Similar to the US, a designated use pattern has been formulated within different types of PAs. By establishing a hierarchy of different uses in law, conflicts between particular interests and claims to use resources, 'resource conflict' in the classification model presented above can be effectively managed.

In nature reserves, the designated use pattern is mainly formulated through the zoning mechanism. According to the Regulations on Nature Reserves (the Regulations), within a nature reserve, different degrees of regulation are applied to different zones, namely, core, buffer and experimental zones:

1   The core zone aims for pristine preservation and represents the most precious ecological value of nature reserves. No type of entry by any individual or any unit is allowed therein, and limited scientific research activities are allowed based on case-by-case approval (Article 27).
2   The buffer zone surrounds the core zone, and scientific research and observation is allowed; however, tourism, commercial activities and the construction of production facilities are prohibited (Article 28 and 32).
3   The experimental zone receives a lower degree of protection than the former two. Activities such as scientific experiments, educational practices, sightseeing, tourism and the domestication and breeding of precious and endangered species are permitted.

No production facilities that cause environmental pollution or damage to the natural resource landscape can be built in the experimental zone (Article 32).

The mandatory percentage of the area of specific zones is not provided in the Regulations. However, according to the Outline of the Overall Planning of Nature Reserves at the National Level issued by the SEPA in 2002,[14] a mandatory provision stated that the area of the core zone of a nature reserve at the national level should be more than one-third of the total area and the area of the experimental zone should be less than one-third of the total area (Article 1.5).

Generally, activities such as felling, grazing, hunting, fishing, collecting medicinal herbs, reclaiming, burning, mining, quarrying and sand dredging are prohibited within nature reserves. These activities are allowed unless exceptional stipulations in laws and administrative regulations are otherwise provided (Article 26).

Unlike nature reserves, a strict zoning system is not explicitly adopted in SHA management. A general distinction between 'core scenic spots' and 'other scenic spots' is provided in the Regulations on SHAs (2006). This distinction can be observed in the scope of 'prohibited activities': Article 27 states that 'any construction of a hotel, hostel, training center, sanitarium or other building irrelevant to the protection of scenic and historic resources is prohibited within the *core scenic spots* of an SHA.' It can be deduced that the construction projects that are prohibited within 'core scenic spots' are allowed in 'other scenic spots', based on examination and approval procedures.

Similar to the congressional instruction to the NPS to 'promote and regulate' the uses of national park resources in the US, agencies are required to 'promote healthy and beneficial sightseeing as well as cultural and entertainment activities within SHAs' (Article 32) and 'improve the transportation, service and tourist facilities' (Article 33). These provisions indicate that the dominant designated use of SHAs is recreational use. In addition to dedicated recreational use, other commercial uses of scenic resources are allowed based on examination and approval procedures. Article 29 states that the following activities need to be approved: the installation and display of commercial advertisements, large-scale entertainment activities, activities that would change the natural state of water resources or water environments, and other activities that affect ecology and the landscape.

Similar to SHAs, there is no strict zoning in forest parks except for the provision that 'no hotel, hostel, sanatorium or other construction project is allowed to be built in precious landscapes, key scenic spots and core scenic areas' (Article 11, Measures of the Administration of Forest Parks of 1993). The main functions of 'forest parks at the national level' are fleshed out by the 2011 Measures: 'to protect forestry scenic resources and biodiversity, to popularize the knowledge of ecological culture and to promote forest-based ecotourism' (Article 5). Timber resources are strictly protected within forest parks: 'felling of trees is only allowed for purposes of cultivation and thinning in order to increase the quality of forest-based scenic resources or conduct forest-based ecotourism' (Article 14). In addition to timber management activities, the 2011 Measures prescribe regulations on film shooting and large-scale performance activities within forest parks. These activities are not prohibited per se, but they are allowed with approval (Article 19).

Based on the discussion above and the model of designated use developed in the context of the US,[15] the respective hierarchy of designated uses within nature reserves, SHAs and forest parks is shown below.

14 SEPA, 国家级自然保护区总体规划大纲 (Outline of Overall Planning of Nature Reserves at the National Level), 2002. Available at http://sts.mep.gov.cn/zrbhq/fzgy/200206/t20020626_90651.htm. Last visited January 2015.
15 See *supra* pp. 122–4 of Chapter 6.

216   Country Studies: China

Table 10.1 Comparison of designated use patterns among nature reserves, SHAs and forest parks

Nature reserves		SHAs	Forest parks
Protection ('natural environment and natural resources')		Protection ('scenic and historical resources')	Protection ('forest-based scenic resources and biodiversity')
Core zone	Preservation	Recreation and tourism	Forest-based recreation and tourism
Buffer zone	Scientific research and observation		
Experimental zone	Scientific experiments, education, sightseeing, tourism, species management		
Commodity use based on explicit exceptional provisions stipulated in laws and administrative regulations (Article 26)		Scenic resource-based commercial activities (e.g. advertising, entertainment activities) (Article 29)	Forestry management activities (e.g. timber thinning and cultivation) (Article 14); forest-based commercial activities (e.g. film shooting and performance) (Article 19)

Source: Adapted from relevant regulations

Compensation and Participation at the Community Level

To mitigate people-park conflicts (i.e. 'development conflict' in the classification model), general principles governing the relationship between conservation and local communities are stipulated. Instruments such as ecological compensation, public participation and community-based management in both substantive and procedural terms are prescribed in legislations and policies.

Ecological Compensation

In the Regulations on Nature Reserves of 1994, a general principle is stipulated that 'in the process of designating and managing nature reserves, local economic development, local residents' production activities and livelihoods should be taken into consideration' (Article 5). In terms of the boundary demarcation of nature reserves, it is prescribed that the 'demarcation of the scope and boundary of nature reserves should take into consideration the integrity and appropriateness of the protected object, and the necessities of local economic construction and residents' producing and living needs' (Article 14). The Regulations state that 'if it is necessary to move out the residents living in the core zone of a nature reserve, local governments should *make proper arrangements* (妥善安置) to settle them down elsewhere' (Article 27). These provisions are principle-based without further elaboration. Disputes arise between local governments and local communities regarding what types of arrangements can be deemed proper and what types cannot.

In the Regulations on SHAs of 2006, the principle of the 'protection of property rights within designated SHAs' is generally provided. The property rights of the owners and users of land, resources and real estate within SHAs are legally protected (Article 11). This is reflected in two aspects:

1   Compulsory consultation procedures before the designation of a SHA: local governments are required to 'fully consult with' property owners and users before designating a SHA (Article 11). The results of such consultation are listed as one of the requisite documents for applying for the designation of an SHA (Article 9).
2   The payment of compensation to the owners and users for their losses arising from the designation of SHAs (Article 11).

The Measures of the Administration of Forest Parks of 1993 have no provisions on coordinating interests between local communities and forest park management or a mechanism for compensation. The Measures of the Administration of Forest Parks at the National Level of 2011 address this gap by providing that 'compensation should be paid to relevant parties within forest parks at the national level for their losses arising from the implementation of the master plans of forest parks at the national level' (Article 16). Furthermore, it is stated that 'agencies should guide those communities living within or near forest parks to conduct endemic and pollution-free farming, husbandry and processing of forest by-products, encourage them to conduct forest resource-management activities and tourism-related activities' (Article 27).

In addition to these provisions on the relevant regulations of PAs, compensation mechanisms have been established in relevant statutes. For example, the Forestry Law of 1998 establishes the 'compensation fund for ecological benefits of forests' (森林生态效益补偿基金), especially for the 'afforestation, cultivation, protection and administration of forest resources and trees within shelter forests and forests for special use' (Article 8). As mentioned earlier, forest-type nature reserves, forests in designated SHAs and forests within forest parks fall into the category of 'forests for special use'. The Regulations for Implementing the Forestry Law issued by the State Council in 2000 explicitly provide that the 'operators of shelter forests and forests for special use have the right to obtain compensation from the compensation fund for the ecological benefit of forests' (Article 15). Furthermore, the Wildlife Protection Law of 2004 provides that 'compensation should be made by local governments to those who suffer from crop loss or other losses due to the protection of wildlife; measures of such compensation should be formulated by governments at the provincial level' (Article 14). This applies to compensation in designated PAs as well.

The new EPL of 2014 explicitly establishes the 'ecological compensation' system. It states that the State should increase financial transfer payments to PAs, and the State guides the governments of ecologically benefited areas and ecologically protected areas in providing compensation through consultation or in accordance with market rules (Article 31).

Local legislation has also made advances in promoting ecological compensation in designated PAs. For example, in 2013, the government of Wuhan City in Hubei Province issued the Provisional Measures on the Ecological Compensation of Wetland Nature Reserves in Wuhan.[16] Ecological compensation is defined as the 'compensation of economic losses due to the restriction of production and operation activities and feeding of avian and other wildlife in order to protect and restore the ecological services provided by wetland nature reserves' (Article 3). The Measures also prescribe principles, including principles regarding 'who loses, who obtains compensation', standards, funding sources and responsibility mechanisms for ecological compensation.

16   People's Government of Wuhan City, 武汉市湿地自然保护区生态补偿暂行办法 (Provisional Measures on the Ecological Compensation of Wetland Nature Reserves in Wuhan), effective on January 1, 2014, *Wuzhenggui* No. 19 [2013]. Full text is available at http://www.whepb.gov.cn/hbZrbhq/104064.jhtml. Last visited January 2015.

Access to Information and Public Participation

Public participation is not explicitly stipulated in the Regulations on Nature Reserves. The Regulations on SHAs require public participation in making the master plans for SHAs. The Regulations state that 'opinions should be fully solicited from relevant departments, the general public and experts; and a hearing should be held when necessary' (Article 18). They also require that solicited opinions and the reasons for adopting or not adopting these opinions should be included in the documents to be submitted for approving the master plans of SHAs (ibid.). Similar to the provisions in SHAs, the Measures of the Administration of Forest Parks at the National Level of 2011 prescribe the requirement of soliciting public opinion in making forest park master plans (Article 10).

The new EPL of 2014 prescribes public participation as one of five fundamental principles (Article 5). An entire chapter of the law specifically addresses the issue of information disclosure and public participation (Chapter 5).[17] However, most of the articles in this Chapter relate to the disclosure of pollution-related information and public participation in the EIA of construction projects. Local communities' participation in PA designation and management is not specifically addressed in the EPL. Other environmental statutes and regulations also provide for citizens' participatory rights in EIA, such as the EIA Law of 2003 and the Regulations on the EIA of Planning of 2009.[18]

In addition to legislation, policy making has paid increasing attention to resolving conflicts between local communities and nature protection. Instruments such as incentive-based mechanisms, public participation and community-based management have been adopted in policies. The Strategy and Action Plan for Biodiversity Protection in China (2011–30), which was issued by the MoEP in 2010,[19] proposed to 'establish incentive mechanisms that combine biodiversity protection and poverty alleviation and to protect local governments and indigenous communities to participate in the construction and management of nature reserves' (Article 3(4)(4)). In this Action Plan, proposals to conduct pilot programs of the community-based co-management of nature reserves were also made (Priority Action 14). Community-based management is considered an effective management strategy that is applauded worldwide.[20] However, although China has carried out some initiatives in the community-based management of PAs, this is not a common practice. According to a survey conducted in 2009 based on approximately 200 nature reserves in China, 42.5 percent of these nature reserves have not conducted such management projects, and 14.7 percent do not incorporate local communities into policy making or decision making.[21]

---

17 For analysis of the public participation provisions in the new EPL, see generally Lang Huanlin, *Public Participation in Environmental Decision-Making in China: Towards an Ecosystem Approach*, PhD dissertation at the University of Groningen, Netherlands, 2014.
18 State Council, 中华人民共和国环境影响评价法 (EIA Law), September 1, 2003, and 中华人民共和国规划环境影响评价条例 (Regulations on EIA of Planning), October 1, 2009.
19 MoEP, 中国生物多样性保护战略与行动计划 (2011–30年) (The Strategy and Action Plan for Biodiversity Protection in China (2011–30)), *Huanfa* No. 106 [2010]. Full text is available at http://www.mep.gov.cn/gkml/hbb/bwj/201009/t20100921_194841.htm. Last visited January 2015.
20 See generally Grazia Borrini-Feyerabend, Shish Kothari and Gonzalo Oviedo, *Indigenous and Local Communities and Protected Areas: Towards Equity and Enhanced Conservation* (Gland, Switzerland and Cambridge, IUCN: 2004).
21 Xu Jiliang et al., 'A Review and Assessment of Nature Reserve Policy in China: Advances, Challenges and Opportunities', 46.4 (2012) *Oryx*, p. 559.

At the legislative level, especially after the enactment of the new EPL of 2014, a preliminary normative framework for access to information and public participation has been established in China. However, gaps still exist in terms of the scope, representation and procedures of participation.[22] The way that local communities can fully access information and effectively participate in the process of PA designation and management is still not firmly guaranteed by law. Existing PA regulations are either silent on this issue or lack specificity and enforceability. What is even more challenging is how to translate law into practice.

Compliance and Enforcement of Law in Practice: A Critical Examination

The issues surrounding the noncompliance and implementation deficits of environmental laws and regulations have been observed by many scholars.[23] It has even been asserted that 'China's problem now is not the absence of environmental laws but the challenge of making them work.'[24] These observations are generally made in the scenario of pollution control. Though the absence of a comprehensive law on PAs is still one of the most formidable challenges at the legislative level, the implementation gap in the field of nature conservation is similar to the case of pollution control. This section examines the implementation of laws and regulations on nature conservation and analyzes the reasons for the deficiencies in implementing conservation law in China.

The preliminary question is how to detect and examine the situation of law enforcement in practice. Relevant authorities in China periodically conduct ad hoc campaigns on the examination of law enforcement to detect and rectify incompliance with laws and regulations. This is deemed a characteristic of the regime of environmental law in China.[25] A discussion of the results of such ad hoc law enforcement campaigns in the field of nature reserves and SHA regulations could help in understanding the problems of law enforcement in reality.

The Examination of the Enforcement of Nature Reserve Regulations

In 2005, by issuing the Notices on the ad hoc Examination on Law Enforcement in Nature Reserves,[26] the MoEP launched a campaign that lasted from March to October 2005 to strengthen law enforcement in nature reserves. This was the first time that such a campaign

---

22 For analysis on whether Chinese legislation on public participation has fulfilled the requirements of participation embodied in sustainable development, see generally Lang Huanlin, *supra* note 17, pp. 163–75.
23 Alasdair MacBean, 'China's Environment: Problems and Policies', 30 (2007) *World Economy*, p. 300; Zuo Keyan, 'Management of Marine Nature Reserves in China: A Legal Perspective', 6.3 (2003) *Journal of International Wildlife Law & Policy*, p. 196; John Zinda, 'Hazards of Collaboration: Local State Co-optation of a New Protected Area Model in Southwest China', 25.4 (2012) *Society & Natural Resources*, pp. 384–99; Charles McElwee, *Environmental Law in China: Mitigating Risk and Ensuring Compliance* (New York: Oxford University Press, 2011), pp. 3–9, and D.Q. Zhou and R. Edward Grumbine, 'National Parks in China: Experiments with Protecting Nature and Human Livelihoods in Yunnan Province, Peoples' Republic of China (PRC)', 144 (2011) *Biological Conservation*, pp. 1314–21.
24 Dan Guttman and Song Yaqin, 'Making Central-local Relations Work: Comparing America and China. Environmental Governance Systems', 1.4 (2007) *Frontiers of Environmental Science & Engineering*, p. 418.
25 Benjamin Van Rooij, *Regulating Land and Pollution in China, Lawmaking, Compliance, and Enforcement; Theory and Cases* (Leiden: Leiden University Press, 2006).
26 MoEP, 关于开展自然保护区专项执法检查的通知 (Notices on Ad Hoc Examination of Law Enforcement in Nature Reserves), *Huanfa* No. 37 [2005].

was specifically launched for nature reserves.[27] According to the circulation released by the MoEP in November 2005, 23 provinces and 2,056 nature reserves were covered in this campaign. In total, 506 cases were filed, 158 entities were required to go through the EIA within a limited period, 260 construction projects were shut down, 136 projects were required to undertake special treatment within a limited period, 10 tourist routes were closed, 66 people were charged, and 23 cases were transferred to other authorities for treatment.[28] The MoEP also circulated seven typical cases of illegal activities that derogated the nature reserves, such as mining, illegal plantation and installment, and construction of hydropower stations and other facilities without EIA and approval.[29]

The MoEP summarized the problems of nature reserve management and the enforcement of nature reserve regulations found in this campaign, which included the following:

1 The approval of applications for designating nature reserves outweighs the construction and management of natural reserves by local governments,
2 The development within nature reserves outweighs the protection of nature reserves and
3 The application to be upgraded to nature reserves at a higher level outweighs the management of nature reserves.[30]

Specifically, noncompliance with laws and regulations is exemplified by the illegal exploitation of mineral resources, the construction of transportation facilities, hydroelectric power stations and forestry-related facilities, and rampant tourism development activities.[31]

In addition to this ad hoc campaign in 2005, the MoEP subsequently launched several more campaigns, such as the campaign in 2010 about the ad hoc examination of law enforcement in nature reserves at the national level[32] and the campaign in 2013 regarding the water sources of the centralized supply of drinking water and nature reserves at the national level.[33] The key points of the 2010 round included the following:

1 Whether there are development and construction activities within nature reserves that derogate environmental quality and ecological services,
2 Whether EIA procedures have been carried out according to the law in terms of construction projects and operational activities,
3 Whether protection, restoration and compensation measures are carried out when construction and development activities are conducted and

---

27 Xinhuanet, 国家环保总局首次开展全国自然保护区专项检查 (The MoEP Launched the Ad Hoc Examination of Nature Reserves for the First Time), April 1, 2005, available at http://news.xinhuanet.com/st/2005-04/01/content_2773209.htm. Last visited January 2015.
28 Gu Ruizhen, 环保总局通报7个破坏自然保护区典型违法案件 (The MoEP Circulates 7 Typical Cases with Regards to Illegal Activities Within Nature Reserves), November 15, 2005, available at http://news.xinhuanet.com/politics/2005-11/15/content_3784206.htm. Last visited January 2015.
29 See Xinhuanet, 环保总局通报2005年破坏自然保护区典型违法案件 (The MoEP Circulates Typical Cases with Regards to Illegal Activities Within Nature Reserves in 2005), November 15, 2005, available at http://news.xinhuanet.com/politics/2005-11/15/content_3785387.htm. Last visited January 2015.
30 Gu Ruizhen, *supra* note 28.
31 Ibid.
32 MoEP, 关于开展国家级自然保护区专项执法检查的通知 (Notices on Ad Hoc Examination on Law Enforcement in Nature Reserves at the National Level), *Huanbanhan* No. 184 [2010].
33 MoEP, 关于开展集中式饮用水水源地和国家级自然保护区专项执法督查的通知(Notice on Ad Hoc Examination on Law Enforcement in Water Source of Centralized Supply of Drinking Water and Nature Reserves at the National Level), *Huanban* No. 77 [2013].

4   Whether the boundary and zoning plan of nature reserves are arbitrarily adjusted, that is, against the stipulation made by the State Council.[34]

These ad hoc campaigns illustrate that problems of law enforcement are not fully rectified by one campaign, as evidenced by repeated and periodic ad hoc campaigns. As Percival comments, these ad hoc campaigns are only 'temporary and undertaken in part to cool down an overheating economy'.[35] Moreover, the main problem of law enforcement lies in the developmental needs of natural resources within reserves. Such needs emerge not only from exploitative commodity use, such as mining and timbering, but also from tourism development activities. A peculiar phenomenon of law enforcement deficiencies in China is the rampant adjustment of nature reserves to circumvent laws and regulations, as discussed below.

The Adjustment of Nature Reserves: Regulations and Enforcement

The phenomenon of the adjustment of nature reserves refers to the de-designation, adjustment of zoning plans, change of boundaries, and change of protected objects in nature reserves. As discussed earlier, due to strict protection within nature reserves, the designation of a PA, especially in the form of a nature reserve, confines the development of the local economy and the exploitation of natural resources. It also imposes burdens on local governments to actively manage the area and monitor it to prevent noncompliance. Therefore, rampant adjustments of reserve boundaries (i.e. the shrinkage of the PA) or even the de-designation of protected status as a nature reserve are frequently exposed by the media. For example, to facilitate the construction of a hydropower station, a conference center and other facilities, the former core zone in the Jinggang Mountain Nature Reserve was adjusted to become a buffer zone and an experimental zone.[36] In 2003, local governments in Yunnan Province received a warning from UNESCO stating that the Three Parallel Rivers Scenic and Historic Area would be delisted from the list of World Heritage Sites if they proceeded with the plan to reduce the total area by 20 percent and to allow mining and hydropower station construction in this area.[37] The negative consequences of these adjustments are explicit, including, but not limited to, the fragmentation of ecosystems, deterioration of habitats for species, and derogation of natural landscapes and enjoyment opportunities.

Strict requirements have been provided in the Regulations on Nature Reserves, which state that the 'de-designation of a nature reserve or any change or adjustment made to its

---

34 Results of the latter rounds of ad hoc campaigns in 2010 and 2013 were not circulated by the MoEP, therefore can only be observed by sporadic information. These four points are summarized from the Department of Environmental Protection in Hubei Province, 湖北省开展国家级自然保护区专项执法检查实施方案 (Implementation Plan of Hubei Province in Conducting Ad Hoc Examination of Law Enforcement of Nature Reserves at the National Level), March 29, 2010, *Ehuanfa* No. 4 [2010]. Full text is available at http://www.hbepb.gov.cn/zwgk/zcwj/shbjwj/201004/t20100402_28846.html. Last visited January 2015.

35 Robert Percival, 'The Challenge of Chinese Environmental Law', 10 (2008) *International Environmental Law Committee Newsletter*, p. 4.

36 See Feng Yongfeng, 中国自然保护区纷纷调整功能，意在经济开发 (Successive Adjustment of Functions of Nature Reserves in China Aiming at Economic Development), June 30, 2009, available at http://culture.gansudaily.com.cn/system/2009/06/30/011154850.shtml. Last visited January 2015.

37 See Yang Min, 云南建议重新划定三江并流，遗产地面积减少20% (Yunnan Suggests Re-drawing the Boundary of the Three Parallel Rivers, the Area of Heritage Site will be Reduced by 20%), October 16, 2006, available at http://www.china.com.cn/city/txt/2006-10/16/content_7245176.htm. Last visited January 2015. See also Guangyu Wang et al., 'National Park Development in China: Conservation or Commercialization?', 41 (2012) *AMBIO*, pp. 252–3.

nature, range or boundaries should be subject to the approval of the people's government which approved the establishment of the nature reserve' (Article 15). However, enforcement of this rule is far from satisfactory in practice. To cope with this problem, in 2002, the State Council issued the Reply to the MoEP Regarding the Provisions on the Administration of Adjustments of Boundary and Functional Zones and the Change of the Title of Nature Reserve at the National Level (the Reply).[38] The MoEP is thus empowered to supervise the mentioned adjustments, and 'other related departments' are in charge of regulating such adjustments based on their respective authorities (Article 4). It is explicitly prescribed that

> ... the scope, the zoning system and the name of nature reserves at the national level should not be adjusted and changed *ad libitum* ... the shrinkage of the scopes of the core zone and buffer zone of nature reserves at the national level should be strictly regulated. (Article 5)

To regulate similar adjustments to nature reserves at local levels, in 2008, the MoEP and six other departments co-issued the Notice on Strengthening the Administration of Adjustments of Nature Reserve,[39] which expanded the examination and approval procedures to nature reserves at the local level (Article 4). Following this notice, the SFA issued a notice in 2008 to address the adjustment of forest-type nature reserves. It added to the previous regulations by stating that 'adjustments are prohibited to those which are titled as nature reserves at the national level in recent years, and strict regulation should be applied to adjustments within nature reserves below the provincial level' (Article 1).

This prohibitive clause by the SFA was further quantified by the State Council in 2010, which explicitly stipulated that 'adjustments to nature reserves are prohibited, in principle, within *five years* of the date on which the establishment of or adjustments to the nature reserve is approved' (Article 2).[40]

In December 2013, the State Council issued Regulations on the Administration of the Adjustment of Nature Reserves at the National Level (the Regulations).[41] Guiding principles were set for the adjustment of nature reserves:

> ... the sizes of core zones and buffer zones should not shrink in principle. The adjustment of nature reserves should guarantee that the main protected objects are effectively protected, the integrity of ecological systems and ecological processes is not derogated, the biodiversity is not impaired, and the nature of a nature reserve is not changed. (Article 5)

According to the official explanation of this new regulation by the MoEP, compared to previous policy documents, the new Regulations made the following changes:

---

38 State Council, 国务院关于环保总局《国家级自然保护区范围调整和功能区调整及更改名称管理规定》的批复, January 29, 2002, *Guohan* No. 5 [2002]. Full text available at http://www.gov.cn/gongbao/content/2002/content_61943.htm. Last visited January 2015.
39 MoEP et al., 关于加强自然保护区调整管理工作的通知 (Notice on Strengthening the Administration of Adjustments of Nature Reserves), April 29, 2008, *Huanfa* No. 30 [2008].
40 State Council, 国务院办公厅关于做好自然保护区管理有关工作的通知 (Notice of General Office of the State Council on Satisfactorily Doing Related Work on the Administration of Nature Reserve), *Guobanfa* No. 63 [2010].
41 State Council, 国家级自然保护区调整管理规定 (Regulations on Administration of Adjustment of Nature Reserves at National Level), *Guohan* No. 129 [2013].

1   Specific causes for adjustment were provided, including a major change of natural conditions, frequent human activities in populated regions inside nature reserves, the need for national major construction projects, and major changes to main protected projects (Article 6).
2   The prohibitive period of adjustment was set: 'adjustments to nature reserves are prohibited, in principle, within five years of the date on which the establishment of or adjustments to the nature reserve is approved' (Article 5). Furthermore, 'a nature reserve at the national level should not be adjusted again if it has been adjusted due to major construction projects' (Article 8).
3   Special protection was provided to those nature reserves with crucial ecological significance. Core zones of these nature reserves could only be enlarged instead of shrunk or exchanged (Article 7).
4   Procedural requirements were added to adjust nature reserves and requirements of consultation to community members, public participation and ecological compensation were incorporated (Articles 8 and 11), and
5   A responsibility mechanism was provided to guarantee compliance (Article 16).[42]

The Regulations are the latest administrative regulations by the State Council on nature reserve management. The initial concern is to reconcile the conflicts between nature reserve protection and the desires of local governments to construct large-scale projects and develop the tourism economy. However, risks remain. The Regulations clearly include 'the necessity for national major construction projects' (国家重大工程) as a legal cause of nature reserve adjustment, which are defined as projects that are examined and approved by the State Council (Article 6). Discretionary power to allow potentially negative influences on nature reserves has not been eradicated but has been shifted from the hands of local governments to the central government. As long as the State Council deems that the economic and social benefits of a proposed project outweigh the benefits of nature conservation, the adjustment of nature reserves can be easily legitimized. In reality, projects that are deemed 'national major construction projects' have more destructive influences on nature than those without national significance, such as the Three Gorges Dam Project, the South-to-North Water Diversion Project (南水北调) and the West-to-East Electricity Transfer Project (西气东输). In this sense, the Regulations may function as a watchdog for local governments' misbehavior. However, it is unclear how to include the central government in the supervision framework.

The Examination of the Enforcement of SHA Regulations

Similar to ad hoc campaigns in nature reserves, in 2003, the MoC (now the MoHURD) launched a campaign for the comprehensive rectification (综合整治) of SHA management nationwide.[43] The rectification of misbehaviors in SHA management was expected to be finished in 2005; however, it was ultimately extended to 2007.[44] The main focus of this five-year long examination included the following:

---

42 MoEP, 环境保护部就国家级自然保护区调整管理规定答问 (Questions and Answers with Regards to the Regulations on the Administration of the Adjustment of Nature Reserves at National Level by the MoEP), December 11, 2013. Available at http://www.gov.cn/jrzg/2013-12/11/content_2545994.htm. Last visited January 2015.
43 MoC, 关于开展国家重点风景名胜区综合整治工作的通知 (Notice on Conducting the Comprehensive Rectification of the Work of National Key Scenic and Historic Areas), March 11, 2003, *Jianbancheng* No. 12 [2003].
44 MoC, 关于做好2005年度国家重点风景名胜区综合整治工作的通知 (Notice on Conducting the Comprehensive Rectification of the Work of National Key Scenic and Historic Area in 2005), August 27, 2005, *Jianbancheng* No. 69 [2005].

224 *Country Studies: China*

1   The placement of the logo and board of National Key SHAs,
2   The establishment of the management bodies of SHAs,
3   The separation of management authority and the commercial operation of SHAs,
4   The demarcation of core protected areas of SHAs and the specific protection plans of these areas,
5   Illegal construction activities and other activities that derogate the environment and
6   The formation of rules and policies for the ground management of SHAs.[45]

According to the circulation of the rectification results released by the MoC in 2007, the management of SHAs demonstrated visible improvements through this five-year campaign in terms of the enactment of local regulations and rules, the formulation of SHA master plans, trans-departmental coordination, and the control of illegal construction.[46] The most prominent problems of the on-the-ground management of SHAs included the following:

1   Some SHAs transferred the administrative functions of management, planning, supervision and the collection of entrance fees to private enterprises;
2   Construction projects were illegally approved and constructed; and
3   The master plans of SHAs were not formulated within the time limit prescribed by law.

Furthermore, the MoC noted that some local governments illegally transfer land within SHAs to enterprises or change the purpose of land use from agricultural land to land for the construction of tourism facilities and real estate development under the banner of developing scenic resources. For example, the administrative agency of the SHA of Wudang Mountain in Shanxi Province transferred 700 *mu* of farmland to commercial land by signing two agreements with local villagers.[47]

Following this five-year renovation campaign from May to October 2012, the MoHURD conducted a series of ad hoc examinations on law enforcement within SHAs at the national level. The circulation of the examination result showed that among the 48 SHAs that were randomly selected for examination, 16 obtained scores higher than 90 and ranked as 'Excellent', 27 obtained scores between 60 and 90 and ranked as 'Qualified or Good' (15 of which were ordered to rectify their problems within a limited period) and 5 SHAs obtained scores lower than 60 and ranked as 'Disqualified' (these SHAs were ordered to be rectified within a limited period).[48] As a result, 20 SHAs out of 48 were deemed to be poorly managed, and they were ordered to be rectified within a limited period. The main problems of law enforcement within these 20 SHAs included the following:

---

45 These points were repetitively mentioned in both the 2003 and 2005 notices issued by the MoC shown in the previous two footnotes.
46 MoHURD, 全国国家级风景名胜区综合整治情况通报新闻发布会文字实录 (Manuscript of the Press Conference on Circulating the Result of the Comprehensive Rectification of the Work on Scenic and Historic Areas at the National Level), December 26, 2007. Available at http://www.mohurd.gov.cn/zxydt/200804/t20080424_162768.html. Last visited January 2015.
47 This case was mentioned by the MoHURD officials in the press conference of the circulation. See ibid.
48 MoHURD, 住房城乡建设部关于国家级风景名胜区保护管理执法检查结果的通报 (Circulation on the Examination Result of Law Enforcement of the Protection and Management of Scenic and Historic Areas at the National Level), December 27, 2012, *Jianchenghan* No. 250 [2012]. Full text is available at http://www.gov.cn/zwgk/2012-12/06/content_2283754.htm. Last visited January 2015.

1   The absence or deficiency of a management agency,
2   Illegal construction projects without undergoing of examination and approval procedures,
3   Delays in formulating master plans or specific resource plans,
4   Illegal transfer of operation rights, management functions and the right to collect entry fees to private enterprises and
5   Deficiencies in the effective monitoring and enforcement of the law.

The Overlapping Designation and Management of PAs: Regulations and Enforcement

Although PAs are categorized into different categories and managed by different departments, the boundary between different designations is not clear. Although inter-agency rivalry, especially between the NPS and the USFS, is also found in public land management in the US, each of its management agencies manages its own system under a specific congressional mandate. At least in terms of geographical boundaries, there is no overlap in their jurisdictions. However, in China, overlapping designation and management is commonplace. The former refers to multiple designations of PAs in the same geographical territory, and the latter refers to multiple management bodies in a particular designated PA. Different institutions manage the same PA based on different standards in accordance with their respective mandates. Therefore, friction and conflicts arise from this overlapping jurisdiction.

Examples of overlapping designations are numerous. The SHA of Wulingyuan at the National Level consists of four components: the Zhangjiajie National Forest Park (the first national forest park in China) and three nature reserves (Suoxiyu, Tianzishan and Yangjiajie).[49] The SHA of Three Parallel Rivers at the National Level in Yunnan Province consists of nine nature reserves and ten SHAs at different levels.[50] According to a 2009 report, there were 102 SHAs at the national level that overlapped with nature reserves, and the boundaries of 18 SHAs were exactly the same as those designated as nature reserves.[51]

Overlapping management is also commonplace in practice. Because management authority for wildlife, water, land, grassland and forestry is given to different departments, a PA is managed by a variety of authorities. This situation is dubbed 'nine dragons co-govern the water' (九龙治水). Taking the SHA of Wulingyuan as an example, there are two main management authorities in this area: the government of Wulingyuan District, which was specifically established based on the geographical scope of Wulingyuan, and the Management Agency of Zhangjiajie Forest Park, which was subordinated to the SFA. Both of these authorities have more than a thousand working staff members in the Wulingyuan area. Furthermore, the MoHURD, the MoEP, the Ministry of Land and Resources and the Tourist Bureau of Zhangjiajie City have authority over the management of Wulingyuan. The problem of overlapping management is dramatically reflected in practice. Taking the SHA of the Lushan Mountain as an example, the management authority is allocated to six different authorities that are in charge of managing the mountain peak, the mountainside and the foot of the mountain. The fragmented allocation of power is epitomized in the charging of fees

---

49 See introduction of Wulingyuan on the website of UNESCO, http://whc.unesco.org/pg.cfm?ID_SITE= 640&CID=31&l=EN. Last visited January 2015.
50 Wang Huanhuan, 保护重叠对贫困影响的法律分析：以云南三江并流区域为例 (Legal Analysis on the Impacts of Overlapping Designation of Protected Areas Over Poverty: A Case Study of the Area of Three Parallel Rivers in Yunnan Province), 4 (2008) 华南理工大学学报(社会科学版) (*Journal of South China University of Technology (Social Science Edition)*), p. 90.
51 The figure is from unpublished data from the SFA. Citing from Xu Jiliang et al., *supra* note 21, p. 558.

at the scenic spot (i.e. 'Three-Layered Waterfall' (三叠泉)), which is split into three layers as the water flows from the peak to the bottom. Because the waterfall is managed by two authorities, visitors who want to enjoy the whole waterfall are required to pay two different fee-charging bodies.[52]

Why is there such an overlap? In addition to the flaws of intuitional arrangement prescribed in the legislation, the preference of SHA designation by local governments may be a reason. This is because nature reserves enjoy stricter legal protection than SHAs. There are more legal obstacles to developing tourism and exploiting resources within nature reserves than within SHAs. After the enactment of the Regulations on SHAs in 2006, many local governments began to designate SHAs over the previous boundary of nature reserves, de-designate nature reserves and re-designate them as SHAs, or shrink the previous boundaries of nature reserves. The problem of overlap has therefore been intensified.

Recognizing the potential for conflict, recent law making and policy making has paid specific attention to the problem of overlap. Measures have been taken *ex ante* and *ex post* to specifically address this problem. The general idea is that, first, overlapping designations should be avoided when a new type of PA is to be designated; and second, the hierarchy of the applicable norms of different PAs should be formulated in the case of an existing overlap.

In terms of *ex ante* measures, the Regulations on SHAs (2006) provide that 'a new SHA should not overlap or intersect a nature reserve' (Article 7). In the Measures of the Administration of National Wetland Parks (Trial) issued by the SFA in 2010, it is also provided that the domain of the national wetland park should not overlap or intersect a nature reserve or a forest park (Article 5). A document issued by the SFA in 2005 stated that new nature reserves, SHAs, or geographical parks cannot be established within the operational scope of the forest parks at the national level. Approval by the SFA should be obtained before such an establishment can be undertaken if the need truly exists (Article 20).[53]

A general solution to existing overlaps is provided under a 'coordination' scenario in the legislation. The Regulations on SHAs (2006) stated that 'where an established SHA overlaps or intersects a nature reserve, planning for SHAs needs to be in harmony with that of nature reserves' (Article 7). Only one existing provision provides an explicit solution to this problem. The Measures on the Administration of Forest Parks at the National Level issued by the SFA in 2011 state that 'concerning the overlap or intersection between forest parks at the national level and nature reserves at the national level, the provisions of nature reserves should prevail' (Article 9).

Analysis of the Reasons for the Enforcement Gap

From the discussion above, it can be observed that the management of nature reserves and SHAs faces similar problems in practice, such as the illegal construction of facilities,

---

52 Huang Hui and Liqing, 共管一座山 庐山何时结束"一山六制"现状 (When will the Situation of 'One Mountain, Six Authorities' End?), in 法制日报 (*Legal Daily*), September 11, 2006. Available at http://news.sohu.com/20060911/n245266581.shtml; see also Liu Jing, Zhang Shuguang and Ye Zaichun, 庐山与黄山的 "体制对话" (Dialogue between Lushan and Huangshan Mountains on Administrative Systems), October 28, 2001, available at http://www.jx.xinhuanet.com/reporter/2001-10/28/content_11982549.htm. Both were last visited January 2015.
53 SFA,国家级森林公园设立、撤销、合并、改变经营范围或者变更隶属关系审批管理办法(Administrative Measures on the Examination and Approval of the Establishment, Revocation, Merger, Change of Business Scope or Change of Subordination Relationship of Forest Parks at the National Level), Order No. 16 of the SFA, June 16, 2005.

the exploitation of resources and rampant commercialization. Generally speaking, noncompliance and the deficiency of law enforcement is commonplace in the ground management of PAs in China. What are the reasons for such a gap?

It has been commonly observed that there are challenges to using the law for environmental protection in China.[54] Numerous studies have discussed the issue of why environmental law cannot be enforced in China. For example, Charles McElwee summarizes nine factors that impede the effective implementation of environmental laws in China:

1. The low status of the law as a means for achieving societal goals,
2. The lack of capacity within the country's bureaucracies and legal institutions,
3. The delegation of responsibility for environmental protection to local authorities,
4. The development the economy outranks protection of the natural environment,
5. The horizontal fragmentation of the responsibility for environmental compliance weakens environmental enforcement efforts,
6. Public oversight of the implementation of environmental laws and regulations is constrained,
7. A strong influence of informal networks on the application and administration of laws and regulations,
8. Environmental policy-making and implementation that are characterized by bureaucratic fragmentation and
9. Structural flaws in existing laws and regulations.[55]

Stefanie Beyer notes that 'enforcement tensions between the center and the periphery [are] a result of decentralization and growing local protectionism, [and are] major obstacles to the implementation process.'[56] Robert Percival states that 'the initial generation of Chinese environmental laws largely consisted of statements of general principles that were ambiguous and difficult to enforce', and 'China's economic boom roared forward faster than these laws could be implemented and enforced.' He adds other factors, such as the highly decentralized nature of China's government, low penalties for environmental violation, the lack of direct enforcement authorities of the MoEP, the lack of education on environmental concerns among the general public, the lack of resources and the influence of environmental NGOs, the lack of an independent judiciary and a tradition of respect for the rule of law.[57]

Although most scholars take the enforcement of pollution control laws as an example to explain the poor implementation of environmental law in China, their explanations for this gap are applicable to nature conservation law. Three reasons that may cause enforcement insufficiencies in PA law have been identified: structural defects in legislation, bureaucratic structures and the underdevelopment of civil society.

First, in terms of the defects of legislation, some scholars argue that the current legislation is not based on a realistic and practical foundation. In terms of the Regulations on Nature Reserves, the regulatory tactic is linear and involves the categorical prohibition of most human activities via zoning. Because nature reserves are managed based on the

---

54 Alex Wang 'The Role of Law in Environmental Protection in China: Recent Developments', 8 (2006–07) *Vermont Journal of Environmental Law*, p. 202.
55 Charles McElwee, *Environmental Law in China: Mitigating Risk and Ensuring Compliance* (New York: Oxford University Press, 2011), pp. 4–9.
56 Stefanie Beyer, 'Environmental Law and Policy in the People's Republic of China', 5.1 (2005) *Chinese Journal of International Law*, p. 185.
57 Robert Percival, *supra* note 35, pp. 3–4.

criteria for different types of resources, such as forests and grassland, the same regulatory standard is applied to all types of reserves. This situation overlooks the complexities of natural and social conditions. The strict regulation of nature reserves 'drain[s] local government budgets'[58] and becomes difficult to enforce. Antagonistic attitudes toward nature reserve designation at the level of local governments and communities can be found. The costs of the implementation of the law increase, and the efficiency of reserve management is limited. Zinda notes that when regulation is consistently implemented, it imposes hardships on local communities. In practice, it disinclines local authorities to undertake effective implementation.[59] Furthermore, the most attractive landscapes and resources are designated as the core zones or buffer zones of a nature reserve, whereas the less interesting scenery in experimental zones suffers from over-construction and overpopulation. Simply, this means that 'core zones tend to be overprotected, and experimental zones go under-protected at the expense of the environment and tourists' enjoyment alike.'[60] In contrast, tourism development is overly emphasized in SHAs, and insufficient attention is paid to nature protection.

Second, in terms of the bureaucratic structure of nature conservation, McBeath notes that 'the organization of China's national bureaucracy is not conducive to effective implementation' of conservation laws.[61] Local protectionism is one of the most identifiable problems of law enforcement in China. The association of local government interests with economic development is deemed the source of local protectionism. Van Rooij stated that 'the main reason for weak natural resource protection enforcement in China, most scholars agree, has been local protectionism, local government protecting local economic, political and social interests while resisting non-local policies and laws.'[62] An interview with one NGO representative reveals that

> ... local governments want to develop the economy. And they want to measure the efficiency of their officials by economic development and not their conservation efforts. So they look at economic development needs first. Each local government administration has only 4–5 years to get promotions, and they focus on economic development. It is short-term, non-sustainable economic development, and that's the main stress to the environment in local areas.[63]

Third, the underdevelopment of civil society and the limited number of environmental NGOs makes sufficient law enforcement difficult to realize. Government's discretionary decision making is not under sufficient supervision by the general public. Citizens are not explicitly empowered with the right to information and the right to participate in PA-related decision making, and they do not have the knowledge or capacity to participate effectively. Government is inclined to close the door to citizens or NGOs, instead of establishing a

---

58 Megan Kram et al., *Protecting China's Biodiversity: A Guide to Land Use, Land Tenure, and Land Protection Tools* (Beijing: The Nature Conservancy, 2012), p. 141.
59 John Zinda, 'Hazards of Collaboration: Local State Co-optation of a New Protected Area Model in Southwest China', 25.4 (2012) *Society & Natural Resources*, p. 388.
60 Paul Mozur, 'Preserving China's Reserves', 171.2 (2008) *Far Eastern Economic Review*, p. 78.
61 Jerry McBeath and Jenifer Huang McBeath, 'Biodiversity Conservation in China: Policies and Practice', 9.4 (2006) *Journal of International Wildlife Law & Policy*, p. 301.
62 Benjamin Van Rooij, *supra* note 25, p. 264.
63 Interview with ENGO representative, Beijing, June 11, 2004. Citing from Jerry McBeath and Jenifer Huang McBeath, *supra* note 61, pp. 308–9.

participatory governance framework. For example, in 2011, the Friends of Nature applied to the MoEP to disclose information on the reason why the Nature Reserve for Rare and Endemic Fish of the Upper Yangtze River was downsized. However, this application was refused because the related information was not fully realized 'process information' (过程性信息) and therefore not necessary to disclose.[64]

The Resolution of Conflicts: The 'Dormant' Role of Courts

Unlike the litigation culture in the US, courts in China are mired in a dilemma. On the one hand, increasing disputes that arise from the transformation of the economy and society call for an efficient judicial mechanism to settle them. On the other hand, the judiciary in general is inferior to other branches and suffers from inappropriate interventions that hinder it from fulfilling its task. This section discusses the role of Chinese courts in adjudicating PA-based conflicts, analyzes the predicament that courts face and presents the latest developments in this field.

The Characteristics and Status Quo *of Conservation-related Lawsuits in China*

Legal suits against polluters have been increasingly found in the courts.[65] However, legal suits regarding conservation issues are still scarce. Courts have played a very limited, even 'dormant' role in this area.

A rough search in *Beidafabao*,[66] a Chinese law database, in September 2014 produced only two civil cases and four administrative cases in which the Regulations on SHAs were *mentioned* in their judgments, six civil cases (one of which involved mass litigation including 21 separate cases with similar causes of action)[67] and one administrative case in which the Regulations on Nature Reserves were *mentioned*, and four civil cases in which Administrative Measures on Forest Parks were *mentioned*. In sum, only 17 cases were found that mentioned the three main conservation regulations.[68] Not all of these judgments directly applied relevant regulations to PAs, let alone the judicial elaboration of specific articles.

The causes of actions in these cases can be classified into the following categories:

1   Administrative litigation against relevant authorities for fines and other forms of administrative punishment due to illegal construction projects within PAs,[69]

---

64 Liu Shixin, 自然保护区面临缩水,环保组织申请信息公开遇阻 (Nature Reserves are Shrinking; Environmental NGOs Encounter Barriers when Applying for the Disclosure of Information), in 中国青年报 (*China Youth Daily*), May 13, 2011. Full text is available at http://cityup.chinasus.org/news/portect/20110513/77489-2.shtml. Last visited January 2015.

65 For more information about pollution-related environmental litigation in China, see generally Alex Wang, *supra* note 54, pp. 195–223.

66 Beidafabao (北大法宝), http://www.pkulaw.cn/, a Chinese law database sponsored by Peking University in Beijing.

67 See the judgment of 余海荣诉江苏盐城国家级珍禽自然保护区管理处等土地承包经营权纠纷案 (*Yu Hairong vs. Yancheng Nature Reserve Administration Bureau of Yancheng, Jiangsu Province*), (2013) 盐民终字第1668号 ((2013) *Yan Min Zhong Zi*, No. 1668), concluded on January 13, 2014, and another twenty cases within the same mass litigation.

68 Since not all judicial judgments are accessible by internet in China, the data collected from *Beidafabao* may not reflect the whole picture in practice. However, it does show the limited number of cases judged by courts.

69 For example, see 朱乃豪诉杭州西湖风景名胜区管理委员会处罚案 (*Zhu Naihao vs. Administrative Committee of the West Lake SHA in Hangzhou*), (2012) 杭西行初字第23号 ((2012) *Hang Xi Xing Chu Zi*, No. 23), concluded on April 28, 2012.

2 Administrative litigation against relevant authorities for undue compensation to villagers due to the designation and management of PAs,[70]
3 Contractual disputes between concessioners (or developers) and local authorities or between different individuals on the usufruct of land and resources within PAs,[71] and
4 Personal injury tort cases relevant to PA management.[72]

Table 10.2 Number of judicial cases on PA-related issues, based on their causes of action

Causes of action	Number of judicial cases			Subtotal
	NR	SHA	FP	
Contract disputes	5	2	3	10
Torts	1		1	2
Administrative punishment		4		4
Administrative compensation	1			1
Subtotal	**7**	**6**	**4**	**17**

Source: Data are collected from *Beidafabao*, September 2014.

Table 10.2 shows that of the limited number of cases, most are related to contract disputes. This is mainly due to negative influences of the validity of existing contracts from the designation of PAs or the adjustment of the zoning and boundaries of designated PAs. In most cases, such contracts use specific types of resources, such as forest land, wetland and mineral resources, for economic purposes. There are also disputable contracts between authorities and concessioners, real estate developers and enterprises engaged in commercially operating PAs. By resolving contractual disputes, courts have interpreted some designated use within PAs. For example, in the case of *Xi'an Baluchuan Ltd. vs. 2nd Branch of Bureau of Geology and Mineral Resources Prospection and Exploitation of Gansu Province*,[73] the High People's Court of Gansu Province ruled that the Forest Law, the Implementation Rules of the Forest Law and the Administrative Measures of Forest Parks did not preclude the right to prospect mineral resources within forest parks. Therefore, though mining activities are prohibited within designated forest parks, valid rights to prospect mineral resources are protected by law. A similar conclusion is drawn from the judgment of *Xi'an Chubuxiang Ltd. vs. 2nd Branch of Bureau of Geology and Mineral Resources Prospecting and Exploitation of Gansu Province*,[74] with regard to the right to prospect mineral resources within designated nature reserves.

70 For example, see 王新明等与浙江省临安市人民政府履行法定职责纠纷再审案 (*Wang etc. vs. The Government of Lin'an City*), (2003)浙行再字第3号 ((2003) *Zhe Xing Zai Zi*, No. 3), concluded on March 15, 2004.
71 For example, see 于学尚与山东黄河三角洲国家级自然保护区大汶流管理站物权保护纠纷上诉案 (*Yu Xueshang vs. Dawenliu Management Station of the Yellow River Delta Nature Reserve at the National Level in Shandong Province*), (2013) 东民四终字第105号((2013) *Dong Min Si Zhong Zi*, No. 105), concluded on December 31, 2013.
72 For example, see 洛阳市文物管理局与汪某等人身损害赔偿纠纷上诉案 (*Luoyang City Bureau of Cultural Relics vs. Wang et al.*), (2008) 洛民终字第1734号 ((2008) *Luo Min Zhong Zi*, No. 1734), concluded on April 27, 2009.
73 西安八路川矿业有限公司与甘肃省地质矿产勘查开发局第二地质矿产勘察院探矿权纠纷上诉案, (2010)甘民二终字第195号 ((2010) *Gan Min Er Zhong Zi*, No. 195), concluded on December 6, 2010.
74 西安初步乡矿业有限公司与甘肃省地质矿产勘查开发局第二地质矿产勘察院探矿权纠纷上诉案, (2010) 甘民二终字第194号 ((2010) *Gan Min Er Zhong Zi*, No. 194), concluded on December 6, 2010.

In the following part, I provide several typical examples of judicial cases and discuss disputes that arise from PA management. These cases are labeled 'typical cases' by *Beidafabao* or the SPC via the SPC's periodic release to guide the adjudication practices of courts at the lower levels.[75]

Case 18: **Wang et al. vs. The Government of Lin'an City *(2003)*[76]**

The plaintiffs, villagers of Baojia village, entered into a contract with the villagers' committee to operate certain areas of bamboo forests in the 1980s. In 1993, parts of the bamboo forests were included in the nature reserve of the Tianmu Mountain due to the expansion of the reserve boundary. This adjustment caused negative impacts on the villagers' utilization and operation of bamboo resources. The reserve management agency established a contract with the plaintiffs in May 1993, confirming the principles of benefit sharing and integrated management, and ensuring that the ownership and usufruct structure would not be changed and that the displacement of villagers would not occur. However, the defendant, the Lin'an government, did not make relevant benefit-sharing arrangements and delayed the compensation of villagers for their losses. The plaintiffs sued the government in 2001 for its inaction and asked for the performance of duties by the defendant.

The court of first instance delivered the judgment in 2001, which ruled that the defendant did not have the authority to promise any compensation to the plaintiffs because this authority was given to the provincial departments or the State Council. Therefore, the defendant's delay in compensating the plaintiffs did not violate the law. The plaintiffs' claims were rejected. The court of second instance sustained the judgment of the first instance in 2002 and added that there was no legal provision at a higher level on the issue of compensation for monetary loss due to the designation and management of nature reserves. Therefore, the formulation of the compensation plan needed to wait for the issuance of relevant regulations by the State Council. The disputes continued, and the re-trial procedure (再审)[77] was initiated in 2003. The High People's Court in Zhejiang Province delivered a retrial judgment that revoked the judgments at the first and second instances. It ruled that the defendant's promise to compensate the villagers' losses was valid and should be implemented, and it ordered the defendant to compensate the plaintiffs within 60 days after the judgment came into force.

The key issue in this case was whether the government's promise to compensate villagers in the absence of specific laws and regulations of ecological compensation was valid and should be implemented. Though the High People's Court finally ruled to implement the promise via an ad hoc re-trial procedure, it can be seen from previous judgments that local courts are inclined to 'defend' the local government's inaction of compensation.

---

75 The 'Guiding Case' system was established by the SPC in 2010. The SPC states that courts at all levels in China should 'refer to' (参照) these guiding cases when delivering a judgment. This initiative by the SPC is deemed a shift towards establishing a precedent system in China. For more details of the 'Guiding Case' project, see Stanford Law School China Guiding Cases Project, available at http://cgc.law.stanford.edu/. Last visited January 2015.

76 王新明等诉浙江省临安市人民政府履行作出经济补偿方案职责行政争议纠纷案, (2001)临行初字第13号 ((2001) *Lin Xing Chu Zi*, No. 13), concluded by the Basic People's Court of Lin'an City; 王新明等与浙江省临安市人民政府履行法定职责行政争议纠纷上诉案, (2002) 杭行终字第12号 ((2002) *Hang Xing Zhong Zi*, No. 12), concluded by the Intermediate People's Court of Hangzhou City in Zhejiang Province, and 王新明等与浙江省临安市人民政府履行法定职责纠纷再审案, (2003) 浙行再字第3号 ((2003) *Zhe Xing Zai Zi*, No. 3), concluded by the High People's Court in Zhejiang Province.

77 The re-trial is an ad hoc legal procedure after the final judgment has been delivered, when new circumstances are found which suffice to overturn the original judgment. It aims at remedying the mistakes made in the final judgment.

Case 19: All-China Environment Federation (ACEF) vs. the Lihu Lake and the Huishan Mountain Management Committee of Wuxi City *(2012)*[78]

This case is the only one that relates to ecological derogation among the nine typical cases released by the SPC about the adjudication of environment- and resource-related cases.[79] Though the court applied the Forestry Law instead of PA regulations in its judgment, it can still be considered a symbolic case in adjudicating conservation-related disputes.

The plaintiff, the ACEF, a government-sponsored environmental NGO in China, sued the defendant, the Lihu Lake and Huishan Mountain Management Committee of Wuxi City (the Committee), in 2012. The plaintiff asserted that the defendant arbitrarily changed the designated use of land from forestry to construction, built a sightseeing elevator and a fire pool on forest land and occupied a vacant lot of up to 10 *mu* that violated the planning of this scenic area. These construction and occupation activities derogated the ecological environment. The ACEF asked the court to order the defendant to restore and compensate the derogated environment. The Measures of Jiangsu Province to Implement the Forestry Law provide that 'the one who changes the designated use of forestry land without approval from relevant forestry authority should restore the land to its original status within a limited period' (Article 41). By interpreting this provision, the court ruled that the dismantling of construction projects in the current case would be against the public interest and was neither economically nor socially efficient. Therefore, the court finally ordered the defendant to plant trees elsewhere that would be equivalent to restoring the derogated landscape in the current case (异地补植).

The court's initiative in choosing the alternative of *ex situ* compensation measures was applauded by the SPC and became the reason for the case to be listed as a 'typical case'.[80]

In addition to the cases included in the database, there were also cases released by media reports. The following cases were not substantively tried by the courts; however, they reveal challenges to the agency's management decision of PAs brought by citizens, and at times they compelled the agency to change its decision due to public pressure.

Case 20: Shi and Gu vs. the Urban Planning Bureau of Nanjing *(2001)*[81]

On October 17, 2001, two teachers from the Law School of the Southeast University lodged administrative litigation against the Bureau of Urban Planning in Nanjing to the Intermediate People's Court (IPC) in Nanjing City. They argued that as the holders of the Park Pass to the SHA of the Sun Yat-sen Mausoleum, they were entitled to enjoy the natural beauty that the defendant was responsible for maintaining. They argued that the construction of the viewing deck at the top of the Zijin Mountain in the SHA 'destroyed the spiritual pleasure of enjoying

---

78 中华环保联合会诉无锡市蠡湖惠山景区管理委员会生态环境侵权案 (2012) 锡滨环民初字第0002号 ((2012) *Xi Bin Huan Min Chu Zi*, No. 0002), concluded by the Basic People's Court of Binhu District of Wuxi City on December 19, 2012. Full text of the judgment is available at the ACEF's website. See ACEF, 我会提起的我国第一例社会组织为原告的生态破坏公益诉讼胜诉 (The ACEF Win the First Public Interest Litigation Against Ecological Derogation which is Brought by Social Organizations in China), December 26, 2012. Available at http://www.acef.com.cn/envlaw/wqdxal/2013/1213/128.html. Last visited January 2015.

79 SPC, 最高法院公布九起环境资源审判典型案例 (The SPC Released Nine Typical Cases about the Adjudication of the Environment- and Resource-related Issues), July 3, 2014. Available at http://www.chinacourt.org/article/detail/2014/07/id/1329697.shtml. Last visited January 2015.

80 See the SPC's explanation of the significance of this case, available at http://www.chinacourt.org/article/detail/2014/07/id/1329702.shtml. Last visited January 2015.

81 For more details of this case, see Huang Xiaowei, 被迫拆除 (Forced Dismantling), 3 (2002) 新闻周刊 (*News Weekly*), p. 13.

the natural beauty of the SHA'. According to the Regulations on the Administration of the Scenic and Historic Area of the Sun Yat-sen Mausoleum in Nanjing City, all of the construction and facilities should be in harmony with the environment within the SHA. Based on this planning principle, the plaintiffs argued that the planning permit for the construction of the viewing deck issued by the defendant was illegal and needed to be revoked.

Six days later, the IPC ruled that the issue that the plaintiffs brought to the court was not a 'significant event'. This was one of the criteria for the jurisdiction of the IPC in receiving administrative cases according to Article 14 of the Administrative Litigation Law (ALL) of 1989, which prescribed that the IPC had jurisdiction over 'significant and complicated cases in areas under its jurisdiction'. The court recommended that the plaintiffs bring the case to the Basic People's Court (BPC) at the district level. Instead of following the recommendation made by the IPC, the plaintiffs brought the case to the High People's Court (HPC) of Jiangsu Province; however, they were again refused. Though this case did not ultimately go through trial proceedings, it drew attention from society and the media. In February 2002, under pressure, the government of Nanjing City decided to dismantle the viewing deck.

Case 21: Jin Kuixi vs. the Bureau of Urban Planning of Hangzhou City *(2003)*[82]

Another case related to the management of the SHA of West Lake addressed the construction permit issued by the Bureau of Urban Planning. On February 25, 2003, Jin Kuixi, who was a resident of Hangzhou City, brought administrative litigation against the bureau to the BPC of the West Lake District of Hangzhou City. He argued that the construction permit issued by the defendant for the project of the University for the Elderly in Zhejiang Province was not in conformity with the law. According to Article 24 of the Regulations on the Administration of the SHA of Hangzhou West Lake, no new construction project or expansion of old construction facilities irrelevant to the management of the SHA of West Lake was allowed. Therefore, the issuance of the construction permit to the university project was illegal and needed to be revoked. Three days later, the BPC rejected his complaints because Jin did not have sufficient interest in this case and was thus unqualified to bring such a lawsuit. According to Article 2 of the ALL of 1989, a person can bring administrative litigation to courts only 'when his or her lawful rights and interests have been infringed upon by a concrete administrative action'. Jin appealed to the IPC of Hangzhou City. On April 17, 2003, the IPC ruled to sustain the original rule made by the BPC by providing the same reason.

This case shows the legislative barriers in terms of the standing requirements for citizens to bring public interest litigation against management agencies' decisions for PAs.

From the cases discussed above, some features of the status quo of conservation-related lawsuits can be summarized as follows:

1 Unlike the explosion of public land-based litigation after the 1970s in the US, there have been very few conservation-related lawsuits in China.
2 Of the limited number of lawsuits, most address contractual disputes due to PA designation and management. This touches upon questions such as compensation and restoration. Most of the disputes are adjudicated on substantive grounds instead of procedural grounds.
3 Though some cases related to public interest litigation are brought to public attention, they are rarely tried by courts in practice. As a result, the fundamental purpose and

---

82 Chinacourt.org, 金奎喜诉杭州市规划局案 (*Jin Kuixi vs. Bureau of Urban Planning of Hangzhou City*), November 29, 2004. Available at http://old.chinacourt.org/public/detail.php?id=92767. Last visited January 2015.

principle of PA regulations is seldom disputed in the courts, and the courts rarely interpret fundamental principles, such as the 'coordination principle' or 'priority of protection'. In reality, controversial issues that might touch upon the interpretation of fundamental principles seldom arrive at the courts. Instead, debates only take place in the media and academia.
4   Generally speaking, the judiciary plays a rather limited or even dormant role in resolving conflicts in PA designation and management.

Analysis of the Predicament of the Judiciary

The dormant role of the courts stands in sharp contrast to the situation in the US. This does not necessarily mean that there are no conflicts in China or that there are fewer conflicts than in the US. The reasons for the dormant role of the judiciary are numerous.

First, potential plaintiffs are limited due to the standing requirement or the limited engagement of civil society. Traditionally, public interest litigation (PIL) is not allowed according to Chinese law. Changes have been made within the new EPL of 2014 that have opened the doors of the courts to NGOs.[83] However, before this, individuals or NGOs that had no direct interest in the disputed issue could not bring the so-called PIL to the courts. Though the Civil Procedure Law was amended in 2012 to allow PIL (Article 55), it has been reported that none of the eight PIL brought by the ACEF in 2013 was accepted by the courts because these PIL did not satisfy the qualification requirements.[84] Furthermore, of the limited number of environmental NGOs in China, most are reluctant to bring lawsuits to courts. They are more inclined to provide education to the public or other activities that can easily obtain support and sponsorship from governments rather than suing governments in the courts. A survey conducted by the ACEF in 2013 shows that only 30 percent of environmental NGOs prefer litigation, 57 percent express caution about bringing PIL, and 11 percent explicitly demonstrate negative attitudes toward PIL. In addition to their unwillingness to bring PIL, in practice, only 14 percent have experience participating in PIL.[85] Furthermore, like the focus of policy making in this field, ecological protection issues are overwhelmed by imperative concerns about pollution problems. Most PIL address pollution control rather than nature conservation. This further limits the number of cases that are actually brought to the courts, let alone the number of cases in which the courts actually deliver judgments.

Second, there is a lack of a right of action provided in legislation. In most environmental statutes, there is no clearly stated dispute-resolution mechanism. Therefore, whether a disputed party can bring a lawsuit to the courts is not fully grounded in law. According to a survey regarding the enforcement of environmental law in China with 12,512 judges and prosecutors who addressed environment-related lawsuits ('the Survey'), in terms of the question, 'what are the reasons at the level of legislation that have impeded the full implementation of environment and resources law?', 92.05 percent of the respondents chose the option that 'the provisions of dispute resolution in environment and resources legislation

---

83 For details, see *infra* pp. 237–8.
84 Zou Chunxia, 中华环保联合会:去年提8起公益诉讼法院均未立案 (ACEF: 8 PIL Claims were Refused by Courts Last Year), March 1, 2014, available at http://news.xinhuanet.com/2014–03/01/c_119559046.htm. Last visited January 2015.
85 ACEF, 《环保民间组织在环境公益诉讼中的角色和作用》调研报告摘要 (Summary of the Survey Report on 'The Role and Function of Environmental NGOs in PIL'), February 28, 2014, available at http://www.acef.com.cn/zhuantilanmu/2013hjwqtbh/huiyinarong/2014/0303/12495.html. Last visited January 2015.

are too simple and lack enforceability', and 3.97 percent chose the option that 'provisions in legislation are too unrealistic to be implemented and do not fit the reality'.[86] Most of the current PA regulations do not provide right of action that authorizes a citizen suit. There is currently no Administrative Procedure Law in China similar to the APA in the US that authorizes citizen suits. Furthermore, the ALL of 1989 prescribes two sets of standards that need to be satisfied before administrative litigation may be heard by the courts: the standard of 'concrete administrative action' and the standard of 'personal and property rights'.[87] Though the newly amended ALL of 2014 changes the term 'concrete administrative action' to 'administrative action' and expands the scope of 'personal and property rights' to include 'other rights' (Article 2 and 12), it still requires a clear identification of the administrative action and legal rights involved. Furthermore, a connection between potential plaintiffs and disputable administration actions is a premise.

Third, the chronic problems that administrative litigation has encountered in general predict the difficulties of environmental lawsuits against management agencies in particular. The lack of judicial independence may be a considerable challenge.[88] According to the Survey, for the question, 'What are the reasons that courts seldom handle pollution-related lawsuits in China?', the answer that ranked highest was 'environmental disputes are numerous; however, local governments have intervened within a short term and settled them for the purpose of maintaining social stability; therefore, few of them are ultimately litigated' (45.76 percent).[89] Because the number of suits is one important indicator to assess social stability by the higher levels of government, local governments are inclined to decrease the rate of litigation, especially group litigation, as much as possible. Though this survey targeted the trial of pollution cases, the rationale is applicable to conservation-related cases. Local governments are the decisive actors that shape PA management policies. Their interests are closely aligned with enterprises that invest and carry out infrastructure construction and PA operation. In addition to inappropriate intervention by local governments, judges may spontaneously align themselves with the policy goals pursued by governments. When discussing Chinese judges' spontaneous alignment with the policy and goals of the Party in environmental cases, Stern cited Feynman's words that 'the people in a big system like NASA *know* what has to be done – *without* being told'.[90]

Fourth, among citizens, petitioning is preferred to litigation. Compared to litigation, the cost to petition governments to settle disputes is much lower. Table 10.3 shows the number of letters and visits (信访), which is similar to the Ombudsman system in some Western countries, and the numbers of administrative reconsiderations and litigations related to environmental issues in recent decades.

---

86 Wang Jing, 我国环保法律实施面临的问题:国家司法机关工作人员的认识 (Problems of Enforcement of Environmental Law in China: A Perspective from Officials Working in the State Judicial Organs), 19.6 (2007) 中外法学 (*Peking University Law Journal*), p. 742.
87 For a discussion of the scope of judicial review in terms of administrative litigation in China, see Yuwen Li and Yun Ma, 'The Hurdle is High: The Administrative Litigation System in the People's Republic of China', in Yuwen Li (ed.), *Administrative Litigation Systems in Greater China and Europe* (Farnham, England and Burlington, VT: Ashgate Publishing, 2014), pp. 15–40.
88 For general discussion about judicial independence in China, see Yuwen Li, *Judicial Independence in China: An Attainable Principle?* (The Hague: Eleven International Publishing, 2013).
89 Wang Jing, *supra* note 86, p. 737.
90 Rachel Stern, 'On the Frontlines: Making Decisions in Chinese Civil Environmental Lawsuits', 32 (2010) *Law & Policy*, p. 82.

Table 10.3 Number of letters and visits related to environmental issues in China (1996–2012)

Year	Number of letters	Number of telephone/ internet complaints	Number of visits	Number of administrative reconsiderations	Number of administrative lawsuits
1996	67,268	–	47,714	–	–
1997	106,210	–	29,677	203	90
1998	147,630	–	40,151	290	621
1999	230,346	–	38,246	263	427
2000	247,741	–	62,059	246	580
2001	367,402	–	80,329	290	696
2002	435,020	–	90,746	285	993
2003	525,988	–	85,028	230	579
2004	595,852	–	86,414	271	616
2005	608,245	–	88,237	211	399
2006	616,122	–	71,287	208	353
2007	–	–	–	520	–
2008	–	–	–	528	–
2009	–	–	–	661	–
2010	–	–	–	694	–
2011	201,631	852,700	53,505	838	–
2012	107,120	892,348	53,505	427	–

Source: MoEP[91]

It can be seen from the table that the number of letters and visits has skyrocketed since the late 1990s. The statistics on the number of administrative reconsiderations and administrative lawsuits are fragmented. Reasonable doubt can be raised regarding how these data are collected because they fluctuate erratically. Though the information is inconsistent, it can be observed that the numbers of reconsiderations and lawsuits do not show a comparable increase to the increase of letters and visits; instead, the number of litigations decreased sharply in the last year in which the data were collected (i.e. 2006). Based on a rough calculation of the 2006 figure, Lv et al. estimate that the ratio of the number of environmental disputes (in the form of letters and visits), the number of cases that underwent administrative procedures (administrative punishment and reconsideration) and the number of cases that underwent judicial procedures is approximately 255:38:1.[92] Thus, a large amount of environmental disputes do not enter judicial procedures. Instead, non-litigation methods, such as letters and visits, are preferred.

Recent Developments in Specialized Justice and Public Interest Litigation: A Critical Review

Recent developments with regard to the adjudication of environmental cases may shed light on and deepen the discussion above. Two developments stand out: the first is the establishment of environmental courts (chambers), and the second is the promotion of PIL in law.

---

91 MoEP,全国环境统计公报 (1996–2012) (Environmental Statistics Bulletin in China (1996–2012)), available at http://www.mep.gov.cn/zwgk/hjtj/qghjtjgb/. Last visited January 2015.
92 Lv Zhongmei, Zhang Zhongmin and Xiong Xiaoqing, 中国环境司法现状调查—以千份环境裁判文书为样本 (Investigation of the *Status Quo* of Environmental Justice in China: Based on a Thousand Samples of Judgments On Environmental Issues), 4 (2011) 法学 (*Law Science*), p. 83.

In June 2014, the SCNPC approved the establishment of a separate chamber, the Environment and Resources Trial Chamber, for adjudicating environment- and resource-related cases within the SPC. In reality, the specialization of environment-related adjudication was promoted at the local level before the final move of the SPC. According to the statistics, in May 2014, 16 provinces had established more than 130 environment chambers, collegial panels, or circuit tribunals around the nation.[93] This initiative of 'specialized justice' in the environment accords with the trend of 'green justice' worldwide,[94] and it was realized as a result of decades of advocacy by Chinese scholars.[95] In June 2014, the SPC issued the Opinions of the SPC on Comprehensively Strengthening Adjudication on Environment and Resources Cases and Providing Potent Judicial Guarantees for Promoting the Construction of Ecological Civilization.[96] These Opinions emphasize the judiciary's role in protecting citizens' legal rights and interests in the environment and resources, unifying the standard of judicial interpretation and the application of law and supervising the exercise of administrative power by trying environment-related administrative litigation.

Both authorities and the media consider the establishment of environmental courts to be a considerable achievement in terms of environmental justice. Wilson asserts that 'the brightest hope for environmental litigation comes in the form of China's newly minted environmental courts.'[97] However, Stern expresses critical opinions by outlining the political logic behind this movement.[98] She argues that these new environmental courts are 'not a step toward judicial empowerments, as international observers might be tempted to conclude, but an effort to enlist courts to serve alongside government bureaus in a multi-pronged environmental campaign'.[99] She lists four functions of environmental courts in China: dispute resolution, policy advocacy, education and social control.[100] Chinese courts are no different from other government bureaus, and 'environmental courts are seen locally as a way to enhance cooperation to solve crises.'[101]

She also notes that these specialized courts need a constant supply of cases to justify their existence.[102] However, the record of the adjudication of these new courts is not satisfying.

---

93 Yan Dingfei, 环保法庭进了最高人民法院 (The SPC Receives the Environment Chamber), in 南方周末(*Southern Weekly*), June 27, 2014. Available at http://www.infzm.com/content/101787. Last visited January 2015.

94 It is said that by 2010, there were 350 environmental courts worldwide. Half of them were created in the previous two years alone. See George Pring and Catherine Pring, *Greening Justice: Creating and Improving Environmental Courts and Tribunals* (Washington, DC: The Access Institute, 2010). Cited from Rachel Stern, 'The Political Logic of China's New Environmental Courts', 72 (2014) *The China Journal*, p. 55 and footnote 12.

95 See generally Wang Shuyi et al., 环境法前沿问题研究 (*Research on the Frontier Issues of Environmental Law*) (Taipei: Yuanzhao Press, 2012), pp. 380–91 (Chapter 12: The Necessity and Feasibility of Specialization of Environmental Adjudication in China); Alex Wang and Jie Gao, 'Environmental Courts and the Development of Environmental Public Interest Litigation in China', 3 (2010) *Journal of Court Innovation*, pp. 37–50, and Tun Lin et al., *Green Benches: What Can the People's Republic of China Learn from Environment Courts of Other Countries?* (Mandaluyong City: Asian Development Bank, 2009).

96 SPC, 最高人民法院关于全面加强环境资源审判工作，为推进生态文明建设提供有力司法保障的意见 (Opinions of the SPC on Comprehensively Strengthening Adjudication on Environment and Resources Cases and Providing Potent Judicial Guarantee for Promoting Construction of Ecological Civilization), *Fafa* No. 11 [2014]. Full text is available at http://www.chinacourt.org/law/detail/2014/06/id/147914.shtml. Last visited January 2015.

97 Scott Wilson, 'Seeking One's Day in Court: Chinese Regime Responsiveness to International Legal Norms on AIDS Carriers' and Pollution Victims' Rights', 21.77 (2012) *Journal of Contemporary China*, p. 871.

98 Rachel Stern, 2014, *supra* note 94, pp. 53–74.

99 Ibid., p. 54.

100 Ibid., pp. 61–3.

101 Ibid., p. 62.

102 Ibid., pp. 71–2.

This relates to the second recent development, lowering the standing requirement and promoting PIL as a means to attract more cases to the courts.

In 2012, the Civil Procedure Law was amended to open the doors to PIL. Article 55 provided that 'lawful authorities' (法律规定的机关) and 'relevant organizations' (有关组织) may initiate PIL against environmental pollution and other activities that violate the social public interest. In defining the term 'relevant organizations', the new EPL of 2014 further provides that an NGO that has satisfied the following requirements may have the standing to bring about an environmental suit:

1. Registered at the civil administration department of the government at the level of a municipality that has sub-districts (设区的市) or above;
2. Specialized in activities relevant to environmental protection for at least five consecutive years with no record of illegal acts (Article 58).

In its interpretations issued in January 2015 (The Interpretations),[103] the SPC further clarified that 'districts of municipalities under the direct control of the central government (直辖市)' can be considered within the level of a 'municipality' stipulated in Article 58 of the new EPL (Article 3). This facilitates those environmental NGOs that are registered at the level of the district of Beijing to bring PIL, for example, Friends of Nature (自然之友) and Nature University (自然大学) that are currently active in PIL in China. Nevertheless, NGOs that are qualified, willing and able to bring lawsuits in China are still scarce.[104]

In addition to the concern about the scarcity of NGOs to bring PIL, scholars have also expressed other concerns about PIL.[105] First, the newly amended ALL of 2014 does not explicitly allow administrative PIL, as the Civil Procedure Law has done. Thus, the administrative PIL, which is the main type of PIL, may be excluded from courts. It is worthy of notice that this situation has been changed recently. In a resolution issued by the SCNPC in July 2015, the SPPC is delegated with the power to bring PIL in areas including protection of ecological environment and natural resources, protection of state-owned assets and others in 13 selected provinces.[106] Following the resolution, the SPPC issued the Pilot Programme of Bringing PIL by Procuratorates in which both civil and administrative PIL are included. Procuratorates are empowered to bring PIL against administrative agencies and other organizations with delegated managerial powers with regard to their inactions or illegal exercise of power.[107] These latest developments indicate that procuratorates have received full sponsorship from the highest authority to be included in the term 'lawful authorities' as prescribed in the 2012 Civil Procedure Law. Such a move also mends the gap in the 2014 ALL that is silent to administrative PIL. Second, more detailed rules and instructions on how the PIL should proceed in the courts are necessary to avoid inconsistencies in handling PIL cases across

---

103 SPC, 最高人民法院关于审理环境民事公益诉讼案件适用法律若干问题的解释 (The SPC's Interpretation on Several Issues Regarding the Application of Law in Public Interest Environmental Civil Litigation), 法释 (2015) 1 号 (Fashi No.1 [2015]), 7 January 2015.
104 Wang Canfa & Cheng Duowei, 新<环境保护法>下环境公益诉讼面临的困境及其破解 (Dilemma of environmental public interest litigation under the new EPL and its solution), 8 (2014) 法律适用 (*Legal Application*), pp. 49–50.
105 Ibid., pp. 47–8.
106 SCNPC, 全国人民代表大会常务委员会关于授权最高人民检察院在部分地区开展公益诉讼试点工作的决定 (Resolution of the SCNPC on Delegating the Supreme People's Procuratorate to Conduct Pilot Work of Public Interest Litigation in Selected Areas), July 1, 2015.
107 SPPC, 检察机关提起公益诉讼试点方案 (Pilot Programme of Bringing PIL by Procuratorates), July 2, 2015.

different courts. Third, a delay in judicial reform may make courts unwilling or unable to accept PIL cases due to inappropriate intervention.

Summary

Chinese law has made gradual progress in resolving PA-based conflicts. This is reflected in the shift of fundamental principles, the formulation of designated-use hierarchy and the adoption of legal instruments on both substantive and procedural grounds.

The shift from the 'principle of coordination' to the 'priority of protection' as the fundamental principle of environmental law indicates a strong resolution and commitment to environmental protection by the nation. Conservation trumps the use of nature, at least in theory. In addition to exhibiting a pro-conservation attitude, relevant statutes and regulations formulate a hierarchical designated use pattern in different types of PAs. This facilitates decision making and judgment when competing interests and claims to use nature emerge. A preliminary normative framework is also established to mitigate development conflicts. Instruments such as ecological compensation, public participation and community-based management have been adopted. However, challenges remain with regard to how to guarantee the enforcement of sufficient compensation, access to information and the participation of local residents in practice.

The greatest challenge lies in how to translate the law in books into law in action. Noncompliance and enforcement deficits in environmental law are paramount in China. Ad hoc law-enforcement campaigns in the fields of SHAs and nature reserves demonstrate the chronic problems of translating conservation law into practice. The rampant adjustment of nature reserves at the local level demonstrates how conservation laws and regulations can be circumvented due to local protectionism. The overlapping designation and management of PAs reveals department interest-based institutional structures and inter-agency rivalry. Structural defects in legislation and local protectionism arising from the bureaucratic structure and underdevelopment of civil society are the three main reasons for insufficiencies in conservation law enforcement.

The role of the judiciary in adjudicating conservation-related disputes remains extremely limited or even dormant. The judiciary faces considerable challenges in realizing its role. The high requirements and underdeveloped civil society have limited the number of potential plaintiffs. The lack of causes of action provided in the legislation does not facilitate the process of bringing lawsuits to the courts. Inappropriate interference by local governments diminishes judicial independence, especially in the case of administrative litigation. There is a lack of a litigant culture among the public in general, and citizens prefer petition to litigation. Recent developments to establish environmental courts and promote PIL signal increasing attention to the role of courts in adjudicating environmental disputes. However, limitations remain with regard to whether courts can be liberated from the bureaucratic goals of policy advocacy and social control, which have a significant influence in changes to the legal landscape of conservation.

11 Pudacuo National Park and Beyond in Yunnan Province

National Parks Envisioned and National Parks in Practice[1]

Introduction

This chapter focuses on the pilot project of national parks in Yunnan Province based on a literature review and on my field research. I chose this project for field research mainly because Pudacuo National Park, which was designated in Yunnan Province in 2007, is applauded for being the 'first national park' in China. During the initial stage of my literature review in early 2012, the national park project in Yunnan Province did not attract my attention because I considered it mainly a local strategy, or even a trick, to attract more visitors and promote the tourism industry. After a search of 'Chinese national parks' online, a media report drew my attention: both Pudacuo National Park in Yunnan Province and Tangwanghe National Park in Heilongjiang Province claimed to be the first national parks in China. It soon became clear that the national park project in Yunnan might entail and indicate more than I had previously perceived. Aiming to conduct field research there, I began to search public information online, especially the contact information for the management authorities of national parks in Yunnan. Unfortunately, this effort was futile. I called several phone numbers provided online, but most of them were not answered. I then established contact with the local office of the Nature Conservancy (TNC) in Yunnan Province. TNC is a US-based environmental NGO that has played a key role in promoting the national park project in Yunnan. One researcher of the national park project, Ms. Jin, chatted with me via Skype. She then put me in contact with Ms. Wang, who was the manager of the national park project. I explained my research interests regarding how TNC collaborated with and mobilized governmental authorities in promoting the national park model in Yunnan. They showed great interest in my research and invited me to visit Yunnan. Initially, I hesitated about whether a visit to Yunnan was worthwhile because I had little contact with governmental officials or scholars there. In the summer of 2012, I presented a paper about the national park project in Yunnan Province, which was mainly based on a literature review, at an environmental law conference held at Wuhan University in China. Afterwards, following a recommendation from a law professor from Wuhan Law School, Ms. Du, I contacted two legal scholars working at a university in Kunming, the capital city of Yunnan Province, who had researched and published articles on the legal issues of national parks in Yunnan. I finally decided to target Yunnan as the object of my field research and paid a visit to Yunnan in September 2012.

To identify the roles of different institutions in the national park project, I listed a number of institutions in Yunnan that I would have liked to visit before my departure. After settling in

---

1 Part of this chapter appeared in my article entitled 'Environmental Reviews and Case Studies: Contextualization of National Parks in the Nature Conservation Scheme in China: A Case Study of Pudacuo National Park in Yunnan Province', published by Cambridge University Press, in 15.3 (2013) *Environmental Practice*, pp. 293–312. However, this chapter has updated the contents of the article with a new structure.

Kunming, I went directly to the Forestry Department of Yunnan Province with a list of questions that I had formulated. Without any contact information or an appointment, I understood that this visit might turn out to be a wild goose chase. After showing my identification card and completing some formalities, the gatekeeper allowed me in. I then found the building directory in the reception hall and searched for the room number of the National Park Management Office, an ad hoc agency established to supervise the national park project in Yunnan. I wrote down the names of the director and other staff members of this office and began to shuttle back and forth in the building to find their offices. When I knocked on the door of the deputy director and expressed my intent to interview her about the issue of national parks, she was surprised but accepted my request. She talked to me for approximately an hour about the motivations of Yunnan to collaborate with TNC and introduced the national park model, the current institutional setting at the provincial and local levels and the status quo of the national park project. I still remember the words she spoke to me before the interview ended:

> We, the Forestry Department, take charge of all the maintenance and management work of Pudacuo; however, there is still suspicion about us regarding how many benefits we have earned from introducing this national park model. I tell you, nothing! I understand you may write down something in your dissertation that foreigners may read. Therefore, I expect you to look at the positive side and the progress we have made when you write. Don't just criticize. It doesn't help at all.

Finding that this type of 'surprise visit' might work, I continued visiting other institutions, including the Legislative Office of the Government of Yunnan Province, the Research Office of the Government of Yunnan Province, the Pudacuo National Park Management Bureau in Shangri-la and the Diqing Prefecture Tourism Investment Company. The interview process went smoothly, and I received insightful information from my interviewees. Moreover, most of the interviewees introduced me to colleagues and provided me with unpublished materials and internal research reports, which I could not have obtained through an online search.

In addition to interviewing officials working in relevant institutions, I joined a tour of Pudacuo National Park led by a local tourist agency. My reason for joining a guided tour was mainly because most tour guides at these agencies were members of the local communities. The scheduled tour also included a visit to local Tibetan guesthouses, where dinner was served and traditional Tibetan song and dance performances were provided as one of the features of their tourist services, though most tourists complained about this visit because it was compulsory and required extra fees. During my visit to Pudacuo, I talked to the tour guides about how their business had been influenced by the designation of national parks, visitors to the park about their personal experiences visiting the park and local community members who were hired by the tourism development company as trash collectors or forest rangers. In this semi-structured way, I obtained a general impression of how tourism-related services proceeded at the community level and how local community members perceived the government's role. For example, the compulsory guesthouse visit was proposed as a method to compensate local communities' losses due to the ban on the horse-riding services they used to provide to visitors. The fees paid by visitors were distributed between tourist agencies and the contracted local households.

After the field visit to Pudacuo, I returned to Kunming and met Mr. Jin and Ms. Wang, whom I had previously contacted at the office of TNC in Kunming. I was warmly received, and I shared with them my field observations and conversations with governmental officials. In turn, I was informed of the process and the status quo of the national park project from an NGO's perspective. In addition, they gave me useful unpublished research reports about the

Laojun Mountain and the Meili Snow Mountain, which were designated as national parks after Pudacuo.

Another source of materials that is worth mentioning is the previous field study conducted by John Zinda during his doctoral work in sociology at the University of Wisconsin-Madison. I contacted Zinda through the reference of a legal scholar working at a university in Kunming. Zinda conducted systemized field studies on the national park project in the Yunnan Province for a total of 17 months from 2008 to 2011, including participant observations, interviews and household surveys. Both qualitative and quantitative data were collected and meticulously analyzed in his PhD dissertation, which was defended in 2013.[2] Due to the nature of my PhD research and the limited time, the observations I obtained during my short visit to Yunnan cannot reflect the full panorama of the national park project, as Zinda's research admirably achieved. By screening the abundant firsthand data he collected and through multiple contacts with him, I further verified my own field observations and complemented my limited field research. In addition to Zinda, other scholars have produced literature and field studies on Yunnan's national park project, including Katherine Fritz,[3] Meryl Burgess,[4] D.Q. Zhou and Edward Grumbine.[5] Based on field studies, Fritz reported her interviews and visits to Pudacuo and provided insightful knowledge regarding the incentives of governments, the purpose of national parks, and the attitudes of park managers. Burgess based her work largely on document analysis and adopted a comparative perspective in analyzing national parks in China and South Africa. Zhou and Grumbine, who were directly involved in Yunnan's national park project, conducted case studies on the establishment of Pudacuo National Park and Laojun Mountain National Park and evaluated whether the new model had improved the existing nature reserve regulations and implementation. In Megan Kram's 2012 book *Protecting China's Biodiversity*, published by TNC, the case study of the establishment of Pudacuo was included as a tool for land and biodiversity protection.[6] Tang Fanglin, who worked on the practice of national parks in China for her PhD dissertation in ecology, provided detailed information on the process of the establishment of national parks in Yunnan.[7]

Based on the literature, field observations and interviews summarized above, this chapter aims to answer the following two questions: how have the different actors involved in the national park project co-shaped the blueprints of national parks in Yunnan ('national parks envisioned'), and how has the crafted national park model been translated into practice ('national parks in practice')? Reasons are provided to explain why a gap exists between these two issues, and possible solutions to mend this gap are presented. Experiences and

---

2 John Zinda, 'Organizing Conservation and Development in China: Politics, Institutions, Biodiversity, and Livelihoods', unpublished PhD dissertation at University of Wisconsin-Madison, 2013.
3 Katherine Fritz, 'National Parks in China: A New Model for Nature Conservation', Independent Study Project (ISP) Collection, Paper 706, Spring 2009. Available at http://digitalcollections.sit.edu/cgi/viewcontent.cgi?article=1708&context=isp_collection. Last visited January 2015.
4 Meryl Burgess, 'The Challenge in Conservation of Biodiversity: Regulation of National Parks in China and South Africa in Comparison', in a series of discussion papers issued by the Centre for Chinese Studies, Stellenbosch University, May 2012. Full text available at http://scholar.sun.ac.za/handle/10019.1/21175. Last visited January 2015.
5 D.Q. Zhou and R. Edward Grumbine, 'National Parks in China: Experiments with Protecting Nature and Human Livelihoods in Yunnan Province, Peoples' Republic of China (PRC)', 144 (2011) *Biological Conservation*, pp. 1314–21.
6 Megan Kram et al., *Protecting China's Biodiversity: A Guide to Land Use, Land Tenure, and Land Protection Tools* (Beijing: The Nature Conservancy, 2012), pp. 171–9.
7 Tang Fanglin, 中国国家公园的理论与实践研究 (Theory and Practice of the Establishment of National Parks in China), unpublished PhD dissertation, Nanjing Forestry University, 2010. See also Tang Fanglin, 中国需要建设什么样的国家公园 (What Kind of National Park does China need?), 5 (2014) 林业建设 (*Forestry Construction*), pp. 1–7.

lessons that can be drawn from Yunnan's pilot project of national parks are summarized in hopes that they can contribute to the ongoing efforts initiated by the central authority to escalate the national park model in China.

The Development of National Parks in Yunnan: Pudacuo and Beyond

Yunnan has the largest number of ethnic nationalities in China and is extremely culturally diversified.[8] At the same time, it remains relatively less developed compared to other regions in China.[9] The significance of Yunnan for nature and biodiversity protection has attracted much attention across the globe.[10] Yunnan is the area with the most environmental NGOs in China and is referred to a 'paradise for NGOs'.[11] Under these circumstances, on the one hand, Yunnan is burdened with the task of effectively protecting biodiversity and conserving nature; on the other hand, it faces considerable challenges in developing the local economy, improving livelihoods and resolving potential cultural and ethnic conflicts. These conditions make Yunnan attractive to international NGOs to bring their ideas, funding and expertise. The birth of national parks is thus facilitated and nourished in this region.

The Birth of National Parks: A Case Study of Pudacuo National Park

Since the late twentieth century, TNC has been actively promoting the introduction of 'national parks' to China together with other NGOs. In 2001, TNC and the Planning Committee of Yunnan Province jointly launched the 'Action Plan of Protection and Development for North-West Yunnan', in which one target proposed was the establishment of the national park system.[12] Since then, TNC has organized a series of study tours composed of high-ranking officials from central and local administrative agencies to visit the field management of national parks in other nations, such as the US, Canada, Australia, Indonesia, New Zealand and Thailand. After more than ten years of lobbying and preparation, Pudacuo National Park was officially inaugurated in Shangri-La County, Diqing Tibetan Autonomous Prefecture of Yunnan Province in 2007.

Designation and Infrastructure

Pudacuo covers approximately 60,000 hectares, encompassing and extending beyond two existing PAs: the Bita Lake Nature Reserve (14,000 hectares), which was designated by the Yunnan government in 1984, and the SHA of Shudu Lake (1,500 hectares), which was one of the scenic spots of the 'SHA of Three Parallel Rivers (三江并流) at the National Level' designated by the State Council in 1988.[13] The remaining 44,500 hectares cover a mixture

---

8   Of the 56 nationalities in China, 52 can be found in Yunnan Province.
9   Throughout the history of China's economy, Yunnan has been ranked in the bottom three in GDP per capita out of 31 provinces and autonomous regions in China. In 2013, the GPD per capita in Yunnan was US$4,050, which equated to approximately 25 percent of that of the top-ranked province, Tianjin, in China. See National Statistics Bureau, 中国统计年鉴 2014 (*China Statistical Yearbook 2014*) (Beijing, China Statistics Press: 2014).
10 It is said that Yunnan 'harbors more plants, animals, and bird species than all of North America'. For example, 243 species of priority protected wild animals are found in Yunnan out of the total number of 335, accounting for 72.5 percent of China as a whole, 15 percent of which are species endemic to Yunnan. See Yuming Yang et al., 'Biodiversity and biodiversity conservation in Yunnan, China', 13.4 (2004) *Biodiversity and Conservation*, p. 813.
11 He Xianghong et al., 滇西北生物多样性保护：政府与NGO共襄大计 (Biodiversity Protection in Northwest Yunnan Province: Cooperation Between Governments and NGO), in 香港文汇报 (*Wen Hui News (Hong Kong)*), April 2, 2009. Available at http://paper.wenweipo.com/2009/04/02/zt0904020049.htm. Last visited January 2015.
12 TNC and Planning Committee of Yunnan Province, 滇西北地区保护与发展行动计划 (Action Plan of Protection and Development for Northwest Yunnan), 2001.
13 See the official website of Pudacuo National Park, available at http://www.puda-cuo.com/. Last visited February 2013.

Figure 11.1 Visitors walking on the trails in Pudacuo National Park, September 2012, © Yun Ma

of collective and state-owned lands, nearly all of which are public-benefit forests (公益林), which means that timber harvesting is prohibited therein.

Within the core zone of Pudacuo is the village of Luorong, which contains approximately 200 residents living in a relatively concentrated area. In total, approximately 6,600 people live in and around Pudacuo.[14] They are allowed to continue using the resources in traditional ways, such as grazing livestock, cultivating crops, and collecting timber and non-timber products. In the past, the local residents around Pudacuo benefited from tourism by providing horse-riding services for tourists, a practice that is now banned. Since the designation of Pudacuo, local residents have received preferential treatment by being hired as forest rangers or trash collectors for the park. Approximately 3.04 million RMB has been disbursed to local communities to designate their collective forests as national parks and to compensate for the loss of horse-riding income.[15]

Visitors to the park are required to board the shuttle eco-buses that connect designated sites that are open to visitors. On the buses, park employees use microphones to describe the biodiversity and geographic conditions of the park. Visitors can leave the bus and walk on two segments of designated trails. These two trails are made of wood planks, one along a wetland and the other with a view of local residents pasturing yaks from a highland meadow. Areas outside the two trails are closed to visitors to minimize the people pressure on the natural landscape. During my two hours walking along the trails, most visitors followed the trail and seldom deviated from the designated route. Signs have been erected that provide information about the flora and fauna of the area.

The Institutional Setting

Multiple levels of government, from central to local, have been involved in the establishment and management of Pudacuo. Aiming to integrate the management authority and avoid overlapping problems, the institutional reconstruction of national parks proceeds at both the provincial and local levels in Yunnan (Figure 11.2).

At the central level, the State Forestry Administration (SFA) approved Yunnan as the pilot province for the designation of national parks and supervised the establishment of Pudacuo

---

14 John Zinda, 'Hazards of Collaboration: Local State Co-optation of a New Protected Area Model in Southwest China', 25.4 (2012) *Society & Natural Resources*, p. 394.
15 D.Q. Zhou and R. Edward Grumbine, *supra* note 5, p. 1317.

National Parks Envisioned and in Practice   245

and other national parks in Yunnan through its subordinate – the Forestry Department of Yunnan Province – in June 2008.

At the provincial level, an ad hoc institution – the National Park Management Office (NPMO) – was established in 2008 within the Yunnan Province Forestry Department. Its main function is to coordinate the establishment and management of national parks around Yunnan – specifically speaking, to develop relevant guidelines and standards and to approve the applications from local authorities for the designation of national parks.

At the local level, the Diqing Prefecture is in charge of supervising and overseeing the basic management of Pudacuo and coordinating with local agencies. Three agencies now run the park on a daily basis, supervised by the prefecture: the Bita Lake Nature Reserve Station within the Diqing Prefecture Forestry Bureau, the Diqing Prefecture Tourism Investment Company within the State Asset Regulatory Commission, and the Pudacuo National Park Management Bureau.[16]

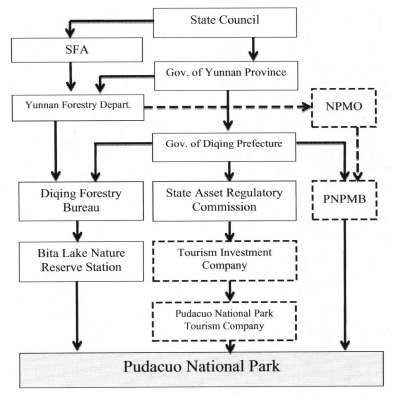

Figure 11.2 Institutional structure associated with the establishment and management of Pudacuo National Park[17]

The Bita Lake Nature Reserve Station was in charge of the management of the area before Pudacuo was designated. It still manages the Bita Lake portion of Pudacuo on behalf of the Forestry Bureau. The Management Bureau of Bita Lake and Shudu Lake, established in May 2005 during the preparatory stage of Pudacuo, was renamed Pudacuo National Park Management Bureau (PNPMB) in October 2006 after the park's debut. Based on the enabling document – 'Interim Measures of Diqing Prefecture on the Management of Meili Snow Mountain and Bita-Shudu

---

16 Megan Kram et al., *supra* note 6, p. 178.
17 The dashed boxes indicate newly established institutions during the national park project.

Lake Scenic Area'[18] – the PNPMB was empowered with 'four unitary' (四统一) functions, including 'unitary management, unitary planning, unitary protection, and unitary development'.

While establishing Pudacuo, Diqing Prefecture set up the Diqing Prefecture Tourism Investment Company (hereafter, 'the Company'), which is wholly owned by the prefecture, in 2006. By using entrance fees from Pudacuo as collateral, the Company obtained a bank loan for up to 730 million RMB to be used as funds for Pudacuo infrastructure projects.

As tourism investment increased, the Company expanded and it is now in charge of the overall tourism financing in Diqing. At the end of 2011, the total assets of the Company, with 806 staff members, reached 2.236 billion RMB.[19] As one of its affiliates, the Pudacuo National Park Tourism Company was established in 2007 to manage the tourism services within Pudacuo, such as collecting entrance fees, paying down investments, paying wages, and disbursing compensation payments to residents for income lost through the curtailment of resident-managed tourism.[20]

Visitation and Income

After the park opened to the public in 2006, the effect of being branded the 'first national park' in China became evident as Pudacuo soon became a major revenue generator for the local government, and both visitation and revenues skyrocketed (Figure 11.3). Compared to the figures in 2005 (prior to the designation), the number of tourists in 2011 increased sevenfold and income 29-fold.

The GDP of Diqing Prefecture benefited from the successful operation of Pudacuo, tripling from 2,797 million RMB in 2005 to 9,640 million RMB in 2011. In terms of Diqing Prefecture's total GDP, the percentage of income from Pudacuo also increased sharply from 0.21 percent in 2005 to 1.8 percent in 2011.[21]

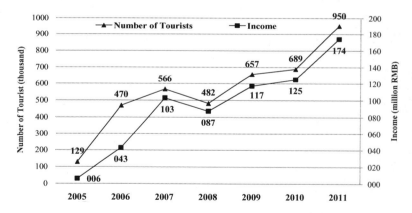

Figure 11.3 Income and tourist visitation of Pudacuo National Park (2005–11)[22]

18 Tibetan Autonomous Prefecture, 梅里雪山、碧塔海属都湖景区管理(暂行)办法 (Interim Measures of Diqing Prefecture on the Management of Meili Snow Mountain and Bita-Shudu Lake Scenic Area), Order No. 6, 2005, Article 6.
19 This information was collected from an interview with Tourism Investment Company staff members on September 24, 2012.
20 John Zinda, *supra* note 14, p. 392.
21 Diqing Prefecture, Statistical Bulletin of National Economy and Social Development of Diqing Prefecture (迪庆州国民经济和社会发展统计公报) (2005–11).
22 The data from 2005 to 2009 are from Megan Kram *et al.*, *supra* note 6, p. 177; the data from 2010–11 are from the official release of 'Construction and Development of Pudacuo National Park', available at http://www.xgll.com.cn/pdcgjgy/5Azl/2012–06/28/content_42902.htm. Last visited January 2015.

Moving beyond Pudacuo: the Dilemma of National Parks in the Context of Central-Local Conflicts

Pudacuo has served as a successful example in at least showing how this new model of PA could be a vast economic success. In December 2009, Yunnan Province identified a goal of creating twelve national parks from 2009 to 2020.[23] From July 2007 to February 2010, TNC obtained funding support from the European Union–China Biodiversity Program (ECBP) to establish another two pilot national parks in Yunnan: Laojun Mountain in Lijiang and Meili Snow Mountain in Deqin. A long-term goal was set by ECBP to 'advocate the national park model of biodiversity conservation to other provinces and central government authorities'.[24] However, the effort to expand was not as smooth as expected. Controversies flourish regarding Yunnan's initiative, which besieges the new model of 'national parks' in a dilemma in China.

Inspired by Yunnan's success, competition about who should be the leader of this new model emerged at the central level among the MoHURD, the MoEP and the SFA. In early 2008, both the MoEP and the SFA informed their counterpart agencies in Yunnan Province that the central government had granted the two agencies the authority to regulate the pilot national parks.[25] However, because of the statutory vacuum at a national level in clearly addressing the issue of national parks, a consensus could not be reached. Yunnan finally took a 'forest' approach to national parks: the SFA approved Yunnan as the province in which to launch the pilot national park in June 2008, and the NPMO was finally established within the Forestry Department in Yunnan Province. However, competition continued to ferment.

Dramatically, in October 2008, the MoEP and the State Tourism Administration jointly approved the establishment of the Tangwang River National Park in Heilongjiang Province in northern China. That park rejected Pudacuo as the first national park in China by claiming to be the first to gain 'official approval'.[26] At the same time, Yunnan officials claimed to be orthodox. One of my interviewees told me, 'They [Tangwang River] just imitate us. They even don't know what a national park is.'[27]

The conflicts finally came to the forefront. Consequently, both the legislation and the administration of the national parks in Yunnan were adversely affected. The issue of national parks became sensitive and contentious. Compared to the fanfare when Pudacuo debuted, the governments in Yunnan became hesitant to openly address the issue of national parks. The pace of the pilot project on national parks slowed. TNC and the ECBP admitted that they had to 'adjust and redevelop' the target they had set to popularize the national park model in other provinces and nationally, and to 'set realistic goals during the project term'.[28] It seemed that such a dilemma could only be resolved by a higher authority. As TNC admitted, 'National parks will not truly be "national" until the central government fully embraces them.'[29]

---

23 Megan Kram et al., *supra* note 6, p. 174.
24 Lu Hefen, *In Search of Harmony: The ECBP Stories* (Hong Kong: Pacific Empire International, 2010), p. 95. Available at http://content.yudu.com/Library/A1nkca/ECBPcompendiumbook/resources/52.htm. Last visited January 2015.
25 *Ibid.*, p. 97.
26 Xinhua News Agency, 我国批准建设首个国家公园黑龙江汤旺河国家公园 (China Approves the Construction of the first National Park in China: Heilongjiang Tangwang River National Park), October 8, 2008. Available at http://www.gov.cn/jrzg/2008-10/08/content_1115528.htm; China Radio International Online, 中国的第一个国家公园到底在哪里? (Where on Earth is the First National Park in China?), October 16, 2008, available at http://gb.cri.cn/18824/2008/10/16/3665s2283606.htm. Both were last visited in January 2015.
27 From an interview with Ms. Zhong, the former director of the NPMO, on September 18, 2012 in Kunming.
28 Lu Hefen, *supra* note 24, p. 101.
29 Megan Kram et al., *supra* note 6, p. 142.

Evaluation of the National Park Model in Yunnan Province

To evaluate the national park model in Yunnan Province, two questions arise: what are the rationale and attributes of the national park model envisioned by its initiators, and whether the practice of national parks has fulfilled the objectives that have been previously established.

National Parks Envisioned

The Attributes of the National Park Model

When TNC lobbied Yunnan Province to introduce national parks, the national park model was perceived as a better model to balance use and conservation. The model of national parks envisioned by TNC largely mirrors the definition and categorization of PA developed by the IUCN. As previously shown, the *primary objective* of a national park is to 'protect natural biodiversity along with its underlying ecological structure and supporting environmental processes, and to promote education and recreation'. The *other objectives* of national parks include managing visitor use, considering the needs of indigenous people and local communities, and contributing to local economies through tourism.[30]

TNC's vision of national parks was first translated into a blueprint for national parks co-developed by TNC and the Planning Committee of Yunnan Province. As previously discussed, in the Action Plan of Protection and Development for North-West Yunnan co-issued by TNC and the Planning Committee, six principles were framed for a model of national parks: 'one park, one enabling legislation', one management agency with unified authority within one particular boundary (i.e. no overlapping management), the participation of multiple stakeholders, the separation of the power between business operation and management by introducing the concession system, the adoption of the management category classified by the IUCN, and coordination and benefit sharing with local communities (section 4.1.3). The Action Plan largely invoked international principles and good practices in other jurisdictions as the source of its legitimacy.

The partnership between TNC and the Planning Committee turned out to be short lived. The Planning Committee broke its promise in funding a subsequent project, and this caused concern about its lack of genuine attention to conservation. In 2002, TNC began to work closely with the World Heritage Office within the Department of Housing and Urban-Rural Development of Yunnan Province, and this collaboration led to the designation of the SHA of Three Parallel Rivers as a World Heritage in 2003. TNC intended to continue its collaboration with the construction department to make it the implementation agency of the national park project. However, after the successful application of the World Heritage designation, the construction department lost interest in carrying on TNC's national park idea.

TNC continued seeking partners within the bureaucracy. At the provincial level, TNC began to work with the Research Office of the Government of Yunnan Province, an ad hoc policy research agency. They co-produced a report on establishing national parks in Yunnan in 2005.[31] This report was written in an orthodox way by repetitively revoking the policy formulas, such as 'scientific development', elaborated by the CPC. In addition to reiterating the perceived national park principles stated above, this report emphasized the advantages of a national park model in elevating the Yunnan region as a world-renowned tourist destination.

---

30 Nigel Dudley (ed.), *Guidelines for Applying Protected Area Management Categories* (Gland, Switzerland: IUCN, 2008), p. 16.
31 Research Office and TNC, 滇西北地区建设国家公园综合报告 (Comprehensive Report on Establishing National Parks in Northwest Yunnan), 2005. This document is cited from John Zinda's PhD dissertation, *supra* note 2, p. 91.

In Zinda's words, TNC began to 'articulate the national park project in language officials were ready to receive'.[32]

At the local level, TNC worked with the Diqing Prefecture to promote the concept of national parks. Diqing showed great interest in embracing this idea. However, the departure of the local government's perception of the idea of national parks from TNC was evident, as demonstrated by the selection of the site for the designation of a national park. The Pudacuo region was not initially promoted by TNC for national park designation. Instead, TNC intended to designate the Shangri-La Gorge as a national park because it was a biodiversity hotspot, and protection of this area did not yet exist. In contrast, Bita Lake, the key component of Pudacuo National Park, was already designated as a nature reserve. TNC's idea was to introduce the 'American' way of recreation to national parks in China, such as the wilderness experience, hiking trails, facilities for backpackers and bed-and-breakfast accommodations. However, the Diqing Prefecture had its own concerns. Shangri-La Gorge was located in a remote area and had hardly any infrastructure. It might attract some backpackers; however, it was not suitable for mass tourism and recreation. National parks needed a stable stream of visitation. Therefore, Shangri-La Gorge was not a desirable choice. TNC compromised, and the first national park was finally established at Pudacuo.

The leading role of the Forestry Department in the national park project was already established when Pudacuo was designated at the local level. TNC considered the Forestry Department a capable and powerful agency to seek support of national parks from the central government after previous unsuccessful collaborations with other departments. A TNC official stated that when they initially approached the Forestry Department, the department was cautious and chary of this project. Until the success of Pudacuo manifested, the Forestry Department decided to lead this project. A swift move was made within the forestry bureaucracy. As previously discussed, the SFA approved Yunnan as the province for the pilot national park in June 2008, and the NPMO was soon established within the Forestry Department in Yunnan Province.

To summarize, TNC has envisioned a national park model based on the IUCN's standard. However, when it sought support at the local level for its national park idea, some trade-offs were made to nudge national parks through local considerations. Nevertheless, TNC and its collaborators have reached some consensus on the attributes of the national park model:

1 Tourism is allowed but should be subject to conservation purposes and based on the concession policy,
2 The administration should be unified with a well-established organizational structure,
3 Community development should be prioritized, and benefits should be shared with local residents and
4 The legal framework should be developed and well implemented, and enabling legislation for each national park should be enacted.

Contextualization of National Parks in the Existing PA Framework

A question that arises with regard to the envisioned national park model is how to contextualize it in the existing PA framework, which entails the issue of the relationship between national parks and existing types of PA designations. The essence of the argument made by TNC and its collaborators is that national parks not only differ from existing types of PA designations but also enable a better balance between use and conservation.

32 John Zinda, ibid.

250 *Country Studies: China*

The purpose of national parks is officially defined as 'to protect nationally and internationally significant natural resources, cultural resources, and magnificent landscapes while providing opportunities for scientific research, recreation, community development, etc.'.[33] An official interpretation indicates that first, the scope of protection for national parks is broader than the scope that natural reserves have protected, and second, that the value of the national resources that national parks have protected is higher than the value of ordinary SHAs.[34] Furthermore, it is believed that national parks can realize the effective protection of larger areas by developing smaller areas.[35] The report co-produced by TNC and the Research Office of Yunnan Province noted that 97 percent of Pudacuo National Park has been effectively protected by developing and exploiting 2.3 percent of its area.[36]

From a qualitative perspective, the perception of the relationship between national parks and existing models with regard to their capacities for income generation and biodiversity protection is reflected in Figure 11.4.

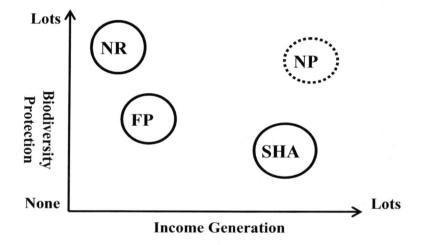

Figure 11.4 Perceptions of the relationship between national parks and other PAs in terms of biodiversity protection and income generation

Note: NR = nature reserve; FP = forest park; SHA = scenic and historic area; and NP = national park
Source: Megan Kram et al.[37]

33 Research Office of the People's Government of Yunnan Province, Yunnan National Park Management Office and The Nature Conservancy, 'Resource Book of Yunnan National Park Policy and Research' (unpublished) (Kunming, China, 2010), p. 46. Cited from D.Q. Zhou and R. Edward Grumbine, *supra* note 5, p. 1316.
34 Project Team for 'An Innovative Model for Biodiversity Conservation and Sustainable Development in Northwest Yunnan', 云南国家公园立法可行性研究 (Research on the Feasibility of Legislation on National Park in Yunnan Province), Research Office of the Yunnan Provincial Government, September 2008, p. 102. This research was conducted by the Research Office of Yunnan Province, the TNC and other institutions in 2007. A copy of this document is at hand with the author.
35 See TNC, 'The Project of Yunnan National Park', available at http://www.tnc.org.cn/NP/. Last visited January 2015. See also Guo Huijun, 云南国家公园建设试点调研报告 (Research Report of Pilot Project of Construction of National Park in Yunnan), 30.2 (2009) 云南林业 (*Yunnan Forestry*), p. 24; Yang Shilong, 云南国家公园建设中的法律难题 (Legal Conundrum during the Construction of National Parks in Yunnan Province), in 2010年全国环境资源法学研讨会 (*Symposium of Environment and Resources Law of China Law Society (2010)*), p. 575.
36 Project Team for 'An Innovative Model for Biodiversity Conservation and Sustainable Development in Northwest Yunnan', *supra* note 34, p. 100.
37 Megan Kram et al., *supra* note 6, p. 143.

As discussed earlier, Pudacuo encompassed and extended beyond previously designated PAs. In this sense, the national park model aimed to integrate and replace the previous models and functioned at a higher level than previous ones. However, in an interview, I was informed that the national parks were designed to function between, instead of above, the approaches of SHAs and nature reserves. When I asked a TNC staff member why TNC did not choose to improve the management of existing nature reserves but rather introduced a new model of national parks, she answered:

> We used to collaborate with local nature reserve managers, but they don't have incentives to work on conservation issues. Only nature reserves at the national level can get financial support from the central government. Local governments have to finance nature reserves at the local level by themselves. We introduced the national park model to complement nature reserves that local governments had no incentives to protect, not to replace them.

TNC's concern echoes the findings in scholarly research that existing PA models, especially SHAs and nature reserves, have irreparable defects that negate a proper balance between the conservation and use of natural resources.[38] SHAs and nature reserves are considered to 'lie at opposite ends of the conservation and income generation spectrum'.[39] No existing PA model lies in between. In this sense, the introduction of a new model that would lie in between was imperative, and national parks were selectively chosen to fill this vacuum. Specifically, a comparison of the attributes of SHAs, nature reserves, and the national park model envisioned by TNC and its collaborators is illustrated in Table 11.1 below.

Table 11.1 Comparison between the models of SHAs, nature reserves and national parks envisioned in Yunnan

	SHAs	*Nature reserves*	*National parks*
Tourism	Allowed in full area	Allowed in experimental zone	Allowed in confined areas (delimited by master plans)
Zoning	No clear zoning	Three zones (core, buffer and experimental zones)	Different zoning systems in individual national parks
Administration structure	Construction department	Environmental protection department (overall supervision); separate departments (corresponding to specific types of nature reserves)	Unified management body (e.g. NPMO)
Provision of visitor services	Concession is not established; monopoly by state-owned enterprises or private enterprises	Concession is not established; monopoly by state-owned enterprises or private enterprises	Concessioners who contract with governments

(continued)

---

38 For the legislative defects, see *supra* pp. 227–8 of Chapter 10.
39 John Zinda, *supra* note 14, p. 388.

Table 11.1 (continued)

	SHAs	Nature reserves	National parks
Benefit sharing and community development	Revenues shared by government and enterprises; complex governance structure; community benefits from tourism disproportionately	Revenues shared by government and enterprises; disenfranchisement of local residents	Community-based tourism; benefit sharing with local communities
Legislation and implementation	Regulation at low legislative hierarchy; insufficiencies of legal implementation	Regulation at low legislative hierarchy; insufficiencies of legal implementation	Management led and supervised by sound legislation and implementation

National Parks in Practice

The actual operation of national parks in Yunnan has been examined in academic discussions. Many scholars have noticed the divergence of national parks in practice from the models envisioned. Zhou and Grumbine summarized three primary problems in Pudacuo: first, the local government focused most of its attention on tourism, not conservation; second, support and compensation for local residents were not appropriate, and third, the relationship between provincial and local government authorities regarding national park management and implementation was problematic.[40] Zinda noted that 'the effort to establish Pudacuo National Park . . . became embroiled in a local strategy to build mass tourism, and as a result the park has not delivered on several of its promoters' promises.'[41] He summarized the divergences from the attributes of the national park model that TNC has espoused:[42]

1 'Tourism underwrites conservation' has been changed to 'tourism dominates management priorities'.
2 'Government direction' is not unified in the way TNC staff had hoped. The authority of the Pudacuo National Park Tourism Company limits the reach of the PNPMB.
3 The legislative process for national parks at the provincial and local levels has stalled.
4 Monitoring and evaluation are restrained by lack of capacity and funding.
5 Instead of a concession program as envisioned, a state-owned monopoly runs the national park.
6 Resident households in and near the park receive the compensation that constitutes a small percentage of the park's revenue.

In accordance with the four previously discussed attributes of the national park model, this section examines the practice of the national park model with regard to the following four aspects: objectives, institutional structure, community development and legislation.

Objective of National Parks: Tourism vs. Conservation

As envisioned, the purpose of tourism is to fund and underwrite conservation activities. After Pudacuo became a major revenue generator for the local government, the title of national park

---

40 D.Q. Zhou and R. Edward Grumbine, *supra* note 5, pp. 1317–18.
41 John Zinda, *supra* note 14, p. 396.
42 John Zinda, *supra* note 14, pp. 393–5.

became a lucrative brand for attracting investment and visitors. This shift can be found in the marketing tool that has been used to advertise Pudacuo. For example, in 2011, the Tourism Investment Company fully sponsored an extravagant wedding party held in Pudacuo for two Chinese pop stars, which attracted broad media coverage as well as harsh criticism from society that the company had abused its power to spend taxpayers' money.[43] The national park concept has become the local government's strategy to compete with other local administrations in the area and make Pudacuo a world-famous tourist destination.

Compared to the unbridled spending on such affairs, investment in nature conservation is far from satisfying. In my interview with a staff member of the PNPMB, I was informed that the Tourism Investment Company obtained a loan from the bank of nearly 730 million RMB. Only 230 million was invested in the park, and Pudacuo must pay off all the loan principal and interest. Zinda's data show that between 2006 and 2009, 78.6 percent of the Company's profits were transferred to the prefecture government.[44] It can be inferred that only a small proportion of revenues were allocated to park management and conservation.

In comparison with the concession-based tourism crafted in the beginning, the practice diverges. Instead of open bidding for its tourism services, the Pudacuo National Park Tourism Company has monopolized all the services, and has operated the whole park. The concession system is not established.

Institutional Capacity: National Park Authority vs. the Operating Company and the Forestry Sector

Institutional reconstruction has begun, including the establishment of the NPMO at the provincial level and the PNPMB at a local level. However, the national park authority's reach is limited at both levels.

Though the NPMO is empowered with regulatory authority, its enforcement capacity is limited.[45] This can be seen from the administrative affiliation of the NPMO. This office is not an independent administrative agency established by an enabling act, unlike the NPS, which was created by the Organic Act in the US. Both the NPMO and the Wetland Protection Management Office are affiliated with the Wild Fauna and Flora Protection and Nature Reserve Administration (hereafter, 'the Administration') within the Forestry Department. According to the 'three fixed plans' (三定方案),[46] the Administration is in charge of the planning, management and supervision of national parks and can formally use the name and stamp of the NPMO when performing duties relevant to the protection of national parks. The NPMO's role is constrained by its institutional capacity. Thus, conflicts between provincial directives and the local government's implementation manifest themselves. When a local government is found to deviate from park regulations and master plans, as in the case of the celebrity wedding party in Pudacuo, it cannot be expected that the NPMO will be capable of rectifying the local government's wrongdoings.

---

43 It was reported that the local government had invested 30 million RMB to sponsor the wedding party. In contrast, the total fiscal revenue in Shangri-La county in 2010 was only 300 million RMB. See Lu Guoping, 张杰谢娜婚礼政府赞助，私事公办岂有此理! (It is Ridiculous for Governments to Sponsor the Wedding Party for Zhang Jie and Xie Na!), available at http://www.sd.xinhuanet.com/blog/2011-09/26/content_23782100.htm. Last visited January 2015.
44 John Zinda's PhD dissertation, *supra* note 2, p. 99.
45 D.Q. Zhou and R. Edward Grumbine, *supra* note 5, p. 1317.
46 The 'three fixed plans' refers to 'fixed functions, fixed internal institutions and fixed staff quotas' (定主要职责,定内设机构,定人员编制). See 云南省林业厅主要职责内设机构和人员编制规定 (Rules on the Main Functions, Internal Bodies and Staff Quotas of the Department of Forestry of the Yunnan Government), *Yunzhengbanfa* No. 247 [2009].

At the local level, in the case of Pudacuo, the PNPMB's authority is also limited. As mentioned earlier, in addition to the PNPMB, two other sectors are currently involved in the management of Pudacuo: the Pudacuo National Park Tourism Company and the Bita Lake Nature Reserve Station. This situation restricts the PNPMB's authority.

First, the PNPMB has the same administrative rank as the Tourism Investment Company and thus lacks the authority to overrule the Company's actions.[47] During my interview with staff members working at the PNPMB, Mr. Bao, the director of the PNPMB, showed me a document that indicated that the PNPMB requested that the prefecture government issue instructions on rationalizing the relationship between the functions of the PNPMB and the Company.[48] This request was made in May 2008, two years after the establishment of the PNPMB. The PNPMB clearly expressed its dissatisfaction with the relationship's status quo in this document: 'The PNPMB devotes nearly all its efforts to coordinating issues that involve community conflicts, but all Pudacuo National Park revenue is held by the Company, which causes the PNPMB great inconvenience in its community management and coordination.' The PNPMB asked the prefecture to clarify the credit and cooperation between the PNPMB and the Company.

Second, the PNPMB's authority is restricted by the forestry sector. In another document that Mr. Bao showed me, the PNPMB requested that the prefecture authorize the PNPMB to perform certain functions currently exercised by the forestry sector in May 2008.[49] The PNPMB argued that the allocation of authority and responsibility to the PNPMB and to the forestry sector was unclear and disorganized, which could be seen in the action of the forestry sector passing the buck to the PNPMB in the case of recent forest fires. Thus, the PNPMB asked the prefecture to grant the PNPMB management authority over the state-owned and collective forests within the park.

Though subsequent responses by the Prefecture Government to the PNPMB's request were not available, from my conversation with the staff of PNPMB, it became evident that the relationships between PNPMB, the Company and the forestry sector have not undergone fundamental changes. In fact, PNPMB does not have the ability to oversee the daily management of Pudacuo. PNPMB is located in the center of the Shangri-La County, whereas Pudacuo is located approximately 50 minutes away from Shangri-La. Both the Company and the Bita Lake Nature Reserve Station are located within Pudacuo. Therefore, PNPMB usually makes phone calls and issues paper documents. The on-the-ground management authority is retained by the Company and the Station.

Community Development: Benefit Sharing vs. Benefit Sidelining

The main forms of community development in Pudacuo are the employment of local residents in park-related jobs and compensation to them for their economic losses. However, both forms are limited in reality.

Compensation to local residents remains a low percentage of the total revenue. As mentioned earlier, approximately 3.04 million RMB in compensation was paid in 2009 to

---

47 John Zinda, *supra* note 14, p. 394.
48 PNPMB, 香格里拉普达措国家公园管理局关于要求理顺管理局与旅游投资公司部份职能关系的请示 (Request for Instructions from the Prefecture Government on Rationalizing the Relationship between Several Functions of the PNPMB and the Tourism Investment Company), *Dipuguanqing* No. 12 [2008].
49 PNPMB, 香格里拉普达措国家公园管理局关于要求将公园规划区内林业部份职能委托给管理局进行管理的请示 (Request for Instructions from the Prefecture Government on Transferring Part of the Management Authority within the Planned Areas of the Park which is currently under the Forestry Sector to the PNPMB), *Dipuguanqing* No. 11 [2008].

residents' households within and around the park. However, that amount accounted for a mere 2.6 percent of the park's 2009 revenue of 117 million RMB. Mechanisms to enhance community-based tourism that were highlighted in various reports have not yet been acted upon by local governments.[50]

Although local residents are given preferential consideration for park jobs, low levels of education often exclude them from better-paying occupations.[51] Thus, inadequate capacity and a lack of knowledge hinder local residents from sharing the benefits. Local governments had more incentives to invest in material capital, such as the construction of infrastructure and facilities, than in human capital, such as the education and training of local residents, with the result that 'while the national park flourishes, residents sit on the sidelines.'[52]

When I interviewed a staff member from the Tourism Company, he expressed his discontent about the residents' desire for more compensation: 'We give them 3,000 yuan, and they will continue asking for 4,000 yuan. If we give them 4,000 yuan, they will ask for 5,000 yuan. They just want to make trouble (闹事).' When I asked a local resident who was hired as a trash collector 'whether your livelihoods improved after the designation of national parks', he told me:

> This place used to belong to us, but the government makes a lot of money from it. Every ten yuan Pudacuo earns, the government takes nine, and we only get one. This is not fair. I only have a small salary from the Company. This is not enough for my whole family.

I continued asking him about the local governments, and he suddenly asked me, 'Are you a journalist? Are you investigating something? If yes, please write down something for us and express our opinions in newspapers so that the government will have to make some changes.' The friction between the authority and local residents in deciding the appropriate proportions in which to allocate tourism benefits is evident.

The Legislative Process of National Parks: A Legal Challenge

As previously mentioned, the model of national parks has been challenged by potential central–local conflicts. This situation is especially reflected in the legislative process of national parks. Although the legislative process for Pudacuo began as early as 2006, an enabling act for Pudacuo has not yet been issued. The draft of the Regulations on National Parks in Yunnan Province was suspended because the Yunnan People's Congress dared not use 'national park' in its local legislation before a national consensus could be reached. The Yunnan Province People's Congress also suggested that the Yulong County People's Congress revise the Regulation of Laojun Mountain National Park by changing its title to Regulation on the Conservation of Laojun Mountain as an interim legislation until the central government had clearer guidance on the designation of national park.[53] The initiator of the project admitted that 'the legislative process for national parks took longer than expected' and referred to this situation in China as 'a legal minefield'.[54]

The Yunnan dilemma touches on a core question related the boundary of legislative power between central and local governments: how much can law-making initiatives supersede

50 D.Q. Zhou and R. Edward Grumbine, *supra* note 5, p. 1317.
51 John Zinda, *supra* note 14, p. 394.
52 Ibid., p. 396.
53 Lu Hefen, *supra* note 24, p. 97.
54 Ibid.

previous legislation? Legal scholars, such as Yang Shilong and Wang Jiangang,[55] have shed light on this question. By exploring whether Yunnan's legislation related to national parks has contravened superordinate laws, it is found that the new zoning system of national parks has bypassed the strict protection formerly provided in the Regulations on Nature Reserves. For example, the special protection zone in Pudacuo, where the designated area accounts for 60 square kilometers, is part of the core zone of the former Bita Lake Nature Reserve, which accounts for 141.33 square kilometers, and the rest of the area is designated as natural habitat zone where the access is open to tourists.[56] The former distinction between the core zone and the buffer zone is thus blurred, and strict protection in the core zone of a nature reserve is degraded. In this sense, the legality of the national park legislation has been challenged, and the Yunnan practices might be overruled. Difficulties are foreseen and compromises are needed in the changing legislative map of Yunnan.

Summary

The national park model that was initially crafted by TNC largely mirrors Category II of PAs elaborated by the IUCN. The new model is promoted as a better model to balance use and conservation that can remedy the defects of existing types of PA designations in China, particularly SHAs and nature reserves. The key attributes of this new model include concession-based tourism, unified administration, community development and benefit sharing and an effective legal framework. However, the process of translating this model into practice in Yunnan demonstrates that the idea envisioned by TNC may be distorted by the power of state agencies. National parks may not be as effective and serviceable as they are meant to be. Instead of using concession-based tourism to fund and underwrite conservation, local governments have transformed national parks into areas for mass tourism without investing sufficiently in conservation activities. The reach of the newly established management authorities is restricted by existing exterior powers, and unified administration only exists on paper. A large percentage of revenue is retained by governments, and local residents remain poorly compensated and only benefit to a limited degree from the flourishing of tourism. The legislative process for national parks is disrupted by inter-agency rivalry at the central level.

Several reasons can be identified to explain this gap. First, as previously demonstrated, economic growth and poverty alleviation are still the paramount concerns in contemporary China. This is especially the case in Yunnan. On the one hand, local governments in Yunnan are willing to cooperate with international organizations and accept funds, technology and experts from them. On the other hand, when implementing these cooperation programs, they are inclined to prioritize tourism development over nature conservation and use national parks to serve their own purposes. Second, the current legal framework for nature conservation may restrain the legislation process for national parks. TNC and its collaborators in Yunnan claim the legitimacy of the national park model largely by revoking the international principles and good practices in other jurisdictions. However, this basis does not suffice to justify the initiative by Yunnan. Instead, the new model must be contextualized in domestic contexts. The legislative vacuum at the central level creates uncertainty and causes dilemmas for national parks.

---

55 Yang Shilong, *supra* note 35, p. 575; Wang Jiangang, 论我国国家公园的法律适用 (Application of Law on National Parks in China), in 2010 年全国环境资源法学研讨会 (*Symposium of Environment and Resources Law of China Law Society (2010)*), p. 532.

56 See Ye Wen, Shen Chao and Li Yunlong (eds.), 香格里拉的眼睛：普达措国家公园规划和建设 (*Eyes of Shangri-La: Planning and Construction of Pudacuo National Park*) (Beijing: China Environmental Science Press, 2008), p. 46.

To proceed with the national park project and achieve the initiators' expectations of effective nature conservation and the improvement of local livelihoods, an explicit endorsement of the new model by the central authority may be a preliminary step. Recently, the central authority released a positive signal related to national park designation in China. In November 2013, the Central Committee of the Communist Party of China (CCCPC) issued the Decisions on Several Major Issues Concerning Comprehensively Deepening Reforms,[57] which clearly proposed to establish a national park system in China (Section 52). This indicates that a comprehensive and fundamental change of the PA scheme will soon occur in China. The National Development and Reform Commission (NDRC) is empowered to take the lead in coordinating between departments and drafting the development plan for national parks. The NDRC maintained a low profile in drawing the blueprint of national parks in the following year, 2014. In contrast, local governments have shown their zeal. In early 2014, the Forestry Department of Hubei Province officially submitted an application to the SFA to be listed as a pilot province of national parks. Tibet also submitted an application to the MoEP.[58] The three main departments at the central level – the MoHURD, the MoEP and the SFA – also began to compete with each other by showing their competences and resolution to the central government to lead the national park project.[59] In early 2015, the NDRC, the MoEP, the SFA, the MoHURD, together with nine other relevant authorities, co-issued the Pilot Scheme for Establishing the National Park System, in which Yunnan, Hubei, Qinghai and six other provinces were designated as the pilot provinces for establishing the national park system; each province was required to choose one area for the pilot project.[60] Later, the NDRC further issued two documents detailing the working focus and the implementation plan for the national park system in 2015.[61] Unfortunately, it is not possible for the public to access any of these documents. Through sporadic information online, it can be seen that there has been a great battle in selecting the pilot provinces and the pilot areas therein.[62] Some symbolic national tourist areas, such as Jiuzhaigou Valley, Zhangjiajie and Yellow Mountain, have opted out of this contest. The reasons behind these decisions are not difficult to understand: these areas already have stable sources of tourist income and the title of 'national park' would not add much luster; indeed, it could be a burden or a threat. Although the way the governance structure of national park management will be formulated remains to be seen, it is unavoidable that some trade-offs will be made between the central and local governments and among different departments and stakeholders.

57 CCCPC, 中共中央关于全面深化改革若干重大问题的决定 (Decisions of the CCCPC on Several Major Issues Concerning Comprehensively Deepening Reforms), November 12, 2013, para.52. Full text in Chinese is available at http://news.xinhuanet.com/politics/2013-11/15/c_118164235.htmm; for an English translation, see http://chinacopyrightandmedia.wordpress.com/2013/11/15/ccp-central-committee-resolution-concerning-some-major-issues-in-comprehensively-deepening-reform. Both were last visited in January 2015.
58 Wen Quan, 多地争抢建设国家公园,专家称很多旨在提速GDP (Many Local Governments Compete to Establish National Parks; Experts say Most of Them Aim at Accelerating GPD), July 19, 2014, available at http://politics.people.com.cn/n/2014/0719/c1001-25301803.html. Last visited January 2015.
59 Ibid.
60 NDRC, etc., 建立国家公园体制试点方案 (Pilot Scheme for Establishing the National Park System), January 2015.
61 NDRC, 建立国家公园体制试点2015年工作要点 (Working Focus of the Pilot Project of Establishing the National Park System in 2015), March 2015； NDRC, 国家公园体制试点区试点实施方案大纲 (Outline of the Implementation Plan of the Pilot Area for Establishing National Parks)，March 2015.
62 See Su Yang, 十说国家公园体制元年（上）(Ten Essays about the First Year of the National Park System Era (Part One)), January 4, 2016. Available at http://www.chinathinktanks.org.cn/content/detail?id=2930628. Last visited February 2016. Su Yang is a researcher at the Development Research Center of the State Council and member of the examination committee of the national park system in NDRC.

Receiving the positive signal released by the central government, the suspended legislative process for national parks in Yunnan was resumed. The Regulations on the Management of National Parks in Yunnan Province (the 'Regulations') were passed and became effective on January 1, 2016, and most of the previous national park practices were finally legalized.[63] However, as a local regulation, the Regulations still need to be coordinated with the legislation at the upper level when it is available.

All these positive moves brighten the future for national parks in Yunnan and in China. It is expected that the establishment o the national park system could be a breakthrough point for the overall reform of the PA management system in China. Effects, challenges, obstacles and pitfalls are to be discovered and conquered by the end of 2017, when the pilot project comes to an end. How the whole picture of PA in China may look like then largely depends on the results and effects of the national park pilot project. At the time being, lessons that the pilot project of national parks in Yunnan can offer are still needed to be drawn.

The situation of Yunnan demonstrates that there may be a gap between the way national parks are envisioned and the way national parks function in practice. A mere shift in the title of a designation is not enough to make 'national parks' become the truth in China. 'National park' is not merely a label to attract tourists or a tool to advertise natural beauty and generate revenue for governments. It indicates an assortment of ideas, objectives, standards and mechanisms of PA management. To mend the gap that has been observed in Yunnan, several steps can be taken. First, the national park model needs to be legalized, and law enforcement needs to be constantly monitored to prevent noncompliance. Second, an integrated management agency needs to be established and fully empowered with the authority of integrated management instead of being a 'shadow agency' of existing institutions. Third, to realize the goal of effective community development in national parks, the knowledge and capacities of local communities need to be increased and enhanced to realize effective participation and benefit sharing. Fourth, a strict threshold for designating national parks may be set by law, such as the 'national significance standard' in the context of US law. Finally, the management of existing types of PA designations needs to be strengthened before hastily transforming them into new designations of national parks. The selection of different types of PA designations needs to be tailored to site-specific conditions and circumstances. National parks are not necessarily a better model per se than existing types of PA designations. As demonstrated by the IUCN, a 'national park' is only one category; it is not necessarily the best type of PA.

---

63 Standing Committee of People's Congress in Yunnan Province, 云南省国家公园管理条例 (Regulations on the Management of National Parks in Yunnan Provinces), January 2016. Full text is available at http://ylxf.yn.gov.cn/Html/News/2015/12/4/127962.html. Last visited February 2016.

12 Comparative Observations, Conclusions and Recommendations

Introduction

Following the investigation in previous chapters on the formation of conflicts and the ways in which they are managed and resolved through institutional interactions in the contexts of the US and China, this chapter aims to draw comparative observations and conclusions and to make legal and policy recommendations for China. First, some comparative observations are provided by identifying the convergences and divergences between the US and China regarding the ways conflicts in PA management are identified and managed within domestic legal regimes. Variables that are engrained in domestic social and economic contexts, governance structures and the stages of legal development in general are identified to explain why divergences exist and how they are formulated. An assessment of the context in which the legal frameworks of PAs are structured from a comparative perspective may provide a better understanding of the transition that is currently occurring in China.

Second, based on the comparative observations, some findings and conclusions are presented in accordance with the research questions proposed in Chapter 1. These include the role of recreation and tourism in shaping the use-conflict framework of PA designation and management; the extent to which a resolution of conflicts has been achieved through institutional interactions in the US and China; whether there is a desirable institutional setting for the management and resolution of conflicts in law; how this desirable setting can be applied in the contexts of the US and China, and finally, how the current research on the resolution of conflicts between conservation and recreation can inform the construction of PA law in general.

Finally, legal and policy recommendations are provided regarding how China can improve its current legal and regulatory framework and better manage and resolve conflicts that arise from PA management in law.

Comparative Observations

In the previous sections, various conflicts in PA designation and management and the contexts in which they are embedded in the US and China were discussed. Institutional interactions, mainly among legislatures, agencies and courts, were observed in the two countries with regard to how these conflicts are identified, managed and resolved. Situating the conflicts in an institutional setting creates the entry point for comparative observations. Following the comparative methodology proposed in Chapter 1, this section summarizes the convergences and divergences by 'analogy, distinction and contrast' and identifies the variables that may give rise to the divergences presented above. By situating China in its current transitional phase, the context of contemporary China is also assessed by referring to the experiences of the US to produce a better understanding of the uniqueness of Chinese problems.

Convergences

The nature conservation schemes in the US and China present some converging features, which are summarized below. This converging process is advanced both by domestic demands, such as increasing recreational activities on public lands, and by international norms, such as the call for sustainable development.

First, based on a review of the evolution of public land policies in the US and China, it is clear that nature conservation and PA management are gaining prevalence in the two countries' political and legal agendas, which can be observed in three aspects. First, both countries have adopted the conservation tool of PA designation and management on their public lands, and a common feature of diversified PA designation can be observed. Public lands in the US are mainly legislated into four distinct systems and are managed by four federal agencies. Overarching designations, such as wilderness areas and national recreational areas, are established across different systems. In China, although the designation of PAs is still undergoing contingent development, diverse types of PA designations have been formulated since the 1980s, and the PA scheme has been continually diversified. Second, PAs have been under intensive management, and exploitative uses of natural resources have been strictly regulated in PAs, such as regulations of mining and timber activities. Third, complicated frameworks of legislation, regulations and policies have been formulated in both countries on conservation-related issues. Although it features a common-law tradition, the US has enacted extensive congressional statutes to regulate the use of PAs. Furthermore, from an academic point of view, increasing academic attention to nature conservation law as a research field separate from pollution control, which is deemed the cornerstone of environmental law, has been observed in both countries.[1]

Second, in terms of public land-use patterns, both countries have ushered in an era of mass recreation and industrial tourism. The US has witnessed a boom of recreational visitation in the post-World War II period. This boom arrived in China in the 2000s along with the liberation of the Chinese economy and a visible increase in disposable personal income. The increase in recreational demand was accompanied by a tendency in terms of both legislation and policy making to promote the recreational use of public land. This tendency is reflected in specific types of PA designations to serve recreational purposes, public-private partnerships in infrastructure construction, and cooperation between agencies and concessioners to provide recreational services to visitors. Recreational use and the conservation of nature have become the two most dominant features of the transformation of public lands.

Third, the effective management of conflicts arising from PA designation and management has become a common task for both countries. Due to the plurality of perceptions of nature, the transformation of land-use patterns and the increasing regulations of the use of natural resources, conflicts have arisen from PA designation and management in both countries. These conflicts have occurred in various forms. Claims on the use of natural resources compete and conflict with each other, and the core of these claims are the commodity use, conservation and the recreational use of natural resources. Conflicts also arise from PAs' competing goals, particularly their development and conservation goals. PA managers must also address various property claims from both individuals and collectives. Interest groups are continually divided, and new forms of conflicts continue to emerge. The identification of potent conflicts has become a crucial step in effectively managing and solving these conflicts.

---

1 For a discussion of the 'natural resource law' in the US, see Robert Fischman, 'What Is Natural Resources Law?', 78 (2007) *University of Colorado Law Review*, pp. 717–825.

Fourth, both countries have endorsed some commonly accepted principles and underpinning values that govern the resolution of conflicts in PA management. These principles and values include the realization of equity between current and future generations, the sustainable use of natural resources, the integration of different interests and the equitable distribution of the benefits and burdens of tourism. These areas of consensus have been largely incorporated into the essence of the principle of sustainable development and its associated principles of sustainable tourism and ecotourism. Although the US and China show different attitudes toward the concept of sustainable development in their domestic legislation, both of their approaches indicate an attempt to realize the requirements of sustainability. Elements that are embodied in sustainability requirements are observed in the legislation of both countries, such as good governance, public participation, access to information and benefit sharing.

Fifth, both countries have adopted common legal instruments to manage PA resources and recreational activities. These instruments have universal applicability and may be transplantable. The environmental impact assessment (EIA) is one such example. The EIA is broadly used as a procedural requirement for decision making concerning the environment. Its instrumental value has been broadly acknowledged across different jurisdictions. Moreover, to address the overcrowding problem produced by mass recreation, the determination of user capacity has become a common method, although whether this indicates a cap on the number of visitors has been debated in the US, as seen in the Merced River case. Both countries have also broadly used the mechanism of comprehensive planning to manage resources and visitors.

Sixth, PA management in the US and China faces some common challenges. The arrival of mass recreation and industrial tourism has threatened PA management. Relentless people pressure has caused a management dilemma regarding how to preserve the unimpaired status of nature while simultaneously satisfying the public's recreational demands. Funding shortfalls have demonstrated deficiencies in the effective management of PAs and the provision of sufficient compensation to those whose interests are affected by PA designation and management. Rampant concessions result in the commercialization of parks, and human-made facilities and recreational amenities need to be attuned to the natural setting. External threats of exploitative commodity use negatively influence the quality of nature conservation at the scale of the ecosystem. These common problems create the need for a question-based and solution-oriented comparative perspective and facilitate a mutual learning process.

Seventh, institutional dynamics and politics in environmental issues can be observed in both countries. There is a record of a connection between law making and policy making regarding PAs and their political environments. In the case of the US, the George W. Bush administration indicated a strong pro-recreation and pro-use attitude, which can be observed from both the drafting of the NPS MP of 2005 and the pro-snowmobiling policy in Yellowstone. The debate between Congress and the president on the allocation of the power to designate national monuments also demonstrates the dynamics and politics of conservation-related issues. In China, political turbulence in the 1970s and 1980s disturbed the development of nature conservation. Subsequently, conservation efforts became vulnerable to changes in administrations. Because most officials of local governments are appointed rather than elected, they are not inclined to make long-term conservation commitments during their tenures in office.

Divergences

Despite the converging features between the US and China, the legislation and practices of PA designation and management in the two countries present different answers to the research questions formulated in Chapter 1. These differences include the role of recreation and tourism, the main forms of conflicts, and the way these conflicts are managed and resolved through institutional interactions. This section examines how the answers to these questions diverge between the US and China.

The Role of Recreation and Tourism in PA Management

In the US, recreation is one of the original justifications of the designation for national parks and the establishment of the NPS. When Yellowstone was designated, national parks were perceived as recreational areas and reservoirs of natural grandeur. By promoting the idea of national parks as recreational paradises, the newly born NPS accumulated its original constituencies, the so-called 'elite recreationists'. This ideal of national parks may not be easily achieved without Americans' desire for outdoor recreation. In this sense, recreation has positive influences on the way certain geographical areas can be protected from exploitative use.

Recreational use is enshrined as one of the two fundamental purposes of national park designation, which is presented in the Organic Act using the term 'enjoyment'. The role of recreation in the designated use patterns of national parks differs from its role in the designated use patterns of other types of public land designations. Under multiple-use mandates, outdoor recreation is one of the seven specifically enumerated types of designated uses of national forestlands and one of the open-ended multiple uses of BLM lands. Under a dominant-use regime, wildlife-dependent recreational use is the priority general public use in the national wildlife refuge system.[2]

In China, recreational uses and the accompanying tourism industry are the major impetuses for diversifying PA designation, especially SHAs and other types of parks. These recreation-oriented designations are distinguished from the original designation of nature reserves that are preservation-oriented. Tourism benefits are a basic means to generate funding for conservation and a major incentive for local governments to generate revenue.

Recreation is enshrined as one of the fundamental purposes of both SHAs and forest parks. In contrast, recreation is not stipulated as part of the fundamental purpose of nature reserves, but it is subject to intensive regulation and is only permissible in experimental zones. According to the national park model envisioned by TNC and its collaborators in Yunnan Province, recreation is deemed a fundamental purpose of national park designations, and tourism benefits are considered the means to realize community development and to improve local livelihoods.

The Dominant Forms of Conflicts in PA Management

In the US, due to the increasing and diversified motorized recreational use of nature, the former alliance between conservationists and recreationists against exploitative commodity use has gradually collapsed. Interests in and claims for the use of nature are diverse and divided. Agencies must manage various conflicts that arise among preservationists, non-motorized recreationists and motorized recreationists. These conflicts are managed by agency rule making and policy making and are translated into numerous lawsuits in the courts. Although recreation has increased as a crucial component of public land use, it has not totally displaced traditional commodity use and become a dominant major use. Conflicts between economic development and conservation still exist. Exploitative activities on adjacent lands and existing mining rights within park boundaries continue to threaten the conservation and recreational use of park resources.

2 For details, see *supra* pp. 122–4 of Chapter 6.

Table 12.1 The main forms of conflict in PA management in the US and China

Typology of conflicts	US	China
Resource conflict	Preservation vs. high-impact, non-motorized recreation vs. motorized recreation	Exploitative use vs. conservation + recreation
	Exploitative use (existing mining rights, adjacent lands) vs. conservation + recreation	Commercialized and industrialized tourism vs. conservation
Development conflict	Conservation vs. Native Americans (ad hoc)	Local communities' livelihoods vs. conservation
Property conflict	Federal ownership vs. non-federal rights (state and individual right-of-way, private inholdings)	State ownership vs. collective ownership vs. private property rights

Because there is no urgent need for poverty alleviation or for the improvement of local communities' livelihoods, development conflicts are not commonly observed in the context of the US, with limited exceptions for Native Americans. Conservation policies in the early period of the US were censured for creating wilderness by removing local people and thus led to concerns about justice.[3] This tension between conservation and Native Americans has been alleviated through compensation to Native Americans and the designation of American Indian reservations.[4]

Although national parks are under the exclusive control of the federal government with little interference from state governments, non-federal rights continue to challenge the conservation and recreational use of national parks. This is apparent in the tension between federal ownership and state and individual rights-of-way and private inholdings inside parks.

In China, conservation is challenged by the encroachment of economic and development activities. This situation is bound by the resource-reliant economic development model in China. The boom of tourism, especially commercialized and industrialized tourism, challenges conservation. Governments, especially those at the local level, are inclined to exploit scenic resources to their maximum in the short term, while sacrificing the interests of nature in the long run and for future generations.

Due to the large number of residents living within PA boundaries and the impoverishment of these areas, development conflicts are evident between local communities and the need for nature conservation. The designation and management of PAs has incurred resentment from local communities due to the strict regulation of these communities' traditional uses of nature and the adverse impacts on their livelihoods. The unbalanced distribution of tourism benefits has caused tension between governments and communities and between communities within PAs and those adjacent to PAs. When economic benefits arise from policy initiatives in adjacent areas, claims arise from community members living within these areas to enjoy these policy benefits. The 'collective forest tenure reform' that liberates forestry resources into the hands of individual households is such an example.[5]

3 Michelle Kalamandeen and Lindsey Gillson, 'Demything "wilderness": implications for protected area designation and management", 16 (2007) *Biodiversity Conservation*, p. 168. See Mark David Spence, *Dispossessing the Wilderness: Indian Removal and the Making of the National Parks* (New York: Oxford University Press, 2000).
4 See Robert Keiter, *To Conserve Unimpaired: The Evolution of the National Park Idea* (Washington, DC: Island Press, 2013), pp. 121–42.
5 See *supra* pp. 28–9 of Chapter 2.

Due to the insufficient protection of participatory rights and the right to information, property rights were not always clearly defined when PAs were originally designated. The designation of PAs sometimes accompanies the 'taking' of collective and individual properties without proper compensation. Therefore, PA management sometimes collides with claims for property rights from collectives and individuals. These so-called 'problems left over by history' (历史遗留问题) create obstacles to the effective implementation of PA regulations.

The Legislative Approach to Conflict Resolution

The US has developed a comprehensive legal system that regulates the use of parklands and resources. Compared to China and most countries in the world, the American legal system regarding national parks is the most extensive and complicated, as noted by American scholars.[6] In contrast, legal development in China lags behind economic and social development. The modernization of law has only occurred in the post-Mao period. Although a comparatively complicated legal framework has been established to control pollution, legislation on nature conservation is preliminary and far from mature. Nevertheless, ecological protection has gained considerable prevalence in policy making. China has formulated a considerably complicated framework of PA-management policies. Problems remain regarding how to *legalize* these policies and to enact an 'Organic Act' in the sense of American law, which functions as the fundamental and governing law for all types of PAs. The ongoing discussion on enacting the Natural Heritage Law is such an effort.

To assess the legislative approaches of these two countries, a general observation is that the US Congress adopts a 'balancing approach', which is particularly reflected in the NPS Organic Act. In contrast, by explicitly embracing the 'priority of protection' as the fundamental principle of the Environmental Protection Law, Chinese legislatures favor a 'thumb on the scale' approach, which prioritizes nature protection.[7]

In terms of the 'balancing approach', there is an age-old debate over the fundamental purpose of national parks as prescribed in the NPS Organic Act, namely, conservation or enjoyment. Congress does not give explicit instructions to the NPS with regard to potential conflicts between the two. In other words, the Organic Act itself does not adjudicate such conflicts. Therefore, considerable room for statutory interpretation is left to the agency. Elaborating on its Management Policies of 2006, the NPS clarifies the priority of conservation in the case of conflict. It further elevates the non-impairment standard by clearly proposing the 'unacceptable impact test' that governs the assessment of a proposed use. The NPS commits itself to conservation-oriented park management by binding itself to a stricter threshold.

Modern environmental statutes, such as the NEPA and the Wilderness Act, burden agencies' decision-making process either in a substantive or a procedural manner. To some extent, these statutes have hardened the softness of the Organic Act in adjudicating conservation–enjoyment conflicts by showcasing a clearer conservation mandate. However, by enabling acts and ad hoc intervention in management conflicts, Congress has shown an inclination to push back toward enjoyment on the scale.

6 Robin Winks, 'The National Park Service Act of 1916: "A Contradictory Mandate"?', 74 (1996–97) *Denver University Law Review*, p. 576 ('legislation passed with respect to the Park System . . . has more extensive application than any other park system in the world').
7 The term of 'thumb on the scale' is referred to by Michael Healy in 'The Sustainable Development Principle in United States Environmental Law', 2 (2011) *George Washington Journal of Energy & Environmental Law*, p. 19. For a discussion about the three approaches to sustainable development in American environmental statutes, see *supra* pp. 55–6 of Chapter 3.

In terms of the 'thumb on the scale' approach, unlike the conservation–enjoyment debate in the context of the US, Chinese legislation has witnessed a shift from 'the principle of coordination' to the 'priority of protection'. The latter proposes to remedy the deficiencies arising from the practices of the principle of coordination. The principle of the priority of protection is the epitome of the elevated role of environmental protection in the nation's legal agenda, although gaps remain regarding how to interpret and apply this principle. This principle has also become a governing principle of PA management.

The Quality of Law Enforcement

Because the US has a good reputation in terms of the rule of law, the law is generally enforced to a satisfactory level in the US. Non-compliance with the law is not commonly observed. In contrast, there is a well-known gap between the 'law in books' and the 'law in action' in China. Non-compliance and deficiencies in law enforcement are commonplace in the ground management of PAs. Efforts toward the effective implementation of conservation law are easily crowded out by driving forces toward continual economic growth, job creation and societal stability. This is observed in the repetitive ad hoc law enforcement campaigns launched by the central government in the field of SHAs and nature reserves discussed in Chapter 10. Some specifically Chinese phenomena also showcase this gap. To develop the economy, local governments tend to adjust the scope and zoning of nature reserves to make way for construction projects. Inter-agency friction and rivalry are commonplace due to the overlapping designation and management of PAs. The case study of the Yunnan National Park Project in Chapter 11 shows that there is a gap between the way national parks are envisioned and the way national parks take shape in practice. National parks, enshrined as a model that facilitates a better balance between conservation and development, have turned out to be part of local governments' strategies to attract visitors and to develop the tourism industry.

The Role of Courts in Adjudicating PA-related Conflicts

In the US, litigation has frequently been used as a method of dispute resolution on public land-related issues since the 1970s. From a quantitative perspective, the courts contribute considerably to resolving conflicts involving public land management through numerous litigations. Although exceptions are found in wilderness-related management decisions, the courts have offered substantial deference to the NPS on its management decisions based on the Organic Act. Situated in the *Chevron* framework, the courts clarify that Congress does not provide a clear-cut answer in terms of the conservation–enjoyment conflict. In other words, courts adopt the *Chevron* step two framework instead of a *Chevron* step one approach to reviewing agency actions. This has a great influence on how the Organic Act should be read: not as a spontaneous preservation mandate but rather as a 'dual mandate'. Furthermore, litigation has limitations in the eradication of conflicts. Therefore, alternative dispute resolution (ADR) mechanisms have been increasingly used to resolve national park-related conflicts.

In China, courts play a limited, even dormant, role in resolving conservation-related disputes. There have been few conservation-related lawsuits. Very few public interest litigations are tried by courts. Consequently, the purpose statements and the principles of PA regulations, such as the previous principle of coordination and the current principle of the priority of protection, are seldom disputed in and rarely interpreted by the courts. In contrast to the litigant culture in the US, there is a lack of a tradition of using litigation as a preferred method to resolve disputes in China. Administrative channels, such as petitions, letters and visits, are the main mechanism for receiving and adjudicating disputes.

Variables

PAs are never merely a separate material sphere; instead, they are interconnected with their surroundings and enmeshed in political, social-economic and legal contexts. Having observed the divergences between the US and China regarding their PA-related legislation and practice, this section identifies several variables in the contexts that may explain the divergences found above.

Recreational Policy-making in Social-economic Contexts

Although both countries have conducted intensive recreational policy making, their starting points differ significantly. In an affluent society such as the US, recreation is deemed an intrinsic component of civic life and a crucial means of achieving public welfare. Recreation is firmly grounded as a fundamental purpose of national parks, whereas the tourism industry is considered a by-product.

In contrast, in China, the social-economic contexts in which PAs are situated are not similarly poetic and opportunistic. When China commenced the implementation of actions to cope with environmental problems, its GDP per capita was less than US$300.[8] The primary goal at that time was economic recovery and poverty alleviation. The GDP-based assessment model of local officials' performance pushes these officials to exploit natural resources to their maximum extent.[9] Therefore, recreation is strongly connected to the incentive to boost the tourism economy, and is used as a means to serve the end of economic development.

Compared with nature conservation in the US, nature conservation in China is more pressured. Well-documented factors of this pressure include the increasing demand on natural resources to develop the national economy, the large population, a poor economic basis and the problem of poverty.[10] The following figures may be illustrative: China possesses 9 percent of the planet's cultivated land, 6 percent of its water supply and 4 percent of its forests and must meet the needs of 21 percent of the earth's population, which is more than 1.3 billion people.[11] The annual GDP growth rate exceeds 10 percent, and the poverty headcount ratio was 13 percent of the total population in 2013.[12] China is facing unprecedented pressure with regard to its conservation agenda.

---

8 Zhang Kunmin and Wen Zongguo, 'Review and challenges of policies of environmental protection and sustainable development in China', 88.4 (2008) *Journal of Environmental Management*, p. 1249.
9 Liu Lingxuan, Zhang Bing and Bi Jun, 'Reforming China's multi-level environmental governance: Lessons from the 11th Five-Year Plan', 21 (2012) *Environmental Science & Policy*, p. 107.
10 See Charles McElwee, *Environmental Law in China: Managing Risk and Ensuring Compliance* (Oxford and New York: Oxford University Press, 2011), p. 2, and Elizabeth Economy, *The River Runs Black: The Environmental Challenge to China's Future* (Ithaca, NY: Cornell University Press, 2010).
11 Benoît Vermander, 'A Growth Engine Reinvents Itself: Towards a Greener China?', in Elvire Fabry and Damien Tresallet (eds.), *Greening Economic Growth: Towards a Global Strategy for Europe* (Paris: Fondation pour l'Innovation Politique, 2008), pp. 85–97.
12 See Li Yuhao, 截止2013年底中国贫困人口仍有8249万 (There were still 82.49 million people living below the poverty standard in China at the end of 2013), October 16, 2014, available at http://cpc.people.com.cn/n/2014/1016/c64387-25850085.html. Last visited January 2015.

The Funding Mechanism

Funding shortfalls for PAs are chronic in China. Similarly, national park managers in the US complain about budget cuts. However, a fundamental difference exists between their funding systems. In the US, the federal budget constitutes the predominant portion of public land management. Only a small portion of funding comes from the collection of entrance fees and private donations. To cope with funding shortfalls, there have been occasional reforms in the US to increase entrance fees and concession royalties.[13] However, these efforts do not change the government funding structure of national parks. Fees and royalties are 'not intended to offset the operational costs associated with a park'.[14] By contrast, most Chinese PAs have to 'fund themselves by themselves'. There is no budget guarantee; only contingent subsidies and allowances flow into PAs.

The consequences of this difference are qualitative rather than quantitative. The funding model in China directly results in the self-funding model for PAs and the follow-up phenomenon of a ticket economy. This is particularly reflected in the fact that in reality, local governments abdicate their management authority and responsibility by including the business sector in the investment and operation of scenic areas. Furthermore, the benefits of tourism have become a huge incentive for local governments to invest in advertising and 'decorating' local scenic resources. Tourism benefits are expected to reimburse these expenditures. This phenomenon is exemplified in local governments' enthusiasm in applying for the World Heritage designation. The expenditure on the application for the 'Chinese Danxia Landform' to be listed as a World Heritage site was nearly 1 billion RMB, most of which came from bank loans. Xinning County in Hunan Province, one of the joint applicants, spent more than 400 million RMB on this project, whereas the fiscal revenue of the whole county was only 200 million RMB in 2008.

The Central-local Relationship in PA Management

The concept of national parks in the US remains a product of the federal government. This concept is 'based upon a strong national sovereign, with little interference by state or local governments'.[15] Compared with other types of public land designations, national parks reveal fewer characteristics of cooperative federalism.[16] As observed by Fischman and King, 'power-sharing arrangements are part of the organic legislation for all of the federal land systems except the national parks.'[17] National park managers have less direct connection with state and local governments with regard to development issues. Other public land-management

---

13 For example, the Concession Management Improvement Act of 1998 was enacted to change the franchise fee distribution pattern between the national park unit and the federal finance authority.
14 NPS Management Policies of 2006, Section 8.2.6.
15 Denise Antolini, 'National Park Law In The US: Conservation, Conflict, And Centennial Values', 33 (2009) *William and Mary Environmental Law and Policy Review*, p. 886; see also M.I. Jeffrey, 'National Parks and Protected Areas – Approaching the Next Millennium', (1999) *Acta Juridica*, p. 172 ('federal control is largely free from interference by the states and allows for a continuity in management style and policy which is much more difficult to achieve in Canada').
16 Cooperative federalism refers to the coordination between the federal government and state governments and co-governance on certain affairs. For a thorough and in-depth discussion of cooperative federalism in natural resources law, see Robert Fischman, 'Cooperative Federalism and Natural Resources Law', 14 (2005–06) *New York University Environmental Law Journal*, pp. 179–231, and Robert Fischman and Angela King, 'Savings Clauses and Trends in Natural Resources Federalism', 32 (2007) *William and Mary Environmental Law and Policy Review*, pp. 129–68.
17 Robert Fischman and Angela King, *ibid.*, p. 129.

agencies must address issues of mining, timbering and hunting that are largely at the hands of state and local governments.[18] It is noteworthy that although this federal approach can prevent interference with the NPS by state interests, the strategy of isolating national parks cannot sustain itself. National park management faces considerable threats from adjacent development, non-federal rights and commercial activities in gateway communities, as discussed in Chapter 5. More cooperation between the NPS, states and gateway communities is needed.

In contrast, PAs in China at both the national and the local levels remain predominantly under the control of local governments. Management agencies are situated under the 'dual leadership' structure in China. Agencies at the ground level are responsible to both the apparatus of PA management at the higher level and the local governments where PAs are located. Studies show that Environmental Protection Bureaus at the ground level are mainly influenced by local governments rather than by the MoEP at the central level.[19] This is also the case for PA management agencies, which have personnel and financial dependence on local governments. Therefore, these agencies tend to side with local governments when conflicts arise between national laws and the goals of local governments.[20]

Similar to other developing countries,[21] China has adopted a decentralizing process in the field of PA management. This process commenced in the early 2000s with the downward transfer of the pricing power of scenic areas, including both SHAs and nature reserves, to local governments.[22] This decentralization process activates local initiatives and boosts the tourism economy at the local level because tourism benefits largely flow to local economies. Local officials are strongly incentivized to boost local economies to obtain promotions. It is said that the central government creates a 'yardstick competition among local officials by rewarding or punishing them on the basis of economic performance'.[23] In this context, local governments, rather than management agencies or departments at the central level,

---

18 All the Organic Acts for the BLM, the USFS and the FWS have prescribed requirements on them to coordinate with state and local governments, especially in terms of planning issues. The FLPMA requires the BLM to coordinate with state and local governments in the development of land-use plans 'to the extent consistent with the laws governing the administration of the public lands', and to consider input concerning land-use decisions from states and other non-federal entities (43 USC 1712 (c)). The National Forest Management Act also requires the Secretary of Agriculture to coordinate with the natural resource 'planning processes of State and local governments'(16 USC 1604 (a)). The National Wildlife Refuge System Improvement Act requires federal long-range plans for national wildlife refuges to be consistent with state wildlife conservation plans, 'to the extent practicable' (16 USC 668 dd(e)(1)(A) (iii)).
19 Liu Lingxuan et al., *supra* note 9, p. 108.
20 Charles McElwee, *Environmental Law in China: Managing Risk and Ensuring Compliance* (Oxford and New York: Oxford University Press, 2011), pp. 5–6.
21 It is said that decentralization reform has been promoted in the developing world 'as the primary means to achieve equitable, efficient and sustainable natural resource management'. See Wolfram H. Dressler, Christian A. Kull and Thomas C. Meredith, 'The Politics of Decentralizing National Parks Management in the Philippines', 25 (2006) *Political Geography*, p. 789; see also Jesse Ribot, Arun Agrawal and Anne Larson, 'Recentralizing while Decentralizing: How National Governments Re-appropriate Forest Resources', 34.11 (2006) *World Development*, p. 1864.
22 State Planning Commission, 国家计委关于印发游览参观点门票价格管理办法的通知 (Administrative Measures of the Price of Entry Fees of Sightseeing Spots), *Jijiage* No. 2303 [2000]. It states that the price department of the State Council is in charge of policy making regarding the prices of all the sightseeing spots in China and macro-control of the general level of prices. The price departments at the level of provincial government or below are in charge of the implementation of the policies relating to the prices of sightseeing spots (Article 4).
23 Zhang Xiaobo, 'Fiscal Decentralization and Political Centralization in China: Implications for Growth and Inequality', 34 (2006) *Journal of Comparative Economics*, p. 714.

play a decisive role in shaping the policy framework and in indicating the direction of PA development.

However, this situation results in aggravated local disparities and the problem of enforcement deficiencies of central regulations. It is argued that the governments at lower levels are ill equipped, with inadequate professionals and capacities, to manage scenic resources with national significance. Considerations such as local interests and the economy impede the long-term objectives of protecting scenic natural resources.[24]

Operation of Administrative Power and Public Trust in General

China has a long history of an omnipotent government. Lacking a separation of powers, the government serves both administrative and judicial functions. In contemporary China, multiple factors impede the exercise of administrative power in an accountable way, including the absence of a unified administrative procedure law (APA, in the sense of the US), a lack of transparency and public participation in the administrative decision-making process, and a lack of awareness about the exercise of administrative power under the rule of law (依法行政) among administrative officials. Therefore, to some extent, the government can freely switch between roles as the exerciser and the supervisor of power, which creates room for rent seeking.

Unlike those in the US, where the NPS is barred from engaging in commercial and profitable activities, scenic resources in China are closely linked to governmental interests, especially governments at the local level. As a result, during the administrative process, potential conflicts embodied in law due to the brevity of legislation or the inherent ambiguities in statutory language are not properly resolved. Instead, these conflicts are intensified and sharpened due to the direct or indirect involvement of the government as the largest stakeholder. The government does not perform as an arbiter but occasionally as a party involved in these conflicts.

Furthermore, public trust in management agencies differs. In the context of the US, the NPS is traditionally deemed a 'white-hat' agency (i.e. the image of a 'good man').[25] The NPS has a reputation for resource stewardship, and it is one of the most popular and well-regarded federal agencies.[26] This positive reputation is not similarly possessed by the Chinese government. Distrust in the government has become a crisis for governance and even for the legitimacy of the ruling party. This is evidenced in the increasing frequency of mass disturbances and social unrest on issues such as pollution and rights related to land and natural resources.[27]

24 Zhang Xiao, 世界遗产和国家重点风景名胜区分权化(属地)管理体制的制度缺陷 (Analysis on the Disadvantages of the Decentralized Administration and Management Model for World Heritage and Key Scenic and Historic Area at the National Level in China), 7 (2005) 中国园林 (*Chinese Garden*), p. 214.
25 Robert Fischman, 'The Problem of Statutory Detail in National Park Establishment Legislation and Its Relationship to Pollution Control Law', 74 (1996) *Denver University Law Review*, 813; see also Denise Antolini, 'National Park Law in the US: Conservation, Conflict, And Centennial Values', 33 (2009) *William and Mary Environmental Law and Policy Review*, p. 852 and footnote 2.
26 Federico Cheever, 'United States Forest Service and National Park Service: Paradoxical Mandates, Powerful Founders, and the Rise and Fall of Agency Discretion', 74 (1996–97) *Denver University Law Review*, p. 626 (noticing the NPS 'one of a very few federal government icons in an anti-government age'); Lindsey Shaw, 'Land Use Planning at the National Parks: Canyonlands National Park and Off-Road Vehicles', 68 (1997) *University of Colorado Law Review*, p. 797.
27 For such cases, see Elizabeth Economy, *supra* note 10. See also Chen Gang, *Politics of China's Environmental Protection: Problems and Progress* (Singapore: World Scientific Publishing, 2009).

Judicial Independence and the Predicament of the Courts

In China, the courts show considerable 'deference' to governments' decisions in administrative litigation in general.[28] This is also the case for conservation-related cases. However, this deferential attitude does not derive from judicial respect for agencies' professional knowledge under the rationale of the separation of powers, as it is in the US. Instead, this attitude derives from the courts' inferior role in terms of administrative power. The courts are supposed to work in tandem with governments for the purposes of policy advocacy and social control. Inappropriate interference in judicial work by governments has led to a phenomenon in which local courts are not willing to handle cases against governments' environmental decision making and do not have the ability to adjudicate such cases independently and neutrally. The predicaments that courts face in China are not found in the US, where constitutionalism and the separation of powers are well respected.

The Role of Civil Society

In the US, public awareness of environmental protection and nature conservation has been raised by constant environmental movements, including the early conservation movements of the late nineteenth century and the modern environmental movement beginning in the 1960s. These have been accompanied by a flourishing of environmental groups and their active participation in all environment-related issues. Furthermore, recreation-based interest groups have emerged as equivalent counterparts to the environmental NGOs that have played key roles in developing conservation schemes. These groups are willing and equipped to assert their rights and interests in the same manner that environmental groups do. Entitled with the standing to bring about public interest litigation, these groups, including both environmental groups and other civic groups, have played a crucial role in elevating the role of the courts in adjudicating disputes.

In China, the awakening of public awareness of the environment occurred later, especially after the occurrence of serious pollution disasters. However, public awareness of nature conservation remains at a considerably low level. The example of Qingdao City may illustrate this. To promote citizens' environmental awareness, some biologists presented the public with information on endangered species, such as their names, shapes and the locations where they were distributed. However, things quickly went awry. Some tourists harvested several plant species, including wild kiwi and lily flowers, according to the directions in the information that was presented.[29] Civil society (i.e. individuals and organizations that are outside the governmental apparatus) is relatively underdeveloped in China.[30] The first environmental

---

28 This is reflected in the low rate of plaintiffs' 'wins' in the courts and the high rate of withdrawal by plaintiffs in administrative litigation. For more general information on the administrative litigation system in China, see Yuwen Li and Yun Ma, 'The Hurdle is High: The Administrative Litigation System in the People's Republic of China', in Yuwen Li (ed.), *Administrative Litigation Systems in Greater China and Europe* (Farnham, England and Burlington, VT: Ashgate Publishing, 2014), pp. 15–40.
29 Yang Lin, 媒体公布崂山濒危野猕猴桃分布，游客按图索骥采了吃 (Media Exposes the Distribution of Endangered Wild Kiwi Fruit in Laoshan Mountain; Tourists Search For and Eat Them According to this Information), in 齐鲁晚报 (*Qilu Evening News*), August 7, 2013. Full text is available at http://politics.people.com.cn/n/2013/0807/c1001-22478743.html. Last visited January 2015.
30 See Yuwen Li (ed.), *NGOs in China and Europe: Comparisons and Contrasts* (Farnham, England and Burlington, VT: Ashgate, 2011).

NGO in China was registered in 1994;[31] as of 2008, this number had increased to 3,539.[32] With such incredible growth, as previously discussed, most of these organizations do not have the intent or capacity to participate in litigation. The reach of environmental groups in the judicial sphere is confined by the standing requirement and the antagonistic judicial culture, as evidenced by the fact that none of the eight public interest litigations brought by the All-China Environment Federation (ACEF) in 2013 was accepted by the courts.[33] Therefore, the role of environmental groups in elevating the role of the courts is not observed in China in the same way that it is in the US.

Assessment of Contexts: Understanding the Transition in China

Having analyzed the convergences, divergences and variables between the US and China, the next question addresses how to assess these contextual similarities and disparities to better understand the distinctive features of the current transition in China.

In recent decades, China has stunned the world with its incredible economic growth. This 'China miracle' closely relates to the development model to which China adheres. Ding summarized the costs of the 'China model' in the thirty years after the reform and opening up as the 'considerable deprivation of vulnerable groups, derogation of ecological environment, systematic corruption and lack of transparency in public policy'.[34] Dubbed 'draining the pond to get all the fish' (竭泽而渔), the current economic development model in China is largely resource-reliant, which has placed environment and natural resources in serious jeopardy. Furthermore, the development path 'pollute first, clean later' (先污染后治理) that most developed countries have followed is insurmountable for China.[35] Environmental interests must currently be sacrificed to accumulate enough money to cope with future environmental problems. China's economic growth is therefore accompanied by striking environmental costs that are estimated to account for 3–8 percent of the country's GDP.[36] Thus, the sustainability of the so-called 'China miracle' is questionable.

Is the development path that China follows inherently 'Chinese'? Is there a sustainable growth model that China can incorporate into its current development discourse?

Examining the public land policies of the US, one can observe a clear shift at the end of the nineteenth century. Throughout that century, the disposal policy, with its core characteristic of 'first in time, first in right', intensively shaped the landscape of the vast West. The Gold Rush and its accompanying infrastructure construction were accompanied by the destruction of watersheds, the extinction of natural resources, the destruction of habitats and a series of pollution problems. The scarcity of natural resources was perceived, in contrast to the previous assumption of an inexhaustible natural bounty. The shift in public land policies from disposal to retention at the end of the nineteenth century signaled an awareness of

---

31 It is the Academy for Green Culture, which is now called Friends of Nature.
32 All-China Environmental Federation, 中国环保民间组织发展状况报告 (Report of the Status of Development of Environmental Non-Governmental Organizations in China), 2008, p. 3.
33 Zou Chunxia, 中华环保联合会:去年提8起公益诉讼法院均未立案 (ACEF: 8 PIL Claims were Refused by Courts Last Year), March 1, 2014. Available at http://news.xinhuanet.com/2014-03/01/c_119559046.htm. Last visited January 2015. For relevant discussion, see *supra* p. 234 of Chapter 10.
34 Ding Xueliang, 辩论"中国模式" (*Debate on the 'China Model'*) (Beijing: Shehui Kexue Wenxian Chubanshe, 2011), pp. 114–39.
35 Alex Wang 'The Role of Law in Environmental Protection in China: Recent Developments', 8 (2006–07) *Vermont Journal of Environmental Law*, p. 198.
36 Ibid., p. 200.

nature conservation that was among the earliest in the world. Consequently, the US preserved a large amount of land and resources, leaving them largely intact and wild. The economy of the US witnessed a sharp increase after the designation of Yellowstone; however, the large-scale destruction of the landscape and resources within national parks is seldom revealed to the public. At the political level, a consensus regarding how national parks should look has not necessarily been achieved. Chapter 5 has shown that national parks are still besieged by various political debates on the commercialization and exploitation of profitable resources.

In contrast, China's turn to develop its economy occurred when its turbulent period of history ended in the 1980s, the same time that awareness of conservation increased. Economic development was then deemed the paramount task of the Chinese government. This task was echoed by the Chinese people, who desperately needed to improve their livelihoods and quality of life. Therefore, the priority of economic development set by the central authority easily obtained legitimacy from society at large. The legitimacy of the CPC's ruling authority was further underpinned by increasing and continual economic growth that produced a substantial increase in the livelihoods of a large percentage of the population in China. In other words, 'the government is "chained" to the imperative of economic growth for the preservation of political stability.'[37] In this sense, nature should be considered not only as a material entity but also as a basis for economic growth and furthermore as a basis for the sovereignty's legitimacy.

However, as society becomes increasingly pluralized and citizens begin to desire a better quality of life and a better environment, economic growth cannot completely sustain the legitimacy challenge in the new era. The derogation of the environment and the depletion of resources are occurring at an alarming rate. To smooth China's transition, the authorities have revitalized and employed traditional ideals and values, such as the 'harmonious society', as the governing ideologies for contemporary China. However, one can assert that harmony may only be a mirage if it is built on the current development model. Making a commitment to nature conservation and delivering on its promise before it is too late might be the foremost task for furthering the unavoidable transition process in China.

Conclusions

Recreation and tourism play a dual role in PA designation and management as a direct cause of the rise of conflicts and a mitigator of conflicts.

On the one hand, recreation and tourism may directly cause the rise of conflicts. As shown in Chapter 3, recreation and tourism are decisive factors that transform public land-use patterns. 'Resource conflicts' arise among competing and conflicting uses of resources, such as motorized use and nature conservation. Recreation and tourism may also cause 'development conflicts'. State policies that promote recreation and tourism in a certain area may be accompanied by the displacement of local people and the expropriation of lands for park designation and expansion purpose.[38] Tourism can be a causative factor that accelerates the marginalization of local people and enlarges the gap between local communities' access to and control of natural resources and external visitors' access to them. McCarthy notes that

---

37 Vic Li and Graeme Lang, 'China's "Green GDP" Experiment and the Struggle for Ecological Modernisation', 40.1 (2010) *Journal of Contemporary Asia*, p. 46.
38 Charles Geisler and Essy Letsoalo, 'Rethinking Land Reform in South Africa: An Alternative Approach to Environmental Justice', 5.2 (2000) *Sociological Research Online*, pp. U3–U14 (this paper discusses human displacement and environmental justice in South Africa due to the expansion of national parks and game refuges).

the growing popularity of nature-based tourism has transformed the environment 'to the detriment or against the will of local users'.[39] Recreation and tourism may also cause 'property conflict'. Private ranchers may be concerned that recreational users encroach on their interests in using their rangelands. Local governments may fear losing recreational constituencies and revenues due to strong preservation mandates from the central authority. This phenomenon can be observed in the claims of 'right of way' by states and individuals on federal lands in the US discussed in Chapter 5 and in the claims of collectives to share tourism benefits with the governmental authority in designated PAs in China, as shown in Chapter 9.

However, recreation and tourism may also serve to mitigate conflicts in PA management. First, recreation helps to build constituencies and protects nature from exploitative use. In the early history of nature conservation, the earliest imperative for conservation arose from the demands of the rich to preserve animals for hunting.[40] The coalition of recreationists and conservationists can counterbalance the exploitation of nature and mitigate conflicts between exploitation and conservation. Second, recreation and tourism can be an incentive for conservation activities. The conservation of natural scenery is a precondition for tourism development. Tourism benefits can contribute to local revenue and generate funding for PA management. In some developing countries such as China, tourism benefits account for a large percentage or constitute the sole source of funding in some PAs. The development of tourism thus becomes a prerequisite for the effective management of PAs. Third, tourism can be a tool for achieving development goals. The benefits of tourism make it a potential development tool. The rise of 'pro-poor tourism' at the end of the 1990s shows that tourism can be a crucial means of alleviating poverty. Pro-poor tourism focuses on 'unlocking opportunities for specific groups within it' rather than 'expanding the overall size of tourism' (tilting the cake, not expanding it).[41] It aims to generate social, economic and environmental benefits from tourism, especially for the poor.[42] Although pro-poor tourism is criticized for failing to '*deliver*' benefits from tourism to the poor', in reality,[43] it shows the potential of tourism to mitigate development conflicts in PA designation and management.

The key to PA management and PA law making rests in how to effectively manage the conflicts between recreation and conservation.

The exploitative use of natural resources has been broadly and intensively regulated within PAs. The future development of PA management and PA law making lies in the reconciliation of conflicts between conservation and recreation. Although conflicts between exploitative use and conservation in PAs may not be easily eradicated in the short run, conflicts between recreation and conservation may be a larger challenge and may represent the dominant form of conflicts in PA management in the future. The previous discussion has shown that a resolution to the conflicts between conservation and recreation is not as simple as favoring conservation while jettisoning recreation or vice versa. In contrast to the traditional focus on

39 James McCarthy, 'First World Political Ecology: Lessons from the Wise Use Movement', 34.7 (2002) *Environment and Planning*, p. 1286.
40 Dan Brockington, Rosaleen Duffy and Jim Igoe, *Nature Unbound: Conservation, Capitalism and the Future of Protected Areas* (London and Sterling, VA: Earthscan, 2008), p. 47.
41 Department for International Development (DFID), *Tourism and Poverty Elimination: Untapped Potential* (London: DFID, 1999), p. 1.
42 Caroline Ashley, Charlotte Boyd and Harold Goodwin, 'Pro-poor Tourism: Putting Poverty at the Heart of the Tourism Agenda', 51 (2000) *Natural Resources Perspectives*, pp. 1–6.
43 David Harrison, 'Pro-poor Tourism: A Critique', 29.5 (2008) *Third World Quarterly*, p. 864.

the regulation of commodity uses within PAs, the regulation of recreational activities necessitates a more delicate balance and a deeper quest for an answer to a fundamental question: what are PAs for?

Previous case studies have shown that most recreational policy making and law making is value-laden. Some trade-offs between conflicting values need to be made to reach a balance between conservation and recreation. In his article 'Fashioning a Recreation Policy for Our National Parklands', Sax argues that fashioning a recreational policy is a profound philosophical choice rather than a mere management decision.[44] The controversy regarding capping the number of visitors to the Merced River raises the question of whether PAs should be protected as enclaves or whether they should accept people. In Runte's words, 'To exclude people, whatever the means, risks loss of support for the national park idea; to accept more people as the price of support jeopardizes the parks themselves.'[45] The Wi-Fi controversy in national parks in the US raises the question of what type of 'park experience' should be provided to visitors. The overflight controversy in the Grand Canyon also raises the question of whether there is a preference for a certain type of experience: do visitors prefer to enjoy the panorama of the Grand Canyon with an aerial view from helicopters or to hike along paved trails or routes? These questions cannot be easily answered through scientific surveys; instead, they necessitate a deeper inquiry into the fundamental purpose of conservation law.

In this sense, competence in managing and resolving conflicts between recreation and conservation can be a touchstone to test whether an existing legal system of PAs is adaptive enough to embrace new challenges, stable enough to accommodate diversified interests and claims, and future-oriented enough to meet the needs of the future generations.

Sustainable development can be used as a benchmark for assessing the legal foundations of PAs in the US and China. A sustainability test of tourism in PAs is both necessary and plausible.

The terms 'sustainability' and 'sustainable development', although currently used imprecisely, can be useful and effective tools for communication between different jurisdictions. These terms provide an integral, holistic and equitable perspective with which to approach environmental issues. The integration requirements embodied in the principle of sustainable development may occur in both procedural and substantive forms. They establish a baseline for legislation and decision making. Governments are required not only to consider the environment, economy and society in their decision-making and adjudication processes, but also to realize and further environmental, social and economic goals in a substantive manner. Countries have translated this baseline into their own legal discourses, as seen in the different attitudes between the US and China regarding the inclusion of this principle in their domestic legislation. Nevertheless, the principle of sustainable development facilitates communication and dialogue between different jurisdictions.

Recreation and tourism have an intrinsic connection to the three pillars upon which the principle of sustainable development is based: the environment, the economy and society. They are closely tied to nature conservation, the tourism industry and environmental justice. The practices in the US and China discussed above have shown that tourism activities may have negative impacts on nature conservation, generate revenue for governments and cause

---

44 Joseph Sax, 'Fashioning a Recreation Policy for Our National Parklands: The Philosophy of Choice and the Choice of Philosophy', 12 (1979) *Creighton Law Review*, pp. 973–85.
45 Alfred Runte, *National Parks: The American Experience* (Lincoln: University of Nebraska Press, 1987), pp. 172–3.

the marginalization of local residents. Therefore, an integral perspective needs to be adopted to examine the interplay and tension among the three pillars of tourism. Similar to the principle of sustainable development, the principles of sustainable tourism and ecotourism may have normative influences on how recreational laws and policies should be made and how tourism activities should be conducted in practice.

Interpretation of law is a crucial means of vitalizing PA-related statutes and ensuring their effectiveness.

Statutory ambiguities are prevalent in PA-related laws. This can be seen in the examples of 'user capacity' in the Merced River case and the 'substantial restoration of natural quiet' in the Grand Canyon overflights case, as discussed in Chapter 7 and the examples of 'transfer of operation rights' and 'concession', as discussed in Chapter 9. These legislative 'deficits' are due either to the unpredictability of conservation practices and management activities, or the intentional delegation of authority from Congress to agencies to realize the flexibility in administration. The existence of statutory ambiguities determines that law must be interpreted to best apply it. Facing an interpretative choice, the resolution of disputes between different parties largely relies on how and by whom the terms stipulated in law are interpreted.

The effect of interpretation on the application of environment law is evidenced by the fact that most leading environmental law cases in the US are also statutory interpretation cases.[46] By adopting a dynamic approach to statutory interpretation, environmental statutes can be applied in difficult situations, and the political controversies surrounding the issues of such situations can be ameliorated. This is clear in the previous discussion about high-profile national park-related controversies in which disputes were settled through the meticulous interpretation of the law. In the context of China, Nagle has keenly noted that unlike their western counterparts, statutory interpretation cases are missing in Chinese environmental law, although a western-style legal system has been adopted in China.[47] The phenomenon of the absence of interpretation cases is closely connected to the enforcement deficit of Chinese law. The 'seemingly beautiful' provisions stipulated in law can only be vitalized and bolstered by being interpreted and applied in a dynamic environment. Therefore, more practices of statutory interpretation are crucial to improve the poorly recorded law enforcement in China.

The quality of a legal institution is engraved in the legal system in which it is embedded. The formula for desirable institutional interactions in legal interpretation needs to be established on a case-by-case basis.

Schmitthoff notes that 'the same institution may hold a key position in the legal system of one country and may be of subordinate character in another system where the corresponding needs are satisfied by other legal institutions.'[48] The divergences between the US and China

---

46 For example, the *Tennessee Valley Authority v. Hill* case (the Supreme Court held that the Endangered Species Act prevented the completion of the dam construction; 437 US 153 (1978)) is not only a leading environmental law case, but also a significant statutory interpretation case due to its adoption of the textualist approach to reading statutes. For relevant discussions of this case by Dworkin and Vermeule, see Adrian Vermeule, *Judging under Uncertainty: An Institutional Theory of Legal Interpretation* (Cambridge, MA: Harvard University Press, 2006), p. 28.
47 John Nagle, 'The Missing Chinese Environmental Law Statutory Interpretation Cases', 5 (1996) *New York University Environmental Law Journal*, pp. 517–55.
48 M. Schmitthoff, 'The Science of Comparative Law', 7.1 (1939) *Cambridge Law Journal*, pp. 97–8.

in terms of their institutional interactions indicate the significance of the context in which a legal institution is situated. Taking courts as an example, the quality of the judicial adjudication of disputes is closely linked to the legal system in which the courts are embedded. Multiple factors may influence the institutional capacity of courts, such as the relationship between courts and extra-judicial bodies, the degree of judicial independence, the development of civil society and the citizens' trust in the judiciary in general. A mere elevation of the courts' role in name, such as the proposal to establish separate environmental courts, does not necessarily increase the courts' institutional capacities. Instead, corresponding measures must be taken to improve the general context in which a particular institution is situated.

Desirable institutional interactions need to be built on the premise of institutional capacity building. This means that legislatures, agencies and courts need to be equipped with their respective institutional functions. In this context, the methodological significance of the statutory interpretation rules proposed by Vermeule, namely, that courts should follow the clear and specific meaning of legal texts or defer to agencies' interpretations in the case of unspecific legislative texts, may be degraded when they are to be transplanted elsewhere. Vermeule's analysis is largely based on empirical studies of the institutional interaction in the context of the US. His argument indicates 'a dramatic shift in interpretative authority from courts to agencies'.[49] His trust in agencies' capacities for statutory interpretation is built on the premises that agencies can perform their function of implementing the law in a satisfactory manner and that agencies have professional knowledge and information that courts do not possess. However, when agencies are tempted or compelled to consider irrelevant factors other than professionalism or when they are involved in the commercial sector, as is the case of China, where the rule of law is not fully established, the institutional capacity of agencies may not receive as much appreciation as Vermeule has argued. In China, public distrust against the bureaucratic government may raise suspicion among the public when courts are expected to 'respect' agencies' interpretative freedom. Furthermore, in the context of the current PA governance structure in China, many different agencies are involved in one statute, and their department-based interests are intertwined. Courts cannot sensibly detect to which agency's interpretation they should defer. Therefore, the deference rule Vermeule has presented cannot be effectively established in the context of China, where the relationship between agencies and courts is different from the one in the US.

Moreover, in the first part of Vermeule's interpretative rule, which argues that judges should interpret statutes according to their 'surface or apparent meaning, eschewing the use of other tools to enrich their sense of meaning, intentions, or purposes',[50] Vermeule urges judges to interpret statutes as simply as possible to minimize decision costs. In the context of China, considering the limited role of courts and the low capacity of judges in adjudicating PA-related disputes, it is doubtful that judges will produce better judgments if they omit the various interpretative tools by adopting Vermeule's approach. Imagine keeping beginners out of the water when they are expected to learn to swim.

Nevertheless, Vermeule's thesis that the capacities of the institution and the systematic effects of a particular interpretative approach should not be overlooked in designing desirable institutional interactions remains inspiring. In Nelson's words, '[Vermeule's] call for decisionmakers in every institution . . . to make honest appraisals of what they do and do not know, is advice that all should heed.'[51]

---

49 Caleb Nelson, 'Statutory Interpretation and Decision Theory', 74 (2007) *University of Chicago Law Review*, p. 331.
50 Adrian Vermeule, *supra* note 46, p. 183.
51 Caleb Nelson, *supra* note 49, p. 368.

In the US, the current institutional interaction among Congress, the NPS and the courts has not produced a productive and unified interpretation of the Organic Act. The courts' institutional capacities are restricted by their deferential attitudes toward agencies and their deficits in eradicating conflicts.

The purpose statement in the Organic Act reveals ambiguities and leaves room for statutory interpretation. It has been claimed that the NPS has received carte blanche from Congress[52] and that it has considerable discretion to make management decisions. The NPS is frequently accused in opposing allegations from both conservationists and recreationists based on the same mandate. Thus, the NPS's discretionary decision making becomes increasingly vulnerable. In Cheever's words, the 'ambiguity which once provided agencies necessary latitude before Congress and the Cabinet now inspire[s] sophisticated western interest groups to challenge agency policy. Mandates which once contributed to the rise of agency discretion now contribute to its decline.'[53]

The focus of national park policy in the US has vacillated between conservation and enjoyment. There is still room for conflicting interpretations of the statute, and there is no clear-cut rule about who should interpret the statutes and in which way. This situation not only creates confusion in academic studies but also leaves room for political maneuvering to tilt the scale toward use and development, which threatens long-term conservation. Statutory vagueness and the delegation of discretion to agencies is a compromise made by Congress to please interested parties. Therefore, Congress is accused of abdicating its responsibility 'to make the tough choices and necessary trade-offs required of it'. In other words, 'delegation gets politicians off the hook – they can promise everything to everyone, and when promises go unfulfilled they have a convenient bureaucratic scapegoat.'[54]

Although the NPS Management Policies of 2006 established the preservation-oriented policy at the National Park System level, inconsistencies and confusion can still be found in the judicial interpretation of the Organic Act. The current Organic Act creates difficulties for courts in 'find[ing] sufficient standards in the statute against which to test the arbitrariness of a park allocation choice [between conflicting uses]'[55] made by the NPS. To some extent, this makes the NPS's management decisions 'largely immune from [judicial] review'.[56] In fact, given their deferential attitudes, the courts prefer this immunity.

By offering substantial deference to agencies, the judiciary shows its reluctance to have the final word on the value judgments made by the NPS, although there are no substantive obstacles that impede it from doing so. Antolini notes that 'courts seem most interested [in] following a principle of great deference rather than in determining if the Organic Act has any substantive guidance.'[57] The finding of substantial deference given to agencies by courts accords with quantitative research by scholars in the field of environmental law in general. For example, Chae reviewed all the environmental judgments delivered by the Supreme Court and found that although the judgments showed both pro-development and pro-environment

---

52 Federico Cheever, 'United States Forest Service and National Park Service: Paradoxical Mandates, Powerful Founders, and the Rise and Fall of Agency Discretion', 74 (1996–97) *Denver University Law Review*, p. 632.
53 Federico Cheever, ibid., p. 630.
54 Martin Nie, 'Statutory Detail and Administrative Discretion in Public Lands Governance: Arguments and Alternatives', 19 (2004) *Journal of Environmental Law & Litigation*, pp. 265–6.
55 A. Dan Tarlock, 'For Whom the National Parks?', 34 (1981) *Stanford Law Review*, p. 266.
56 Ibid.
57 Denise Antolini, *supra* note 25, p. 895.

278 Country Studies: China

results, in general, the Supreme Court showed strong deference to agency decision making.[58] Farber also concluded that 'the persistent theme in the Court's environmental decisions of the last twenty years has been deference to administrative agencies.'[59]

In addition to showing a reluctant attitude toward agencies' management decisions, the judiciary shows its limitations in fundamentally *resolving* conflict. Litigation on public land issues is protracted, repetitive and costly. As a result, there has been a rise in ADR mechanisms to end disputes and eradicate conflicts. Courts are not totally value-free. They are not immune from and are vulnerable to political changes, which is reflected in the conflicting rulings between the D.C. court and the Wyoming court in the Yellowstone snowmobile case.

In the US, a congressional solution may be the best alternative to reconstruct the institutional framework of statutory interpretation in managing national parks.

Although the National Park System has evolved over nearly a century, the NPS is still governed by the Organic Act, which has not been significantly amended. The fundamental purpose of the National Park System remains intact. Is the Organic Act adaptive and elastic enough to meet current and future challenges? Is there a need to overhaul the Organic Act?

Scholars have different opinions about the need for such an amendment. Keiter holds that there is no need to re-write the Organic Act. The gloss that has accumulated on the Act, including judicial precedents and agency policies, should be sufficient to enable the NPS to promulgate new policies and strategies needed to address the new challenges that national parks will face. Specifically, five reasons are provided:

1. Congress has adopted several amendments to address changing conditions and crises instead of rewriting the Act;
2. The Organic Act has proven to be flexible and adaptable, which enables the NPS to identify and implement new policies to address changed conditions, enhanced knowledge and new values;
3. The Act's non-impairment standard is the strongest found in contemporary public land law, and it has been used to provide important legal protection for park resources;
4. Judicial precedents have acknowledged that resource conservation is the NPS's first management priority, and
5. Political compromises and trade-offs in the legislative process may not result in the expected result of rewriting the Act.[60]

In contrast, Antolini states that 'the dual mandate has created an unpredictable system of judicial review.'[61] She suggests that there should be a reinforced national commitment to conservation by national parks. To reach this goal, Congress should clarify the conservation mandate by amending the purpose statement of the Organic Act. She suggests adding

---

58 Young-Geun Chae, 'The US Supreme Court's Policy Preference and Institutional Restraint in Environmental Law', 7 (2000) *Wisconsin Environmental Law Journal*, p. 68.
59 Daniel Farber, 'Is the Supreme Court Irrelevant – Reflections on the Judicial Role in Environmental Law', 81(1996) *Minnesota Law Review*, p. 558.
60 Robert Keiter, 'Revisiting the Organic Act: Can It Meet the Next Century's Conservation Challenges?', 28.3 (2011) *The George Wright Forum*, pp. 246–8.
61 Denise Antolini, *supra* note 25, p. 858.

the phrase 'where proven compatible' before the word 'enjoyment'.[62] In this way, the Organic Act would read as follows:

> ... the fundamental purpose ... [is] <u>giving highest priority</u> ~~which purpose is~~ to conservinge the scenery and the natural and historical objects and the wildlife therein and <u>allowing, where proven compatible,</u> ~~to provide for~~ the enjoyment of the same in such manner and by such means as will leave them unimpaired for ~~the enjoyment of~~ future generations.[63]

Cheever also supports a clearer clarification of the mission statement by Congress. Such a clarification may facilitate the conveyance of 'the same message to all interested parties' and may not 'guarantee enhanced agency stature and discretion, but would at least make it possible'.[64]

This research concludes that a simple amendment, as suggested by Antolini, would be both theoretically and practically beneficial; at least, such an amendment would be harmless. This might be the simplest way to bring national parks out of the current muddy situation. The argument for a congressional solution must be primarily based on reconstructing the questions that the Organic Act has raised.

In terms of reading the Organic Act, the core question in the current literature and judicial deliberation is which one should be prioritized if conservation and enjoyment conflict. Courts deem the issue of balancing the two conflicting purposes of conservation and enjoyment to be within the scope of administrative discretion, and they have provided considerable deference. However, it needs to be clarified that there are actually two sets of questions embodied in the Organic Act:

1 Whether conservation is the ultimate goal of national park designation and management, and
2 Whether the proposed enjoyment is the type of enjoyment that will not cause impairment and whether a particular conservation activity is the type of conservation that will not cause impairment.

Not only may enjoyment cause impairment, but impairment may also be caused by conservation activities in which affirmative management behaviors are conducted, such as the culling of animals and the clear-cutting of trees. Wilderness-management activities, such as restoration projects, can also cause impairment to the 'wilderness' value protected by law. These management activities are frequently challenged in courts for not complying with the Organic Act.[65] Therefore, both conservation and enjoyment must be subjected to the 'non-impairment test'. Enjoyment may conflict with the unimpaired condition of national parks, not conservation.

The first question, 'what are national parks for?', is more or less a public policy issue; in Nie's words, it is a 'value and interest-based political question'. The institutional capacity of agencies is limited to making a final judgment on this issue. They are not 'the most legitimate

---

62 Ibid., pp. 911–21.
63 Ibid., p. 912.
64 Federico Cheever, *supra* note 52, p. 646.
65 For example, *WildEarth Guardians v. National Park Service*, 804 F. Supp. 2d 1150 (Colo. D.C. 2011) (the NPS's elk management plan in which it uses public volunteers to cull elk in the Rocky Mountain National Park is challenged by environmental groups); *Californians for Alternatives to Toxics v. United States Fish & Wildlife Serv.*, 814 F. Supp. 2d 992 (E.D. Cal. 2011) (the agencies' trout restoration project is challenged for its use of pesticide to eradicate non-native trout in order to restock the native species of trout).

arbiters of the public good',[66] and they are 'usually ill-equipped to resolve what are often deeply divisive and intractable political conflicts'.[67] Nor is the judiciary the proper institution to make such a choice. The judiciary's deferential attitude, as shown above, has already reflected the limitations of its institutional capacity to answer this question. Instead, this question is most appropriate for legislative debate and resolution.[68] Congress is *the* institution that has both the authority and the institutional capacity to perform this task. In addition to the theoretical reasoning, from a practical point of view, there is an increasing tendency in Congress to become involved in solving particular management conflicts, as shown in examples of the detailing of management instruction in enabling acts and the ad hoc intervention in conflict resolution by enacting specific statutes, as discussed previously.

In contrast, agency expertise is best reflected in the second question, carrying out the non-impairment test. The NPS has expertise in assessing the possible negative influences of a particular type of recreational activity on nature. The NPS delivers its conclusion regarding whether an 'impairment' is caused based on the facts and data available to it. This is a process in which the judiciary lacks knowledge and expertise and should provide judicial deference.

As implied by Vermeule, a desirable institutional design can only be achieved when the capacities and limitations of each institution are sufficiently considered and properly balanced. As Coggins urges, 'all interests will be better off if Congress actually decides the political resource allocation questions, the executive carries out the letter and spirit of the law, and the courts make sure the executive does just that.'[69]

In China, institutional interactions do not yield a stabilized conflict resolution mechanism but a crisis-based approach. Institutional building may be the foremost task for China.

The dynamics of institutional interactions in statutory interpretation in the context of the US are not similarly observed in China. Institutional interactions among Congress, the central government, local governments and courts do not necessarily lie in who interprets the law and how, at least not in the current phase of legal development, but in how to make the law work. Discretion is not intentionally delegated to agencies for the flexibility of administration; instead, the brevity and vagueness of statutory provisions leave room for maneuvering and the abuse of power. Agencies' decision-making processes are not always a prudent construction or interpretation of the law but are sometimes a process to deviate from the law by taking advantage of statutory loopholes. Departments at the central level – the legislators of 'administrative regulations' – have sporadically clarified ambiguous statutory provisions for conservation purposes, as seen in the examples interpreting whether the prohibition of assigning or transferring land and resources within an SHA includes the prohibition of transferring its operational rights and whether the scope of concessions covers the operation of the whole area of SHAs or a specific item of services.[70] However, prevalent non-compliance with the central regulations at the local level weakens the practical significance of these interpretative efforts. Although the principle of the priority of protection is embodied in legislation, legal enforcement bodies have neither the incentive nor the capacity to carry out these 'seem-

---

66 Martin Nie, *supra* note 54, p. 225.
67 Ibid., p. 225.
68 Ibid., p. 275.
69 George Coggins, 'Regulating Federal Natural Resources: A Summary Case Against Devolved Collaboration', 25 (1999) *Ecology Law Quarterly*, p. 610.
70 See *supra* p. 192 et seq. of Chapter 9.

ingly beautiful' provisions in legislation. Inter-agency rivalry has resulted in a piecemeal and counter-productive regulatory and management framework of PAs. A frail and weak judiciary is unable to genuinely supervise the government's exercise of administrative power or to effectively resolve disputes. Lacking judicial independence and capacity, the judiciary plays a limited role in resolving conservation-related disputes.

However, these discussions are not meant to downgrade the significance of statutory interpretation and its applicability in China. As mentioned above, statutes need to be meticulously interpreted to be best applied. More statutory interpretation practices need to be conducted by both agencies and courts in China. In this way, the statutory language can be sharpened, examined, tested and revived to be adapted to new challenges. Considering the more general language used in Chinese statutes, Nagle even asserts that China should have '*more* statutory interpretation disputes than the United States, not fewer'.[71]

Instead of resolving disputes in an interactive institutional setting, a crisis-based approach is generally followed when conservation conflicts are identified and resolved in China. When there is a crisis that threatens the stability of the state, there is always some 'strong reactive regulation'. Apart from such crises, 'there are only weak proactive policies that do not substantially mitigate the continuing decline of the nation's environment.'[72] Potential conflicts are addressed through petitions or whistle blowing by those whose interests are affected. The media selectively intervene, and the conflict becomes a public event. Responses from the central and/or local authorities follow the public debate. Finally, a site-specific decision or solution is made. Such a crisis-based approach is intrinsically ad hoc. A stabilized and normalized mechanism to discover potential conflicts and to manage and resolve these conflicts is not well established. There is no doubt that such a mechanism must be law-based. Rebuilding each institution's capacity is a preliminary step. Specific legal and policy recommendations are made in the following section.

Legal and Policy Recommendations for China

The following recommendations are mainly made on three bases:

1 The observation of intrinsic Chinese problems and possible solutions;
2 The experiences and lessons of the US that may be beneficial in resolving similar problems in China, and
3 Guidelines and good practices at the international level, especially the guidelines from the IUCN on PA management.

The following recommendations are generally made in accordance with the logic of enhancing and improving each legal institution's capacity and performance. There is no hierarchy or sequence to these recommendations. Together, they form an interconnected vision of and route for necessary reforms in China.

To Elevate the Role of Law in General and Conservation Law in Particular

The process of realizing sustainability is a joint effort by different fields with specific concerns and perspectives. For instance, politics emphasize representativeness, responsiveness

---

71 John Nagle, *supra* note 47, p. 548.
72 Graeme Lang, 'Forests, Floods, and the Environmental State in China', 15.2 (2002) *Organization & Environment*, pp. 109–30.

and responsibility; management involves efficiency and effectiveness, and the core values of the law are public interests, due process, justice and equity. Such co-efforts are of crucial importance for China to realize sustainable development. In this direction, the law can and should make a difference.

The law plays a vital role in translating policy into practice. In the field of nature conservation, the law establishes the institutional framework for PA management, allocates access to resources among stakeholders, provides oversight on agencies' decision making, regulates the use of nature, sets environmental standards, provides compensation to those affected and prescribes responsibility mechanisms for non-compliance.

Given the value of the rule of law, law is employed as the principal tool for managing and resolving conflicts over land use in the US. The lack of a historical legal culture makes the realization of the rule of law a daunting task for contemporary China. Gradually, China has recognized the pivotal role that law can play in coping with the deteriorating environment. However, despite visible achievements in the legal system, limitations remain. Governments are still inclined to use administrative measures of a command-and-control nature instead of legal measures. Officials still have limited awareness of the rule of law. Some mechanisms with a policy nature are still not legalized and lack legal supervision. Citizens prefer to petition and protest outside the established legal channels due to their general distrust of governments and courts.

In addition to elevating the role of law, more attention needs to be paid to developing the legal system of nature conservation in addition to increasing the awareness of pollution control law. In China, serious pollution problems arising from urbanization and economic development have gained considerable attention among the public. To some extent, this has dwarfed the urgency of nature conservation.

Moreover, legislation is not an end in itself. The law must be enforced. The gap between 'law in books' and 'law in action' has already become one of the largest problems that China currently faces. Although fundamental principles such as the priority of protection and strict regulations have been stipulated in the law, the way these provisions are translated into practice must be monitored and rectified in the long run.

To Formulate an Interconnected Legislative System for PAs

The American experience demonstrates that the legislative framework for PAs is complex and interconnected. In China, the development of the legal framework for nature conservation could not be accomplished simply by enacting a Natural Heritage Law or a Protected Areas Law, regardless of how it is named by the legislature. Instead, legislative vacancies in other fields, such as administrative procedure law and ecological compensation law, also need to be mended to supplement the legal framework of nature conservation in general.

In terms of legislative design, it seems that the proposal to enact the Law on Protected Areas as the governing statute of nature conservation law is preferable to the Law on Natural Heritage or the Law on Nature Reserves. This Law on Protected Areas would cover existing types of PA designations, including SHAs, nature reserves, forest parks and others. Based on the concept of the 'Organic Act' in the American sense, this law may function for PAs in China similarly to how the Organic Act functions for PAs in the US. Fischman identified five requisite components of modern organic acts, including a purpose statement, designated use, comprehensive planning, substantive management criteria and public participation requirements.[73] These requisite components can also guide the enactment of the Law on Protected Areas in China.

To specify the contents of PA legislation, first, because the principle of priority of protection was stipulated in the Environmental Protection Law of 2014, the proposed Law on Protected Areas may also consider explicitly incorporating this principle.

Second, designated use patterns should be formulated based on different types of PAs. A dominant use pattern may be a preferable choice to establish a hierarchy of different types of uses. The determination of a designated use needs to correspond with the goals for a particular type of PA. Some good practices can be adopted from the IUCN, such as the definition and categorization of PAs, the delineation of the 'primary objective' and 'other objectives' of each type of PA and the hierarchical relationship among these objectives.

Third, statutes may detail their constructions to managers in accordance with different types of PAs. In this way, agency discretion may be reduced to prevent room for undesirable maneuvering. New legislations and amendments of existing regulations may consider adopting more substantive and specific management criteria. The existing requirement that the area of the experimental zone should be less than one-third of the total area of nature reserves is an example of a substantive criterion.[74] Lessons can also be learned from the NPS regarding its definitions of terms such as 'appropriate use', 'unacceptable impact' and 'preferred public enjoyment' in its MP of 2006.[75]

Fourth, statutes may prescribe explicit procedural requirements for management decision making, such as public participation and the disclosure of information. Responsibility and accountability mechanisms for the violation of these requirements need to be stipulated accordingly. In this way, before the unified Administrative Procedure Law can be enacted, individual statutes can provide minimal procedural guarantees.

Fifth, statutes may add the provision of providing rights of action to private individuals and organizations. The previous discussion has shown that the lack of the explicit provision of rights of action has led to a limited number of cases being heard in courts.[76] Adding such provisions may facilitate lawsuits being brought to courts and may strengthen the authority of courts in receiving and trying such cases.

Sixth, because contingencies and unpredictability have been observed in the allocation of the budget for PAs, a legal provision on budget guarantees for PA management may be added. It may be argued that the effectiveness of PA management cannot necessarily be increased due to a budget increase. However, this is a preliminary step that is likely to yield desirable outcomes. Without fundamentally changing the funding structure, the commercial operation of PAs will be unavoidable.

Seventh, the statute may consider finalizing and unifying the regulatory standard for concession practices. Some loopholes and intentional ambiguities in existing regulations need to be mended and clarified. For example, the Regulations of Scenic and Historic Areas of 2006 hesitate to use the term 'concession' and do not explicitly distinguish between 'concession' and the 'transfer of operation rights'. The regulations only require that tickets should be exclusively 'sold' by administrative agencies, but this does not necessarily mean that

---

73 Robert Fischman, 'National Wildlife Refuge System and the Hallmarks of Modern Organic Legislation', 29 (2002) *Ecology Law Quarterly*, pp. 510–13.
74 Article 1.5 of the Outline of Overall Planning of Nature Reserves at the National Level issued by the SEPA in 2002. See *supra* p. 215 of Chapter 10.
75 *Supra* p. 120 et seq. of Chapter 6.
76 See *supra* pp. 234–5 of Chapter 10.

entrance fees should be exclusively 'retained' by agencies. These provisions leave room for maneuvering. 'Good practices' in concession regulations, such as the Regulations of Scenic and Historic Areas in Guizhou Province, can be examined and used as examples for other provinces and for central legislation.

Eighth, to cope with the problem of overlapping designations and management, the following provision may be added to statutes: 'the management authority of newly designated PAs should not overlap with those of existing designations. With regard to existing overlap between different types of PAs, those legal provisions that provide for stricter protection shall prevail.'

Finally, in addition to enacting an Organic Act for PAs, the legislative model of 'enabling acts for each park unit' in the US can be transferable. Currently, the 'one reserve, one act' (一区一法) goal has been recognized in both the literature and policy documents. However, most existing enabling legislation repeats the laws and regulations of a higher level without showing site-specific features. Local conditions and necessities may be taken into account in future legislation to facilitate site-specific management. Moreover, because all enabling acts in the US are enacted by Congress, the legislative authority may not necessarily be the NPC in the context of China. Local legislatures may take the lead in producing enabling legislation for the units of PAs. Situated in the legislative hierarchy in China, enabling legislation by local legislatures should not contravene with the governing 'Organic Act' by the central legislature, which means that the precedence of enabling legislation over the general Organic Act in the US does not apply. In this way, the uniformity of management standards can be provided without significantly jeopardizing the divergent needs of each unit.

To Build Efficient, Professional and Accountable Agencies

A healthy and productive institutional interaction among legislatures, agencies and courts necessitates an efficient, professional and accountable agency to carry out and enforce the law. Three steps are proposed to enhance the institutional capacity of PA management agencies.

The first step is to establish an efficient institutional structure. The current institutional setting of PA management, either at the vertical or the horizontal level, demonstrates irreconcilable problems, such as local protectionism, non-compliance with central regulations at the local level and inter-agency rivalries. To solve these problems, reforms to streamline management authority may be necessary. Although these reforms have not been placed on the reform agenda, some proposals have been made, such as the establishment of an ad hoc department or committee at the central level to unify the conservation authority and the reform of the SFA by separating its productive and protective functions and merging its protective function with the MoEP.[77] At the local level, there has been an ongoing effort toward the establishment of ad hoc management agencies at the ground-management level and the strengthening of their authority over integrated management. As shown in Chapter 11, 'integrated management' is one of the key attributes of the proposed national park model that is currently under deliberation. Cooperation among different departments is of crucial importance to assist these agencies in performing their functions. Therefore, empowering the

---

77 Obtained from the panel discussion during the Annual Conference of the Environmental and Nature Resource Law Society of 2014, held on August 21–22 in Guangzhou. Cai Shouqiu and Luo Ji hold different opinions on how to re-allocate the productive functions of the SFA. Cai proposes establishing a state-owned enterprise that is responsible for timber production and Luo argues for privatization of timber rights in China.

ground-level agencies through the legislation and monitoring of law enforcement is a crucial step. To cope with the problem of interference in agencies by local governments, a plausible solution is to elevate the level that is in charge of 'leading' the management agencies. Some nature reserves have adopted the institutional structure 'under direct control of governments or departments at the provincial level' and thus have lessened the improper interference from governments at lower levels.[78]

The second step is to build a professional agency. Science is the basis for effective nature conservation. Professional knowledge is therefore a prerequisite for managers to conduct effective PA management and genuinely enforce the law. Professionalism is the preliminary step in building an agency's legitimacy, and it is the entry point for the judicial review of an agency's management decisions. The quality of PA management in China remains at a considerably low level due to insufficiencies in professionalism. Even worse, PAs in China are pushed into tourism markets. PA management institutions are not ready to face the challenges that tourism may bring. Wang and Buckley note that forest parks in China are managed by forestry agencies whose expertise lies in timber production and trade, not environmental management.[79]

The third step is to build an accountable government. As previously shown, Chinese governments do not possess the reputation of a 'good man', as the NPS does in the US. Instead, Chinese citizens are often suspicious of policies and decisions made by the government for fear of corruption and 'black box' operations. This fear is validated by the rampant abuse of power by local governments in tourism development. The lack of accountability of governments to the public may be a crucial reason for this fear. The mechanisms of accountability generally refer to the legal mechanisms through which the exercise of public power is confined. Three sets of accountability questions arise: who should be accountable? To whom and for what should an account be given?[80] First, all subjects that exercise public power need to be accountable. In addition to governments and agencies, enterprises, especially those that are 'improperly' delegated with the power to operate and manage PAs by contracting with governments, should be held accountable. Second, in a constitutional sense, the government that exercises the power to dispose of and manage natural resources in PAs should be accountable to the original source of its authority, namely, the owners of PAs, which are, according to the Constitution, the people or the collectives. On a micro scale, governments should account for their actions to those who might be adversely impacted by these actions. Third, governments need to make their management decisions in a transparent and participatory way, justify their decision-making processes, serve the public interest and receive oversight from legislatures, courts and society. The abuse of power in PA development observed in the previous discussion can be curbed and controlled only when those who hold this power are held accountable.

To Activate the Courts' Role in Adjudicating Resource-related Conflicts

Although some defects in the judicial approach to dispute resolution in the US can be observed in the previous discussion, the current task for China is to strengthen, not weaken,

---

78 For example, Wuyishan Nature Reserve at the National Level is under the direct control of the Forestry Department of Fujian Province, instead of the government of Wuyishan city.
79 Chao-Hui Wang and Ralf Buckley, 'Shengtai Anquan: Managing Tourism and Environment in China's Forest Parks', 39 (2010) *AMBIO*, p. 452.
80 See generally Colin Scott, 'Accountability in the Regulatory State', 27.1 (2000) *Journal of Law and Society*, p. 41.

the role of courts. The courts' role needs to be activated to better adjudicate conservation- and recreation-related disputes.

As previously discussed, in addition to their original functions of dispute resolution, environmental courts in China serve other functions, such as policy advocacy, public education and social control.[81] The paramount task ahead is to establish and enhance the judiciary's authority in general and newly established environmental courts' authority in particular. Three steps can be taken to accomplish this goal:

1. Depoliticize the political functions of the judiciary, particularly the newly established environmental courts, to align with the government's policy goals and empower the judiciary with the independence to adjudicate disputes;
2. Lower the standing requirements and encourage the use of litigation tools to provide a stable case supply to the courts, and
3. Increase the level of professionalism of the judiciary in dealing with specific environmental issues to enhance its authority.

There are concerns among legislators and policy makers regarding whether the opening of courts may lead to a litigation explosion and the abuse of the right to sue. Concerns also arise regarding whether governments may lose the ability to control, thereby reducing social stability. These concerns have slowed judicial reform in this field. However, in contemporary China, the main reason for social unrest is the abuse of administrative power and the resulting paramount public distrust of government in general. Empowering the courts to solve disputes and exercise their supervision of governments may rectify government's wrongdoing. Furthermore, removing the barriers that courts face can be a continuous and daunting process. The cultivation of civil society and citizens' willingness and desire to use the tool of litigation cannot be realized overnight. Therefore, although there is a possibility that a litigation explosion may emerge, it will not occur in the short run. The eradication of unnecessary concerns about litigation is a preliminary step toward establishing the role that courts should play.

To Cultivate Civil Society and Increase Public Awareness

Citizens' awareness of environmental protection is a prerequisite for effective nature conservation. In recent years, public awareness of environmental protection has been raised due to horrendous pollution problems. This is partly because air and water quality directly relates to people's daily lives. In contrast, the importance of biodiversity protection, such as the protection of 'ugly' species of toads or snakes, is not well acknowledged. The American experience shows that environmental NGOs play a crucial role in participating in governments' environmental decision making or in lodging suits in courts. In China, because the amended Civil Procedure Law and Environmental Protection Law have embraced public interest litigation and empowered environmental NGOs to bring cases to courts, the cultivation of civil society, including various grassroots environmental NGOs, would be a crucial step toward guaranteeing the effective implementation of these provisions.

As previously shown, in the US, recreational groups have emerged as a powerful counterpart to environmental groups in shaping conservation and recreation policies. In China, these recreational groups are also emerging, such as the Association for Self-driving Tours.

---

81 Rachel Stern, 'The Political Logic of China's New Environmental Courts', 72 (2014) *The China Journal*, p. 61.

These associations and clubs release data, reports and industrial standards and represent the interests of specific groups of citizens. The establishment of a participatory framework for the administrative process requires the equal representation of interests. Therefore, more attention needs to be paid to the cultivation and development of these special user groups.

Final Remarks

In contemporary China, multiple factors have emerged simultaneously, including increasing recreational demands, unprecedented pollution problems, rigid targets for continuous economic growth, developmental goals for poverty alleviation, the maintenance of social stability and a growing environmental community. Each of these factors holds a particular position on the country's development agenda. The transition that China is undergoing has given rise to the further pluralization and polarization of interests, which has intensified the pre-existing tension in both society and law. Due to the underdevelopment of the legal system in general, it seems that the rate at which conflicts are managed and resolved by the law lags far behind the rate at which new conflicts arise. Furthermore, although new legislation is continually being enacted, in practice, the efficacy of laws remains at a considerably low level. Currently, the scheme of PAs in China is still undergoing experimental and contingent changes. It is difficult to determine China's current path or the path it may follow in the future. It is conceivable that the path toward a full-fledged legal system for nature conservation and the effective implementation of such laws in practice will be formidable and frustrating.

It seems that any effort by a single institution to effectively identify, manage and resolve conflicts is ultimately insufficient. The long-perceived image of an almighty government in China has been continually challenged, and it is losing its legitimacy. Methods such as ad hoc law enforcement campaigns and strong reactive regulations no longer suffice. The US context reveals a telling process of how different institutions interact with each other in a developed legal system. Some adjustments to each institution's niche in the overall frame of a legal regime may be necessary, as previously argued. In contrast, for the time being, the foremost task for China is still to build each institution's capacity instead of dismantling it. This capacity-building process is a prerequisite for a normative institutional setting and for the realization of the rule of law in the long run in China. Carving a new path is not easy. Following the path that is already paved may be a promising step for China. Let Congress make good laws; let law enforcement bodies genuinely apply the law; and let the courts decide whether the government has done wrongs. These suggestions propose a simple truth. As a result, any effort to search for an alternative may be futile.

Appendix I

The List of Applicable Laws on Protected Area Management in China

Enactment date (amendments)	Title	Main purposes and relevant provisions
1979 (amended in 1989, 2001 and 2014)	Environmental Protection Law	To protect and improve environment; to prevent and control pollution and other public hazards; to safeguard human health; to promote construction of ecological civilization and promote economic and social sustainable development (Article 1)
1982 (amended in 1999)	Marine Environmental Protection Law	To protect the marine environment
1984 (amended in 1998)	Forest Law	To protect, cultivate and rationally utilize forest resources and speed up afforestation of lands
1985 (amended in 2002, 2013)	Grassland Law	To protect, construct and rationally use grassland, improve eco-environment, maintain biodiversity, develop modern husbandry, and promote economic and social sustainable development
1986 (amended in 2000, 2004)	Fisheries Law	To protect and rationally use fishery resources, and protect legal rights and interest of fishery producers
1986 (amended in 1996)	Mineral Resources Law	To develop mining industry; to strengthen the exploration, development and protection of mineral resources
1986 (amended in 1988, 1998 and 2004)	Law on Land Administration	To protect and develop land resources, rationally use lands and protect cultivated lands
1988 (amended in 2002)	Water Law	To undertake the rational development, utilization, saving and protection of water resources; to prevent and control water disasters; to conduct the sustainable use of water resources; to meet the needs of national economic and social development
1988 (amended in 2004)	Wildlife Protection Law	To protect and save the rare and endangered species of wild animals, to protect, develop and rationally utilize wild animal resources and to maintain ecological balances
1989 (annulled in 2007)	City Planning Law	To conduct city planning and construction

1991 (amended in 2011)	Law on Water and Soil Conservation	To prevent and control soil and water erosion, to protect and reasonably use soil and water resources, to reduce natural disasters, to improve the ecological environment, and to ensure the sustainable development of the economy and society.
1993 (amended in 2002, 2009 and 2012)	Agricultural Law	Protection of agricultural resources and agricultural environment
2001	Law on Prevention and Control of Desertification	To prevent land desertification, rehabilitate desertificated land, maintain ecological safety Requirement of reasonable financial compensation on designating nature reserves on rehabilitated land (Article 35)
2002	Law on Environmental Impact Assessment	To regulate EIA in planning and construction projects; compulsory EIA in special plans, such forestry, tourism and natural resources exploitation (Article 8)
2005	Animal Husbandry Law	Construction of livestock farm is forbidden in SHAs, core zone and buffer zone of nature reserves (Article 40)
2008	Law on Urban and Rural Planning	Consideration of preservation and rational use of scenic resources in making urban and rural plans (Article 32); prohibition of alteration of purpose of land use for natural reserves in urban and rural plans (Article 35)
2013	Law on Tourism	To protect and rationally use tourist resources

Bibliography

Selected Bibliography (English)

Aagaard, Todd S. 'Environmental Harms, Use Conflicts, and Neutral Baselines in Environmental Law'. *Duke Law Journal* 60.7 (2011): 1505–64.

Agee, James K. 'Issues and Impacts of Redwood National Park Expansion'. *Environmental Management* 4.5 (1980): 407–23.

Alford, William P., and Yuanyuan Shen. 'Limits of the Law in Addressing China's Environmental Dilemma'. *Stanford Environmental Law Journal* 16 (1997): 125–48.

Aman, Alfred C. *Administrative Law and Process: Cases and Materials*. Newark, NJ: LexisNexis Matthew Bender, 2006.

Anderson, James E. *The Emergence of the Modern Regulatory State*. Washington, DC: Public Affairs Press, 1962.

Ansson Jr., Richard J. 'Our National Parks – Overcrowded, Underfunded, and Besieged with a Myriad of Vexing Problems: How Can We Best Fund Our Imperiled National Park System?' *Journal of Land Use & Environmental Law* (1998): 1–52.

—— and Dalton L. Hooks Jr. 'Protecting and Preserving our National Parks in the Twenty First Century: Are Additional Reforms Needed above and beyond the Requirements of the 1998 National Parks Omnibus Management Act'. *Montana Law Review* 62 (2001): 213–68.

Antolini, Denise E. 'National Park Law in the U.S.: Conservation, Conflict, and Centennial Values'. *William and Mary Environmental Law and Policy Review* 33 (2009): 851–922.

Appel, Peter A. 'Wilderness and the Courts'. *Stanford Environmental Law Journal* 29 (2010): 62–129.

Araiza, William D. 'Democracy, Distrust, and the Public Trust: Process-Based Constitutional Theory, the Public Trust Doctrine, and the Search for a Substantive Environmental Value'. *UCLA Law Review* 45 (1997–98): 385–452.

Ashley, Caroline, Charlotte Boyd, and Harold Goodwin. 'Pro-Poor Tourism: Putting Poverty at the Heart of the Tourism Agenda'. *Natural Resources Perspectives* 51 (2000):1–6.

Atapattu, Sumudu. 'Sustainable Development, Myth Or Reality: A Survey of Sustainable Development Under International Law and Sri Lankan Law'. *Georgetown international Environmental Law Review* 14 (2001): 265–300.

Baker, Randall. *Environmental Law and Policy in the European Union and the United States*. Westport, CT: Praeger, 1997.

Barnard, Michelle. 'The Role of International Sustainable Development Law Principles in Enabling Effective Renewable Energy Policy – A South African Perspective'. *PER: Potchefstroomse Elektroniese Regsblad* 15.2 (2012): 1–40.

Barral, Virginie. 'Sustainable Development in International Law: Nature and Operation of an Evolutive Legal Norm'. *European Journal of International Law* 23.2 (2012): 377–400.

Beyer, Stefanie. 'Environmental Law and Policy in the People's Republic of China'. *Chinese Journal of International Law* 5.1 (2006): 185–211.

Bhat, Sairam. *Natural Resources Conservation Law*. Los Angeles, CA: SAGE, 2010.

Blumm, Michael C., and Lynn Schaffer. 'The Federal Public Trust Doctrine: A Law Professors' Amicus Brief'. Lewis & Clark Law School Legal Studies Research Paper No. 2014–18 (2014).

Borrini, Grazia et al. *Indigenous and Local Communities and Protected Areas: Towards Equity and Enhanced Conservation*. Gland, Switzerland and Cambridge: IUCN – the World Conservation Union, 2004.

Boyle, Alan E., and David Freestone. *International Law and Sustainable Development: Past Achievements and Future Challenges*. Oxford and New York: Oxford University Press, 1999.

Brockington, Dan, Rosaleen Duffy and Jim Igoe. *Nature Unbound: Conservation, Capitalism and the Future of Protected Areas*. London and Sterling, VA: Earthscan, 2008.

Budowski, Gerardo. 'Tourism and Environmental Conservation: Conflict, Coexistence, Or Symbiosis?' *Environmental Conservation* 3.01 (1976): 27–31.

Burgess, Meryl. *The Challenge in Conservation of Biodiversity: Regulation of National Parks in China and South Africa in Comparison*. Stellenbosch University. Centre for Chinese Studies, 2012.

Burnham, William. *Introduction to the Law and Legal System of the United States*. St. Paul, MN: West, 2011.

Callicott, J. Baird. 'Contemporary Criticisms of the Received Wilderness Idea'. *Wilderness Science in a Time of Change: Changing Perspectives and Future Directions*. Eds. David Cole et al. Ogden, UT: US Department of Agriculture, Forest Service, Rocky Mountain Research Station, 2000. 24.

Calvert, Kori, et al. 'Recreation on Federal Lands', *Congressional Research Service Report for Congress*, RL33525, September 22, 2010. Full text is available at http://cnie.org/nle/-crsreports/10Oct/RL33525.pdf. Last visited April 2015.

Camargo, Blanca, Katy Lane, and Tazim Jamal. 'Environmental Justice and Sustainable Tourism: The Missing Cultural Link'. *The George Wright Society Forum*. 24.3 (2007): 70–80.

Campbell, Scott. 'Green Cities, Growing Cities, just Cities?: Urban Planning and the Contradictions of Sustainable Development'. *Journal of the American Planning Association* 62.3 (1996): 296–312.

Carr, Ethan. 'Park, Forest and Wilderness'. *The George Wright Forum*. 17.2 (2002): 16–30.

Carter, Bill, and Gordon Grimwade. 'Balancing use and Preservation in Cultural Heritage Management'. *International Journal of Heritage Studies* 3.1 (1997): 45–53.

Cass, Ronald A. *Administrative Law: Cases and Materials*. New York: Wolters Kluwer Law & Business, 2011.

Cater, Erlet, and Gwen Lowman. *Ecotourism: A Sustainable Option?* Chichester: Wiley, 1994.

Cathcart-Rake, John. 'The Friends of Yosemite Valley Saga: The Challenge of Addressing the Merced River's User Capacities'. *Environmental Law* 39 (2009): 833–66.

Ceballos-Lascuráin, Héctor. *Tourism, Ecotourism, and Protected Areas: The State of Nature-Based Tourism Around the World and Guidelines for its Development*. Gland, Switzerland and Cambridge: IUCN, 1996.

Chae, Young-Geun. 'The US Supreme Court's Policy Preference and Institutional Restraint in Environmental Law'. *Wisconsin Environmental Law Journal* 7 (2000): 41–92.

Cheever, Federico. 'British National Parks for North Americans: What we can Learn from a More Crowded Nation Proud of its Countryside'. *Stanford Environmental Law Journal* 26.2 (2007): 7–36.

Chen, Gang. *Politics of China's Environmental Protection: Problems and Progress*. Singapore: World Scientific Publishing, 2009.

Chen, Jianfu. *Chinese Law: Context and Transformation*. Leiden: Nijhoff, 2008.

Coburn, Tom. 'PARKED! How Congress' Misplaced Priorities are Trashing Our National Treasures', www.novoco.com/.../resource.../coburn_parked_how_congress_misplaced . . . , October 2013, p. 15. Last visited January 2016.

Coggins, George Cameron. 'Regulating Federal Natural Resources: A Summary Case against Devolved Collaboration'. *Ecology Law Quarterly* 25.4 (1998): 602–10.

——— and Robert L. Glicksman. 'Concessions Law and Policy in the National Park System'. *Denver University Law Review* 74 (1996): 729–1281.

———, Charles F. Wilkinson, and John D. Leshy. *Federal Public Land and Resources Law*. New York: Foundation Press, 2007.

Comay, Laura, Carol Vincent, and Kristina Alexander, 'Motorized Recreation on National Park Service Land', *Congressional Research Service Report for Congress*, February 8, 2013. Full text is available at http://www.fas.org/sgp/crs/misc/R42955.pdf. Last visited April 2015.

Costanza, Robert, et al. 'The Value of the World's Ecosystem Services and Natural Capital'. *Ecological Economics* 25.1 (1998): 3–15.

Davis, Kenneth Culp. *Discretionary Justice; a Preliminary Inquiry*. Baton Rouge: Louisiana State University Press, 1969.

Dernbach, John C. 'Sustainable Development as a Framework for National Governance'. *Case Western Reserve Law Review* 49.1 (1998): 1–103.

Dilsaver, Lary M. *America's National Park System: The Critical Documents*. Boston, MA: Rowman & Littlefield, 1994.

Dressler, Wolfram H., Christian A. Kull, and Thomas C. Meredith. 'The Politics of Decentralizing National Parks Management in the Philippines'. *Political Geography* 25.7 (2006): 789–816.

Drexhage, John and Deborah Murphy, 'Sustainable Development: From Brundtland to Rio 2012', background paper prepared for consideration by the High Level Panel on Global Sustainability at its first meeting, September 19, 2010. Full text is available at http://www.un.org/wcm/webdav/site/climatechange/shared/gsp/docs/GSP1-6_Background%20on%20Sustainable%20Devt.pdf. Last visited April 2015.

Dudley, Nigel. *Guidelines for Applying Protected Area Management Categories*. Gland, Switzerland: IUCN, 2008.

Duncan, Thomas M. 'Driving Americans' Perception of Recreation: Awaiting the Park Service's Long-Term Solution to Access in Yellowstone National Park'. *Villanova Sports & Environmental Law Journal* 19 (2012): 699–783.

Eagles, Paul F.J. 'Governance of Recreation and Tourism Partnerships in Parks and Protected Areas'. *Journal of Sustainable Tourism* 17.2 (2009): 231–48.

Economy, Elizabeth. *The River Runs Black : The Environmental Challenge to China's Future*. Ithaca, NY: Cornell University Press, 2010.

Edmonds, R.L. *Patterns of China's Lost Harmony : A Survey of the Country's Environmental Degradation and Protection*. London and New York: Routledge, 1994.

Engel, Antonia, and Benedikt Korf. *Negotiation and Mediation Techniques for Natural Resource Management*. Rome: Food and Agriculture Organization of the United Nations, 2005.

Eskridge Jr., William N. 'Dynamic Statutory Interpretation'. *University of Pennsylvania Law Review* (1987): 1479–555.

Fabry, Elvire, and Damien Tresallet. *Greening Economic Growth: Towards a Global Strategy for Europe*. Paris: Fondation pour l'innovation politique, 2008.

Farber, Daniel A. 'Is the Supreme Court Irrelevant – Reflections on the Judicial Role in Environmental Law'. *Minnesota Law Review* 81 (1996): 547–69.

Fischman, Robert L. 'From Words to Action: The Impact and Legal Status of the 2006 National Wildlife Refuge System Management Policies'. *Stanford Environmental Law Journal* 26.1 (2007): 77–135.

——. 'Cooperative Federalism and Natural Resources Law'. *NYU Environmental Law Journal* 14 (2005): 179–231.

——. 'The National Wildlife Refuge System and the Hallmarks of Modern Organic Legislation'. *Ecology Law Quarterly* 29 (2002): 457–622.

——. 'The Problem of Statutory Detail in National Park Establishment Legislation and its Relationship to Pollution Control Law'. *Denver University Law Review* 74 (1997): 779–814.

Fischman, Robert L. and Angela M. King. 'Savings Clauses and Trends in Natural Resources Federalism'. *William and Mary Environmental Law and Policy Review* 32 (2007): 129–68.

Flintan, Fiona, and Ross Hughes. *Integrating Conservation and Development Experience: A Review and Bibliography of the ICDP Literature*. London: International Institute for Environment and Development, 2001.

Frey, Bertram C., and Andrew Mutz. 'The Public Trust in Surface Waterways and Submerged Lands of the Great Lakes States' *University of Michigan Journal of Law Reform* 40 (2006): 907–93.

Bibliography 293

Fritz, Katherine. 'National Parks in China: A New Model for Nature Conservation'. *Independent Study Project Collection*, Paper 706, 2009.

Gamborg, Christian, Clare Palmer and Peter Sandøe. 'Ethics of Wildlife Management and Conservation: What Should We Try to Protect?' *Nature Education Knowledge* 3.10 (2012): 8.

Gates, Paul W. and United States Public Land Law Review Commission. *History of Public Land Law Development*. Washington, DC: Government Printing Office, 1968.

Geisler, Charles and Essy Letsoalo. 'Rethinking Land Reform in South Africa: An Alternative Approach to Environmental Justice'. *Sociological Research Online* 5.2 (2000).

Gillespie, Alexander. *Protected Areas and International Environmental Law*. Leiden and Boston, MA: Martinus Nijhoff Publishers, 2007.

Gilpin, Alan. *Environmental Impact Assessment: (EIA): Cutting Edge for the Twenty-First Century*. Cambridge: Cambridge University Press, 1997.

Ginther, Konrad, Erik Denters, and P.J.I.M. Waart. *Sustainable Development and Good Governance*. Dordrecht: M. Nijhoff, 1995.

Gordon, Robert W., Horwitz, Morton J. *Law, Society, and History: Themes in the Legal Sociology and Legal History of Lawrence M. Friedman*. Cambridge and New York: Cambridge University Press, 2011.

Gorte, Ross, et al., 'Federal Land Ownership: Overview and Data', *Congressional Research Office Report for Congress*, R42346, February 8, 2012. Full text is available at https://www.fas.org/sgp/crs/misc/R42346.pdf. Last visited April 2015.

Graham, John, et al. *Governance Principles for Protected Areas in the 21st Century*. Parks, Canada: Canadian International Development Agency, 2003.

Greiber, Thomas, IUCN – The World Conservation Union, and IUCN Environmental Law Centre. *Conservation with Justice: A Rights-Based Approach*. Gland, Switzerland and Bonn, Germany: IUCN, in collaboration with the IUCN Environmental Law Centre, 2009.

Guttman, Dan, and Yaqin Song. 'Making Central-Local Relations Work: Comparing America and China. Environmental Governance Systems'. *Frontiers of Environmental Science & Engineering in China* 1.4 (2007): 418–33.

Han, Nianyong, and Ren Zhuge. 'Ecotourism in China's Nature Reserves: Opportunities and Challenges'. *Journal of Sustainable Tourism* 9.3 (2001): 228–42.

Harkness, James. 'Recent Trends in Forestry and Conservation of Biodiversity in China'. *The China Quarterly* 156, Special Issue: *China's Environment* (1998): 911–34.

Harrison, David. 'Pro-Poor Tourism: A Critique'. *Third World Quarterly* 29.5 (2008): 851–68.

Hays, Samuel. *Conservation and the Gospel of Efficiency: the Progressive Conservation Movement, 1890–1920*. Cambridge, MA: Harvard University Press, 1959.

He, Miao, and An Cliquet. 'Sustainable Development through a Rights-based Approach to Conserve Protected Areas in China'. *China-EU Law Journal* 3.3–4 (2014): 143–63.

Healy, Michael P. 'The Sustainable Development Principle in Untied States Environmental Law'. *George Washington Journal of Energy & Environmental Law* 2 (2011): 19–41.

Hees, Sander. 'Sustainable Development in the EU: Redefining and Operationalizing the Concept', *Utrecht Law Review* 10.2 (2014): 60–76.

Herman, Dennis J. 'Loving them to Death: Legal Controls on the Type and Scale of Development in the National Parks'. *Stanford Environmental Law Journal* 11 (1992): 3–67.

Higham, James E. S. *Critical Issues in Ecotourism: Understanding a Complex Tourism Phenomenon*. Amsterdam and Boston, MA: Butterworth-Heinemann, 2007.

Hirschl, Ran. 'On the Blurred Methodological Matrix of Comparative Constitutional Law'. *The Migration of Constitutional Ideas*. Ed. Sujit Choudhry. Cambridge: Cambridge University Press, 2007. 40–47.

Hodas, Voir David R. 'The Role of Law in Defining Sustainable Development: NEPA Reconsidered'. *Widener Law Symposium Journal* 3 (1998): 1–60.

Hoover, Katie, Kristina Alexander and Sandra Johnson, 'Wilderness: Legislation and Issues in the 113th Congress', *Congressional Research Service Report* R41610, April 17, 2014. Full text is available at http://nationalaglawcenter.org/wp-content/uploads/assets/crs/R41610.pdf. Last visited April 2015.

Bibliography

Horner, Susan Morath. 'Embryo, Not Fossil: Breathing Life into the Public Trust in Wildlife'. *Land & Water Law Review* 35 (2000): 23–75.

Huffman, James L. 'Speaking of Inconvenient Truths – A History of the Public Trust Doctrine'. *Duke Environmental Law & Policy Forum* 18 (2007): 1–103.

———. 'The Inevitability of Private Rights in Public Lands' *University of Colorado Law Review* 65 (1993): 241–78.

International Law Association. 'New Delhi Declaration of Principles of International Law Relating to Sustainable Development'. April 2, 2002. Full text is available at http://cisdl.org/tribunals/pdf/NewDelhiDeclaration.pdf. Last visited April 2015.

Jabareen, Yosef. 'A New Conceptual Framework for Sustainable Development'. *Environment, Development and Sustainability* 10.2 (2008): 179–92.

Jafari, Jafar. 'Research and Scholarship: The Basis of Tourism Education'. *Journal of Tourism Studies* 1.1 (1990): 33–41.

James, Alexander, Michael Green and James Paine. *A Global Review of Protected Area Budgets and Staffing*. Cambridge: WCMC-World Conservation Press, 1999.

Jeffrey, M.I. 'National Parks and Protected Areas-Approaching the Next Millennium'. *Acta Juridica* (1999): 163–87.

Jiang, Hong. 'Grassland Management and Views of Nature in China since 1949: Regional Policies and Local Changes in Uxin Ju, Inner Mongolia'. *Geoforum* 36.5 (2005): 641–653.

Jim, C.Y., and Steve S.W. Xu. 'Recent Protected-Area Designation in China: An Evaluation of Administrative and Statutory Procedures'. *Geographical Journal* 170.1 (2004): 39–50.

Kahr, Byron. 'The Right to Exclude Meets the Right to Ride: Private Property, Public Recreation, and the Rise of Off-Road Vehicles'. *Stanford Environmental Law Journal* 28 (2009): 51–108.

Kalamandeen, Michelle, and Lindsey Gillson. 'Demything "Wilderness": Implications for Protected Area Designation and Management'. *Biodiversity and Conservation* 16.1 (2007): 165–82.

Kamba, Walter Joseph. 'Comparative Law: A Theoretical Framework'. *International and Comparative Law Quarterly* 23.03 (1974): 485–519.

Kass, Madeline June. 'The National Park Service Management Policies Controversy'. *Natural Resources & Environment* (2006): 68–70.

Keele, Kamron. 'Preservation and Use: Road Building, Overcrowding, and the Future of our National Parks'. *Tulane Environmental Law Journal* 11 (1997): 441–59.

Keiter, Robert B. *To Conserve Unimpaired: The Evolution of the National Park Idea*. Washington, DC: Island Press, 2013.

———. 'Revisiting the Organic Act: Can it Meet the Next Century's Conservation Challenges?'. *The George Wright Forum*. (2011): 240–53.

———. 'Public Lands and Law Reform: Putting Theory, Policy, and Practice in Perspective'. *Utah Law Review* 3 (2005): 1127–226.

———. 'Preserving Nature in the National Parks: Law, Policy, and Science in a Dynamic Environment'. *Denver University Law Review* 74 (1996): 649–95.

Keith, Mackenzie S. 'Judicial Protection for Beaches and Parks: The Public Trust Doctrine Above the High Water Mark'. *Hastings West-Northwest Journal of Environmental Law & Policy* 16 (2010): 165.

Klass, Alexandra B. 'Modern Public Trust Principles: Recognizing Rights and Integrating Standards'. *Notre Dame Law Review* 82 (2006–07): 699–754.

Klemm, Cyrille de, Clare Shine, IUCN Environmental Law Centre and IUCN Biodiversity Programme. *Biological Diversity Conservation and the Law: Legal Mechanisms for Conserving Species and Ecosystems*. Gland, Switzerland: IUCN – the World Conservation Union, 1993.

Kline, Benjamin. *First Along the River: A Brief History of the U.S. Environmental Movement*. Lanham, MD: Rowman & Littlefield Publishers, 2011.

Knight, Richard L. and Sarah F. Bates. *A New Century for Natural Resources Management*. Washington: Island Press, 1995.

Kotzé, Louis J. and Alexander R. Paterson. *The Role of the Judiciary in Environmental Governance: Comparative Perspectives*. Alphen aan den Rijn, The Netherlands and Frederick, MD: Kluwer Law International, 2009.

Kram, Megan, et al. *Protecting China's Biodiversity : A Guide to Land use, Land Tenure & Land Protection Tools*. Arlington, VA: The Nature Conservancy, 2014.

Lacey, Michael James. *Government and Environmental Politics: Essays on Historical Developments since World War Two*. Washington, DC and Lanham, MD: Wilson Center Press, 1989.

Lafferty, William M. and James Meadowcroft. *Implementing Sustainable Development: Strategies and Initiatives in High Consumption Societies*. Oxford: Oxford University Press, 2000.

Laitos, Jan G. and Rachael Reiss. 'Recreation Wars for our Natural Resources'. *Environmental Law*. 34.4 (2004): 1091–122.

Laitos, Jan G. and Thomas A. Carr. 'The Transformation on Public Lands'. *Ecology Law Quarterly* 26.2 (1999): 140–242.

Laitos, Jan G. and Rachael Gamble. 'The Problem with Wilderness'. *Harvard Environmental Law Review* 32 (2008): 503–97.

Lang, Graeme. 'Forests, Floods, and the Environmental State in China'. *Organization & Environment* 15.2 (2002): 109–30.

Lausche, Barbara J. *Guidelines for Protected Areas Legislation*. Gland, Switzerland: IUCN, 2011.

Lazarus, Richard J. 'Changing Conceptions of Property and Sovereignty in Natural Resources: Questioning the Public Trust Doctrine'. *Iowa Law Review* 71 (1985–86): 631–716.

Lee, Sangkwon, and Tazim Jamal. 'Environmental Justice and Environmental Equity in Tourism: Missing Links to Sustainability'. *Journal of Ecotourism* 7.1 (2008): 44–67.

Lele, Sharachchandra M. 'Sustainable Development: A Critical Review'. *World Development* 19.6 (1991): 607–21.

Lemons, John, and Dean Stout. 'A Reinterpretation of National Park Legislation' *Environmental Law* 15 (1984): 41–65.

Leshy, John D. 'Contemporary Politics of Wilderness Preservation'. *Journal of Land Resources & Environmental Law* 25 (2005): 1–13.

Levi-Faur, David. 'The Odyssey of the Regulatory State: From a "Thin" Monomorphic Concept to a "Thick" and Polymorphic Concept'. *Law & Policy* 35.1–2 (2013): 29–50.

Lewis, Connie Diane, et al. *Managing Conflicts in Protected Areas*. Gland, Switzerland: IUCN – the World Conservation Union, 1996.

Li, Jing-wen, Cui Guo-fa, and Li Jun-qing. 'Income and Managing Problems of the Protected Areas in China'. *Journal of Forestry Research* 12.3 (2001): 195–200.

Li, Ping, and Zhu Keliang, *A Legal Review and Analysis of China's Forest Tenure System with an Emphasis on Collective Forestland*. Washington, DC: Rights and Resources Initiative, 2007.

Li, Yanbo, et al. 'Current Status and Recent Trends in Financing China's Nature Reserves'. *Biological Conservation* 158 (2013): 296–300.

Li, Yuwen. *Administrative Litigation Systems in Greater China and Europe*. Farnham, England and Burlington, VT: Ashgate Publishing, 2014.

——. *Judicial Independence in China: An Attainable Principle?* The Hague: Eleven International Publishing, 2013.

——. *NGOs in China and Europe: Comparisons and Contrasts*. Farnham, England and Burlington, VT: Ashgate, 2011.

Li, Vic, and Graeme Lang. 'China's "Green GDP" Experiment and the Struggle for Ecological Modernisation'. *Journal of Contemporary Asia* 40.1 (2010): 44–62.

Liang, Bin. *The Changing Chinese Legal System, 1978–Present: Centralization of Power and Rationalization of the Legal System*. New York: Routledge, 2008.

Lin, Justin Yifu. 'The Household Responsibility System in China's Agricultural Reform: A Theoretical and Empirical Study'. *Economic Development and Cultural Change* (1988): S199–224.

Lin, Tun, and Asian Development Bank. *Green Benches: What can the People's Republic of China Learn from Environment Courts of Other Countries?*. Mandaluyong City: Asian Development Bank, 2009.

Liu, Lingxuan, Bing Zhang, and Jun Bi. 'Reforming China's Multi-Level Environmental Governance: Lessons from the 11th Five-Year Plan'. *Environmental Science & Policy* 21 (2012): 106–11.

Locke, John. *Two Treatises on Government*. London: Awnsham Churchill, 1690.

Lu, Hefen. *In Search of Harmony: The ECBP Stories*. Hong Kong: Pacific Empire International Ltd., 2010.

Ma, Xiao-Long, Chris Ryan, and Ji-Gang Bao. 'Chinese National Parks: Differences, Resource use and Tourism Product Portfolios'. *Tourism Management* 30.1 (2009): 21–30.

Ma, Yun. 'Working in Concert: Regulation and Incentives for Private Land Conservation in the United States'. *When Private Actors Contribute to Public Interests: A Law and Governance Perspective*. Eds. A. McCann et al. The Hague: Eleven International Publishing, 2014. 155–76.

———. 'Contextualization of National Parks in the Nature Conservation Scheme in China: A Case Study of Pudacuo National Park in Yunnan Province'. *Environmental Practice* 15.3 (2013): 293–312.

MacBean, Alasdair. 'China's Environment: Problems and Policies'. *The World Economy* 30.2 (2007): 292–307.

Mantell, Michael. 'Preservation and Use: Concessions in the National Parks'. *Ecology Law Quarterly* 8.1 (1979): 1–54.

Mappes, Harmony A. 'National Parks: For Use and "Enjoyment" Or for "Preservation" and the Role of the National Park Service Management Policies in that Determination Note'. *Iowa Law Review* 92 (2007): 601–36.

Marong, Alhaji. 'From Rio to Johannesburg: Reflections on the Role of International Legal Norms in Sustainable Development'. *Georgetown International Environmental Law Review* 16 (2003): 21–76.

Marx, Axel. 'Towards Sustainability? The Case of Tourism and the EU'. *European Energy and Environmental Law Review* 6.6 (1997): 181–6.

Mashaw, Jerry L. 'Norms, Practices, and the Paradox of Deference: A Preliminary Inquiry into Agency Statutory Interpretation'. *Administrative Law Review* 57.2 (2005): 501–42.

McBeath, Jerry, and Jenifer Huang McBeath. 'Biodiversity Conservation in China: Policies and Practice'. *Journal of International Wildlife Law and Policy* 9.4 (2006): 293–317.

McCarthy, James. 'First World Political Ecology: Lessons from the Wise Use Movement'. *Environment and Planning A* 34.7 (2002): 1281–302.

———. 'Snowmobiles: Environmental Standards and Access to National Parks', *Congressional Research Service Report*, RL 31149, 2002, p.CRS6, available at http://cnie.org/NLE/CRSreports//RL31149.pdf. Last visited April 2015.

McCloskey, Michael. 'The Emperor has no Clothes: The Conundrum of Sustainable Development'. *Duke Environmental Law and Policy Forum*. 9 (1998): 153–60.

McElwee, Charles R. *Environmental Law in China: Managing Risk and Ensuring Compliance*. New York: Oxford University Press, 2011.

McShane, Katie. 'Anthropocentrism vs. Nonanthropocentrism: Why should we Care?' *Environmental Values* 16.2 (2007): 169–86.

Michaels, Ralf. 'The Functional Method of Comparative Law'. *The Oxford Handbook of Comparative Law*. Eds. Mathias Reimann and Reinhard Zimmermann. Oxford: Oxford University Press, 2006. 339–82.

Moss, Kenneth R. 'The Public Trust Doctrine in South Carolina'. *South Carolina Environmental Law Journal* 7 (1998): 231–93.

Mozur, Paul. 'Preserving China's Reserves'. *Far Eastern Economic Review* 171.2 (2008): 77–9.

Nagle, John Copeland. 'How National Park Law really Works'. *University of Colorado Law Review* 86 (2015): 861–926.

———. 'Wilderness Exceptions'. *Environmental Law* 44 (2014): 373–414.

———. 'The Spiritual Values of Wilderness'. *Environmental Law* 36 (2005): 5–19.

———. 'The Missing Chinese Environmental Law Statutory Interpretation Cases'. *N.Y.U. Environmental Law Journal* 5 (1996): 517–55.

Nelson, Caleb. 'Statutory Interpretation and Decision Theory'. *University of Chicago Law Review* 74 (2007): 329–68.

Nie, Martin. 'Statutory Detail and Administrative Discretion in Public Lands Governance: Arguments and Alternatives'. *Journal Environmental Law & Litigation* 19 (2004): 223–91.

———. 'Drivers of Natural Resource-based Political Conflict'. *Policy Sciences* 36.3–4 (2003): 307–41.

Nie, Martin and Michael Fiebig. 'Managing the National Forests through Place-based Legislation'. *Ecology Law Quarterly* 37 (2010): 1–52.

Norton, Bryan G. *Sustainability: A Philosophy of Adaptive Ecosystem Management*. Chicago, IL: University of Chicago Press, 2005.

NPCA (National Park Conservation Association). 'A Responsible Process: Using Master Leasing Plans to Balance Sensible Energy Development and the Protection of National Parks'. 2013. Full text is available at http://www.npca.org/assets/pdf/A-Responsible-Process-web-spreads.pdf. Last visited April 2015.

OECD (Organization for Economic Co-operation and Development). *Governance in China*. Paris: OECD Publishing, 2005.

Orr, Shannon K., and Rebecca L. Humphreys. 'Mission Rivalry: Use and Preservation Conflicts in National Parks Policy'. *Public Organization Review* 12.1 (2012): 85–98.

Otto, Jan Michiel, et al, eds. *Law-making in the People's Republic of China*. The Hague and Boston, MA: Kluwer Law International, 2000.

Pearson, Eric. 'The Public Trust Doctrine in Federal Law'. *Journal of Land Resources & Environmental Law* 24 (2004): 173–7.

Percival, Robert V. *Environmental Regulation: Law, Science, and Policy*. New York: Aspen Publishers, 2009.

———. 'The Challenge of Chinese Environmental Law'. *International Environmental Law Committee Newsletter* 10 (2008): 2–6.

Plater, Zygmunt J.B. *Environmental Law and Policy: Nature, Law, and Society*. New York: Aspen Publishers, 2004.

Plummer, Ryan, and David A. Fennell. 'Managing Protected Areas for Sustainable Tourism: Prospects for Adaptive Co-Management'. *Journal of Sustainable Tourism* 17.2 (2009): 149–68.

Posner, Richard A. 'Reply: The Institutional Dimension of Statutory and Constitutional Interpretation'. *Michigan Law Review* (2003): 952–71.

———. *Law, Pragmatism, and Democracy*. Cambridge, MA: Harvard University Press, 2003.

Rabin, Robert L. 'Federal Regulation in Historical Perspective'. *Stanford Law Review* (1986): 1189–326.

Rasband, James R., et al. *Natural Resources Law and Policy*. New York: Foundation Press and Thomson Reuters, 2009.

Redclift, M.R. *Sustainable Development: Exploring the Contradictions*. London and New York: Methuen, 1987.

Ribot, Jesse C., Arun Agrawal, and Anne M. Larson. 'Recentralizing while Decentralizing: How National Governments Reappropriate Forest Resources'. *World Development* 34.11 (2006): 1864–86.

Rooij, Benjamin van. *Regulating Land and Pollution in China: Lawmaking, Compliance and Enforcement: Theory and Cases*. Leiden: Leiden University Press, 2006.

Ross, Heather E. 'Using NEPA in the Fight for Environmental Justice'. *William and Mary Journal of Environmental Law* 18 (1993): 353–74.

Ross, Molly. 'The Requirement to Leave Park Resources and Values "Unimpaired"'. *The George Wright Forum* 30–1 (2013): 68–9.

Runte, Alfred. *National Parks the American Experience*. Lincoln: University of Nebraska, 1987.

Sax, Joseph L. 'Fashioning a Recreation Policy for our National Parklands: The Philosophy of Choice and the Choice of Philosophy'. *Creighton Law Review* 12 (1978): 973–85.

———. 'The Public Trust Doctrine in Natural Resource Law: Effective Judicial Intervention'. *Michigan Law Review* 68 (1969–70): 471–566.

Scheg, Nathan L. 'Preservationists vs. Recreationists in our National Parks'. *Hastings West-Northwest Journal of Environmental Law and Policy* 5 (1998): 47–61.

Scherl, Lea M., et al. *Can Protected Areas Contribute to Poverty Reduction? : Opportunities and Limitations*. Gland, Switzerland and Cambridge: IUCN – The World Conservation Union, 2004.

Scherr, S. Jacob, and R. Juge Gregg. 'Johannesburg and Beyond: The 2002 World Summit on Sustainable Development and the Rise of Partnership'. *Georgetown International Environmental Law Review* 18 (2005): 425–63.

Scheyvens, Regina. 'Ecotourism and the Empowerment of Local Communities'. *Tourism Management* 20.2 (1999): 245–9.
Schmitthoff, M. 'The Science of Comparative Law'. *Cambridge Law Journal* 7.01 (1939): 94–110.
Scholten, Miroslava. *The Political Accountability of EU and US Independent Regulatory Agencies.* Leiden: Koninklijke Brill NV, 2014.
Schrijver, Nico. *The Evolution of Sustainable Development in International Law: Inception, Meaning and Status.* Leiden: Martinus Nijhoff, 2008.
Schrijver, Nico and Friedl Weiss. *International Law and Sustainable Development: Principles and Practice.* Leiden: Martinus Nijhoff Publishers, 2004.
Schwartz, Mark W. 'The Performance of the Endangered Species Act'. *Annual Review of Ecology, Evolution, and Systematics* 39 (2008): 279–99.
Scott, Colin. 'Accountability in the Regulatory State'. *Journal of law and society* 27.1 (2000): 38–60.
Seerden, René. *Administrative Law of the European Union, its Member States and the United States : A Comparative Analysis.* Antwerp: Intersentia, 2007.
Shafer, Craig L. 'The Unspoken Option to Help Safeguard America's National Parks: An Examination of Expanding US National Park Boundaries by Annexing Adjacent Federal Lands'. *Columbia Journal of Environmental Law* 35 (2010): 57–125.
Shapiro, Judith. *Mao's War Against Nature: Politics and the Environment in Revolutionary China.* Cambridge and New York: Cambridge University Press, 2001.
Sharpley, Richard. 'Tourism and Sustainable Development: Exploring the Theoretical Divide'. *Journal of Sustainable Tourism* 8.1 (2000): 1–19.
Shaw, Lindsey Kate. 'Land Use Planning at the National Parks: Canyonlands National Park and Off-Road Vehicles'. *University of Colorado Law Review* 68 (1997): 795.
Shutkin, William Andrew. 'The National Park Service Act Revisited'. *Virginia Environmental Law Journal* 10 (1991): 345–70.
Singer, Joseph William. 'Legal Theory: Sovereignty and Property'. *Northwestern University Law Review* 86 (1991): 1–56.
Smil, Vaclav. *China's Environmental Crisis: An Inquiry into the Limits of National Development.* Armonk, NY: M.E. Sharpe, 1993.
Smith, Sarah C. 'A Public Trust Argument for Public Access to Private Conservation Land'. *Duke Law Journal* (2002): 629–50.
Smyth, Paul. 'Conservation and Preservation of Federal Public Resources: A History'. *Natural Resources & Environment* 17 (2002): 77–114.
Sneddon, Chris, Richard B. Howarth, and Richard B. Norgaard. 'Sustainable Development in a Post-Brundtland World'. *Ecological Economics* 57.2 (2006): 253–68.
Spence, Mark David. *Dispossessing the Wilderness: Indian Removal and the Making of the National Parks.* Oxford: Oxford University Press, 2000.
Squires, Matthew L. 'Federal Regulation of RS 2477 Rights-of-Way'. *NYU Annual Survey of American Law* 63 (2007): 547–612.
Steiger, John W. 'The Consultation Provision of Section 7 (a)(2) of the Endangered Species Act and its Application to Delegable Federal Programs'. *Ecology Law Quarterly* 21 (1994): 243–328.
Stern, Rachel E. 'On the Frontlines: Making Decisions in Chinese Civil Environmental Lawsuits'. *Law & Policy* 32.1 (2010): 79–103.
———. 'The Political Logic of China's New Environmental Courts'. *China Journal* 72 (2014): 53–74.
Stevens, Jan, and Richard Asher Frank. *Current Policy and Legal Issues Affecting Recreational Use of Public Lands in the American West.* Washington, DC: Resources for the Future, 2009.
Stewart, Richard B. 'The Reformation of American Administrative Law'. *Harvard Law Review* (1975): 1667–813.
Stonich, Susan C. 'Political Ecology of Tourism'. *Annals of Tourism Research* 25.1 (1998): 25–54.
Su, Dan, Geoffrey Wall, and Paul F.J. Eagles. 'Emerging Governance Approaches for Tourism in the Protected Areas of China'. *Environmental Management* 39.6 (2007): 749–59.
Sunstein, Cass R. 'Chevron Step Zero'. *Virginia Law Review* (2006): 187–249.

——. 'Is Tobacco a Drug? Administrative Agencies as Common Law Courts'. *Duke Law Journal* (1998): 1013–69.

Tarlock, A. Dan. 'For Whom the National Parks?' *Stanford Law Review* 34 (1981): 255–74.

Terborgh, John, et al. *Making Parks Work: Strategies for Preserving Tropical Nature*. Washington, DC: Island Press, 2002.

Tosun, Cevat. 'Limits to Community Participation in the Tourism Development Process in Developing Countries'. *Tourism Management* 21.6 (2000): 613–33.

Unrau, Harlan D., et al. *Administrative History: Expansion of the National Park Service in the 1930s*. Denver, CO: Denver Service Center, 1983.

Vermeule, Adrian. *Judging Under Uncertainty: An Institutional Theory of Legal Interpretation*. Cambridge, MA: Harvard University Press, 2006.

Vincent, Carol. 'National Park System: Establishing New Units'. Congressional Research Service Report for Congress, RS20158, July 22, 2010. Full text is available at http://crs.ncseonline.org/nle/crsreports/10Aug/RS20158.pdf. Last visited April 2015.

Voigt, Christina. *Sustainable Development as a Principle of International Law: Resolving Conflicts between Climate Measures and WTO Law*. Leiden: Martinus Nijhoff Publishers, 2009.

Wang, Alex. 'The Role of Law in Environmental Protection in China: Recent Developments'. *Vermont Journal of Environmental Law* 8 (2006): 195–223.

Wang, Alex and Jie Gao. 'Environmental Courts and the Development of Environmental Public Interest Litigation in China'. *Journal of Court Innovation* 3 (2010): 37–50.

Wang, Chao-Hui, and Ralf Buckley. 'Shengtai Anquan: Managing Tourism and Environment in China's Forest Parks'. *Ambio* 39.5–6 (2010): 451–3.

Wang, Guangyu, et al. 'National Park Development in China: Conservation or Commercialization?' *Ambio* 41.3 (2012): 247–61.

Williams, A. 'Reconciling Tourism and the Environment: A Task for International Environmental Law?'. *Vermont Journal of Environmental Law* 9 (2007): 23–70.

Wilson, Scott. 'Seeking One's Day in Court: Chinese Regime Responsiveness to International Legal Norms on AIDS Carriers' and Pollution Victims' Rights'. *Journal of Contemporary China* 21.77 (2012): 863–80.

Winkler, Ralph. 'Why do ICDPs Fail?: The Relationship between Agriculture, Hunting and Ecotourism in Wildlife Conservation'. *Resource and Energy Economics* 33.1 (2011): 55–78.

Winks, Robin W. 'The National Park Service Act of 1916: A Contradictory Mandate?' *Denver University Law Review* 74.3 (1997): 575–624.

Woodward, Karen. '"Loving the Environment to Death": Can Law Protect the Environment from the Leisure Threat?' *European Energy and Environmental Law Review* 5.5 (1996): 148–52.

World Commission on Environment and Development. *Our Common Future*. Oxford and New York: Oxford University Press, 1987.

Xu, Haigen, Shunqing Wang, and Dayuan Xue. 'Biodiversity Conservation in China: Legislation, Plans and Measures'. *Biodiversity & Conservation* 8.6 (1999): 819–37.

Xu, Jianchu, and David R. Melick. 'Rethinking the Effectiveness of Public Protected Areas in Southwestern China'. *Conservation Biology* 21.2 (2007): 318–28.

Xu, Jiliang, et al. 'A Review and Assessment of Nature Reserve Policy in China: Advances, Challenges and Opportunities'. *Oryx* 46.04 (2012): 554–62.

Xu, Jintao, Andy White and Uma Lele, 'China's Forest Land Tenure Reforms: Impacts and Implications for Choice, Conservation, and Climate Change', *Rights and Resources Initiative*, 2010. Full text is available at http://www.rightsandresources.org/documents/files/doc_1403.pdf. Last visited February 2015.

Yochim, Michael. 'The Development of Snowmobile Policy in Yellowstone National Park'. *Yellowstone Science* 7.2 (1999): 2–10.

Zellmer, Sandra. 'A Preservation Paradox: Political Prestidigitation and an Enduring Resource of Wildness' *Environmental Law* 34 (2004): 1015–89.

Zhang, Kun-min, and Wen Zong-guo. 'Review and Challenges of Policies of Environmental Protection and Sustainable Development in China'. *Journal of Environmental Management* 88.4 (2008): 1249–61.

Zhang, Xiaobo. 'Fiscal Decentralization and Political Centralization in China: Implications for Growth and Inequality'. *Journal of Comparative Economics* 34.4 (2006): 713–26.

Zhou, D.Q., and R. Edward Grumbine. 'National Parks in China: Experiments with Protecting Nature and Human Livelihoods in Yunnan Province, Peoples' Republic of China (PRC)'. *Biological Conservation* 144.5 (2011): 1314–21.

Zinda, John. 'Organizing Conservation and Development in China: Politics, Institutions, Biodiversity, and Livelihoods'. Unpublished PhD dissertation. University of Wisconsin-Madison, 2013.

——. 'Hazards of Collaboration: Local State Co-Optation of a New Protected-Area Model in Southwest China'. *Society & Natural Resources* 25.4 (2012): 384–99.

Zou, Keyuan. 'Management of Marine Nature Reserves in China: A Legal Perspective'. *Journal of International Wildlife Law and Policy* 6.3 (2003): 173–204.

Zweigert, Konrad, and Hein Kötz. *Introduction to Comparative Law*. Oxford and New York: Clarendon Press and Oxford University Press, 1998.

Selected Bibliography (Chinese)

All-China Environmental Federation.《环保民间组织在环境公益诉讼中的角色和作用》调研报告摘要 (Summary of the survey report on 'The Role and Function of Environmental NGOs in PIL'), February 28, 2014, available at http://www.acef.com.cn/zhuantilanmu/2013hjwqtbh/huiyinarong/2014/0303/12495.html. Last visited April 2015.

——.中国环保民间组织发展状况报告 (Report of the Status of Development of Environmental Non-Governmental Organizations in China), 2008.

Cai, Shouqiu, and Wang Huanhuan. 改革开放30年：中国环境资源法、环境资源法学与环境资源法学教育的发展 (30 Years after the Open-up Policy: Development of Legislation on Environment and Natural Resources, Environment and Natural Resources Law and Legal Education on Environment and Natural Resource Law in China). 甘肃政法学院学报 (*Journal of Gansu Institute of Political Science and Law*) 3 (2009): 1–9.

Cao, Mingde. 论生态法的基本原则 (Analysis on the Fundamental Principles of Ecological Protection Law). 法学评论 (*Law Review*) 6 (2002): 60–68.

CCCPC (Central Committee of the Communist Party of China). 中共中央关于全面深化改革若干重大问题的决定 (Decisions of the CCCPC on Several Major Issues Concerning Comprehensively Deepening Reforms), November 12, 2013.

Ding Xueliang. 辩论'中国模式' (*Debate on the 'China Model'*). Beijing: Shehui Kexue Wenxian Chubanshe, 2011.

Du, Jiang. 论中国旅游产业功能与产业政策的转变 (Analysis on the Transformation of the Function and Industrial Policy of Tourism in China). 北京第二外国语学院学报 (*Journal of Beijing International Studies* University) 5 (2005): 1–6.

Du, Qun. 我国生态综合管理的政策与实践：生态功能区划制度探索 (Policies and Practices of Integrated Ecosystem Management in China: Exploration of the System of Ecological Functional Zoning), 2007年全国环境资源法学会（年会）论文集（第三册）(*Symposium of the Annual Conference of National Environmental Law and Natural Resources Law in 2007(Volume 3)*). 2007.

Friends of Nature. 中国环境发展报告 (2013) (*Annual Report on Environment Development of China (2013)*). Beijing: Social Sciences Academic Press, 2013.

Gao, Lihong, and Cheng Fang. 我国自然遗产保护的立法合理性研究-兼评《自然遗产保护法》征求意见稿草案 (Research on the Appropriateness of the Legislation on Protection of Natural Heritage in China: Comments on the Draft of the Natural Heritage Law). 江西社会科学 (*Social Science in Jiangxi*) 1 (2012): 153–62.

Gong, Gu. '环评风暴'的制度困境解析—以水电项目为例 (Analysis on the Institutional Dilemma of the 'EIA Storm': The Example of Hydro-electric Projects). 法商研究 (*Studies in Law and Business*) 6 (2009): 122–30.

Guo, Huijun. 云南国家公园建设试点调研报告 (Research Report of Pilot Project of National Park Construction in Yunnan). 云南林业 (*Yunnan Forestry*) 30.2 (2009): 24.

Han, Nianyong. 中国自然保护区可持续管理政策研究 (Research on the Policies of Scientific Management of Nature Reserves in China). 自然资源学报 (*Journal of Natural Resources*) 15.3 (2000): 201–7.

Jiang, Bixin. 行政诉讼法与抽象行政行为 (Administrative Litigation Law and Abstract Administrative Actions). 行政法学研究 (*Administrative Law Review*) 3 (2009): 13.

Jiang, Ming'an, ed. 中国法学三十年(1978–2008) (*Thirty Years of China Law (1978–2008)*). Beijing: Zhongguo Renmin Daxue Chubanshe, 2008.

Jin, Ruilin, ed. 环境法学 (*Textbook of Environmental Law*). Beijing: Peking University Press, 1999.

Ke, Shuifa and Zhao Tiezhen. 中国的自然保护区 (Nature Reserve in China). 地理教学 (*Geographical Teaching and Study*). 11 (2001): 10.

Li, Jianquan, et al. 我国自然保护区林权改革问题与对策探讨 (Problems and Countermeasures on Collective Forest Tenure Reform in the Nature Reserves in China). 林业资源管理 (*Forest Resources Management*) 12 (2009): 1–8.

Liu, Min. 中国景区经营权转让研究综述 (Literature Review of the Research on the Transfer of Operating Rights of Scenic Areas in China). 地理科学进展 (*Progress in Geography*) 31.11 (2012): 1492–502.

Liu, Wenjing, et al. 我国自然保护区集体林现状问题与分析 (Problems and Analysis of the Status Quo of Collectively Owned Forest Lands in Nature Reserves in China). 世界林业研究 (*World Forestry Research*) 24.3 (2011): 74.

Liu, Yang, and Lv Yihe. 旅游活动对卧龙自然保护区社区居民的经济影响 (The Economic Impact of Tourism on Local Residents in Wolong Nature Reserve). 生物多样性 (*Biodiversity Science*) 16.1 (2008): 68–74.

Lv, Zhongmei, Zhang Zhongmin and Xiong Xiaoqing. 中国环境司法现状调查–以千份环境裁判文书为样本 (Investigation of the *Status Quo* of Environmental Justice in China – Based on a Thousand Samples of Judgments on Environmental Issues). 法学 (*Law Science*) 4 (2011): 82–93.

Ma, Huaide, ed. 行政程序立法研究:《行政程序法》草案建议稿及理由说明书(*Studies on legislation of administrative procedure: recommended draft of the Administrative Procedure Law and its explanations*) . Beijing: Falv Chubanshe, 2005.

Ma, Yun. 美国公共信托理论评介(Review of the Public Trust Doctrine in the United States). Unpublished master's dissertation. China University of Political Science and Law, 2011.

Ministry of Housing and Urban-Rural Development. 中国风景名胜区事业发展公报 (1982–2012) (*Bulletin of the Development of Scenic and Historic Areas in China (1982–2012)*), December 2012. Full text is available at http://www.mohurd.gov.cn/zxydt/w020121204199374149717193750.doc. Last visited April 2015.

Peng, Decheng. 中国旅游景区治理模式研究 (*Research on the Governance Models of Tourist Spots in China*). Beijing: Zhongguo Lvyou Chubanshe, 2003.

Project Team for 'An Innovative Model for Biodiversity Conservation and Sustainable Development in Northwest Yunnan'. 云南国家公园立法可行性研究 (Research on the Feasibility of Legislation on National Park in Yunnan Province). Research Office of the Yunnan Provincial Government, 2008.

Ran, Jingcheng. 中国自然保护56年 (56 Years of Natural Protection in China). 中国国家地理 (*China National Geography*) 7 (2012): 70.

Shen, Kui. 行政诉讼确立'裁量明显不当'标准之议 (Analysis on Establishing the Standard of 'Obvious Inappropriate Discretion' in Administrative Litigation). 法商研究 (*Studies in Law and Business*). 4 (2004): 27–37.

Shen, Qiaohong. 85名专家联名建议修改自然遗产保护法 (85 Experts Jointly Recommended to Revise the Natural Heritage Protection Law. 南方周末 (*Southern Weekly*). September 15, 2012. Full text is available at http://www.infzm.com/content/80785. Last visited April 2015.

Tang, Fanglin. 中国国家公园的理论与实践研究 (Theory and Practice of the Establishment of National Parks in China). Unpublished PhD dissertation. Nanjing Forestry University, 2010.

——. 中国需要建设什么样的国家公园 (What Kind of National Park does China Need?). 林业建设 (*Forestry Construction*) 5 (2014): 1–7.

Tang, Ling. 风景名胜区产权制度变迁研究 (Research on the Evolution of the Property Rights System of Scenic and Historic Areas). Unpublished PhD dissertation. Sichuan University, 2007.

———. 论公共资源类旅游景区所有权与经营权分离 (Analysis on the Separation of Ownership and Operation Right of Public Resource-based Tourist Scenic Areas). 西南民族大学学报 (*Journal of Southwest University for Nationalities*) 7 (2005): 275–7.

Tian, Shizheng, and Yang Guihua. 中国国家公园发展的路径选择：国际经验与案例研究 (Path Selection for the Development of China's National Parks: International Comparison and Case Study). 中国软科学 (*China Soft Science*) 12 (2011): 6–14.

———. 国家公园旅游管理制度变迁实证研究–以云南香格里拉普达措国家公园为例 (An Empirical Study on the Changes in Management Systems of National Parks – A Case Study of Pudacuo National Park in Shangri-La, Yunnan Province). 广西民族大学学报 (*Journal of Guangxi University for Nationalities*) 31.4 (2009): 52–7.

Wang, Canfa, and Cheng Duowei. 新<环境保护法>下环境公益诉讼面临的困境及其破解 (Dilemma of Environmental Public Interest Litigation under the new EPL and its Solution). 法律适用 (*Legal Application*) 8 (2014): 46–51.

Wang, Huanhuan. 保护重叠对贫困影响的法律分析：以云南三江并流区域为例 (Legal Analysis on the Impacts of Overlapping Designation of Protected Areas Over Poverty: A Case Study of the Area of Three Parallel Rivers in Yunnan Province). 华南理工大学学报(社会科学版) (*Journal of South China University of Technology(Edition of Social Science)*) 4 (2008): 88–99.

Wang, Jiangang. 论我国国家公园的法律适用 (Application of Law on National Parks in China). 2010 年全国环境资源法学研讨会 (*Symposium of Environment and Resources Law of China Law Society (2010)*). (2010): 532.

Wang, Jiheng. 论生态环境保护优先原则 (Analysis on the Principle of Priority of Ecological Protection). 河南省政法管理干部学院学报 (*Journal of Henan Administrative Cadre Institute of Politics and Law*) 5.6 (2011): 79–85.

Wang, Jing. 我国环保法律实施面临的问题:国家司法机关工作人员的认识 (Problems of Enforcement of Environmental Law in China: A Perspective from Officials Working in the State Judicial Organs). 中外法学 (*Peking University Law Journal*) 19.6 (2007).

———. 从环境基本法的立法特征论我国《环境保护法》的修改定位 (Analysis on the Strategy of Amending the Environmental Protection Law of China Considering the Characteristics of the Fundamental Law). 中外法学 (*Peking University Law Journal*) 16.4 (2004): 472–84.

Wang, Shuyi, et al. 环境法前沿问题研究 (*Research on the Frontier Issues of Environmental Law*). Taipei: Yuanzhao Press, 2012.

Wu, Weixing. 从协调发展到环境优先–中国环境法制的历史转型 (From 'Coordinated Development' to 'Priority of Environment': The Historical Turn of Chinese Environmental Law System). 河海大学学报(哲学社会科学版) (*Journal of Hehai University*). 10.3 (2008): 29–31, 48.

Xie, Ninggao. 国家风景名胜区功能的发展及其保护利用 (Development of Functions of Scenic and Historic Areas at the National Level and Their Protective Use), 中国园林 (*Journal of Chinese Landscape Architecture*) 4 (2002) : 16–20.

———. 索道对世界遗产的威胁 (Threats of Ropeways on World Heritage). 旅游学刊 (*Tourism Tribune*). 6 (2000): 57–60.

Xu, Haigen. 中国自然保护区经费政策探讨 (Discussion on the Funding Policy of Nature Reserves in China). 农村生态环境 (*Rural Ecological Environment*) 17.1 (2001): 13–16.

Yan, Shipeng, and Luo Ying. 国家级自然保护区'-区–法'立法模式的理论分析 (The Theoretical Analysis on the Legislative Model of 'One Reserve, One Enabling Act' in Nature Reserves at the National Level. 世界林业研究 (*World Forestry Research*) 20.5 (2007): 68–72.

Yan, Youbing, and Zhao Liming, 旅游景区经营权转让探析 (Analysis of Transfer of Operational Right of Scenic Areas). 西北农林科技大学学报 (*Journal of Northwest A&F University*). 5.3 (2005): 92–6.

Yang, Chaofei, ed. 通往环境法制的道路:<环境保护法>修改思路研究报告 (*Path to Environmental Rule of Law: Research Report on Amending the Environmental Protection Law*). Beijing: Zhongguo Huanjing Chubanshe, 2013.

Yang, Haikun. 论我国行政立法 (Analysis on Administrative Rule-making in China). 北京社会科学 (*Beijing Social Science*) 1 (1992): 138–47.

Yang, Qunfang. 论环境法的基本原则之环境优先原则 (Analysis of the Principle of Priority of Environment as a Fundamental Principle of Environmental Law). 中国海洋大学学报(社会科学版) (*Journal of Ocean University of China (Social Science Edition)*) 2 (2009): 62–5.

Yang, Shilong. 云南国家公园建设中的法律难题 (Legal Conundrum during the Construction of National Parks in Yunnan Province). 2010 年全国环境资源法学研讨会 (*Symposium of Environment and Resources Law of China Law Society (2010)*). 2010: 575.

Yao, Jiawei. 第一个自然保护区50年'保卫战' (Fifty Years' 'Guardian War' for the First Nature Reserve). 南方周末 (*Southern Weekly*). February 14, 2007. Full text is available at http://www.infzm.com/content/5913. Last visited April 2015.

Ye, Wen, Shen Chao and Li Yunlong, eds. 香格里拉的眼睛：普达措国家公园规划和建设 (*Eyes of Shangri-La: Planning and Construction of Pudacuo National Park*). Beijing: China Environmental Science Press, 2008.

Zhang, Qianfan. 司法审查的标准与方法-以美国行政法为视角 (Tests and Methods of Judicial Review: A Perspective from the Administrative Law of the United States). 法学家 (*The Jurist*) 6 (2006): 36–44.

Zhang, Xiao. 世界遗产和国家重点风景名胜区分权化(属地)管理体制的制度缺陷 (Analysis on the Disadvantages of the Decentralized Administration and Management Model for World Heritage and Key Scenic and Historic Areas at the National Level in China). 中国园林 (*Chinese Garden*) 7 (2005): 214.

Zhao, Xudong, and Huang Jing. 俄罗斯"环境保护优先性"原则：我国环境法'协调发展'原则的反思与改进 (Analysis on the Principle of 'Priority of Environmental Protection' in Russia: Rethinking and Improvement of the 'Coordination Principle' in China). 河北法学 (*Hebei Law Science*) 6 (2000): 131.

Zheng, Chunyan. "隐匿"司法审查下的行政裁量观及其修正-以《最高人民法院公报》中的相关案例为样本的分析 (Judicial Perception of Administrative Discretion and its Rectification, from the Perspective of 'Hidden' Judicial Review: An Analysis based on Relevant Cases Released in the Supreme People Court's Gazette). 法商研究 (*Studies in Law and Business*) 1 (2013): 61.

——. 取决于行政任务的不确定法律概念定性-再问行政裁量概念的界定 (The Nature of 'Indefinite Legal Term' Inferred from Administrative Tasks – Re-questioning the Definition of Administrative Discretion). 浙江大学学报 (*Journal of Zhejiang University*). 37.3 (2007): 166–74.

Zhong, Linsheng, and Wang Jing. 我国保护地生态旅游发展现状调查分析 (Investigation and Analysis on Situation of Ecotourism Development in Protected Areas of China). 生态学报 (*Acta Ecologica Sinica*) 31.24 (2011): 7450–457.

Zhou, Ke, and Hou Jiaru. 我国自然保护区分类体系的立法完善 (Improvement of Legislation on the Categorization System of Nature Reserves in China). 首都师范大学学报（社会科学版）(*Journal of Capital Normal University (Social Sciences Edition)*) 2 (2007): 58–63.

Zhu, Xiao. 论中国环境法基本原则的立法发展与再发展 (Analysis on the Development and Further Development of the Fundamental Principles of Environmental Law in Legislation in China). 华东政法大学学报 (*Journal of East China University of Political Science and Law*) 3 (2014): 4–16.

Index

accountability 283, 285
adjacent development 74–5, 97–8, 262
administrative agency (definition) 21–2, 33–4, 62–3
administrative litigation 167, 229–30, 235, 238–9
Administrative Procedure Act 62, 84, 127–8, 140, 142, 147
alternative dispute resolution 145, 152–3, 265, 278
arbitrary and capricious standard 65, 84, 128, 136, 145

benefit sharing 16, 206–7, 231, 248, 252, 254–5
Bush administration 98, 120, 135, 140, 261

campaign 30, 201, 210, 219–26, 265, 287
central-local relationship 40, 247, 267–9, 284; cooperative federalism 71, 267
Chevron deference 65, 115, 129, 265; step zero 130
civil society 228, 234, 238, 243, 270–1, 286–7
commerce clause 72
common law 72, 84–6
Communist Party of China 172, 204, 257, 272
communities: local (gateway) 48, 105, 205–8, 216–18; community-based management 216, 218, 252
comparative method 6–9, 259–71
compatibility standard 78, 123, 279
compliance and enforcement 219–29, 265, 280–1
comprehensive planning 73, 122, 261, 282
concession 123–4, 168, 200–2, 261, 283; Concession Policy Act 76; Concession Management Improvement Act 76; Guizhou province 200–1
conflict (definition) 43; resource 49–50, 189–92, 262–3; development 49–50, 205–8, 262–3; property 27–9, 49–50, 100–3, 206–7, 216–17, 262–4

conserve (conservation) 41–3, 112–13, 120
constitution 53; U.S. 71–2; P.R.C. 157–9, 160–1, 210–11, 285
Convention on Biological Diversity 16, 31

damming 25, 117–18, 190; *see also* Hetch Hetchy valley
deference 64–5, 277–8; *see also Chevron* deference
department-based legislation 177
derogation standard 74–5, 120–1
designated use 122–3, 214–16, 283
development-conservation paradox 48; *see also* people-park conflict
discretion 63–5, 124, 130–8, 152, 283
dispute (definition) 43
dominant use 77, 89, 262
Duck Stamp Act 77–8

ecological compensation 207, 216–17
ecosystem management 45, 105, 174
ecosystem service 17, 42, 48
enabling act (legislation) 77, 86–7, 118, 169, 284
Endangered Species Act 56, 83–4, 275
environmental court 236–7, 286
environmental impact assessment 54, 82–3, 163, 190–1, 261
environmental philosophy 44–6, 274

Federal Land Policy and Management Act 79–80, 100, 124
forest park 34–5, 38–9, 214–16
forest tenure 28–9, 39, 263

good governance 61–2
Grand Canyon national park 108, 112; overflight 143–6, 152, 274–5

hard look 124, 128, 136–8
Hetch Hetchy Valley 25–6
hunting 46, 77, 106, 133

impairment standard 73, 111–14, 120–2, 278–80; permanent 80
informal rulemaking 84, 128
information: access (right) to 53, 61, 208, 218, 228; disclosure 218, 283
inholding 102–3, 110, 263
institution: capacity building 227, 253, 276, 287; theory 65–7, 276, *see also* legal interpretation
inter-agency rivalry 33–4, 60, 225–6, 247, 256–7, 281, 284
International Court of Justice 54
International Union for Conservation of Nature and Natural Resources (IUCN) 17–9, 39, 58, 248–9, 256, 281

judicial independence 234–6, 270, 281, 286

Land and Water Conservation Fund 27, 92–3, 96, 102
legal interpretation 65, 275; institutionary theory 65–7, 276
legal transplantation 9, 261
Leopold Report 105
letters and visits 235–6, 266
local protectionism 227–8, 239, 284

Maoist era 30, 261
mass recreation 2, 91–4, 106, 109, 260
Master Leasing Plans 98
Mead standard 129–30, 132
Merced river 146–51, 261, 274–5
motorized recreation 2, 46–50, 88–90, 103–4, 182
multiple-use 42, 78–90, 123–4, 262
Multiple-Use Sustained-Yield Act 79–80, 124

National Park Service 21, 25, 119–22, 269
national park system 26, 73–5
national recreation areas 23
National Environmental Policy Act 56, 82–3, 101, 116, 122, 127, 137–8
national forest system 21–2, 113–14
national park: IUCN 17–19; U.S. 24–6; China 35–6, 240–58
National Park Omnibus Management Act 27, 75
National Park Service General Authorities Act 26, 73–4
National Park Service Organic Act 73, 111–15, 278–80, 282–3

national park system 18, 21
national wilderness preservation system 22–3, 81
national wildlife refuge system 21–2
natural heritage 36, 163–5
norm 54, 60; *see also* sustainable development
nuisance 84

Obama administration 22, 27, 95, 98, 102, 121
off-road vehicle 46, 100, 107–9, 138
overcrowding 94–5, 182, 261

people-park conflict 50, 216
paper park syndrome 177, 185–8
paradigm 9
place-based legislation 77, 169
plan 178; Five-Year Plan 170–8
policy-making: NPS Management Policies 120–2, 277; China 169–76, 178–9, 264
pollution control 72, 171, 177–8, 227
poverty reduction 49–51, 55, 273
preemption 71
preserve (preservation) 41–3, 74, 112–14, 120, 124
principle: coordination 210–13; priority of protection 57, 210–14, 265, 283; precautionary 53–4, 213
professional (expert) 5, 67, 119, 121, 144, 276, 285
progressivism 20–1, 47, 67
property clause 72
protected area (definition) 15–9, 39–40, 164–5, 260
public domain 1, 20–1
public interest litigation 233–4, 238
public participation 53, 61, 63, 208, 218–19, 228
public trust 269, 276, 286
public trust doctrine 84–6

rails-to-trails 101–2
recreation (definition) 43; recreational tourism 182
Redwood Amendment 27, 74–5
regulation 47, 106–9; regulatory state 47
right of action 127, 167, 283
rights of way 100–1

scientific development 57, 171–2
Skidmore deference 130
Southern Utah Wilderness Association case 130–3
standing 127, 233–4, 270–1, 286
substantive management criteria 76, 215, 283
sustainable development 49, 51–62, 171–2, 261, 274; Brundtland Report 51–2; *see also* tourism

target responsibility system 178
The Nature Conservancy 240–58

ticket economy 180, 185, 188, 207, 267
tourism 46–7, 180–5; sustainable tourism 57–8, 183–4; ecotourism 58–9, 184–5
transfer of operation rights 176, 192–202, 283

unacceptable impact 122–3, 125
underfunding 96–7, 185–9, 267
United Nations Conference on the Human Environment (Stockholm, 1972) 30, 51
use (definition) 41–3
user capacity 146–51, 261
utilitarian 25, 45, 79, 113–14

Visitor Experience and Resources Protection 147–50

western development 20, 172, 190
Wild and Scenic Rivers Act 117–18, 146–51
wilderness 45, 124; Wilderness Act 80–2, 114, 116–17, 137, 264; wilderness area 18, 22, 81
wildlife-dependent recreation use 78, 122–3, 262
wise uses 16, 45

Yellowstone national park 1, 15, 21–4, 95, 119, 262; Yellowstone model 45; snowmobile 108–9, 139–42

zoning 167, 214–16; ecological functional 173–4; primary functional 173